An Introduct ics

Also by Nick Wilkinson

MANAGERIAL ECONOMICS: A Problem-Solving Approach

An Introduction to Behavioral Economics

Nick Wilkinson
Richmond, The American International University in London

First published 2008 by
PALGRAVE MACMILLAN

Palgrave Macmillan in the UK is an imprint of Macmillan Publishers Limited,
registered in England, company number 785998, of Houndmills, Basingstoke,
Hampshire RG21 6XS.

Palgrave Macmillan in the US is a division of St Martin's Press LLC,
175 Fifth Avenue, New York, NY 10010.

Palgrave Macmillan is the global academic imprint of the above companies
and has companies and representatives throughout the world.

Palgrave® and Macmillan® are registered trademarks in the
United States, the United Kingdom, Europe and other countries.

ISBN-13: 978–0–230–53259–5
ISBN-10: 0–230–53259–4

This book is printed on paper suitable for recycling and made from fully
managed and sustained forest sources. Logging, pulping and manufacturing
processes are expected to conform to the environmental regulations of the
country of origin.

A catalogue record for this book is available from the British Library.

A catalog record for this book is available from the Library of Congress.
Library of Congress Catalog Card Number: 2007052306

10   9   8   7   6   5
16   15   14   13   12   11

Printed and bound in Great Britain by
CPI Antony Rowe, Chippenham and Eastbourne

Contents

Part IV Strategic Interaction

7 Behavioral Game Theory

Part V Conclusion

List of Tables and Figures

Tables

Figures

Preface

There should really be no need for a book entitled "Behavioral Economics." All economics is behavioral in the sense of examining how people allocate resources in different types of situation. However, over the last three decades the standard neoclassical model, based largely on the assumption of expected utility maximization, has come under increasing criticism from both outside and inside the economics profession. There are a large number of empirical anomalies which the standard model fails to explain.

Yet, in spite of this situation and the considerable interest and debate in the profession, there is not a single current text available on behavioral economics. There are books on behavioral aspects of other disciplines, such as marketing, finance, and even managerial accounting; there are collections of papers on behavioral economics; and there are books on particular aspects of behavioral economics, such as behavioral game theory. Thus there appears to be both high demand and low supply for a text in this area.

Many undergraduate students are now starting to study aspects of behavioral economics. The book is particularly appropriate for students in the third or fourth years of undergraduate study, or in a postgraduate program, once they have become familiar with the standard neoclassical model, its assumptions and methods, and to some extent its limitations. For postgraduate students in particular the text should serve as a foundation for linked themes and materials, providing a jumping-off point for further reading of the original papers on which the book is based.

The text has the following objectives:

1. To present the principles and methods of behavioral economics in a logical and amenable manner, contrasting them with those of the standard economic model (SEM).

2. To illustrate how a behavioral economic model (BEM) is superior to the SEM in terms of power of explanation and prediction, using a wide variety of empirical examples from both observational and experimental studies.

3. To provide a critical examination of the existing literature relating to the BEM.

4. To explain the policy implications of the BEM, particularly when these differ from those of the SEM.

5. To provide a coherent psychological framework underpinning the findings of behavioral economics.

6. To indicate the way forward for the subject, in terms of future challenges and areas meriting further research.

It should not be inferred from this that there is a single behavioral model which has universal acceptance. Within particular areas, like intertemporal choice and social preferences, there is often a profusion of models. Indeed, one main criticism of behavioral economics is that there is an excessive number of different models, many of which may apply in a given situation. This criticism will be discussed in the first chapter of the text.

A vital theme of the book is that it is intended to be highly cross-disciplinary in nature. Any book on behavioral aspects must of course involve psychology, but there are two aspects included which some behavioral economists tend to ignore: evolutionary psychology and neuroscience. Both are relatively new disciplines and both arouse considerable controversy.

Many economists and psychologists reject the theories of evolutionary psychology as being largely speculative. They are frequently dismissed in the social sciences as being "just-so" stories, meaning that they are not true scientific theories in terms of proposing testable hypotheses. This view is because of two main factors: (1) it is impossible by definition to perform experiments on the past; and (2) the past record of facts is highly incomplete. We will show that this dismissal is largely unjustified and that evolutionary psychology can indeed produce testable hypotheses, many of which have been confirmed by substantial empirical evidence. Furthermore, the tendency of many economists to limit explanations to economic phenomena is even more unsatisfactory as far as "just-so" stories are concerned. For example, many readers would not be satisfied with the explanations that people tend to succumb to temptation because they have short time horizons in decision-making and that they make bad decisions when they are angry. These can also be regarded as "just-so" stories because they both beg the questions regarding *why* people have short time horizons and *why* we have seemingly harmful emotional responses like anger.

The fast-developing area of neuroscience can also be of great benefit to economics. The conjunction of the two disciplines has led to the birth of neuro-economics. Economists have traditionally relied on "revealed preference," meaning choice, in market behavior to develop their theories, but this approach has significant limitations. We will examine situations where choice and preference do not coincide and where intertemporal choice and framing effects cause preference reversals. These anomalies have important welfare implications. New techniques, like fMRI and PET scans, combined with a greater understanding of the operation of genes, neurotransmitters, and hormones can lead to greater insights into human behaviour, both in terms of universalities and in terms of individual differences. We now know, for example, that different types of cost and benefit are processed in different areas of the brain and that both altruistic and spiteful behaviour, in the form of punishment, give pleasure, in spite of what the doer might say about their motivation. Neuro-economics, like evolutionary psychology, has attracted some strong criticism from within the economics profession, and this debate is reviewed in the first chapter.

In summary, the intention is to provide a book which is (1) comprehensive, rigorous, and up-to-date in terms of reviewing the latest developments in the field of behavioral economics; (2) multidisciplinary in approach; and (3) user-friendly in terms of exposition, discussing a large number of examples and case studies to which the average reader can relate. Typically three case studies are included at the end of each chapter, with questions reviewing the relevant material. Finally, here is a note of apology: readers may find some repetitiveness in the materials in the various chapters. I offer three excuses: (1) some readers or instructors may wish to skip certain chapters, like the more technical chapter on game theory; (2) many of the themes in different chapters are linked, with the features of prospect theory and mental accounting in particular applying in many different areas; and (3) it seems appropriate to hammer home certain points, especially when these are at variance with other commonly held theories or beliefs.

Acknowledgements

The following publishers kindly granted permission to reprint the material that appears in the book.

The Economist magazine:

Loss Aversion in Monkeys. June 23, 2005.
The Rational Response to Terrorism. July 21, 2005.
Soothing the Savage Breast. January 12, 2006
Brothers in Arms. June 29, 2006.
Pursuing Happiness. June 29, 2006.
The Joy of Giving. October 12, 2006.

The American Economic Association:

Frederick, S., Loewenstein, G., and O'Donoghue, T. (2002). Time discounting and time preference: A critical review. *Journal of Economic Literature, 40*(2), Table 1, 378–9.
Fehr, E. and Gächter, S. (2001). Fairness and retaliation. *Journal of Economic Perspectives, 3*, Figure 2, p. 167.

Cambridge University Press:

Camerer, C.F. (2000). Prospect theory in the wild; Evidence from the field. In D. Kahneman and A. Tversky (Eds), *Choices, Values, and Frames*, Table 16.1, 289.

Princeton University Press:

Camerer, C.F. (2003). *Behavioral Game Theory*, Table 6.3, 272.

I also thank the following authors for granting personal permission to reproduce their work:

Colin Camerer, Ernst Fehr, Shane Frederick, Simon Gächter, George Loewenstein, and Ted O'Donoghue.

Finally, I thank Dr Sanjit Dhami of Leicester University for his constructive comments regarding the manuscript.

Part I
Introduction

1

Nature of Behavioral Economics

1.1 Behavioral economics and the standard economic model

What is behavioral economics?

Economic phenomena relate to any aspect of human behavior that involves the allocation of scarce resources; thus it is very wide-ranging in its subject area. For example, all of the following can be described as economic phenomena, although they may also of course involve other disciplines of study: searching for a sexual partner on the Internet, watching a documentary on television, making a charitable donation, giving a lift to one's neighbor in order to make it easier to ask them for a favor later, deciding to take a nap rather than mow the lawn, teaching one's child to play tennis, and going to church.

Economics, like all sciences, is concerned with developing theories. Theories attempt to describe and explain relationships between phenomena we observe. In order to do this they need to proceed on the basis of a number of assumptions or premises. Sometimes these assumptions are made explicit, but in many cases they are implicit, and it is often important to tease out these implicit assumptions because if a theory proves to be inaccurate it is usually because the assumptions on which it is based are incorrect.

This is where behavioral economics is relevant. As Camerer and Loewenstein (2004) succinctly put it,

> Behavioral economics increases the explanatory power of economics by providing it with more realistic psychological foundations.
>
> (p. 3)

Ho, Lim, and Camerer (2006) also state,

> It is important to emphasize that the behavioral economics approach *extends* rational choice and equilibrium models; it does not advocate abandoning these models entirely.
>
> (p. 308)

In order to understand these claims, and also to understand various critiques of behavioral economics, we now need to examine the major assumptions underlying the standard economic model (SEM), and then consider various important and widespread phenomena that this model is unable to explain.

The standard economic model

Throughout this book we will make comparisons between the SEM and various theories that relate to behavioral economics that we can summarize for the sake of brevity into a Behavioral Economic Model (BEM). This is not to imply that all the aspects of either the SEM or the BEM are complementary and nonconflicting; we will encounter various controversies within the BEM, where different theories are based on different premises and make different predictions. However, in spite of such conflicts, there are greater similarities between the different theories within each model than there are when comparing the two main models in general.

In some ways the contrast between the two models above parallels the contrast that is often drawn between what is sometimes referred to as the Standard Social Science Model (SSSM) and the Evolutionary Psychology Model (EPM), first described by Tooby and Cosmides (1984). The relationship between behavioral economics and evolutionary psychology (EP) is discussed further in the section on objectives later in this chapter.

The key components of the SEM that are relevant from the point of view of behavioral economics include the following assumptions:

- Economic agents are rational.
- Economic agents are motivated by expected utility maximization.
- An agent's utility is governed by purely selfish concerns, in the narrow sense that it does not take into consideration the utility of others.
- Agents are Bayesian probability operators.
- Agents have consistent time preferences according to the discounted utility model (DUM).
- All income and assets are completely fungible.

We will examine the meaning and implications of these assumptions in detail in the relevant chapters, since in some cases this will merit a considerable amount of discussion. However, at this point there are two fundamental and related issues that need some discussion, and these concern the role and interpretation of the "assumptions." In a highly influential article, Friedman (1953) claimed that the scientific worth of a theory is determined purely in terms of congruence with reality (discussed in more detail later in this section). According to Friedman, testing the reality of a theory's assumptions is fundamentally wrong and productive of much mischief... [I]t only confuses the issue, promotes misunderstanding about the significance of empirical evidence for economic theory, produces a misdirection of much intellectual effort... The relevant question to ask about the "assumptions" of theory is not whether they are descriptively "realistic", for they never are, but whether they are sufficiently good approximations for the purpose at hand.

According to this view, a good theory that makes accurate predictions means that individuals behave "as if" they follow the behavioral assumptions. Most economists, even critics of the SEM, agree regarding this aspect of the role of assumptions, and concede that economic theories cannot be falsified on the basis of their assumptions alone, however unrealistic these may appear to be; they can only be falsified on the basis of their inability to make accurate predictions.

The second and related issue concerns the interpretation of the term "assumptions." Some economists, notably Gul and Pesendorfer (2005), have argued that the assumptions described above are not to be treated as **axioms** or fundamental premises that are "self-evident." They claim instead that, as far as rationality is concerned, this is not an assumption in economics but a **methodological stance**. Their paper also implies that at least some of the other "assumptions" need to be treated in a similar manner. Expanding this claim they state,

> This stance reflects economists' decision to view the individual as the unit of agency and investigate the interaction of the purposeful behaviours of different individuals within various economic institutions. One can question the usefulness of this methodological stance by challenging individual economic models or the combined output of economics but one cannot disprove it.
>
> (p. 42)

However, we must take issue with Gul and Pesendorfer when they compare the situation of critics of the rationality assumption with the situation of critics of experimental economics. In this context they claim that "a critic cannot expect to disprove the usefulness of experimental methods for understanding choice behaviour." In principle it is possible to demonstrate the *usefulness* or lack of usefulness of experimental methods. If various types of experiment fail to predict behavior in the real world then it could be claimed that such methods are not useful. These methods are also discussed in more detail later in the chapter, in the section on methodology. The important point here is that, although theories cannot be falsified simply on the basis of their assumptions, these assumptions, or methodological stance, may be shown not to be useful, at least in certain circumstances. We will see numerous examples of this throughout the remaining chapters, but a simple one will suffice here for illustration. It is generally assumed in the SEM that people use exponential discounting when evaluating future preferences. This results in the normatively desirable behavior of having time-consistent preferences. However, empirical evidence shows that people frequently display inconsistent preferences, for example by overestimating future utilities. Thus gym members often overestimate future usage when they join a club; gyms are aware of this and structure their membership fees accordingly, with high start-up costs or initiation fees and low peruse charges. In this situation, discussed in more detail in Chapter 6, the assumption of exponential discounting in the SEM is not *useful*, since it cannot explain the behavior of either consumers or producers.

Shortcomings of the standard economic model

Over the last two or three decades behavioral economists have drawn increasing attention to various problems in the standard model. Consider the following questions:

- Why is the return on stocks so much higher on average than the return on bonds?
- Why do sellers often value their goods or assets much higher than buyers?
- Why are people willing to drive across town to save $5 to purchase a $15 calculator but not to purchase a $125 jacket?
- Why are people delighted to hear they are going to get a 10 % raise in salary, and then furious to find out that a colleague is going to get 15 %?
- Why do people forever make resolutions to go on a diet or stop smoking, only to give in later?
- Why do people go to the ATM and withdraw a measly $50?
- Why do people prefer to postpone a treat like a luxury dinner rather than have it sooner?
- Why is someone unwilling to pay $500 for a product, but then delighted when their spouse buys them the same product for the same price using their joint bank account?

- Why is someone willing to drive through a blizzard to go to see a ball game when they have paid for the ticket, but not when they have been given the ticket for free?

- Why are people willing to bet long odds on the last race of the day, but not on previous races?

None of these questions are answerable using the SEM, because of the restrictive nature of the assumptions involved. In some cases there are anomalies, meaning that the SEM makes inaccurate predictions; in other cases the SEM is incomplete or silent, meaning that it cannot make predictions at all. However, as will be seen, the questions are all answerable using the richer BEM. Before moving on to discuss the development of behavioral economics it is necessary to examine the nature of theories and their evaluation, in order to gain a better understanding of the advantages and disadvantages of different approaches and models.

Evaluating theories

There are various criteria that scientists in general propose as being relevant in terms of evaluating theories. For example, Stigler (1965) proposes three essential criteria for judging economic theories: congruence with reality, generality, and tractability. The evolutionary biologist E.O. Wilson adds a further criterion, parsimony, which ironically is particularly pertinent for the SEM. These criteria are now discussed in more detail.

1. *Congruence with reality*
   This factor is generally recognized as being the most important for any scientific theory. Good theories are able both to explain or fit existing observations and to make testable predictions which later prove to be correct. In this respect Newton's laws of motion represent a good theory, but not as good as Einstein's theory of relativity, since they do not fit reality as well on a cosmic scale. It is notable that such theories are sometimes referred to as "laws," in the sense that they represent regularities; this is particularly applicable when such "laws" involve general principles with widespread application, which leads us on to the second criterion.

2. *Generality*
   Good theories apply to a wide selection of phenomena; Newton's and Einstein's theories qualify again, although again Einstein's is better, in terms of applying to a larger range of situations. Theories of quantum mechanics and evolution by natural selection are further examples of general

theories. Examples from economics are the law of diminishing returns, the law of demand regarding the inverse relationship between quantity and price, and the law of comparative advantage.

3. *Tractability*

This criterion refers to how easy it is to apply theoretical models to different situations in terms of making testable predictions. In practice this relates in particular to the complexity of the theory involved. More complex theories take into account more parameters (usually by making fewer assumptions) and are therefore more difficult to represent as models. In many sciences, including economics, these models are often best represented in mathematical form. There are two reasons for this: first, mathematics allows the theory to be represented most concisely and unambiguously, including the assumptions involved; second, it allows manipulation to be performed, resulting in precise predictions for given values of the parameters involved in the model. However, highly complex theories may prove to be somewhat intractable if the resulting mathematical analysis becomes unmanageable. In practice there is often a trade-off between tractability and the final criterion, parsimony.

4. *Parsimony*

This criterion refers to the principle of Occam's razor, named after the philosopher William of Occam, and first expressed in the 1320s. He said, "What can be done with fewer assumptions is done in vain with more." In the words of E.O. Wilson (1998), "Scientists attempt to abstract the information into the form that is the simplest and aesthetically the most pleasing – the combination called elegance – while yielding the largest amount of information with the least amount of effort." This criterion is particularly relevant as far as the SEM is concerned, since parsimony is one of its great virtues. By assuming that economic agents are selfish utility maximizers the SEM is able to derive a large number of predictions regarding the behavior of individuals and firms. However, there may be another trade-off here: if a theory is too parsimonious, it may not satisfy the first criterion so well, since it may make too many assumptions to apply to real-world situations. This is the main criticism behavioral economists level at the SEM, since it cannot explain the anomalies described earlier, or indeed many others.

The behavioral economists Ho, Lim, and Camerer (2006) propose a somewhat different list of desirable properties of theories. They include generality and congruence with reality (they refer to this as "empirical accuracy"), but they add the features of **precision** and **psychological plausibility**. Precision refers to the ability to give exact numerical predictions about behavior, and they give the example of Nash equilibrium analysis in game theory, which is discussed in Chapter 7. Ho, Lim, and Camerer also argue that generality and precision are particularly important in economic models, while empirical accuracy and psychological plausibility have been given more importance in psychology. The authors then claim that the goal in behavioral economics is to have all four properties. As we have already argued, psychological plausibility is likely to lead to more accurate and useful models, albeit more complex ones. Numerous examples will be given of such models in the remainder of the book.

1.2 History and evolution of behavioral economics

The classical and neoclassical approaches

There tends to be a widespread belief that the economists of the eighteenth and nineteenth centuries who pioneered the discipline had no time for psychology. The neoclassicists in particular are often portrayed as systematizers who wanted to bring some mathematical rigour to their subject by imposing some simplifying assumptions regarding motivation. A good example is the work of Daniel Bernoulli (1738), who might be regarded as the originator of the theory of choice under risk, explaining risk-aversion in terms of the diminishing marginal utility of money. However, the portrayal of the classicists and neoclassicists as mathematical systematizers actually gives somewhat of a false impression, obscuring some important realities. Although Adam Smith, the father of economics, is best known for his work *The Wealth of Nations*, in 1776, he was also the author of a less well known work, *The Theory of Moral Sentiments*, in 1759. The latter work contains a number of vital psychological insights and foreshadows many more recent developments in behavioral economics, particularly relating to the role of emotions in decision-making.

Similarly, Jeremy Bentham, best known for introducing the concept of utility, had much to say about the underlying psychology of consumers. Francis Edgeworth wrote *The Theory of Mathematical Psychics* in 1881, the title indicating his concern with psychology; this is reflected in his well-known "Edgeworth Box," which relates to two-person bargaining situations and involves a simple model of social utility. However, psychology was in its infancy at this time as an academic discipline, and many economists wanted the also-new science of economics (it was still largely referred to as political economy) to have a surer and more rigourous grounding, similar to that of the natural sciences. Hence sprang the neoclassical revolution, and the birth of the concept of *Homo economicus*, that rational self-interested utility maximizer.

Post-war economic approaches

In the first half of the twentieth century there were still economists who considered and discussed psychological factors in their work, for example Irving Fisher, Vilfredo Pareto, and John Maynard Keynes. The latter famously speculated, both figuratively and literally, on the stock market, with notable success. However, the general trend during this time was to ignore psychology, and by World War II psychologists were *persona non grata* in economists' circles.

This trend continued after the war, aided in many ways by the advent of better computational methods. As computers became more powerful it became possible to build and estimate mathematical models of both markets and the economic system as a whole. The sub-discipline of econometrics became a vital tool for economists as a means of both developing and testing theories. Economists became obsessed with mensuration, meaning the measurement of variables, and the estimation of economic parameters using mathematical equations and econometric methods. Much progress was made in terms of theoretical development, and the emphasis on mathematical treatment led to greater rigour and more precise, if not accurate, results.

Some economists realized that the behavioral assumptions underlying their models were unrealistic, but we have seen earlier that there was a methodological approach, typified by Milton Friedman, that economic theory had little to do with the accuracy of these behavioral assumptions or with understanding why individuals behave as they do.

The resurgence of psychology

Some heretics, like Herbert Simon, viewed this approach as somewhat blinkered. He was not prepared to accept the host of ready excuses that were offered when predictions went astray: temporary "blips," the introduction of new and unpredictable factors, measurement discrepancies, and so on. He believed it important to understand the underlying motivation behind the behavior of economic agents in order to improve existing theories and make more accurate predictions. Simon (1956) introduced the term "bounded rationality" to refer to the cognitive limitations facing decision-makers in terms of acquiring and processing information.

There were a number of seminal papers written in the 1950s and 1960s which complemented the work of Simon and pointed to various anomalies, suggesting some theoretical improvements. Notable contributions were made by Markowitz (1952), Allais (1953), Strotz (1955), Schelling (1960), and Ellsberg (1961). However, it was really at the end of the 1970s that behavioral economics was born. Two papers were largely responsible for this. The first, in 1979, was entitled "Prospect theory: An analysis of decision under risk" and was written by two psychologists, Daniel Kahneman and Amos Tversky, being published in the prestigious and technical economic journal *Econometrica*. These two researchers had already published a number of papers relating to heuristic decision-making, but prospect theory (PT) introduced several new and fundamental concepts relating to reference points, loss-aversion, utility measurement, and subjective probability judgments. All of these are discussed in detail in Chapter 3, and repeated references are made to them throughout this work.

The second paper, "Toward a positive theory of consumer choice," was published by the economist Richard Thaler in 1980. In particular he introduced the concept of "mental accounting," closely related to the concepts of Kahneman and Tversky, and this is discussed at length in Chapter 4.

Since 1980 the field of behavioral economics has become a burgeoning one, as both economists and psychologists have expanded and developed the work of the pioneers mentioned above. As more success has been achieved in explaining the anomalies of the SEM and in developing a more complete body of theory, the field has now become a more respectable one, with a variety of journals publishing relevant research.

However, it should be made clear that behavioral economists do not conform to a uniform school of thought. Although they all are concerned with the psychological foundations of economic behavior, they may have quite conflicting beliefs regarding fundamental aspects. For example, we will see that the views of Kahneman and Tversky, Vernon Smith, and Gigerenzer all differ substantially regarding the role and nature of assumptions, appropriate methods of investigation, the value of various kinds of empirical evidence, and conclusions regarding such issues as rationality, efficiency, and optimization.

Behavioral economics, experimental economics, and neuroeconomics

These three areas of economics are all relatively new, taking off in the 1980s, and there are significant overlaps between them. The relationships between these subjects need to be explained in order to appreciate the methodological issues discussed in the following section. We have already covered the subject area of behavioral economics in general terms, so let us now consider experimental economics. This is not a distinct area of study, as are most categories of economics; rather it is a method of study that can be applied to any subject area. However, it has particular application to behavioral economics, since the latter is concerned with psychological processes that are difficult to observe directly in terms of revealed preference. By using controlled experiments and asking hypothetical questions researchers can gain more insight into such psychological processes.

The field of experimental economics was largely pioneered by Vernon Smith, who believed that economics could be enriched by experimental methods that would not only lend insight into psychological processes, but also enable a tighter control over the relevant variables in order to come to more specific and reliable conclusions than is often possible with conventional observational studies. These aspects, and examples, are discussed in more detail in the following section.

Neuroeconomics refers to the use of empirical evidence relating to brain activity in order to come to conclusions relating to economic behavior. It has been made possible by a number of recent technological developments, particularly in terms of brain scanning and imaging techniques like PET (positron emission tomography), fMRI (functional magnetic resonance imaging), EEG (electroencephalography), and rCBF (regional cerebral blood flow). These methods detect brain activity in particular areas in terms of electrical activity or increased blood flow, and this can shed considerable light on various topics of interest in behavioral economics. The findings are especially relevant in terms of decision-making heuristics, learning processes, and the role of the emotions. Researchers are discovering that different types of thinking or mental process are performed in different parts of the brain, indicating the importance of brain structure or anatomy. They are also finding that different chemicals and hormones have dramatic effects on behavior. Various examples of neuroeconomic studies will be given throughout the book, the first being Case 1.3 at the end of this chapter, which examines altruistic activity in terms of the different parts of the brain that may be stimulated. This in turn enables conclusions to be drawn regarding motivation, since it is largely known what parts of the brain are associated with certain types of process or emotion. Thus it appears that giving to others may in turn give joy to the giver, while other acts we perform are designed to punish.

The relevance and application of both experimental economics and neuroeconomics have been controversial issues, and this controversy is discussed in the next section.

1.3 Methods

Economists' methods

Traditionally there has been a contrast between the methods used by economists and those used by psychologists, and this has sometimes caused a considerable degree of mutual suspicion and distrust. Fudenberg (2006) gives an apocryphal quotation at the beginning of a recent paper evaluating the status of behavioral economics:

> The difference between economics and psychology is that we psychologists never start our talks with assumptions that are wrong.
>
> That's because you psychologists never make any assumptions at all.

Economists would then go on to claim that when scientists claim to be proceeding on the basis of not making any assumptions, this means that they are unwittingly making implicit assumptions and that these are probably stupid ones.

It is important for students of behavioral economics to be familiar with the historical differences between the two disciplines and their implications if they are to understand the critical attitudes that are sometimes expressed by the different camps.

Although both branches of social science make use of empirical studies in order to test their theories, economists have tended to rely more on observational studies while psychologists have relied largely on experimental studies. There have been three main reasons for this.

1. Economists are primarily concerned with studying behavior, what people do; this is shown by their revealed preference in terms of what products they buy. Psychologists are primarily concerned with studying motivation, why they behave as they do.

2. It has often been impossible or impractical to use experiments in economic situations, for the researcher may lack the relevant control. Even when such control is possible, as when an economic adviser is able to influence or determine government policy, experimentation may have damaging or unethical consequences. Governments may be unwilling to experiment with tax levels (for example, based on the infamous Laffer curve) or with using different policies for different groups (for example, by giving educational vouchers to one group and general subsidies to another). Although observational studies do not allow the kind of manipulation of

relevant variables that is possible in experimental studies, economists have often been able to overcome the resulting problems by using sophisticated statistical or econometric techniques that enable them to isolate the effects of specific variables.

3. Economists have also been more concerned with studying the behavior of groups of agents, in particular markets, rather than single individuals.

As a result of these factors economists tend to shrug off criticisms of psychologists who claim that their experiments show that individuals do not act according to the assumptions of the SEM. Economists have various counter-arguments here:

1. The assumptions are merely a methodological stance; the SEM makes no claim to say anything about the underlying psychological processes of agents. This argument was discussed earlier.

2. Markets average out individual deviations in behavior; individuals who deviate will tend to be eliminated from the market by competitive forces similar to natural selection.

3. The experiments of psychologists tend to be flawed. This last accusation is discussed in the next subsection.

As already stated, the result of these differences in approach has been a significant parting of the ways between economics and psychology for much of the twentieth century. Only in the last 25 years or so has some degree of *rapprochement* been achieved, as discussed in the subsection relating to consilience.

Psychologists' methods

The experimental approach traditionally used by psychologists has significant advantages over the observational approach in terms of control over the relevant variables, allowing investigators to manipulate them in order to determine their influence directly. Thus one group of subjects may play a game of chance against a player who is shabbily dressed and deliberately acts diffidently, while another group may play the same game against a professionally dressed and confident opponent. Evidence indicates that subjects bet more against the first type of player, even though the outcome of the game is entirely governed by chance.

It is thus possible to design experiments and divide subjects into different groups to reveal a large amount of information regarding the influences of different factors that would be impossible or impractical to achieve in observational studies. However, such experiments, including those performed under the rubric of behavioral economics, are often viewed by economists as being flawed, for a variety of reasons. We now need to discuss the methodological issues related to behavioral economics in general terms.

Methodological issues

There are five main issues that have been raised relating to the methods used in behavioral economics. The first issue follows on from the discussion above, that mainstream economists often view behavioral experiments as flawed. A second issue relates to assumptions. The other three issues relate specifically to neuroeconomics, which we have mentioned as being a key tool in behavioral economics. Two of these issues are raised by Gul and Pesendorfer (2005) in their article entitled "The case for 'mindless economics,'" and the final issue has been raised by Fudenberg (2006).

1. *Experimental design*

There are three main issues here. These relate to the use of financial incentives, the use of deception, and lack of control.

a) *The use of financial incentives*

These incentives are used in order to motivate participants. They are widely used in economic experiments, but not in psychological ones. Economists tend to believe that financial incentives are vital in order to ensure that subjects behave in the same manner that they would in the real world and that they invest appropriate cognitive attention to the demands of the experiment. Psychologists frequently counter that such incentives may distort the results, by vitiating the intrinsic interest that subjects may have in participating in the experiment. Evidence is mixed here, but let us give one example that will illustrate the importance of the issue. A study by Hoffman, McCabe, and Smith (1996), using unearned rewards, had found that people acted more generously in dictator games than the SEM predicts, sharing on average 40 % of their wealth when acting in complete anonymity. However, a later study by Cherry, Frykblom, and Shogren (2002) found that when subjects earned rewards, as opposed to receiving them "as manna from heaven," the majority of them behaved in a significantly different way, acting as pure self-interested agents as the SEM would predict. Ninety-five percent of them shared none of their wealth with their partners under conditions of complete anonymity. These experiments and the nature of dictator games are discussed in more detail in Chapter 8, in terms of their implications for the concept of fairness.

b) *The use of deception*

Another criticism of many psychological experiments is that the necessary manipulation involves a deception of at least some of the subjects. A number of studies, in particular by Hertwig and Ortmann (2001), have indicated the widespread use of deception in experimental studies, with between 30% and 50% of studies published in top journals like the *Journal of Personality and Social Psychology* and the *Journal of Experimental Social Psychology* using deception.

Deception is often justified by practitioners on two grounds. First, it allows investigators to create situations that they would not otherwise be able to observe under normal circumstances, such as how people react in emergencies. Second and more important, it enables the investigator to camouflage the real purpose of the experiment from the subjects, in order to prevent them reacting strategically and producing a misleading result. This is particularly important when researching people's behavior and attitudes on sensitive social issues. For example, a study involving racial prejudice may need to be disguised in order to prevent people realizing the purpose of the experiment and reacting with a political correctness that they might not otherwise observe.

The main problem arising from the widespread use of deception is that it becomes common knowledge that psychologists use such methods, and this also influences the behavior of subjects who tend to react cynically in the knowledge that they may be deceived. Psychologists are then forced to continually search for new and naïve pools of subjects in order to obtain reliable results from their experiments. The studies of Hertwig and Ortmann indicate the increasing use of freshman students for such experiments.

c) *Lack of control*

A final problem relating to experimental design is that economists often criticize experiments performed by behaviorists for their lack of control, resulting in a misinterpretation or confounding of effects. This is particularly important when the objective is the elicitation of subjects' preferences. A good illustration of this relates to the endowment effect, discussed in Chapter 3. We will see that some studies show a strong endowment effect, with sellers demanding twice the price that buyers are willing to pay, while other studies with different experimental protocols show no endowment effect at all. Another example concerns the issue of discounting, discussed in Chapters 5 and 6. Many studies show that people discount heavily over the short-term time frame compared with the long-term one, but this effect may arise because of greater transactions costs for delayed payments compared with immediate payments. The higher short-term discount rate may therefore be a result of confounding two different effects: "pure" time preference and transactions costs. We will see that this problem can be eliminated by greater experimental control, involving the comparison of two delayed payments.

2. *A set of assumptions needs to be evaluated as a whole*

This is a recommendation of Fudenberg (2006) in his article "Advancing beyond 'Advances in Behavioral Economics.'" He observes that the normal approach in developing theories in behavioral economics has been to modify one or two assumptions in the SEM in the direction of greater psychological realism. Fudenberg points to the dangers of this step-by-step approach, particularly in the analysis of equilibrium and strategic interaction and in self-control theories. Relaxing one assumption may have a "knock-on" effect on other assumptions, making the new set inconsistent, and this needs to be taken into consideration. Therefore modelers need to take all the assumptions as a set and see how many need to be modified in order to end up with a new set that is self-consistent. This problem is examined in more detail in Chapters 6 and 7.

3. *Neuroeconomic studies are irrelevant to economics*

Gul and Pesendorfer take issue in particular with the approach of Camerer, Loewenstein, and Prelec (2005), expressed as follows:

> First, we show that neuroscience findings raise questions about the usefulness of some of the most common constructs that economists commonly use, such as risk-aversion, time preference, and altruism.
>
> (pp. 31–32)

Gul and Pesendorfer then state, "The argument that evidence from brain science can falsify economic theories is . . . absurd" (p. 10). The basis for their view is that economics makes no claims regarding the psychological or neurological processes involved in making choice decisions. They draw an analogy, by considering the reverse situation, concluding that an economic study cannot invalidate a theory relating to neuroscience, on the similar grounds that neuroscience takes no position regarding economic axioms like revealed preference.

There appears to be some misunderstanding here regarding the claims of the behaviorists. Gul and Pesendorfer are correct in saying that economics makes no claims regarding psychological processes and also that evidence from brain science cannot falsify economic theories. Models in the SEM tend to involve "as if" statements, meaning that agents behave as if a particular mental calculus was being performed. Gul and Pesendorfer explain that this is "an expositional device not meant to be taken literally." They then give an example relating to consumer behavior, where it is predicted that consumers will buy the amount of a good which equates the marginal utility of the last dollar spent with the marginal utility of the last dollar spent on other goods. This does not imply that consumers actually perform the mental processes involved, but it does make the implicit assumption that consumers aim to maximize their total utility.

This is all fine; I remarked earlier that economists and most behaviorists have no problem with such "as if" models *provided that* they make accurate predictions. However, behaviorists do not generally claim that evidence from brain science can falsify economic theories. Instead the behaviorist claim is that economic theories are often falsified by empirical studies involving economic data relating to revealed preference; in other words, they are falsified on their own terms. Where studies in brain science are useful is in understanding *why* the theories are falsified, in terms of the underlying psychological or neurological processes. These studies may then indicate that certain implicit assumptions in the "as if" statements of the SEM may be bad assumptions to make because they lead to false predictions.

A good illustration of this issue concerns credit card spending. People spend more on credit cards than if they pay cash, contradicting the SEM. Evidence falsifying the model comes from economic data. However, brain studies, like that conducted by Knutson *et al.* (2007), can help us to understand why people act in this way. There is also evidence from neuroeconomic studies that neural imaging data can be used to predict future behavior. For example, the Knutson *et al.* study shows that brain activity in different regions can predict purchasing behavior above and beyond self-report variables. Relationships between consumer preferences, prices, spending, and brain activation are discussed in more detail in Chapter 4, in connection with mental accounting.

Further evidence of the ability of neural imaging to predict economic behavior comes from a study by De Quervain *et al.* (2004). This indicated that activation of a particular neuron during one game was correlated with punishment in a different game. The De Quervain *et al.* study is discussed in more detail in Chapter 8 in relation to fairness. The finding here may have large implications for economics, since it indicates that data relating to neural states can be a better predictor of behavior than other aspects of subjects' behavior.

Although Gul and Pesendorfer (2005) maintain that brain scans are not economic phenomena and are therefore not relevant to economic theory, it seems fair to say that if they can be used to predict economic phenomena better than existing economic models then they may suggest how to construct better economic models.

We will return to the apparent conflict of claims between the two schools of thought in the next subsection related to consilience, but before that we should discuss two other main areas of dissent.

4. *Neuroeconomics is not relevant in discussions of economic welfare*
Gul and Pesendorfer argue that behaviorists not only make invalid claims of a positive nature regarding the value of neuroscientific studies, but also make invalid normative claims, in particular that the economic choices people make do not maximize their happiness. In particular they dispute the claim by Kahneman (1994) that "the term 'utility' can be anchored in the hedonic experience of outcomes, or in the preference or desire for that outcome." They also challenge the following claim of Camerer, Lowenstein, and Prelec (2005):

> If likes and wants diverge, this would pose a fundamental challenge to welfare economics.
>
> (p. 36)

behaviorists therefore tend to form conclusions regarding rationality based on this divergence, and these are discussed in detail in Chapter 9, once we have a large number of examples on which to draw.

Gul and Pesendorfer respond by saying,

> Welfare in economics is a *definition* and *not a theory* (of happiness). Therefore, the divergence between "liking and wanting" does not pose any challenge to the standard definition of welfare, no matter how the former is defined.

As a consequence of their view, behaviorists tend to take a paternalistic approach to welfare policy, according to Gul and Pesendorfer, since people need to be "prodded" in order to take actions that will make them happier.

Once again, Gul and Pesendorfer are correct in saying that the SEM has nothing to say about happiness and that it makes no normative or "therapeutic" claims in terms of helping decision-makers to make choices that will make them happier. However, contrary their claim, neuroeconomics does not try to improve an individual's objectives. It can clarify the different implications of pursuing different objectives, for example happiness and welfare, but it does not as a science propose any moral philosophy regarding what people "should" do. Individual behaviorists may of course make normative statements, as do other economists, but this is not an element of neuroeconomics *per se*. Furthermore, defining welfare purely in terms of revealed preferences does narrow down the scope of economic analysis. We will see examples in later chapters of situations where the difference between liking and wanting is significant and where preference and choice are not identical. There are important policy implications here. It is not just a matter of people making "mistakes," in terms of bad judgments based on bounded rationality, for example looking the wrong way when crossing the road in a foreign country. There are other reasons why individuals may take actions that they regret afterwards in terms of not maximizing their welfare. Decisions involving intertemporal choice frequently involve this situation; for example, experimenting with drugs and then becoming an addict, or choosing a lump-sum pension instead of an annuity. If we can analyze the reasons for these nonoptimal decisions, this can help both the individuals involved and the policy-makers. Some may still regard this is being outside the scope of economics, but, if we are concerned with the study and achievement of the optimal allocation of resources, it seems curious not to extend the SEM in ways that may better enable us to attain this end.

5. *Neuroeconomic studies may be inconclusive*
   There are many problems involved in applying and interpreting brain scans, certainly with the current level of technology. One particular problem, described by Fudenberg (2006), concerns the relationship between behavior and neural correlates. Because there is a high level of interactivity between different brain areas, it is difficult to unravel cause from effect in terms of neural processes and functions. Correlation does not imply causation. Therefore, just because there is activity in a certain part of the brain, this does not mean that this part of the brain is initiating the activity; there may be an underlying cause elsewhere, involving "upstream" neurons. Thus it is difficult to draw conclusions regarding the neural causes of behavior.

Consilience

From the birth of behavioral economics the methods used by researchers in the area have tended to combine the traditional methods used by economists with those more commonly used by psychologists. In particular, experiments have become more popular, and this has led to the development of the field of experimental economics discussed earlier. The advantages of control are clear compared with the ambiguity often resulting from observational studies. A good example is the study of bargaining situations that often result in deadlock or impasses, such as the failure of legal cases to settle before trial and labor strikes, where the concept of fairness is relevant. Mere observation of such situations in the real world often cannot lead to definite conclusions. Failure to reach agreement could be caused by agency problems, by reputation-building effects in repeated negotiations, or simply by a lack of cognitive understanding by the participants. However, by modeling the negotiation process into an ultimatum bargaining game experiment (discussed at length in Part III), it is possible to eliminate the last three possibilities and test in isolation the nature of people's concept of fairness.

So what does consilience mean, and why is it relevant? First, it is necessary to explain the origin of this term. It is perhaps best known as the title of a book by the sociobiologist E.O. Wilson, although he borrowed it from the philosopher of science Whewell, who in 1840 defined consilience as follows:

> The Consilience of Inductions takes place when an Induction, obtained from one class of facts, coincides with an Induction, obtained from another different class. This Consilience is a test of the truth of the Theory in which it occurs.

Consilience thus involves horizontal integration between disciplines, and it can relate not only to the sciences, both natural and social, but also to philosophy and the humanities in general. A couple of examples will aid an understanding of its practical application.

An example illustrated by Wilson himself concerns the problem of regulating forest reserves. Many different disciplines can provide input as far as solving this problem: ecology, economics, biology, geography, history, ethics, sociology can all aid an informed environmental policy. If any one of these disciplines is ignored, the policy is likely to prove less than optimal. Of course, given an issue of such worldwide scale, one can question the use of the term "optimal," and its meaning must be clarified in this context.

A different kind of example, more in keeping with Whewell's definition and more relevant in terms of the traditional conflict between economics and psychology, is provided by research into the role of the emotions in human decision-making. The majority of philosophers in the past, notably Kant, have held that the emotions should be kept out of decision-making, as being an enemy of reason. However, recent empirical evidence from different disciplines questions this assertion. Frank (1988), an economist, has used an essentially game-theoretic approach to conclude that emotions are a valuable aid in making optimal decisions, because they provide credible commitments. Pinker (1997), an evolutionary psychologist and psycholinguist, has arrived at the same conclusion in terms of emotions having evolved as adaptive psychological mechanisms. Damasio (1994), a neuroscientist, has again arrived at the same conclusion regarding the value of the emotions in decision-making, by studying patients with brain damage and developing a "somatic marker" hypothesis. These different kinds of approach, all making use of independent facts and methodologies, provide strong evidence against the traditional Kantian model.

The examples above indicate first that the disciplines of economics and psychology can complement each other, as the pioneering studies of Kahneman and Tversky, and Thaler have demonstrated, along with many more recent studies in behavioral economics. They also indicate that both disciplines can be further enriched by research from other new disciplines, notably evolutionary psychology and neuroscience. It is important to stress that the relationship is one of *complementarity* here, not *substitution*. This appears to be one of the concerns of Gul and Pesendorfer. Brain scans are not a substitute for studies involving revealed preference or actual behavior, but the latter cannot substitute for brain scans either in terms of the information revealed. This is not to say that brain scans are some panacea for understanding human behavior, for we have seen that their interpretation is problematic.

We can gain a further insight into the relationship between different disciplines by considering another example discussed by Gul and Pesendorfer. Section 3 of their 2005 article is entitled "Different objectives demand different abstractions." They claim that economics and psychology have different rather than similar objectives and that therefore they use different concepts and different methods. I am in agreement with this, because I do not believe it detracts from the complementarity of the different disciplines. In order to discuss this issue further we need to explore the concept of reductionism.

Reductionism

Ernest Rutherford once famously said, "All science is either physics or stamp-collecting." This statement pithily summarizes a reductionist approach to science. However, the term "reductionism" has come to take on many different interpretations over the years; thus we have, for example, ontological reductionism, explanatory reductionism, eliminative reductionism, classical reductionism, derivational reductionism, hierarchical reductionism, precipice reductionism, and "greedy" reductionism. The type of reductionism that is espoused in this book can be labeled as "explanatory and hierarchical." This version proposes that complex entities and concepts are best explained in terms of entities and concepts only one level down the hierarchy; these in turn may be explained in terms related to one level further down, and so on. An example from economics will aid an understanding of this approach, in particular what is meant by the term "hierarchy" in this context. We may seek an explanation for the poor level of economic performance of a country. The immediate cause may be the low level of productivity. We then ask why productivity is low; maybe the reason is a lack of investment. In turn, the main reason (there may be multiple causal factors here) for the lack of investment may be poor managerial practices. So far the explanations have related to phenomena at the economic level of hierarchy. When we ask why managerial practices have been poor, the explanation is likely to lie in social, political, or institutional factors, which are at a lower level of the hierarchy. These in turn may need to be explained in terms of social psychology; then explanations may become biological, then chemical, and finally we get down to physics at the bottom of the hierarchy. However, by reducing things one level at a time we can obtain explanations for phenomena at the appropriate level. Similarly, if someone wants an explanation for how an internal combustion engine works, normally they are looking for an explanation at the mechanical level, not one in terms of chemistry or particle physics.

This hierarchical approach has proved extremely successful in the physical sciences. For example, the phenomenon of light can now be explained in terms of electromagnetic radiation, and the outstanding achievement of Maxwell was in providing a unified explanation for visible light, heat, x-rays, ultraviolet rays, and radio waves.

Social scientists have been more reluctant to accept reductionism, perhaps fearing encroachment on their specialist areas by outsiders who show a cavalier disrespect for the formalities of the subject. However, to others it is unsatisfactory to be told that, for example, procrastination is just a human psychological failure, without asking why procrastination should be such a widespread phenomenon. In view of this problem behavioral economists are sometimes accused of ignoring the psychological underpinnings of their findings and presenting their accounts of people's behavior as "just-so stories." In other cases, when they do venture psychological explanations for different aspects of economic behavior, the explanations seem to be of an *ad hoc* nature, with no coherent universal framework that can embrace the different psychological phenomena. This is a problem referred to by Fudenberg (2006), when commenting that there were "too many behavioral theories, most of which have too few applications." Fudenberg compares this situation with the evolution of game theory, which until the 1970s, when the work of Nash, Harsanyi, and Selton became appreciated, had the same *ad hoc* status. This challenge is discussed further in the concluding chapter, but it is suggested at this point that the discipline of evolutionary psychology, described in more detail in the following section, may hold the key to providing a more unifying framework for behavioral economics in terms of relating the underlying psychological mechanisms.

1.4 Objectives, scope, and structure

Objectives

In view of the foregoing discussion, this book has the following major objectives:

1. Present the principles and methods of behavioral economics in a logical and amenable manner, contrasting them with those of the SEM.
2. Illustrate how the BEM is superior to the SEM in terms of power of explanation and prediction, using a wide variety of empirical examples from both observational and experimental studies.
3. Provide a critical examination of the existing literature relating to the BEM.
4. Explain the policy implications of the BEM, particularly when these differ from those of the SEM.
5. Provide a coherent psychological framework underpinning the findings of behavioral economics.
6. Indicate the way forward for the subject, in terms of future challenges and areas meriting further research.

Evolutionary psychology

While it may be hazardous to try and condense all psychological explanations into a universal protocol, there is one aspect of psychological analysis, again controversial, that we believe can be a significant aid in understanding and relating many of the different findings from empirical studies. This is the relatively new discipline of evolutionary psychology. The foundation of this area of science is that, just as our anatomical and physiological systems evolved over millions of years in the crucible of natural selection, so did the anatomy and physiology of our brains, resulting in evolved psychological mechanisms (EPMs) which are essentially mental adaptations. Our preferences and decision-making processes are therefore heavily shaped by our evolutionary past. One important implication of this, which will be explored in various aspects of the book, is that some of our EPMs may be obsolete and even harmful in our current vastly changed social and natural environment;

an often-quoted example is our nearly universal desire for sweet and fatty food. This may indeed have aided the survival of our Pleistocene ancestors, but when food is plentiful it causes obesity and disease. Readers who are interested in learning about evolutionary psychology in more detail should peruse one of the many good texts on the subject, for example that by Buss (1999). The more casual reader can be referred to *Mean Genes*, an eminently readable bedside book, written by Burnham and Phelan (2001), who combine the disciplines of economist and biologist.

Now it should be made clear from the start that it is certainly not proposed that every psychological mechanism determining behavior is of genetic origin resulting from natural selection. This caricature of evolutionary psychology, combined with the misleading label of "genetic determinism," is one that is unfortunately both pervasive and pernicious in many social sciences. There are many differences between individuals, groups, and societies that have obviously arisen for cultural reasons, and no evolutionary psychologist denies this. However, what is also striking in many of the empirical studies that will be examined throughout this book is that there are certain universal features of human, and even primate, psychology, which lend themselves to an evolutionary explanation. Such explanations will not be attempted here in terms of argument; suggestions will be made, but it is not appropriate to delve at length into the various factors that relate to whether psychological mechanisms are likely to be evolutionary or cultural.

Many economists and psychologists reject the theories of evolutionary psychology as being largely speculative. They are frequently dismissed in the social sciences as being "just-so" stories, meaning that they are not true scientific theories in terms of proposing testable hypotheses. This view is caused by two main factors: (1) it is impossible by definition to perform experiments on the past; and (2) the past record of facts is highly incomplete. I will show that this dismissal is largely unjustified and that evolutionary psychology can indeed produce testable hypotheses, many of which have been confirmed by substantial empirical evidence. Furthermore, the tendency of many economists to limit explanations to economic phenomena is even more unsatisfactory as far as "just-so" stories are concerned. For example, many readers would not be satisfied with the explanations that people tend to succumb to temptation because they have short time horizons in decision-making and that they make bad decisions when they are angry. These are also fundamentally "just-so" stories because they both beg the questions regarding *why* people have short time horizons and *why* we have seemingly harmful emotional responses like anger.

Normative aspects

Unfortunately the term "normative" is used in two main different senses by economists, causing confusion. Sometimes it is used in the sense of being opposite to positive. **Positive statements** relate to descriptions involving factual information. Such statements can be judged to be correct or incorrect, often with a margin of error, based on empirical observation. **Normative statements** in this context relate to value judgments, which are necessarily subjective and cannot be judged to be correct or incorrect empirically. An example is statement 1:

Statement 1   It is not fair that Firm A pays its workers such a low wage.

Such statements often include the words "ought" or "should"; for example, we might modify the above statement by saying as follows:

Statement 2   Firm A ought to pay its workers a higher wage.

However, care must be exercised here, because statements including these words are not always normative in the sense of involving a value judgment. An example is statement 3:

Statement 3   Firm A ought to pay its workers a higher wage if it wants to maximize profit.

Statement 3 does not involve a value judgment, and can be evaluated empirically. Of course one can question the social value of profit, but that is a separate issue.

Confusion can arise because the last type of statement is also often referred to as normative. It is perhaps preferable to label it as prescriptive, as opposed to descriptive. **Prescriptive statements** can be considered as policy implications, for individuals, firms, or governments, in terms of being guides to behavior, *assuming* a particular objective or set of values. Thus such statements, or "normative theories" as they are often referred to, tend to involve some kind of optimization. A fundamental example is the theory of expected utility maximization. Prescriptive statements in the above sense always follow logically from descriptive statements; for example, Statement 3 can be restated as follows:

Statement 4   In Firm A's situation a higher wage will maximize profit.

A more precise prescription would determine the specific level of wage that would maximize profit. Thus such prescriptive statements can also always be evaluated empirically.

Sciences in general, including social sciences like economics, are not in any privileged position in terms of making normative statements in the sense of value judgments. The privilege which scientists enjoy is that they are better able to understand the factual implications of value judgments. Thus while an economist may not have any superior "moral authority" in judging whether Firm A is acting fairly, she may be able to point out that its existing low wage strategy is likely to cause more labor unrest, higher labor turnover, and higher recruiting and training costs.

As a final point in this discussion, it is relevant to mention that there is a third category of statement that can be made, apart from positive and normative. These are **coherent statements**. A coherent statement is one that "makes sense" in terms of obeying the rules of logic and conveying some meaning. Self-contradictory statements, for example, are said to be incoherent. Good theories obviously have to be coherent; however, the coherence of a statement or theory is not judged by empirical evidence.

As far as this book is concerned we will not be concerned with the validity of normative statements as value judgments. However, we will be concerned with the question *why* people make certain value judgments; this is a psychological issue that has important policy implications in the prescriptive sense. We will also see that the SEM is essentially a normative model in this prescriptive sense, while the BEM is essentially a descriptive model. Indeed, Tversky and Kahneman (1986) claim that no theory of choice can be both normatively adequate and descriptively accurate. This statement will have to be explained and discussed in the remainder of the book.

Structure

In order to achieve the objectives described at the beginning of the section, the book is divided into five parts. Following the introduction there is a part on foundations of behavioral economics, in which the fundamental concepts of preference, decision-making under risk and uncertainty, and mental accounting are discussed. The third part of the book examines intertemporal decision-making, where costs and benefits of decisions are incurred in different time periods. The fourth part examines strategic interaction and the applications of game theory. The final part involves a discussion of rationality and a conclusion; in particular we are concerned here with achieving the sixth objective stated earlier, looking at the future of the discipline.

Within each chapter there is also frequently a typical structure. The principles and assumptions of the relevant aspects of the SEM are examined first, with a description of shortcomings or anomalies. Various behavioral models are then introduced, and these are evaluated in the light of the empirical evidence available, with comparisons being made between different models. Normative or policy implications are also discussed. Finally, some important applications of the BEM are examined in more detail in case studies at the end of each chapter.

1.5 Summary

- Behavioral economics is concerned with improving the explanatory power of economic theories by giving them a sounder psychological basis.
- The BEM relaxes the restrictive assumptions of the SEM in order to explain a wide variety of anomalies in the SEM.
- There are four main criteria for evaluating and comparing theories: congruence with reality, generality, tractability, and parsimony.
- Behavioral economics is a relatively new discipline, becoming recognized around 1980; before that time psychology had largely been ignored by economists for many decades.
- Behavioral economists use a variety of methods or approaches, based on both traditional economics and psychology, and also borrowing from those commonly used in other sciences as well. Thus both observational and experimental studies are used, and sometimes computer simulations and brain scans. This relates to the concept of consilience.
- There are various methodological issues related to the behavioral approach, and in particular to the application of neuroeonomics.
- Reductionism is a vital key to success in developing science in spite of its bad press. It is a means of relating explanations at different levels of science to each other and integrating them into a whole.
- Evolutionary psychology is an important discipline in helping to provide a unifying psychological framework for understanding the findings of behavioral economics.

1.6 Applications

Three situations where the BEM can be usefully applied are now presented. In each case it is not appropriate at this stage to engage in a detailed discussion of the issues involved, since these are examined in the remainder of the book;

instead a summary of the important relevant behavioral issues is given in an outline form. However, these applications should serve to give the reader a flavor of what behavioral economics is about in general terms.

Case 1.1   Loss-aversion in monkeys

Monkeys show the same "irrational" aversion to risks as humans

ECONOMISTS often like to speak of *Homo economicus*—rational economic man. In practice, human economic behaviour is not quite as rational as the relentless logic of theoretical economics suggests it ought to be. When buying things in a straight exchange of money for goods, people often respond to changes in price in exactly the way that theoretical economics predicts. But when faced with an exchange whose outcome is predictable only on average, most people prefer to avoid the risk of making a loss than to take the chance of making a gain in circumstances when the average expected outcome of the two actions would be the same.

There has been a lot of discussion about this discrepancy in the economic literature—in particular about whether it is the product of cultural experience or is a reflection of a deeper biological phenomenon. So Keith Chen, of the Yale School of Management, and his colleagues decided to investigate its evolutionary past. They reasoned that if they could find similar behaviour in another species of primate (none of which has yet invented a cash economy) this would suggest that loss-aversion evolved in a common ancestor. They chose the capuchin monkey, *Cebus apella*, a South American species often used for behavioural experiments.

First, the researchers had to introduce their monkeys to the idea of a cash economy. They did this by giving them small metal discs while showing them food. The monkeys quickly learned that humans valued these inedible discs so much that they were willing to trade them for scrumptious pieces of apple, grapes and jelly.

Preliminary experiments established the amount of apple that was valued as much as either a grape or a cube of jelly, and set the price accordingly, at one disc per food item. The monkeys were then given 12 discs and allowed to trade them one at a time for whichever foodstuff they preferred.

Once the price had been established, though, it was changed. The size of the apple portions was doubled, effectively halving the price of apple. At the same time, the number of discs a monkey was given to spend fell from 12 to nine. The result was that apple consumption went up in exactly the way that price theory (as applied to humans) would predict. Indeed, averaged over the course of ten sessions it was within 1 % of the theory's prediction. One up to *Cebus economicus*.

The experimenters then began to test their animals' risk aversion. They did this by offering them three different trading regimes in succession. Each required choosing between the wares of two experimental "salesmen". In the first regime one salesman offered one piece of apple for a disc, while the other offered two. However, half the time the second salesman only handed over one piece. Despite this deception, the monkeys quickly worked out that the second salesman offered the better overall deal, and came to prefer him.

In the second trading regime, the salesman offering one piece of apple would, half the time, add a free bonus piece once the disc had been handed over. The salesman offering two pieces would, as in the first regime, actually hand over only one of them half the time. In this case, the average outcome was identical, but the monkeys quickly reversed their behaviour from the first regime and came to prefer trading with the first salesman.

In the third regime, the second salesman always took the second piece of apple away before handing over the goods, while the first never gave freebies. So, once again, the outcomes were identical. In this case, however, the monkeys preferred the first salesman even more strongly than in the second regime.

What the responses to the second and third regimes seem to have in common is a preference for avoiding apparent loss, even though that loss does not, in strictly economic terms, exist. That such behaviour occurs in two primates suggests a common evolutionary origin. It must, therefore, have an adaptive explanation.

What that explanation is has yet to be worked out. One possibility is that in nature, with a food supply that is often barely adequate, losses that lead to the pangs of hunger are felt more keenly than gains that lead to the comfort of satiety. Agriculture has changed that calculus, but people still have the attitudes of the hunter-gatherer wired into them. Economists take note.

Issues

This ingenious experimental study illustrates three particularly important aspects of behavioral economics:

1. *Methods*
   The experimental approach, traditionally followed by psychologists, is used here, in order to achieve a degree of control that would be impossible to gain through mere observation. Three different trading regimes are used in order to compare responses and test the basic hypothesis of loss-aversion. Note the use of deception, although it is unlikely in this case to cause a general increase in cynicism among the population of capuchin monkeys available as subjects.

2. *Evolutionary psychology*
   The purpose of the experiment is not just to test whether capuchin monkeys have loss-aversion, but more importantly to test whether the widely observed loss-aversion in humans is likely to have an evolutionary explanation. The fact that loss-aversion has been observed in many different countries and societies constitutes evidence of an evolutionary origin, but the observation of the same characteristic in a fairly closely related species is even stronger evidence. This is a typical type of experiment carried out by evolutionary psychologists to test their hypotheses. It is also notable that the issue regarding why loss-aversion should be an evolved psychological mechanism or adaptation is also raised. This issue will be discussed in more detail in Chapter 3 on PT.

Case 1.1 *continued*

3. *Rationality*

This concept is examined in detail in Chapter 9, and we will see that it is a highly ambiguous term, which can be used in many different senses. However, in the current context, a "rational" individual behaving according to the SEM should have no preference between the two "salesmen" in the second and third trading regimes, since the outcomes from each are ultimately identical. The "irrationality" observed in the monkeys is explained by the concept of loss-aversion, an important aspect of PT. Thus the BEM is better able to explain the behavior observed in the experiment.

Source: *The Economist,* June 23, 2005

Case 1.2 Money illusion

The issue of money illusion is one that has been much discussed by economists, since the days of Irving Fisher (1928). It has been defined in various ways, which has been the cause of some confusion, but a brief and useful interpretation has been given by Shafir, Diamond, and Tversky (1997) in a classic article:

A bias in the assessment of the real value of transactions induced by their nominal representation.

It should be noted that such an interpretation does not limit money illusion to the effects of inflation, as will be seen.

Economists have tended to take an attitude to the assumption of money illusion that Howitt describes in the *New Palgrave Dictionary of Economics* (1987) as "equivocal." At one extreme there is the damning quotation by Tobin (1972): "An economic theorist can, of course, commit no greater crime than to assume money illusion." The reason for this view is that money illusion is basically incompatible with the assumption of rationality in the SEM. Thus a rational individual should be indifferent between the following two options:

Option A   Receiving a 2% yearly pay increase after a year when there has been inflation of 4%.

Option B   Receiving a pay cut of 2% after a year when there has been zero inflation.

In each case the individual suffers a decrease in pay in real terms of 2%. However, some empirical studies indicate that people do not show preferences that are consistent with rationality in the traditional sense and that money illusion is widespread.

Perhaps the best-known study of this type is the one quoted earlier by Shafir, Diamond, and Tversky (SDT). This used a questionnaire method, asking people questions about a number of issues related to earnings, transactions, contracts, investments, mental accounting, and fairness and morale. We will concern ourselves here with questions related to earnings and contracts, since these will illustrate the main findings.

An earnings-related situation was presented as follows:

Consider two individuals, Ann and Barbara, who graduated from the same college a year apart. Upon graduation, both took similar jobs with publishing firms. Ann started with a yearly salary of $30 000. During her first year on the job there was no inflation, and in her second year Ann received a 2 % ($600) raise in salary. Barbara also started with a yearly salary of $30 000. During her first year on the job there was a 4 % inflation, and in her second year Barbara received a 5 % ($1500) increase in salary.

The respondents were then asked three questions relating to economic terms, happiness, and job attractiveness:

1. As they entered the second year on the job, who was doing better in economic terms?
2. As they entered the second year on the job, who do you think was happier?
3. As they entered the second year on the job, each received a job offer from another firm. Who do you think was more likely to leave her present position for another job?

Seventy-one per cent of the respondents thought that Ann was better off, while 29 % thought that Barbara was better off. However, only 36 % thought Ann was happier, while 64 % thought that Barbara was happier. In the same vein, 65 % thought that Ann was more likely to leave her job, with only 35 % thinking Barbara was more likely to leave.

A contracts-related question was designed to test people's preferences for indexing contracts for future payment to inflation. From a seller's viewpoint this would be preferred by decision-makers who were risk-averse in real terms, while those who were risk-averse in nominal terms would prefer to fix the price now. The situation featured computer systems currently priced at $1000; sellers could either fix the price in 2 years at $1200, or link the price to inflation, which was expected to amount to 20 % over the 2 years. The options were framed first of all in real terms (based on 1991 as the current year) as follows:

Contract A   You agree to sell the computer systems (in 1993) at $1200 a piece, no matter what the price of computer systems is at that time. Thus, if inflation is below 20 % you will be getting more than the 1993-price; whereas, if inflation exceeds 20 % you will be getting less than the 1993-price. Because you have agreed on a fixed price your profit level will depend on the rate of inflation.

Contract B   You agree to sell the computer systems at 1993's price. Thus if inflation exceeds 20 % you will be paid more than $1200, and if inflation is below 20 % you will be paid less than $1200. Because both production costs and prices are tied to the rate of inflation, your "real" profit will remain essentially the same regardless of the rate of inflation.

When the options of fixing the nominal price and index-linking were framed as above in real terms, a large majority of the respondents (81 %) favored the option of index-linking, indicating risk-aversion in real terms. However, when the equivalent options were framed in nominal terms, as shown below, a different result was obtained:

Case 1.2 *continued*

Contract C   You agree to sell the computer systems (in 1993) at $1200 a piece, no matter what the price of computer systems is at the time.

Contract D   You agree to sell the computer systems at 1993's price. Thus instead of selling at $1200 for sure, you will be paid more if inflation exceeds 20%, and less if inflation is below 20%.

In this case a much smaller majority (51%) favored the index-linking option, which now seemed more risky.

When the contract situation was reversed, so that respondents were now in a buying situation, it was also found that the framing of the options affected the responses. Once again respondents were risk-averse in nominal terms when the options were framed in nominal terms and risk-averse in real terms when the options were framed in real terms.

Issues

The discussion of money illusion raises a number of important issues in behavioral economics. Some of these are similar to the previous case:

1. *Methods*
   Economists have criticized the validity of the SDT results on two main grounds. First, they have doubts about the questionnaire methodology, suspecting that there may be considerable differences between what people say they might do in a hypothetical situation and what they would actually do in the real world when motivated by economic incentives. Second, they point out that it is not sufficient to show money illusion at the level of individual behavior; it must also be present at the aggregate level in order to have real economic significance. Individual differences may cancel each other out, thus resulting in no overall economic effect.

2. *Rationality*
   It is usually argued that money illusion is not rational at the level of the individual. However, it is notable from the SDT study that the majority of the respondents realized that Ann was better off in economic terms, even though a majority thought that Barbara was happier. This perceived decoupling of absolute economic welfare from happiness is not necessarily irrational, and will be discussed further in the Chapter 9. Furthermore, it may well happen that a majority of individuals do not themselves suffer from money illusion at the individual level, but may believe that others do. Therefore, in order to understand the existence of money illusion at the aggregate level, it is necessary to examine the strategic interaction of individuals in the economy.

3. *Mental accounting*
   It is notable that the SDT study not only attempts to test for money illusion in a descriptive sense, it also goes some way toward trying to explain its existence in psychological terms. This involves in general aspects of mental accounting, more specifically the theory of multiple representations. These aspects are discussed in detail in Chapter 4, but at this stage we can outline the theory

by saying that it proposes that people tend to form not just a single mental or cognitive representation of information, but several simultaneously. Thus we may form both a nominal and a real mental representation of different options, but, depending on how they are framed, one or other may be salient. Thus the concepts of framing effects and saliency are important. The SDT study maintains that normally the nominal representation tends to be salient, since it is cognitively easier to handle, demanding less information. This therefore tends to give rise to money illusion. Later on we will see that there are similarities here with types of optical illusion.

4. *Strategic interaction*
As already stated, it is important to consider strategic interaction in order to understand money illusion at the aggregate level. If some economic agents act irrationally, for example by raising prices without any inflationary cause, then it may be optimal for other agents who are rational to react in the same way and "follow the crowd." This effect is of vital importance in stock markets, as noted by many authors. Strategic interaction also has to take into account the possible existence of "super-rationality," as discussed by Fehr and Tyran (2003). These aspects are all examined in Chapter 7.

Case 1.3 Altruism

The Joy of giving

Donating to charity rewards the brain

PROVIDING for relatives comes more naturally than reaching out to strangers. Nevertheless, it may be worth being kind to people outside the family as the favour might be reciprocated in future. But when it comes to anonymous benevolence, directed to causes that, unlike people, can give nothing in return, what could motivate a donor? The answer, according to neuroscience, is that it feels good.

Researchers at the National Institute of Neurological Disorders and Stroke in Bethesda, Maryland, wanted to find the neural basis for unselfish acts. They decided to peek into the brains of 19 volunteers who were choosing whether to give money to charity, or keep it for themselves. To do so, they used a standard technique called functional magnetic resonance imaging, which can map the activity of the various parts of the brain. The results were reported in this week's *Proceedings of the National Academy of Sciences*.

The subjects of the study were each given $128 and told that they could donate anonymously to any of a range of potentially controversial charities. These embraced a wide range of causes, including support for abortion, euthanasia and sex equality, and opposition to the death penalty, nuclear power and war. The experiment was set up so that the volunteers could choose to accept or reject choices such as: to give away money that cost them nothing; to give money that was subtracted from their pots; to oppose donation but not be penalised for it; or to oppose donation and have money taken from them. The instances where money was to be taken away were defined as "costly". Such occasions set up a conflict

---

Case 1.3 *continued*

between each volunteer's motivation to reward themselves by keeping the money and the desire to donate to or oppose a cause they felt strongly about.

Faced with such dilemmas in the minds of their subjects, the researchers were able to examine what went on inside each person's head as they made decisions based on moral beliefs. They found that the part of the brain that was active when a person donated happened to be the brain's reward centre—the mesolimbic pathway, to give it its proper name—responsible for doling out the dopamine-mediated euphoria associated with sex, money, food and drugs. Thus the warm glow that accompanies charitable giving has a physiological basis.

But it seems there is more to altruism. Donating also engaged the part of the brain that plays a role in the bonding behaviour between mother and child, and in romantic love. This involves oxytocin, a hormone that increases trust and co-operation. When subjects opposed a cause, the part of the brain right next to it was active. This area is thought to be responsible for decisions involving punishment. And a third part of the brain, an area called the anterior prefrontal cortex—which lies just behind the forehead, evolved relatively recently and is thought to be unique to humans—was involved in the complex, costly decisions when self-interest and moral beliefs were in conflict. Giving may make all sorts of animals feel good, but grappling with this particular sort of dilemma would appear to rely on a uniquely human part of the brain.

Issues

1. *The nature of economic behavior*

   Economic behavior is not just about monetary transactions. "Altruistic" acts and spiteful acts also are relevant. We need to understand the basis of such acts in order to explain and predict human behavior in a wide variety of different situations, such as donating to charity, labor strikes, lending the neighbor one's car, and remonstrating with people who litter the streets.

2. *Fairness and social preferences*

   This aspect is closely related to the first one. We need to understand the importance of inequality-aversion, the perceived kindness of others, reciprocity, and the intentions of others if we are to predict behavior in social situations when strategic interaction is important. This area is covered in Chapter 8.

3. *The role of neuroscience*

   The study described above demonstrates clearly how useful neuroscience can be in explaining behavior that cannot easily be explained by the SEM. In particular it shows that "self-interest" needs to be understood in a broad context. Charitable acts are thus self-interested acts because they make us feel good, contrary to the common narrow understanding of self-interested acts. It is important to realize that only by performing neuroscientific studies involving techniques like fMRI can we establish firm evidence regarding the real motivations behind "altruistic" and spiteful acts, since people often deny these motivations, and even "honest" introspection may not reveal them. This aspect is discussed in more detail in the next chapter and also in the concluding chapter.

Source: *The Economist* print edition, October 12, 2006

Part II
Foundations

2 Values, Attitudes, Preferences, and Choices

2.1 The standard economic model

Consumer behavior

The standard model of consumer behavior is very simple. As Varian (2006) expresses it, "people choose the best things they can afford" (p. 33). This is essentially a constrained optimization situation in mathematical terms. The objects of consumer choice are referred to as consumption bundles, and these relate to a complete list of the goods and services that are involved in the particular choice problem being considered. In a generalized situation we also need a description of when, where, and under what circumstances these goods would become available. People care not only about what goods are available now, but what will be available at a later date; they also care more for a bottle of water if they are in the middle of a desert than if they are in the Antarctic. Any bundle of goods can be described in the most simple terms as (x_1, x_2) or just X, where x_1 denotes the amount of one good and x_2 the amount of another good, or the amount of all other goods. By limiting the number of parameters to just two it is possible to use a graphical method of representation and analysis.

Preferences

In the standard model it is assumed that consumers can rank bundles according to their desirability. If a consumer definitely wants an x-bundle rather than a y-bundle then it is said that he or she **strictly prefers** the x-bundle to the y-bundle. This can be written as $(x_1, x_2) \succ (y_1, y_2)$. Alternatively, if a consumer is **indifferent** between the two bundles, this means that they have no preference for either bundle over the other. This relationship is usually described by the expression $(x_1, x_2) \sim (y_1, y_2)$. Finally, if a consumer prefers or is indifferent between the two bundles, we say that he or she **weakly prefers** (x_1, x_2) to (y_1, y_2), and this is written as $(x_1, x_2) \succeq (y_1, y_2)$.

Preference relations are meant to be operational notions. Thus it is also assumed in the SEM that choice is determined by preference; this is important since it is choice that is directly observable, not preference. If a consumer chooses a particular bundle, it is assumed that this bundle is preferred to another bundle if that other bundle was both available and affordable. This is what is meant by the concept of **revealed preference**.

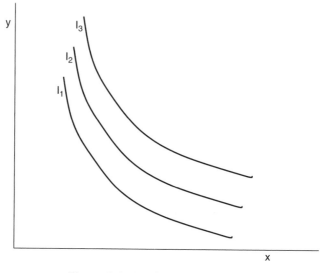

Figure 2.1   Indifference curve map

Indifference curves

The theory of consumer choice is often illustrated using a graphical approach involving indifference curves. An indifference curve represents different combinations of two goods to which the consumer is indifferent, that is which yield the same total utility. Figure 2.1 is an indifference map, showing a number of indifference curves, with curves further away from the origin representing bundles involving greater quantities of goods; these bundles are therefore preferred to those on lower indifference curves. Thus any combination of goods on curve I_2 is preferred to any combination on curve I_1. However, nothing is specified regarding how much more these goods are preferred; thus we can say nothing regarding the relative sizes of the difference between I_2 and the difference between I_3 and I_2. Indifference curves are normally drawn as downward-sloping and convex to the origin; this is because of certain assumptions that are described in the next section.

Equilibrium

Indifference curve maps can be used to illustrate the notion of consumer equilibrium. It is assumed that consumers have a **budget constraint** relating to the amount of money that they have available to spend on the relevant consumption bundles. This budget constraint can be represented in terms of the following inequality:

$$p_x x + p_y y \leq m$$

where m is the available budget. The budget constraint is shown in Figure 2.2 as the line going through points A, C, and B. Although the budget is sufficient to buy combinations A and B, these are not optimal combinations since they are not on the highest indifference curve that can be reached. Combination C is the optimal combination, where the consumer purchases the bundle (x_1, y_1). This situation can be generalized: any optimal point of consumption will occur at a point of tangency between an indifference curve and a budget constraint line. Setting the slopes of these two curves equal gives the condition that the consumer should spend so that the marginal utility of the last dollar spent on each good is the same. This condition can be further generalized to apply to any number of goods in a consumption bundle.

The exposition of consumer equilibrium in the standard model often uses the term "marginal utility," but in fact this is not essential. The slope of an indifference curve can also be expressed in terms of the marginal rate of substitution (MRS) of one good for another. The MRS_{xy} represents the amount of y that a consumer is prepared to give up in order to get one more unit of x. Thus the equilibrium condition amounts to consuming a combination such that the MRS is equal to the ratio of the prices: $MRS_{xy} = p_x/p_y$. The advantage of this form of exposition is that it avoids the thorny concept of utility. A detailed discussion of utility is deferred until a later section.

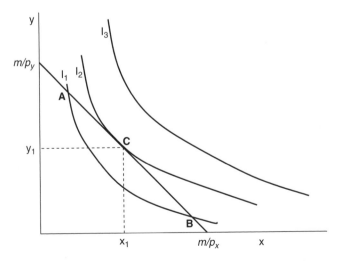

Figure 2.2 Indifference curves and consumer equilibrium

2.2 Axioms, assumptions, and definitions

Axioms

In discussing the foundation of the SEM, in particular in terms of how it relates to consumer preference, it is essential to distinguish between the basic axioms of the model and other important assumptions that often accompany it. While the former are fundamental to the model, the latter are somewhat flexible and are varied in different circumstances. This distinction is relevant in discussing the weaknesses of the SEM in the following section. We will also see that there is a distinction between descriptive and normative axioms. This aspect is discussed in the next chapter.

There are four main axioms relating to consumer preference:

1. *Completeness*
   A person can compare any two consumer bundles, X and Y. Such a comparison must lead to one of three possible mutually exclusive outcomes:

   a) Basket X is preferred to basket Y; we have seen that this can be written as $(x_1, x_2) \succeq (y_1, y_2)$.
   b) Basket Y is preferred to basket X; we have seen that this can be written as $(y_1, y_2) \succeq (x_1, x_2)$.
   c) The consumer is indifferent between the two baskets; we have seen that this can be written as $(x_1, x_2) \sim (y_1, y_2)$.

   This is referred to as the completeness principle because the preferences cover all possible outcomes.

2. *Transitivity*
   If three different baskets, X, Y, and Z, are considered, a consumer who prefers basket X to basket Y and who prefers basket Y to basket Z must also prefer basket X to basket Z. This can expressed as follows:

   $$\text{if } (x_1, x_2) \succeq (y_1, y_2) \text{ and } (y_1, y_2) \succeq (z_1, z_2), \text{ then } (x_1, x_2) \succeq (z_1, z_2)$$

   Similarly, if a consumer is indifferent between basket X and basket Y and who is also indifferent between basket Y and basket Z must also be indifferent between basket X and basket Z.

3. *Reflexivity*
   Any bundle is at least as good as itself: $(x_1, x_2) \succeq (x_1, x_2)$. This axiom is generally regarded as being trivial.

4. *Revealed preference*

This axiom can come in either weak or strong forms: If (x_1, x_2) is revealed directly/indirectly as preferred to (y_1, y_2), and the two bundles are not the same then (y_1, y_2) cannot be revealed to be directly/indirectly preferred to (x_1, x_2).

Assumptions

In addition to the above axioms there are four other main assumptions, often referred to as principles, which frequently accompany the SEM. These assumptions are particularly relevant in situations where there is uncertainty; they are therefore discussed in more detail in the next chapter in relation to expected utility theory (EUT), which is the aspect of the SEM that is relevant in such situations. We will also see that EUT involves certain additional assumptions, apart from the ones discussed below. Tversky and Kahneman (1986) claim that the following substantive assumptions can be ordered in terms of a hierarchy of increasing importance as far as their normative appeal is concerned. Thus the cancellation condition has been challenged by many theories, but the invariance condition is absolutely necessary for any normative theory.

1. *Cancellation*

This is the principle that any state of the world that results in the same outcome regardless of one's choice can be cancelled or ignored. It is sometimes referred to as a minimal approach to decision-making, as opposed to a topical or comprehensive approach (discussed later). Thus, if X is preferred to Y then the prospect of winning X if it rains tomorrow (and nothing otherwise) should be preferred to the prospect of winning Y if it rains tomorrow, because the two prospects both result in the same outcome (nothing) if there is no rain tomorrow. This assumption is also consistent generally with the marginalist approach of the neoclassical economists.

2. *Dominance*

This condition is simpler and stronger than the first one, and therefore is more fundamental to the SEM. It states that if option X is better than option Y in one state and at least as good in all other states then option X is dominant over option Y and should be chosen. This is related to the reflexivity axiom discussed earlier, but is not as strong a condition.

3. *Extensionality*

The SEM generally assumes that people have the same attitude to a particular object and attribute the same value to it, however that object is described, given a certain level of information about that object. Thus people should have the same attitude to a particular kind of packaged meat, whether it is described as having 5 % fat or as 95 % fat-free. This is again related to the reflexivity axiom.

4. *Invariance*

This condition is essential for any normative theory. It states that different representations of the same choice problem should yield the same preference. This therefore rules out "framing effects," discussed at length in the next few chapters. It states that the relation of preference should not depend on the description of the options (**description invariance**) or on the method of elicitation (**procedure invariance**). Without stability across equivalent descriptions and equivalent elicitation procedures, a person's preferences cannot be represented as utility maximization in the standard EUT.

There is also the assumption in the SEM that consumers maximize utilities. This is usually taken as both a descriptive and a normative statement: people *do* behave in this way, and *ought* to behave in this way, to maximize their welfare. This normative aspect is related to the concept of rationality. However, rationality is a highly complex issue, incorporating many factors, so I am deferring its discussion until Chapter 9. The assumption of utility maximization is implied in the discussion of equilibrium conditions earlier. Under conditions of uncertainty the assumption is extended to become **expected utility maximization**, discussed in the next chapter. Of course, bearing in mind the discussion in the previous chapter regarding the nature of assumptions, this condition does not imply that consumers consciously evaluate utilities in a quantitative manner in all decisions. For economists the model is satisfactory so long as consumers behave *as if* they are maximizing utilities.

Certain other assumptions are invoked in particular situations; these are discussed in the relevant context in the remaining sections and chapters. However, we need to be aware of the differing status of these assumptions; some are really not a necessary component of the SEM and can easily be relaxed without compromising the model. For example, the SEM is sometimes said to involve assumptions regarding three characteristics of indifference curves. The first of these has already been stated as an axiom, involving transitivity of preferences. The second characteristic is that the curves are downward-sloping; this implies that more of a good is always preferred to less of a good. This principle is referred to as the **monotonicity** of preferences, and can be expressed in technical terms thus: if (x_1, x_2) is a bundle of goods and (y_1, y_2) is a bundle of goods with at least as much of both goods and more of one, then $(y_1, y_2) \succ (x_1, x_2)$. This assumption follows directly from the definition of a **good** that it is a commodity where more of it is preferred to less. Some commodities, like pollution and garbage, are referred to as "**bads**." The assumption of monotonicity is not essential to the SEM; for example, when people reach satiation the principle no longer applies. The third characteristic of indifference curves is that they are convex to the origin. This is sometimes referred to as the assumption of **convexity** of preferences, but it is not really an essential assumption either; rather it follows from the **law of diminishing marginal utility**. This law states that, as more of a good is consumed within a certain time period, additional units of consumption will eventually yield less marginal utility. The law is in the nature of an empirical regularity rather than being an assumption in analysis. It is this characteristic of convexity which determines the inverse relationship between price and quantity demanded in the conventional demand curve, although such a relationship can also be derived by other means (Becker 1976).

Definitions

Before discussing the weaknesses of the SEM in terms of consumer preference, it will help to clarify the situation if definitions are now given of the four terms that form the title of this chapter: "attitude," "value," "preference," and "choice." It should be stated at the start that the definitions which follow are not universally agreed upon or followed by either economists or psychologists, but they are widely shared.

1. *Attitude*

    This has been usefully defined as "a psychological tendency that is expressed by evaluating a particular entity with some degree of favour or disfavour" (Eagly and Chaiken 1996). This concept has a broader range of application than the concept of preference, as will be seen shortly. Attitudes relate to any entity that people can like or dislike. Entities include physical objects, living beings, and abstract concepts, involving anything that can elicit an affective response. It is important to realize that objects of attitudes are **mental representations**, not objective states of affairs. This helps us to understand the violations of the invariance and extension principles discussed above. People have a different mental representation of meat with 5 % fat compared with meat that is 95 % fat-free.

    A related characteristic of attitudes is that they tend to involve **judgment by prototype**. This refers to the phenomenon that global judgment of a category is determined primarily by the relevant properties of a prototype and is based on the older concept of a **representation heuristic** (Tversky and Kahneman 1971, 1983; Kahneman and Tversky 1972, 1973). This kind of judgment leads to various kinds of extension bias, as we will see. An example, discussed in more detail in the next section, involves **duration neglect**: people tend to recall past experiences in terms of a prototypical moment, rather than as the total experience. Thus they may ignore the length of an unpleasant experience like a colonoscopy, recalling instead the moment of most intensive pain.

2. *Value*

This is a problematical term, for it is widely used in two different senses. In one sense our values determine our attitudes, while in the other sense our attitudes determine our values. In the first sense, values refer to tastes or likes/dislikes: we may have a taste for cauliflower, a taste for roller coasters, or a taste for making charitable donations. Thus values in this sense include moral values. One can of course take the question further back, following a reductionist theme, and ask what determines a person's values; however, important as this issue is, it goes beyond the scope of this book and into the details of evolutionary psychology.

The second sense of the term "value" refers to the quantitative evaluation of an object which results from an attitude. The determination of value involves judgment. This sense of the term "value" is what economists conventionally mean by the term "utility", whether referring to experienced or decision utility. These terms will be discussed in more detail in the following two sections.

3. *Preference*

As we have already discussed, economists are conventionally more concerned with preferences, in particular so-called "revealed preferences," while psychologists may be more concerned with attitudes. In the standard SEM it is assumed that attitudes determine preferences, but that is not necessarily true.

4. *Choice*

This involves an action on the part of the subject/consumer, involving some kind of decision. The SEM generally assumes that choice is simply revealed preference. We will see, however, that preferences and choices are not necessarily identical and that choices need not be a reflection of attitudes and judgments (Tversky, Sattath, and Slovic 1988; Tversky and Griffin 2000).

There are other terms related to these that also need to be clarified, such as "pleasure," "happiness," and "well-being." These were discussed briefly in the previous chapter, but to shed further light on them, and on the four terms above, we need to examine the different types of utility. This is done after a discussion of the weaknesses of the SEM.

2.3 Weaknesses of the standard economic model

At this point we can now consider weaknesses of the SEM, in terms of both anomalies and incompleteness. As explained in the previous chapter, it is important to distinguish between these two problems. The first relates to situations where the SEM makes inaccurate predictions, while the second relates to situations where the SEM has nothing to say, making no predictions at all. The second area is more controversial, since some economists argue that these areas of "silence" do not represent a weakness at all; as we have also seen in the previous chapter, it is claimed that economics has no interest in such areas. This issue is not a matter of testing a theory by empirical evidence; it involves a subjective value judgment regarding what economics *should* be concerned about. The first area discussed below involves one such area.

Happiness is a three-act tragedy

Perhaps the most obvious weakness in terms of omission concerns the nature of happiness. The evolutionary psychologist and psycholinguist Steven Pinker (1997) has described happiness as a three-act tragedy. This claim has the following elements:

1. Happiness involves an interpersonal comparison of one's perceived well-being with that of others. Although self-reported happiness appears to increase sharply with income at any point in time (Easterlin 2001), studies in both the United States (Myers and Diener 1995) and Japan (Easterlin 1995) indicate that self-reported happiness in general has not increased over several decades in spite of a several-fold increase in real income. Pinker quotes the words of Gore Vidal: "it is not enough to succeed. Others must fail."

2. Happiness also involves an intrapersonal comparison of one's perceived well-being with one's previous well-being. This observation therefore invokes the notion of a **reference point**, a key element of Prospect Theory which is discussed in detail in the next chapter. A frequently quoted study regarding this issue is that of Brickman, Coates, and Janoff-Bulman (1978), which found that, after a period of adjustment, lottery winners were not much happier than a control group, and paraplegics not much unhappier.

3. Happiness and unhappiness are not symmetrical reflections of gain and loss. The impact of losses is greater than equivalent gains. This observation invokes the concept of **loss-aversion**, another key element of PT. Pinker quotes tennis star Jimmy Connors: "I hate to lose more than I like to win."

As discussed in the previous chapter, this weakness does not represent an anomaly of the SEM, since economists generally issue disclaimers as far as the concept of happiness is concerned, only being concerned with a particular definition of welfare.

In the SEM there is much consideration of **Pareto efficiency**. This measure of efficiency is typically expressed that nobody can be made better off without making anyone else worse off. However, it is normally assumed in the SEM that **Pareto efficiency** is a desirable goal. As Varian (2006) states,

> If there is some way to make some group of people better off without hurting other people, why not do it?

> (p. 613)

The second act of the happiness tragedy indicates why we might not want to do it. Making some people better off will automatically make others worse off in terms of happiness, if not in terms of welfare in the narrow sense. This has very important political implications as far as government policy is concerned. The growing gap between the pay of bosses and that of workers in the United States is a case in point. In general the economic welfare of workers has not suffered over the last 20 years, but they feel worse off knowing that their bosses are so much better off than they are. Although the disparity is largest in the United States, resentment at "fat cat" CEO pay has been expressed in many other countries also.

Discrepancies between objective causes and subjective effects

There appear to be discrepancies between objective measures of sources of comfort/discomfort and reported measures of subjective feelings. Again, many defenders of the SEM would argue that reported measures of subjective feelings are not economic phenomena and that therefore they are of no concern to economists (Gul and Pesendorfer 2005, p. 40). However, when such feelings do or can affect later decisions, this is of relevance to economics. A study by Redelmeier and Kahneman (1996) of patients undergoing colonoscopies illustrates this phenomenon well. The patients were asked to report the intensity of current pain on a scale of 0–10 at minute intervals over a period up to 69 minutes. However, those patients who suffered more pain for longer periods did not necessarily have a worse recollection of the experience as a whole. Instead it seemed that the most important determinant of post-experience evaluation was a combination of the maximum pain suffered at any point and the mean pain suffered during the last three minutes. This finding has become known as the **Peak-End rule**. It has been confirmed by later studies, including one by Katz, Redelmeier, and Kahneman (1997), where the examining physician left the colonoscope in place for a minute after the end of the examination in half of the sample of patients. This extended the duration of the totality of discomfort of the procedure, but was in itself not very painful. Those patients with the extended treatment involving more total discomfort and pain gave a more favorable retrospective evaluation of the experience. This would affect later preferences in terms of type of treatment, and this is contrary to the predictions of the SEM, supporting instead behavior predicted by the Peak-End rule.

Expectations effects

Another weakness concerns the effect of expectations. There is some evidence, mentioned in the last chapter, that high expectations of happiness can lead to disappointment. This emerges in particular from the study by Schooler, Ariely, and Loewenstein (2003) regarding people's plans for the millennium celebration of 2000. Those people who spent the most time, effort, and money tended to be the least satisfied. It seems that the reference point phenomenon is again relevant here. Of course in this case it can be argued that the disappointment, or lower utility, after the event may be more than offset by the higher utility associated with the anticipation of the event. This leads to a consideration of a further related omission from the SEM, relating to **anticipatory utility**. This issue is discussed in more detail in Chapters 5 and 6, since it involves discounting, but the essential point is that anticipation of pleasure can itself be pleasurable, with the result that people may defer the pleasurable experience in order to prolong the anticipatory utility. It is this factor that may at least partly explain the saying that revenge is a dish that is better served cold (it is also better for being planned rather than hastily delivered in an emotional state, as will be explained in Chapter 9).

Addiction and abstention

In the conventional model it is assumed that more consumption of a good gives more total utility. The SEM does take into account "bads," like garbage or pollution, where more consumption decreases total utility, but these are phenomena where increasing consumption is monotonically bad, meaning increasingly bad throughout the range of consumption. For some people, however, there are goods which give *too much* pleasure, and *excessive* consumption is associated with various problems in terms of health, and time and money spent. Addiction is a major factor in this context. The phenomenon of addiction can cover a wide range of goods: alcohol, tobacco, and other recreational drugs are the most commonly cited examples, but one can also include food in general (or particular types of food like junk food), gambling, sex, computer games, and indeed any activity involving a significant degree of excitement.

The psychological mechanisms relating to enjoyment of these goods are complex, being of a double-edged nature. However, one factor that deserves mention at this point is the concept of **diagnostic utility**. A number of studies have found that people infer their happiness from their actions in a **self-signaling** manner (Campbell and Sawden 1985; Elster 1985, 1989; Bodner and Prelec 1997, 2001). The last study quotes as an example a person who takes a daily jog in spite of the rain, who may view that activity as a gratifying signal of willpower, dedication, or future well-being. Bodner and Prelec continue, "For someone uncertain about where he or she stands with respect to these dispositions, each new choice can provide a bit of good or bad 'news.'" One implication of this concept is that people who fear that they may be, or become, addicted to a good may be better off, and feel themselves better off, abstaining from consumption completely. To indulge even slightly may reveal themselves to indeed have an addictive personality, and the acknowledgment of such weakness may make it impossible to break the addiction. These concepts of diagnostic utility and self-signaling may well help to explain the unfortunate and all-too-common phenomenon of "falling off the wagon," with its vicious circle of low self-esteem and compensatory indulgence. The issue is discussed in more detail in Case 2.1.

Endowment effects

These effects are discussed in more detail in the next chapter, but the essence of the phenomenon is that utility is not independent of possession. Those people who have acquired a good in some way, through either purchase or gift, tend to value it more highly than others. For example, a study by Kahneman, Knetsch, and Thaler (1990) endowed subjects with either a mug or a pen on a random basis. Both groups were allowed to switch their good for another at a minimal transaction cost, and if preferences were independent of endowment, one would expect the sums of the fractions of subjects swapping their mug for a pen and vice versa to be equal to one. One extreme situation would be where everyone valued the mug more than the pen, with 100 % switching from pens to mugs and 0 % switching in the other direction, and the other extreme would be where everyone valued the pen more than the mug, with 100 % switching from mugs to pens and 0 % switching in the opposite direction. However, it was observed that only 22 % of the subjects traded. This experiment confirms the finding of Knetsch (1989), where subjects were reluctant to exchange mugs for chocolate bars and vice versa. The main psychological factor underlying endowment effects is **loss-aversion**, discussed in the next chapter in the context of PT. We will also see that the evidence regarding endowment effects is mixed (List 2004; Plott and Zeiler 2005).

Framing effects

These effects, which are discussed in more detail in the next two chapters, are one of the most important phenomena in behavioral economics, violating the invariance principle. Numerous studies have found that people's responses, in terms of values, attitudes, and preferences, depend on the contexts and procedures involved in eliciting these responses. For example, when subjects have been asked to rate their overall level of happiness, their responses have been influenced by a prior question regarding the number of dates they have had in a recent time period. This is an example of an **anchoring effect**, another phenomenon discussed in later chapters, where people's responses are "anchored" to other phenomena in their consciousness, however irrelevant these might appear to be.

Framing effects are particularly important since they account for a high incidence of **preference reversal** (Slovic and Lichtenstein 1983; Tversky, Slovic, and Kahneman 1990). This phenomenon relates to situations where people favor option A when a question or problem is posed or framed in one way but favor option B when the same problem is posed in a different way. In order to illustrate preference reversal, we will take a classic example, sometimes referred to as the "**Asian disease**" problem. People are informed about a disease that threatens 600 citizens and asked to choose between two undesirable options (Tversky and Kahneman 1981). In the "positive frame," people are given a choice between (A) saving 200 lives with certainty, and (B) a one-third chance of saving all 600 with a two-thirds chance of saving nobody. Most people prefer A to B here. In the "negative frame," people are asked to choose between (C) 400 people dying with certainty, and (D) a two-thirds chance of 600 dying and a one-third chance of nobody dying. In this case most people prefer D to C, in spite of the fact that A and C are identical results or "prospects," and B and D are identical results. As well as illustrating framing effects and preference reversal, this example also illustrates loss-aversion (saving lives is seen as a gain, while dying is seen as a loss). We will see in the next chapter that the nature and implications of the Asian disease problem are a controversial subject area, because of the confounding of framing and reflection effects.

2.4 Nature of utility

In order to shed light on the weaknesses of the SEM, we now need to examine the concept of utility. This involves a discussion of the concept's evolution over time, the issue of measurement, and the different types of utility that are relevant in decision-making.

Historical evolution

The concept of utility is one of the most basic building blocks in economic theory. In particular, it underlies the theory of consumer choice. In this chapter, however, we will only be concerned with riskless choice; the effects of risk and uncertainty will be discussed in the next chapter.

The assumption that the objective of consumers is expected utility maximization is the most fundamental single component of the SEM, dating back to Jeremy Bentham (1789). It should be noted that, strictly speaking, the term "expected" implies an element of risk or uncertainty, the discussion of which is deferred until the next chapter. In Bentham's original usage, the term "utility" referred to the experiences of pleasure and pain, which "point out what we ought to do, as well as what we shall do." Thus utility has a **hedonic** characteristic, which later researchers, notably Kahneman (2000), refer to as **experienced utility**. We shall see later in this section that the meaning of the term "utility" has changed since Bentham's time and is now regarded as outmoded by many economists who tend to favor the concept of **decision utility**. As discussed in more detail later, this meaning of utility refers to the weight assigned to an outcome in a decision and is revealed by people's choices. It is this revealed preference meaning of utility that is generally used in the SEM.

This modern concept of utility appears to have two obvious advantages over Bentham's concept. First, it is easier to measure, since decision utility can be inferred from the choices and actions that people take. Second, it no longer implies a commitment to a hedonistic philosophy. Sen (1987) in particular has been at pains (excuse the hedonistic pun!) to point out that the maximization of experienced utility is not always what people are trying to achieve, and his opinion is shared by many economists and psychologists. Indeed, some economists would go further and say that the study of people's objectives is outside the realm of economics and belongs in psychology or even philosophy. This issue is discussed further later in the chapter and in particular in Chapter 9, since it relates to the concept of rationality.

So where does this leave us as far as the concept of utility is concerned? The main point is that Bentham's hedonistic concept of utility may well still be appropriate in terms of determining our choices and actions, as well as conferring the additional advantage of allowing a more parsimonious model of behavior. This argument will become clearer as we examine the various types of utility later in the section.

Cardinal and ordinal utility

Early economists believed that utility could be measured quantitatively, in terms of an aribitrary unit called "utils," using a ratio scale with a zero point. Thus if consumption of basket A yielded 10 utils and basket B yielded 20 utils then it could be said that basket B yielded twice as much utility as basket A. Some economists even considered that utility could be added interpersonally, meaning that a utility for John of 10 utils could be added to a utility for Jane of 20 utils, yielding a total utility of 30 utils.

Modern economists tend to disfavor any **cardinal** measure of utility, meaning a measure involving an interval scale. Instead, they favor an **ordinal** measure, where baskets of commodities are simply ranked according to preference. This view implies that statements like "basket A has twice as much utility as basket B" are meaningless, and certainly interpersonal additions of utility are invalid. The use of an ordinal measure as opposed to a cardinal measure has the advantage of involving fewer assumptions regarding the nature of utility. We have already seen that the equilibrium condition relating to the behavior of consumers in terms of utility maximization can be expressed in terms of ordinal utility using the concept of the MRS. The law of diminishing marginal utility can also be expressed in ordinal terms.

We will now see that the concept of utility is a complex one, having many differentiated meanings and determinants. By examining these we will attain a much greater understanding of observed behavior, and in particular the shortcomings described in Section 2.3.

Decision utility

This is the type of utility usually discussed by economists, since it is easiest to measure in terms of revealed preference. It is important to note that decision utility does not therefore necessarily reflect attitudes or judgments. A study by Tversky and Griffin (2000) illustrates this point. Sixty-six undergraduate students were presented with the following information:

Imagine that you have just completed a graduate degree in communications and you are considering 1-year jobs at two different magazines.

(A) At Magazine A, you are offered a job paying $35 000. However, the other workers who have the same training and experience as you do are making $38 000.

(B) At Magazine B, you are offered a job paying $33 000. However, the other workers who have the same training and experience as you do are making $30 000.

Approximately half the students were asked which job they would choose, while the other half were asked which job would make them happier. The first question relates to decision utility while the second relates to hedonic or experienced utility. In this case the experienced utility is expected in the future, and it appears that people try to imagine what it would feel like to experience those states, involving the formation of an attitude. However, when people are asked to make a choice or decision, they tend to search for reasons or arguments to justify their choice. This difference was reflected in the survey results: 84 % of the subjects chose (A), the job with the higher absolute salary and lower relative position, but 62 % of the subjects thought that (B), the job with the lower absolute salary and higher relative position, would make them happier. In this sense, then, it could be claimed that people preferred (B), thus indicating a distinction between choice or revealed preference on the one hand and actual preference in terms of happiness on the other. Why do people choose an option that they think will make them less happy? There are various possible reasons that we will have to explore.

Another discrepancy between choice (decision utility) and attitude (experienced utility) arises when the object of choice/attitude has many attributes. For example, the consideration of a car may involve the attributes of safety, fuel economy, size, durability, and performance (to name just a few). The standard decision-making approach involves two steps: (1) determine values for each attribute, using some kind of scale; and (2) determine weights for each attribute, in order to compare them. For example, a loss of one mile to the gallon in terms of fuel economy may be equivalent to two cubic feet of boot space. There may also be certain minimum requirements for each attribute. However, it has been shown, for example by Tversky, Sattath, and Slovic (1988), that this procedure is more relevant in determining attitudes or judgments; when it comes to preference, the most important attribute is weighted more heavily, presumably because it is a more convenient rationale for choice (Tversky and Kahneman 1973). This bias is sometimes referred to as the **prominence effect**.

This effect may also be explained by the **Somatic-Marker Hypothesis (SMH)**, proposed by the neuroscientist Damasio (1994). He points out the problems involved in the conventional utility maximization model, in terms of both the amount of time involved and the other cognitive difficulties described by Tversky and Kahneman, and concludes that people can still make good, and quick, decisions based on "gut feeling." In essence, Damasio is referring to the existence of visceral factors that are discussed in Chapter 9 in the context of rationality; his SMH proposes that these factors create a "somatic marker," an unpleasant gut feeling when a bad outcome connected with a given response option comes to mind. The somatic marker

> forces attention on the negative outcome to which a given action may lead, and functions as an automated alarm signal which says: Beware of danger ahead if you choose the option which leads to this outcome. The signal may lead you to reject, *immediately*, the negative course of action and thus make you choose among other alternatives. The automated signal protects you against future losses, without further ado, and then allows you *to choose from among fewer alternatives*.

Thus this mechanism is a first stage in the decision-making process, which Damasio believes probably increases both the accuracy and the efficiency of the process. He has observed that patients with damage to the prefrontal cortex of the brain, where this process appears to occur, tend to be handicapped in many real-life decisions; for example, the choice of who to befriend, who to have as a marriage or business partner, and what to pursue as a career. By using only "pure reason" as opposed to "practical reason" they take too long to make many decisions, and end up making many mistakes which ultimately reduce their well-being.

In conclusion it can be said that sometimes decision utility, as illustrated by revealed preference, will cause us to make bad decisions in terms of our happiness. However, in other circumstances, taking into account the SMH, and indeed any subconscious factors involved in decision-making, people may make good decisions even though utility maximization may not be involved as a conscious mental process at all. Of course this particular phenomenon does not contradict the SEM; people may be performing in an "as if" manner.

Experienced utility

So far experienced utility has been described as a unified concept. However, Kahneman (2000) draws a useful distinction between **remembered utility**, after the experience, and **real-time utility**, during the experience. These are measured in different ways and are relevant for different purposes.

a) Remembered utility is measured using a **memory-based approach**; this involves a retrospective evaluation of past experience. The concept is therefore subject to bias, in particular the application of the Peak-End rule. As already seen in connection with the colonoscopy studies by Katz, Redelmeier, and Kahneman (1997), a prolongation of the duration of pain at a lower level of intensity can lead to a more favorable evaluation, violating the principle of dominance. This can also be relevant in decision-making, if people base decisions on remembered past utility or disutility.

b) Real-time utility is measured using a **moment-based approach**; this is a more difficult procedure to implement, since it involves a continuous monitoring of the subjects. For example, in the colonoscopy studies the subjects were asked to rate their pain on a scale of 0 (no pain at all) to 10 (intolerable pain) every 60 seconds. An example relating to two patients is given in Figure 2.3. This moment-based approach can also be used to derive what Kahneman refers to as **total utility**, which in turn can be used as a measure of "objective happiness," under certain assumptions, as will be discussed in the next section.

Endowment and contrast effects

An important theory regarding happiness and well-being (not necessarily the same thing as we will see) is that people judge their level of these based on the concepts of **endowment** and **contrast** effects (Tversky and Griffin 2000). It should be noted that the endowment effect in this context is not the same kind of endowment effect referred to earlier, where the acquisition of goods causes the acquirer to value the goods more highly than expected. In the words of Tversky and Griffin,

> The endowment effect of an event represents its direct contribution to one's happiness or satisfaction. Good news and positive experiences enrich our lives and make us happier; bad news and hard times diminish our well-being.

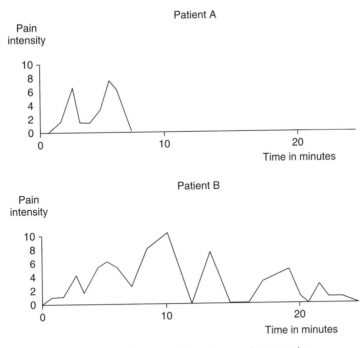

Figure 2.3 Moment utility of two colonoscopies

The contrast effect is an indirect effect that works in the opposite direction:

> A positive experience makes us happy, but it also renders similar experiences less exciting. A negative experience makes us unhappy, but it also helps us appreciate subsequent experiences that are less bad.

Contrast effects are particularly important in societies where people are generally becoming more affluent over time, and in this context are often referred to as **treadmill effects**. They are responsible for the second act of Pinker's three-act tragedy described earlier.

There are two main theories explaining the existence of treadmill effects. The oldest theory explains them in terms of **adaptation** (Helson 1964; Brickman and Campbell 1971). This is a hedonic response, which can be most easily seen in physiological terms. When subjects immerse one hand in cold water and the other in hot water for a period of time, and then immerse both hands in the same container of lukewarm water, they experience the strange sensation of one hand feeling warm (the one that was previously in cold water) and the other hand feeling cold (the one that was previously in hot water).

This theory has been used to explain why both lottery winners and paraplegics appear to adjust rapidly to their changes in circumstances.

However, not everyone is convinced by the adaptation theory as far as such explanations are concerned. Frederick and Loewenstein (1999) have proposed a number of reasons why reported happiness may not be reliably measured on the scales used. Kahneman (2000) proposes a different mechanism by which treadmill effects can be explained, using the term "**satisfaction treadmill**." This explains the phenomenon in terms of an **aspiration effect**. Kahneman explains this effect by using an example of a graduate student who is constrained by her income to eating mediocre dishes when she goes to a restaurant. When she takes a lucrative job she can afford to consume food of a higher quality, and her overall utility increases for a time. However, after a transition period, we observe that her satisfaction returns to its previous level. Her aspiration level has increased, and her utility is influenced by her aspiration level; other things being equal, the higher the aspiration level, the lower the utility. Alternatively, we can say that there is no longer a contrast between the dishes she is consuming now and the ones that she was consuming a while ago, just after her income had increased.

Two points should be noted regarding this aspiration effect. Kahneman refers to the satisfaction treadmill as being distinct from the hedonic treadmill. However, while the mechanism involved is different, it can also be claimed that the aspiration effect is still hedonic in nature. The second point is that the aspiration effect may involve a **ratchet effect**. Further research needs to be done in this area, but it may be that people find it easier to adjust their aspirations upwards rather than downwards. The concept of loss-aversion is relevant here.

The endowment and contrast theory (ECT) has some interesting applications. For example, room surroundings have been found to affect people's general satisfaction and their satisfaction with their current housing situation in a way that is incompatible with conventional theory but compatible with the ECT (Schwarz et al. 1987). Subjects were required to spend an hour either in an extremely pleasant room (spacious, nicely furnished, and decorated with posters and flowers) or in an extremely unpleasant room (small, dirty, smelly, noisy, and overheated). Subjects who were placed in the pleasant room reported higher overall life satisfaction than those in the unpleasant room, showing the dominance of the endowment effect as far as general satisfaction or well-being is concerned. However, subjects placed in the unpleasant room reported higher satisfaction with their housing than those in the pleasant room, showing the dominance of the contrast effect in the context of a relevant standard of comparison. Thus Tversky and Griffin conclude,

A specific event, therefore, is likely to have a significant contrast effect in the domain to which it belongs, and little or no contrast effect in others.

Anticipatory utility

As mentioned earlier, people gain hedonic utility from the anticipation of events in the future, for example by looking forward to a holiday or dreading a visit to the dentist. This anticipatory utility is based on a person's expected or **predicted utility**, meaning their belief about the future experienced utility of an event. Again endowment and contrast effects are relevant. Playing the lottery presents an interesting application, since this type of behavior is not readily explained by EUT, as discussed in more detail in the next chapter. Unrealized hopes and fears can give rise to positive or negative endowment in terms of anticipatory utility. The probability of winning a lottery is very low, which means that the failure to win does not cause much disappointment. Therefore, as Tversky and Griffin (2000) state, "the dream of becoming an overnight millionaire could produce enough pleasure to offset the mild disappointment of not winning the lottery." When the positive endowment effect outweighs the negative contrast effect, people can enjoy playing the lottery even when they do not win. Another possible explanation of people playing the lottery is given in the next chapter. It should be noted that the contrast effect appears to be highly sensitive to the probability of winning or losing. As the probability of winning increases, the costs of the disappointment of losing (the contrast effect) appear to increase more quickly than the benefits of hope of winning (the endowment effect). The implication of this is that, for a given expected value, people should tend to prefer long-odds situations rather than short-odds – they have sweeter dreams and milder disappointment.

Residual utility

Whereas anticipatory utility looks forward to future events, residual utility relates to pleasure or pain felt at later periods of time in separate episodes. This phenomenon arises because utility profiles may be concatenated or disjunctive. For example, a person may gain anticipatory utility regarding going on holiday in Hawaii for a month before the actual event, then enjoy the holiday for a week, and then maybe suffer a contrast effect when they return to work. In addition, maybe a month later, they may feel another "utility boost" related to the same holiday experience, when they reminisce with friends. These later episodes may be repeated at various intervals after the original experience to which they relate.

Diagnostic utility

This aspect of utility has already been mentioned as an anomaly in the SEM. Diagnostic utility refers to the situation where people infer their utility from their actions. It was seen that the phenomenon that is relevant here is the process of self-signaling, which is particularly important for people who are uncertain where they stand in terms of certain personal attributes, for example the possession of strong willpower. Thus, when we consider the situation of someone deciding whether they should have an alcoholic drink, we should not just consider the experienced or hedonic utility of the good consumed, we should also consider the utility to be inferred from the action of consumption, in terms of signaling the vice of a weak will or the virtue of a strong will. It may be that the negative diagnostic utility of an action may outweigh the positive expected experienced utility related to the good consumed. In this case the person will abstain from consumption. It will be seen in the first case study at the end of the chapter that this concept has widespread applications.

2.5 Measurement of utility

Total utility and objective happiness

Ultimately, it would be desirable if an enriched model of consumer preferences could be developed; this model would have to be considerably more complex than the SEM, to take into account the shortcomings and different types of utility so far described. The model must also take into account the relationship between utility and happiness, and this necessitates using some kind of conversion scale as far as measurement is concerned. The principles involved in this process will now be examined, before moving on to discuss the very considerable practical difficulties.

Kahneman (2000) argues that it is the concept of **objective happiness** that is relevant for many policy decisions, at the individual, group, or governmental level. Objective happiness is based on the concept of total utility, which in turn can be derived from the summation of moment utility, assuming a number of important conditions or criteria for measurement. We have already seen that remembered utility is not a good guide to actual experienced utility because of biases like the Peak-End rule. Before examining the criteria for measurement, it is worthwhile considering the significance of this difference between remembered and moment-based utility. It is generally argued that people base their decisions on predicted utility, or future expected utility, and in familiar situations this tends to be based on past experienced remembered utility. Thus people's decisions may be biased, failing to achieve maximum real-time utility measured using a moment-based approach. For example, a person may remember a particular colonoscopy (the longer one profiled in the lower graph in Figure 2.3) as being less painful than another one (the shorter one profiled in the upper graph in Figure 2.3), and if they are unfortunate enough to have to decide which type to have on a further occasion, they may choose the longer type, in spite of the shorter type causing less total real-time pain. Therefore we can say that remembered utility may be more relevant in terms of explaining actual decision-making, meaning that remembered utility is more relevant in a **descriptive model**. However, it is moment-based utility that is more relevant in a **prescriptive or normative model**, when we are interested in what people *ought* to do in order to maximize utility. We shall return to this point in the discussion of policy implications in the next section.

Dimensions of utility

The conventional SEM model treats utility as being a one-dimensional variable. There are a number of objections to this. For one thing, neurological research has shown that pain and pleasure are registered and processed in different parts of the brain (Cacioppo, Gardner, and Berntson 1999), and can be activated simultaneously. They do not simply cancel each other out, but there is evidence that they inhibit each other. For example, it has been shown that watching pleasant pictures of food or smiling babies reduces the startle response to a loud sound, whereas watching disgusting pictures increases the startle response (Lang 1995).

Furthermore, a major finding of research on hedonic or affective experience is that two dimensions are relevant. Apart from the valence (good to neutral to bad), the degree of arousal (from actively frenetic to passively lethargic) is important (Russell 1980; Stone 1995; Plutchik and Conte 1997; Russell and Carroll 1999; Warr 1999). There is a difference, for example, between the experience of joyful enthusiasm one might derive from a roller-coaster ride and the serene pleasure one might derive from a hot tub after a hard day at the office. Both experiences confer positive utility, but of a different nature. We will return to this issue shortly in the discussion of criteria, specifically relating to independence.

At this point we can note that hedonic or affective state can be reported in terms of an **affect grid**. This is a two-dimensional diagram in which subjects report their state by marking a particular point on the two dimensions of valence and arousal; such a grid is represented in Figure 2.4, with four different examples of affective states, one in each quadrant.

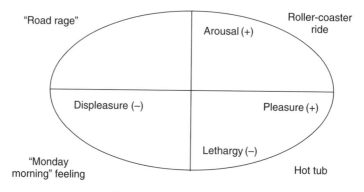

Figure 2.4 An affect grid

Criteria for measurement

We can now concern ourselves with measuring the total utility of a particular experience, since it has been persuasively argued, notably by Kahneman (2000), that this is the relevant variable representing objective well-being. The term "objective" will be explained at the end of this section. Kahneman describes six conditions that must be satisfied in order to make intrapersonal and interpersonal comparisons of experiences.

1. *Inclusiveness*

   All aspects of an experience that affect utility should be taken into account. This means that anticipatory utility from looking forward (or dreading) an event and residual utility from reminiscing about a past event should be taken into account. Diagnostic utility should also be factored into the measurement.

   It is often objected at this point that defining happiness in terms of the above utilities does not capture all the elements of well-being; in particular it is claimed that such a narrow hedonic view does not take into account any moral conception of what constitutes "the good life" (Nussbaum and Sen 1993). Kahneman (2000) concludes, "Objective happiness is only one constituent of the quality of human life, but it is a significant one." The problem here is that some commentators are not considering the concept of happiness in a sufficiently broad context. Many writers are prepared to include various psychological criteria of well-being in a measure of "good mood" or "enjoyment of life," such as the maintenance of personal goals, social involvement, intense absorption in activities, and a sense that life is meaningful (Czikszentmihalyi 1990; Argyle 1999; Cantor and Sanderson 1999; Fredrickson 2000). If such criteria are considered relevant for happiness, why exclude the feeling of living a virtuous life? There is no reason to consider feelings of being virtuous, or sinful, as being in any important respect different from other psychological factors. The guilt one may feel resulting from not helping a friend causes a similar uneasy sensation of loss of self-esteem to the guilt that may ensue from not taking one's usual daily exercise. Ultimately, moral feelings must also make themselves conscious through neurophysiological processes of the same kind as other psychological factors. This is of course a contentious issue, but it is argued that there is a tendency for people in the social sciences, and even more in the humanities, to have an approach that is insufficiently reductionist; indeed reductionism is often explicitly and vigorously opposed in these disciplines. It is suggested here that the reason for this is that the "reductionist program" is frequently misunderstood. Describing or explaining moral sensations in terms of physiological processes does not in any way deny the existence of these sensations, or explain them away, any more than describing the internal combustion engine in terms of molecular interactions denies the fact that the pistons drive and rotate the crankshaft. It is a question of explaining phenomena at a different level. The essential problem of the anti-reductionists is that by divorcing our "higher" moral feelings from physiological processes in a dualistic manner they fail to explain how such feelings come to be felt in the first place. This issue of dualism is discussed further in Chapter 9.

As a final point here I should say that current progress in neuroscience is beginning to provide physiological correlates of moment utility (affective valence). The difference between levels of electrical activity in the left and right hemispheres of the prefrontal cortex appears to meet most criteria for such a measure (Davidson 1998). It has been found that positive and negative affect are associated with greater activity in the left and the right prefrontal regions respectively. It has also been shown that stable individual differences in the characteristic value of this difference are highly correlated with measures of temperament and personality, both in adults (Davidson and Tomarken 1989; Sutton and Davidson 1997) and in babies (Davidson and Fox 1989). These observations are also relevant to the fourth condition below.

2. *Ordinal measurement across situations*

It must be possible at least to rank experiences as far as moment utility is concerned. This means that it must be possible to compare different types of experience, like burning one's finger on a stove and becoming irritated in a traffic jam, on a common scale. This causes us to return to the concept of the affect grid with its two dimensions. It may be difficult enough to compare and rank two kinds of pain, physiological and psychological, without the additional complication of taking degree of arousal into account. Ultimately, as Kahneman (2000) states, this issue can only be determined empirically.

Ideally, a cardinal scale of measurement would be desirable. In this case total utility could be derived from moment-based utility by calculating the area under a utility profile, as in Figure 2.3, representing the temporal integral of the utility function. However, in order to perform the necessary calculation, it is necessary to have an equivalency scale so that pain intensity and time can be conjoined into a single measure. For example, it may be that 1 minute at pain intensity 6 is equal to 2 minutes at pain intensity 5. This type of calculation is performed in certain practical situations, like medical decision-making, which uses the concept of QALYs (Quality Adjusted Life Years). QALYs are derived from judgments of equivalence between periods of survival that vary in duration and in level of health. For example, 2 years of survival at a QALY of 0.5 are considered equally desirable as 1 year in normal health (Broome 1993). The introduction of a cardinal scale also involves an assumption that is possible to find an "idealized observer" who can make appropriate judgments of equivalence. Although the problems here appear great, the point is that in reality decisions like what type of medical treatment to give must be made. The challenge is to make these decisions on the basis of criteria that will maximize the happiness of those involved. It is not really very helpful for economists to throw their hands up in dismay and say that they are not actually concerned with this aspect of the allocation of resources.

3. *Distinctive neutral point*
A neutral point means that there is no pleasure and no pain. In the colonoscopy studies discussed there is a natural neutral or zero point. This feature anchors the scale and is vital for a cardinal measurement of utility using a ratio scale. Under the latter assumption it is meaningful to say that two time-pleasure units give twice as much utility as one time-pleasure unit.

4. *Interpersonal comparability*
The scale must allow comparisons between individuals and groups. This is vital for public policy decisions. However, there are a number of complications that have to be considered. Perhaps the most obvious is the subjectivity problem: different subjects may register affect on different personal scales. However, once again neurophysiological studies come to our aid. Research has shown that there is substantial agreement between subjects when it comes to giving self-reports of pain associated with an objectively measured

intensity of stimulus. For example, different women gave similar self-reports of pain related to the measured strength of labor contractions during childbirth (Algom and Lubel 1994).

Another problem that arises with interpersonal comparisons relates to the first part of Pinker's three-act tragedy: if one individual or group gains utility, this may automatically confer disutility to other individuals or groups in a nonobvious way. Increasing the salaries of one group of workers may make others feel less satisfied, even though their salaries may be unchanged in absolute terms.

5. *Time neutrality*
All moments are equally weighted in measuring total utility. This treatment is dissimilar to the treatment of time in either decision utility or remembered utility. With decision utility the utility of later experiences is weighted less heavily because it is discounted, as explained in Chapters 5 and 6. On the other hand, with remembered utility the utility of later experiences may be weighted more heavily, due to the bias of the Peak-End rule.

6. *Independence of experiences*
Kahneman (2000) refers to this feature as **separability**, but there is actually a broader condition that is involved here. Kahneman refers specifically to the phenomenon where the ordering of events has an effect on utility. For example, the utility of a tennis game may be greater before a heavy lunch compared with afterwards. In this case the separability or independence condition is violated, since the utility of the experience is not independent of the time when it is experienced. The fact that utility is best represented in at least a two-dimensional manner aggravates this problem, since the active–passive dimension is particularly sensitive to time sequence. For example, when I am at the gym I derive pleasure from listening to music with a high level of energy at the upper end of the active scale. When I am driving home such music would be overstimulating; instead I prefer something relaxing and calming (which in turn would be wholly inappropriate in a gym environment). Thus our preferences can change significantly according to time of day, and in more general terms according to our mood. The assumption that is generally made in the SEM is that intrapersonal judgments and preferences are fairly stable. This does not seem to be justified in terms of practical experience, and this has very important implications that need to be explored in the next section.

2.6 An expected psychological utility model

It is now necessary to come to certain conclusions regarding the status of the SEM in terms of consumer preferences. It is obviously easier to criticize the model and point out weaknesses than it is to replace it with a superior model. In fact current researchers in behavioral economics have not attempted to do this in any comprehensive way, and it is not intended to do such a thing here. However, what can be achieved is to indicate what kind of model or models would prove to be a worthy successor. The term "expected" is used in this context because when we make decisions the utility gained from them is realized in the future. It should be noted, however, that we are still making some simplifying assumptions at this stage; in particular we are ignoring risk and uncertainty, the effects of intertemporal factors on choice, and strategic interaction, all of which are discussed in the remaining parts of the book.

Foundations in evolutionary neurobiology

As explained earlier, it is necessary to take a reductionist approach in order to understand the ultimate causes of the various behavioral aspects observed. The brain did not evolve in order to maximize utility, well-being, or hedonic pleasure. The forces of natural selection have caused the brain to be designed as a system that maximizes **biological fitness**. This term can be understood as meaning our ability to survive and reproduce. Evolutionary biologists also use the term "inclusive fitness," where the ability extends to our kin, since that increases the overall likelihood of "spreading our genes." Thus we can state that the individual is prompted to maximize hedonic pleasure as a means to the ultimate end of maximizing biological fitness. Actions that result in hedonic pleasure have in the past generally improved biological fitness, while actions causing displeasure or pain have been an indication that our biological fitness is threatened. Furthermore, it is important to understand that this hedonic pleasure relates not only to conventional goods, but also to what we can call "moral sentiments." If we do not recognize this, we will become entangled in the problem of dualism, which, as we will see in Chapter 9, still bedevils the thinking of some neuroscientists, as well as economists and philosophers.

There are two essential problems caused by the mechanistic nature of the evolutionary process, causing our hedonic systems to be easily hijacked:

1. *Time lags*

   Lags exist between the optimal design and the demands of the current environment. A good example is our liking for fatty foods, which improved our biological fitness in the past, but is now a serious threat given their easy availability and the sedentary nature of many of our lives.

2. *Use of heuristics*

These rules are useful shortcuts to decision-making, particularly given time constraints and bounded rationality, but they are prone to error. For example, after several consecutive tosses of a coin come up heads, many people think that a tail is then more likely on the next toss.

After this summary of the underlying evolutionary factors, we can now turn our attention to consider more specific aspects of an appropriate behavioral model.

Nature of the model

There are a number of important features of a desirable model that emerge from the preceding discussions:

1. *All-inclusivity*

The most fundamental point is that there is a unifying theme to all the factors we have so far considered. **Psychological utility** can be viewed as an all-inclusive concept that takes into account all different affects we may feel, whether due to purely physical pleasures or displeasures or whether due to aspects of self-esteem, fulfillment, belonging, or having a purpose in life. Ultimately, all these factors have to be weighed against each other on a single scale when we make decisions. For example, on leaving a restaurant we have to decide whether to tip the waiter or save the money; is our guilt for not tipping worth the money saved? The decision-making process can be reduced to a neurophysiological level, for after the decision is made, even if it is made unconsciously, a stream of actions or physiological responses will ensue (reaching for one's wallet, or not). Of course, with the current state of knowledge in neuroscience, there is an enormous amount that is still unknown regarding these highly complex processes, but we do know that they must occur, and research is gradually uncovering more about them.

2. *Dynamic preferences*

Our preferences are not stable, in particular because affect is not a one-dimensional variable. Although we always prefer pleasure to displeasure (even masochists gain pleasure from pain), the kinds of activities and goods that confer pleasure constantly vary according to our mood, time of day, and preceding activities.

3. *Distinction between attitudes and preference*

Any model must take into account this difference if it is to successfully explain and predict behavior. We have to be able to explain why it is that people appear to make choices that they think may make them less happy, such as choosing a job with a higher absolute salary but lower relative salary. Although much further research needs to be done in this area, one speculation is offered here. The higher absolute salary may be chosen because of the certainty factor; we know that it will make us better off, but we may only think it possible that we will come to be unhappy later. Thus there are elements of both risk and uncertainty and intertemporal choice that may be involved in this type of decision.

4. *Distinction between descriptive and prescriptive models*

The appropriate model to use depends on the purpose of its use. If we wish to describe or predict actual decisions then a descriptive model is appropriate, and we have seen that this involves the concepts of decision utility or predictive utility, often based on remembered utility, and preference rather than attitude. However, for policy decisions aiming to maximize welfare, it is more appropriate to use a prescriptive or normative model, involving moment utility and total utility, based on attitudes rather than preferences.

2.7 Policy implications

The factors discussed in this chapter have a number of implications for public policy which may not be intuitive, and often contradict current legal practices and government policies in many countries. Some areas that have been investigated by empirical studies are discussed below.

Jury awards of punitive damages

The psychology underlying these awards was investigated by Kahneman, Schkade, and Sunstein (1998). Three main questions were asked about scenarios relating to compensatory damages in product liability cases:

1. How outrageous was the defendant's behavior?
2. How severely should the defendant be punished?
3. How much should the defendant be required to pay in punitive damages?

The first two questions required a rating on a seven-point scale, while the third question required a dollar amount to be stated. It is notable that correlations between the evaluations are high, always at least 0.80. Since the outrage rating appears to be a direct measure of the affect evoked by cases of personal injury, the implication is that the amount of punitive damages awarded is determined largely by the outrage factor, determined by attitude rather than economic preference.

In addition to this general finding, the same authors found that respondents experienced a degree of outrage that was independent of the amount of harm caused. Thus it seems that we judge behavior in terms of outrageousness, regardless of its consequences. However, when it comes to judging punitive intent and assessing damages, the second and third questions, the consequences of the behavior are of great importance. This finding does seem intuitive, since punishment contains a retributive element based on the harm caused. A further finding of the study was that the defendant's ability to pay was relevant as far as the third question is concerned. Large firms with more resources were penalized more heavily in terms of damages, although the size of the firm had no effect on evaluations of outrageousness or punitive intent. This finding again seems plausible, since a $10 million payment represents a large amount for a small firm, whereas it is a small one for a large firm.

A further finding illustrates the importance of **context-dependence,** which can cause preference reversals. It is commonly observed that there is a high correlation between punitive awards and compensatory damages awarded. When there is a large amount of financial harm, compensatory damages tend to be high, leading to high punitive damages. This is likely to be caused by the anchoring effect of the high compensatory damages. On the other hand, in cases of personal injury punitive damages tend to be low, since compensatory damages are also low. It should be noted that in real life these cases are determined in isolation, by different juries. However, it is very probable that outrage is higher in cases of personal injury (such as a child being burned by a faulty product) than in cases of business fraud. This presents a possibility of testing the theory that degree of outrage is relevant in evaluating the size of punitive award. An experiment by Kahneman, Schkade, and Sunstein (1998) placed subjects in the position of having to judge two cases together as well as independently; in both situations compensatory damages had already been awarded, $500 000 for the personal injury case and $10 million for the financial harm. As predicted, subjects who only judged one case awarded more punitive damages in the financial case (median = $5 million) than in the personal injury case (median = $2 million). However, a large majority (75%) of the respondents who judged the two cases together assessed larger awards in the personal injury case, resulting in a significant preference reversal (median of $2.5 million for personal injury, $0.5 million for the financial harm). This result confirms two important theories in behavioral economics: the existence of context-dependence and anchoring effects, and the influence of affect on attitudes and evaluations.

In response to these anomalies, Sunstein, Kahneman, and Schkade (1998) have proposed certain reforms which "would require jurors to do what they can do well, not what they can do poorly." Their conclusion was that jurors are good at combining normative evaluations with empirical facts, meaning that they have sound intuitions about the appropriate severity of punishment. However, their ability to translate these intuitions into dollars appears to be weak; therefore the authors proposed that the jury make graded recommendations relating to the severity of punishment to the judge, who would then perform the task of translating this intent into a dollar amount.

The Contingent Valuation Method (CVM) and public goods

The **CVM** is often used as a means of eliciting the value the people place on public goods, including nonuse goods such as the continued existence of rare species. The valuation produced is then used as a basis for public policy decisions. CVM sometimes relies on asking people to report their **stated willingness to pay** (**SWTP**) to achieve various results, although more recently superior indirect techniques of valuation have been used, which may reduce some of the problems discussed below. Although asking people to value public goods, like cleaning up a lake, may superficially seem quite dissimilar to asking jurors to estimate punitive damages, there are important similarities and problems.

Studies have shown similar results in terms of high correlations between various evaluation methods when attitudes toward protecting the environment are involved (Kahneman and Ritov 1994; Payne *et al.* 1999). For example, Kahneman and Ritov (1994) used four different measures to evaluate an intervention to protect the peregrine falcon from pollution:

1. Stated willingness to pay (SWTP) for the intervention.
2. Degree of political support for the intervention.
3. Personal satisfaction expected from making a voluntary contribution.
4. Importance of the problem as a public issue.

The last three measures were all based on a rating scale. As with the punitive damages situation, the high correlations between the different measures suggest that the measures are all a reflection of an underlying attitude or affect. There are two important implications of this relating to the use of SWTP in terms of obtaining biased and unreliable results:

1. *Anchoring effects*

   As we have already seen, these are prominent in a number of situations, for example the estimation of punitive damages. A further example is given in Case 2.2 involving environmental protection.

2. *Insensitivity to scope*

   This is a form of extension bias. Kahneman (1986) found that Toronto residents were willing to pay only a little more to clean up all the polluted lakes in Ontario than to clean up polluted lakes in a particular region of Ontario. Jones-lee, Loomes, and Philips (1995) found that the SWTP of UK respondents to a program to reduce the risk of nonfatal head injuries increased by only 29 % when the number of prevented injuries increased by 200 %. Further examples relating to environmental protection are again given in Case 2.2.

An important consequence of this bias is that when CVM uses the technique of asking for people's SWTP it is highly misleading to use the **add-up principle**, whereby the values of different results are simply added together. For example, one cannot reliably conclude that the value of saving two species A and B from extinction is the value of saving species A plus the value of saving species B, even in the situation where the two events may seem quite independent from each other (the species being unrelated).

Some improvements to the SWTP technique of CVM have been proposed, notably the **referendum protocol**. This involves asking people simply to vote on an issue; the wording of the question for a particular respondent would therefore only quote a single value; for example, "Would you vote for a proposition requiring you to pay $20 to clean up Lake Ontario?" Different groups of respondents are given different values to respond to, and the responses allow a distribution of willingness-to-pay to be estimated. However, although this survey protocol may alleviate the problem of anchoring effects, the general problems of framing effects, extension bias and insensitivity to scope remain. When values are based on attitudes, the standard rules of economic theory regarding preference no longer apply. Kahneman, Ritov, and Schkade (1999) propose a somewhat similar solution in general terms to the problem of CVM to the solution proposed for jury awards: elicit and measure public opinion regarding their attitudes to the relevant issue using psychometric criteria, and then use expert opinion to convert these judgments into monetary terms.

Crime and Punishment

A contentious area of application of some of the research findings concerns the devising of punishments for crimes. There are various purposes of punishment, including retribution, the achievement of justice, removal of danger, deterrence, and even festival, but it is the function of deterrence that is relevant at this point. Current legal practices in most countries prescribe lengthy prison sentences for serious crimes. These tend to involve a painful period of initial shock (most prison suicides occur in the first 24 hours), because of the prominent contrast effect. After that there is a long period of adjustment and habituation. Inmates may even become institutionalized to the extent that they come to prefer the security and routine of prison existence, as dramatized in the film *The Shawshank Redemption*. According to the Peak-End rule, released prisoners may look back on their experience with little fear and regret. This may account for the high observed levels of re-offending or recidivism for many offences. Of course there may be other reasons for this, related to a lack of emphasis on rehabilitation by the authorities, or lack of job opportunities, or even an increase in criminal skills while inside prison. However, as far as deterrence is concerned, the Peak-End rule would suggest that short sharp punishment might be more effective than relatively lengthy prison terms. It is difficult to uncover revealing evidence regarding this issue, since few countries or societies make use of the former type of punishment any more.

One aspect of the punishment issue that is particularly contentious, at least in the United Kingdom, concerns the smacking of children. Smacking is an example of a short sharp punishment, which may be effective in causing an unpleasant memory, although not necessarily effective as a deterrent. In many countries, however, smacking is illegal, and it is frowned on by the European Court of Justice. It is not intended here to give any normative judgment on this issue; the purpose is merely to point out two flaws in the arguments put forward by those who oppose smacking, based on behavioral factors discussed in the chapter. The following is an excerpt from the *London Times* (2006):

> Historically, polls asking parents if they want to ban smacking have come up with a majority response of "no". But more recent work by the Children Are Unbeatable Alliance, a coalition of charities opposed to smacking, asking if children should have the same legal protection as adults from assault, has elicited a resounding "yes" from parents.

The information is presented as though there has been some change of opinion on the issue, but this is an obvious example of the framing effect. The mental representation conjured up by smacking a child may well involve a reasoned, controlled, and disciplined act performed after some "crime" has been committed, with the primary objective of deterrence. On the other hand, the mental representation of an assault is likely to be entirely different: it may involve a vicious, heated and violent attack, maybe with a weapon, and unprovoked, with the intention of causing some serious harm. It is therefore hardly inconsistent that people should want children to have the same legal protection as adults against such attacks, while at the same time not wanting to ban smacking.

The second flaw in the argument is that children are not treated as adults by the law in a number of ways. Most countries now have a minimum age for criminal responsibility and have laws protecting children against exploitation of various kinds, while prohibiting them from driving motor vehicles, consuming alcohol and tobacco, and having sex. It is widely accepted that the child's mind does not function in the same way as that of an adult. In particular, children are less likely to consider the likely consequences of their actions when they perform them, and they are less likely to realize such consequences. These factors are generally viewed as justifying such restrictions. It is therefore contradictory to insist that children should be treated as adults when it comes to punishment.

There is another issue raised here as far as punishment is concerned, and that concerns whether it is an effective deterrent; the Peak-End rule suggests that some forms of punishment may cause more unpleasant memories than others, but that does not necessarily make them effective deterrents. This topic will therefore be discussed further in the context of game theory and strategic interaction.

2.8 Summary

- The SEM relating to consumer preferences uses the analytical framework of indifference curves and budget constraints.

- The SEM is based on axioms related to completeness, transitivity, reflexivity, and revealed preference.

- In addition to the above axioms, the assumptions of cancellation, dominance, extension, and invariance are frequently made, in a hierarchical order of importance.

- There are many shortcomings in SEM as it relates to consumer preferences, indicating that the nature of utility is much more complex than the model supposes.

- Shortcomings can relate to either anomalies or incompleteness.

- There are many different concepts of utility, all of which have developed from the original hedonic concept of Bentham.

- There are five types of utility that can be distinguished: decision utility, experienced utility, anticipatory utility, residual utility, and diagnostic utility.

- Endowment and contrast effects are important in determining utility.

- Objective happiness can be measured in terms of total utility, which involves a moment-based measurement approach.

- There are different dimensions of utility: it is not just the valence that is relevant, but also the level of arousal. Experiences can thus be represented on an affect grid.

- There are six main conditions for measuring utility in terms of practical applications: inclusiveness, measurement on an ordinal scale, distinctive neutral point, interpersonal comparability, time neutrality, and independence of experiences.

- Dualism refers to the idea that the operations of the human mind cannot be reduced to neurophysiological processes. It therefore tends to exclude "moral sentiments" or emotions from the concept of utility, in contrast to the principle of inclusivity.

- A successful and realistic utility model must recognize the evolutionary origins of the human brain. This organ evolved to maximize biological fitness, and is prompted to maximize hedonic utility as a means to this end.

- Many anomalies arise from the nature of this evolutionary process; two problems in particular are time lags and the use of heuristics.

- A successful theory must contain four features: all-inclusivity, dynamic preferences, the distinction between attitudes and preferences, and the distinction between descriptive and prescriptive models. Therefore different models may be appropriate in different situations.

- There are a number of policy implications of the behavioral aspects discussed in the chapter. Three examples are jury awards of punitive damages, the CVM approach to valuation, and attitudes to crime and punishment.

2.9 Applications

Case 2.1 When abstention is better than moderate consumption

Addictive behavior is of great interest to anyone studying utility. Of particular relevance here are the concepts of self-signaling and diagnostic utility. The psychology involved goes back to the James – Lange theory of emotions, where people infer their own states from their behavior.

According to Bodner and Prelec (1997) there are many situations where it is useful to consider both the outcome utility and the diagnostic utility of a decision, with the total utility being a combination of the two types. For example, a person may have the preferred disposition of not being addicted to a particular "vice"; the list of such vices could be extensive: alcohol, cigarettes, recreational drugs, eating unhealthy foods, gambling, and hiring prostitutes are some of the more obvious examples. People have only a limited knowledge of this disposition; it is largely unknown and inferred from behavior. Therefore a person may refrain from indulging in such a vice if the payoff in terms of diagnostic utility (having higher self-esteem) exceeds the loss of outcome utility in terms of immediate pleasure. Alternatively, they may reduce their indulgence below the "natural consumption level," which relates to the level of activity when only outcome utility is considered.

However, Bodner and Prelec point out that the above conclusion is only a "face-value" interpretation. If we are to achieve a more realistic explanation and prediction of behavior, we have to consider the "true" interpretation of such situations, where the subject is more sophisticated. In their words,

> In the true interpretations case, the signalling value of good actions is discounted for the diagnostic motive, which creates an escalating pressure for behavioural perfection. The generic result is that either diagnostic utility wins, and the person does the same "perfect" thing irrespective of disposition, or natural impulses win, and the person simply ignores the diagnostic component of the utility structure.

We will consider the implications of face-value interpretations first, using an example where a person may have three different natural dispositions: "low," "moderate," and "high," and each is assumed to be equally likely. It is also assumed that even with a low disposition there is a tendency to consume a light amount rather than abstain completely. This situation is illustrated in Figure 2.5. The first set of arrows indicates the optimal actions for each disposition, which can be derived mathematically from certain basic assumptions; the second set of arrows indicates the corresponding face-value interpretations. Two conclusions can be drawn here:

1. In equilibrium a person cuts back on the vice by one step from the natural level.
2. Face-value interpretations induce a self-image that is too good by one step, except for the best disposition, which is correctly diagnosed.

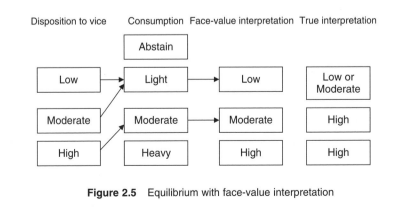

Figure 2.5 Equilibrium with face-value interpretation

Case 2.1 *continued*

The face-value interpretations ignore the diagnostic motive for reducing consumption. However, the true interpretations show that the consumption levels shown in Figure 2.5 will not be optimal, or in equilibrium, since the true interpretations do not match the actual disposition. Therefore we now need to complicate the situation by determining the consumption levels that would be consistent with true interpretations.

There are three possibilities here, depending on the strength of the diagnostic utility. When this is zero or weak, consumption will be at natural levels. People with high dispositions to the vice will not be persuaded to reduce consumption to moderate levels since this will not convince them that their disposition is only moderate. The situation is shown in Figure 2.6.

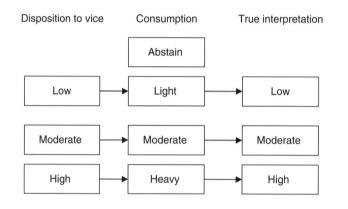

Figure 2.6 Equilibrium with weak diagnostic utility

As diagnostic utility becomes stronger, a different equilibrium emerges in which consumption falls to zero (abstention) for the two better dispositions, but remains heavy for those with a high or unfavorable disposition. This is referred to as a partially separating equilibrium and is shown in Figure 2.7. It should be noted that abstention does not maximize outcome utility for any of the dispositions (under our assumptions), but it emerges as an optimal outcome when diagnostic utility becomes sufficiently high. This is an example of "excessive virtue," caused by the harsh interpretation of even a light level of consumption. Bodner and Prelec express the reasoning as follows, in terms of gambling:

> A person who is concerned about his inclination to gamble, and who has, as a result, never ventured into a casino, would treat even one lapse as evidence of a strong gambling urge. The person might say – "given how much I care not to discover that I have a taste for gambling, then I must indeed have a strong taste for it if I succumb on this occasion!" Moderation is not an option.

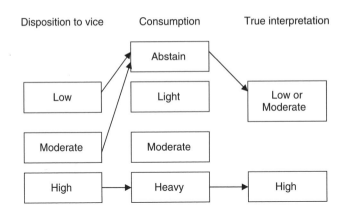

Figure 2.7 Equilibrium with moderate diagnostic utility

Finally, when diagnostic utility is sufficiently strong, even people with a high disposition will abstain. The result is a pooling equilibrium, shown in Figure 2.8.

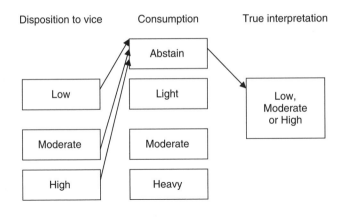

Figure 2.8 Equilibrium with strong diagnostic utility

It is interesting that in this situation when everyone abstains, the abstention provides no information about a person's underlying disposition. The conclusion here is somewhat paradoxical: the fact that the abstention rule is not informative actually enforces the rule. If a person could be sure that their disposition was perfect, they could afford to relax and consume a light amount, for example gamble occasionally.

As Bodner and Prelec are at pains to point out, even though the true-interpretation situations may be more "realistic," this does not mean that they provide the best empirical model of how people actually behave. As we will see in Chapter 9, self-deception is common, and, in particular, many people have a misplaced confidence in their own abilities. Bodner and Prelec make the following comment relating to the study by Quattrone and

---

Case 2.1 *continued*

Tversky (1984), involving the use of a cold-pressor test to diagnose heart function:

> The subject population apparently divided into a self-satisfied, face-value interpretations majority and a pessimistic, true-interpretations minority.

Questions

1. Explain why there may be another good reason for abstention from a "vice," in terms of "enforced ignorance."
2. Explain why, when diagnostic utility is strong, it is not possible to have an equilibrium that pools on light or moderate consumption. Consider in particular the likely behavior of those with the best disposition.
3. Explain why it can be best to follow a rule even if that rule is not informative.

Case 2.2 Environmental protection

In many research studies subjects are asked to indicate their willingness to pay (WTP) for a specified amount of a relatively homogeneous good. This method (SWTP) varies the amount of the good across groups of respondents. A good example of this experimental design was the study by Desvousges *et al.* (1992). The basic question that the respondents were asked can be paraphrased as follows:

> 2,000/20,000/200,000 migrating birds die each year by drowning in uncovered oil ponds, which the birds mistake for bodies of water. These deaths could be prevented by covering the oil ponds with nets. How much money would you be willing to pay to provide the needed nets?

This kind of question is evoking an attitude (as opposed to a preference) in the respondents which in turn involves a mental representation of a prototypical incident. We have all seen pictures in the media of exhausted birds, feathers soaked in black oil, unable to fly.

As far as the results of the survey are concerned, the mean SWTP for saving 2000 birds was $80, the mean SWTP for saving 20 000 birds was $78, and the mean SWTP for saving 200 000 birds was $88.

Questions

1. Explain why it is important to distinguish between attitudes and preferences. Does the referendum format of CVM address this problem?

2. Explain the cause of the inconsistencies in the results of the study. Give some similar examples.

3. Explain how more reliable methods may be used in terms of determining the optimal amount of public expenditure to be allocated to issues like environmental protection.

Case 2.3 Anti-Social Behaviour Orders (ASBOs), punishment and happiness

Soothing the savage breast

Tough rhetoric aside, Britain's war on incivility is entering a surprisingly conciliatory phase

TONY BLAIR is back in the bully pulpit. On January 10th, he declared that he was jettisoning centuries of legal precedent. He lambasted the criminal justice system, which, he said, protects the accused better than their victims. Then he quietly unveiled a plan to tackle petty criminality and anti-social behaviour that was startling for its moderation, at least by comparison with what has come before.

Britons may not suffer more from incivilities such as graffiti, spitting and verbal abuse than other nations, but they certainly make more of a fuss about them. MPs hear so many complaints from their constituents that Tony Banks, a former left-wing MP who died on January 8th, described one legislative attempt to tackle the problem as a "letting-off-steam bill". Since coming to power in 1997, the Labour government has honed weapons against anti-social behaviour that are unmatched for severity in the western world.

The most potent of these is the Anti-Social Behaviour Order (ASBO). This can be handed out for conduct that causes, or even contributes to a general sense of, "harassment, alarm or distress". On the slenderest evidence (including hearsay), perpetrators as young as ten years old can be banned from entering an area, wearing particular clothing or even speaking certain words. Breach the terms of the order, and the maximum sentence is five years in prison. Some 6,500 ASBOs have been imposed since they became available in 1999.

They are enormously popular, as are other powers, such as curfews and "dispersal orders", which can be used to break up groups. MORI, a pollster, found last year that ASBOs were opposed by just 4% of people. The government is confident that Liberal Democrat and Conservative MPs, who oppose the new measures (the Tories almost to the point of sounding like hand-wringing liberals), are on the wrong side of public opinion.

This week's plans would not, in truth, greatly strengthen powers against anti-social behaviour. That would scarcely be possible, given the fierceness of the current laws. "Short of bringing back the stocks, there's not much more we could do," says Les Carter of Leeds City Council.

Case 2.3 *continued*

The toughest-seeming of the powers announced this week (and the one that attracted most media coverage) would allow the police to evict disorderly households from their homes. It is unlikely that such a power would be used often. The law would be hedged with safeguards and restrictions: it is almost impossible deliberately to make children homeless, for example. Besides, any family thrown out of its home would be likely to turn up at a nearby housing office, demanding accommodation—and would often be given it. Local authorities, which work closely with the police, may not be keen on that.

Quietly, almost stealthily, the government's action plan ushers in more sympathetic tools for dealing with misbehaviour. The government plans to set up a parenting academy where social workers and other professionals can learn how to instruct others in the arts of child-rearing. Parents will be invited (or, if their children are really troublesome, ordered) to attend classes. In extreme cases, households will be removed to flats where the children will be fed nutritious food.

Such methods are already being tested in some unlikely places. No British city took a harder line on anti-social behaviour than Manchester, which, by the end of 2004, had dished out four-and-a-half times as many ASBOs per head as London. But Eddy Newman, a Manchester city councillor, says the enforcement drive has reached a plateau. The city is now going in for more touchy-feely stuff—mediation between neighbours, intensive support for troubled youths and leaflets encouraging parents to read to their children at night.

Similar initiatives are under way in Camden, a London borough notorious for tough policies. Camden now has five "youth-inclusion support panels" which try to quell anti-social tendencies before they reach the point where tougher measures are required. It used ASBOs more sparingly last year than in the previous 12 months. That may be the beginning of a trend. The English courts doled out ten fewer ASBOs in the second quarter of 2005 (the most recent period for which figures are available) than they did in the first. It was the first decline yet recorded.

Why the reluctance to use such a powerful and popular weapon? Partly because ASBOs have proved unwieldy. Leeds got the courts to hand out 66 in a single purge, but, according to Mr Carter, would not do so again. Blanket use meant less stigma for the recipients. And ASBOs are not cheap: the council had to defend one in court, at a cost of some £25,000 ($44,000). When granting orders against children, the courts increasingly tack on training programmes, which must also be paid for.

A more serious problem is that tough measures do not appear to placate the public. The British Crime Survey shows that worry about loitering teenagers, noisy neighbours and drunken louts—the sort of menaces the laws are designed to tackle—has barely abated in the past five years. Last year, anxiety actually increased.

It is not that the war on incivility has fallen flat, say those who led the campaigns in the cities. In the most troubled places, tough measures helped to restore order. But levels of tolerance changed, too. Once word got out that the police and local authorities had a powerful new weapon for dealing with annoyances, people began to spot more problems in their neighbourhoods that they wanted sorted out.

Mark Harris, of Leeds City Council, compares the campaign against anti-social behaviour with the birth of the National Health Service in the 1940s. The architects of the NHS assumed that demand would die down after lingering ailments were cleared up. Instead, public expectations simply increased. So it has proved with the war on incivility. As Neil Pilkington, the principal solicitor of Salford City Council, puts it: "The more you do, the more people develop high expectations of you, and the more they complain."

Questions

1. ASBOs are an attempt to use public opinion as a means of valuing a "bad" that causes disutility. In principle this may appear to be desirable in a democracy. What problems may arise in practice?

2. Do ASBOs act as an effective punishment in terms of the behavioral principles discussed in this chapter?

3. Explain why the tough measures relating to anti-social behavior enacted by the Blair government since 1997 have not had the intended effect of placating the public.

Source: *The Economist* print edition, January 12, 2006

Decision-Making under Risk and Uncertainty

3.1 Background

Expected utility theory

The SEM of decision-making under risk is EUT. This has been widely accepted and applied both as a descriptive model of economic behavior and as a normative model of rational choice; this means that it assumes that rational people would want to obey the axioms of the theory and that they do actually obey them in general.

The concept of utility was discussed in the previous chapter, and we have seen that we can think of it in terms of subjective value. Decision-making under risk can be considered as a process of choosing between different **prospects** or gambles. A prospect consists of a number of possible outcomes along with their associated probabilities. Thus any theory of decision-making under risk will take into account both the consequences of choices and their associated probabilities. In keeping with the rest of this text, situations will often be explained in words or in terms of examples first, before using mathematical notation, even though the latter is often both more concise and more precise, in terms of avoiding ambiguity. As explained in the preface, this sequence should help the reader to relate abstract terms to real concepts more easily. This is particularly important in the initial stages of analysis, until the reader becomes familiar with mathematical notation. A simple example of a situation involving decision-making under risk is given below, where an individual is required to choose between two alternative courses of action, resulting in two prospects:

Prospect A: 50 % chance to win 100 50 % chance to win nothing
Prospect B: Certainty of winning 45

It will be convenient to denote prospects with bold case letters. In general terms a prospect can be described mathematically as follows:

$q = (x_1, p_1; \ldots; x_n, p_n)$ where x_i represents outcomes and p_i represents associated probabilities. Riskless prospects yielding a certain outcome x are denoted by (x). Thus prospect A above can be expressed as $q = (100, .5; 0, .5)$, but for simplicity null outcomes can be omitted, thus reducing prospect A to $(100, .5)$. Prospect B can be expressed as $r = (45)$.

The axioms underlying EUT were originally developed by von Neumann and Morgenstern (1944), and are related to the axioms of preference described in the previous chapter:

1. *Completeness*

   This requires that for all q and r

   $$\text{either } q \succeq r \text{ or } r \succeq q \text{ or both.}$$

2. *Transitivity*

   If we take any three prospects, q, r, and s,

   $$\text{if } q \succeq r \text{ and } r \succeq s, \text{ then } q \succeq s$$

   Sometimes the two above axioms are combined together and referred to as the **ordering** axiom.

3. *Continuity*

   This principle guarantees that preferences can be represented by some function that attaches a real value to every prospect. In formal terms this can be expressed as follows:

   For all prospects, q, r, and s, where $q \succeq r$ and $r \succeq s$, there exists some probability p such that there is indifference between the middle-ranked prospect r and the prospect $(q, p; s, 1-p)$. The latter is referred to as a **compound prospect**, since its component outcomes q and s are themselves prospects. We will see that such prospects are important in experimental studies, since they often lead to violations of EUT.

   The majority of economists have assumed that the existence of some preference function involving the above axioms is the starting point for constructing any satisfactory model of decision-making under risk. Essentially, the assumption amounts to consumers having well-defined preferences, while imposing minimal restrictions on the precise form of those preferences.

   A further axiom of EUT is the independence axiom; this imposes quite strong restrictions on the precise form of preferences. It is described below, and examples will be given in the following subsection related to anomalies in EUT.

4. *Independence*

   This axiom relates to the cancellation principle described in the previous chapter that any state of the world that results in the same outcome regardless of one's choice can be canceled or ignored. Kahneman and Tversky refer to this axiom as the **substitution axiom** in their 1979 paper. Let us illustrate the independence axiom with a simple numerical example first, before giving the formal representation. If prospect $q = (\$3000)$ is preferred to prospect $r = (\$4000, .8)$, then prospect $q' = (\$3000, .25)$ is preferred to prospect $r' = (\$4000, .2)$. The reader should note that the last two prospects have 25 % of the probabilities of the first two prospects. The independence axiom can be generalized in the following formal representation:

For all prospects, q, r, and s:

$$\text{if } q \succeq r \text{ then } (q, p; s, 1-p) \succeq (r, p; s, 1-p), \text{ for all } p \qquad (3.1)$$

It can be seen that there is a common component of the compound prospects $(s, 1-p)$; according to the cancellation principle this component can be ignored in the comparison.

EUT also is based on the **expectation principle** that the overall utility of a prospect is the expected utility of its outcomes. In mathematical notation,

$$U(x_1, p_1; \ldots; x_n, p_n) = p_1 u(x_1) + \cdots + p_n u(x_n)$$

Based on the four axioms above and the expectation principle, EUT states that consumers will behave in such a way that they will maximize the following preference function:

$$V(q) = \sum p_i \cdot u(x_i) \qquad (3.2)$$

Where q is any prospect, and $u(.)$ is a utility function defined on the set of consequences $(x_1, x_2, \ldots, x_n)$.

EUT provides a simple model for combining probabilities and consequences into a single measure of value that has various appealing qualities. One particularly important property is commonly referred to as the **monotonicity** principle. Although we have discussed "monotonicity" in the previous chapter in the context of indifference curves, in EUT the term implies that objective improvements to a prospect, meaning increasing some of its payoffs while holding others constant, should make it at least as attractive if not more so than before. It is thus related to the principle of dominance described in the previous chapter, but in this situation we say that the dominance is **stochastic** since we are comparing not just outcomes but also probabilities. Again an example from Tversky and Kahneman (1986) will aid understanding before giving a formal representation.

Consider the following pair of lotteries, described by the percentage of marbles of different colors in each box and the amount of money you win or lose depending on the color of a randomly drawn marble. Which lottery do you prefer?

Option A				
90 % white $0	6 % red win $45	1 % green win $30	1 % blue lose $15	2 % yellow lose $15
Option B				
90 % white $0	6 % red win $45	1 % green win $45	1 % blue lose $10	2 % yellow lose $15

The reader can verify that option B will be preferred to option A because it **stochastically** dominates it. For white, red, and yellow marbles the situation is the same, but for both green and blue marbles the outcomes are more favorable, with the probabilities remaining the same.

It has been generally held by economists that the monotonicity principle is fundamental to any satisfactory theory of consumer preference, both descriptive and normative. Therefore its formal representation as an axiom is necessary:

5. *Monotonicity*

Let $x_1, x_2, \ldots, x_n$ be outcomes ordered from worst (x_1) to best (x_n). A prospect $q = (p_{q1}, \ldots, p_{qn})$ stochastically dominates another prospect $r = (p_{r1}, \ldots, p_{rn})$ if for all outcomes $i = 1, \ldots, n$:

$$\sum_{j=1}^{n} p_{qj} \geq \sum_{j=i}^{n} p_{rj} \tag{3.3}$$

with a strict inequality for at least one i.

In addition to the above axioms various assumptions are commonly made in EUT, in similar manner to that described in the previous chapter.

1. **Asset integration**

A prospect is acceptable if and only if the utility resulting from integrating the prospect with one's assets exceeds the utility of those assets alone. Thus it is final states that matter, not gains or losses. In mathematical notation,

$(x_1, p_1; \ldots; x_n, p_n)$ is acceptable at asset position w if
$U(w + x_1, p_1; \ldots; w + x_n, p_n) > u(w)$

2. **Risk-aversion**

A person is said to be risk-averse if he prefers the certain prospect (x) to any risky prospect with expected value x. In EUT, risk-aversion is caused by the concavity of the utility function. This characteristic is in turn explained by the law of diminishing marginal utility, as discussed in the previous chapter. The concave utility function is represented and compared with other functions in the section on the shape of utility functions. The relationship between attitude to risk and the shape of the utility function is also explained in this section.

A number of anomalies have been observed relating to these axioms and assumptions, arising both from laboratory experiments and from field data. Some of these observations predate Kahneman and Tversky's classic paper on PT of 1979, some relate specifically to the paper, and others have come to light since then. At this point we will move on to discuss the last category of observations first; this will give the reader a general feel for the problems of EUT, since all the observations come from field data. We will then examine two examples predating PT; both date back to Allais (1953), although both are also discussed in the 1979 PT paper. Finally, the specific results from Kahneman and Tversky (KT) and other studies are discussed in more detail in later sections, examining the components of PT and adopting a more rigorous analysis.

Anomalies in expected utility theory

Many of these anomalies have been described, categorized, and analyzed by Camerer (2000). A useful summary is given in Table 3.1, which is adapted from Camerer. This table names and describes the phenomena involved, classifies the anomalies according to domain, and indicates which elements of PT are relevant in terms of explaining the anomalies. These anomalies are discussed in more detail in later sections of the chapter and also in the following chapter on mental accounting, after the elements of PT have been explained.

Let us now examine a more detailed example of an anomaly in EUT, this time from experimental data. This is sometimes referred to as the **Allais paradox**, and dates back to 1953. This is illustrated in the payoff matrix in Table 3.2. Each row represents an act involving a prospect, while each column represents a "state of the world," with the associated probabilities at the top of each column. The values in the matrix represent payoffs to each act (in $ for example) given a certain state of the world. Subjects are first presented with a choice between options A and B. The independence axiom implies that since these two acts have the same consequence in the third state of the world, the third state should be irrelevant to that choice. The same argument applies when subjects are then presented with a choice between options C and D. It should now be seen that, when the third state of the world is ignored, the choice

Table 3.1 Phenomena inconsistent with EUT

Phenomenon	Domain	Description	Elements in PT
Equity premium	Stock market	Stock returns are too high relative to bond returns	Loss-aversion
Disposition effect	Stock market	Hold losing stocks too long, sell winners too early	Loss-aversion reference points
Downward-sloping labor supply	Labor economics	New York City cab drivers quit around daily income target	Loss-aversion
Asymmetric price elasticities	Consumer goods	Purchases more sensitive to price increases than to price cuts	Loss-aversion
Insensitivity to bad income news	Macroeconomics	Consumers do not cut consumption after bad income news	Loss-aversion reference points
Status quo bias Default bias	Consumer choice	Consumers do not switch health plans; choose default insurance	Loss-aversion
Favorite-long shot bias	Horse race betting	Favorites are underbet, long shots are overbet	Decision weighting (overweighting low probabilities)
End-of-the-day effect	Horse race betting	Shift to long shots at the end of the day	Reference points Diminishing marginal sensitivity
Buying phone wire insurance	Insurance	Consumers buy overpriced insurance	Decision weighting (overweighting low probabilities)
Demand for Lotto	Lottery betting	More tickets sold as top prize rises	Decision weighting (overweighting low probabilities)

Table 3.2 The Allais paradox

	Option	.1	.01	.89
Choice 1	A	500	500	500
	B	2500	0	500
Choice 2	C	500	500	0
	D	2500	0	0

between A and B is identical to the choice between C and D, that is a choice between (500, .11) and (2500, .1). Therefore, according to the independence axiom, if A is preferred to B, C should be preferred to D, and vice versa. However, there is evidence from numerous studies that many people faced with similar pairs of choices choose A over B, but D over C, violating the independence axiom. This phenomenon is an example of what is called the **common consequence effect**.

Table 3.3 Same payoffs but different probabilities of winning

	Option	
Choice 1	A	(6000, .45)
	B	(3000, .90)
Choice 2	C	(6000, .001)
	D	(3000, .002)

Another anomaly in EUT is described in the KT paper, again relating to the independence or substitution axiom. This situation is shown in the payoff matrix in Table 3.3. It can be seen that the choices between A and B and between C and D involve the same payoffs, and also the same relative probabilities, with the probability of the lower payoff being twice the probability of the higher payoff. Once again the independence axiom implies that if A is preferred to B then C should be preferred to D, and vice versa. The KT paper found a very contrasting result, with only 14 % of their subjects preferring A to B, but 73 % preferring C to D. This is an example of a phenomenon called the **common ratio effect**, since the ratio of the probabilities in each option is the same in both choices.

These preliminary examples should give the reader a flavor of the anomalies related to EUT. Furthermore, the observed departures from the theory were **systematic**, meaning that they were in a predictable direction, rather than being random errors. Now we can turn our attention to various attempts that have been made since the late 1970s to account for these violations of EUT in terms of proposing a more satisfactory theory.

It is useful here to use the broad classification proposed by Starmer (2000), who distinguishes between **conventional** and **nonconventional** theories. The former accepted the first three axioms of completeness, transitivity, and continuity, but were prepared to allow violations of the independence axiom, since these violations had been widely observed since the work of Allais. However, these conventional theories proposed that preferences should still be **well-behaved**; in particular, this characteristic involves maintaining monotonicity or dominance, and also the principle of invariance described in the previous chapter. Nonconventional theories do not insist on preferences being well-behaved in these ways. We will consider the conventional theories first, since these represent both the earlier departure and the least modification of EUT.

3.2 Conventional approaches to modifying expected utility theory

There are a large number of different theories that have been proposed in this category, and it is not intended to review all of them here. Instead the leading contenders are described in terms of their main features, advantages, and disadvantages. It is not possible to conduct such a review on an entirely chronological basis, since many theories have been developed over some period of time by several writers. Instead, theories are presented largely in the order that corresponds to the extent of their departure from EUT, with those theories that depart least being presented first.

Weighted utility theory

One of the earliest extensions of EUT was termed "weighted utility theory" (Chew and MacCrimmon 1979). The preference function is represented as follows:

$$V(q) = \left[\sum p_i \cdot g(x_i) \cdot u(x_i) \right] / \left[\sum p_i \cdot g(x_i) \right] \tag{3.4}$$

Where $u(.)$ and $g(.)$ are two different functions assigning nonzero weights to all outcomes. This model incorporates EUT as a special case when the weights assigned by $g(.)$ are identical for every outcome. The model has been axiomatized by various economists, including Chew and MacCrimmon (1979), Chew (1983), and Fishburn (1983). These all involve a weaker form of the independence axiom; for example,

if $q \succ r$ then for each p_q there exists a corresponding p_r such that $(q, p_q; s, 1 - p_q) \succ (r, p_r; s, 1 - p_r)$, for all s.

A similar model, which generalized this approach, was proposed by Machina (1982). In behavioral terms these theories proposed that people became more risk-averse as the prospects they face improve. The main advantage of such theories was that they explained the violations of independence in the common consequence and common ratio cases, but they lacked intuitive appeal because there was no psychological foundation. They were empirically rather than theoretically grounded.

Disappointment theory

Later theories had a better psychological foundation. An example is the disappointment theory developed by Bell (1985) and Loomes and Sugden (1986).

In the latter version the preference function is represented as follows:

$$V(q) = \sum p_i.\{u(x_i) + D[u(x_i) - \underline{U}]\} \qquad (3.5)$$

where $u(x_i)$ refers to a measure of "basic" utility, meaning the utility of x_i considered in isolation from the other outcomes of q, and $\underline{U}$ is a measure of the prior expectation of the utility of the prospect. It is assumed in the model that if the outcome of a prospect is worse than expected, meaning if $u(x_i) < \underline{U}$, a sense of disappointment will be experienced. On the other hand, if an outcome is better than expected, there will be a sense of elation. When $D(.) = 0$, the model reduces to EUT. However, the extension to the EUT model is intended to capture the psychological intuition that people are disappointment averse; this entails the disappointment function $D(.)$ being concave in the negative region and convex in the positive region.

Betweenness models

Theories of this type have been proposed by Gul (1991)'and Neilson (1992). Again they involve a weakened form of independence. Betweenness can be described as follows:

$$\text{if } q \succ r \text{ then } q \succ (q, p; r, 1-p) \succ r \text{ for all } p < 1$$

In behavioral terms this implies that any probability mixture of two lotteries will be ranked between them in terms of preference and, given continuity, an individual will be indifferent to randomization among equally valued prospects.

Nonbetweenness models

Other models do not impose restrictions as strong as betweenness. **Quadratic utility theory**, proposed by Chew, Epstein, and Segal (1991), is based on a weakened form of betweenness called **mixture symmetry**. This can be represented as follows:

$$\text{If } q \sim r \text{ then } (q, p; r, 1-p) \sim (q, 1-p; r, p)$$

The lottery-dependent utility model of Becker and Sarin (1987) has even weaker restrictions, assuming nothing regarding independence (although still assuming completeness, transitivity, continuity, and monotonicity).

Decision-weighting theories

All the theories described so far assign *subjective* weights, or utilities, to outcomes. The value of any prospect is then determined by a function that combines these subjective weights with *objective* probabilities. Decision-weighting theories involve the use of probability transformation functions which convert objective probabilities into subjective decision weights. Betweenness does not generally hold in these cases.

These theories are empirically grounded in that there is much evidence that people tend to systematically underestimate probability in some situations and overestimate it in others. For example, Pidgeon *et al.* (1992) found that people underestimate the probability of dying from common causes, like heart disease and cancer, and overestimate the probability of dying from rare causes, like an airline accident. This evidence is reviewed in more detail in the next section on PT. The effects of this phenomenon can be captured by incorporating decision weights in the preference function. An early version of this kind of model was proposed by Edwards (1955; 1962), being called **subjective expected value**. This model used subjective probabilities but objective outcomes, meaning that outcomes were entered into the model in a "raw" form with $u(x_i) = x_i$. The resulting preference function is given by

$$V(q) = \sum w_i.x_i \tag{3.6}$$

A later version, developed by Handa (1977), employed a probability weighting function $\pi(p_i)$, which transforms the individual probabilities of outcomes into weights. $\pi(.)$ is assumed to be increasing, with $\pi(0) = 0$ and $\pi(1) = 1$. Variations of this model were proposed that allowed nonlinear transformations of probabilities; both probabilities and outcomes are measured subjectively. Starmer (2000) refers to such forms as **simple decision weighted utility** models, and the corresponding preference function is shown below:

$$V(q) = \sum \pi(p_i).u(x_i) \tag{3.7}$$

Since nonlinear transformations of probabilities did not satisfy the monotonicity principle as far as preferences were concerned these models were generally not taken seriously by most economists. For example, Machina (1983) argued that any such theory will be "in the author's view at least, unacceptable as a descriptive or analytical model of behaviour" (p. 97).

Rank-dependent expected utility theory

Rank-dependent models were first developed by Quiggin (1982) in response to the problem described above. They proposed decision weighting with more sophisticated probability transformations designed to ensure monotonicity in the preference function. In this type of model the weight attached to outcomes depends not only on the true probability of the outcome but also on its ranking relative to the other outcomes of the prospect. It is more complex to describe mathematically than previous models, but the starting point is to rank the outcomes $x_1, x_2, \ldots, x_n$ from worst (x_1) to best (x_n). The model then proposes the preference function:

$$V(q) = \sum w_i . u(x_i) \tag{3.8}$$

where the weights are given by the weighting function:

$$w_i = \pi(p_i + \cdots + p_n) - \pi(p_{i+1} + \cdots + p_n)$$

The interpretation of this function is that $\pi(p_i + \cdots + p_n)$ is a subjective weight attached to the probability of getting an outcome of x_i or better, while $\pi(p_{i+1} + \ldots + p_n)$ is a weight attached to the probability of getting an outcome of better than x_i. In this theory, therefore, $\pi(.)$ is a transformation of **cumulative probabilities**.

Rank-dependent models have become popular among economists because they have both empirical and theoretical appeal. Empirically they take into account the psychological tendency to overestimate and underestimate probabilities related to particularly good or bad outcomes. Theoretically the appeal has been the preservation of monotonicity.

The form of $\pi(.)$ is critical in determining the predictions of the model. For example, convexity of $\pi(.)$ implies a pessimistic outlook in that it attaches relatively high weights to lower ranking outcomes compared with higher-ranking ones. A favorite form, employed by Quiggin (1982), involves a more complex inverted S-shape, illustrated in Figure 3.1.

This function has $\pi(p) = p$ when $p = p^*$; it is concave below p^* and convex above it. These forms of weighting function can be obtained using a variety of mathematical forms, some using one parameter and some using two. It goes outside the scope of this book to discuss these in detail, but the single-parameter model of Tversky and Kahneman (1992) is described in the next section.

As with other conventional extensions of EUT, rank-dependent EUT relies on a weakened form of the independence axiom called **co-monotonic independence**. This imposes the restriction that preferences between prospects

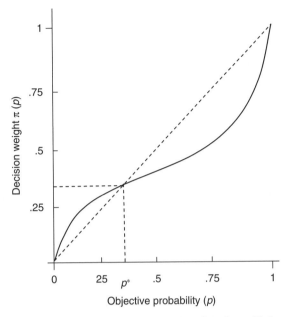

Figure 3.1 Rank-dependent probability weighting function with inverted S-shape

will be unaffected by substitution of common consequences so long as these substitutions do not affect the rank order of the outcomes in either prospect. Other variations of the rank-dependent model have proposed similar axioms, like **ordinal independence** (Green and Jullien 1988).

Conclusions

These more complex extensions to EUT have without doubt explained some of the observed violations, in particular those relating to independence. Over the last 50 years a very large body of studies has built up evidence that can discriminate between the theories described above in terms of their predictive ability. In particular, studies by Conlisk (1989), Camerer (1992), Harless (1992), Gigliotti and Sopher (1993), and Wu and Gonzalez (1996) tend to support the decision-weighting models in favor of other conventional models. Furthermore, those models involving an inverted S-shaped weighting function tend to have better empirical fit than those using other functional forms of the weighting function (Lattimore, Baker, and Witte 1992; Tversky and Kahneman 1992; Camerer and Ho 1994; Abdellaoui 1998; Gonzalez and Wu 1999). These more sophisticated models show significant predictive improvement over EUT.

However, even these models are still unable to explain widely observed violations of monotonicity, as well as violations of transitivity and invariance.

These violations have been observed not only in experiments but also in the field, and include the various anomalies described by Camerer (2000) and illustrated in Table 3.1. The nature of these violations is described in the next section, which is concerned with the exposition of PT; this is classified by Starmer (2000) as a nonconventional theory.

3.3 Prospect theory

The first question at this stage is, what constitutes the difference between a conventional and a nonconventional theory? All the theories described so far, including EUT, have essentially been models of preference maximization, assuming that agents behave *as if* optimizing some underlying preference function. As we have noted in the previous two chapters, the form of the function makes no claim regarding underlying psychological mechanisms or processes. On the other hand, as we have also seen, behavioral models try to model the psychological processes that lead to choice, and Starmer (2000) refers to these as **procedural theories**. Prominent features of these models include the existence of **bounded rationality** and the consequent use of decision **heuristics**. Bounded rationality implies that the agent has both imperfect information in a complex and dynamic decision environment, and limited computational ability; the agent's objectives may also be imperfectly defined. Thus the concept of optimization becomes more complex, with constraints of time, computational resources, and often-conflicting objectives. In such situations the use of heuristics becomes necessary; these are computational shortcuts that simplify decision-making procedures. Since the late 1970s a variety of these nonconventional theories have been developed, but without any doubt PT has been by far the most influential of these. Thus this section concentrates on a detailed discussion of this particular theory. In the concluding section of the chapter some of the other procedural theories are discussed and compared.

The PT was originally developed in the KT paper of 1979 and then extended in a later paper by the same authors in 1992, being renamed "cumulative prospect theory." We shall see, however, that most of the elements of the theory have important precedents, in particular the work of Markowitz (1952) and Allais (1953). PT models choice as a two-phase process: the first phase involves editing, while the second involves evaluation. The use of an editing phase is the most obvious distinguishing characteristic of PT from any of the theories discussed in the previous section. The second feature that distinguishes PT from these theories is that outcomes are measured as gains or losses relative to some reference point. These features and the other features of PT are now discussed.

Editing

This phase consists of a preliminary analysis of the offered prospects, which has the objective of yielding a simpler representation of these prospects, in turn facilitating the evaluation process. Certain heuristic rules and operations may be applied, not necessarily consciously, to organize, reformulate, and narrow down the options to be considered in the next phase. These operations include coding, combination, segregation, cancellation, simplification, and the detection of dominance.

1. *Coding*

   Empirical evidence suggests that people normally perceive outcomes as gains or losses relative to some reference point, rather than as final states of wealth or welfare. This aspect is discussed in more detail in the next section on evaluation.

2. *Combination*

   Prospects can sometimes be simplified by combining the probabilities associated with identical outcomes. For example, the prospect (100, .30; 100, .30) will be reduced to (100, .60) and evaluated as such.

3. *Segregation*

   Some prospects contain a riskless component that can be segregated from the risky component. For example, the prospect (100, .70; 150, .30) can be segregated into a sure gain of 100 and the risky prospect (50, .30). Likewise, the prospect (−200, .8; −300, .2) can be segregated into a sure loss of 200 and the risky prospect (−100, .2).

4. *Cancellation*

   This aspect was described earlier in relation to the independence axiom. When different prospects share certain identical components, these components may be discarded or ignored. For example, consider a two-stage game where there is a probability of .75 of ending the game without winning anything and a probability of .25 of moving onto the second stage. In the second stage there may be a choice between (4000, .80) and (3000). The player must make the choice at the start of the game, before the outcome of the first stage is known. In this case the evidence in the KT study suggests that there is an **isolation effect**, meaning that people ignore the first stage, whose outcomes are shared by both prospects, and consider the choice as being between a riskless gain of 3000 and the risky prospect (4000, .80). The implications of this effect, in terms of inconsistency in decision-making, are considered later, in the section on decision weighting.

5. *Simplification*

Prospects may be simplified by rounding either outcomes or probabilities. For example, the prospect (99, .51) is likely to be coded as an even chance of winning 100. In particular, outcomes that are extremely improbable are likely to be ignored, meaning that the probabilities are rounded down to 0. This part of the editing phase is often performed first, and the sequence of the editing operations is important, because it can affect the final list to be evaluated. As we shall see, the sequence and method of editing can depend on the structure of the problem.

6. *Detection of dominance*

Some prospects may dominate others, meaning that they may have elements in common, but other elements involve outcomes or probabilities that are always preferable. Consider the two prospects (200, .3; 99, .51) and (200, .4; 101, .49). Assume that the second component of each prospect is first of all rounded to (100, .5), then the second prospect dominates the first, with the outcome of the first component being the same, but its probability being greater.

As has already been stated with regard to the isolation effect, there are various aspects of the editing process that can cause anomalies such as inconsistencies of preference, which will be discussed later. The KT editing heuristic has therefore been criticized on various grounds. For example, Quiggin (1982) has argued that the editing process is redundant if the preference function is appropriately specified. He has also argued that the final stage of detecting dominance, while it may induce monotonicity, has the side effect that it admits violations of transitivity. Quiggin refers to this as an "undesirable result." Starmer (2005) argues that this comment, and other criticisms of PT, is motivated by "a pre-commitment to preference theories which satisfy normatively appealing criteria such as transitivity and monotonicity" (p. 282). He further argues that such a pre-commitment is misplaced in the light of direct empirical evidence. This issue will be discussed further later when more examples have been examined.

Evaluation

Once the editing phase is complete, the decision-maker must evaluate each of the edited prospects, and is assumed to choose the prospect with the highest value. According to PT, the overall value of an edited prospect, denoted V, is expressed in terms of two scales, v and π. The first scale, v, assigns to each outcome x a number, $v(x)$, which reflects the subjective value of that outcome.

The second scale, π, associates with each probability p a decision weight $\pi(p)$, which reflects the impact of p on the overall value of the prospect.

The first scale entails an explanation of **reference points, loss-aversion**, and **diminishing marginal sensitivity**, while the second scale entails an explanation of **decision weighting** or weighted probability functions. These four aspects of PT are discussed at length in the next four sections, since they are core concepts to which repeated reference is made throughout the remainder of the text. There is one other element that is often ascribed to PT, concerning the framing of decisions, but this aspect is discussed in the next chapter, in the context of mental accounting.

A mathematical exposition of the basics of the KT model can now be given, which is essentially taken directly from the 1979 paper. The original KT model was concerned with simple prospects of the form $(x, p; y, q)$, which have at most two nonzero outcomes. In such a prospect, one receives x with probability p, y with probability q, and nothing with probability $1 - p - q$, where $p + q \leq 1$. A prospect is **strictly positive** if its outcomes are all positive, that is if $x, y > 0$ and $p + q = 1$; it is **strictly negative** if its outcomes are all negative. A prospect is **regular** if it is neither strictly positive nor strictly negative.

The basic equation of the theory describes the manner in which v and π are combined to determine the overall value of regular prospects.

If $(x, p; y, q)$ is a regular prospect (i.e., either $p + q < 1$, or $x \geq 0 \geq y$, or $x \leq 0 \leq y$), then

$$V(x, p; y, q) = \pi(p)v(x) + \pi(q)v(y) \tag{3.9}$$

Where $v(0) = 0$, $\pi(0) = 0$, and $\pi(1) = 1$. As in utility theory, V is defined on prospects, while v is defined on outcomes. The two scales coincide for sure prospects, where $V(x, 1.0) = V(x) = v(x)$. Equation (3.9) generalizes EUT by relaxing the expectation principle described earlier.

As a simple example, take the situation of tossing a coin where the outcome of heads results in a gain of $20 while the outcome of tails results in a loss of $10. We can now express the utility of this regular prospect below:

$$V(20, .5; -10, .5) = \pi(.5)v(20) + \pi(.5)v(-10)$$

The evaluation of strictly positive and strictly negative prospects follows a different rule. In the editing phase, as described earlier, such prospects are segregated into two components: (i) the riskless component, that is the minimum gain or loss which is certain to be obtained or paid; (ii) the risky component, that is the additional gain or loss which is actually at stake. The evaluation of such prospects is described in the next equation.

If $p+q=1$ and either $x > y > 0$ or $x < y < 0$, then

$$V(x, p; y, q) = v(y) + \pi(p)[v(x) - v(y)] \tag{3.10}$$

That is, the value of a strictly positive or strictly negative prospect equals the value of the riskless component plus the value-difference between the outcomes, multiplied by the weight associated with the more extreme outcome. For example,

$$V(400, .25; 100, .75) = v(100) + \pi(.25)[v(400) - v(100)]$$

The essential feature of Equation (3.10) is that a decision weight is applied to the value-difference $v(x) - v(y)$, which represents the risky component of the prospect, but not to $v(y)$, which represents the riskless component.

The following four sections discuss the main elements of the KT model of PT, including the additions of cumulative PT, which relate to the last of the elements. In each case PT is compared with other theories, and the relevant empirical evidence from various laboratory and field studies is examined.

3.4 Reference points

Nature

In PT outcomes are defined relative to a reference point, which serves as a zero point of the value scale. Thus the variable v measures the value of deviations from that reference point, that is gains and losses. As Kahneman and Tversky (1979) say,

> This assumption is compatible with basic principles of perception and judgement. Our perceptual apparatus is attuned to the evaluation of changes or differences rather than to the evaluation of absolute magnitudes. When we respond to attributes such as brightness, loudness, or temperature, the past and present context of experience defines an adaptation level, or reference point, and stimuli are perceived in relation to this reference point.
>
> (p. 277)

It should be noted that this element of PT was not an innovation of the KT model. It has a considerably longer history, involving in particular aspects of the work of Markowitz (1952) and Helson (1964), although we will see later that the Markovitz model differs in other important respects from the KT model. The concept of reference points is indeed part of folklore in some respects. For example, readers who are familiar with the children's story "A Squash and a Squeeze" will recognize the wisdom of the old man in advising the woman who complains that her house is too small. After cramming all her animals into the house, and then clearing them all out again, she finds that her house now seems large.

It is often assumed in analysis that the relevant reference point for evaluating gains and losses is the current status of wealth or welfare, but this need not be the case. In particular, the relevant reference point may be the expected status rather than the current status, an example being given in the discussion of anomalies. We will return to this aspect of the determination of the reference point later.

As with the other three central components of PT, it is now useful to consider the psychological foundation of the concept and then to explain its application by means of a number of examples, discussing how the concept helps to explain certain anomalies in the EUT.

Psychological foundation

Evolutionary psychologists attempt to go beyond describing mental attributes and try to explain their origins and functions in terms of adaptations. It can be seen that the psychological concept of a reference point is related to the broader biological mechanisms of **homeostasis** and **allostasis**. Both of these have fundamental functions that appear to have evolved as adaptations. **Homeostasis** is a well-known biological principle, whereby various systems in the body have an optimal set point, and deviations from this point trigger negative feedback processes that attempt to restore it. Examples are body temperature, the level of blood sugar, and electrolyte balance. The term **allostasis** was introduced by Sterling and Eyer (1988) to refer to a different type of feedback system whereby a variable is maintained within a healthy range, but at the same time is allowed to vary in response to environmental demands. Heart rate, blood pressure, and hormone levels are variables in this category. Thus when we exercise, both heart rate and blood pressure are allowed to rise in order to optimize performance. Wilson, Gilbert, and Centerbar (2003) suggest that happiness is also a variable in this category; this issue is discussed further in Chapter 9.

A simple physical or biological illustration of the phenomenon of reference points is the experiment where a person places one hand in cold water and the other in hot water for a certain time, before placing both hands in the same container of lukewarm water. The subject experiences the strange sensation of one hand now feeling warm (the one that was in cold water), while the other hand feels cool (the one that was in hot water). It appears that the visible evidence from the eyes that both hands should feel the same is unable to override the separate reference points of previous temperature in the brain. We shall see that these fundamental evolved adaptation mechanisms underlie many of the anomalies in the SEM.

Empirical evidence

It is now time to analyze the effects of the reference point phenomenon on decision-making under risk, applying PT to various real-life situations. At this stage the examples are limited to situations where the reference point phenomenon can be isolated from other elements of PT. Further examples, including those given in Table 3.1, involve a combination of elements, and a discussion of these situations is therefore deferred until later in the chapter.

One of the best-known anomalies in EUT is a phenomenon sometimes referred to as the "**happiness treadmill,**" which was mentioned in the previous chapter. The average income in the United States has increased by more than 40 % in real terms since 1972, yet in spite of having far greater income and wealth, Americans regularly report that they are no happier than previously. Similar findings have occurred in other countries. Furthermore, the phenomenon does not appear to be caused by the unreliability of self-reporting data; if other indicators of happiness or unhappiness are examined, such as suicide rates and the incidence of depression, we see the same story. Suicide rates are at least as high in rich countries, like the United States, Japan, Sweden, and Finland, as they are in poor countries. Similarly, within the same country, suicide rates tend to be at least as high among affluent groups as they are among poor groups.

Even in situations like winning the lottery, where a large and sustained increase in happiness would be expected, at least according to EUT, empirical evidence indicates that winners report average satisfaction levels no higher than that of the general population within as little time as a year (Brickman, Coates, and Janoff-Bulman 1978).

There is a happier side to the story with this phenomenon, and that is that it works in both directions. People who have suffered some kind of major personal tragedy, such as the loss of a loved one or serious injury, also tend to recover quickly in terms of reported happiness level. As indicated in the previous chapter, both of these regressions to normal levels of satisfaction tend to be unexpected by those involved, certainly as far as their rapidity is concerned. It is notable that half of prison suicides occur on the first day of imprisonment. Inmates generally adapt quickly to their new environment, in spite of their fearful expectations.

Expectations have an important role to play as far as the reference point phenomenon is concerned. When people expect a pay rise of 10%, for example, and then they are awarded just 5%, they tend to be disappointed. Their reference point in this case is not their current pay level but their expected pay level; thus they code and evaluate the pay award as a loss, not as a gain.

Reference points are also strongly influenced by the status of others. We may be delighted with a pay rise of 5%, until we find out that a colleague has been awarded 10%, when we react with fury. In this case the new information shifts the reference point, turning what was initially coded as a gain into a loss. Again, EUT is unable to explain this phenomenon, which will be discussed in more detail in Chapter 8 in connection with fairness and social utility functions.

Another situation where the reference point may not correspond to the current level of wealth is where a person has not yet adapted to the current asset position. The KT paper gives the example:

> Imagine a person who is involved in a business venture, has already lost 2,000 and is now facing a choice between a sure gain of 1,000 and an even chance to win 2,000 or nothing. If he has not yet adapted to his losses, he is likely to code the problem a choice between $(-2,000, .50)$ and $(-1,000)$ rather than as a choice between $(2,000, .50)$ and $(1,000)$.

As will be explained later in the chapter, the phenomena of loss-aversion and diminishing marginal sensitivity cause the person who has not yet adapted to be more likely to take a risk than the person who has adapted to the recent loss.

Shifts in reference points may also arise when a person formulates his decision problem in terms of final assets, as proposed in EUT, rather than in terms of gains and losses. This causes the reference point to be set to zero wealth, and we will see later that this tends to discourage risk-seeking, except in the case of gambling with low probabilities, for example entering lotteries.

3.5 Loss-aversion

Nature

In the words of Kahneman and Tversky (1979),

> A salient characteristic of attitudes to changes in welfare is that losses loom larger than gains. The aggravation that one experiences in losing a sum of

money appears to be greater than the pleasure associated with gaining the same amount.

(p. 279)

For example, most people would not bet money on the toss of a coin, on the basis that a heads outcome gives a specific gain, while a tails outcome gives an equal loss. In mathematical terms, people find symmetric bets of the form $(x, .50; -x, .50)$ unattractive. The phenomenon can be expressed in more general mathematical terms as follows:

$$v(x) < -v(-x) \text{ where } x > 0 \qquad (3.11)$$

Again, this element of PT is not an innovation; it is discussed, for example, by Galanter and Pliner (1974).

As with the previous element of PT, it is useful to consider the psychological foundation of the phenomenon first, before moving on to examine a more detailed analysis of examples, indicating how these explain anomalies in EUT.

Psychological foundation

Evolutionary psychologists have speculated on the origins of the phenomenon, in terms of its adaptationary usefulness. Pinker (1997) has proposed that, whereas gains can improve our prospects of survival and reproduction, significant losses can take us completely "out of the game." For example, an extra gallon of water can make us feel more comfortable crossing a desert; a loss of a gallon of water may have fatal consequences. While such conjectures regarding the origins of the phenomenon are by necessity in the nature of "just-so" stories, there is no doubt of the existence of the asymmetry in real life, as will be shown in the following subsection.

Empirical evidence

As with the discussion of reference points, it is helpful to start with a phenomenon where loss-aversion can be isolated from other elements of PT. An example is the observation of asymmetric price elasticities of demand for consumer goods. Price elasticities indicate price sensitivity, measuring the percentage change in quantity demanded divided by the percentage change in price. Loss-averse consumers dislike price increases more than they like the gains from price cuts, and will reduce purchases more when prices rise than they will increase purchases when prices fall. Therefore loss-aversion implies that price elasticities will be asymmetric, with demand being more elastic in response to price rises than in response to price reductions. Such asymmetric responses have indeed been found in the case of eggs (Putler 1992) and orange juice (Hardie, Johnson, and Fader 1993).

The extent of loss-aversion can be measured in terms of a coefficient of loss-aversion, which is calculated by taking the ratio of the loss and gain disutilities. For example, the study by Hardie, Johnson, and Fader found this coefficient to be around 2.4 for orange juice.

An anomaly in finance, particularly in stock markets, is a phenomenon known as the **disposition effect** (Shefrin and Statman 1985), where investors tend to hold on to stocks that have lost value (relative to their purchase price) too long, while being eager to sell stocks that have risen in price. This involves both loss-aversion and reference points, with the purchase price acting as a reference point in this case. EUT is unable to explain this phenomenon easily, since according to this aspect of the SEM people should buy or sell based on expectations of the future price, not the past price. Furthermore, tax laws encourage selling losers rather than winners, in order to reduce capital gains tax liability. Although investors sometimes claim that they hold on to losers because they expect them to "bounce back," a study by Odean (2004) indicated that unsold losers only yielded a return of 5 % in the following year, compared with a return of 11.6 % for winners that were sold later. Genesove and Mayer (2001) have reported a similar disposition effect in the housing market; owners appear to be unwilling to sell their properties for less than they paid for them, and therefore tend to hold on to them too long before selling when the market goes into a downturn.

Another anomaly of EUT which can be explained by PT concerns the **end-of-the-day effect** observed in racetrack betting. Bettors tend to shift their bets toward long shots, and away from favorites, later in the racing day (McGlothlin 1956; Ali 1977). In this case again both loss-aversion and reference points are involved. Because the track stacks the odds against bettors in order to make a profit, by the last race of the day most of them are suffering losses. It appears that most bettors also use zero daily profit as a reference point; they are therefore willing to bet on long shots in the last race, since a small bet can generate a sufficiently large profit to break even for the day. Some studies indicate that this effect is so large that conservatively betting on the favorite to show (a first, second, or third place finish) in the last race is profitable, even allowing for the track's biasing of the odds. It is important to note that EUT cannot account for this phenomenon if bettors integrate their wealth, meaning that they regard gains and losses from the last race on one day as being in the same category as gains and losses on the next outing.

Further anomalies involving loss-aversion, combined with other effects, are discussed in more detail in the first two case studies at the end of the chapter, and also in the first two case studies in the next chapter. These involve endowment effects, insensitivity to bad income news, the equity premium puzzle, and the downward-sloping labor supply curve. Endowment effects are also discussed in Section 3.8, since this is an area where PT has attracted significant criticism.

There have been a number of recent studies investigating and reviewing the factors determining loss-aversion and its boundaries (Ariely, Huber, and Wertenbroch 2005; Camerer 2005; Novemsky and Kahneman 2005a, b). It is appropriate to discuss these more fully in the context of mental accounting in the next chapter.

3.6 Shape of the utility function

Nature

There is an ongoing debate in the literature regarding this issue. We will consider four main possibilities here: (1) The traditional concave function of the SEM; (2) The Friedman–Savage (FS) function; (3) The Markowitz (M) function; and (4) the Prospect Theory (PT) function.

1. *The SEM utility function*

   As already discussed, this has a concave shape, caused by the law of diminishing marginal utility. The implication of this is that there is risk-aversion at all levels of wealth. Nobody would ever want to make a fair bet, meaning one where the expected value of the prospect is zero, for example betting on the toss of a coin.

   It can be seen in Figure 3.2 that this utility function is monotonically increasing, meaning that u is increasing throughout the range of x; in mathematical terms, du/dx or $u' > 0$. However, the slope of the utility function decreases, meaning that the second derivative of u with respect to x is negative. In mathematical notation, $u'' < 0$.

2. *The Friedman–Savage utility function*

   Friedman and Savage (1948) observed that the traditional concave function failed to explain various widely observed phenomena, such as gambling. They proposed a function that had two concave regions, with a convex region between them, in order to explain these anomalies. This is shown in Figure 3.3.

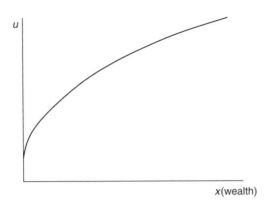

Figure 3.2 Standard economic model utility function

Although the FS utility function does explain some anomalies of the SEM function, it still fails to explain various empirical observations. For example, it predicts that in the middle region of wealth people will be willing to make large symmetric bets, for example betting $10 000 on the toss of a coin. In reality people do not like such bets, as was pointed out by Markowitz (1952).

3. *The Markowitz utility function*

Markowitz proposed various amendments in order to remedy the failings of other functions to explain empirical data. He anticipated the work of Kahneman and Tversky by including both reference points and loss-aversion in his analysis. The shape of his utility function was S-shaped in the regions of both gain and loss. However, as can be seen in Figure 3.4, in the middle region of small gains and losses between points A and B, the function has a reversed S-shape. The implications of this shape of function

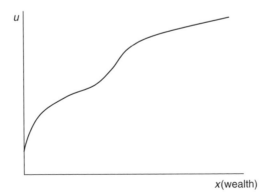

Figure 3.3 Friedman–Savage utility function

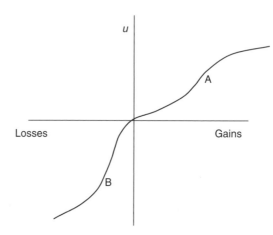

Figure 3.4 Markowitz utility function

are that people tend to be risk-seeking for small gains (explaining most gambling) and risk-averse for small losses (explaining why many people take out insurance). However, people would be risk-averse for large gains and risk-seeking for large losses.

It should be noted that this graph also takes into account the other two elements of Markowitz, that are also features of PT: reference points (measuring outcomes in terms of gains and losses) and loss-aversion (the function is steeper in the loss domain than in the gain domain).

4. *The Prospect Theory utility function*

In PT, risk-aversion may be caused by two factors. One factor is the nature of the decision-weighting factor (π), discussed in the next section. The other factor is the phenomenon of diminishing marginal sensitivity, which determines the shape of the function $v(x)$. Kahneman and Tversky proposed a utility function that featured diminishing marginal sensitivity in the domains of both gains and losses. The marginal value of both gains and losses generally decreases with their magnitude (Galanter and Pliner 1974); this is essentially an aspect of the well-known feature of the SEM, the law of diminishing returns. The relationship is shown graphically in Figure 3.5.

It can be seen that in PT the value function for changes of wealth is normally concave above the reference point and usually convex below it. In mathematical terms this can be expressed as follows:

$$v''(x) < 0 \text{ for } x > 0 \text{ and } v''(x) > 0 \text{ for } x < 0 \qquad (3.12)$$

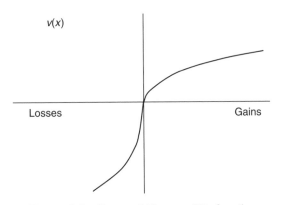

Figure 3.5   Prospect Theory utility function

This type of function implies that diminishing marginal sensitivity generally causes risk-aversion in the domain of gains and risk-seeking in the domain of losses. For example, when faced with the prospects of (200, .5) and (100) people generally choose the latter, since the gain of 200 does not usually have twice as much utility as the gain of 100. In mathematical terms, $v(200) < 2v(100)$. However, if we reverse this situation in order to consider people's attitudes to losses we find that people generally prefer the prospect $(-200, .5)$ to (-100). They are prepared to gamble in this situation, since the loss of 200 does not usually have twice as much disutility as the loss of 100. In mathematical terms, $-v(200) < -2v(100)$. Kahneman and Tversky named this phenomenon the **reflection effect**, meaning that the preference between negative prospects is the mirror image of the preference between positive prospects.

Psychological foundation

In the words of Kahneman and Tversky (1979),

> Many sensory and perceptual dimensions share the property that the psychological response is a concave function of the magnitude of physical change. For example, it is easier to discriminate between a change of 3° and a change of 6° in room temperature, than it is to discriminate between a change of 13° and a change of 16°. We propose that this principle applies in particular to the evaluation of monetary changes.
>
> (p. 278)

As with the other elements of the KT model, evolutionary psychologists like to go beyond the descriptive statement above and speculate on how such a mental adaptation can have evolved. It appears that in many situations it is relative changes, rather than absolute changes, that are the key to survival and reproduction. For example, when one is hungry, a kilogram of meat is extremely useful (compared with zero or a very small amount); ten kilos is not much more useful, unless there are a lot of mouths to feed, since the additional amount could not be stored in our ancestral environment.

However, there does appear to be one exception to diminishing marginal sensitivity, in the loss region. As was mentioned in the discussion of loss-aversion, a really large loss can have fatal consequences. The implication of this is that people may be risk-averse for very large losses, while being risk-seekers in the case of smaller losses. Examples of such situations are given in the discussion of anomalies below.

Empirical evidence

We will start by comparing EUT and PT as far as the shape of utility functions is concerned. Diminishing marginal sensitivity is also a feature of EUT as well as PT, but when combined with reference points and loss-aversion it has different implications in PT compared with EUT.

Let us consider the reflection effect. As an empirical demonstration of this effect, the KT paper examined the attitudes of a sample of 95 respondents to positive and negative prospects and found the following results: when choosing between the prospects (4000, .80) and (3000), 80 % preferred the second prospect (a sure gain), but when choosing between the prospects (−4000, .80) and (−3000), 92 % preferred the first prospect, taking a risk of making a greater loss. The reflection effect had also been observed by other researchers before the KT study, for example Markowitz (1952) and Williams (1966).

The EUT regards diminishing marginal utility and the concavity of the utility function as being the cause of risk-aversion. It tends to explain risk-aversion in terms of expected values and variances. However, when the prospects of the losses in the previous example, (−4000, 0.8) and (−3000), are compared, the second choice has both higher expected value and lower variance, and therefore should be preferred according to EUT. As seen earlier, the empirical evidence of the KT study contradicts this prediction, with 92 % of their sample preferring the first prospect.

The EUT also has problems explaining various attitudes toward insurance. It may seem initially that taking out insurance implies risk-aversion, as implied by EUT. However, by assuming a concave utility function throughout the domain of the level of assets, EUT implies risk-aversion is universal. This is contradicted by the fact that many people prefer insurance policies that offer limited coverage with low or zero deductible over comparable policies that offer higher maximal coverage with higher deductibles. Thus taking out insurance may be risk-averse compared with not taking out any insurance at all, but some policies, which may be popular, may be risk-seeking compared with others.

There is one phenomenon related to insurance which may appear to be an anomaly for both PT and EUT. This concerns attitudes to **probabilistic insurance**. This type of policy involves the purchaser paying a fraction of the premium of full insurance, but only gives the probability of the same fraction of paying out if an accident occurs. It appears that such a policy involves more risk than standard insurance. Empirical evidence from the KT study indicates that such insurance would not be popular, which appears to contradict the predictions of the PT model. This apparent anomaly in PT, along with certain tendencies for risk-seeking in the gain domain mentioned earlier, can only be explained after a discussion of decision weighting in the next section.

So far we have compared the EUT and PT utility functions in terms of empirical evidence. However, it can also be seen that there are important differences between the PT function and the Markowitz (M) function. Markowitz noted the presence of risk-seeking in preferences among positive as well as negative prospects, and, as we have seen, he proposed a utility function that has convex and concave regions in both the gain and the loss domains. The Markowitz function has received some empirical support from a study by Jullien and Salanié (1997), which related to racetrack betting. This study found that the utility function for small amounts of money was convex. Another study by Levy and Levy (2002) has also claimed to contradict the PT function and support the Markowitz model.

These studies raise some important issues:

(1) How does the PT model explain activities like gambling? This widely observed empirical phenomenon appears to imply risk-seeking in the gain domain.

(2) How does the PT model explain why people take out insurance? This is also a common activity, and seems to imply risk-aversion in the loss domain.

It is possible to discuss the Jullien and Salanié, and Levy and Levy studies, and examine the apparent anomalies in the PT model, only after a discussion of the remaining element of the model, decision weighting.

3.7 Decision weighting

Nature

As with some of the previous elements of PT, which feature in other theories prior to the original KT paper, decision weighting is not a unique element of PT. Various conventional theories incorporate decision weighting, notably rank-dependent EUT. This is also the area where there are some substantive differences between the original 1979 paper and the revised 1992 paper, which introduces the term **cumulative prospect theory**. The latter version is more complex, but more satisfactory in a number of ways. In particular, it is more general, applying to situations involving uncertainty as well as those involving risk, and it is also better supported empirically, fitting a wide number of studies by different researchers in different countries. However, in order to better understand the development of the theory, we will discuss the original version first before extending it.

As with the other elements of the KT model, it is appropriate to start with a quotation from the 1979 paper:

> In prospect theory, the value of each outcome is multiplied by a decision weight. Decision weights are inferred from choices between prospects much as subjective probabilities are inferred from preferences in the Ramsey–Savage approach. However, decision weights are not probabilities: they do not obey the probability axioms and they should not be interpreted as measures of degree or belief.
>
> (p. 280)

There are actually two reasons why decision weights may be different from objective probabilities, and it is important to distinguish between them, even though they may have the same biasing effect, as we will see. These reasons relate to **estimation** and **weighting**. The first aspect relates to situations where objective probabilities are unknown, while the second relates to situations where these probabilities are known but do not necessarily reflect decision preferences according to EUT.

1. *Estimation of probabilities*

   People are often lousy at estimating probabilities of events occurring, especially rare ones. They overestimate the probability of dying in plane crashes, or in pregnancy, or suffering from violent crime. An often-quoted example of overestimating low probabilities concerns playing the lottery.

The California lottery, one of the biggest in the world, requires matching six numbers between 1 and 51 in order to win the main prize. The odds against doing this are over eighteen million to one. In other words, if one played this lottery twice a week, one could expect to win about every one hundred and seventy-five thousand years. It was found by Kahneman, Slovic, and Tversky (1982) that people overestimated the odds of winning by over one thousand percent.

Another example of situations where people are often bad at estimating probabilities is where conditional probabilities are involved. A simple example is where, after several consecutive coin tosses turning up heads, people are inclined to think that tails is more likely on the next toss (in this case the objective probability should be known but appears to be rejected). A more complex example involving conditional probabilities is given by Casscells, Schoenberger, and Grayboys (1978), and relates to a situation where a person takes a medical test for a disease, like HIV, where there is a very low probability (in most circumstances) of having the disease, say one in a thousand. However, there is a chance of a false prediction; the test may only be 95 % accurate. Under these circumstances of having a positive test people tend to ignore the rarity of the phenomenon (disease) in the population and wildly overestimate the probability of actually being sick. Even the majority of Harvard Medical School doctors failed to get the right answer. For every thousand patients tested, one will be actually sick while there will be fifty false positives. Thus there is only a one in fifty-one chance of a positive result meaning that the patient is actually sick.

2. *Weighting of probabilities*

The 1979 paper by Kahneman and Tversky concentrates on the discussion of those decision problems where objective probabilities, in terms of stated values of p, are both known and adopted by respondents. In such situations decision weights can be expressed as a function of stated probabilities: $\pi(p) = f(p)$. These decision weights measure the impact of events on the desirability of prospects and not the perceived likelihood of these events, which was discussed above in the context of estimation. As an illustrative example, consider the tossing of a fair coin, where there is an objective probability of .50 of winning 100 or nothing. In this case it is usually observed empirically that $\pi(.50) < .50$, meaning that there is risk-aversion.

There are a number of important characteristics of the weighting function that were observed by Kahneman and Tversky. Most obviously, π is an increasing function of p, with $\pi(0) = 0$ and $\pi(1) = 1$; this means that impossible events are ignored and the scale is normalized so that $\pi(p)$ is the ratio of the weight associated with the probability p to the weight associated with a certain event. In addition there are three important characteristics of π which violate the normal probability axioms in EUT: **subadditivity, subcertainty**, and **subproportionality**. These are now discussed in turn.

The characteristic of subadditivity relates to situations where p is small. For example, the KT paper found that the prospect (6000, .001) was preferred to (3000, .002) by 73 % of the respondents. This contravenes the normal risk-aversion for gains and diminishing marginal sensitivity described in earlier elements of PT, and can only be explained by a weighting function involving subadditivity.

In the above example, $\pi(.001)v(6000) > \pi(.002)v(3000)$

Since $v(3000) > .5v(6000)$ because of diminishing marginal sensitivity (concavity of v)

$$\pi(.001)v(6000) > \pi(.002)v(3000) > \pi(.002).5v(6000)$$

Canceling $v(6000)$ from both sides of the first and last terms,

$$\pi(.001) > .5\pi(.002)$$
$$\pi(.5 \times .002) > .5\pi(.002)$$

In general terms the subadditivity principle can be expressed as follows:

$$\pi(rp) > r\pi(p) \text{ for } 0 < r < 1 \tag{3.13}$$

The overweighting of probabilities illustrated above was also observed by KT in the domain of losses. They observed that 70 % of their respondents preferred the prospect (−3000, .002) to the prospect (−6000, .001), which shows the reflected preferences of the previous example. However, they did not find that this principle applied to larger probabilities, for example where $p = .90$. The significance of these findings is discussed in the section relating to anomalies.

The second principle of subcertainty can be illustrated by a couple of examples coming from studies by Allais (1953). Allais noted that people tend to overweight outcomes that are considered certain, relative to outcomes that are merely probable. He found that 82 % of his respondents preferred the prospect (2400) to the prospect (2500, .33; 2400, .66). Yet 83 % of his respondents preferred (2500, .33) to (2400, .34).

Thus in the first case, $v(2400) > \pi(.66)v(2400) + \pi(.33)v(2500)$
While in the second case, $\pi(.33)v(2500) > \pi(.34)v(2400)$
Thus $v(2400) > \pi(.66)v(2400) + \pi(.34)v(2400)$
Dividing by $v(2400)$,
$1 > \pi(.66) + \pi(.34)$

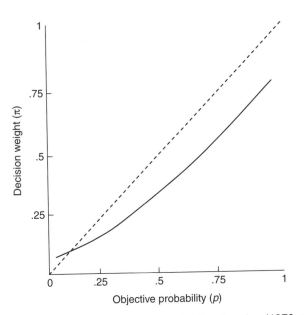

Figure 3.6   A typical Prospect Theory weighting function (1979 version)

In general terms the subcertainty principle can be expressed as

$$\pi(p) + \pi(1-p) < 1 \qquad (3.14)$$

One main implication of subcertainty is that preferences are generally less sensitive to variations in probability than EUT would suggest. This is illustrated in the graph in Figure 3.6, where $\pi(p)$ is less steep than the 45° line.

The discontinuities of the function at low and high probabilities reflect the phenomenon that there is a limit to how small a decision weight can be attached to an event, if it is given any weight at all. The implication is that events with very low probabilities are ignored, or given a weight of zero, and there is then a discrete quantum jump to a minimum decision weight that is applied to events that are regarded as just sufficiently likely for them to be worth taking into consideration. A similar effect occurs at the upper end of the probability spectrum, where there is a discrete jump between certainty and uncertainty.

A final characteristic of decision-weighting functions is that they involve subproportionality. This means that they violate the independence or substitution axiom of EUT. For example, the KT study found that 80% of respondents preferred the certainty of (3000) to the uncertain prospect (4000, .8), but when these outcomes had their probabilities reduced by a common factor of a quarter, the situation was reversed. Thus 65 % of their respondents preferred the prospect (4000, .2) to the prospect (3000, .25).

The independence axiom was stated in formal terms near the beginning of the chapter. In more simple terms this principle states that if a prospect A (x, p) is preferred to prospect B (y, q) then it follows that any probability mixture (A, r) must be preferred to the mixture (B, r). In the example above $r = 1/4$. In contrast the subproportionality principle of PT states the following:

$$\frac{\pi(pq)}{\pi(p)} \leq \frac{\pi(pqr)}{\pi(pr)} \quad 0 < p, q, r \leq 1 \tag{3.15}$$

This means that, for a fixed ratio of probabilities, the ratio of the corresponding decision weights is closer to unity when the probabilities are low than when they are high. In more simple terms, people judge probabilities that are the same compared in relative terms (1 to .8 and .25 to .2) to be more similar when probabilities are small (.25 is judged more similar to .2 than 1 is to .8).

This completes the description of the original version of decision weighting in the 1979 paper. However, certain empirical anomalies were later observed, described in the final subsection, and the revised "cumulative prospect theory" was developed in the 1992 paper. The essential difference in general terms is that the principle of diminishing marginal sensitivity is now applied to weighting functions as well as the utility function. In the words of Tversky and Kahneman (1992),

Diminishing sensitivity entails that the impact of a given change in probability diminishes with its distance from the boundary. For example, an increase of .1 in the probability of winning a given prize has more impact when it changes the probability of winning from .9 to 1.0 or from 0 to .1, than when it changes the probability of winning from .3 to .4 or from .6 to .7. Diminishing sensitivity, therefore, gives rise to a weighting function that is concave near 0 and convex near 1.

(p. 303)

The weighting function, for both gains and losses, therefore has an inverted S-shape, shown in Figure 3.7. This is again similar to the weighting function used in many conventional rank-dependent EUT models. Instead of using the symbol π to denote decision weights, the symbol $w(p)$ is used, and the general shape of the function is described by the following mathematical form:

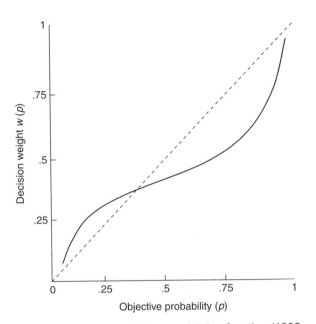

Figure 3.7   A typical Prospect Theory weighting function (1992 version)

$$w(p) = \frac{p^{\gamma}}{[p^{\gamma} + (1-p)^{\gamma}]^{1/\gamma}} \qquad (3.16)$$

The parameter γ determining the curvature of the function may be different for losses compared with gains. As Tversky and Kahneman point out, this form has several useful features: it has only one parameter, γ, thus maintaining parsimony; it is versatile, in accommodating weighting functions with both convex and concave regions; and it does not require $w(.5) = .5$ as a point of symmetry for the curve. Related to this last feature, the most important advantage of the form is that it fits empirical data well, as we will see shortly.

The practical implications of these modifications to the weighting function are that, instead of having a simple twofold attitude to risk, involving risk-aversion for gains and risk-seeking for losses, there is now a more complex fourfold pattern: risk-aversion for gains and risk-seeking for losses of high probability; risk-seeking for gains and risk-aversion for losses of low probability. As we will see in the last part of this section, this refined model fits better with empirical observations.

This 1992 model has in turn been modified by various authors, notably Prelec (1998). The most important amendment has been to eliminate the discontinuities at each end of the curve, thus addressing situations involving very low probabilities. An axiomatic foundation for the Prelec model is provided by al-Nowaihi and Dhami (2006).

Psychological foundation

There are various puzzles regarding the attitudes to risk described above. First, there is the issue concerning why we are bad at estimating probabilities, particularly those of rare events. Second, there is the issue regarding why we are usually risk-averse when gains are at stake, but risk-seeking when losses are involved. Finally, there is the issue of exceptions: why are we sometimes risk-seeking for gains, particularly when probabilities are low? Evolutionary psychologists have ventured a number of theories relating to these issues, and there is some interesting evidence both from other species and from neuroscientific studies.

As far as the first issue is concerned, it appears that we are bad at estimating probabilities for events that have no resemblance to those that have occurred in our evolutionary past. Betting on the lottery is obviously in this category. Complex problems involving conditional probabilities would also often fall into this category of unfamiliarity. On the other hand, events that were a high risk in our evolutionary past, such as death in pregnancy or through violent assault, tend to be overestimated in importance in our current environment (Slovic, Fischhoff, and Lichtenstein 1982; Glassner 1999).

As an interesting corollary, there is evidence that some animals are extremely good at estimating probabilities in situations that directly affect their survival. One might not expect woodpeckers to be exceptionally good mathematicians, but in one respect they seem able to solve a problem that would stump many skilled humans (Lima 1984). In a laboratory experiment, woodpeckers were presented with two kinds of artificial trees, both of which had 24 holes. In one group they were all empty, while in the other 6 of the holes contained food. The problem facing the woodpeckers was similar to the one facing oil wildcatters: to determine how many holes to try before moving on. If they left too soon they would be deserting a tree that may still contain food, but if they stayed too long they missed out on opportunities elsewhere. Using sophisticated mathematics it can be calculated that the woodpeckers would maximize their food intake by leaving a tree after encountering six empty holes. In the study it was found that the average number of holes tried by the woodpeckers was 6.3, remarkably close to perfect. Furthermore, when the number of empty holes was varied in the experiment, the woodpeckers changed their behavior accordingly.

What is the implication of this? It is not that woodpeckers are better mathematicians than humans. However, the process of natural selection has honed the instincts of woodpeckers over millions of years. Those ancestral wood-peckers who were better at solving this problem, through some neurological superiority, were more likely to pass on their genes, with the same capacity, to future generations. Over time, competition between woodpeckers would ensure that only the most successful would survive and breed, so that today's woodpeckers have adapted extremely well to solving their perennial problem. We shall see that this process, which the evolutionary biologist and ethologist Richard Dawkins has titled the *Blind Watchmaker* (1986), can lead to the building of extremely effective mechanisms for solving problems, particularly in the domain of behavioral game theory (BGT).

However, returning to human behavior, there is at least one other important factor that is relevant in terms of explaining our poor estimation of probabil-ities. Our senses of perception have become attuned through natural selection to become highly selective, filtering out "noise" and trivia, and external events have to compete for our attention. We tend to give more weight to events that attract our attention for whatever reason. In modern times the media play an important role here. Because events like plane and train accidents receive much media coverage, they attract our attention more than car accidents, and this affects our estimation of probabilities, causing us to overestimate them.

Let us now consider the second issue mentioned above. What explains the general pattern of risk-aversion for gains? Once again animal studies are instructive. In general, animals often appear to be risk-averse, for example in competition for mates. Such competition rarely results in fatal injuries. Often there are displays and shows of strength to begin with; if this fails to discourage one of the contenders, the situation may escalate to some form of sparring. This preliminary "sizing up" usually results in one or other contender backing down, except when the rivals are very evenly matched. This rarity of intraspecies lethal combat was once explained by biologists in terms of group selection, meaning that the phenomenon was good for the species as a whole. However, this group selection explanation has been long discredited, at least in this context (Williams 1966), with biologists now favoring individual selection, at the level of the "selfish gene", to use another expression from Dawkins (1976). In simple terms, the aphorism "those who fight and run away live to fight another day" is appropriate.

This leads us to the third main issue. There are obviously situations where humans are risk-seeking in the region of gains. What can account for this? Again it is necessary to consider animal studies and neurological research, as well as human studies. A study of macaque monkeys by Platt and McCoy (2005) has demonstrated that, like humans, they are fond of a gamble. An experiment indicated that they preferred an unpredictable reward of fruit juice to a reward of a certain amount, where the expected values of both prospects were the same. The experiment also showed that the monkeys still preferred to gamble even when the unpredictable prospect delivered a series of miserly portions. Platt's conclusion was that ". . . it seemed as if these monkeys got a high out of getting a big reward that obliterated any memory of all the losses that they would experience following that big reward." It is also notable that the gambling behavior was mirrored by neuronal activity in the brain region associated with the processing of rewards.

In simple terms, there are situations where it does pay most species to take risks, even life-threatening ones. Were it not for this propensity to take such risks, the human race would never have ventured forth to populate the whole planet and would have stayed concentrated in Africa, where *Homo sapiens* originated about a hundred thousand years ago. There are still a few tribal societies in existence today where life is very much as it was then. The Yanomamö in South America are such a tribe, surviving by hunting and small-scale farming. Violence is a way of life for this tribe, with a quarter of the men dying from this cause. The killers in turn are often killed by relatives of their victims. The question therefore arises: why do Yanomamö men risk killing each other? An extensive, long-term study by the anthropologist Chagnon (1988) has revealed that those who kill and survive end up having more wives and babies. The study compared 137 Unokais (men who had killed at least one other man) and 243 nonUnokais in the tribe. The Unokais had on average 1.63 wives and 4.91 children, while the nonUnokais averaged only 0.63 wives and 1.59 children.

Therefore taking risks can obviously pay dividends. Our brains thus require mechanisms built into them over the course of evolution which provide rewards for taking risks. These mechanisms are biochemical in nature, and the most important one involves the neurotransmitter dopamine. As discussed in the chapter on rationality, some people have a variation of the dopamine D4 receptor gene, sometimes referred to as the "novelty-seeking" gene. This variation can lead to a number of variations in behavior patterns (Benjamin *et al.* 1996). Studies have shown how such variations affect migration (Chen *et al.* 1999) and sexual behavior (Hamer 1998). A discussion of how far such a gene might spread throughout a population is deferred until the chapter on BGT, since it involves an explanation of the concept of an evolutionarily stable strategy (ESS). At this stage it just needs to be noted that such a gene bestows not only certain advantages on its possessor (the tendency to take more opportunities), but also certain disadvantages (the tendency to come to grief when taking such opportunities).

Empirical evidence

Some of the anomalies in EUT have already been discussed in the previous sections. However, some further explanation of these phenomena is necessary, and a number of others can also be discussed. In particular we are now in a position to show that PT is in general better at explaining various real-life phenomena than EUT, or any of the conventional models extending EUT. As Camerer (2000) has observed in a review and comparison of PT with other theories, PT, and in particular cumulative PT, can explain not only the same observations that EUT can explain, but also the various anomalies that cannot be explained by EUT.

Let us begin by examining empirical evidence supporting the inverted S-shaped weighting functions for both gains and losses. Tversky and Kahneman (TK) (1992) performed a study with graduate students to reveal their preferences in terms of certainty equivalents (CEs) for a number of prospects. Table 3.4 gives a sample of results that were observed, showing the expected values (EVs), median CEs, and attitudes to risk for each prospect.

Thus with the first prospect the subjects were prepared to pay an average of $78 dollars to obtain an EV of $95, showing risk-aversion. In general, if the CE >EV this indicates risk-seeking for both gains and losses, while if the CE < EV this indicates risk-aversion for both losses and gains.

This data can be transformed in order to draw a decision-weighting function. We do not have to take into account diminishing marginal sensitivity as far as the utility function is concerned in this case, since all the amounts of money involved are the same in this example, $100. Thus attitude to risk is affected only by diminishing marginal sensitivity in the decision-weighting function. The plotting of this function requires the calculation of the ratios of the certainty equivalents of each prospect (c) to the nonzero outcome (x). Thus for the first prospect in Table 3.4 this ratio $c/x = .78$. One can interpret this ratio as a subjective or weighted probability, in that a subject may know the objective probability of gaining $100 is .95, but because of risk-aversion

Table 3.4 Empirical results related to weighting function

Prospect	Description of Prospect	EV ($)	Median CE ($)	Attitude to Risk
(0, .05; $100, .95)	Gain, high probability	95	78	Averse
(0, .05; −$100, .95)	Loss, high probability	−95	−84	Seeking
(0, .50; $100, .50)	Gain, medium probability	50	36	Averse
(0, .50; −$100, .50)	Loss, medium probability	−50	−42	Seeking
(0, .95; $100, .05)	Gain, low probability	5	14	Seeking
(0, .95; −$100, .05)	Loss, low probability	−5	−8	Averse

they really perceive the probability as .78 in terms of decision-making. From the small sample of results above a decision-weighting function is drawn, in this case for gains, shown in Figure 3.8. It should be noted that the 45° line, where $c/x = p$, represents risk-neutrality; points above the line occur where $c/x > p$, implying risk-seeking, while points below the line occur where $c/x < p$, implying aversion. In the case of decision-weighting functions for losses, the situation is reversed: points above the line represent risk-aversion and points below the line represent risk-seeking. It should also be noted that the curve is not symmetrical, since $w(.5) = .36$.

The graph above relates only to a very small sample of observations for the sake of simplicity. However, when applied to a much larger sample of the TK observations, the general shape of the function fits well for both gains and losses. The graph confirms the predictions of PT in terms of risk-seeking for gains of low probability and risk-aversion for gains of high probability, with this pattern being reversed for losses. In the TK sample as a whole, 78 % of the subjects were risk-seeking for gains of low probability, while 88 % were risk-averse for gains of high probability; and 80 % were risk-averse for losses of low probability, while 87 % were risk-seeking for losses of high probability.

The empirical observations of the 1992 TK study have been replicated in a number of other studies. A particularly notable study was carried out by Kachelmeier and Shehata in 1992, and was one factor leading to a revision

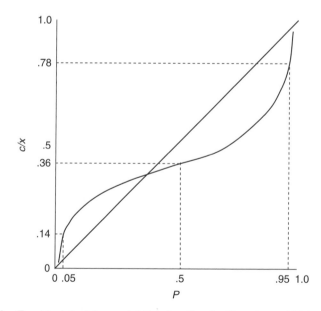

Figure 3.8 Empirical decision-weighting function for Tversky and Kahneman data

of the original version of PT. This study was carried out in China, and due to the prevailing economic conditions there, the investigators were able to offer substantial rewards of up to three times the normal monthly income. The main finding was that there was a marked overweighting of low probabilities; this resulted in pronounced risk-seeking for gains. In the highest payoff condition described above, and with a probability of winning of .05, certainty equivalents were on average three times larger than expected values.

Many other studies, in a variety of different fields, provide general support for cumulative PT when it is compared with EUT. Insurance is a good example of a field where appropriate comparisons can be made. According to EUT, people buy insurance at a cost greater than the expected monetary loss because they have a utility function that is concave throughout, making them risk-averse in the domain of losses. Thus they dislike large losses disproportionately compared to the small losses of paying insurance premiums. The problem with this explanation is that in many situations people do not buy insurance voluntarily. For example, car insurance is compulsory by law in many countries or states (and even then many people drive uninsured). This failure to buy insurance is easier to reconcile with PT, where the utility function is convex for losses. Furthermore, cumulative PT can also explain why people *do* sometimes buy insurance in terms of the overweighting of low probabilities, or risk-aversion for low probabilities of loss, rather than in terms of the large disutility of loss, as with EUT.

One aspect of insurance provides crucial evidence regarding the validity of the two theories, and this concerns probabilistic insurance, described earlier. According to EUT, if there is a small probability, r, that the policy will not pay out, then a person should be prepared to pay approximately $(1 - r)$ times as much as the full premium for probabilistic insurance. For example, if there is a 1 % chance that the claim will not be paid in the event of an accident, then a person should be prepared to pay about 99 % of the full premium. However, empirical evidence indicates that people have a strong dislike of probabilistic insurance. A study by Wakker, Thaler, and Tversky (1997) showed that people were only willing to pay 80 % of the full premium in the situation above. On the other hand, cumulative PT can explain this once again in terms of the overweighting of low probabilities; since probabilistic insurance does not reduce the possibility of loss to zero, such a prospect is unappealing. Thus, in the words of Camerer (2000),

> Prospect theory can therefore explain why people buy full insurance *and* why they do not buy probabilistic insurance. Expected utility cannot do both.

We find a similar problem for EUT when it comes to explaining the popularity of gambling and the equity premium on stocks compared with bonds. EUT can explain the former by assuming a convex utility function for money, causing risk-seeking, but, given this assumption, stocks should return *less* than bonds, which is patently untrue over the long term. The equity premium is discussed in detail in the first case study in the next chapter. Gambling is explained by PT once again in terms of the overweighting of low probabilities. This can apply to all forms of gambling, from horse racing to playing the lottery.

Various aspects of playing the lottery have already been discussed. There is one further phenomenon here that adds support to the PT model. People like big prizes disproportionately. Although EUT can explain this with the additional assumption of a convex utility function, the overweighting of low probabilities in PT can also be relevant. Larger states or countries tend to find that their lotteries are more appealing and more widely played. One might expect that the larger prizes offered would be offset by the lower probability of winning, but this appears not to be the case.

As far as gambling on horse racing is concerned, there is further interesting evidence available. There is a significant bias toward betting on long shots rather than on favorites. This bias can be measured in terms of the proportion of total money bet on long shots and comparing this with the proportion of times such horses actually win. Studies by Thaler and Ziemba (1988) and Hausch and Ziemba (1995) indicate that long shot horses with 2% of money bet on them only win about 1% of the time. The overweighing of low probabilities appears to be a relevant factor here. However, if one takes account of the study by Jullien and Salanié (1997) mentioned earlier, the convexity of the utility function for some amounts of gain may also be relevant.

There is another side to the story above, and that is the aversion toward betting on heavy favorites. In this case the Jullien and Salanié (1997) study found that there was a highly nonlinear weighting function for losses, causing probabilities of losses to be strongly overweighted. For example, it was found that $\pi(.1) = .45$ and $\pi(.3) = .65$. Thus it seems that, while people like to gamble, they are disproportionately afraid of the small possibility of losing when they bet on a heavy favorite.

There is one final aspect to this racetrack betting situation which has broader implications, and this is sometimes referred to as "the gambler's fallacy," or **the law of averages**. Long shots are frequently horses that have lost several races in a row. Gamblers often believe that they are therefore "due" for a win in these circumstances. The phenomenon is the same as the situation where a coin comes up heads on several consecutive tosses and people believe that there is then a greater chance that the coin will come up tails on the next toss.

There is an interesting explanation for this apparently irrational phenomenon in terms of evolutionary psychology (Pinker 1997). It is proposed that in our past evolutionary environment there was often good reason to believe that a series of common outcomes would be likely to be broken at some point. This was particularly true for meteorological events like rain or sunshine. Of course the expected length of the series would depend on the circumstances, but, just as a cloud eventually blows past the sun, at some point the probability becomes higher that in the next time period the sun will come out again.

It seems fitting to end this section with an example of a phenomenon that involves all the elements of prospect theory: tax evasion. Dhami and al-Nowaihi (2007) have shown that PT is superior to EUT in explaining various puzzles in this area, in particular why tax evasion is so low given its low detection rate, and why evasion is positively correlated with the tax rate.

While this subsection reviews some of the evidence supporting PT in terms of probability weighting, Section 3.8 will provide a more extensive review of empirical evidence in general terms, comparing PT with EUT and other conventional theories.

3.8 Criticisms of prospect theory

The PT has now been around for nearly three decades; during that time, not surprisingly considering its nonconventional nature and radical implications, it has attracted numerous criticisms. We will discuss six of them here: the lack of normative status; the nature of the utility function; the determination of reference points; endowment effects and market experience; the discovered preference hypothesis (DPH) and misconceptions; and the nature of framing effects. We will also see that the third, fourth, and fifth factors are related.

Lack of normative status

The most fundamental criticism relates to the normative aspects of the theory. Kahneman and Tversky propose PT as a descriptive rather than a normative theory. The authors treat the EUT model as the normative model to be used as a benchmark, but in rejecting its usefulness as a descriptive model, they do not propose any norm or norms to replace it. While the editing phase of the model adds explanatory power to the model in the descriptive sense, by introducing elements of bounded rationality and decision heuristics it not only makes the model less parsimonious, but also makes it **indeterminate**. Thus the model loses the simplicity and tractability of EUT and some conventional models which optimize a single variable.

Let us now consider the nature of this indeterminacy. In general terms this is caused by the fact that, like other procedural models, there are features of the model that are underdetermined by the theory, such as the order in which certain operations are performed in the editing phase, the location of reference points, and the shape of the probability weighting function. The issue of the determination of reference points is discussed later in the section. As far as the weighting function is concerned, the cumulative function in Figure 3.8 is unlikely to be accurate in detail. In the words of the 1992 study,

> We suspect that decision weights may be sensitive to the formulation of the prospects, as well as to the number, the spacing and the level of outcomes. In particular, there is some evidence to suggest that the curvature of the weighting function is more pronounced when the outcomes are widely spaced.
>
> (p. 317)

The evidence referred to here comes from Camerer (1992).

However, the main problem related to normative status concerns violations of both monotonicity and transitivity. Examples of these are given in the concluding section. Many economists would question whether it is even possible to have theories of "preference" that violate transitivity. Certainly it becomes more difficult to talk about people maximizing any preference function, although not impossible as we will see.

The nature of the utility function

A study by Levy and Levy (2002) claimed to have found evidence contradicting one aspect of PT in a series of experiments which compared the PT and Markowitz utility functions. The Levy and Levy (LL) study argued that the original KT data did not provide a reliable indicator of the shape of utility functions because it always asked subjects to compare prospects that were both either positive or negative. In reality, the LL study claimed, most prospects are mixed, involving situations where there is a possibility of either gain or loss, for example in investing on the stock market. Their study included a number of experiments, asking respondents to choose between such mixed prospects. The main objective was to test whether the data supported the PT model, with the S-shaped utility function, or the M model, with the reversed S-shaped function throughout most of the range. The study used a total of 260 subjects, consisting of business students and faculty from a number of institutions, along with a number of professional practitioners. One of the tasks in the experiments will serve as an example of the methodology.

The subjects were asked to consider that they had invested $10 000 in stock and were evaluating the possible returns, choosing between the following two mixed prospects:

Prospect F: $(-3000, .5; 4500, .5)$ Prospect G: $(-6000, .25; 3000, .75)$

Both prospects are not only mixed, involving the possibility of either gain or loss, but their expected values are the same, 750, and the same for both the gain and the loss components, 2250 and -1500. According to the PT model, people are risk-averse in the domain of gains; therefore they should prefer the gain of 3000 with a probability of .75 in prospect G to a gain of 4500 with the probability of .5 in prospect F. Similarly, the PT model proposes that people are risk-seeking in the domain of losses; thus they should prefer a loss of 6000 with a probability of .25 in prospect G to a loss of 3000 with a probability of .5 in prospect F. Therefore prospect G is dominant over prospect F according to the PT model, while the situation is reversed according the M model. The LL study found that 71 % of their subjects preferred F while only 27 % preferred G. They interpreted this finding as showing strong evidence against the PT model, and, combined with the results of other tasks in their experiments, they concluded that the M model was better supported.

However, the LL study has been criticized in a paper by Wakker (2003). Wakker claims that the data of the LL study can still be used to support the PT model, since the LL study ignored the element of decision weighting. The LL study justified this on the grounds that the probabilities involved in their experiments were always at least .25 in magnitude and that probabilities in this range should involve a linear weighting function. Wakker disputes this, claiming that nonlinearities in this range can have a significant distorting effect, enough to make the results compatible with PT. When we consider the finding of Jullien and Salanié reported above, with losses involving $\pi(.3) = .65$, Wakker's conclusion seems to have some justification.

The determination of reference points

Some economists view it as a weakness of PT that reference points are not determined endogenously. The determination of reference points is necessary in order to estimate the incidence and effects of loss-aversion; a good example of this problem relates to the endowment effect, discussed next. If subjects are given something for free in an experiment, they are likely to value this object differently than if they had "earned" it in some way (Cherry, Frykblom, and Shogren 2002). In practice, however, it is difficult to construct an experimental design where subjects can experience real losses without destroying the incentive to take part. The Cherry, Frykblom, and Shogren study overcame this problem by allowing subjects to "earn" wealth by taking part in a quiz and answering questions correctly. This study is discussed in more detail in Chapter 8 in the context of fairness games.

Kahneman and Tversky, and other supporters of PT, generally use either the existing situation as a reference point, or some anticipated or expected situation. However, more precision regarding the determination of reference points would be an aid to constructing better models of behavior. Certainly more research into how reference points are determined in different situations would be valuable. For example, it would be useful to know if different types of saver or investor have the same reference points. Furthermore, an understanding of the process of the dynamic adjustment of reference points over time would aid the analysis of various psychological phenomena; an example is the "writing off" of sunk costs, discussed in more detail in the next chapter.

Endowment effects and experience in the market

There has been considerable laboratory evidence from numerous studies over many years that supports the existence of **endowment effects**. These effects relate to the situation where an owner of a good, or seller, places a higher value on it than a nonowner, or buyer. According to PT this phenomenon arises through a combination of reference points and loss-aversion. The owner's or seller's reference point involves possessing the item, while the buyer's reference point does not involve possession; the seller's loss in a transaction is greater than the buyer's gain in the transaction.

However, there have also been some economists who have expressed the belief that the endowment effect is merely the result of a mistake made by inexperienced consumers and through time these consumers will learn "better" behavior that conforms to the neoclassical SEM (Knez, Smith, and Williams 1985; Brookshire and Coursey 1987; Coursey, Hovis, and Schulze 1987; Shogren et al. 1994). Some of these researchers have also reported empirical findings that do not support the endowment effect hypothesis. Most recently List (2004) has conducted a large-scale study involving more than 375 subjects who actively participated in a well-functioning marketplace. The purpose of the study was to test the predictions of PT in terms of the endowment effect against the predictions of the SEM. Further details of the study are described in Case 3.1, but here it is sufficient to note that all subjects actively traded sportscards and memorabilia. In the experiment they were endowed with either a candy bar or a mug of similar market value, and asked whether they would like to trade. List found that both inexperienced and experienced consumers did not trade as much as predicted by the SEM, revealing an endowment effect as people tended to value the good they were endowed with more than the other product. However, for "intense" consumers who traded in their usual market at least 12 times monthly, and for dealers, there was no reluctance to trade and therefore no evidence of an endowment effect. List's conclusion was that experience in the market did indeed tend to eliminate the endowment effect and that furthermore there was a transference of this experience, meaning that experience in the subjects' normal market of sportscards and memorabilia transferred its effects to trading other goods.

I will not comment on these results as yet, since the final criticism of PT and endowment effects involves some similar results.

The discovered preference hypothesis and misconceptions

There are some studies that combine a number of objections. The **DPH** developed by Plott (1996) proposes that people's preferences are not necessarily revealed in their decisions. They have to be discovered through a process of information gathering, deliberation, and trial-and-error learning. Subjects must therefore have adequate opportunities and incentives for discovery, and it is claimed that studies lacking these factors are unreliable. Plott argues that most studies that support the endowment effect are in this category, lacking the necessary elements of experimental design that ensure reliability. Binmore (1999) makes a similar claim.

Plott and Zeiler (2005) pursue this issue further by performing experiments to test whether subject misconceptions, rather than PT preferences, can account for the gap between willingness to pay (WTP) and willingness to accept (WTA) that PT refers to as the endowment effect. It should be noted that the methodology in this study was different from that in List (2004) and many other studies, because it did not focus on willingness to trade as such, but on the concepts of WTA and WTP, which entail various problems in terms of analysis. Plott and Zeiler (PZ) draw attention in particular to the concept of "**subject misconceptions**," and point out that this is not operationally defined or quantified. It is in effect a compound effect of several effects that PZ identify: misunderstanding an optimal response; learning effects; lack of subjects' attention because of inadequate incentives to give an optimal response; and giving a strategic response. Since these problems apply to much research in experimental economics, it is worth giving some explanation regarding each of them and discussing the PZ approach to solving these problems. This approach incorporates the following four elements.

1. *Use of an incentive compatible elicitation device*

   When subjects are asked to state a WTP or WTA they are essentially in a kind of auction scenario, and this is not the same buying/selling scenario as the normal marketplace. This lack of familiarity may cause subjects to misunderstand how to give an optimal response. Therefore an important principle in the PZ study was to use an **incentive compatible elicitation device**. A common technique used in experimental economics in such situations to elicit valid responses is the **Becker–DeGroot–Marschand (BDM)** mechanism. This mechanism pits each buyer and seller against a random bid, which determines the price paid by the buyer and that received by the seller. All sellers stating bids lower than the random bid sell the good, and all buyers stating bids higher than the random bid buy the good. Sellers bidding higher than the random bid and buyers bidding lower do not transact. The purpose of this mechanism is to elicit bids that reflect the true value to each party. The optimal response is to state a bid equal to the subject's true value.

2. *Training*

   Since it is not obvious to subjects that stating one's true value is an optimal response, especially given that the random bid is determined by a lottery, PZ took time in their study to fully explain the mechanism using numerical examples. An illustration here will clarify the situation. Say a seller's true value is $6, but they overbid, stating $7, maybe under the misapprehension that this may cause the buyer to bid higher, as in many real-life situations. This is an example of a **strategic response**, where one party to a transaction takes into account the behavior and reactions of the other party. If the random bid is $6.50, they will not transact, and there is an opportunity cost of $0.50, because they are forgoing a transaction that would give them a consumer surplus of $0.50. Now take the situation where a buyer's true value is $6. They may underbid, stating $5, maybe under the misapprehension that this may cause the seller to come down in price, again as in real-life situations. If the random bid is $5.50, they will not transact and will again forgo $0.50. The training was therefore designed to ensure that subjects understood the nature of the BDM mechanism, and therefore stated bids that represented their true values.

3. *Practice rounds*

   This procedure allows subjects to "learn through using the mechanism while still educating themselves about its properties." Subjects can also ask questions, and the experimenter can check that subjects are understanding the nature of the task.

4. *Anonymity*

Anonymity in decisions and payouts is important because otherwise subjects may again be inclined to make strategic responses, either to impress other subjects or to impress the experimenter.

PZ found that while they could replicate the WTA–WTP gap in the study of Kahneman, Knetsch, and Thaler (1990) using an experimental procedure lacking in controls, they couldn't observe the gap when they implemented the full set of controls described above. PZ concluded that this ability to "turn the gap on and off" constituted a rejection of the PT interpretation of the gap as being an endowment effect, in favor of the theory of subjects' misconceptions as being the cause.

The PZ study is certainly a valuable and informative one in many ways, but its conclusion has one main weakness. This is that the methodology is "all-or-nothing," in the sense that either there is very little experimental control, or various controls are combined together. The result is that a number of effects are confounded together in the "subjects' misconceptions" category. Plott and Zeiler admit this, giving five possible interpretations of these misconceptions (some of which they reject) in their conclusion. Further research is needed, using various degrees of control in the experimental design, to establish whether the switching off of the WTA–WTP gap is mainly due to misunderstanding the optimal response, learning effects, giving some kind of strategic response, or misinterpreting the intentions of the experiment or experimenter. It may be that learning effects, through practice rounds, could be the main factor; this would support the findings of List (2004) reported earlier.

It has been argued that the best type of experimental design to ensure that the requirements of the DPH are met is a **single-task individual-choice** design (Cubitt, Starmer, and Sugden 2001). Such a design can ensure that subjects get an opportunity to practice a single task repeatedly, with the requisite learning effect, and it can also ensure simplicity and transparency, which are difficult to achieve in market-based studies, where tasks are more complex and involve interactions with others. However, when Cubitt, Starmer, and Sugden reviewed the results of nine different experiments involving such a design, they found that the results still violated the independence axiom for consistent choices in Allais-type situations, discussed earlier. Another study by Loomes, Starmer, and Sugden (2003) also questioned the interpretation of the disappearance of the WTA–WTP gap under market experience. These researchers note that even after repeated trading, individuals' valuations of given lotteries remain subject to a high degree of stochastic variation, arguably reflecting many subjects' continuing uncertainty about what these lotteries are really worth to them.

(c166)

Having mentioned these results and conclusions, we can now consider an associated problem with the PZ conclusion. If subjects did not have a clear understanding of the experiment they may have been inclined to state certain values which did not reflect their true values, perhaps still giving a strategic response. Although Plott and Zeiler think this unlikely, it would mean that their results do not provide evidence rejecting the occurrence of the endowment effect in the real world outside the laboratory.

The nature of framing effects

Inconsistent results have been reported as far as the ability of PT to explain framing effects. Different types of framing effect have been demonstrated by Levin, Schneider, and Gaeth (1998): standard risky choice, attribute framing, and goal framing. This study claimed that PT probably best explains the first type of effect, but not the other two. It also doubted that PT could interpret the empirical evidence of risky choices in different contexts. A similar conclusion was reached by Wang and Johnston (1995), who indicated that framing effects are context-dependent, rather than being a generalized phenomenon. Other evidence suggests that a framing effect depends on task, content and context variables inherent in the choice problem (Wang 1996; Fagley and Miller 1997).

A further body of research criticizes the original approach of Tversky and Kahneman (1981) in using the Asian disease problem as an illustration of framing effects. Several studies have argued that this approach actually confounded two different effects: a framing effect and a reflection effect (Arkes 1991; Kühberger 1995; Levin, Schneider, and Gaeth 1998; Chang, Yen, and Duh 2002). This distinction now needs to be explained in some detail in order to understand the implications.

A framing effect depends on whether the problem is framed in a positive or negative *frame*, which depends on the negation "not." A reflection effect depends on the *domain* of the problem, meaning whether it relates to a gain or loss. Illustrating this difference, statement A, "200 people will be saved," represents both a positive frame and a positive domain, whereas statement C, "400 people will die," involves both a negative frame and a negative domain.

It is therefore argued that, because frame and domain correlate perfectly in the TK treatment of the Asian disease problem, it is impossible to disentangle the framing and reflection effects. On the other hand, it can be claimed that statement B, "400 people will not be saved," although identical in meaning with statement A, involves a negative frame but a positive domain. Similarly, statement D, "200 people will not die" is identical in meaning with statement C, but involves a positive frame with a negative domain. Thus, by restating A and C, it is possible to test PT against other theories as far as explaining framing effects is concerned.

This is the approach taken by Chang, Yen, and Duh (2002), who test PT against two competing models: **probabilistic mental models** (Gigerenzer, Hoffrage, and Kleinbolting 1991) and **fuzzy-trace theory** (Reyna and Brainerd 1991). PT explains the Asian disease problem by using different reference points for different comparisons. Statements A and B are worded in terms of people being saved, both involving a *perceived* positive domain (the actual domain is negative since people are still dying); thus in the domain of gains people are risk-averse and prefer option A to B. On the other hand, statements C and D are expressed in terms of people dying, involving a negative perceived domain, or losses. In this domain people are risk-seeking, and therefore prefer option D to C.

According to the theory of probabilistic mental models (PMM) people first attempt to construct a local mental model (LMM) of the task given to them, and then utilize it to solve the problem using long-term memory and elementary logical operations. If, as in any complex problem, this process is not possible, then a PMM is constructed using probabilistic information generated from long-term memory. Thus PMM theory suggests that a decision-maker solves a problem by applying inductive inference, meaning that they put the specific decision task into a larger context. The theory explains framing effects in terms of the inferences people make when presented with incomplete information. When people edit the statement "200 people will be saved" they may infer that maybe over time more than 200 will be saved. On the other hand, the statement "400 people will die" may be edited so that it is inferred that maybe more than 400 people will eventually die. Thus when statements A and C are expressed differently, with negative frame and positive domain and vice versa, it is possible to test PMM theory against PT. For example, when asked to compare A', "400 people will not be saved" with B, "1/3 chance that 600 will be saved, and 2/3 chance that 0 will be saved," PT predicts that A' will be favored, while PMM theory predicts that B will be preferred, interpreting A' to mean that maybe more than 400 people will not be saved.

Fuzzy-trace theory (FTT) proposes that people prefer to reason using simplified representations of information, that is the gist of the information, rather than using exact details. For example, both numerical outcomes and probabilities are represented dichotomously; this means that the Asian disease options can be simplified as follows:

Statement A: Some people will be saved.
Statement B: Some people will be saved or nobody will be saved.
Statement C: Some people will die.
Statement D: Nobody will die or some people will die.

In choosing between A and B, the first part of the statement is common to both options, thus the choice centres on the difference "nobody will be saved," and A is preferred to B. Similarly, in choosing between C and D the difference is "nobody will die," and D is preferred to C. Therefore, given the original four options, FTT makes the same predictions as PT. However, option A' now becomes "some people will not be saved," which cannot be compared directly with B. Likewise, option C' becomes "some people will not die," which cannot be compared directly with D. Under these circumstances, according to FTT, people are forced to think in more detail about the problem, calculating expected values and choosing according to their attitudes to risk.

The study by Chang, Yen, and Duh (2002) attempts to test the different theories against each other by performing two experiments. In both cases the experiments are expressed in terms of an investment decision problem, but in the first case the options are presented in the same way as the original Asian disease problem, with A being compared to B and C being compared to D. The results confirm all three theories and it is impossible to test for differences between them. However, in the second experiment A' is compared to B and C' is compared to D. In this case all three theories make different predictions. Chang, Yen, and Duh find that FTT explains the results best, since there is no significant difference between responses according to whether the frame is positive or negative. Thus they conclude that there is no framing effect in the situation where domain and frame are different, confirming the study of Stone, Yates, and Parker (1994). They find further evidence in favor of FTT in the comments of subjects relating to the scenario. In the first experiment only 18 % of the subjects (undergraduate business students) mentioned the calculation of expected values in their comments. By contrast, in the second experiment they find that 35 % of the subjects refer to the calculation of expected values.

However, there is one main shortcoming of the Chang, Yen, and Duh study, which is admitted by the authors. This is that the subjects are not asked to indicate their perceived problem domain or problem frame. For example, the study assumes that option A′ (400 people will not be saved) involves a perceived problem domain of gain. This assumption is certainly questionable, since it can be argued that the reference point used here may be that all people will be saved and that therefore A′ involves a perceived loss. If this is indeed the case then the predictions of PT are confirmed. More research needs to be done in this area to ascertain how people perceive problem domains.

There are important policy implications of framing effects, in particular in the type of accounting situation described by Chang, Yen, and Duh. Over the last few years there have been numerous accounting scandals in both the United States and Europe involving the reporting of financial information to both shareholders and auditors. If framing effects are better understood, this may enable government legislators and standard setters, like the International Accounting Standards Board, to better determine both the kind of information and the presentation of information so as to prevent fraud and deception.

3.9 Conclusions

It should not be inferred from the discussion above that these have been the only criticisms of PT; we have concentrated on these issues since they have attracted the most discussion in the literature. However, in this chapter we have seen that PT is able to explain various anomalies in EUT, even if there are a number of areas where further research needs to be done in order to clarify how PT compares with other theories like the DPH and PMM and FTT. This applies in particular to the issues of experimental design, context-specificity, and framing effects. It should be noted, though, that all these theories involve the use of heuristics, and are therefore compatible with the general Tversky–Kahneman approach to the psychology of decision-making.

There are three areas in particular where PT not only proves a better predictor than EUT, but also proves superior to other conventional models. These relate to violations of monotonicity, violations of transitivity, and event-splitting effects (Starmer 2000). None of these well-observed empirical phenomena can be explained by other theories so far discussed.

Violations of monotonicity

As we have seen, economists have generally constructed models that have been designed to ensure this "desirable" feature. Why has it been regarded as desirable? It seems intuitive that people would not choose an option that was obviously stochastically dominated by another option. In order to understand the issue better, I will repeat the example given earlier in the chapter from Tversky and Kahneman (1986):

Consider the following pair of lotteries, described by the percentage of marbles of different colors in each box and the amount of money you win or lose depending on the color of a randomly drawn marble. Which lottery do you prefer?

Option A				
90 % white	6 % red	1 % green	1 % blue	2 % yellow
$0	win $45	win $30	lose $15	lose $15

Option B				
90 % white	6 % red	1 % green	1 % blue	2 % yellow
$0	win $45	win $45	lose $10	lose $15

It is transparent in this example that Option B dominates Option A, as we saw earlier. However, there are situations where stochastic dominance is not so obvious. Consider the following example, from the same study by Tversky and Kahneman, which is a slightly modified version of the above problem.

Option C			
90 % white	6 % red	1 % green	3 % yellow
$0	win $45	win $30	lose $15

Option D			
90 % white	7 % red	1 % blue	2 % yellow
$0	win $45	lose $10	lose $15

In this version, Option C is basically the same as Option A, but combines blue and yellow marbles into the same category because they both result in a loss of $15. Similarly, Option D is basically the same as Option B, but combines red and green marbles, since they both result in a win of $45. However, the framing of the options makes it more difficult to detect the dominance of D over C. Kahneman and Tversky found that 58 % of subjects preferred the dominated Option C. Thus it can be seen that the editing phase is an important feature of the choice process.

Violations of transitivity

These violations again relate to the editing phase of the choice process, involving framing effects, and in particular preference reversal. This phenomenon was examined in the previous chapter, but is a widespread empirical finding under conditions of risk. Loomes and Sugden (1982; 1987) develop a model called **regret theory** that is explicitly designed to take into account both violations of monotonicity and transitivity. This theory has the further advantage that it posits a preference function that can be maximized, giving the model normative status. However, experiments by Starmer and Sugden (1998) suggest that regret theory does not explain all the observed violations. Loomes and Sugden (1995) also propose a **random preference** model, which proposes that people act on preferences based on a core theory, but the parameters to be applied in any context vary randomly, for example the degree of risk-aversion. Such a model may account for the common finding that subjects make preference reversals even when faced with the same pair-wise choice problem twice within the same experiment. Studies by Starmer and Sugden (1989), Camerer (1989), Hey and Orme (1994), and Ballinger and Wilcox (1997) indicate that between one quarter and one-third of subjects switch preferences on repeated questions.

As Starmer (2000) states,

> The bottom line is that economists do not have a theory of non-transitive behaviour that is consistent with available evidence.
>
> (p. 363)

However, Starmer does say that some of the evidence is suggestive of the kind of theory that would be needed. In this respect he reports (1999) an experiment that tests for the specific form of intransitivity implied by PT and finds it.

Event-splitting effects

These effects are actually discussed in more detail in the next chapter, since they relate to the issue of mental accounting and the principle of the segreg-ation of gains. They again involve the editing phase of the choice phase and associated framing effects. We will see that in many situations, like selecting a portfolio for a pension, people tend to use a **1/n heuristic**, where they tend to ascribe probabilities and make choices which are approximately evenly spread over the range of options presented. We will also see that this phenomenon extends beyond the area of risk.

Other factors

Apart from the three cases above, there are other anomalies in EUT, and other theories, that are not easily explained by any additional assumptions that are consistent with the SEM. One is that people appear to value control, even when this conveys no rational advantage. A study by Langer (1982) indicated that people who were allowed to choose their entries in a lottery valued their tickets more highly than those who were simply assigned entries at random. When researchers offered to buy the tickets back from the subjects they found a huge difference: those subjects who were assigned tickets were willing to sell them for an average of just under $2, while those who selected their own entries demanded more than $8. Another anomaly that is discussed in Langer's study involves the same factor of illusory control over events. When people played a game of chance against an opponent, the appearance of the opponent affected the amount that players were willing to bet. The game simply involved drawing a playing card, with the higher card winning. Half the bettors played against a well-dressed and confidently acting opponent, while the other half played against opponents who acted in a bumbling manner and wore ill-fitting clothes. Of course the chance of winning is a half in either situation, yet bettors were willing to bet 47 % more when faced with opponents who appeared inferior.

This factor of control, however illusory, is likely to be one factor why people regard car travel as less risky than train or air travel. PT can accommodate this apparently irrational tendency in terms of the overweighting of certain probabilities, although it should be noted that in this case again the probabilities are not necessarily low. A different weighting function may be involved in these situations, in the same way that the Jullien and Salanié study found different weighting functions for losses compared with gains.

In more general terms, the strong desire to be in control appears to be an important reason why the majority of people still believe in the phenomenon of free will (Wegner 2002). Again, evolutionary psychology has proposed an explanation for this emphasis on control. In our past, our ancestors developed a very useful cause-imputing mental adaptation which enabled them to impute and analyze causes of events. It was often better from a survival point of view to impute an incorrect cause of an event than to consider the event as being causeless. For example, if one's goods disappeared overnight, it might have been better for one's future prospects to blame the wrong person for stealing the goods than to believe that the goods just vanished without a cause. A strong desire for accountability has always been a prominent feature of most criminal justice systems in all kinds of different societies. This aspect of social fairness and punishment is discussed in detail in Chapter 8.

It seems fitting to end this conclusion by commenting on the main criticism of PT discussed earlier, its lack of normative status. In the past there has been too much reliance on axioms like monotonicity and transitivity in spite of mounting empirical evidence of their violation. Models like PT have been rejected because they permit such violations. For example, Quiggin (1982) commented that the implication in PT that certain choices may violate transitivity was "an undesirable result."

Economics as a science needs to reject assumptions that are proved invalid, and in turn reject theories based on these assumptions which are incapable of accurate prediction. It should not be rejecting theories that disavow such assumptions and by doing so predict well. As Starmer (2000) states,

> there should be no prior supposition that the best models will be ones based on the principles of rational choice, no matter how appealing those may seem from a normative point of view.
>
> (p. 363)

Therefore it is inappropriate to use normative criteria, as many economists have done, to evaluate a descriptive model. PT may be less neat and parsimonious than EUT and conventional extensions of EUT, and it may make less precise predictions, but it is undoubtedly a better predictor. In time a normative version of PT may be developed, once economists obtain a better understanding of phenomena like the learning process and reactions to incentives, but lack of normative status is not necessarily a weakness of the theory.

3.10 Summary

- PT is about decision-making under risk.
- A prospect consists of a number of possible outcomes along with their associated probabilities.
- EUT rests on three main axioms: transitivity, continuity, and independence. In addition, assumptions are usually made regarding expectation, asset integration, and risk-aversion.
- In EUT, risk-aversion is caused by the utility function being concave.
- Conventional extensions to EUT relax the independence axiom in a number of ways, but still maintain monotonicity and transitivity.
- Some conventional models incorporate probability weighting, thus including subjective evaluations of both outcomes and probabilities.
- PT states that decision-making under risk involves two phases: editing and evaluation.

- The editing process involves coding, combination, segregation, cancellation, simplification, and detection of dominance.

- The evaluation of prospects in PT involves four main principles: reference points, loss-aversion, diminishing marginal sensitivity, and decision weighting.

- Reference points are points denoted as zero on the value scale, with outcomes having values measured as deviations from this reference point, that is in terms of gains and losses.

- Reference points are often the current level of assets or welfare, but may also involve expectations of the future. Sometimes people may not have yet adjusted to the current situation, so their reference point may relate to a past situation.

- The biological basis of reference points is related to the processes of homeostasis and allostasis.

- Reference points can explain the anomaly of EUT referred to as the "happiness treadmill."

- Loss-aversion means that the disutility from losses is greater than the utility from gains of the same size.

- Loss-aversion can explain anomalies like the "disposition effect" and the "end-of-the-day" effect.

- Diminishing marginal sensitivity means that people become increasingly insensitive to larger gains and losses. Thus the value function is S-shaped, being concave in the region of gains and convex in the region of losses. This may cause risk-aversion for gains and risk-seeking for losses, depending on decision weighting.

- The Markowitz function has a reversed S-shape throughout the normal range of gains and losses, implying risk-seeking for gains and risk-aversion for losses.

- Decision weighting means that outcomes are weighted not according to objective probabilities, as in EUT, but according to decision weights.

- Decision weights may differ from objective probabilities for two reasons: people are often bad at estimating probabilities; and even if such probabilities are known or stated, people may weight them subjectively.

- People frequently overweight low probabilities.

- Decision weighting can explain many anomalies in EUT, such as gambling and insurance, in particular probabilistic insurance.

- PT has been criticized on various grounds: lack of normative status, the nature of utility functions, the relationship between endowment effects and market experience, the DPH and subjects' misconceptions, and framing effects.

3.11 Applications

Three case studies are included in this chapter, all relating to anomalies in EUT. The first two cases both involve reference points and loss-aversion, while the last case involves decision weighting.

Case 3.1   The endowment effect

According to the SEM, ownership or entitlement should not affect the value of goods. This assumption relates to the Coase theorem, which states that the allocation of resources will be independent of property rights. There are two main exceptions to the Coase theorem: (1) income effects may affect tastes; and (2) transaction costs may discourage trade. In addition to these exceptions, there are certain other situations where economists have proposed that value may be affected by ownership: (3) where ownership has conveyed experiential effects, causing people to value items they have owned for some time; and (4) where buyers and sellers need time to adjust to and learn market conditions, which may have recently changed.

Apart from the above exceptions, the SEM predicts that buyers and sellers should not on average demand different prices for the same good, that is the WTP of buyers should not differ significantly from the WTA of sellers. Stated in different terms, the SEM assumes that indifference curves are unaffected by ownership. However, many anomalies have been observed over the years. For example, a number of hypothetical surveys have shown that in the case of hunting and fishing rights the WTA of sellers has been between 2.6 and 16.5 times as large as the WTP of buyers. In a real exchange experiment, it was found that the ratio for deer hunting rights was 6.9 (Heberlein and Bishop 1985). Another such experiment found that the ratio for lottery tickets was 4.0 (Knetsch and Sinden 1984).

A particularly comprehensive and detailed study was performed by Kahneman, Knetsch, and Thaler in 1990. One important objective of this study was to isolate any endowment effect from any of the other circumstances mentioned above that might cause discrepancies between WTP and WTA. For example, the researchers carried out a number of experiments with tokens first, to accustom the subjects to the situations. As expected, these induced-value experiments showed no difference between the WTP and the WTA for tokens. However, when the experiments were repeated with consumer goods, using mugs and pens, significant differences appeared. Four trials were performed with the subjects (Cornell University students) in order to eliminate any learning effect over time, but it was found that there was very little difference between the trials. There were 44 subjects involved, divided into two equal groups, one with the property right to the good which they could sell, and the other without the property right initially but in a position to bid for it. It was also stressed to the subjects that it was in their interest to state their true WTP and WTA in the questionnaires, because after the four trials one trial would be taken at random, the market-clearing price (MCP) would be calculated from the responses, and the relevant transactions would then take place. Thus, if the subjects with the property right indicated a WTA at or below the MCP they would then sell at this price, while subjects without the property right who indicated a WTP at or above the MCP would then buy at this price.

The following results were recorded:

Mugs – The median WTP soon settled to $2.25 after the first trial, while the median WTA was a constant $5.25 throughout all the trials. An average of 2.25 trades took place with each trial, compared with an expected 11 (50 % of the 22 pairs of subjects would be expected to have the potential buyer value the good more than the seller).

Pens – The median WTP was a constant $1.25, while the median WTA varied between $1.75 and $2.50. An average of 4.5 trades took place per trial, compared with the expected 11.

The authors of the study came to the following conclusions:

1. There was evidence contradicting the SEM – People's preferences do depend on entitlements.

2. Indifference curves depend on the direction of trade – An indifference curve showing acceptable trades in one direction may cross another indifference curve showing acceptable exchanges in the opposite direction.

3. Endowment effects reduce the gains from trade – The volume of trade will be lower than predicted by the SEM. This is not because of inefficiencies like transaction costs, but because there are less mutually advantageous trades available.

4. Endowment effects will be different for different goods – They are unlikely to exist at all for money tokens, or for goods that are purchased explicitly for the purpose of resale, or for goods for which perfect substitutes are available at a lower price. The effects are likely to be strongest "when owners are faced with an opportunity to sell an item purchased for use that is not easily replaceable." Examples given are tickets to a sold-out event, hunting licenses in limited supply, works of art, and a pleasant view.

5. Endowment effects can also apply to firms and other organizations – For example, firms may be reluctant to divest themselves of divisions, plants, or products, and they may be saddled with higher wage levels than newer competitors.

Questions

1. Explain how PT can explain endowment effects.

2. Explain, with aid of a graph, how the endowment effect may cause indifference curves to cross, contrary to the SEM.

3. Wimbledon tickets are allocated by a lottery process. Given that there is a secondary market for such tickets, what implications does the endowment effect have in this situation?

4. We have seen that studies by List (2004) and Plott and Zeiler (2005) argue that the endowment effect is not present under various circumstances. What circumstances may eliminate the endowment effect?

Case 3.2   Insensitivity to bad income news

There are various versions of the SEM as far as the relationship between income and spending over time is concerned, for example the Friedman "permanent income hypothesis." These models are used to predict how much consumers will spend now and how much they will save, depending on their current income, anticipations of future income, and their discount factors. However, all these models assume that consumers have separate utilities for consumption in each period and that they use discount factors that weight future consumption less than current consumption. Moreover, these models make many predictions that seem to be contradicted by empirical evidence. They generally predict that people should plan ahead by anticipating future income, estimating their average income over their lifetime, and then consuming a constant fraction of that total in any 1 year. Since most people earn increasing incomes over their lifetime, the SEM predicts that people will spend more than they earn when they are young, by borrowing, and will save when they are older. In fact, however, consumer spending tends to be close to a fixed proportion of current income and does not vary across the life cycle nearly as much as the SEM predicts. Also, consumption falls steeply after retirement, which should not be the case if people anticipate retirement and save enough for it.

There are a number of aspects of behavioral economics that are relevant in examining the relationship between income and spending. Some of these were discussed in the previous chapter, and some are discussed further in Chapters 6 and 7 on intertemporal choice. At this point we are concerned with applications of PT. In particular, the concepts of reference points and loss-aversion are relevant.

It is therefore instructive to focus on a study by Shea in 1995. This yielded another result that contradicted the predictions of the SEM. Many groups of workers have their wages set in advance for the following year. According to the SEM, if next year's wage is unexpectedly good then the workers should spend more now, and if next year's wage is unexpectedly low then the workers should reduce their spending now. Shea examined the behavior of unionized teachers and found a ratchet effect: the teachers did spend more when their future wages were unexpectedly high, but they did not reduce spending when their future wages were unexpectedly low.

This ratchet effect was explained by a model developed by Bowman, Minehart, and Rabin (BMR) in 1999. Whereas in the SEM consumers have separate utilities for consumption in each period, represented as $u(c_t)$, the BMR model was a two-period consumption-savings model in which workers have reference-dependent utility, $u(c_t - r_t)$, where r_t represents a reference level of consumption for time period t.

Case 3.2 *continued*

In the next time period the reference point is an average of their previous reference point and their previous level of consumption. Thus $r_t = \alpha r_{t-1} + (1-\alpha)c_{t-1}$. This means that the pleasure workers get from consumption in any time period depends on how much they consumed in the previous time period through the effect of previous consumption on the current reference point. If workers consumed a lot in a previous time period, their current reference point will be high, and they will be disappointed if their current consumption and standard of living fall, that is if $c_t < r_t$.

Furthermore, the BMR model proposes loss-aversion, meaning that the marginal utility of consuming just enough to reach the reference point is always larger than the marginal utility from exceeding it. There is also a reflection effect so that if people are consuming below their reference point, the marginal utility of consumption rises as they get closer to it.

Given these features in the BMR model, we can see how it explains the ratchet effect observed in the behavior of the teachers in Shea's study. If teachers are currently consuming at their reference point and then get bad news about future incomes, they may not reduce their current consumption at all for two reasons:

1. Loss-aversion implies that cutting current consumption will cause their consumption to fall below their reference point, which results in great displeasure.

2. Reflection effects imply that workers are willing to gamble that next year's incomes may be better. They would prefer to gamble on the prospect that they will either consume far below their reference point or consume right at it than accept the certain prospect of consuming a relatively small amount below their reference point.

Questions

1. Explain what is meant by a "ratchet effect" in the context of Shea's study.
2. Explain in words the meaning of the expression: $r_t = \alpha r_{t-1} + (1-\alpha)c_{t-1}$
3. Explain the reflection effect described above in terms of a numerical example.
4. What implications do you think there might be for government policy arising from the Shea study and the BMR model?

Case 3.3 Fears of terrorist attacks

The rational response to terrorism

How people respond to terrorist attacks

CARRIED out by fanatics intending to kill, maim and spread fear, suicide-terrorism is not an obvious subject for economic analysis. The greatest costs are paid in blood, not mere money. Yet terrorists aim not only to kill, but also to disrupt ordinary life. How far do they succeed? Lots of pundits try to gauge the public mood after an attack, and it often seems that one man's guess is as good as another's. Are the citizenry defiant, resigned or intimidated? Here, economists can help, for it is their instinct to look at what people do, not what they say; to trust numbers, not anecdotes; and to look for clues in the inflections of mass behaviour, not the hasty reflections of the mass media.

Gary Becker, a Nobel laureate at the University of Chicago, is well known for applying economic methods to realms of life that most of his colleagues consider off limits. Terrorism is one such area. In a working paper circulated last year, he and Yona Rubinstein, of Tel Aviv University, examine how the general public responds to the threat posed by suicide-bombers.

The response is sometimes plain. The number of miles clocked up by passengers on America's domestic airlines fell by 16 billion, or 32%, between August and October 2001, according to America's Bureau of Transportation Statistics. Even two years after the attacks of September 11th, air travel had yet to regain its 2001 peak.

Was this an overreaction? The response certainly appears greater than the objective risks would warrant. According to Mr Becker, the public reacts to terrorism much as it responds to outbreaks of rare but fearsome diseases, such as BSE or "mad-cow disease". The chances of infection may be slight, but that does not stop people shunning beef *en masse*.

While such reactions are easy to understand, they are difficult for economists to explain. Perhaps people are simply ignorant of the true probabilities involved. But this argument, say Mr Becker and Ms Rubinstein, misunderstands the way terrorism works. Killing is a means of spreading fear. Terrorists introduce a small risk of violent death into humdrum daily activities, such as taking a bus. Even if that tiny risk is never realised, people suffer from the terror it sows. Mr Becker and Ms Rubinstein argue that it is not the risk of physical harm that moves people; it is the emotional disquiet. People respond to fear, not risk.

On November 29th 2001 a suicide-bomber killed three Israelis and wounded nine others on a public bus heading for Tel Aviv. According to Mr Becker and Ms Rubinstein, Israel's public buses suffered an average of one such attack a month in the year that followed. Not surprisingly, the bombs had a profound effect on passengers, reducing the use of public buses by about 30%, the two economists calculate.

But this large overall response masks some pronounced differences between passengers. Casual users, who bought their tickets on the day of travel, were much likelier to stay away after bombings: each attack cut their use of buses by almost 40%. But regular travellers, who bought weekly or monthly bus passes, were largely undeterred.

This is puzzling. It appears that neither the casual users nor the regular passengers calibrated their response to the added risk they faced. Suppose the frequency of attacks on buses doubled from one month to the next. Passengers could take half as many trips and restore the same objective risk they tolerated a month earlier. This is as true for people who normally travel twice a day as it is for people who normally travel twice a month. But passengers do not react in this way. Some abandon buses altogether, others take as many trips as before.

Case 3.3 *continued*

Perhaps regular passengers ride out of necessity, not choice. If they cannot afford a car or a taxi, they will take the bus whatever their feelings about it. But Mr Becker and Ms Rubinstein found a similar reaction to terrorism among patrons of big-city cafés, which are also common targets of suicide-bombers. As the number of fatalities increased, casual users stayed away; habitués spent as much money in cafés as ever.

Habitual bravery

Fear of terrorism may or may not be irrational. But it is not irresistible, Mr Becker and Ms Rubinstein conclude. With some effort, people can overcome their fear, but they will do so only if it is worth their while. For the dedicated patron of coffee shops, it is worth conquering their qualms, since the effort pays off every time they enjoy their favourite haunts. For the casual user, it is not. The threat of terrorism spoils something they only enjoyed on occasion anyway. Likewise, for someone who takes the bus twice a day, overcoming a fear of terrorism is an "investment" well worth undertaking.

The behaviour of bus riders and café customers suggests that this investment in courage is a fixed cost, not a variable one. People do not fight their fear each time they step on a bus; they choose to overcome it once and for all, or not at all. Once a person has come to terms with terror, it makes little difference to him whether he gets on a bus twice a day or once a day. He may be subjecting himself to a slightly higher risk of actual attack, but he is not adding anything to his fear of such a catastrophe. And it seems to be the fear, not the risk, that sways people.

In the morning rush hour, 500 tube trains serve London. Every weekday, 6,800 buses are scheduled to run in the city. Only three trains and one bus were bombed on July 7th. But anyone who rode on public transport on July 8th will have thought about the danger. Even if only a tiny proportion of Londoners ever fall victim to terrorism, they are all touched by it. Whether or not they are terrorised by it is a choice only they can make.

Questions

1. In what ways do people's reactions to terrorism conform to the PT model?
2. Explain the statement that "investment in courage is a fixed cost, not a variable one." How is the statement related to the claim that it is fear, not risk, that sways people?
3. What are the implications of both PT and the study by Becker and Rubinstein as far as government policy relating to terrorist attacks is concerned?

Source: *The Economist* print edition, July 21, 2005

Mental Accounting

4.1 Nature and components of mental accounting

The term "mental accounting" was introduced by Thaler's landmark article "Mental accounting and consumer choice" (1985); just as the previous chapter drew heavily on the two papers by Kahneman and Tversky on PT, this chapter draws heavily on two papers by Thaler, the original 1985 paper and the update, "Mental accounting matters," in 1999. Thaler draws parallels between the accounting process as used by firms and the mental accounting process used by individuals, defining mental accounting as follows:

> Mental accounting is the set of cognitive operations used by individuals and households to code, categorize and evaluate financial activities.

Thus mental accounting encompasses a broad range of human behavior, which as we shall see is not just restricted to financial activities. Like PT, mental accounting theory (MAT) was developed to overcome descriptive anomalies in the SEM, and it incorporates the basic elements of PT in its formulation. It helps us to develop a better understanding of the psychological processes that underlie choices and decisions.

Thaler's papers refer to three components of the mental accounting process:

- the perception of outcomes and the making and evaluation of decisions;
- the assignment of activities to specific accounts;
- the determination of the time periods to which different mental accounts relate.

These three components are now discussed, summarizing the material in Thaler's papers, while adding certain other relevant material and reorganizing the content so that some of the original material covered in the first area, such as opening and closing accounts, is now discussed under the third area.

4.2 Framing and editing

Implications of prospect theory

Mental accounting is concerned with how people perceive and evaluate situations when there are two or more possible financial outcomes, in particular with how people combine these outcomes. For example, purchase decisions, even for a single item, always involve both a cost and a benefit. Such decisions become more complex when there are special offers like discounts, prize draws, or two-for-one offers. Multiple purchases, when the items are complementary, like buying a holiday with airfare, hotel, car rental, meals, and so on, are also more complex. Sequential outcomes also need to be evaluated. For example, do people prefer to win two separate lotteries paying $50 and $25, or a single lottery paying $75? EUT, based on the invariance principle, would indicate that people would be indifferent between the two outcomes. However, Thaler found that in a survey 64 % of subjects predicted that the two-time winner would be happier.

PT contains some important implications as far as this process of evaluating joint outcomes is concerned. Thaler summarized these in his 1985 paper:

1. Segregate gains (because the gain function is concave due to diminishing marginal sensitivity).
2. Integrate losses (because the loss function is convex, again due to diminishing marginal sensitivity).
3. Integrate smaller losses with larger gains (to offset loss-aversion).
4. Segregate small gains from larger losses (the utility of a small gain can exceed the utility of slightly reducing a large loss, again due to diminishing marginal sensitivity).

Thus the first principle can explain the finding regarding lottery preferences. These principles have some important implications for marketing strategy, in terms of what Thaler refers to as "hedonic framing." For example, instead of marking down a price from $20 to $18, and framing this reduction as "new low price" or "now only $18," it may be better to use a **reference price** of $20, and emphasize the $2 discount. This is based on the fourth principle above, sometimes referred to as the "silver lining" principle. There is a further reason for framing the discount in this way, as will be seen in the subsection "**Evaluation of outcomes and decision-making**" in relation to transaction utility.

Hedonic editing

Whereas framing is concerned with the external description of events that is given to a subject, editing is concerned with the internal process whereby the individual codes or "parses" the information. The lottery example above can be used as an illustration. People tend to evaluate the outcomes separately, coming to the following conclusion:

$$v(\$50) + v(\$25) > v(\$50 + \$25)$$

or in more general terms:

$$v(x) + v(y) > v(x + y)$$

The principles of hedonic editing can also be applied to another well-known anomaly in EUT, the "jacket-calculator saving" situation mentioned at the beginning of the first chapter. It appears anomalous that people are prepared to drive for 20 minutes to save $5 on an item when the normal cost is $15, but not when it is $125. If people use the "minimal" account frame of EUT related to the cancellation principle then the issue is simply one whether it is worth traveling for 20 minutes to save $5, and the normal cost of the item is irrelevant. Similarly, if the "comprehensive" account frame is used, where all other factors such as current wealth and expected future earnings are taken into consideration, the cost of the item whose price is reduced is irrelevant. This is another application of the invariance principle.

The editing process of MAT, however, can account for the difference in choice. Whereas EUT considers $v(\$5)$ as the value of the saving regardless of the item whose cost is reduced, MAT regards the savings on each item as a difference between two values. Thus the saving on the $15 item is coded as $v(-\$15) - v(-\$10)$, whereas the saving on the $125 item is coded as $v(-\$125) - v(-\$120)$. Because of the diminishing marginal sensitivity of the loss function, the first saving has a greater utility than the second. We shall see in the next section, as with the framing of discounts, that there is another possible explanation for this phenomenon in terms of transaction utility.

As stated earlier, the concept of hedonic editing has important implications for marketing strategy. Much research has been carried out regarding the effectiveness of different types of sales promotions, comparing consumer response to price versus nonprice promotions, but until recently there has been an inadequate theoretical explanation for the differential response. Jha-Dang and Banerjee (2005) utilize a mental accounting theoretical framework to explain observed differences in effectiveness. They test in the laboratory consumer response to three different types of promotions of the same monetary value:

1. *Extra product promotion* – an additional amount of the product is provided at the same price.
2. *Price off promotion* – a temporary price reduction below the regular price is given.
3. *Premium promotion* – a separate complementary product is provided free.

The first method does not segregate gains, since the gain is in the same form as the product bought, whereas the other two methods do segregate gains, with the gain from the promotion being either monetary or in the form of a complementary product. The authors had hypothesized that the second and third types of promotion would prove more effective and found that their experimental evidence supported this hypothesis.

Another important area of application of the concept of hedonic editing is in the insurance industry. People generally dislike the idea of deductibles because of loss-aversion. The use of rebates or no-claims bonuses is preferred by the consumer, since rebates appear as a gain, or silver lining, while the extra premium paid may not be valued that highly because of diminishing marginal sensitivity. A study by Johnson *et al.* (1992) asked subjects to compare two offers of auto insurance cover, one with a deductible frame and one with a rebate frame. The results are shown below:

1) Deductible frame – premium of $1000 for 1 year

   This policy has a deductible of $600 which will be subtracted from the total claims against the policy. In other words, if you make any claims against the policy, the company will give you the total amount of the claims minus the deductible. If your claims in 1 year total less than $600, the company will pay nothing. If your claims exceed $600, the company will pay all of the amount above $600.

2) Rebate frame – premium of $1600 for 1 year

   With this policy, a rebate of $600 minus any claims paid will be given to you at the end of the year. In other words, if you have no claims against the policy, the company will give you $600 back at the end of the year. If you do file one or more claims, you will get back $600 minus the amount the company paid out for your claims. Should the total claims exceed $600, the company will give you no rebate but will pay the claims.

The reader can verify that the two policies offer the same financial terms, in the sense that the subject will end up with the same state of wealth regardless of whether they make claims and how much they claim. In fact the first policy should be preferable if the discounting of future values is taken into account, since the second option essentially involves giving the company an interest-free loan of $600 for a year. However, the study found that only 44 % of subjects would accept the first option, while 68 % of subjects would accept the second option.

Hedonic editing is also relevant in the phenomenon of endowment effects, described in the previous chapter. The key issue here is the location of the appropriate reference point; any gains above this will be valued less highly than losses below the reference point. Again the insurance industry provides some instructive examples. In this case we do not need to rely solely on survey or experimental evidence, but can refer to empirical observations from naturally occurring situations. Johnson *et al.* (1992) compare the situations in New Jersey and Pennsylvania, where changes in insurance laws allow us to examine real choices. Both states introduced the option of a reduced right to sue in case of pain and suffering, in return for lower insurance rates. However, the laws in the two states differed in terms of the default option. In New Jersey the default option was the reduced right, so motorists had to pay extra for the full right. In Pennsylvania the default option was the full right, so motorists had to opt out in order to get a discount. The result was that in New Jersey only about 20 % of motorists chose to acquire the full right, whereas in Pennsylvania about 75 % of motorists retained the full right to sue (Insurance Information Institute 1992). While other factors that affect this decision may vary between the two states, the huge difference in results appears to provide important evidence in favor of this aspect of MAT.

There are also other significant implications of this kind of endowment effect for public policy. One of the most important current issues relates to contributions to pension funds and provision for the elderly. Although there are a number of factors that are relevant here, for example moral hazard, it has been found in many countries that the majority of people do not make sufficient contributions to allow for a comfortable retirement, because of the self-control and discounting problems discussed in Chapter 6. There is some evidence that suggests that if higher contributions are presented as a default option in employment contracts, people are more likely to accept them. On the other hand, they tend to be unwilling to actively opt to pay higher contributions when lower contributions are presented as the default option.

Generally speaking, empirical evidence supports the Hedonic Editing Hypothesis (Thaler and Johnson 1990) that people edit multiple outcomes in a manner that is optimal, in other words that they behave according to the four principles outlined above. The only exception concerns the second principle: people appear to prefer to segregate rather than integrate losses. Thaler and Johnson established this by asking questions regarding people's temporal preferences regarding losses, on the basis that a preference for two outcomes on the same day implied integration while a preference for the outcomes being a week or two apart implied segregation. They inferred from this that a loss a short time prior to another one would *increase* the sensitivity of the person to another loss rather than decrease it. A short time period to recover from a loss would reduce the sensitivity to the second loss. It should be noted that this exception does not imply that people are behaving in a nonoptimal manner in terms of the maximization of hedonic utility, but rather that the loss-aversion factor in PT needs to be refined to take into account the observed behavior.

Evaluation of outcomes and decision-making

It was stated earlier that even the simplest purchase decision, involving a single item with no special offers, involves multiple outcomes: the benefit or value from consumption and the cost paid. The SEM frames the net value of the purchase in terms of benefit minus cost. In reality the phenomenon of loss-aversion makes this coding of the purchase hedonically inefficient. Both Kahneman and Tversky (1984) and Thaler (1985) therefore reject the idea that costs are necessarily viewed as losses.

Thaler proposes instead that there are two types of utility that consumers gain from a transaction:

1) *Acquisition utility* – This represents the value of the good obtained relative to its price, equivalent to the concept of consumer surplus.

2) *Transaction utility* – This corresponds to the perceived value of the "deal," in other words the difference between the reference price and the price paid.

Thaler notes two important implications of the transaction utility component. The first is that people are often tempted to buy "deals," where transaction utility dominates acquisition utility; we then often find that these items are seldom used. Marketing strategies skilfully manipulate the framing of offers, using reference prices and emphasizing savings ("silver linings"). Examples of such goods are clothing, household gadgets, and health club memberships (Wilkinson 1996; 2003). In the last case self-control factors are also relevant, and these will be discussed in the next section. The other implication relates to the opposite situation, where people forgo goods that have the potential to benefit the consumer in terms of acquisition utility, but are rejected because of a high perceived transaction disutility. Thaler gives the example of a thirsty beer drinker who will pay $4 for a beer from an expensive resort, but refuse to pay $2.50 for the same beer from a grocery, on the grounds that he has a reference price of only $2 in the latter case. We will see later, in Chapter 8, that there is an additional dimension that may also be involved in these sorts of decisions: our notion of fairness may be violated.

The evaluation process becomes more complex when product components are bundled together in a **product bundle**. Sometimes this happens naturally; for example, when computers are bought with screens and cars with stereo systems. Other times sellers deliberately bundle products together which not only may be complementary, but may also be substitutes if the intention is to offer the consumer variety. Thaler (1999) claims that in this situation using a **consolidated price** for the bundle is preferable to using a **partitioned price** in terms of consumer evaluation. He states two advantages of this form of framing: first, it integrates losses in terms of the costs to the consumer; and second, it prevents raising the salience of the expense of individual items. He uses examples of luxury packages to illustrate this, like a Club Med vacation or a *prix fixe* dinner.

There is conflicting empirical evidence regarding the evaluation of consolidated prices versus partitioned prices (Drumwright 1992; Wang 1996; Johnson, Herrmann, and Bauer 1999). Actually this should not be surprising in the light of the notion of Kahneman and Tversky (1984) that prices are "legitimate exchange for value received" and should be treated as proxies for the goods and services acquired. Thus prices do not merely represent a cost or loss, they can also be viewed as proxy for a benefit. With this in mind, price partitioning may segregate losses, reducing consumer evaluations, but at the same time it may segregate gains, improving evaluations. Therefore price partitioning may have a net effect on evaluations that is either good or bad, depending on the circumstances.

Chakravarti *et al.* (2002) have investigated the circumstances which may influence overall consumer evaluations of product bundles. They agree with Thaler regarding the general point that partitioning raises the salience of the price of the components, but add that it also differentially raises the salience of different aspects of the product depending on the component that is partitioned. They conduct an experiment with refrigerators, which are bundled with an icemaker and a warranty. The icemaker is a consumption-related accessory, while the warranty is a performance-related accessory. They found that partitioning both the icemaker and the warranty significantly improved consumer evaluations, but the effect was greater with the consumption-related accessory. However, the investigators warn that in other circumstances partitioning a performance-related accessory could have unfavorable consequences, drawing attention to a factor that may cause negative associations for the consumer.

Evidence supporting the mental accounting approach to the editing of consumer preferences comes from various neural imaging studies (Bechara *et al.* 1996; Kuhnen and Knutson 2005; Knutson *et al.* 2007). These show that distinct neural circuits related to anticipatory affect provide critical input into subsequent purchase decisions, indicating that there is a trade-off between the potential pleasure of acquisition and the pain of paying. Knutson *et al.* (2007) used event-related fMRI to investigate how consumers weigh preferences and prices in a three-phase dynamic process: consumers see the product first, then the price, and then have to make a choice whether to buy or not. Their results indicate that the first phase involves the nucleus accumbens (NAcc), indicating that this brain region is involved in the subjects' reaction to products. Subjects' subsequent reaction to price information was reflected in activation of the mesial prefrontal cortex (MPFC) and the insula. More specifically it was observed that excessive prices deactivated the MPFC while activating the insula. The authors note,

> ... price alone could not account for the correlation between MPFC activation and the price differential ... These findings are consistent with the idea that people do not react as much to absolute price as to the price relative to what they think is acceptable for a given product (Thaler 1985) (making it difficult to determine whether prices are high or low without knowing their associated product).
>
> (p. 152)

Thus, rather than there being a general sense of arousal during a purchase decision process, different parts of the brain are activated or deactivated at different times in response to different stimuli. The authors conclude that

> The findings are consistent with the hypothesis that the brain frames preference as a potential benefit and price as a potential cost.
>
> (p. 153)

As noted in the first chapter, this study also shows that brain activation can be used to predict purchase decisions above and beyond self-report variables. The authors furthermore conclude that "fMRI prediction methods may eventually prove most useful in situations where people's behaviour and self-reported preferences diverge."

4.3 Budgeting and fungibility

Just as firms set budgets or targets for spending in various categories, and allocate expenses to different categories, so do individuals. However, for individuals the budgets do not just relate to spending, they also relate to other monetary categories such as income and wealth. Studies also indicate that people appear to maintain different accounts for time (Leclerc, Schmidt, and Dube 1995; Rha and Rajagopal 2001). The characteristic of **fungibility** relates to the substitutability of different budget categories; if budgets are fungible, overspending in one category can be compensated by underspending in another category and vice versa. We now need to consider the consequences of this and the implications regarding the BEM compared with the SEM.

Consumption budgeting

Thaler (1999) suggests that the allocation of spending to different categories serves two purposes. The first is to facilitate comparisons or trade-offs between different uses of funds; for example, should I spend the money I saved this last three months on a holiday or a new computer? The second purpose is to act as a self-control device, for example, if I have already spent my weekly budget on eating out at restaurants then I will have to wait until next week before I eat out again.

Evidence suggests that different individuals and households conduct this budgeting of spending in quite different ways. Sometimes the allocation can be very strict and formalized; for example, involving the putting of certain sums of money into different labeled envelopes on a regular basis. In other cases the allocation can be looser, less formalized, and less frequent. In general, poorer individuals or families tend to have budgets defined over shorter periods, like weeks or months, whereas wealthier individuals and families may have annual budgeting periods. For example, Heath and Soll (1996) find that most of their MBA student subjects had weekly food and entertainment budgets.

The fungibility of spending categories has also been investigated by observing the reactions of consumers to unexpected price changes and in-store coupons. Both of these would be expected to have a wealth effect according to the SEM, but observed behavior indicates that the effects are greater than those predicted by the SEM, operating through the perceived liquidity of consumers. Janakiraman, Meyer, and Morales (2002) find that unanticipated price increases reduce consumers' tendencies to buy discretionary goods, while unanticipated price reductions increase it. Furthermore, they find that the mechanism is different in each case. The unexpected price increases cause increased small-deal sensitivity whereby consumers dislike buying goods at the regular price, but tend to buy goods on offer at small discounts. However, unexpected price reductions appear to cause a simpler illusory wealth effect, with increased purchases but no change in small-deal sensitivity.

Unexpected coupons also appear to have the effect of increasing the number of unplanned purchases. Heilman, Nakamoto, and Rao (2002) find that surprise coupons increase consumers' basket size by about 12%, in terms of both items purchased and dollars spent. Moreover, the incremental purchases tend to be either "treats," products that are cognitively related to that which was promoted, or products shelved in close proximity to that which was promoted.

A paradox regarding consumption budgeting, at least according to the SEM, is that people are often delighted to receive gifts that they would never buy for themselves. According to the SEM, if the marginal utility of a good or service is greater than its marginal cost then it should be worth buying. Thus the standard advice for gift-giving is that gifts of cash are best, since a gift in kind can only be as good as cash at best, and then only if it is something that the recipient would have bought anyway. Yet people are delighted to receive gifts like iPods, holidays, clothing items, and expensive bottles of wine. Of course, there are various explanations regarding why people enjoy receiving gifts:

1. *The marginal cost of the gift to the recipient is zero* (ignoring any complications like feelings of reciprocal obligations, discussed in Chapter 8). Therefore, as long as the marginal utility is positive, it will improve the welfare of the recipient. However, many people appear to experience feelings of joy on receiving gifts that indicate that the marginal utility may exceed the marginal cost even if the recipient were to pay it.

2. *There is a marginal utility associated with gratitude.* The receiver of the gift may be gratified that the giver has such a good opinion of them that they choose to buy them a gift. This is again assuming that the receiver does not believe the giver was acting in a strategic way, for example expecting a favor in return.

3. *The recipient may be "liquidity constrained."* Therefore the recipient is unable to afford the good or service, even by borrowing funds. However, there are many situations where this is obviously not the case.

The appropriate psychology of giving and receiving gifts takes into account lack of budget fungibility and self-control factors. People tend to have specific budgets for the items mentioned above: expensive consumer durables, holidays, clothing, and wine. If these budgets are exceeded in any time period, consumers do not trust themselves to keep to their budgets in later time periods. For example, a person may have a weekly budget of $100 for eating out at restaurants. This may involve one good meal per week. It would be dangerous for the consumer to exceed this, as this would set a new reference point at a higher level of consumption. If this reference point were to become established, it would cause not only the budget to be exceeded, but would also make it hard to revert to the original consumption level because of loss-aversion. However, a free meal or voucher would not allow a new reference point to become established, as this would be regarded as a special occasion. There are a number of applications of this psychology. Examples are sales contests and prize draws, where prizes tend to have high value relative to most people's budgets.

Some research into the mental accounting process suggests that, rather than being a rigid and categorical process, it tends to be a pliant, malleable, and self-serving process (Soman and Gourville 2001; Cheema and Soman 2002; 2006). In particular, many small and routine expenses are either not coded, or are allocated to a miscellaneous category equivalent to "petty cash." This means that they are not subject to normal accounting controls. Cheema and Soman (2006) find that people are more likely to incur expenses when they are ambiguous to the extent that they can be allocated to more than one expenditure category at the discretion of the consumer. The policy implications of this effect will be discussed at the end of this section.

Income budgeting

People often find it difficult to classify transactions in terms of income or wealth. For example, should one treat a windfall gain as a source of income or as an addition to wealth? In other situations there may be a clear distinction; a tax refund or an increase in salary obviously fall into the income category. However, there appear to be some common "rules" that apply to both situations. Evidence suggests that people classify both sources and uses of funds on a serious–frivolous scale (O'Curry 1997). Windfall gains may be regarded as frivolous, whereas a pay rise would be serious. Going to the cinema may be frivolous, but paying the rent is serious. Furthermore, O'Curry finds that people match the seriousness of the source of gain with the use to which it is put, again indicating a lack of fungibility. This finding is also supported by Kooreman (1997), who reported that spending on children's clothing is much more sensitive to changes in the designated child allowance than to other income sources.

Another finding regarding the fungibility of income categories relates to the payment of dividends by firms. In principle, firms could return profits to shareholders either by paying dividends or by repurchasing shares. If dividends are taxed at a higher rate than capital gains, as in the United States, tax-paying shareholders should prefer the repurchase of their shares to receiving dividends. The SEM would thus predict that firms would never pay dividends under these tax conditions. Shefrin and Statman (1984) have proposed a mental accounting explanation for the payment of dividends.

This explanation involves self-control aspects, and a principal-agent model of self-control developed by Thaler and Shefrin (1981) and discussed in detail in Chapter 6. Dividend payments make it easier to follow the rule: it is OK to spend the payments but do not touch the principal. When shares are repurchased it is more difficult for shareholders to determine how much of the resulting cash inflows they can afford to spend without dipping into capital.

Shefrin and Thaler (1992) also explain another observed anomaly in the SEM, where many people simultaneously borrow and yet take too few income tax exemptions in order to receive a large tax refund from the IRS. Again this is a self-control device to prevent overspending, and in particular to allow saving. The tax refund would be classified as a "serious" source of funds on O'Curry's scale, making it easier to use the funds for saving.

Wealth budgeting

There is considerable evidence that people classify wealth into different categories in two main ways. The most obvious classification is according to liquidity. Cash in hand is most liquid, followed by money in checking and money market accounts. Savings and time deposits are less liquid, and then come stocks and bonds. Next in the hierarchy is home equity. This has become more liquid in recent years, with the prevalence of home equity loans, but most people still aim to pay off their mortgage by the time they retire. This aspect of home equity is discussed in more detail in Case 4.3. At the far end of the scale comes the "future income" account, which relates to future expected earnings and long-term savings like retirement accounts, or whole-life policies. The marginal propensity to consume (MPC) from these different categories varies enormously: for current assets the MPC is nearly unity, while for future income it is close to zero. This indicates a clear lack of fungibility, which is totally in contrast with the life-cycle hypothesis of the SEM (Modigliani and Brumberg 1954; Friedman 1957). According to the life-cycle hypothesis any change in wealth should produce an identical effect on consumption, no matter what is the source of the wealth change. A pay rise, a lottery win, a capital gain on the stock market, and an expected inheritance would all cause the same effect, assuming they were all of the same discounted net value (see Chapter 5 for more detail on discounting).

Soman and Cheema (2002) have also attacked the life-cycle hypothesis on different grounds. They claim that their research reinforces other findings that "consumers are unable to correctly value their future incomes and that they lack the cognitive capability to solve the intertemporal optimization problem required by the life-cycle hypothesis." Of course the conventional argument in the SEM is that people do not necessarily need to consciously solve this problem; they may still behave *as if* they have solved the problem, maybe under the constraints of market forces. However, Soman and Cheema go on to argue that consumers, particularly inexperienced ones, use information such as their credit limit as a signal of their future earnings potential. Credit limits are not the kind of market constraint that is likely to lead consumers to optimizing behavior. One reason for this concerns self-control problems discussed in the next two chapters.

A second method of classifying wealth concerns the distinction between "realized" and "paper" wealth gains and losses. "Paper" gains and losses are mainly caused by changes in the values of stocks or real estate, but may also be caused by revaluations of inventory. In general the MPC tends to be much lower with "paper" gains, especially if these are reversible, as with a stock market gain (Cheema and Soman 2002).

There is now an abundance of studies that indicate various anomalies in the SEM related to the fungibility of wealth. These anomalies relate to the use of credit cards, attitudes toward stock returns, segregation of asset types as investments, and the impact of social interactions. These issues are now discussed.

1. *Use of credit cards*

There are a number of studies showing that ways in which people use credit cards violate the assumptions of the SEM in terms of perfect fungibility of assets and utility maximization. Prelec and Simester (2001) report that with real transactions of high value, WTP is substantially higher when credit card use is required compared with the situation when cash is required. More specifically they observe that in a sealed bid auction for tickets to a Boston Celtics basketball game WTP was up to 100 % higher when credit cards were required for the transaction rather than cash. This phenomenon is related to payment decoupling, discussed later.

There is also evidence that the simultaneous use of credit cards and savings accounts violates the SEM. Bi and Montalto (2005) observe that the average debt of US households with credit cards was over $8000 in 2004, yet most of these households with credit cards also hold financial assets, with nearly 40 % of them holding positive liquid assets of more than one month's income. Why do people borrow funds at 10 % while they are accumulating funds in liquid accounts yielding less than 2 %? It appears that this use of revolving credit means that some people view liquid assets as a special or emergency fund, but do not view a line of credit in the same way. Once more a lack of fungibility is demonstrated, and again the explanation may lie in self-control factors. Thaler and Shefrin (1981) claim that people may have a rule that they save at least a given proportion of their salary, maybe for their children's education, and never withdraw from this fund. Such a rule prevents the usual type of internal arbitrage that characterizes the SEM. Yet, as Shefrin and Statman (1984) state, "The underlying rationale is straightforward. By prohibiting withdrawals from the 'college fund', the possibility of not replenishing that fund because of a weak will is avoided."

2. *Attitudes toward stock returns*

It has been reported that a combination of loss-aversion and narrow framing explains the behavior of stock returns and volatility (Barberis and Huang 2001). This study also finds that this behavior is better explained by "individual stock accounting," rather than by "portfolio accounting." This means that investors are loss-averse over individual stock fluctuations rather than over the fluctuations of their portfolios as a whole.

3. *Segregation of asset types*

It also appears that investors tend to allocate funds among different portfolio assets as if the individual assets are independent parts of the investment portfolio. Rockenbach (2004) performed a controlled laboratory study to test whether investors split their funds between safe and risky assets as if each of the two asset types represented separate portfolio layers or mental accounts. The subjects in the experiments, who consisted of both students and investment professionals, repeatedly allocated funds among stocks, call options, and risk-free bonds. The main finding was that the pricing of the option suggested that subjects saw stocks and options as substitutes and in a separate class from risk-free bonds.

4. *Social interactions*

People often acquire assets as a result of a social interaction of some type. Some researchers have investigated the reactions of subjects who were asked to value either the purchase or the sale of items possessing some social significance, under various different social circumstances. It appears that reactions in these situations are often emotionally charged and that some trade-offs are regarded as taboo (Fiske and Tetlock 1997; Tetlock *et al.* 2000). For example, people do not like to value friendships in terms of improved living conditions. The effects of these social interactions are discussed in detail in Chapter 8, but at present it is sufficient to note that they appear to induce people to posit a social or emotional value to objects that is quite independent of the item's monetary value. For example, a person may be highly reluctant to sell a ring that was bequeathed to them by a parent. This phenomenon reinforces endowment effects and reduces the fungibility of assets.

Time budgeting

This is one area where research findings appear to be conflicting. Rha and Rajagopal (2001) investigate whether people do perform mental accounting regarding time; they find that people do appear to maintain separate accounts for time based on the context. For example, people view time spent driving or waiting differently depending on the context; there is a significant difference between perceptions of work-time versus nonwork-time. Furthermore, they find that "people attempt to match the time spent on different activities based on source of gain of time." Thus people try to utilize time received from a particular category within the category itself. This finding is analogous to that of Kooreman (1997) described earlier, indicating that people try to match expenditure category with income category in the case of children's welfare benefits. There is a further analogy with consumption accounting in that people appear to have a miscellaneous category that can be used as a "buffer source." Thus sleep time can be used to finish activities that are relatively under more time pressure.

A more recent study (Duxbury et al. 2005) appears to have contrary findings. The authors report similar results to those discussed earlier in terms of the trade-off between time spent and money saved; for example, in the classic jacket-calculator situation where subjects react differently to saving $5 for a 20-minute drive depending on the normal price of the item on sale. However, when the direction of the effect is reversed, so that the trade-off is between money spent and time saved, the authors report an absence of mental accounting effects. Their conclusion is that "mental accounting effects may be context-specific and suffer from a lack of generality."

Policy implications

There are a number of policy implications of a normative nature which follow from the findings described above. These relate to individuals, firms, and governments. Many of the implications relate to self-control problems which involve the discounting of future welfare effects, and these are discussed further in Chapters 5 and 6.

One major implication is that people should allocate expenses to unambiguous categories to avoid overspending. The study by Cheema and Soman (2006) indicates that people are more likely to spend if there is ambiguity in the categories used. An extreme example of such a self-control device is where cash is placed in labeled envelopes for specific uses. There are also implications here for gift-giving; we have seen that people may be delighted to receive a gift that they would never buy for themselves, being outside their budget for that category of expenditure.

Another type of self-control device for consumption relates to the restriction of cash withdrawals from banks or ATMs to small amounts. This may be an effective commitment if there is no opportunity to withdraw more cash in the near future. In a similar manner consumers may limit their purchases to small amounts. Smokers may buy packs of ten cigarettes, for example, which again may be an effective commitment if there is no opportunity, or if it is inconvenient, to buy further cigarettes later. This last example is interesting because it violates two economic principles. First, it is normally cheaper to buy most goods in larger quantities. Second, it contradicts a principle of PT described earlier that losses should be aggregated because of diminishing marginal sensitivity. The fact that people do violate both of these principles in reality is a testimony to the importance of self-control problems and the lengths that people will go to in order to overcome them. Wertenbroch (1996) neatly sums up this tendency: "To control their consumption, consumers pay more for less of what they like too much." According to Prelec and Simester (2001), we should always leave home without our credit cards; their use causes us to overspend and under-save. This issue is discussed further later in the context of payment decoupling.

As far as firms are concerned, marketing strategies may pursue exactly the opposite practice of the "unambiguity" policy described above, in order to induce consumers to buy when they might otherwise demur. A common marketing ploy for selling relatively expensive durables and services is to express the price in terms of an amount per day (Gourville 1998). Thus a $500-per-year health club membership might be expressed as "only $1.37 per day." At first sight this may again seem to violate the principle from PT that small losses should be aggregated because of diminishing marginal sensitivity. However, in this situation there is a more dominant mental accounting principle that small expenses may be allocated to a miscellaneous or petty cash category and therefore not be scrutinized so carefully.

There are also implications for government policy in situations where there is an issue of aggregation versus disaggregation. Governments may want to achieve the opposite of firms, in terms of discouraging the consumption of goods regarded as undesirable. Therefore, instead of expressing costs in terms of an amount per day or week, the government may want such costs to be evaluated by consumers over a period of a year or longer. Government antismoking campaigns may thus stress yearly costs. As a result, instead of viewing the cost of smoking as £5 per day, which may fall into the petty cash category, the consumer may come to view the cost as nearly £2000 per year, a more daunting expense.

A well-documented self-control problem relates to saving for retirement. Although the reasons for this are discussed later, one important implication follows from what has already been said regarding the liquidity of assets. People are more likely to leave their savings alone if such savings are in unambiguous illiquid accounts, like retirement accounts. Furthermore, governments can encourage savings in this form by providing the relevant tax incentives, like individual savings accounts (ISAs) in the United Kingdom. Another implication for government policy concerns framing. Until recently the "default option" in many pension schemes has been to opt out. A recent report by the Pensions Commission in the United Kingdom recommends establishing a new national savings scheme where the default option is to contribute; studies have indicated that this might double the enrollment rate.

However, this does not answer the question: how can we save more in the first place? One method of achieving this is to integrate savings plans with spending accounts. For example, credit card plans exist whereby not only must the whole balance be paid in full each month, but an additional payment is included to be placed in a savings account. This method takes advantage of the principle of integrating losses due to diminishing marginal sensitivity.

We have seen so far that policy implications may involve either integration or segregation, depending on the circumstances and the objectives. Another area where this issue is relevant is in the evaluation of portfolios. The studies discussed earlier indicate that people tend to evaluate portfolio items individually rather than in total when the issue concerns risk and volatility. However, there is some conflicting evidence here. When the issue concerns the evaluation of lottery portfolios, people often prefer an aggregated evaluation rather than a segregated one. A good example is the one originally formulated by Redelmeier and Tversky (1992). This involves a simple lottery with outcomes ($2000, .5; −$500, .5). If this lottery is played twice, the outcomes can be represented as ($4000, .25; $1500, .5; −$1000, .25). The framing effect here is that people are more likely to play this repeated lottery if the outcomes are aggregated than if they are segregated. However, the effects of aggregation appear to be context-specific. Langer and Weber (2001) report that people also prefer "venture" lotteries when the outcomes are aggregated; such lotteries involve a high probability of loss, but a chance of a big gain. On the other hand, "loan" lotteries, where there are low-moderate probabilities of large losses, tend to be evaluated better when the outcomes are segregated. There are as yet no conclusive studies regarding situations where the "lotteries" in the portfolio are heterogeneous rather than being identical. This issue regarding the representation and evaluation of outcomes has important implications for the policies of investment funds and hedge funds, since they want to know how their client investors will view different methods of representing the outcomes of the same portfolio.

There are also policy implications regarding time budgeting. Again people may budget time into different categories for self-control reasons. The author, for example, may have a time budget related to writing five pages a day. Other tasks such as doing housework, repairing the table, or paying a bill may be foregone in achieving this target. Furthermore, it should be stressed that it is not only onerous tasks that may be foregone; playing sudoku may also have to go by the wayside. However, some of the activities foregone may actually have a greater productivity in financial terms than the writing of the five pages. The fifth page may have an estimated marginal revenue of £20, but the time taken to write this page may mean being late with paying a bill at a cost of £50. This time budgeting may not appear to be rational according to the SEM. The issue here, discussed further in Chapter 9, concerns self-signaling. If the author slips behind the five-page target, this may be viewed as a lack of self-control, with a resulting loss of self-respect; if the target is repeatedly missed, this loss of self-respect may possibly lead to the abandonment of the writing project altogether. Thus, seemingly irrational allocations of time budgets may in the long term serve an important purpose.

4.4 Choice bracketing and dynamics

The evaluation and decision-making situations so far considered have essentially related to either single transactions or product bundles. We can consider this approach as essentially a cross-sectional one in terms of examining different components of a transaction at the same period of time. However, it has already been seen that, especially in self-control situations, evaluations can be made over different time frames. Therefore it is now necessary to take a time-series approach to evaluation and decision-making. "Choice bracketing" refers to how people segregate or aggregate choices over time periods.

Opening and closing accounts

In any accounting system, decisions have to be made when to leave accounts open and when to close them. A number of examples from different decision situations will be discussed here: buying and selling stock, reporting earnings, sunk costs, and payment decoupling.

1) *Buying and selling stock*

If a stock in one's portfolio has fallen in value, but is retained, that is the account is left open, then there is a "paper" loss. Not surprisingly such losses are less painful than "realized losses" that occur when the account is closed and the stock sold. Decisions in this area are particularly interesting when an investor needs to raise cash, maybe to buy new stock, and has to choose between selling a stock that has fallen in value and a stock that has risen in value. The SEM predicts that a rational investor should sell the stock that has fallen, since losses are tax-deductible while gains are subject to capital gains tax. However, Odean (1998) finds that investors were more likely to sell stocks that had increased in value rather than stocks that had decreased; this phenomenon is referred to as the **"disposition effect."** In addition, he finds that the stocks sold subsequently outperformed the stocks bought, underlining further the irrationality (in the conventional sense) of the strategy. It thus appears that unrealized losses in particular are not coded as losses in the same way as realized losses, and do not cause the same degree of loss-aversion.

Oehler *et al.* (2003) report similar findings in their experiments as far as the general preference to sell winners rather than losers. They find that the disposition effect is only reduced under the strong pressure of mechanisms like a dealer market, when the last price is assumed as a reference point, rather than the purchase price. In this kind of situation, market forces can overcome the mental accounting bias. The authors comment colorfully that when investors use purchase price as a reference point "they die hard in all market settings." However, the authors also note that markets do not collapse in their experiments due to disposition investors' reluctance to trade. Their explanation is that there is a coexistence of two or more groups of investors, including both disposition investors and momentum traders.

2) *Reporting earnings*

Firms as well as individuals make use of discretion when reporting earnings in official announcements. Such discretion is created in a number of ways, but in particular involves the timing of the recording of revenues and expenses. If a firm wants to boost its reported earnings, it can "pre-book" revenues that it has not yet received, and delay recording costs or spread them over several time periods. A study by Burgstahler and Dichev (1997) indicates that firms are reluctant to announce losses or decreases in earnings. Small reported gains and increases are much more common than small reported losses and decreases, conforming to the predictions of PT regarding loss-aversion.

This is not the only aspect of PT corroborated by the above study. Large gains appear to be trimmed down in order to allow more scope for improvement in the following accounting period, confirming the predictions of having diminishing marginal sensitivity to gains and the use of reference points. Furthermore, whereas small losses may be massaged into small gains, moderate losses tend to be somewhat inflated, again as predicted by the diminishing marginal sensitivity characteristic.

3) *Sunk costs*

Consumers frequently have to decide when to open and close mental accounts when the purchase decision and consumption are separated in time. This can happen for a number of reasons: some goods have to be booked in advance, like theater or airline tickets; some goods and services are durables, yielding benefits over a substantial period of time; some goods are bought on credit, and therefore purchased first, then consumed, and finally paid for later.

If payment is made before consumption, and there is no rebate if the consumer changes his mind later, as is usually the case in the first two situations above, then the consumer is faced with a sunk cost. Economists define such costs as being those which do not vary according to a particular decision; they do not have to occur before the decision is made. According to the SEM, sunk costs should not affect the decision to consume. For example, the decision to drive through a blizzard to watch a game should not be affected by whether a ticket has already been purchased or not. Similarly, the decision to buy a theater ticket should not be affected by whether one has just lost a ticket and needs to buy another one. However, there is considerable evidence that sunk costs do affect decisions (Kahneman and Tversky 1984; Arkes and Blumer 1985; Gourville and Soman 1998; Prelec and Loewenstein 1998).

Kahneman and Tversky (1984) find that consumers are less willing to replace a lost theater ticket than if they had lost an equivalent amount of money. This is in keeping with the fungibility research described earlier; replacing a lost ticket involves further spending in the same category, while losing money does not. Arkes and Blumer (1985) find that season ticket holders to a theater group who paid full price were initially more regular attenders than those who had received a discount, but that there was no difference in attendance in the second half of the season. Gourville and Soman (1998) find that members of a health club who pay dues twice a year attend more frequently in those months when the dues are paid.

Thus it appears that sunk costs do affect consumer behavior, but are eventually written off. What is the mental accounting explanation for this? Again, as with product bundling, it appears that salience is the relevant factor. If a cost has just been paid, it is salient in the mind, and if the payer does not consume the relevant good or service the cost is then edited as a loss. Loss-aversion thus leads to consumption. There are important marketing implications of this finding that are discussed shortly.

Another situation where sunk costs are relevant is the decision to replace a durable. Heath and Fennema (1996) show that consumers tend to depreciate durables on a linear basis over time, but mental depreciation depends not just on time but on frequency and the quality of past usage (Okada 2001). Okada finds that people are more likely to prefer a trade-in for their existing good than to buy a new good with an equivalent discount. Okada's experimental study gave consumers a choice between trading in an existing camera for $80 and buying the new one for a $80 discount from the regular price of $200. The SEM predicts that people would prefer the second option since they get to keep their old camera. However, in the experiment 56 % of the subjects preferred the first option, and only 44 % the second. It might be claimed that this result is caused by a general "trade-in effect," where people prefer trade-ins to discounts, but this explanation is eliminated by the study showing that there is no bias toward the first option when the old camera was won by lottery. Therefore it appears that a mental accounting explanation is required. This allows consumers to depreciate items purchased based on their endowment value and receive a transaction value on trade-in that more than offsets the transaction value of the discount in the second option.

4) *Payment decoupling*

As noted above, there are many situations where payment and consumption are separated in time. Additionally we have seen that payment and consumption can also be separated or "decoupled," even when they are basically simultaneous in time but the product consists of a bundle so that consumers are unable to allocate costs directly to particular components. Thaler (1999) comments that in general consumers do not like the experience of "having the meter running," since this draws unwelcome salience to the cost of specific components of a product bundle. This **flat rate bias** is particularly prominent in telecommunications. Most telephone customers prefer a flat rate service than paying by call when the bill would be the same under both circumstances (Train 1991), and even when paying by call would cost them less (Prelec and Loewenstein 1998). America Online (AOL) found that when they introduced a flat rate Internet service in 1996 they were so swamped by demand that customers had trouble logging on to the service, earning the company bad publicity.

Payment decoupling also has effects on usage of durables and services. Soman and Gourville (2001) find that in an experimental situation skiers with a four-day lift pass are more likely to miss the last day skiing than if they buy the pass on a daily basis. Furthermore, in a field study they find that customers with multi-performance theater tickets are more likely to miss performances than those buying tickets separately. Decoupling is particularly important in the health club industry, where self-control problems are evident. If people pay an annual fee, this first of all creates a mental commitment on the part of the consumer. From that point for the rest of the year the marginal cost per visit is zero, thus making it easier to make the decision to exercise than in the pay-per-visit scenario.

Decoupling is particularly obvious with the use of credit cards. It has already been noted that willingness to pay can be significantly increased by the use of credit cards rather than cash (Prelec and Simester 2001). Stores also would not be willing to pay 3% or more of their revenues to card companies unless credit cards were effective in increasing spending. The most obvious effect of credit card use is that it enables liquidity-constrained individuals to buy goods they would otherwise be unable to purchase. Also the SEM predicts that payment later rather than in the present should be preferred on a discounting basis, provided that the card is paid in full and no interest is charged. However, in practice the average household with credit cards has an outstanding debt that is not paid off monthly, as we have already noted. Furthermore, Prelec and Loewenstein (1998) make the point that, other things being equal, consumers prefer to pay before rather than after. Therefore there must be some mental accounting factors related to decoupling that are relevant in the preference for credit cards. Two different effects can be identified:

1. The use of credit cards reduces the salience of the costs of the purchase. Thus Soman (1997) finds that students leaving the campus bookstore were much more accurate in remembering the amount of their purchases if they paid in cash than if they paid by credit card.

2. Credit card bills aggregate a number of items together so that each individual item loses salience. As Thaler (1999) notes, the impact of

an individual purchase of $50 is less than the impact of an additional $50 item in a bill for $843. This reduction in salience is related to the principle in PT and mental accounting regarding the integration of losses due to diminishing marginal sensitivity.

In neural terms, this reduction in salience is likely to be related to the deactivation of the insula. As seen earlier in the discussion of the study by Knutson *et al.* (2007), insula activation seems to be related to the anticipation of pain, or the displeasure of paying an excessive price. Further neuroeconomic research in this area of paying by credit card rather than cash, although presenting methodological difficulties, would be revealing. It may ultimately suggest certain policy implications in terms of solving this self-control problem.

Prior outcome effects

We have already seen that in certain gambling situations, like betting on racehorses, prior outcomes can affect attitudes to risk. For example, people are more likely to bet on long shots in the last race of the day (the "end-of-the-day effect"). The mental accounting explanation is that people tend to close their betting accounts at the end of the day and are loss-averse. Since the majority of punters are in a loss position by the time of the last race, they are often prepared to take a risk on a long shot in order to break even by the end of the day. Thaler and Johnson (1990) find similar results in their experiments with MBA students playing with real, but small, stakes. Gamblers in casinos are often observed to keep money that they have won during the day in a separate pocket (or mental account) from their "own" money; Thaler and Johnson refer to this phenomenon as the **house money effect**, and gamblers tend to be risk-seeking with such funds. On the other hand, they tend to be risk-averse if they are in a losing position and probabilities and possible gains are moderate; only if there is a chance to break even, usually with a low probability of a relatively high gain, do they seek risk.

Experiments tend usually to be limited to small stakes relative to overall wealth, but Gertner (1993) has found supporting evidence regarding the daily closing of accounts by observing the behavior of contestants in a television game show called "Card Sharks." Winners of the show on a particular day had to predict whether a card picked at random from a deck would be higher or lower than a card that was showing. The odds of winning vary from certainty to about even. After making the prediction the contestant can then make a bet on the outcome of between 50 % and 100 % of the amount they have won that day (on average about $3000). Gertner finds that the present day's winnings strongly influence the size of the bet; in contrast cash won on previous days has virtually no effect. Thus cash won today is treated in a separate account from cash won the day before, a finding even more remarkable considering the difference in time between the shows in real time may be only a few hours, and previous winnings have not yet been collected.

Myopic Loss-Aversion (MLA)

We have already seen that when gambles or lotteries are combined they are evaluated differently from when their outcomes are presented singly. In general, people tend to be more willing to take risks if they combine many bets together than if they consider them one at a time. It is therefore useful to examine how the process of repetition affects the evaluation of gambles given the phenomenon of loss-aversion. We can then consider the many real-life situations where people, especially investors, have to determine how frequently they should evaluate their positions and close their mental accounts.

A good example to illustrate the effect of repetition of gambles is the one described by Thaler (1999) and originally analyzed by Samuelson (1963). The outcomes of an individual bet are represented as ($200, .5; −$100, .5). If an individual has a loss-aversion factor of 2.5, they would reject this bet, since it would give them a loss-aversion-adjusted expected value of −$25. However, if the bet is played twice, the outcomes become ($400, .25; $100, .5; −$200, .25). In this situation the loss-aversion-adjusted expected value is +$25, and the combined bet would be acceptable. Therefore in order to explain why many people reject attractive small bets, it is necessary to consider both loss-aversion and a segregated mental accounting approach.

Benartzi and Thaler (1995) have adopted such an approach in analyzing what has become known as the **equity premium puzzle** (EPP) (Mehra and Prescott 1985). This situation is discussed in more detail in Case 4.1, so a mere outline of it is given here. The equity premium is the difference in the rate of return on equities (stocks) and a safe investment such as treasury bills. The puzzle is that this difference has historically been very large. The equity premium has averaged about 6 % per year over the last 80 years. Part of this difference can be attributed to risk, but Mehra and Prescott show that the level of risk-aversion necessary to explain such a large difference in returns is implausible. They estimate that a coefficient of relative risk-aversion of about 30 would be necessary to explain the historical equity premium.

Benartzi and Thaler explain the puzzle in terms of loss-aversion rather than risk-aversion. They note the risk attitude of loss-averse investors depends on the frequency with which they close their accounts and reset their reference points. They hypothesize that investors have preferences described by PT, and then ask how often people would have to evaluate the changes in their portfolios to make them indifferent between the (US) historical distributions of returns on stocks and bonds. Their simulations suggest that a period of about 13 months would achieve this, implying that if most people evaluate their portfolios once a year the EPP is solved.

This attitude toward evaluation is termed "myopic loss-aversion," since such a strategy is not in the long-run interests of investors. Many studies have shown that if a longer evaluation period is enforced then investors take more risks (Gneezy and Potters 1997; Thaler *et al.* 1997; Benartzi and Thaler 1999; Gneezy, Kapteyn, and Potters 2003). The study by Thaler *et al.* manipulated the frequency with which subjects make investment decisions between stocks and bonds, with three different possibilities: eight times a year, once a year, and once in every 5 years. In the two longer-term situations subjects invested about 67 % of their funds in stocks, while with the more frequent evaluation subjects only invested about 41 % of the funds in stocks. Benartzi and Thaler (1999) asked university staff members how they would invest retirement funds, choosing between stocks and bonds. The authors this time manipulated the method of representing returns, either displaying the distribution of 1-year rates of return or showing the distribution of 30-year rates of return. Subjects who viewed the 1-year rates invested the majority of their funds in bonds, while those shown the 30-year rates invested 90 % of their funds in stocks.

Some studies of MLA indicate that professionals are as prone to the phenomenon as more naïve or inexperienced investors. Gneezy, Kapteyn, and Potters (2003) find that "market prices of risky assets are significantly higher if feedback frequency and decision flexibility are reduced." They conclude that "market interactions do not eliminate such behavior or its consequences for prices." Haigh and List (2005) find that, although there are differences between the behavior of professionals (from the CBOT) and students, the behavior of the traders actually displayed a greater tendency to MLA than that of the students. There is therefore something of a conflict between these studies and the study of Oehler *et al.* (2003) discussed earlier. The latter study indicated that the strength of market forces may suppress behavioral anomalies such as the disposition effect, but this does not appear to be applicable to MLA. The Haigh and List study is also interesting in that it contrasts with the List (2004) study discussed in the previous chapter, where there was evidence that market experience reduces the endowment effect.

There are also some recent studies that question the applicability of MLA in general. Langer and Weber (2005) argue that the relation between myopia and the attractiveness of a lottery sequence is less general than suggested in previous research. They extend the concept of myopic loss-aversion to myopic prospect theory, providing experimental evidence that for specific risk profiles myopia will not decrease but increase the attractiveness of a sequence. Another study by Aloysius (2005) claims that the results obtained in the study by Benartzi and Thaler (1999) can be explained in terms of ambiguity-aversion caused by bounded rationality rather than MLA.

MLA is an example of the more general phenomenon of **narrow framing**, where prospects are evaluated singly rather than as part of an overall portfolio. Similarly, the term **narrow bracketing** refers to the phenomenon where evaluation periods for decision-making are short. It appears to be a common phenomenon in various fields of activity, and an example involving the labor supply of cab drivers is discussed in Case 4.2.

The diversification heuristic

A further anomaly in consumer behavior is observed when simultaneous choices between goods are compared with sequential choices. The diversification heuristic was first observed by Simonson (1990). He gave students the opportunity to choose between six snacks under two different conditions: (1) sequential choice: subjects picked one of the snacks at each of three class meetings held a week apart; and (2) simultaneous choice: on the first class meeting subjects selected three snacks to be consumed over the next three weeks. Simonson observed that there was much more variety-seeking in the simultaneous choice condition than in the sequential choice condition: in the former, 64 % of the subjects chose three different snacks, whereas in the latter only 9 % of the subjects made this choice. Simonson suggests that this anomaly can be explained by variety-seeking serving as a choice heuristic. This may be a useful evolutionary psychological mechanism in many situations when consumption is in the immediate future. However, the heuristic may be misapplied in other situations where consumption is over a longer period. The error represents a failure of predicted utility to accurately forecast future experienced utility.

The effect has been referred to as **diversification bias** by Read and Loewenstein (1995), who observed a similar phenomenon among trick-or-treaters on Halloween night. An experiment involved children calling at two adjacent houses. At one house the children were allowed to choose between two treats (sequential choice), whereas at the other they were told to choose whichever two they liked (simultaneous choice). The results showed strong diversification bias in the simultaneous choice condition: every child selected one of each treat. However, in the sequential choice condition only 48 % of the children selected different treats. The contrast is particularly notable since in each condition the treats are put into the same bag, or portfolio, and consumed later.

Diversification bias is not restricted to children and students. A similar kind of diversification bias has been observed in investors by Benartzi and Thaler (1998). There appears to be a general tendency to divide retirement funds fairly evenly over the range of assets on offer. This is sometimes referred to as the **1/n heuristic**, on the basis that if there are n assets on offer then the amount $1/n$ will be invested in each. The result is that the composition of people's portfolios can be easily skewed by manipulating the range of assets on offer. For example, with just two funds, one for stocks and one for bonds, there would tend to be a 50/50 split; but if another fund for stocks is added to the range of possible assets, the proportion of the portfolio invested in stocks would tend to jump to two-thirds. A more recent study by Hedesström, Svedsäter, and Gärlin (2004) investigated the behavior of a large sample of citizens in the Swedish premium pension scheme; the authors find evidence of the same diversification bias and use of the $1/n$ heuristic.

4.5 Summary

- Mental accounting is the set of cognitive operations used by individuals and households to code, categorize and evaluate financial activities.

- There are three main aspects of mental accounting: (1) the perception of outcomes and the making and evaluation of decisions; (2) the assignment of activities to specific accounts; and (3) the determination of the time periods to which different mental accounts relate.

- PT has various implications for mental accounting, in particular four principles: (1) segregate gains; (2) integrate losses; (3) integrate small losses with larger gains; and (4) segregate small gains from large losses.

- Transactions confer two different types of utility: acquisition utility and transaction utility.

- Products are frequently sold as bundles of components, in which case the price may be consolidated or partitioned.

- Determining whether the price should be consolidated or partitioned is important in marketing strategy since it affects consumer responses. Each method may prove preferable in different circumstances, depending on how it increases the salience of particular product characteristics.

- Various neural imaging studies provide supporting evidence for the mental accounting process in terms of editing and evaluating outcomes.

- There is a large body of evidence that mental accounts for consumption, income, wealth, and time are not fungible, as is assumed in the SEM.

- In consumption budgeting some people may have fixed budgets for particular categories of spending, while others may have more flexible budgets and categories. More flexibility tends to cause people to spend more than they would with less flexibility.

- People often classify types of income on a serious–frivolous scale, and match increases in income in one category with increases in spending in the same category.

- In wealth budgeting, anomalies relate to the use of credit cards, attitudes toward stock returns, segregation of asset types as investments, and the impact of social interactions.

- There are a number of normative or policy implications of lack of fungibility relating to individuals, firms, and governments. Many of these relate to self-control problems like controlling credit card spending and saving for retirement.

- Like any accounting system, mental accounting requires making decisions regarding when to open and close accounts.

- Typical situations when such decisions have to be made are buying and selling stock, reporting earnings, depreciating sunk costs, and payment decoupling.

- Prior outcomes affect attitudes to risk in subsequent situations. The "house money effect" appears to be common, where gains encourage risk-seeking but only in regard to recent gains.

- MLA also appears to be a common phenomenon, where people evaluate their portfolios too frequently, leading them to be too risk-averse in the long-run and forgoing returns.

- Diversification bias is observed in a number of situations, especially notable where investors use the $1/n$ heuristic in selecting from a range of assets to include in their portfolios.

4.6 Applications

Three case studies will be discussed now. The first two relate to different aspects of MLA, while the last one relates to fungibility and consumption budgeting.

Case 4.1 The equity premium puzzle

The EPP is that over the long-term stocks have consistently outperformed bonds by a large margin. It is certainly one of the most hotly debated topics in financial economics. The debate was largely sparked off by a paper by Mehra and Prescott (1985). They reported that, on the basis of US data for about 100 years from 1889 to 1978, the average annual real return to stock was 7 %, while the average annual return to Treasury bills was 1 %, indicating a risk premium between risky and safe assets of about 6 %. The authors claim that such a large premium is a puzzle because, according to conventional economic models, it implies an astronomical coefficient of risk-aversion in excess of 30. In order to aid an interpretation of this value, Mankiw and Zeldes (1991) provide an example: a person with such a degree of risk-aversion would be indifferent between a gamble with a 50 % chance of a consumption of $100 000 and a 50 % chance of a consumption of $50 000, and a certain consumption of $51 209. This does not seem reasonable in the light of other empirical data. Furthermore, the puzzle does not seem confined to the United States. A study by Canova and De Nicoló (2003) finds that "the basic features of the equity premium and risk-free puzzles remain regardless of the sample period and the country considered." The risk-free puzzle can be viewed as the converse of the EPP, as it poses the apparent anomaly of why the risk-free rate is so low.

At present, investigators are divided into three main camps: those who do not believe that there is a puzzle at all, those who have proposed some kind of explanation, and those who have reviewed the different explanations and believe that the puzzle remains. The purpose here is not to discuss all these different approaches in any detail, but rather to focus on one particular explanation by Benartzi and Thaler (1995), which involves the behavioral aspects of PT and mental accounting. Before explaining this approach, however, it is worthwhile gaining an overall perspective by giving a brief overview of the three main camps mentioned above.

Those investigators who do not believe in the existence of the premium point to various problems and ambiguities related to measurement. Perhaps the most fundamental issue here is the distinction between the historical premium and the expected or *ex ante* premium. Ibbotson and Chen (2003) estimate that the *ex ante* premium over the period 1926–2000 in the United States was about 1.25 % lower than the historical premium. A second issue relates to the choice of risk-free asset. Most studies use either Treasury bills or long-term Treasury bonds, usually with a maturity of 20 years. Jones and Wilson (2005) estimate that over the period 1871–2003 the historical equity premium was 4.79 % on bonds and 3.85 % for bills. However, in certain periods the difference has been much larger. In the period 1990–2003 the equity premium was only 2.05 % for bonds, but 6.32 % for bills. Jones and Wilson also discuss a third measurement issue: the use of geometric means versus arithmetic means. They use the former measure on the basis that they are more appropriate in a long-term time series study. The difference is notable: Jones and Wilson estimate that arithmetic means, as used in the Mehra–Prescott study, tend to be 1.6–1.8 % higher than geometric means. A final measurement issue concerns whether returns should be described in nominal or real terms. Benartzi and Thaler (1995) argue that nominal measures are often more appropriate, for two reasons: first, returns are usually reported in nominal terms; second, simulations suggest that investors cannot be thinking in real terms, otherwise they would not be willing to hold Treasury bills over any evaluation period, since they always yield negative prospective utility. Although these measurement issues muddy the waters as far as obtaining a precise measure of the size of the equity premium, most researchers still believe that the historical premium is significantly large.

Over the last 20 years there have been many attempts to explain the puzzle. Some of the better known models are as follows:

(1) Generalized expected utility (Epstein and Zin 1989; Weil 1989).

(2) Habit formation (Constantinides 1990; Ferson and Constantinides 1991; Hung and Wang 2005; Meyer and Meyer 2005).

(3) Imperfect markets or market frictions (He and Modest 1995; Luttmer 1996; Zhou 1999).

(4) Ambiguity or uncertainty (Olsen and Troughton 2000; Aloysius 2005).

(5) Delayed consumption updating (Gabaix and Laibson 2001).

(6) Fluctuating economic uncertainty or consumption volatility (Bansal and Yaron 2004).

Finally, there are a considerable number of commentators who have surveyed the above models and results, and conclude that the EPP is still a puzzle, for example Kocherlakota (1996), Chapman (2002), Mehra (2003) and Oyefeso (2006).

The Benartzi and Thaler (BT) approach combines two important elements:

(1) A utility function described by PT, involving reference points, diminishing marginal sensitivity, a weighted probability function, and loss-aversion. The authors note that this function has something in common with the habit formation explanation in that both models involve reference points.

(2) A mental accounting process whereby portfolios are evaluated at regular intervals and accounts are "closed."

The authors then proceeded to ask two questions:

(1) What evaluation period would investors have to use in order to be indifferent between a portfolio consisting entirely of stocks and a portfolio consisting entirely of 5-year Treasury bonds?

(2) Given the evaluation period determined above, what combination of stocks and bonds would people hold in order to maximize prospective utility?

The authors based their answers to the above questions on simulations using historical data for the United States from 1926 to 1990 involving monthly returns on stocks, bonds, and bills. They find that the evaluation period in the first question was about 13 months, in terms of nominal returns, and about 10 months for real returns. They then find that the optimal position for investors involves 30–55 % of the portfolio invested in stock. The prospective utility function is virtually flat over this range. These results broadly match empirical findings; institutional investors

Case 4.1 *continued*

have about 53 % of their portfolios in stocks, while individuals allocate their funds between stocks and bonds on about a 50–50 basis.

Having derived results to these two questions, the authors proceed to ask two further questions:

(1) Which aspects of PT drive the results?

(2) How sensitive are the results to alternative specifications?

They find that loss-aversion is the main determinant of the outcomes, whereas the specific functional forms of the value function and weighting functions are not critical. When the parameters in the model are changed in specification this also does not appear to significantly affect the length of the evaluation period. For example, if actual probabilities are used instead of a weighting function, the period is reduced by one or two months.

The BT study also examines the relationship between the equity premium and the length of evaluation period. They find that the premium falls from 6.5 % for a 1-year period to about 3 % for a 5-year period, 2 % for a 10-year period and 1.4 % for a 20-year period. The authors then comment that investors with a 20-year horizon are able to reap the reward of an economic rent of 5.1 % if they are able to resist the temptation to count their money often: "in a sense, 5.1 % is the price for excessive vigilance."

These reduced premiums estimated by the BT study are matched by calculations by Jones and Wilson (2005). The risks of loss in terms of investing in stocks rather than bonds are reflected in the probability of a negative premium for the period of evaluation. This probability is particularly relevant in the BT model, which is driven strongly by loss-aversion. Jones and Wilson estimate that the probability of a negative premium falls from 41 % for a 1-year period to 33 % for a 5-year period, 25 % for a 10-year period, and 17 % for a 20-year period.

The final element in the BT paper contains a solution to the puzzle of organizational MLA. While individuals may be strongly tempted to count their money frequently, why should this apply to institutional investors like pension funds who should have every reason to take a long-term evaluation period? The answer given is that the reason for organizational MLA lies in an agency problem. The fund managers in such institutions have to report results on an annual basis, and are held accountable for these short-term results. Bearing in mind the competitive nature of these funds, there may be a "tragedy of the commons" here in that managers may be tempted to trade off better short-term results for better long-term results, knowing that their rivals are in the same situation. Such game theory considerations are discussed in Chapter 7.

Questions

1. Explain the statement "in a sense, 5.1 % is the price for excessive vigilance."

2. What is the significance of the probability of a negative premium?

3. Is the equity premium likely to remain at the historical level in the future?

Case 4.2 Why you can't find a cab on a rainy day?

The theory of labor supply in the SEM predicts that the supply curve will be a standard upward-sloping one, where workers will work longer hours at higher wages. This theory is based on the concept of intertemporal substitution, meaning that when wages are high workers will substitute work for leisure, as the opportunity cost of leisure is higher at the higher wage. If people have diminishing marginal utility of leisure time then they will be inclined to give up more leisure as the wage increases.

In practice, however, the theory has been difficult to test empirically, since a number of conditions need to be satisfied. An ideal testing situation would involve the following factors:

1. *The increase in wages should be temporary.* Otherwise the effect of the increase will be compounded with other effects related to future expected wealth.

2. *Wages are relatively constant within a day.* This allows workers to use the level of wages earlier in the day to act as a guide in prompting them how many hours to work later in the day.

3. *Wages vary from day to day and are uncorrelated.* This allows an investigation into how workers adjust their hours to the wage rate on a daily basis, without being able to use the previous day's wage rate as a guide to how long to work the next day.

These conditions are satisfied well by one particular group of workers: cab drivers. On some days they are busy, and their hourly wage rate is higher, while other days are quieter, causing a lower rate. Drivers are in a position to determine the number of hours they work on a daily basis, depending on their average hourly wage for that day. A study by Camerer *et al.* (1997) examined data relating to New York City cab drivers between 1988 and 1994, using three different samples totaling 1826 observations. These observations related both to different drivers and to the same drivers on different days. The investigators relied on data from trip sheets that drivers fill out daily, checked against the records of the meters inside the cabs. Hours worked were calculated by measuring the time taken from when the first customer was picked up to when the last customer was dropped-off. Daily wage rates were calculated by dividing total daily revenue (not including tips) by hours worked.

The objective of the study was to test two competing hypotheses:

1. SEM – upward-sloping supply curve, with positive wage elasticity.

2. BEM – downward-sloping supply curve, with negative wage elasticity.

The latter model involves the supposition that workers are target workers, meaning that they aim for a daily income target, and stop working when they reach that target. This implies a more specific hypothesis regarding wage elasticity. Wage elasticity measures the percentage change in hours worked in response to a 1% change in the wage rate. If workers aim for a daily income target then the wage elasticity should be -1. The implications of this behavior in terms of economic theory are discussed later.

Case 4.2 *continued*

The investigators used ordinary least squares regression to estimate the relationship between hours worked against the wage rate, using logarithms of both variables in order to estimate the wage elasticity. Thus their model is in the form as follows:

$$\ln H = a + b \ln W$$

where H represents the number of hours worked per day, W represents the hourly wage rate, and b represents the wage elasticity.

They obtained separate results for each sample and certain sub-samples. The simple correlations between log hours and log wages are all negative for the three main samples: $-.503$, $-.391$, and $-.269$. Although these correlations are not very high, for the two largest samples, totaling 1506 observations, the regression coefficients are not only negative but statistically significant at the 5 % level. Furthermore, the two estimates of wage elasticity are $-.926$ and $-.975$, both very close to -1.

The study also investigated how elasticities varied with both experience and payment structure. Drivers were divided into two groups, according to whether they had more or less than 3 years of experience. The hypothesis relating to experience was that the more experienced drivers would learn that they could earn more by driving more on high-wage days and driving less on low-wage days. This would cause them to have a more positive elasticity. This hypothesis was indeed confirmed: there is a marked difference between the elasticities for experienced and inexperienced drivers. Indeed in two of the samples the elasticity is positive.

It was also hypothesized that the way drivers pay for their cabs would affect elasticity. Drivers fall into three main categories here: those who rent daily for a 12-hour shift; those who rent weekly or monthly; and those who own their cabs. The first group has a relatively low negative elasticity ($-.197$), while the elasticities for the other two groups are $-.978$ and $-.867$ respectively, suggesting that they are target workers.

The issue of optimality is also raised in the study. It is estimated that if drivers worked the same number of hours in total, but redistributed on the basis of working a constant number of hours per day, they could increase their earnings by an average of 5 %. Furthermore, assuming that their utility function for leisure is concave, this fixed-hours rule would also improve total leisure utility. It was also estimated that, if drivers reallocated their total driving hours as if the wage elasticity were $+1$, they could increase earnings by 10 % on average.

The study concludes by considering different explanations for the results. Four possible explanations are rejected:

1. *Drivers are "liquidity-constrained."* This means that they do not have enough cash to pay daily expenses and cannot borrow. If this is the case, they could not afford to stop driving on low-wage days. However, cab owners are not liquidity-constrained (the medallion licenses they own are now valued at about $250 000), and yet their wage elasticities are still negative.

2. *The calculation of the working hours and wage rate does not take into account actual hours worked.* It may be that on quiet days drivers finish late, but take a lot of unrecorded breaks. This would cause total hours worked to be lower and the wage rate to be higher. However, in one of the samples the breaks were recorded and excluded; this made no difference to the results.

3. *Drivers finish early because being busy and carrying a lot of passengers is tiring.* However, a survey of the cab fleet managers revealed that most of them thought that fruitlessly searching for fares on a low-wage day was more tiring than carrying passengers.

4. *The data is biased, since it only takes into account days worked, or "partcipation," not the days when drivers chose not to work at all.* It may be that there is a tendency to work unexpectedly on some days, this being correlated with working long hours. However, drivers usually operate on a fixed shift schedule, with penalties for not showing up, making unexpected participation of little importance.

Having rejected the four explanations above, the authors conclude that daily income targeting is the best explanation for the results obtained. As with the previous case study relating to the equity risk premium, the essential behavioual factor here is MLA. Drivers have a reference point in terms of a daily income target, and are averse to any shortfalls or losses compared to this target. Any gains have progressively less marginal utility because of the concavity of the utility function. The question then is, why do they have an evaluation period of such a short time as one day? This seems an extreme example of "narrow bracketing." The authors of the study propose two explanations for this:

1. *Daily income targets serve as a useful heuristic.* It is easier to use this rule than to try to estimate the marginal utility of work time and compare it with the marginal utility of leisure time for each day.

2. *Daily income targets serve as a useful self-control device.* If longer evaluation periods are used, it becomes easy for drivers to slack off and finish early, with the intention of making up for lost time and income later in the week or month. The situation is similar to that of an author with a daily target of pages written, discussed earlier in the chapter. Furthermore, as the study notes, "a drive home through Manhattan with $200–$300 in cash from a good day is an obstacle course of temptations for many drivers, creating a self-control problem that is avoided by daily targeting."

As a final point the authors of the study comment on the difference between experienced and inexperienced drivers. Experienced drivers are less likely to be target earners, and closer to being optimizers. The study suggests that there may be two reasons for this:

1. Drivers learn to optimize through experience.
2. Non-optimizing target-earners are weeded out by a selection process.

Questions

1. Why can't you catch a cab on a rainy day?
2. Explain the differences between the predictions of the SEM and those of the BEM.
3. Explain why target earners have a wage elasticity of -1.

Case 4.2 *continued*

4. Explain the meaning of the statement "furthermore, assuming that their utility function for leisure is concave, this fixed-hours rule would also improve total leisure utility."
5. Explain why daily targeting is "myopic."
6. Explain why daily targeting is related to self-control factors.
7. Explain the major similarities and differences between this case and the case relating to the EPP.

Case 4.3 Consumer spending and housing wealth

There is a considerable amount of evidence at present (October 2006) that the United States is heading for a property bust. After several years of growth rates in excess of 10 % per year, house prices have slowed sharply, and some measures indicate that they are already falling. This is highly significant for economists who want to make forecasts of consumer spending and GDP growth based on the relationship between consumer spending and housing wealth. Such forecasts are vital for macroeconomic policy, given the time lags involved. This is the big question: is consumer spending likely to fall considerably, forcing the economy into a deep recession, or is the effect likely to be much smaller, with a soft landing? Economists, as is so often the case, are divided on the issue.

Of particular relevance here is the huge increase in mortgage-equity withdrawal in recent years, as real estate prices have soared. This withdrawal refers to the amount of cash people extract from their homes through bigger mortgages and home equity loans. In the 1990s this averaged about 2 % of personal income, but reached a peak of 10 % in 2005, before falling back to 6 % by the end of the year (Greenspan and Kennedy 2005). This phenomenon makes forecasts more difficult, in particular involving a number of behavioral factors.

Let us start by considering the SEM treatment of the issue of the relationship between consumer spending and housing wealth. The most important theory here, as we have seen, is the permanent income hypothesis (PIH). This assumes rational expectations regarding future income and wealth. According to this hypothesis people would estimate the likely increase in their property wealth over their lifetimes and adjust their spending by averaging this increase over a long time period. However, we already know that this prediction is incorrect since it cannot explain the large increase in mortgage-equity withdrawal in recent years. In particular, it cannot explain survey evidence that people spend about half of the cash they release from their homes.

In order to better understand the issue, and make more reliable forecasts, we need to take into account behavioral factors. There are three of these that are of particular importance here: 1) nonstandard discounting; 2) lack of fungibility of wealth accounts; and 3) loss-aversion. We will now discuss each in turn.

1. *Nonstandard discounting*

   Discounting is discussed in the next two chapters, so we will not examine detailed aspects of it here. It is sufficient to say at this point that people tend to find it hard to save (see Case 6.2), and therefore they may be forced to withdraw equity from their homes, especially when they retire, in order to fund spending.

2. *Lack of fungibility of wealth accounts*

   There are various recent studies that suggest that people have different MPCs for different types of wealth, in contradiction to the PIH. Carroll, Otsuka, and Slacalek (2006) have estimated that in the United States an increase in housing wealth of $100 eventually results in a rise in spending by $9, whereas a similar increase in stock-market wealth would only boost spending by $4. These results are broadly confirmed by a study by Bostic, Gabriel, and Painter (2006), which has estimated that the wealth effect from housing is about three times bigger than that of financial assets. Case, Quigley, and Shiller (2005) also found the wealth effect from housing to be larger than that from the stock market. Furthermore, Slacalek (2006) has found that the effect of housing wealth on spending has risen since 1990 in industrial countries as a whole. The effect appears to be particularly large, bigger than for financial assets, in the United States and United Kingdom, since these economies have more sophisticated markets and instruments for mortgage-equity withdrawal. These findings all suggest that, other things being equal, a property bust in the United States (or United Kingdom) would cause a sharp fall in spending.

3. *Loss-aversion*

   However, other things are not equal, since the studies mentioned above describe situations where house prices have been rising. As we have seen, loss-aversion can often cause asymmetries in consumer behavior, depending on whether a particular variable is rising or falling; asymmetric price elasticities are an example of such behavior. The MPCs represent another situation where asymmetries are relevant. Consumers find it easier to increase spending than to reduce it, hence their preference for rising consumption profiles, as discussed in Case 6.3. Once new reference points for higher levels of consumption become established, consumers find it difficult to adjust to lower levels. The significance of this is that a fall in house prices might not affect spending very much, as consumers try to maintain spending levels. Thus a deep recession might be avoided. However, this is not the end of the story. In order to maintain such spending levels consumers may be forced to burden themselves with greater debts in forms other than home equity. Standard bank loans and credit card debt could increase, maybe causing strains on the banking system with increasing default levels.

Questions

1. What is the significance of home-equity withdrawal for the relationship between housing wealth and consumer spending?

2. What does the PIH predict regarding the effects of a property bust?

3. Would the effects of a property bust in the United Kingdom and other countries be similar to the effects in the United States?

Part III
Intertemporal Choice

The Discounted Utility Model

5.1 Introduction

Intertemporal choices relate to decisions involving trade-offs between costs and benefits occurring in different time periods. Governments, firms, and individuals are all faced with such decisions on a frequent and ongoing basis: for example, investing in roads, schools, and hospitals; building a new factory or launching a new product; buying a new car; spending on a vacation; or joining a health club. Economists have been interested in such decisions since at least the days of Adam Smith, but the current model that is generally used by most economists, as well as by governments and firms, is the DUM, originally proposed by Samuelson in 1937. The widespread use of the model seems strange to many practitioners in behavioral economics, in view of the fact that Samuelson himself had significant reservations regarding both the normative and descriptive aspects of the model and that many anomalies have been observed over the last few decades.

Because the topic of intertemporal choice is so broad in scope, the structure in the previous chapters is somewhat modified. Up to this point we have started with the fundamental aspects of the SEM, observed the anomalies, and then extended the model, introducing behavioral modifications. In this chapter, however, we will concentrate entirely on describing the DUM (as the relevant aspect of the SEM), and examining its implications and anomalies. Only in the next chapter will we move on to discuss alternative behavioral models. At that point we will see that various factors discussed in previous chapters are relevant in terms of formulating such models.

In this chapter, therefore, we begin by considering the historical origins of the DUM, before describing the essential features of the model. The discussion of origins is important, since many of the more recent behavioral developments are in many ways a reversion to much earlier work involving psychological and sociological factors. After the features of the DUM are described, its many anomalies are discussed. The nature and causes of these anomalies involve a discussion of the complex concept of time preference. Finally, various policy implications of the DUM are considered.

5.2 Origins of the discounted utility model

Although Adam Smith was the first economist to discuss the importance of intertemporal choice as far as the wealth of nations was concerned, it was Rae who essentially provided a psychological foundation for a theory of intertemporal choice.

John Rae and the desire for accumulation

In the early nineteenth century, Rae (1834) identified "the effective desire for accumulation" as being the key psychological factor determining a society's decisions to save and invest, which in turn determined a country's rate of economic productivity and growth. Rae also identified four psychological factors that either promoted or inhibited this desire, and which varied across different societies. The two promoting factors were as follows:

The bequest motive – to accumulate resources for one's descendants.
The propensity to exercise self-restraint – this involves the intellectual capacity to foresee probable future outcomes of decisions, and the willpower to put long-term interests ahead of short-term ones.

The two inhibiting factors described by Rae were as follows:

The uncertainty of human life – there is no point in saving for the future if it is unlikely that we will have much of one. Rae summed this up by saying that

> When engaged in safe occupations, and living in healthy countries, men are much more apt to be frugal, than in unhealthy, or hazardous occupations, and in climates pernicious to human life.

The urge for instant gratification exacerbated by the prospect of immediate consumption – Rae again expresses this in vivid terms:

> The actual presence of the immediate object of desire in the mind by exciting the attention, seems to rouse all the faculties, as it were, to fix their view on it, and leads them to a very lively conception of the enjoyments which it offers to their instant possession.

Two different approaches

Later theorists developed two different views of time preference stemming from Rae's work. One view took the approach that the default situation was that people weighted the present and future equally, but the discomfort of delaying gratification caused people to weigh future outcomes less heavily than present ones (Senior 1836). The second view took the opposite approach, proposing that people generally only considered immediate utility, but the anticipation of future utility might on occasion more than offset any loss of current utility, causing them to delay gratification (William Jevons 1888; Herbert Jevons 1905). Both approaches emphasize the importance of current feelings, but explain variations in time preference between people in different ways. According to the first approach, people vary in terms of the discomfort they experience in delaying gratification. According to the second approach, variations in time preference arise because people have different abilities to anticipate the future.

Böhm-Bawerk and trade-offs

The next major development in the theory of intertemporal choice came from Böhm-Bawerk (1889). He, and later Pigou (1920), introduced the notion that people generally underestimate future wants, leading to a time preference pattern biased toward the present. It should be noted at this stage that this notion does not involve a discounting of future outcomes; instead it is the utility of these outcomes that is underestimated. This is a key distinction that will be discussed in more detail later.

Böhm-Bawerk introduced another important innovation in the theory of intertemporal choice. Such choices were seen as trade-offs in terms of allocating resources to oneself in different periods of time, similar to trade-offs in allocating resources between consuming different current goods.

Irving Fisher and indifference curve analysis

The final development before the introduction of the DUM came from Irving Fisher (1930). He formalized much of the work outlined above, extending the Böhm-Bawerk framework of analysis in terms of using indifference curves. Current consumption was plotted on the horizontal axis and future consumption (usually for the following year) was plotted on the vertical axis. The concept of the MRS between current and future consumption was also applied; this depended on both time preference and diminishing marginal utility.

It should also be emphasized that Fisher discussed at length the psychological factors affecting time preference. Thus he not only took account of future wealth and risk, but also referred to the four factors described by Rae, and to foresight, which is the other side of the coin of Böhm-Bawerk's notion of the underestimation of future wants. Fisher also stressed the importance of fashion:

This at the present time acts, on the one hand, to stimulate men to save and become millionaires, and, on the other hand, to stimulate millionaires to live in an ostentatious manner.

The reason for underlining the fact that these early pre-DUM developments in the theory of intertemporal choice all took different psychological factors into account is that the DUM itself swept away the explicit consideration of these psychological factors, condensing them into a single construct: the discount rate. The implications of this "revolution" need to be discussed at some length in the remainder of this chapter.

Samuelson and the discounted utility model

Samuelson introduced the DUM in 1937 in a short article modestly titled "A Note on Measurement of Utility." Apart from commenting that the comparison of intertemporal trade-offs required a cardinal as opposed to ordinal measure of utility, it extended Fisher's indifference curve analysis, essentially limited to the comparison of two periods, to multi-period situations. However, as noted above, it combined all the psychological factors involved in time preference into the single parameter of the discount rate. The nature of the model can be best described in mathematical terms. It specifies an intertemporal utility function $U^t(c_t, \ldots, c_T)$, which describes the utility at time t of the consumption profile $(c_t, c_{t+1}, c_{t+2}, \ldots)$ starting in period t and continuing to period T. The model incorporates the general axioms of the SEM described in previous chapters regarding the completeness, transitivity, and independence principles. The DUM then goes on to assume that a person's intertemporal utility function can be described by the following specific functional form:

$$U^t(c_t, \ldots, c_T) = \sum_{k=0}^{T-t} D(k)u(c_{t+k}) \quad \text{where } D(k) = (1/1+\rho)^k$$

The term $u(c_{t+k})$ can be interpreted as the person's instantaneous utility function, meaning their perceived well-being in period $t+k$. The term $D(k)$ refers to the person's discount function, meaning the relative weight that the person attaches in time period t to their well-being in period $t+k$. Finally, the term ρ refers to the person's discount rate, meaning the rate at which they discount expected future utilities. This term therefore combines all the various psychological factors involved in time preference that were discussed earlier.

It will aid an understanding of the workings of the model, as well as the implications and anomalies discussed later, if a simplified example is examined at this stage. Let us take the following consumption profile, measured in thousands of dollars per year over a period of the next 3 years: (20, 20, 20). We will also assume for simplicity that these consecutive equal amounts of consumption yield equal amounts of utility. It should be noted that this assumption violates some of the behavioral factors considered in earlier chapters, such as the effects of reference points, habit formation, and the desire for increasing consumption profiles (the "happiness treadmill"). These complicating factors will be discussed later in terms of their implications for the DUM.

Since the measurement of utility is in arbitrary units of "utils," we can consider the utility profile as consisting of the terms (20, 20, 20). It is assumed that the model is discrete and that the utilities are all received at points in time at the end of each period, rather than being continuous flows throughout each period. This may appear unrealistic but the DUM can be modified to transform it into a continuous-time model; the utility function becomes an integral of a negative exponential function. For simplicity we will use the discrete form of the model. If the consumer discounts future utility at the rate of 10 % per year, the current utility of the consumption and utility profiles can now be calculated as follows:

$$U'(20, 20, 20) = \frac{20}{1+0.1} + \frac{20}{(1+0.1)^2} + \frac{20}{(1+0.1)^3} = 49.74 \qquad (5.1)$$

This calculation illustrates an important feature of the DUM: it closely resembles the compound interest formula used in calculating net present values. This analogue with the common technique for evaluating financial investments has been largely responsible for the rapid assimilation of the model by economists, particularly after Koopmans (1960) showed that the model could be derived from a set of axioms or basic principles that are superficially plausible. The model also gained normative status, as it was shown that an exponential discounting function was consistent with rationality, in the sense that it resulted in dynamically consistent choices. Other economists, including Lancaster (1963), Fishburn (1970), and Meyer (1976), have since provided alternative axiom systems for the DUM, further increasing its perceived legitimacy and popularity.

5.3 Features of the discounted utility model

There are a number of features of the DUM that now need to be examined, since these relate to the implicit psychological assumptions underlying the model. These features have been analysed and their validity critically reviewed by Frederick, Loewenstein, and O'Donoghue (2002), and the following discussion draws extensively from that review.

Integration of new alternatives with existing plans

It is a common assumption in most decision or choice situations relating to the SEM that people evaluate new alternatives by integrating them with existing plans. This means that if a person is offered a prospect A (say, investing $10 000 now to gain $15 000 in 3 years), the effects of this prospect on the person's whole consumption profile must be considered. Thus, if the person currently has the consumption profile $(c_t, \ldots, c_T)$ then they must estimate their new consumption profile if they were to accept prospect A, for example $(c'_t, \ldots, c'_T)$. Prospect A would then be accepted if $U^t(c'_t, \ldots, c'_T) > U^t(c_t, \ldots, c_T)$.

Although this approach may seem logical from a normative point of view, meaning that people should want to integrate new alternatives in order to maximize welfare, we have already seen in previous chapters that this places unrealistic demands on people's mental capacities. People may not have well-formed consumption profiles relating to all future periods, and they may be unable or unwilling to reformulate such plans every time that new prospects are encountered. The next section relating to anomalies in the DUM will examine empirical evidence regarding people's behavior in this regard.

Utility independence

It is assumed in the DUM that it is simply the sum of all the discounted future utilities, for example the value of 49.74 in Equation 5.1, which is relevant in terms of making intertemporal choices. This ignores the possibility that the distribution of utilities over time may be relevant. As we shall see, people may prefer a flat or rising utility profile to a falling one, or a pattern of dispersion of utilities rather than a concentrated pattern. This assumption is also related to the next one.

Consumption independence

It is assumed in the DUM that a person's welfare in any time period is independent of consumption in any other period. This means that preferences over consumption profiles are not affected by the nature of consumption in periods in which consumption is identical in the two profiles. It is therefore analogous to the independence axiom in EUT. As Frederick, Loewenstein, and O'Donoghue state,

> Consumption independence says that one's preference between an Italian and Thai restaurant tonight should not depend on whether one had Italian last night nor whether one expects to have it tomorrow.

It should be noted that neither Samuelson nor Koopmans proposed that this assumption had either normative or descriptive validity. Indeed we will review a number of empirical anomalies in the remainder of this chapter and the next.

Stationary instantaneous utility

The DUM generally assumes that the instantaneous utility function is constant over time, meaning that the same activity yields the same utility in the future, viewed from the future, as now. For example, if activity A is expected to yield 20 utils in 3 years' time, the current utility of A, which can be written as $u^0(A)$, will be discounted to about 15 utils (at a 10% discount rate). However, it is assumed that the utility of A in 3 years' time, $u^3(A)$, will still be 20 utils. This implies that people's preferences do not change over time, an obviously unrealistic assumption.

Evidence suggests that people tend to exaggerate the degree to which their future preferences will resemble their current ones, a phenomenon referred to as **projection bias** (Loewenstein, O'Donoghue, and Rabin 2003). Thus they may expect to like the music of Oasis in 20 years because they like it now, but then find in 20 years' time that they cannot stand it.

Stationary discounting

It is assumed in the DUM that people use the same discount rate over their lifespan. In contrast, there is considerable evidence that discounting rates vary according to age. Mischel and Metzner (1962) have found that willingness to delay gratification increases with age, implying that older people have a lower discount rate. However, the relationship between discounting and age appears to be a complex one. In an experimental study of respondents between the ages of 19 and 89 it was found that older people discount more than younger ones and that middle-aged people discount less than either group (Read and Read 2004). Similar results were found by Harrison, Lau, and Williams (2002). It would appear therefore that young people are more impatient than their parents, but discount less than their grandparents, whose future involves a greater degree of uncertainty.

Constant discounting

The DUM assumes that at any period of time the same discount rate is applied to all future periods. In mathematical terms this means that, given the discount function,

$$D(k) = (1/1 + \rho)^k$$

at time period t. The same per-period discount rate ρ is applied to all periods in the future. This condition ensures time-consistent preferences; since the SEM views time-consistent preferences as being rational, and inconsistent preferences are usually seen as irrational, this feature of the DUM is often perceived to be legitimate. However, there is plentiful empirical evidence that discount rates are not constant over time, but rather tend to decline. Inconsistent time preferences have been widely observed. This evidence, and alternative models of accommodating it, is reviewed in the next chapter.

It should also be noted at this stage that constant discounting is not a sufficient condition for consistent time preferences to exist. Stationary discounting is also necessary. If discounting is not stationary then in the following time period $t+1$ one may observe the different, but still constant, discount function

$$D_{t+1}(k) = (1/1 + \rho')^k$$

where $\rho' \neq \rho$. For example, the evidence in the Read and Read study mentioned above suggests that as people enter middle age, $\rho' < \rho$. In this situation discounting is constant in both periods t and $t+1$, but the discount rate changes with the passage of time. The consequence of this is that once again time preferences will be inconsistent.

Independence of discounting from consumption

Another assumption of the DUM is that all forms of consumption are discounted at the same rate. Without this assumption it is impossible to reduce the discount rate to a single parameter or to talk about a uniform time preference. As Frederick, Loewenstein and O'Donoghue put it,

We would need to label time preference according to the object being delayed – "banana time preference," "vacation time preference," and so on.

There is indeed evidence that different products are discounted at different rates and even that different attributes of products are discounted differently. For example, Soman (2004) has found that perceived effort and perceived price are discounted differently. Do-it-yourself products involve effort in terms of consumption and appear more attractive when the purchase is planned for sometime in the future. When purchase is immediate such products appear less attractive, implying that perceived effort is discounted more heavily than price. Once again the consequence is preferences that are inconsistent over time.

Diminishing marginal utility and positive time preference

Although these two features are not essential elements of the DUM, in practice most analyses involving intertemporal choice assume that both conditions exist. In actuality both elements predate the DUM, since Fisher (1930) emphasized the importance of each of them in his indifference analysis approach. Indifference curves generally require the assumption of diminishing marginal utility or concave utility functions. The implication of this condition is that it might cause people to delay consumption until later time periods. For example, when we eat a delicious and generously portioned meal we may prefer to leave some of it for the next day, or, if at a restaurant, take the remaining portion home in a doggy bag.

It should be noted that this effect of diminishing marginal utility operates in the opposite direction to the normal direction of time preference. Normally, time preference is positive, meaning that people apply a positive discount rate to future utilities. For this reason many economists have not been happy with Fisher's approach, on the grounds that it confounds the effect of diminishing marginal utility with "pure" time preference. However, we shall see in a later section that it is very difficult to define the term "pure time preference," since there are in reality a number of confounding factors, not just the phenomenon of diminishing marginal utility.

5.4 Methodology

Before discussing anomalies in the DUM, it is necessary to consider the methodology used by investigators in empirical studies that measure discount rates. Many aspects of the methodology described also apply to other areas of research, but this discussion is particularly important in the current context, given the enormous variation in results reported: studies have computed discount rates varying from minus 6% (delayed rewards are preferred) to infinitely positive. An understanding of the different methods employed by researchers will in turn aid an understanding of the sources of these variations, as well as the anomalies and alternative models to the DUM described later. Two aspects of methodology need to be discussed: type of study and method of calculation of the discount rate.

Types of empirical study

There are two main types of study in general terms that can be conducted. Both of these were briefly described in the introductory chapter, since they apply to all aspects of research in behavioral economics. One type of study is a **field study**, and the other type is an **experimental study**. Before discussing each of these in detail it should also be mentioned that either type of study can be between subjects or within subjects. A **between-subjects** study examines differences between two or more groups of people, each of which is given a different task or series of tasks. For example, one group may be asked to state preferences relating to rewards a week from now, while another group is asked to state preferences relating to rewards a month from now. A **within-subjects** study examines different responses from the same subjects, which necessitates each subject performing a series of at least two tasks. For example, subjects may be asked to state preferences relating to rewards both 1 week from now and 1 month from now. As will become evident from the following discussion, in some circumstances the first type of study is preferable or is the only practical possibility, while in other circumstances the second type of study is preferred.

1. *Field studies*

    In the context of researching intertemporal choice these studies involve observing real decisions that people make in their lives. The following are examples of situations involving such types of study:

    - choices involving buying different electrical appliances, where some are more expensive, but save electricity and reduce costs during their lifetime;
    - life-cycle saving behavior;
    - choices at retirement between receiving a lump sum or receiving an annuity;

- choices between receiving income in 10 or 12 installments during the year;

- choices of smokers and drug addicts which involve trade-offs between current benefits and long-term costs;

- comparisons between individuals' credit card repayments and income payments.

The advantage of field studies compared with experimental studies is their high level of **ecological validity**. This means that there is no concern that the results do not apply in reality, for the simple reason that the results are by necessity real. However, this does not mean that the results are **conceptually valid**, meaning that they actually succeed in measuring what they are supposed to measure. This is because field studies (and experimental studies also to a lesser extent) may be subject to a number of **confounds**. A confound occurs when a result or reported value is a conflation of two or more effects which are not, or cannot be, isolated from each other. The confounds that are involved in measuring time preference generally are discussed in a later section, but at this stage it will suffice to give one example. When people buy inefficient but cheaper electrical appliances this may not be because they discount future cost savings at a high rate. Various other factors may be relevant: (1) people may be ignorant of the future cost savings; (2) people may be informed about future cost savings but disbelieve them or regard them with a large amount of uncertainty; (3) people may have cash constraints that do not permit a higher current expenditure; (4) there may be hidden costs related to buying more efficient appliances, in terms of greater maintenance or reduced reliability; and (5) people may be incapable of translating the relevant monetary information into a basis for decision-making and simply make a random choice, or choose out of habit or current convenience.

2. *Experimental studies*

These studies involve asking subjects to evaluate either real or hypothetical prospects that are manipulated by the investigator. They tend to be more common than field studies in intertemporal research, because field studies limit the flexibility of the investigator and tend to present more problems with interpretation, due to the existence of unavoidable confounds. In experimental studies confounds can often be avoided by careful experimental design.

In experimental studies either real or hypothetical rewards and costs can be used. These do not have to be monetary in nature, but may relate to health or levels of comfort and discomfort. The obvious advantage of using real rewards is that subjects are more motivated to act in ways that correspond closely to their behavior in real life, and such studies are therefore more likely to yield accurate predictions. However, there is also an advantage of using hypothetical outcomes in terms of flexibility; it is possible to use both large rewards and losses in this case, as well as using longer-time delays. A study by Kirby and Marakovic (1995) compared discounting under both kinds of situation, using 30 permutations of 5 different rewards (between $14.75 and $28.50) and 6 different delays (between 3 and 29 days). The conclusion was that discount rates were lower for hypothetical rewards, and this was also the conclusion of Coller and Williams (1999) in a different type of study, although in this case the results were more ambiguous.

Four experimental procedures tend to be used: choice tasks, matching tasks, rating tasks, and pricing tasks.

a) *Choice tasks*

This is the most common experimental method for eliciting discount rates. Subjects are typically asked to choose between a smaller, more immediate reward and a larger, more distant reward. The obvious disadvantage of this technique is that it only provides a lower or upper limit to the discount rate. For example, if people prefer a sum of $110 in 1 year to $100 now, this merely tells us that their discount rate is less than 10%. In order to yield more precise results, investigators have to offer a series of many different choices, so that if people prefer $110 in 1 year, they are then asked if they prefer $105, and so on. Thus usually a bracket can be calculated for each subject. Apart from the complications and length involved, another problem with the technique is that it is subject to an anchoring effect, discussed in more detail in Chapter 9. Subjects tend to be influenced unduly by the first option offered. One way in which this problem can be countered is by using **titration procedures**. These present subjects with responses that are successively at opposite ends of a spectrum. For example, a first question might ask subjects to choose between $100 now and $101 in 1 year, while the next question asks them to choose between $100 now and $1000 in 1 year; then the next question might compare $100 now with $102 in a year, followed by $100 now and $500 in a year, as the procedure gradually narrows down to a central range.

b) *Matching tasks*

With this method subjects give open-ended responses which equate two intertemporal options. For example, they may be asked how much money they would require in 1 year to be equivalent to receiving $100 now. Such a technique has two advantages over the procedure of choice tasks. First, an exact discount rate can be computed from a single response, without the need for asking a series of questions. Second, there is no anchoring problem, since the responses are open-ended.

However, there are various problems that arise with the matching task procedure, which can lead to misleading results. One prominent problem is that subjects tend to use crude rules for making judgments. For example, it is quite common for people to use a "times *n*" rule for generating future reward equivalents, meaning that they multiply the present amount by the number of years to obtain an equivalent delayed reward. Thus subjects may state that $100 now is equivalent to $500 in 5 years' time. Such a rule does not necessarily mean that subjects are responding in ways that do not correspond to real-life behavior, but this suspicion is confirmed by a second problem that results are highly inconsistent according to the method of matching used. When subjects are asked to state the future reward that is equivalent to a specified current reward they tend to use a much higher discount rate than when they are asked to state the current reward that is equivalent to a specified future reward. For example, Frederick and Read (2002) have found that when subjects were asked to state the amount that would be equivalent in 30 years to $100 now, the median response was $10 000, implying a discount factor over the 30-year period of 0.01. However, when subjects were asked to state the amount now that would be equivalent to receiving $100 in 30 years the median response was $50, implying a discount factor over the same period of only 0.5.

The same kind of inconsistency has been found when questions have been framed in terms of matching amount of reward and time of delay. For example, a study by Roelofsma (1994) asked one group of subjects to state the amount of money they would require to compensate for delaying the delivery of a purchased bicycle by 9 months, obtaining a median response of 250 florins. However, when another group of subjects were asked how long they would be willing to delay the delivery of the bicycle in return for the compensation of 250 florins, the mean response was only 3 weeks, implying a discount rate twelve times as high.

These highly inconsistent results obtained with matching procedures shed doubt on the reliability of the procedure in general, while simultaneously demanding some kind of psychological explanation. As with other cases of inconsistency and preference reversal one of the consequences is that normative models of behavior become problematical to develop. This aspect is discussed in more detail in the next chapter in the section related to policy implications.

c) *Rating tasks*

With this procedure subjects are asked to rate outcomes in different time periods in terms of either like or dislike. Thus an ordinal scale is used as opposed to a cardinal and ratio-based scale. The advantage is that this imposes less of a computational strain on subjects, but the disadvantage is that results are less well differentiated. For example, if a person rates $150 in 1 year as being preferable to $100 now, it is not clear if the difference in preference is large or small.

d) *Pricing tasks*

This procedure involves eliciting a WTP by respondents in order to receive or avoid a particular outcome in the future, expressed in either monetary or nonmonetary terms (like an extra year of life or a specified amount of pain). Like rating tasks, this procedure allows the manipulation of time between subjects, since each individual may evaluate either the immediate or the delayed outcome in isolation.

Methodological issues

It can be seen from Case 5.1 that even experimental studies have produced a wide variation in reported discount rates. This is because, although controls have been used, different controls have been used in different studies. To give a flavor of this we will take one of the most controlled studies, performed by Harrison, Lau, and Williams (2002), and examine the principles underlying its experimental design and the issues raised. They asked a representative sample of 268 people from the Danish population the basic question: do you prefer $100 today or $100 + x tomorrow? The format of their experiment modified this question in six ways:

1. *Use of choice tasks*

Twenty different amounts were offered as the B option to compare with a standard A option in order to estimate narrow boundaries for an individual's discount rate.

2. *Random payments used as incentives*

Subjects were simultaneously asked several questions with varying amounts of x, with one question being selected at random for actual payment after the end of the experiment. The objective was to avoid income effects that might affect the answers to later questions. This is a standard mechanism among researchers for ensuring participation, motivation, and reliable responses. The main problem with this method is that it does not allow for learning effects to take place (Starmer 2000).

3. *Use of "front-end delay"*

Both early and later options were in the future. Thus, instead of asking, for example, whether subjects preferred $100 *now* or $100 + *x* in 6 months, the investigators asked whether subjects preferred $100 *in 1 month* or $100 + *x* in 7 months. This avoids the problem, mentioned in the first chapter, that there could be a confound between the effects of "pure" time preference and transactions costs in the future. Receiving money in the future always involves some transactions cost, as it has to be collected in some way and there is a possibility of the experimenter defaulting. If both options involve future payment, this effect is controlled for. This is an important control device, which has not been used in many studies. Comment on the results is given later.

4. *Use of different time horizons*

Four time horizons were used: 6 months, 12 months, 24 months, and 36 months. Some subjects were randomly assigned to answer questions relating to a single time period while others were asked questions relating to all periods. Using both methods allows the evaluation of the effect of the subjects' consideration of multiple time periods.

5. *Information relating to the subjects' market rate of interest is elicited*

The objective here was to examine the possibility that subjects' discount rates were censored by market rates. This means that the interest rates reported by subjects do not reflect "pure" time preference, but are determined by the market rates they face. For example, if someone can borrow at 6% they might prefer $105 in 1 year to $100 now, since borrowing the $100 would be more expensive.

6. *Provision of the annual interest rates associated with delayed payment*

This facilitates comparisons between the options in the experiment and external or market options.

The format of this experimental design does not permit the testing of all the effects discussed in Section 5.5 on anomalies, for example the "sign effect" and the "magnitude effect," but it does succeed in controlling for some important problems relating to misconceptions and confounds. However, there is one issue that merits some further discussion here. The authors report that

> Our results indicate that nominal discount rates are constant over the one-year to three-year horizons used in these experiments.

Some commentators have concluded from this that the use of front-end delay, by eliminating the confound related to transactions cost, provides supporting evidence in favor of the constant discounting characteristic of the DUM and against hyperbolic discounting. The issue of hyperbolic discounting is discussed in the next chapter, but the merits of this claim need some clarification. Closer inspection of the study's results indicates that the 6-month discount rate was actually 34.9 %, the 12-month rate was 29.0 %, and the 24-month and 36-month rates were 27.4 % and 27.9 % respectively. Thus the claim that a constant discounting rate applies throughout the *whole* period is misleading. What would be revealing here is the use of a shorter front-end delay, of a day or a week, and an estimation of discount rates for periods shorter than 6 months. This kind of empirical evidence would facilitate the evaluation of the constant discounting claim.

Calculation of the discount rate

It is also a worthwhile exercise at this point to review the mathematics behind the calculation of discount rates, since different methods can be used here. The simplest method involves the standard compounding formula used in net present value and internal rate of return calculations in evaluating investment decisions. This formula can be represented below:

$$F = P(1+r)^n \tag{5.2}$$

where F = future value, P = present value, r = discount rate, and n = number of time periods. For example, if subjects match the value of $500 in 10 years to $100 now, the method above would calculate the discount rate as follows:

$$500 = 100(1+r)^{10}$$

This yields a discount rate of about 17 % a year.

However, most empirical studies do not use the above method of calculation because it involves **discrete compounding**, usually with yearly periods, as in the above example. Instead it is usually preferred to use **continuous compounding**. This involves using an exponential function:

$$F = Pe^{nr} \tag{5.3}$$

This formula can be manipulated to solve for the value of r as follows:

$$r = \frac{\ln(F/P)}{n} \tag{5.4}$$

If the same values in the discrete example above are substituted into the exponential function, the implied discount rate is 16%. When continuous compounding is used the implied discount rates are always lower than with discrete compounding, and the difference between the two methods becomes greater as discount rates increase. For example, if the future equivalent in the above situation was $1000 instead of $100 (as would happen if a subject was using the "times n" rule) then discrete compounding would yield a discount rate of 26% while continuous compounding yields 23%.

Discount rates can also be calculated on either an average or a marginal basis. For example, subjects might be indifferent between receiving $100 now, receiving $120 in 1 year, and receiving $160 in 5 years. Using continuous compounding this implies a discount rate of 18.2% over the next year (between year 0 and year 1), and an average discount rate of 7.8% per year over the next 5 years (between year 0 and year 5). However, it may be useful in some situations to consider the marginal discount rate per period. In the situation above the marginal discount rate between year 1 and year 5 is 7.2% per year.

5.5 Anomalies in the Discounted Utility Model

Many anomalies in the DUM have already been noted, in terms of the features of the model described earlier and the manner in which such features do not appear to be confirmed by empirical evidence. Many other anomalies arise due to factors discussed in the previous two chapters, relating to PT and mental accounting. These further anomalies relate to the "sign effect," the "magnitude effect," the "delay-speedup" asymmetry, the "date/delay effect," preference for improving sequences, and violations of independence and preference for spread. These factors are now discussed in turn.

The "sign effect"

This effect means that gains are discounted more than losses, as proposed by PT. For example, a study by Thaler (1981) asked subjects how much they would be willing to pay for a traffic ticket if payment could be delayed for periods of 3 months, 1 year, or 3 years. The responses indicated that people used much lower discount rates than in situations where monetary gains were involved. This study was an experimental and hypothetical one, but in this situation it should be practical to conduct a field study, since local government authorities maintain records of fines and dates of payments. In many cases the implied discount rate used by such authorities is very large, with fines often doubling in a matter of a few weeks. The main problem with analyzing such a study would be the existence of confounding factors discussed in the previous section. In this case people may forget to pay, or delay payment in the hope of evading the fine altogether (if authorities fail to follow up on all tickets issued).

At the extreme end of the loss-discounting spectrum, there are several studies that indicate that many people prefer to incur a loss immediately rather than delay it (Mischel, Grusec, and Masters 1969; Yates and Watts 1975; Loewenstein 1987; Benzion, Rapoport, and Yagil 1989; MacKeigan *et al.* 1993; Redelmeier and Heller 1993). This implies a zero discount rate for losses. The general psychological explanation for such loss-aversion may be somewhat different from other types of loss-aversion where the loss is immediate, in the sense that there is an additional factor involved: anticipatory utility or, in this case, disutility. As we have seen in Chapter 2, people do not like the idea of a loss "hanging over" them, and may prefer to endure the pain of the loss immediately and "get it over and done with."

The "magnitude effect"

Studies that vary outcome size often find that large outcomes are discounted at a lower rate than small ones (Thaler 1981; Ainslie and Haendel 1983; Loewenstein 1987; Benzion, Rapoport, and Yagil 1989; Holcomb and Nelson 1992; Green, Fry, and Myerson 1994; Kirby, Petry, and Bickel 1999). For example, in Thaler's study subjects were indifferent between $15 immediately and $60 in a year, $250 immediately and $350 in a year, and $3000 immediately and $4000 in a year. These matching preferences indicated discount rates of 139 %, 34 %, and 29 % respectively.

This phenomenon requires a psychological explanation, which appears to be lacking in the literature where the effect has been observed. It should be noted that the effect works in the opposite direction to the effect of diminishing marginal utility. The discount rates calculated for Thaler's study above are based on the monetary values, not the actual utilities. If utilities were used to calculate discount rates instead of monetary values then, assuming the law of diminishing marginal utility applies, the differences in discount rates between small and large amounts would be even greater.

The "delay-speedup" asymmetry

Studies have also investigated the effect of changing the delivery time of outcomes. These changes can be framed either as delays or as accelerations from some reference point in time. For example, Loewenstein (1988) has found that subjects who did not expect to receive a VCR for another year would pay an average of $54 to receive it immediately (a perceived gain). However, those subjects who thought they would receive the VCR immediately demanded an average of $126 to delay its receipt by a year (a perceived loss). Other studies have confirmed these findings in situations where the outcomes involved payments, that is negative outcomes, rather than positive ones like the delivery of a product. In these situations subjects demand more to accelerate payment (a perceived loss) than to delay it (a perceived gain).

We can note that these results are predicted by PT. Two elements of the theory are involved: reference points and loss-aversion.

Preference for improving sequences

The DUM predicts that, total undiscounted utility being equal, people will prefer a declining sequence of outcomes to an increasing sequence, since later outcomes are discounted more heavily. Thus, given the two consumption profiles (50, 60, 70) and (70, 60, 50) over three consecutive time periods, the DUM predicts that people will prefer the latter to the former. In contrast, many studies have shown that people prefer improving profiles. For example, Loewenstein and Sicherman (1991) have found that, for an otherwise identical job, most subjects prefer an increasing wage profile to a declining or flat one. Hsee, Abelson, and Salovey (1991) have found that an increasing salary sequence was rated as highly as a decreasing sequence that conferred a much larger monetary amount. In addition to these studies involving gains, some investigators have examined sequences of losses. Varey and Kahneman (1992) have found that subjects strongly preferred a sequence of decreasing discomfort to a sequence of increasing discomfort, even when the overall sum of discomfort over the interval was otherwise identical. Chapman (2000) investigated the responses of people to hypothetical sequences of headache pain, with the sequences being matched in terms of total pain; durations varied from one hour to as long as 20 years. For all durations, between 82% and 92% of the subjects preferred sequences of pain that were declining rather than increasing.

These findings are in line with various effects reported in Chapter 2; for example, expectations effects and anticipatory utility, and reference points. In particular, it is worth recalling the colonoscopy studies of Katz, Redelmeier, and Kahneman (1997), where remembered utility, which in turn may determine decision utility, may differ from real-time utility. Remembered utility, or disutility, may depend more on utility at the end of the sequence rather than at the start, as predicted by the Peak-End rule.

The "date/delay effect"

While all the effects described above involve objective changes and manipulations of outcomes and time periods, recent research has also indicated that people may make different intertemporal choices when logically identical situations are presented or framed in different ways. Studies by Read *et al.* (2005) and LeBoeuf (2006) find that people use lower discount rates in situations when time periods are described using end dates than when the same time periods are described as extents. For example, the LeBoeuf study asked subjects the following two questions (on February 15):

1. How much money would you want to receive *in eight months* to be equivalent to receiving $100 now?
2. How much money would you want to receive *on October 15* to be equivalent to receiving $100 now?

Although the two questions are equivalent in logical terms, it was found that people generally demanded a larger amount in answering the first question, implying a higher discount rate when a future gain is framed in terms of extent. Similar results are reported when outcomes are expressed as losses rather than gains, and in a number of experiments when the time intervals until outcomes occur vary between 2 months and 2 years.

LeBoeuf proposes a psychological explanation for this phenomenon, utilizing aspects of both PT and mental accounting:

When consumers consider an interval demarcated by a date, the date may be construed as a relatively abstract point in time, and consumers may not even compute the interval's length. In contrast, when that same interval is described as an extent, by definition, the amount of time is highlighted . . . Thus consumers may attend more to interval length when facing an extent.

If the interval length is perceived as being longer, it follows that a higher discount rate will be used. There are various policy implications of this finding, and these are discussed in the next chapter.

Violations of independence and preference for spread

As mentioned in the previous section, the assumption of consumption independence implies that preferences between two consumption profiles should not be affected by the nature of consumption in periods in which consumption is identical in the two profiles. Again, there is evidence that suggests that consumers may respond differently in situations that are logically equivalent. For example, Loewenstein and Prelec (1993) have found that when people are given a "simple" choice – (A) dinner at a fancy French restaurant next weekend; or (B) dinner at the same restaurant on a weekend 2 weeks later – most people prefer the first option, the sooner dinner. This is predicted by the DUM, as people discount the utility of the later event more heavily. However, the investigators observed different results when subjects are offered an "elaborated" choice: (C) dinner at a fancy French restaurant next weekend and dinner at home on a weekend 2 weeks later; or (D) dinner at home next weekend and dinner at the French restaurant on a weekend in 2 weeks. In this decision situation most people prefer the second option. Since the most likely event for subjects is to have dinner at home, the "elaborated" options (C) and (D) amount to the same as the "simple" options (A) and (B). Thus there appears to be a framing effect, causing preference reversal.

The psychological explanation here appears to be that the "elaborated" options draw attention to the sequence of outcomes over time, and, as seen above, people prefer an improving sequence.

Loewenstein and Prelec (1993) also observe a preference for spreading outcomes, again a violation of independence. An experiment involved subjects hypothetically receiving two coupons for fancy restaurant dinners, and asking them when they would use them. Two different conditions were used, one involving a 2-year time limit and the other involving no time limits. Results indicated that subjects scheduled the two dinners later with the 2-year limit (8 weeks and 31 weeks) than when there were no limits (3 weeks and 13 weeks). It appears that framing the offer with a 2-year limit causes the subjects to spread their outcomes over a longer period if the 2-year horizon is longer than the implicit time horizon used by subjects who face no time limits. This is another example of an anchoring effect.

There is also evidence that people have a preference for spreading incomes as well as consumption, a phenomenon referred to as "income smoothing."

A natural experiment occurs in California, where about a half of the United School Districts give teachers the choice of receiving their annual salaries in 10 or 12 monthly payments. The DUM would predict that teachers should choose 10 payments and earn interest on their savings. However, in reality about 50% of the teachers choose 12 installments, even though over a long period of time the interest foregone is considerable (Mayer and Russell 2005). The psychological explanation, supported by a survey of the teachers, is that the 12-payment option, by spreading the receipt of incomes, facilitates self-control over spending.

Implications of anomalies

With other aspects of the SEM, violations of the model, for example preference reversals, are often perceived by subjects as being mistakes once they are pointed out. However, this is frequently not the case with the anomalies described above. A few examples will illustrate this important point:

1. *The "sign effect"*
   When within-subjects studies are compared with between-subjects studies, the size of the sign effect is greater with the first type of study. Thus, when subjects are exposed to both gains and losses the disparity in discount rates is greater than when subjects are only exposed to either gains or losses but not both. If the "sign effect" were regarded as a "mistake" by subjects, one would expect the disparity to be smaller or nonexistent in within-subjects studies where subjects could directly compare their responses to losses and gains.

2. *The "magnitude effect"*
   The evidence here is similar to that relating to the "sign effect." Frederick and Read (2002) have found that when subjects evaluate both small and large amounts the disparity in discount rates is greater than when they evaluate only small or large amounts. Once again this runs contrary to what one would expect if the anomaly was regarded as a "mistake," since the comparison of the small and large amounts would provide an anchoring effect.

3. *Preference for improving sequences*
   In the study by Loewenstein and Sicherman (1991) it was explained to subjects that a decreasing wage profile ($27 000, $26 000, . . . , $23 000) would enable them to consume more in every period than the corresponding increasing wage profile ($23 000, $24 000, . . . , $27 000) with the same nominal total. However, this did not affect the behavior of the subjects, who continued to prefer the increasing profile.

The significance of this behavior is that, at least in many situations, people do not regard the anomalies described as being mistakes, or errors of judgment. Actually, this should not be surprising, since at the outset the DUM was not presented as either a valid descriptive or a normative model. Unfortunately, as it has gained rapid and widespread acceptance by economists and other practitioners, the DUM has covertly gained a reputation in terms of descriptive and normative validity.

Therefore, after reviewing the DUM and its shortcomings, the task is now to examine other models of intertemporal choice which have better descriptive and normative validity. This is the subject of the next chapter.

5.6 Summary

- Early scholarship relating to intertemporal choice emphasized the importance of psychological factors in determining preferences.

- The DUM compressed the influences of all factors affecting time preference into a single parameter, the discount rate.

- The originator of the DUM, Samuelson, never intended the model to be either normative or descriptive in terms of validity.

- The DUM has eight primary features: integration of new alternatives with existing plans; utility independence; consumption independence; stationary instantaneous utility; stationary discounting; constant discounting; independence of discounting from consumption; diminishing marginal utility; and positive time preference.

- Empirical research may involve either field studies or experimental studies. The latter may involve either real or hypothetical rewards/losses. Either type of study may be between subjects or within subjects.

- Experimental studies may involve choice tasks, matching tasks, pricing tasks, and rating tasks. The first two techniques are most common.

- Discount rates can be calculated on either a discrete or a continuous compounding basis. The latter method, involving an exponential function, is more common.

- There are a large number of anomalies in the DUM: the "sign effect," the "magnitude effect"; the "delay-speedup" asymmetry; preference for improving sequences; the "date/delay effect"; and violations of independence and preference for spread.

- The anomalies in the DUM should not be regarded as mistakes or errors in judgment. Instead they imply that the model lacks both descriptive and normative validity.

5.7 Applications

At this stage of our analysis of intertemporal choice we are not really in a position to examine and evaluate individual situations, since we have not yet discussed alternative behavioral models that aim to overcome the shortcomings of the DUM. Therefore the analysis of particular specific situations will be delayed until the next chapter. There is therefore only one application included here; this is a general overview of empirical studies measuring discount rates conducted over a 25-year period.

Case 5.1   Empirical estimates of discount rates

In a landmark article in 2002 entitled "Time Discounting: A Critical Review," the authors Frederick, Loewenstein, and O'Donoghue summarized in a table the implicit discount rates from all the studies that they could find between 1978 and 2002 where such discount rates were reported or could easily be calculated. The table lists 42 studies, and describes the type of study, the good involved, whether real or hypothetical rewards/losses were involved, the elicitation method, the time range, the annual discount rate, and the discount factor. The discount (δ) is calculated by using the expression $\delta = 1/(1 + r)$. As we shall see in the next chapter, it can be more convenient mathematically to use the discount factor instead of the discount rate in expressing various phenomena. The table is reproduced below (Table 5.1):

Questions

1. What factors might account for the huge variability in the estimates of discount rates?
2. Does there appear to be any relationship between the size of discount rates and whether rewards are real or hypothetical?
3. What is the implication of a negative discount rate, and what might cause this?
4. Is there any evidence of methodological progress, in terms of a convergence of estimates as time goes on? What is the significance of any lack of progress?

Table 5.1 Empirical estimates of discount rates

Study	Type	Good(s)	Real/Hypo Rewards	Elicitation Method	Time Range	Annual Discount Rate (%)	δ
Maital and Maital (1978)	Experimental	Money and coupons	Hypo	Choice	1 year	70	0.59
Hausman (1979)	Field	Money	Real	Choice	Undefined	5–89	0.95–0.53
Gateley (1980)	Field	Money	Real	Choice	Undefined	45–300	0.69–0.25
Thaler (1981)	Experimental	Money	Hypo	Matching	3 months to 10 years	7–345	0.93–0.22
Ainslie and Haendel (1983)	Experimental	Money	Real	Matching	Undefined	96 000–∞	0.00
Houston (1983)	Experimental	Money	Hypo	Other	1 year to 20 years	23	0.81
Loewenstein (1987)	Experimental	Money and pain	Hypo	Pricing	Immediate to 10 years	–6–212	1.06–0.32
Moore and Viscusi (1988)	Field	Life years	Real	Choice	Undefined	10–12	0.91–0.89
Benzion, Rapoport, and Yagil (1989)	Experimental	Money	Hypo	Matching	6 months to 4 years	9–60	0.92–0.63
Viscusi and Moore (1989)	Field	Life years	Real	Choice	Undefined	11	0.90
Moore and Viscusi (1990a)	Field	Life years	Real	Choice	Undefined	2	0.98

Study	Field/Experimental	Commodity	Real/Hypo	Method	Time range	Number	Discount rate
Moore and Viscusi (1990b)	Field	Life years	Real	Choice	Undefined	1–14	0.99–0.88
Shelley (1993)	Experimental	Money	Hypo	Matching	6 months to 4 years	8–27	0.93–0.79
Redelmeier and Heller (1993)	Experimental		Hypo	Rating	1 day to 10 years	0	1.00
Cairns (1994)	Experimental	Money	Hypo	Choice	5 years to 20 years	14–25	0.88–0.80
Shelley (1994)	Experimental	Money	Hypo	Rating	6 months to 2 years	4–22	0.96–0.82
Chapman and Elstein (1995)	Experimental	Money and health	Hypo	Matching	6 months to 12 years	11–263	0.90–0.28
Dolan and Gudex (1995)	Experimental	Health	Hypo	Other	1 month to 10 years	0	1.00
Dreyfus and Viscusi (1995)	Field	Life years	Real	Choice	Undefined	11–17	0.90–0.85
Kirby and Marakovic (1995)	Experimental	Money	Real	Matching	3 days to 29 days	3678–∞	0.03–0.00
Chapman (1996)	Experimental	Money and health	Hypo	Matching	1 year to 12 years	Negative to 300	1.01–0.25
Kirby and Marakovic (1996)	Experimental	Money	Real	Choice	6 hours to 70 days	500–1500	0.17–0.06
Pender (1996)	Experimental	Rice	Real	Choice	7 months to 2 years	26–69	0.79–0.59
Wahlund and Gunnarsson (1996)	Experimental	Money	Hypo	Matching	1 month to 1 year	18–158	0.85–0.39

Table 5.1 (Continued)

Study	Type	Good(s)	Real/Hypo Rewards	Elicitation Method	Time Range	Annual Discount Rate (%)	δ
Cairns and van der Pol (1997)	Experimental	Money	Hypo	Matching	2 years to 19 years	13–31	0.88–0.76
Green, Myerson, and McFadden (1997)	Experimental	Money	Hypo	Choice	3 months to 20 years	6–111	0.94–0.47
Johanneson and Johansson (1997)	Experimental	Life years	Hypo	Pricing	6 years to 57 years	0–3	1.00–0.97
Kirby (1997)	Experimental	Money		Pricing	1 day to 1 month	159–5747	0.39–0.02
Madden et al. (1997)	Experimental	Money and heroin	Hypo	Choice	1 week to 25 years	8–∞	0.93–0.00
Chapman and Winquist (1998)	Experimental	Money	Hypo	Matching	3 months	426–2189	0.19–0.04
Holden, Shiferaw, and Wik (1998)	Experimental	Money and corn	Real	Matching	1 year	28–147	0.78–0.40
Cairns and van der Pol (1999)	Experimental	Health	Hypo	Matching	4 years to 16 years	6	0.94
Chapman, Nelson, and Hier (1999)	Experimental	Money and health	Hypo	Choice	1 month to 6 months	13–19000	0.88–0.01
Coller and Williams (1999)	Experimental	Money	Real	Choice	1 month to 3 months	15–25	0.87–0.80

Kirby, Petry, and Bickel (1999)	Experimental	Money	Real	Choice	7 days to 186 days	50–55 700	0.67–0.00
van der Pol and Cairns (1999)	Experimental	Health	Hypo	Choice	5 years to 13 years	7	0.93
Chesson and Viscusi (2000)	Experimental	Money	Hypo	Matching	1 year to 25 years	11	0.90
Ganiats et al. (2000)	Experimental	Health	Hypo	Choice	6 months to 20 years	Negative to 116	1.01–0.46
Hesketh (2000)	Experimental	Money	Hypo	Choice	6 months to 4 years	4–36	0.96–0.74
van der Pol and Cairns (2001)	Experimental	Health	Hypo	Choice	2 years to 15 years	6–9	0.94–0.92
Warner and Pleeter (2001)	Field	Money	Real	Choice	Immediate to 22 years	0–71	1.00–0.58
Harrison, Lau, and Williams (2002)	Experimental	Money	Real	Choice	1 month to 37 months	28	0.78

Alternative Intertemporal Choice Models

6.1 Time preference

The most obvious characteristic of the table at the end of the previous chapter is the very wide disparity between different measures of the discount rate, even within the same study as well as between studies. Thus it is not simply differences in methodology in terms of experimental design that account for these variations. The primary reason for the variability is the existence of confounding factors in the measurement of time preference. This raises the fundamental issue of what constitutes time preference. Before discussing this issue, let us examine the various confounding factors involved.

Consumption reallocation

Most studies use monetary rewards as payoffs rather than consumption. When discount rates are calculated it is normally assumed that rewards and losses are consumed immediately at the same point in time that they are received, and that they do not affect the pattern of consumption at other time periods. For example, if a reward of $100 is to be received in 1 year, it is assumed that this amount will be consumed immediately rather than causing a stream of higher consumption over a prolonged time period after 1 year. Furthermore, it is assumed that this reward is not anticipated, in terms of increasing consumption in time periods before it is received. It is obvious from empirical observation that both aspects are unrealistic. Ideally, the calculation of discount rates should take into account the effects of rewards and losses on the whole lifetime pattern of consumption.

Intertemporal arbitrage

When rewards are tradable, like money, intertemporal choices may not reflect time preference directly, but may be caused by intertemporal arbitrage. For example, if a person prefers $100 now to $150 in 5 years' time, this may be because they can invest $100 now at the market rate of interest and make it worth more than $150 in 5 years. When financial markets are efficient it can be argued that discount rates will converge on the market rate of interest, rather than being a direct reflection of time preference. Of course market interest rates are affected by time preference, but they are also influenced by many other factors such as default risk, uncertainty, liquidity, and so on.

However, there is a heavy weight of empirical evidence that financial markets cannot explain intertemporal choices, since discount rates generally are much higher than market interest rates. For example, people with substantial savings earning 4 % interest per year should not prefer $100 today to $120 in 1 year if financial markets are efficient, yet many do. Such choices and preferences imply either that people are ignorant about the operations of the markets, or that they are unable to use the markets properly for some reason. It appears, therefore, that discount rates do take into account time preference, and other factors, in ways that the market interest rate does not.

Concave utility

As can be seen from Table 5.1, the majority of empirical studies involve monetary rewards, and base the calculation of discount rates on the monetary amounts. As was mentioned briefly in the last chapter, it is misleading to calculate discount rates on this basis, since it is implicitly assumed that utility increases linearly with monetary amounts. This assumption is in direct contradiction to both the SEM and the principles of PT. An example will illustrate the effects of relaxing this assumption and instead incorporating a concave utility function, as proposed by PT. Say that the average response of a group of subjects is that they are indifferent between $100 now and $150 in 5 years. The imputed discount rate (assuming no consumption reallocation) is 8.1% a year on the basis of the monetary amounts. However, it may be that the $150 has only 30% more utility than $100 (this is also ignoring the effect of inflation, which is considered later). Using utility as the basis for discounting, the imputed discount rate is only 5.2%. This shows that utility discount rates are lower than monetary discount rates when utility functions are concave.

In terms of empirical findings, Chapman (1996) attempted to allow for the concavity of the utility function by estimating a utility function from the monetary amounts, and found that the discount rates calculated from the utility function were indeed substantially lower than the monetary discount rates. However, it is difficult empirically to conduct a reliable study to estimate utility discount rates, bearing in mind the problem of consumption reallocation discussed earlier. For example, although it may be possible to estimate that $150 has only 30% more utility than $100, what is relevant are the streams of utility that flow from the reward of $150. A consumer may respond by spending an extra $30 a year over the next 5 years, and a person's utility function may not be concave over such small amounts.

Uncertainty

Future rewards and costs are almost invariably associated with uncertainty in practice. Thus in field studies it is particularly difficult to avoid this confound, regardless of whether rewards and costs are expressed in monetary terms or in other ways. For example, even if we can be sure that a particular electrical appliance will save us a certain amount of electricity in the future (which is unlikely in itself), we cannot be sure what will be the future price of electricity.

In experimental studies it might appear that investigators could avoid this confound by assuring subjects that delayed rewards will be delivered with certainty. This is indeed the common practice in such studies, but whether respondents can accept this situation from a subjective point of view is questionable. It may be that there is an unconscious psychological mechanism that automatically relates delay to uncertainty. One reason for such a mechanism is that even if rewards are certain in monetary or other terms, our valuation of these may change over time, since utilities change as tastes change in ways that are not entirely predictable. For example, in the future we come to value money less and health more than we do today. Therefore there will always be an element of uncertainty relating to future tastes and utilities.

Furthermore, some experimental studies have compounded this problem by introducing ambiguity into the situation. For example, a study by Benzion, Rapoport, and Yagil (1989) asked respondents to imagine that they had earned money, but when they arrived to receive payment they were told that the "financially solid" public institution that had promised to pay them was "temporarily short of funds." They were then asked to specify future amounts of money that would make them indifferent to receiving the amount of money that they had been promised immediately, with varying amounts of delay. The methodological problem here is that there is an inconsistency in terminology: financially solid institutions should not become temporarily short of funds. The latter expression introduces an element of uncertainty into the subject's consideration.

One finding that seems beyond doubt here is that discount rates are significantly affected by uncertainty. This is established by studies that introduce objective uncertainty. For example, in a study by Keren and Roelofsma (1995), one group of subjects was asked to choose between 100 florins immediately and 110 florins in one month, while another group was asked to choose between a 50% chance of 100 florins immediately and a 50% chance of 110 florins in 1 month. With the first group 82% preferred the smaller immediate option, but, when rewards were uncertain, only 39% of the second group preferred the smaller immediate reward. Thus a much higher discount rate is implied when rewards are certain compared with the uncertain situation.

Inflation

Most studies ignore the effect of inflation in the calculation of discount rates, assuming that the utility of $100 now is the same as the utility of $100 in 10 years at the times they are received. In practice, people are likely to discount future monetary rewards according to their experiences with and expectations of inflation. Furthermore, there is another element of uncertainty here, as the effect of future inflation on purchasing power becomes more uncertain as the duration of delay increases.

Expectations of changes in utility

It was stated above that our tastes often change in unpredictable ways. However, some of these changes are partially predictable. Again, we have seen earlier that people often prefer rising consumption profiles, and this preference is anticipated. The factors underlying this phenomenon are examined in Case 6.3, along with the implications. At this point we can observe that it has two effects on preferences and discounting, which operate in opposite directions. The more obvious effect is that if we expect to have higher consumption levels in the future, the marginal utility of $100 of consumption now is greater than the marginal utility of $100 of consumption in 5 years, because of the effect of the law of diminishing marginal utility. This effect exerts an upward bias on discount rates.

However, there is another effect at work here. People may wish to defer consumption to later periods in order to have a rising consumption over time, but they may lack the self-control to save sufficient income earned now to provide for this future consumption. In such a situation, people may welcome some sort of commitment device that allows them to have more money in the future without the opportunity to spend it earlier, in the same sort of way that they may commit to paying into a pension fund. We have already seen something of this effect in the case of the teachers who preferred to be paid 12 times a year rather than 10. In this situation people may prefer to receive the money in the future rather than immediately. This effect exerts a downward bias on discount rates.

Anticipatory utility

This is another phenomenon that has been discussed earlier, in Chapter 2. For example, people may wish to defer consumption of a restaurant dinner, since the anticipation of the future utility may increase total utility. The modeling of this factor is discussed in a later section, but at this stage we can observe that the effect is to exert a downward bias on discount rates.

Visceral influences

Visceral factors relate to desire states, emotions and sentiments, and cravings. The prospect of an immediate reward (the "actual presence of the immediate object of desire" in Rae's terms) may stimulate visceral factors that temporarily increase the attraction of the reward. However, like uncertainty, it is difficult to unravel these influences from time preference. It is argued by Frederick, Loewenstein, and O'Donoghue (2002) that if the visceral factors increase the attractiveness of the immediate reward without affecting its enjoyment (decision utility rather than experienced utility) then "they are probably best viewed as a legitimate determinant of time preference." On the other hand, if visceral factors do affect experienced utility then "they might best be regarded as a confounding factor."

What is time preference?

The presence of the various confounding factors described above raises the fundamental issue concerning the definition of time preference. In particular, the issue involves whether time preference is a unitary construct. This has aroused much debate in the psychology literature. There is a general consensus that psychological constructs or traits must satisfy the following three criteria:

1. *Constancy*
   Constructs tend only to be useful when they remain constant within the same person over time. For example, many studies have shown that people's scores on intelligence tests change little over time.

2. *Generality*
   Constructs or traits should be able to predict a wide range of behaviors, rather than just a single narrow aspect of behavior. Intelligence is again a good example of such a trait. Impulsiveness is another example. Impulsive people make rash decisions without much (or any) thought, like purchase decisions, which they frequently regret afterwards.

3. *Correlation between different measures*
   Valid constructs can be measured in different ways that correlate highly with one another. In the case of intelligence it is difficult to devise tests that measure a cognitive skill where test results are not correlated. Tests of personality characteristics such as impulsiveness are similar. People who rate as impulsive on one question are likely to rate as impulsive on other questions.

The construct of time preference does not satisfy these criteria well. In terms of constancy, there is some evidence that the ability of children to delay gratification is significantly correlated with other variables much later in life, such as academic achievement and self-esteem (Mischel, Shoda, and Peake 1988; Shoda, Mischel, and Peake 1990; Ayduk *et al.* 2000). However, this only constitutes evidence of construct validity to the extent that these other variables are expressions of time preference, which some people would question.

On the other hand, there is a considerable body of evidence that discount rates for different rewards and costs are at best only weakly correlated. Fuchs (1982) found no correlation between experimental studies involving hypothetical monetary rewards and real-world behaviors involving time preference, such as seat-belt use, smoking, credit card debt, and the frequency of exercise and dental checkups. Chapman and Elstein (1995) and Chapman, Nelson, and Hier (1999) have found only weak correlations between discount rates for money and for health. Furthermore, Chapman and Elstein found no correlation between discount rates for losses and rates for gains. The main evidence of correlations involves addictive behavior: smokers tend to invest less in human capital, having flatter, as opposed to rising, income profiles (Munasinghe and Sicherman 2000); heroin addicts tend to have higher discount rates for monetary rewards (Kirby, Petry, and Bickel 1999).

It should be noted here that low correlations between different aspects of behavior involving time preference do not necessarily provide definitive evidence that time preference is not a unitary construct. For example, people may show a low discount rate for monetary rewards, implying that they value future revenues highly, but show a high discount rate for health-related factors, because they do not exercise. There are many possible explanations why people might engage in such seemingly inconsistent behavior: (1) they may have a strong aversion for exercise; (2) they are too busy earning income for their future to exercise; (3) they may value monetary rewards more than their health, maybe because they can bequeath them to their children; and (4) they do not believe that exercise is necessary for good health.

Furthermore, one should add that high correlations would not provide definitive evidence for a unitary construct either. As is the case with other social phenomena, time preference and time-related behaviors may themselves be correlated with other factors such as intelligence and social class. These factors would have to be identified and controlled in order for a study to provide proper evidence.

What can be concluded regarding time preference from such diverse and incomplete findings? It is suggested by Loewenstein *et al.* (2001) and Frederick, Loewenstein, and O'Donoghue (2002) that a useful approach may be to revert to a pre-DUM model and "unpack" time preference into its more fundamental psychological components: **impulsivity**, **compulsivity**, and **inhibition**. The advantage of doing this is that each of these characteristics can be measured reliably, and each explains and predicts different aspects of behavior. These terms and their influences are now discussed.

Impulsivity refers to the extent to which people act in a spontaneous, unplanned manner. Impulsive people may act without making conscious decisions, and their behavior tends to reveal a high discount rate for many types of activity such as credit card use. Compulsive people tend to make plans and stick to them. Thus they may exercise regularly, get medical checkups regularly, always use a seat belt, and pay bills on time. Generally such repetitive behaviors imply low discount rates for the relevant activities. Inhibition involves the ability to inhibit "knee-jerk" responses or impulsive behavior that may follow visceral stimuli. People who are inhibited may be criticized for not following their instincts, for example in terms of sexual behavior, but they may also be praised for their willpower, when it comes to refraining from eating junk food. The ability to resist visceral influences implies a low discount rate for the relevant behaviors, with more importance being attached to the future effects of such behaviors. The relevance, and indeed the very meaning of the term "willpower," is discussed in the next section.

A final observation regarding time preference is that, as with aspects of behavior discussed in other chapters, research in neuroscience is making progress in terms of locating specific areas in the brain which influence or determine the three psychological factors described above (Damasio 1994; LeDoux 1996). The fact that different brain areas appear to be involved in affecting these factors would seem to be sufficient justification for unpacking the concept of time preference. Further progress in the neuroscientific field may shed more light on the interrelationships between these psychological characteristics and their relationships with other aspects of behavior. This issue is discussed further in the third section.

Now that the concept of time preference has been discussed in some detail, and its component factors examined, we can turn our attention to the consideration of various alternative models to the DUM.

6.2 Hyperbolic discounting

Time-inconsistent preferences

When the DUM was examined in the previous chapter it was seen that the model assumed both constant discounting (at any period the same discount rate was used to discount outcomes in all future periods) and stationary discounting (the same discount rate was used in all future periods as in the current period). Under these assumptions people would have preferences that were time-consistent. In practice, both field studies and experimental studies have shown that inconsistent time preferences are common. For example, we may decide now that at the restaurant this evening we will resist the temptation to have a tasty dessert, because that would not be good for our future health. Yet later, when the dessert trolley comes round (better restaurants know the power of visceral influences, and therefore display the tempting goods under our noses), we yield to temptation and indulge ourselves.

Experimental studies have shown the phenomenon of time-inconsistent preferences in a more precise and quantitative manner. For example, Ainslie and Haslam (1992) reported that "a majority of subjects say they would prefer to have a prize of a $100 certified check available immediately over a $200 certified check that could not be cashed before 2 years; the same people do not prefer a $100 certified check that could be cashed in 6 years to a $200 certified check that could be cashed in 8 years." It is important to see how this would affect a subject's behavior. When presented with the second choice they will prefer to wait for the larger amount in 8 years, but sometime later, within the next 6 years, their preference will switch to the smaller amount being received sooner. This implies that the discount rate used by the subjects is greater over the short time horizon than over the long time horizon. Similar results have been found with choices involving a wide range of goods apart from both real and hypothetical cash rewards, for example health, food, and access to video games.

Studies using matching tasks as opposed to choice tasks have confirmed these findings, as discussed by Thaler (1981) and Benzion, Rapoport, and Yagil (1989). Subjects were asked to state the money amounts where they would be indifferent between x at time t and y immediately, with both x and t being variables. This permits the direct computation of discount rates for different time periods, and it has been repeatedly found that the discount rate is a decreasing function of t. Of course, as we saw in the previous chapter, this kind of methodology lends itself to the confound influence of transactions costs, since there is no front-end delay with the payment of y.

Nature of hyperbolic discounting

The first economist to discuss alternatives to the constant discounting approach of the DUM was Strotz (1955), who did not see any normative value in the approach. Strotz also realized the implication of relaxing the assumption of

constant discount rates in terms of the existence of time-inconsistent preferences. Although he did not propose any specific mathematical form of discount
function as an alternative, he did draw attention to the case of declining
discount rates. The first formal models involving hyperbolic discounting were
constructed by Chung and Herrnstein (1967) and Phelps and Pollak (1968).
This work has later been developed, in particular by Ainslie (1975; 1986;
1991; 1992) and by Laibson (1996; 1997; 1998).

In order to clarify the terminology and facilitate the understanding of the
mathematics of the various models, let us begin by distinguishing between
the terms **discount rate**, **discount factor**, **per-period discount factor**, and
discount function. In the conventional discounting model of the DUM, the
discount rate ρ is constant and corresponds to the interest rate at which future
utilities are discounted. The discount factor is the proportion by which each
period's utility is multiplied in order to calculate the present value of the utility.
In the constant discounting model the discount factor is given by $1/(1+\rho)^t$.
The per-period discount factor δ represents the proportion by which each
discount factor is multiplied to compute the discount factor for the following
period. In the DUM this is again constant, being given by $1/(1+\rho)$. The
discount function describes the relationship between the discount factor and
time, showing the total effect of discounting over a range of time periods. The
discount function in the DUM can therefore be described as $D(t) = \delta^t$, and
this is referred to as an exponential discount function. Thus if a person has a
utility function $u(x_0, x_1, x_2, \ldots, x_0)$, the utilities in the periods $0, 1, 2, \ldots, t$
are discounted by $1, \delta, \delta^2, \ldots, \delta^t$. It should be noted that the time variable is
treated as being discrete in this case, only assuming whole numbers.

These concepts are best illustrated by an example and a graph. In the
DUM we will assume that the value of $\rho = 0.1$. It follows that $\delta = 0.9091$.
After 10 time periods the discount factor will have the value of $0.9091^{10} =
0.3856$. Thus a utility of 100 units expected in 10 years will have a discounted
present utility of 38.56 units. A graph of this discount function is shown in
Figure 6.1.

The original hyperbolic discount function introduced by Chung and
Herrnstein (1967) was based on experimental studies with animals, and took
the form $D(t) = 1/t$. Herrnstein (1981) also developed another special case of
hyperbolic function, where $D(t) = (1 + \alpha t)^{-1}$.

Phelps and Pollak (1968) used a modified version of this function, referred
to as a **quasi-hyperbolic function**. This is described below:

$$D(t) = 1 \quad \text{if } t = 0$$
$$\beta\delta^t \qquad \text{if } t > 0$$

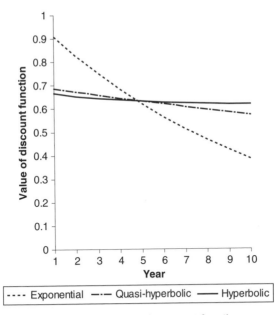

Figure 6.1 Shapes of discount functions

In general $\beta < 1$, implying that the discount factor between the current period and the next is lower than the discount factor in later periods. In the limiting case where $\beta = 1$ the quasi-hyperbolic function reduces to the exponential function of the DUM.

Therefore, in contrast to the DUM, the utilities in the periods $0, 1, 2, \ldots, t$ are discounted by $1, \beta\delta, \beta\delta^2, \ldots, \beta\delta^t$. The advantages of this model are as follows:

1. It fits empirical findings well, mimicking the qualitative property of the hyperbolic discount function. This can be seen in Figure 6.1, where hyperbolic, quasi-hyperbolic, and exponential functions are compared. The reason for its effectiveness lies in its assumption of a higher discount rate between the current period and the next, but a constant discount rate thereafter. The per-period discount rate between now and the next period is $(1 - \beta\delta)/\beta\delta$, whereas the per-period discount rate between any two future periods is $(1 - \delta)/\delta$, a smaller value.

2. It maintains most of the analytical tractability of the exponential model. It is again a discrete function, and after period 1 the per-period discount factor is δ, the same as the exponential function. In Figure 6.1 it is assumed that $\beta = 0.7$ and $\delta = 0.98$, since this produces a function that crosses the exponential function halfway through the 10-year period for ease of comparison.

Phelps and Pollak (1968) originally introduced this functional form in order to study intergenerational altruism, and the function was first applied to individual decision-making by Elster (1979).

The pure, generalized hyperbolic function was originally introduced by Harvey (1986) and has been further developed by Prelec (1989) and Loewenstein and Prelec (1992). It has also been discussed in various contributions by Ainslie and Laibson mentioned earlier. This is a continuous function, taking the form $D(t) = (1 + \alpha t)^{-\beta/\alpha}$. The α-coefficient determines how much the function departs from constant discounting. The limiting case, as α goes to zero, is the exponential discount function $D(t) = e^{-\beta t}$, in its continuous form. In Figure 6.1 it is assumed that $\alpha = 100\,000$ and $\beta = 3500$, again to give a function that intersects the others halfway through the 10-year period.

Implications of hyperbolic discounting

The primary implication of hyperbolic discounting is that time preferences will be inconsistent. We have already seen that there is a large body of empirical evidence that supports the theory of dynamic inconsistency in preferences. The manner in which such inconsistency affects behavior depends on the degree of self-awareness of subjects, in terms of how aware they are that their preferences will change over time. There are two extreme situations. One extreme is where people may be completely "**naïve**," believing that their future preferences will be identical to their current ones. This would imply that people do not learn at all from past experience of changing preferences. Such people think that they will use a constant discount rate in the future, but will actually discount hyperbolically. If we refer to the person's belief regarding the value of their β as b then $\beta < b = 1$.

The opposite extreme is where people are completely "**sophisticated**," and can predict accurately how their preferences will change over time. In this case $\beta = b < 1$. In reality it appears that most people lie somewhere in the middle of the spectrum, meaning that $\beta < b < 1$, although there is limited empirical evidence regarding this aspect.

A good illustration of the differences between the behaviors of exponential, naïve and sophisticated hyperbolic discounters is given by Ho, Lim, and Camerer (2006). They give a hypothetical numerical example relating to the situation of buying and consuming potato chips. They use a three-period model as follows:

1. *Purchase decision*: this involves a choice between a small (one serving) bag or a large (two servings) bag which involves a quantity discount.

2. *Consumption decision*: this involves a choice between consuming one serving or two, and an instantaneous utility related to consumption. If the smaller bag is purchased in the first period, only one serving can be consumed, but purchase of the larger bag offers the choice between consuming a single serving and leaving the other to a later period, or consuming both servings in the same period.

3. *Health outcome*: this is adverse because chips are bad for you, but is much worse if two servings are consumed rather than one.

Under these conditions, and using reasonable parameters for discounting and outcomes, the authors conclude that each group of discounters may behave differently:

1. *Exponential discounters*: these may buy a large bag to benefit from the quantity discount, but only consume a single serving in the second period to avoid the worst health outcome.

2. *Naïve hyperbolic discounters*: these may buy a large bag, believing that they will behave like the exponential discounters and only consume one serving in the next period. However, in the second period they discount hyperbolically, applying a high discount factor to the adverse health effects in the third period, and they end up consuming both servings.

3. *Sophisticated hyperbolic discounters*: these may choose the small bag as a self-control or commitment device, knowing that in the next period they would be unable to resist the temptation of consuming both servings if they bought the large bag.

If the utilities of actual behavior are measured from the viewpoint of the first period then the exponential discounters end up with the most utility in this example, because they benefit from the discount. The naïve hyperbolic discounters end up worst off, because of the adverse health effects which they discount heavily when they get to the second period. However, we should not conclude that sophisticated hyperbolic discounters will always end up better off than naïve ones. If they anticipate that they will eventually succumb to temptation, they are more likely to succumb earlier (in an "unravelling" effect) than naïve discounters. This phenomenon is discussed again in Chapter 9, in view of its implications regarding rationality.

In order to understand the significance of the self-awareness factor, it is useful to consider the effect of dynamic inconsistency on the psychology of the subject. Taking the example of the dessert trolley described earlier, the subject finds that their earlier preference starts to leave them, being replaced by an opposite one, often exacerbated by visceral influences. In folk psychology the terms "temptation" and "willpower" are often used in this context. We shall see that such concepts have no psychological basis unless there is dynamic inconsistency in preferences. With the DUM and constant discounting, one will at all times either want the dessert or not want it; there is no scope for the exertion of willpower. If the discounted benefits of eating the dessert exceed the discounted costs then one will indulge, and if they do not then one will not indulge.

We are now in a position to begin to understand the nature of "willpower" and of "virtues" and "vices," key concepts in philosophy, but frequently misunderstood because of the lack of an adequate framework of analysis. A full analysis cannot be given at this stage, since this involves the use of a "multiple-self" model discussed in a later section and the application of intrapersonal game theory discussed in the next chapter. However, we can still achieve a grasp of the situation in general terms. "Virtues" involve the willingness to suffer short-term costs (or sacrifice short-term benefits) in order to achieve greater long-term benefits. "Vices" involve the inability to delay gratification, often termed a "self-control problem," yielding to the temptation of short-term benefits, but suffering long-term costs that more than outweigh these benefits. With the constant discounting model, as stated earlier, there is no conflict between short term and long term: one path of action will at all times seem preferable. The important implication here, discussed extensively by Ainslie (2001) in his book *Breakdown of Will*, is that in the DUM the concepts of temptation and willpower are redundant.

However, with hyperbolic discounting a person will reach a point in time when the instantaneous utility of a "vice," such as indulging in an unhealthy dessert, will make it attractive, meaning that discounted benefits exceed discounted costs at that period of time. The conflict arises because the subject will normally remember that their preference in the past was different, and, if the subject is sufficiently self-aware, they will also realize that in the future they will come to regret their action if they indulge, because from that future standpoint, discounted costs exceeded discounted benefits.

The main implication of self-awareness is that people will make commitments to prevent them from taking later actions that fall into the category of "vices." We have already seen one hypothetical example, relating to buying a small bag of chips rather than a large one. Plentiful evidence of such commitments provides a "smoking gun" as far as hyperbolic discounting, time-inconsistent preferences, and self-awareness are concerned. Ancient references to such commitment devices include the story of Ulysses ordering his shipmates to tie him to the mast so that he could listen to the song of the sirens without being lured onto the rocks and shipwrecked. Burnham and Phelan (2001) provide some off-the-wall modern examples: smearing one's brownie with mayonnaise when given lunch on a plane, and posting one's Internet cable to oneself. Both actions are designed to prevent later indulgence when preferences have changed, but obviously they are only possible if a certain degree of self-awareness is present. Other common forms of commitment involve the use of whole life insurance policies and illiquid savings accounts, paying health club memberships for a year where there is no refund or cancellation option, and leaving one's credit card at home when going shopping.

A good example of commitment from sophisticated subjects concerns an experiment conducted by Ariely and Wertenbroch (2002). This involved executive education students at MIT, who had to write three papers in a semester for a particular class. One group was given evenly spaced deadlines throughout the semester for the three papers, while the other group was allowed to select their own deadlines. The penalty for an overdue paper was the same in each case. Although it was possible for the second group to have made all their papers due at the end of the semester, in the experiment many did in fact commit to spacing out their deadlines. It was also notable that those who did have evenly spaced deadlines, whether externally or internally imposed, performed better than those who did not. Thus it appears that the more sophisticated subjects, who foresaw self-control problems, made the commitment involving evenly spaced deadlines, and as a result improved their welfare.

As already stated, people generally lie somewhere in the middle of the spectrum of self-awareness, and O'Donoghue and Rabin (2001) introduced a model of partial self-awareness that accounts for various aspects of observed behavior, although it was specifically designed to account for the phenomenon of procrastination. In this model, people are aware that they will have self-control problems in the future, but they underestimate the magnitude of the problems. The authors observe that, when people choose from a menu of options involving costs and benefits at different times in the future, they may now eschew an option involving immediate action and relatively small benefits in favor of an option involving action and greater benefits in the long term. However, later on, they may forsake the latter option in favor of another option that involves action and even greater benefits still further in the future. Thus preferences may constantly shift, with actions continuously being delayed. For example, we may decide not to tidy the garage this week because we plan to redecorate it next month. Next month we may decide that redecoration of the garage is not as important as fencing the garden. While this model cannot explain all types of procrastination, for example where a given task is continuously delayed, it does have important policy implications that are discussed in a later section.

Another interesting example of commitment has been researched by Frank and Hutchens (1993), and involves the preference for rising wage profiles. This preference has been discussed earlier, and is also the subject of Case 6.3. It is argued that the main pressure for rising wage and consumption profiles is a social one and that if the workers involved can commit to restricting their wages in the short term in return for the promise of higher wages later in their careers, they can improve their welfare. Although the authors admit that their evidence is insubstantial quantitatively, it is highly suggestive. To our knowledge there has been no extensive study of the phenomenon discussed by Frank and Hutchens, and it is probable that the primary reason for this is the lack of available data for a wide range of professions.

All of the examples of commitment described to this point involve deliberate actions. There have also been a number of studies, particularly in the psychology literature, where commitment does not involve such action, but instead involves the automatic involvement of the emotions. Although economists such as Becker and Akerlof had broached this subject earlier, Hirshleifer (1987) and Frank (1988) were the first economists to develop a formal theory of the emotions as commitment, based on game theory. Since that time there has been considerable input from various fields, including political scientists, psychologists, and neuroscientists. Until the work of Hirshleifer and Frank there had been much puzzlement regarding the usefulness of emotions such as anger, envy, and hatred, all of which are commonly viewed as "negative" emotions, in contrast to the "positive" emotions such as love, joy, and pride. Negative emotions often caused people to take actions that were self-destructive, and therefore they seemed to serve no Darwinian purpose, meaning that it was difficult to see why they had evolved. The main contribution of Hirshleifer and Frank was to propose a theory that such emotions served as a credible commitment, deterring others from taking advantage of us. Thus, although such emotions might cause short-term harm (and long-term harm in individuals where they are excessive), in most individuals they serve to promote our long-term welfare.

A number of misunderstandings tend to occur regarding the Hirshleifer–Frank model. First of all, there is a difference between the capacity to feel an emotion and the actual feeling of the emotion. As Elster (1998) has observed, an irascible person may rarely feel anger, because others may take care not to provoke the person's anger. To correct another misunderstanding, the theory does not mean that the capacity for anger is always "good" for us, anymore than the capacity for pain is always good for us; it simply means that on average it has served people well in the past, or in biological terms it has improved our inclusive fitness. The theory also does not mean that we should always display anger when it is provoked; sometimes it is better to keep calm, particularly in view of social conventions.

Finally, it should be noted that emotions would not be necessary as commitment devices if the DUM and constant discounting were applicable. According to the DUM, if someone offends us, a "rational" calculation of self-interest will tell us how to react, in terms of whether to punish the offender, how and when; there is no conflict between short-term and long-term interests.

Criticisms of the hyperbolic discounting approach

It is fair to say that hyperbolic discounting has entered into the mainstream of behavioral economics, largely due to its well-documented empirical superiority over the exponential model and its analytical convenience. However, it has not been without its critics. It should be noted that these critics are largely not defenders of the traditional DUM, but are proponents of newer and more radical models.

Let us examine criticisms from defenders of the DUM first. These fall mainly into three categories, all of which have been mentioned earlier:

1. *Failure to use front-end delay.* This results in a confound with transaction costs explained in the previous chapter.
2. *Use of hypothetical rewards.* This may lead to unreliable results due to a lack of incentives compared with the use of monetary rewards.
3. *Failure to provide information relating to the annual interest rates implied in the different options.* Most studies simply give the options in terms of choice or matching tasks without such information. Coller and Williams (1999) found that discount rates were significantly lower when annual interest rate information is provided.

As far as this last criticism is concerned, it has been sometimes suggested that there are legal requirements in many countries that require the provision of such information, and that this makes the provision of interest rate information a realistic condition. This may be true in different types of lending/borrowing situation, but the majority of intertemporal choice decisions are not of this type. When we are debating whether to eat a dessert, or join a health club, or tidy the garage, these are not situations where interest rate information is realistically going to enter the decision process.

Furthermore, as was discussed at the end of the previous chapter, studies that have incorporated the desired control elements, such as that by Harrison, Lau, and Williams (2002), have not eliminated the nonconstant discount rate phenomenon. While rates did not vary much between 1 and 3 years, rates were higher for the 6-month time frame. Many hyperbolic discounting studies show higher rates for periods less than a year.

We will now move on to consider criticisms from proponents of newer discounting models. One more recent theory that has been proposed as being superior to hyperbolic discounting is **subadditive discounting**. The concept of subadditivity has been discussed in Chapter 3, and when applied to discounting it implies that people are less patient (i.e. have higher discount rates) per unit of time over shorter intervals regardless of when they occur. Thus the theory suggests that people would have a higher discount rate for a daily period than for a monthly period, even if the daily period were at a relatively distant point in the future. Read and Roelofsma (2003) conclude that subadditive discounting is superior to hyperbolic discounting in terms of explaining empirical results for both choice and matching tasks.

However, the main problem with hyperbolic discounting, which applies also to subadditive discounting, is that it lacks a psychological foundation. It is basically a descriptive theory rather than an explanatory one. Even though the phenomenon has been widely observed among animals as well as humans and has been studied by researchers in many disciplines, its strongest proponents have struggled to provide a good psychological foundation for it. Although most have entirely ignored this aspect, some have been conscious of this failure. For example, Ainslie (2001), a psychiatrist, has considered the possible evolutionary origins of such a psychological mechanism, in terms of how it might have increased inclusive fitness compared with the more intuitively appealing exponential discounting approach. Ultimately, he admits that he has no idea how a hyperbolic discounting mechanism could have evolved. Fehr (2002) sounds a more positive note, suggesting that in evolutionary history risks faced by both humans and animals have varied over time, thus leading to the application of different discount rates to future events and inconsistent behavior. Dasgupta and Maskin (2005) also take an evolutionary approach, proposing that uncertainty regarding the timing of payoffs accounts for hyperbolic discounting. This psychological foundation is examined again in the section on more radical models.

6.3 Modifying the instantaneous utility function

In the previous chapter we described various anomalies observed in the DUM, and in the first section of this chapter many of these are viewed as confounds as far as measuring time preference and discount rates are concerned. It can be argued that it is more appropriate to treat these confounding factors as additional aspects of the instantaneous utility function. Models that attempt to achieve this are now discussed.

Habit-formation models

There is a long tradition of habit-formation models in economics, going back to Duesenberry (1949). His hypothesis that the level of consumption depended on a past peak of consumption was based on the idea that current utility depends not only on current consumption, but on past consumption:

$$U_t = f(C_t, C_{t-1}, C_{t-2}, \dots) \tag{6.1}$$

In most models all the values of past consumption are combined together into a composite variable, Z_t, that may be exponentially weighted to give more importance to more recent periods, and that is increasing with past consumption. The utility function then becomes

$$U_t = f(C_t, Z_t) \tag{6.2}$$

Thus the more a person has consumed in the past the more utility current consumption will yield, causing the person to consume more now. It should be noted that this ignores the possibility of shifting reference points, discussed shortly, which would have the opposite effect. This model can be applied in macroeconomic terms to all consumers and all goods, or on a microeconomic basis to particular goods. For example, Becker and Murphy (1988) have used a habit-formation model to examine the effects of past and future prices on the current consumption of addictive goods. These models have also often been used to explain the EPP discussed in Case 4.1. We will examine their relevance again in Case 6.2, which concerns the relationships between savings, consumption, and growth.

Prospect Theory models

Perhaps the single most salient characteristic of PT is its use of reference points, as explained in Chapter 3. When a person's reference point for current consumption is past consumption, a reference-point model is identical with a habit-formation model. However, this is only a special case of the more general reference-point model. Reference points can also be dependent on expectations of the future, or on social comparisons, as we have seen. The importance of social comparisons is considered in Case 6.3, in connection with the preference for rising consumption profiles.

Other important features of PT that affect the instantaneous utility function are loss-aversion and diminishing marginal sensitivity. Loewenstein and Prelec (1992) have used a utility function incorporating such features in order to explain the anomalies of the "magnitude effect," the "sign effect," and the "delay-speedup" asymmetry discussed in the previous chapter. The factor that is particularly important in their analysis is the concept of the **elasticity of the utility function**. The elasticity concept "captures the insight that people are responsive to both differences and ratios of reward amounts" (Frederick, Loewenstein, and O'Donoghue 2002). Thus a person may be indifferent between receiving $10 now and $20 in a year, but prefer $200 in a year to $100 now. It may appear that a lower discount rate is being used for the larger amounts; however, in reality the person may have a constant time preference in the two options but may be more responsive to the difference between $100 and $200 than to the difference between $10 and $20.

Similarly, the Loewenstein–Prelec model can explain both the "sign effect" and the "delay-speedup" asymmetry in terms of loss-aversion, with people discounting gains more than losses. In the case of the "delay-speedup" situation it needs to be recognized that any shift in consumption either forward or backward in time is made less desirable by loss-aversion, since although one gains consumption in one period, one also loses consumption in another period (when it was originally expected). Thus the gains from accelerating consumption are not as great as the losses from delaying it. Reference-point models incorporating loss-aversion have also been applied to draw conclusions regarding the PIH (Friedman 1957). According to the conventional log-linear version of the PIH model, changes in future income, while affecting the level of consumption, will not affect the rate of consumption growth; consumption in all future periods will be increased or decreased by the same proportion in every period. However, as shown by Bowman, Minehart, and Rabin (1999), a decrease in future incomes may not reduce current consumption very much because of loss-aversion, thus causing future consumption to fall by a greater amount as people are forced to adjust. Consumption growth may therefore respond more to future income decreases than to future income increases, and two studies by Shea (1995a,b) lend some support to this hypothesis.

Anticipatory utility models

We have seen in Chapter 2 that people derive utility from anticipation of future consumption as well as from current and past consumption. This effect can be expressed in a manner parallel to the habit-formation model and Equation (6.1):

$$U_t = f(C_t, C_{t+1}, C_{t+2}, \dots) \tag{6.3}$$

This phenomenon works in the opposite direction to the normal direction of time preference, for both gains and losses. Thus we may prefer to delay consumption of certain products where anticipatory rewards are important, and accelerate bad outcomes rather than have them hanging over us (Loewenstein 1987). There are certain exceptions to this: waiting for a good outcome can be frustrating, while one may prefer to delay the possibility of a bad outcome to avoid spoiling the weekend (for example when students take a test). It should be noted that if there is uncertainty regarding the outcomes, this adds another dimension to the situation, as the emotions of hope and anxiety enter the picture. Such visceral influences are discussed shortly. If a normal discounting approach is taken, without modifying the utility function, the result is that different discount rates will be calculated with different goods, as is often observed in empirical studies. In this case the reality is that the utilities have not been modified to allow for anticipation and that if this is done the discount rates may actually be constant.

Visceral influence models

The nature of visceral influences has been discussed earlier in the chapter. In particular, we have seen that the temporal proximity of an outcome may increase its desirability. This may cause a higher rate of discount to be computed for near-future outcomes when factors like anger, hunger, lust, and sleeplessness are involved, thus seeming to support the hyperbolic discounting approach. However, it may be more appropriate to modify the instantaneous utility function to allow for a momentary increase in utility in certain circumstances (Loewenstein 1996; 2000). It should be noted that temporal proximity of the outcome is only one of these circumstances. Other cues may also be important, for example spatial proximity, or the presence of associated sights, sounds or smells.

The influence of visceral factors is more complicated than just the effect on the instantaneous utility function. It has been found, for example, that when people are under their influence they tend to overestimate how long their effect will last, while when people are not under their influence they tend to underestimate the magnitude of their effect in the future. This phenomenon is discussed further in Chapter 9. People may also not want to want certain things, even expressing their preference for not doing something while they are actually doing it, like taking drugs. Obviously, self-control factors are relevant here, and the concepts of temptation and willpower again. These will be further discussed in the next section, in the context of multiple-self models.

6.4 More radical models

In Chapter 3, we saw that it was possible to distinguish between conventional modifications to EUT and nonconventional alternatives. However, even these nonconventional alternatives, like PT, are really best viewed as extensions of the SEM rather than outright rejections of it. Similar considerations apply to the DUM, but it is more difficult here to draw the line between the conventional and the nonconventional. So far the alternative models to the DUM that we have examined have involved modifying either the discount function or the instantaneous utility function. Even here, though, some of the modifications involve nonconventional factors related to PT. The models examined in this section involve more radical differences from the DUM, although in some cases they are still often considered conventional models, like the dual-self model of Fudenberg and Levine (2006). The reason for this lack of clarity, or blurring of distinctions, is that intertemporal models are more complex than static models of preference, consisting of more components. This has led to a hybridization of models, in that some components of a model may be "conventional" while other components may be "non-conventional." This issue is best explained in more detail as we examine the individual models.

Projection bias

This is an example of a phenomenon that has been discussed earlier. People's tastes change over time, and there is a general tendency to underestimate the magnitude of these changes. The presence of visceral influences, discussed above, is only one of the factors that can cause this; habit formation and the shifting of reference points are two other important factors that can cause the same phenomenon. This bias is contrary to the assumption of rational expectations in the SEM, which implies that people can forecast changes in their tastes accurately. It has been modeled by Loewenstein, O'Donoghue, and Rabin (2003), who review extensive evidence for the phenomenon. In the case of habit-formation the utility function in Equation (6.2) may be appropriate as the instantaneous utility function at time t is $U_t = f(C_t, Z_t)$. This can be expressed more simply as $U_t(C_t, Z_t)$, where Z_t again represents a composite variable reflecting past consumption. At time $t + 1$ an individual's true instantaneous utility function may be $U_{t+1}(C_{t+1}, Z_{t+1})$, and their expectation of this function at time t may be $\tilde{U}_{t+1}(\hat{C}_{t+1}, Z_{t+1}, Z_t)$. This represents expected utility in time $t + 1$ of expected consumption in time $t + 1$ and past consumption up to that period, given the current level of past consumption at time t. According to the projection bias model,

$$U_t(C_t, Z_t) < \tilde{U}_{t+1}(\hat{C}_{t+1}, Z_{t+1}, Z_t) < U_{t+1}(C_{t+1}, Z_{t+1})$$

This can be modeled more precisely using a weighted function to indicate how accurately people forecast future utilities:

$$\tilde{U}_{t+1}(\hat{C}_{t+1}, Z_{t+1}, Z_t) = \alpha[U_t(C_t, Z_t)] + (1-\alpha)[U_{t+1}(C_{t+1}, Z_{t+1})] \qquad (6.4)$$

where $0 \leq \alpha \leq 1$.

The higher the value of α, the greater the degree of projection bias, meaning that there is a greater tendency to underestimate future utilities.

This phenomenon, which resembles myopia, has important policy implications for individuals, firms, and governments. For example, people may consume more of a good now, underestimating the effect that this will have on future utility, and therefore underestimating future consumption, or the desire for future consumption, of the good. In this situation, people may discount future consumption too highly as far as the maximization of welfare in terms of experienced utility is concerned. The policy implications are discussed in the next section.

Mental accounting models

The features of mental accounting were discussed extensively in Chapter 4, and it was seen that these involved the aspects of framing and editing, fungibility, and choice bracketing. We now need to examine the effects of these behavioral aspects on intertemporal choice and discounting.

One of the main implications of lack of budget fungibility is that different discount rates are applied to different goods. We have seen that small purchases may be classified as "petty cash," with the result that people may be more inclined to spend on these, using a higher discount rate. Goods involving a larger expenditure, such as durables, may be evaluated more carefully using a lower discount rate.

There are also a number of implications of choice bracketing which contradict the predictions of the DUM. We have seen that people often prefer to prepay for various expenses to avoid the "pain of paying" later for something they have already consumed (Prelec and Loewenstein 1998), whereas the DUM predicts a preference for paying later. Furthermore, they may prefer to receive payment for work after, rather than before, performing it, again in contradiction to the DUM. We have also discussed the preference for payment decoupling, which may lead to fixed-fee pricing with zero marginal costs, as for example with many health club membership schemes. This is another contradiction of the DUM, which predicts a dislike for up-front fees. This situation is examined in more detail in Case 6.1.

Another anomaly of the DUM observed earlier, which relates to choice bracketing, is the preference for spread of consumption. Loewenstein and Prelec (1993) found that people tend to prefer to spread the "treats" of dining at a fancy French restaurant, although in this case there was also a preference for an improving sequence of outcomes, as predicted by PT. The preference for spread is a separate phenomenon, and appears to be related to anticipatory utility.

Multiple-self models

The term "multiple-self" has an element of ambiguity that needs to be clarified from the outset. First, the concept can be applied to the situation where the "self" is a dynamic and ever-changing entity over time. This is most clear when we compare our current self, in terms of attitudes, values, and beliefs, with our self in some period well in the past; sometimes we have difficulty understanding our past selves and may indeed be embarrassed by them. However, the term "multiple-self" can also be applied to situations at a particular point in time, when there appear to be conflicts between our short-term "self" and our long-term "self." Models of this situation are often referred to as dual self models, for example that of Fudenberg and Levine (2006) discussed later.

All these models are inspired by the observation that self-control problems are commonplace, and often involve forms of commitment described in the discussion of hyperbolic discounting. Indeed the term "self-control" can be considered meaningless *unless* there is more than one "self." It begs the following questions:

1. Who is doing the controlling, if not the self?
2. Why is there a need for self-control, if there is just a single self seeking to maximize some kind of preference function?

Furthermore, there is significant neuroscientific evidence that we have two separate systems that are involved in intertemporal decision-making. Using the fMRI technique, McClure et al. (2004) found that decisions relating to immediately available rewards involve the preferential activation of parts of the limbic system associated with the midbrain dopamine system, including the paralimbic cortex. In contrast, with intertemporal choices generally, regions of the lateral prefrontal cortex and posterior parietal cortex are engaged uniformly. The study also found that

> The relative engagement of the two systems is directly associated with the subjects' choices, with greater relative fronto-parietal activity when subjects choose longer term options.
>
> (p. 503)

The authors hypothesize that

> short-run impatience is therefore driven by the limbic system, which responds preferentially to immediate rewards and is less sensitive to the value of future rewards, whereas long-run patience is mediated by the lateral pre-frontal cortex and associated structures, which are able to evaluate trade-offs between abstract rewards, including rewards in the more distant future.
>
> (p. 504)

This evidence is also supported by comparisons with advanced primates, who have substantially smaller prefrontal cortexes than humans, and with subjects with prefrontal brain damage. In both cases individuals are heavily influenced by the availability of immediate rewards and are unable to delay gratification or plan ahead.

There are a variety of multiple-self models. Some models involve a near-sighted or myopic self and a far-sighted self who are in conflict and alternately take control of behavior (Winston 1980; Schelling 1984; Ainslie and Haslam 1992). These models are criticised by Frederick, Loewenstein, and O'Donoghue (2002) on the grounds that they fail to explain why either type of self gains control, and they do not capture the fundamental asymmetry between the far-sighted and near-sighted selves. Far-sighted selves can make commitments to control the behavior of near-sighted selves, but not vice versa.

As noted by Frederick, Loewenstein, and O'Donoghue (2002), "few of these multiple-self models have been expressed formally, and even fewer have been used to derive testable implications that go much beyond the intuitions that inspired them in the first place." However, as they also point out, this is not so much a failure of the models themselves as an indication of the complexity of the underlying phenomena. Certainly the models do help to explain the existence of various self-control strategies, and can also, with the aid of game theory, provide a much-needed psychological foundation for hyperbolic discounting.

Dual-self models

A variation of the above model has been proposed by Thaler and Shefrin (1981), along the lines of principal-agent theory. The far-sighted self is the principal or "planner," while there is a sequence of near-sighted selves who constitute the agent or "doer." Thus the model captures the asymmetry aspect. The far-sighted planner is concerned with future utilities, whereas the near-sighted doer is only concerned with the instantaneous utility function at a particular point in time. The planner is at least partially aware of the conflicts that will occur in the future, for example when the dessert trolley comes around, and can adopt commitment strategies to control the behavior of doer, by perhaps only going to restaurants that do not serve tempting desserts. This type of principal-agent model involves aspects of game theory discussed in the next chapter.

A further type of dual-self model is also based on game theory, in this case relating to social interaction and the choice between cooperation and defection (Elster 1985). This is fundamentally a prisoner's dilemma (PD) situation on a repeated basis. Self-control requires the continued cooperation of a series of instantaneous selves. As we will again see in the next chapter, there is a tendency for an unraveling sequence of defection whereby sequential selves repeatedly give in to temptation. There is also a self-signaling effect here, which has been discussed earlier, whereby giving in to temptation signals the next self that they lack the self-control to commit themselves to avoiding temptation in the future, thus destroying confidence and "willpower."

The most well developed model of this type is arguably the dual-self model of Fudenberg and Levine (2006). This actually rejects hyperbolic discounting and for this reason may be termed a "conventional model." However, it also incorporates elements of PT and mental accounting which are unconventional. The Fudenberg–Levine (FL) model is based on the neuroscientific evidence of McClure *et al.* (2004) described above, in that it posits a patient long-run self and a sequence of myopic short-run selves. These selves are involved in playing a game in a sequence of stages. The long-run and short-run selves share the same preferences over the outcomes in each stage, but they regard the future differently. The short-run self is impatient and has "baseline preferences" only for the current stage, while the long-run self also has preferences for future stages. Each stage consists of two phases. In the first phase the long-run self can choose a self-control action that influences the utility of the short-run self.

This means that, at some cost in utility for both selves, the long-run self can choose preferences other than the baseline preferences. In the second phase, once its preferences have been determined, the short-run self takes the final decision. This whole process is illustrated in Case 6.1 related to joining a gym and exercising.

Fudenberg and Levine emphasize the advantages of their model over hyperbolic discounting, in that it produces a single equilibrium for behavior, rather than the multiple equilibria that are associated with hyperbolic discounting and the multiple-self model. While being analytically simpler and making more precise predictions, they claim that it can explain empirical facts just as well.

There are a number of predictions or implications of this model. For example, the authors find that self-control costs lead to longer delays. They also develop a banking-savings model where it is predicted that people will use self-control in limiting the amount of pocket cash that they have available to spend later in a nightclub scenario. It is notable that this aspect of the model incorporates mental accounting concepts, in that bank cash is regarded differently from pocket cash in terms of the MPC. The concept of a reference point is also used in that the amount of pocket cash is used as the reference point for spending, not one's total wealth. It is important that the constraint on spending here is not liquidity, since in principle one could write a check or use a credit card in the nightclub. However, these are "non-anonymous" accounts, meaning that spending from them will result in an identifiable transaction later, which may cause self-recrimination or recrimination from one's partner. Cash on the other hand is an anonymous account, as we discussed in the chapter on mental accounting. Fudenberg and Levine also explain Rabin's "risk paradox" in a similar way: people are averse to taking small risks which involve pocket cash, but do not have similar risk-aversion for large gambles that involve bank cash.

One final implication of the model is important. It proposes that the costs of self-control are nonlinear, meaning that an increase in self-control involves an increasing marginal cost. The underlying principle here is that self-control is an exhaustible resource and that therefore the law of diminishing returns applies, as discussed in more detail in Chapter 9. The consequence is that increasing cognitive load reduces self-control. The FL paper reports an experiment by Shiv and Fedorikhin (1999), where subjects were asked to memorize either a two- or a seven-digit number, and then walk to a table with a choice of two desserts, chocolate cake, and fruit salad. In one treatment the actual desserts were on the table, whereas in a second treatment the desserts were represented by photographs. It was hypothesized that

1. Subjects would face a self-control problem regarding the cake, in the sense that it would have a higher emotional or visceral appeal, but be less desirable from a "cognitive" viewpoint.

2. Subjects' reactions were more likely to be determined by emotional reactions when cognitive resources were constrained by the need to remember the longer number.

3. The "cognitive overload effect" would be greater when subjects were faced with actual desserts rather than with their pictures.

All three hypotheses were supported by the experimental results. When faced with real desserts, subjects who were asked to remember the longer number chose the cake 63 % of the time, while subjects given the two-digit number only chose the cake 41 % of the time, a statistically significant difference. However, when faced with pictures of the desserts, the choices were 45 % and 42 % respectively, an insignificant difference. These results can also be explained by the dual-self model, in that the long-run self, faced with increasing cognitive costs, is less well able to exert self-control. The FL paper also notes that the increasing marginal cost of self-control implied by the Shiv and Fedorikhin study contravenes one of the axioms proposed by Gul and Pesendorfer (2001) in relation to self-control, specifically the axiom relating to set-betweenness. This axiom was discussed in the context of EUT in Chapter 3, where we saw that evidence did not support it in that context either.

The procedural approach

In the discussion of hyperbolic discounting it was noted that its most important failing was the lack of a psychological foundation. Rubinstein (2003) both disputes the empirical evidence for hyperbolic discounting, and provides an alternative framework for decision-making which he claims does have a legitimate psychological foundation. Like various other models we have seen, Rubinstein's approach is based on a heuristic process. This proposes that the decision-maker uses a procedure that applies similarity relations, involving a money dimension and a time dimension, in a series of three steps.

The objects of choice in intertemporal situations can be described as being in the form (x, t), where $\$x$ is received with a delay of t units of time. Thus a decision-maker may have to compare two choices: $A = (x, t)$ and $B = (y, s)$. According to Rubinstein (2003), many decision-makers go through the following three steps:

1. *Search for dominance*

   If $x > y$ and $t < s$ then A dominates B, since it is preferable in both dimensions (a larger reward is received sooner).

2. *Search for similarities in the two dimensions*

   If the decision-maker finds similarity in one dimension only, he or she determines his or her preference using the other dimension only. For example, if x is similar to y, but $t > s$, then B is preferred to A, since the rewards seem similar, but B involves less delay.

3. *Use of a different criterion*

   If the first two stages do not give a result, some different criterion must be used (Rubinstein is not specific regarding the nature of this).

Rubinstein conducts three experiments to test how the procedural approach explains behavior compared with hyperbolic discounting. It is worth describing the first experiment here, since it will aid an understanding of the different models and how they compare. This experiment was performed in 2002 with a total of 456 students on a between-subjects basis involving choice tasks and money. Different students were asked to answer either Question 1 or 2 below:

Q1   Choose between the following two options:

   a) Receiving $467.00 on June 17, 2004
   b) Receiving $607.07 on June 17, 2005

Q2   Choose between the following two options:

   a) Receiving $467.00 on June 16, 2005
   b) Receiving $467.39 on June 17, 2005

Fifty-five percent of the subjects chose delay in Question 1, while only 46 % chose delay in Question 2. According to the procedural approach the 39 cents difference in Question 2 is too small to be meaningful, causing subjects to tend to prefer the shorter delay, even by only one day. In Question 1, however, neither amount nor time period are similar, so subjects have to resort to the third step of the approach. Rubinstein comments that the results contradict any hyperbolic discounting approach. The 1-day discount rate implied by the preference for earlier delivery in Question 2 is lower than the 1-year discount rate implied by the preference for delay in Question 1.

   While this example does not provide conclusive evidence in favor of the procedural approach, when combined with the results of the other two experiments, it does pose significant questions regarding the hyperbolic discounting model. It can also be observed that Rubinstein's results contradict the subadditive model of discounting, which predicts a greater 1-day discount rate.

Conclusion

While the hyperbolic discounting model undoubtedly fits empirical data better than the DUM and is analytically tractable, it may not fit some evidence as well as the procedural approach. However, we have seen that the main problem with the hyperbolic discounting model is that it lacks a psychological foundation, a factor that is at least partially remedied by the procedural approach. Three further observations are in order by way of conclusion:

1. *Responses of subjects are often best considered in terms of elasticities*
   This point has been mentioned before in connection with reward amounts, but it is also relevant with delay times. When rewards are immediate, for example a tasty dessert is 5 minutes away, delays of even 1 day are long in terms of relative time compared with the current reference point, 28 700 % in this case. On the other hand, when we compare a reward in 2 years with a reward in 4 years, the 2-year delay is only 100 % in relative terms. If our psychological decision-making mechanisms are attuned to elasticities rather than absolute measures, this could explain many of the hyperbolic discounting findings.

2. *There is a close resemblance between the heuristic psychological mechanisms involved in the procedural approach and fuzzy-trace theory*
   There is an important similarity between Rubinstein's approach and aspects of fuzzy-trace theory discussed in Chapter 3. According to both theories decision-makers use crude heuristics rather than sophisticated quantitative calculations and comparisons. This is also in keeping with much of the work by Kahneman and Tversky (1973; 1982).

3. *Many of the models described are not mutually exclusive, but are best considered as complementary*
   Although for the sake of exposition and simplicity we have considered each of the models throughout this chapter in isolation, it is actually more appropriate to consider them in possible combinations. An example of this is given in Case 6.1, where elements of hyperbolic discounting, modifying the instantaneous utility function, visceral influences, projection bias and the multiple-self models are all relevant.

6.5 Policy implications

There are a number of normative aspects as far as policy implications are concerned that arise from the models of intertemporal choice discussed here. These relate to individuals, firms, and governments.

Individuals

We have seen that the main implication of the various models presented in this chapter is that dynamic conflicts occur over time causing preference reversals, and in turn causing people to make commitments regarding future behavior. Two particularly widespread problems in this field involve dieting and saving, and these are examined more closely in the first two case studies.

Hyperbolic discounting models may describe such situations well in many cases, but as far as lending insight into their nature and normative aspects, multiple-self models have a significant advantage. This is because they can highlight the essential asymmetry involved between the current or myopic self and the meta-self that is at least partially aware of future changes in preferences. As already stated, the meta-self can make strategic commitments to constrain the later behavior of the myopic self, but the reverse cannot happen. For example, the person who finds it difficult to rise in the morning may place the alarm clock on the other side of the room to ensure that the myopic self does not simply slam it off immediately it rings the next morning, but the myopic self cannot reply in any strategic manner to such a commitment.

For individuals, therefore, the key to maximizing experienced utility over the long run may be the use of appropriate strategic commitment devices that constrain the future desires of the myopic self. It is also important, as we have seen, that the meta-self is aware of the changing preferences that inevitably occur. Of course, it will never be possible for any meta-self to have rational expectations to the extent that all future preferences will be accurately predicted; however, the more able people are to learn from past experience regarding such changes, the more likely it is that they will be successful in anticipating future changes and conflicts, and taking appropriate action.

Commitments can be either external or internal. External commitments, once made, become uncontrollable by the individual, and therefore are most effective because they do not depend on the person's willpower. Putting money into an illiquid life insurance policy is an example. The disadvantage is that they lack flexibility if a person's circumstances change. Internal commitments involve making personal rules, for example saving 10 % of one's salary every month, but these are more vulnerable to temptation.

A further implication of the fact that agents have only incomplete information about future preferences is that abstinence may be a better policy than moderate consumption, as illustrated in Case 3.1. In situations involving the possibility of addiction, such as gambling, smoking, or drinking, an abstinence rule, though a second-best rule, can act as a commitment device against inefficient learning that would lead to future excesses (Carillo 2004).

However, there is a final twist to this situation that we have also touched on earlier, and this relates to self-signaling. When the self-control problem is repeated, as is often the case, a yielding to temptation (or "defection") in the first round can lead to a loss of self-confidence, thus making defection more likely in the next round and so on. Thus a far-seeing self may envisage the likely succession of failures if too harsh a rule is made initially, and decide instead to adopt a less strict policy as far as commitment is concerned.

It is therefore difficult to draw definite conclusions regarding how individuals should make commitments in self-control situations. The main general conclusion is that those agents who know themselves, and can predict their future selves, best are also best able to maximize their own welfare in terms of experienced utility.

Firms

There has not been as much research relating to policy implications for firms as there has been for individual agents or governments. However, DellaVigna and Malmendier (2004) have shown that dynamic inconsistencies and other anomalies regarding timing of rewards and payment have important implications for contract design in the case of both **investment goods** and **leisure goods**. Investment goods are defined as those where there are immediate costs, in terms of money and effort, and delayed benefits, for example health club memberships. Leisure goods involve immediate benefits and delayed costs, such as credit card financing. DellaVigna and Malmendier (2004) construct sophisticated models of consumer and firm behavior, the mathematics of which are omitted here, and investigate various possibilities according to the degree of naiveté of consumers and different market conditions. They find that empirical evidence from various industries confirms the predictions of the models. The authors summarize their findings in terms of three main implications:

1. *Firms should price investment goods below marginal cost.*
   Naïve consumers tend to overestimate usage of such goods, and therefore overestimate the value of the discount on marginal cost. For example, in the health club industry it is common to have a zero marginal cost for users, who

mainly pay annual or monthly fees (DellaVigna and Malmendier 2003). Price discrimination cannot explain such a practice, since more frequent users with less elastic demand would be charged a higher per-usage price, and this type of strategy by firms is not commonly observed. As far as sophisticated consumers are concerned, they can use the high initial cost as a form of commitment. This situation is examined in more detail in Case 6.1.

2. *Firms should price leisure goods above marginal cost.*
   In this case naïve consumers underestimate future usage, for example credit card financing. They are therefore attracted by offers that have favorable initial terms. Sophisticated consumers can take advantage of this by paying off their outstanding balances each month, and therefore borrowing for up to 6 weeks free of charge, since many card companies do not charge annual fees. Mobile phone companies have similar charging schemes, with free minutes per month, but high charges for excess time. Naïve consumers may be attracted by the free minutes, but tend to underestimate their phone usage and may therefore end up paying high monthly bills. Mail order firms use similar attractive offers with free books or CDs, but high charges for additional items. DellaVigna and Malmendier (2004) note a slightly different strategy in the gambling industry. In this case, hotels, notably in Las Vegas, charge attractive low rates for accommodation and dining, since naïve gamblers underestimate their gambling activity and losses. Thus for the hotels the gambling activity subsidizes their core business. Again, sophisticated consumers can take advantage of this strategy by staying and dining in the hotels, but take in shows or play golf rather than gamble.

3. *Firms should charge back-loaded fees and introduce switching costs for all goods.*
   It is common for credit card companies to have introductory or "teaser" offers, like zero interest rate charges on balance transfers for limited periods like 6 months. After the initial period the interest rates usually rise very significantly, typically to about 10 % above prime or base rates. Such a strategy is profitable since naïve consumers underestimate the amount of their borrowing after the teaser period is over (Ausubel 1999). **Switching costs** relate to the costs, both in money and in effort, of either switching to a new provider or canceling the agreement. For example, health clubs typically offer automatic renewal, and allow members to cancel their memberships only in person or by letter, rather than by email or by phone. The result is that users tend to remain members longer than otherwise. DellaVigna

and Malmendier (2004) found that there was an average period of over 2 months between a member's last usage and the cancellation of their membership.

DellaVigna and Malmendier also draw conclusions regarding the welfare effects of these policy implications. They observe that for sophisticated consumers market interactions need not reduce their welfare. In fact they may gain if they are in effect being subsidized by naïve consumers, as is the case with credit card financing. In addition, market mechanisms encourage firms to create commitment devices that allow sophisticated consumers to increase their long-run welfare, for example by investing in life insurance policies. However, for naïve consumers who have nonrational expectations, two adverse welfare effects are noted. First, there is an overall reduction in efficiency in terms of net surplus to consumers and producers. Second, in monopoly there is a redistribution of surplus from consumers to producers, who are able to take advantage of the lack of consumer awareness to increase their profits. In perfect competition the second effect is eliminated, but this situation rarely arises in reality.

These adverse effects on the welfare of naïve consumers also have implications for government policy. This general aspect is now discussed.

Government

The models of intertemporal choice presented in this chapter have significant implications for a number of areas of government policy. The following aspects are now discussed: (1) incomplete self-knowledge, (2) addiction, (3) savings, (4) investment, (5) social security, (6) social projects, and (7) environmental policy.

1. *Incomplete self-knowledge*

DellaVigna and Malmendier (2004) have shown that naïve consumers are not able to maximize their welfare, even if there is perfect competition. There is a role for a paternalistic government to intervene in such situations, if it can obtain more information regarding the future preferences of these consumers than the consumers themselves. While this may be possible in some circumstances, the information requirements for policy intervention are large, and even then intervention may not be a complete remedy. It may well be that, as DellaVigna and Malmendier recommend, the best policy is to educate naïve consumers as far as possible regarding their lack of self-awareness.

2. *Addiction*

Addiction is of course one specific area where incomplete self-knowledge is relevant. However, there are certain tax implications in this case that have been ignored by the main body of public finance literature. Of particular interest here is a study by Gruber and Köszegi (2001), which arrives at two main conclusions. First, there is evidence that smokers are forward-looking in their smoking decisions, in that announced but not yet effective tax increases lead to both increased sales and reduced consumption. Second, given the empirical evidence regarding time-inconsistent preferences, there is a justification for basing taxes not only on the external costs imposed by smokers, but also on the internalities that they impose on themselves. Internal costs for smoking are far greater than external ones, with the study estimating that a pack of cigarettes costs $30.45 in terms of lost life expectancy. The authors estimate that optimal internality taxes are probably at least $1 per pack in the United States.

When it comes to other recreational drugs, the US laws have historically been very strict regarding sales, imposing severe penalties, but not so strict regarding possession. This policy may have a perverse effect on behavior, as noted by Fudenberg and Levine (2006). Severe penalties have the effect of increasing the fixed cost of making a transaction, causing consumers to buy larger quantities in each transaction. Such stockpiling is likely to lead to greater consumption, as we saw in the hypothetical example involving potato chips. Fudenberg and Levine, along with other economists, have therefore recommended legalization of such "temptation" goods, combined with a high excise tax, similar to the policies used in many countries in relation to cigarettes. This type of policy provides a greater incentive to reduce consumption of harmful products.

By contrast, Gul and Pesendorfer (2007) argue that taxing goods involving harmful addiction decreases welfare, while prohibitive policies may increase welfare. They draw a distinction between two types of policy: those that increase the price and opportunity costs of consumption (like taxes) and those that reduce the availability and feasibility of consumption (prohibitive policies). The problem, as they point out, is that most prohibitive policies, like making possession illegal, also in effect increase price and opportunity costs.

3. *Savings*

Naïve individuals tend to overestimate their ability to save for the future and do not take advantage of available commitment devices to help them save more. Laibson (1997) has argued that as new and liquid financial instruments have proliferated since the 1980s, due to the deregulation of banking systems in various countries, this problem has been aggravated. While dereg-ulation may have increased competition and efficiency, one undesirable result has been that many automatic commitment devices in the form of illiquid savings instruments have disappeared. The policy implications are further complicated by changes in mandatory retirement laws in many countries. Diamond and Köszegi (2003) use a multiple-self model to argue that recent changes may cause people to save more in order to retire earlier. Govern-ments, however, often want people to retire later in order to reduce the financial burden on public finances. Trying to encourage people both to save more and to retire later is a major problem facing many governments.

4. *Investment*

We have seen that time-inconsistent preferences can lead to procrastina-tion. Entrepreneurs who are sophisticated in terms of being aware of this tendency may make the commitment of foregoing free information in order to avoid procrastination and invest now. Brocas and Carrillo (2004) argue that this phenomenon may lead to excessive investment in the economy and entry mistakes. They further argue that government intervention, forcing investors to acquire information before making investment decisions, may reduce interest rates and lead to an overall improvement in welfare in the economy as a whole.

5. *Social security*

People receiving social security benefits, in cash or in other forms, tend to receive these benefits on either a weekly or a monthly basis. Cash benefits are usually paid weekly. However, the food stamp program in the United States operates on a monthly basis. Providing benefits in the form of food stamps is in itself an automatic commitment mechanism, since it prevents recipients from using the benefits to buy goods regarded as undesirable by the government. However, given a self-control problem and a lack of other forms of commitment, monthly provision may lead to excessive consumption in the first part of the month. Shapiro (2005) provides evid-ence that caloric intake declines by 10–15 % over the food stamp month, providing further evidence for time-inconsistent preferences and against the permanent income hypothesis. It may therefore be that this program would improve welfare if it operated on a weekly basis, although these improvements would have to be balanced against the increased transaction costs for both recipients and government.

6. *Social projects*

Such projects relate to major infrastructure investments like building roads, schools, hospitals, power stations, and railways. Governments must determine an appropriate official discount rate to apply to costs and benefits in order to make optimal investment decisions. Evans and Sezer (2004) observe that countries have used very different approaches in this area. For example, Germany bases its 3% real rate on financial market data, while France has applied an 8% real rate based on the marginal product of capital. In 2003 the United Kingdom switched from a 6% real rate, based mainly on the cost of capital, to a 3.5% real rate based entirely on social time preference, which Evans and Sezer argue is the appropriate rate to use. For public investment decisions it might initially seem that time-inconsistent preferences and self-control problems may not apply, but governments may also be inclined to place short-run electoral benefits before longer-run budgetary considerations. In this case they might use high official discount rates. Evans and Sezer examined official discount rates and estimated social time-preference rates (STPRs) in six major countries: Australia, France, Germany, Japan, United Kingdom, and United States. The only major country where the official discount rate is less than the estimated STPR is Germany, where the 3% official discount rate is less than the estimated STPR of 4.1%. France appears to have a large discrepancy, applying the rate of 8% while the estimated STPR is only 3.5%. Such a policy could lead to severe public underinvestment, to the cost of future generations.

7. *Environmental policy*

This is another area where bad decisions can harm future generations. Once again procrastination is a major problem. There are on the one hand good reasons for waiting until reliable evidence is available before making major global decisions that could impose large and immediate costs. However, some authors have argued that time-inconsistent preferences have been one of the main problems of enforcing and enlarging the scope of the Kyoto protocol (Winkler 2006). Additional problems are involved here, relating to the "tragedy of the commons" situation, discussed in Chapter 7, and the degree of uncertainty. It is argued by Newell and Pizer (2003) that this uncertainty also relates to appropriate future interest rates used for discounting purposes and that such rates should be much lower than the present rate, being only a half of this rate in a hundred years. These authors estimate that such a procedure would nearly double the net present value of the benefits of environmental protection policies.

6.6 Summary

- There are many confounding factors involved in the measurement of time preference.

- Time preference does not appear to be a unitary psychological construct, since it does not satisfy the three main criteria of constancy, generality, and correlation between different measures.

- It may be more useful to decompose time preference into three main elements: impulsivity, compulsivity, and inhibition.

- Hyperbolic discounting involves applying higher discount rates to time periods nearer in the future, and lower ones to periods further away.

- Hyperbolic discounting has become widely applied in behavioral economics because it describes empirical data much better than the exponential discounting of the DUM. In particular, it explains time-inconsistent preferences, which are an anomaly in the DUM.

- The existence of time-inconsistent preferences is the cause of self-control problems. This is particularly true when visceral factors are present.

- The main strategy used by individuals confronted with self-control problems is to make commitments. This is only possible for self-aware or sophisticated agents. External commitments involve less willpower than internal ones.

- The concepts of temptation and willpower are redundant in the DUM, since a particular path of action will always dominate preferences.

- Emotions are an important form of commitment. These are internal, but to a large extent uncontrollable. The expression of emotion is the controllable element.

- The main criticism of the hyperbolic discounting approach is that it lacks a psychological foundation.

- Alternative behavioral models involve modifying the instantaneous utility function. Such models also can explain time-inconsistent preferences.

- More radical models involve the concepts of projection bias, mental accounting models, multiple-self models, dual-self models, and the procedural approach.

- Models should not be seen as being mutually exclusive; many can be complementary to each other.

- There are a number of policy implications of these behavioral models for individuals, firms, and governments. These relate particularly to self-control problems and commitment.

6.7 Applications

The applications considered here all involve time-inconsistent preferences, self-control problems, and the making of effective commitments. The first two cases involve the common problems of exercising and saving. The last problem, related to the preference for rising consumption profiles, also involves social preferences.

Case 6.1   Price plans for gym memberships

We have already mentioned various policy implications following from studies by Della Vigna and Malmendier (2004). One particular situation these authors examined was the optimal pricing structure for firms facing consumers with hyperbolic preferences for gym memberships. They developed a three-stage model as follows:

Period 1
> The firm offers the consumer a membership plan with a membership fee F and a per-use fee p. The consumer either accepts or rejects the contract.

Period 2
> If the consumer accepts the contract, he or she pays F and then makes the decision whether to exercise (E) or not (N). If the consumer chooses E, he or she incurs a cost c, which relates to the personal effort of exercising, and also pays the firm the usage fee p. If the consumer chooses N, then there is no cost c or usage fee p.

Period 3
> If the consumer chooses E then there is the delayed health benefit b; this is obviously not received if the consumer chooses N.

The firm incurs a setup cost of K whenever a consumer accepts the contract, and a unit cost a if the consumer chooses E. The consumer is also assumed to be a hyperbolic discounter with parameters β, b, and δ, as explained in the section on hyperbolic discounting. For simplicity, the firm is assumed to be time-consistent with a discount factor δ.

For the naïve hyperbolic discounter choosing to exercise, the decision process can be described as follows:

Period 1
> The utility from choosing E is $\beta\delta (\delta b - p - c)$, and the payoff from N is 0. Therefore the consumer chooses E if $c \leq \delta b - p$.

Period 2
> Choosing E only gives a utility of $\beta\delta b - p - c$, so the consumer actually chooses E only if $c \leq \beta\delta b - p$, a smaller amount than in period 1.

Thus we can see that the naïve hyperbolic discounter, by misinterpreting his or her own future discounting process, overestimates the net utility of E when buying the membership. Such consumers choose to exercise less often than they planned to when buying the membership.

Case 6.1 *continued*

The sophisticated consumers on the other hand are under no illusions regarding their propensity to exercise and correctly predict their choice of E.

Assuming profit maximization, DellaVigna and Malmendier predict that for time-consistent consumers (with $\beta=1$) the firm simply sets p^* (the optimal per-use fee) equal to the marginal cost a. However, for hyperbolic discounters with $\beta < 1$, the optimal pricing contract involves setting the per-use fee below marginal cost ($p^* < a$), and the membership fee F^* above the optimal level for time-consistent consumers. There are two reasons for this result:

1. Sophisticated consumers like the lower per-use fee because it serves as a commitment device for increasing the probability of exercising. They know that they will be tempted to skip going to the gym unless the per-use fee is low.
2. The higher membership fee allows the firm to exploit the overconfidence of naïve consumers. They will be willing to pay the higher membership fee because they overestimate their frequency of usage and the resulting benefits.

DellaVigna and Malmendier also present empirical evidence in support of their model. They showed that firms in the health club industry typically charged high membership fees and low, often zero, per-use fees. More specifically, they found that the average membership fee was about $300 per year. Most gyms also have the option of paying no membership fee but paying a higher per-use fee (about $15 per visit) instead. The study found that the average gym member goes to the gym so rarely that their actual per-use cost works out at about $19 per visit. These consumers would be better off not buying the membership and just paying on a per-use basis. Therefore this forecasting mistake allows us to conclude that many gym members behave like they are naïve hyperbolic discounters.

Questions

1. Compare and contrast the purchasing decision in the health club situation with the purchasing situation modeled earlier in the chapter relating to buying potato chips.
2. If naïve consumers learn to become more sophisticated, how is this likely to affect their buying behavior and firms' strategy in the health club industry?
3. Explain the implications if a health club were to abandon a fixed fee structure and just charge a relatively low per-use fee of $10.

Case 6.2 The savings problem

Over the last 20 years, household savings rates in many of the rich OECD countries have fallen sharply. The so-called "Anglo-Saxon countries" – America, Canada, Britain, Australia, and New Zealand – have the lowest rates of household saving. Americans, on average, save less than 1 % of their after-tax income today compared with 7 % at the beginning of the 1990s. In Australia and New Zealand, personal saving rates are negative, as people borrow in order to consume more than they earn. The general pattern can be seen in Figure 6.2.

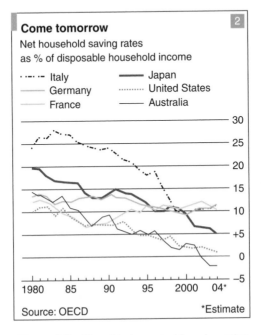

Figure 6.2   Trend in household saving rates

Other countries with rapidly aging populations, especially Japan and Italy, have also seen their personal saving rates plummet, though from a higher level. The Japanese today save 5 % of their household income, compared with 15 % in the early 1990s. Only a few of the rich countries, notably France and Germany, have avoided this pattern of reduced saving. Germans saved around 11 % of their after-tax income in 2004, up slightly from the mid-1980s.

This general trend in the rich countries raises a number of issues:

1. What is the appropriate way to measure a country's savings?
2. Are rich countries saving enough?
3. What kinds of government policy are effective in encouraging saving?

All of these issues involve certain aspects of behavioral economics, although some of the aspects are not directly related to intertemporal choice. We will focus on those aspects that are related to intertermporal choice, observing differences between the SEM and the BEM.

Case 6.2   *continued*

The appropriate way to measure savings

The most fundamental point here is that as far as countries are concerned it is the total amount of savings by households, firms, and governments that is important. Thus saving by firms in the form of retained profit and budget surpluses by governments can in principle make up for any deficit by households. However, there appears to be at least some interrelationship between these different categories. A theory called **Ricardian equivalence** holds that increases in public saving are cancelled out by falls in private saving as individuals anticipate future tax cuts. An OECD study (2004) of 16 rich countries between 1970 and 2002 has found that, on average, about half of any improvement in public finances is offset by lower private saving in the short term, and about two-thirds in the long term. However, in the United States, one of the most extreme cases of low national saving, the offset was smallest. This raises policy issues discussed later.

As far as the household saving rate is concerned, this is calculated by subtracting consumption spending from after-tax income. One measurement problem is that the definitions of both income and spending that statisticians use in the national accounts often bear little resemblance to what people think of as saving and spending. Realized capital gains, for instance, are not included in income, even though the taxes paid on capital gains are deducted from income. There is an aspect of mental accounting that is relevant here. As seen in Chapter 4, people tend to classify income and wealth into different accounts and their marginal propensities to spend and save from these different accounts are also very different. For example, people tend to have a high MPC with current income, but a much lower one for various categories of wealth, like capital gains. We shall see that this lack of fungibility has important implications for government policy.

Adequacy of saving

There are both macro- and microeconomic aspects of this issue, and both have become the subject of highly controversial debate amongst economists and policy-makers in recent years. The macroeconomic aspects relate to the function of saving in the economy as a whole, and in particular its role in funding investment and stimulating growth. We are not so much concerned with this issue here, although many economists would say that, with a current net national savings rate of only 2 %, the US economy would definitely benefit from a boost in saving as far as economic growth is concerned. Even with a large amount of borrowing from overseas, as seen in its current-account deficit approaching 7 % of GDP, investment tends to be low, and the sustainability of this overseas borrowing is questionable.

The main issue from a behavioral point of view concerns the microeconomic aspects of saving: are individuals saving enough? In order to answer this question we must consider the three main motives for individual saving:

1. *Precautionary* – people want to insure against a sudden drop in income.
2. *Consumption smoothing* – people often wish to consume more than their income when they are both young and old, and therefore save most in their middle age.
3. *Bequest motive* – people want to leave assets to their children.

Therefore the issue whether people are setting aside enough from their current income depends on assumptions regarding what those people will want to consume or bequeath in future, what wealth they have already accumulated, and what the returns on those assets will be.

In the 1990s many economists argued that in the United States individual saving was insufficient, notably Bernheim and Scholz (1993). However, more recent studies have argued the opposite case, for example Engen, Gale, and Uccello (1999) and Scholz, Seshadri, and Khitatrakun (2003). The last of these studies concluded that 80 % of US households had accumulated adequate saving.

However, the main weakness of these more optimistic studies lies in the assumptions made. First, they include individuals' equity in their house as part of their financial assets. Again the fungibility issue is relevant here. While there is some evidence in both the United States and the United Kingdom that increases in property values have fuelled increased consumption, people still do not treat such wealth in the same way as other forms of wealth. Not only are such unrealized paper gains subject to reversal, but there is also an endowment effect here; many old people are reluctant to sell their house to finance their retirement consumption. If only half an individual's house equity is included, the most optimistic study suggests that just under 60 % of US households have adequate savings.

A second important assumption in the studies mentioned is that future state pension benefits will be paid as promised. Given the budgetary pressures posed by the baby-boomers in many countries, a reduction in benefits is quite probable, particularly in the United States. For poorer Americans, any cut in promised pension benefits would significantly reduce the adequacy of their current saving. Projected payments from social security exceed the value of all other financial assets for the bottom one-third of the income distribution.

In the United Kingdom, where the government's level of pension provision is set to replace a much smaller proportion of earnings than in the United States, the situation is similar. A recent report by Britain's Pension Commission argued that given the downward trends in the occupational pensions provided by employers and the erosion of state pensions, 60 % of workers over 35 are not saving enough.

A third assumption concerns the rate of return on savings. In recent years, the biggest difference between high-saving and low-saving OECD countries has been the return on assets. A recent report from the McKinsey Global Institute observes that between 1975 and 2003 asset appreciation was responsible for almost 30 % of the increase in the value of household financial assets in the United States, whereas in Japan high saving rates made up for negative returns on assets. Based on current rates of return and saving patterns in big industrial economies, the McKinsey study is not optimistic regarding the adequacy of global wealth accumulation. There is currently much uncertainty regarding future rates of asset appreciation.

Case 6.2 *continued*

Implications for government policy

How can governments increase the amount households save? Tighter monetary policies would certainly help. In the United States, in particular, policy has been loose by most standards for many years, encouraging borrowing at the expense of saving. Most governments also use tax incentives to some extent. The simplest incentive would be to switch from an income-tax structure, where tax is deducted twice (once from company profit and again when people receive investment income), to a consumption-based structure. However, governments tend to limit such a switch because it is regressive in nature, shifting the tax burden from rich to poor.

Some government policies have the effect of reducing saving rather than encouraging it. For example, in the United States eligibility for welfare assistance such as food stamps is phased out if a couple has assets over $3000. In the United Kingdom, the means-tested pension credit, designed to help pensioners, has the perverse result of making saving for workers on low incomes an unattractive proposition: for every pound of savings income they can incur marginal tax rates of at least 40 %.

One major alternative tax incentive has been to shelter retirement accounts, in effect subsidizing them. In the United States, the subsidy on retirement-saving accounts is 27 % of the value, amounting to 1 % of GDP in terms of foregone tax revenue. There is a debate regarding the effectiveness of this policy (Yoo and de Serres 2004), with some economists arguing that it merely displaces saving from one form to another, without increasing overall saving. However, a study by Venti and Wise (1987) concluded that "the vast majority of IRA (Individual Retirement Account) saving represents new saving, not accompanied by a reduction in other saving." These results were confirmed using a different methodology by Feenberg and Skinner (1989).

In summary, there are three main aspects of behavioral economics that have important policy implications in terms of the adequacy of saving:

1. *Fungibility*
   Different forms of saving and wealth are not treated as being fungible or substitutable. This is demonstrated by the evidence from the Venti and Wise study and the Feenberg and Skinner study. Governments can make use of this lack of fungibility to encourage more saving.

2. *Self-control and commitment*
   IRAs, like other retirement accounts, are illiquid, since they involve a 10 % tax surcharge if money is withdrawn before the investor reaches 59$\frac{1}{2}$ years old. Venti and Wise (1987) commented, "Some persons of course may consider the illiquidity of IRAs an advantage: it many help to insure behaviour that would not otherwise be followed. It may be a means of self-control." As stated earlier, the general trend in global financial markets toward greater liquidity may have discouraged saving by removing such commitment devices. Therefore governments can encourage more saving by creating additional commitment devices in the form of illiquid savings accounts with tax incentives, such as Individual Savings Accounts (ISAs) in the United Kingdom.

3. *Framing*

The desire to save, particularly for retirement, can be much influenced by the way in which the options in retirement plans are framed, as noted in Chapter 4. Poorer people, for example, are more likely to be enrolled in private retirement plans if that is the employer's default option than if workers have to elect to enroll. A study by Madrian and Shea (2001) indicated that shifting to automatic enrollment raised participation among poorer workers from just over 10 % to 80 %.

Questions

1. Explain why the putting of money in a retirement account might not reduce other forms of saving.
2. Explain why fungibility is an issue as far as increasing saving is concerned.
3. In what circumstances is illiquidity of assets a desirable characteristic?

Case 6.3 The desire for rising consumption profiles

Frank and Hutchens (1993) have investigated the factors that may cause wage profiles to rise in ways that are not explained by increases in productivity. In particular they examined the cases of airline pilots and intercity bus drivers, both of whom have relatively constant productivity over most of their careers, but who have average annual earnings at the end of their careers 600 % higher and 50 % higher respectively than at the start of their careers. The authors rejected four existing explanations of the rising wage profiles, relating to investment in firm-specific capital, binding contracts, risk-aversion, and adverse selection, before proposing a theory relating to commitment. The workers involved had to commit to accepting lower earnings than was justified by their productivity in the early years of their careers. It was further argued that such commitment is more likely in circumstances where much of the social activity of the workers involved is with fellow workers, and they showed that this is indeed the case with the two groups of workers they studied. Although the evidence in the study was by no means conclusive, being limited to only two groups of workers, it is highly suggestive.

Questions

1. What are the behavioral factors underlying a preference for rising wage and consumption profiles?
2. Explain why pilots and bus drivers have relatively constant productivity over their career.
3. Explain why investment in firm-specific capital cannot satisfactorily account for rising wage profiles as far as airline pilots and intercity bus drivers are concerned.
4. Explain the role of commitment in causing rising wage profiles, and why social activity with fellow workers is important as far as the likelihood of commitment is concerned.

Part IV
Strategic Interaction

7

Behavioral Game Theory

7.1 Nature of behavioral game theory

In the previous chapter we considered some aspects of game theory in general, since some of these concepts were necessary in order to understand how intertemporal preferences affect behavior. In particular we have seen that game theory is relevant whenever there is interdependence in decision-making. In some cases the game was played between a firm and consumers, as in Case 6.1 involving price plans for gym memberships; in other cases the game was played between different "selves," specifically an impatient short-run self and a patient long-run self. We have also come across some of the important concepts in game theory, such as strategies, sequence, commitment, and payoffs. In this chapter we consider more general applications of game theory. In order to discuss these applications it is necessary to have a more solid foundation as far as the basic elements of game-theoretic analysis are concerned.

The essence of interdependent decision-making situations is that when A makes a decision (for example regarding price, entry into a market, whether to take a job), it will consider the reactions of other persons or firms to its different strategies, usually assuming that they act rationally, and how these reactions will affect their own utility or profit. It must also take into account that the other parties (from now on called "players"), in selecting their reactive strategies, will consider how A will react to their reactions. This can continue in a virtually infinite progression. In this situation there is often a considerable amount of uncertainty regarding the results of any decision.

These kinds of situation occur in all areas of economics; some examples are the setting of interest rates by the central bank in macroeconomic policy; oligopolistic pricing in microeconomics; wage negotiations and strikes in labor economics; bidding in financial economics; and trade negotiations in international economics. Game theory situations also occur in politics, sociology, warfare, "games" and sports, and biology, which make the area a unifying theme in much analysis. Game theorists have therefore come from many different walks of life, although the main pioneers were von Neumann and Morgenstern (1944) and Nash (1951), who were essentially mathematicians.

Elements of a game

The concept of a game, as we are now using it, therefore includes a large variety of situations that we do not normally refer to as games. A good example is the standard PD game, shown in Figure 7.1. The classic PD situation involves two prisoners who are held in separate police cells, accused

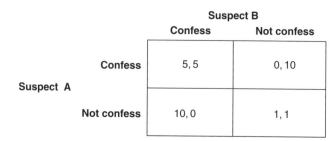

Figure 7.1 Prisoner's Dilemma

of committing a crime. They cannot communicate with each other, so each does not know how the other is acting. If neither confesses, the prosecutor can only get them convicted on other minor offences, each prisoner receiving a 1-year sentence. If one confesses while the other does not, the one confessing will be freed while the other one receives a 10-year sentence. If both confess, they will each receive a 5-year sentence.

The values in the table represent payoffs, in terms of jail sentences; the payoffs for Suspect A are the left-hand values, while the payoffs for Suspect B are the right-hand values. The objective for each suspect in this case is obviously to minimize the payoff in terms of jail time.

Thus we can say that chess, poker, and rock-paper-scissors are games in the conventional sense, as are tennis and football (either American football or soccer). However, games in the technical sense used in this chapter also include activities like going for a job interview, a firm bargaining with a labor union, someone applying for life insurance, a firm deciding to enter a new market, a politician announcing a new education/transport/health policy, or a country declaring war. What do these diverse activities have in common?

The following are the key elements of any game:

1. *Players* – These are the relevant decision-making identities, whose utilities are interdependent. They may be individuals, firms, teams, social organizations, political parties, or governments.

2. *Strategies* – These can be defined in different ways. In some cases the term "strategy" refers to a complete plan of action for playing a game. In other cases a strategy simply involves the choice of a single action, like "confessing" in a PD game. It is important to understand that in many games there may be many actions involved. A complete plan means that every possible contingency must be allowed for. In this chapter, in keeping with common convention, we will use the term "rule" for a complete plan of action, and reserve the term "strategy" for a specific action or move.

3. *Payoffs* – These represent changes in welfare or utility at the end of the game, and are determined by the choice of strategy by *each* player. It is normally assumed that players are rational and have the objective of maximizing these utilities or expected utilities. Notice that the word *each* is important; what distinguishes game theory from decision theory is that in the latter outcomes only depend on the decisions of a single decision-maker.

The **normal-form representation** of a game specifies the above three elements, as shown in Figure 7.1. Players are assumed to move simultaneously, so these kinds of situation can be represented by tables or matrices. The normal-form representation helps to clarify the key elements in the game.

When the players do not move simultaneously, and the sequence of moves is important, it is necessary to use an **extensive-form representation**, which usually involves a **game tree**. The concept of a game tree is illustrated in Figure 7.2; this is an example of an ultimatum game. In this type of game there are two players, and as with many games, there is a proposer (P) and a responder (R). In its standard form, a certain sum of money, frequently $10, represents a value of the gain to exchange, or surplus, that would be lost if no trade was made. P offers the sum x to R, leaving themselves $10 – x$. R can either accept the offer, or reject it, in which case both players receive nothing. In the game shown in Figure 7.2 it is assumed that if A determines an even split out of 10 the game ends and that the only possible uneven split is (8, 2).

The extensive-form representation involves five elements:

1. a configuration of **nodes** and branches running without any closed loops from a single starting node to its end nodes;
2. an indication of which node belongs to each player;
3. probabilities that "nature" (an external force) uses to choose branches at random nodes;
4. collections of nodes, which are called **information sets**;
5. payoffs at each end node.

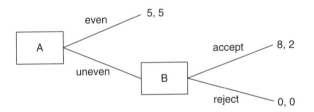

Figure 7.2 Extensive form of ultimatum game

Nodes therefore represent decision points for a particular player, or for nature (for example, it may decide to rain or not). Information sets are collections of nodes where a player has the move at every node in the information set, and when the play in the game reaches a particular node, the player with the move does not know which node in the information set has been reached. There are two decision nodes, the first for A and the second for B. The second node has an information set. The equilibria for both this game and the PD are discussed in the next section.

Types of game

There are many different types of game theory situation, and different methods of analysis are appropriate in different cases. It is therefore useful to classify games according to certain important characteristics.

1. *Cooperative and noncooperative games*
   In cooperative games the players can communicate with each other and collude. They can also enter into third-party enforceable binding contracts. Much of this type of activity is expressly prohibited by law in developed countries, thus most of the games that are of interest in economic situations are of the noncooperative kind. This type of game involves forming self-enforcing reliance relationships, which determine an equilibrium situation. The nature of such equilibria is discussed in the next section.

2. *Two-player and multi-player games*
   The PD situations are obviously two-player games. However, this kind of game is capable of being extended to consider more than two parties, as we will see in the next chapter, in the context of public goods games. Having more players tends to increase the likelihood of defection, particularly in the "one-off" situation. One version of such a situation is sometimes referred to as **the tragedy of the commons**. This applies in cases where property rights are untradable, insecure, or unassigned, for example where pollution is involved. The reasoning is that with more players it is important to defect before others do; only if defectors are easily detected and punished will this be prevented. The depletion of fish stocks in the North Sea due to overfishing and the resulting conflicts are an example of the tragedy of the commons. In other situations, instead of the resource being overused, it is undersupplied, as with public goods like streetlights and hospitals. With multi-player games there is also the opportunity for some of the players to form coalitions against others, to try and impose strategies that would otherwise be unsustainable.

3. *Zero-sum and nonzero-sum Games*

With zero-sum games, sometimes called "constant-sum games," the gain of one player(s) is automatically the loss of another player(s); thus the sum of the gains (or losses) of the players is constant. This can apply, for example, in derivatives markets, where certain transactions occur between two speculators. However, most situations involve nonzero-sum games; furthermore, even when monetary gains and losses offset each other, the utilities of such gains and losses may not do so, because of loss-aversion.

4. *Perfect and imperfect information*

In the version of the PD presented earlier in the chapter it was assumed that all the players knew for certain what all the payoffs were for each pair of strategies. In practice this is often not the case, and this can also affect strategy. In some cases a player may be uncertain regarding their own payoffs; in other cases they may know their own payoffs but be uncertain regarding the payoffs of the other player(s). For example, an insurance company may not know all the relevant details regarding the person applying for insurance, a situation leading to adverse selection. Likewise, bidders at an auction may not know the valuations that other parties place on the auctioned item. Games with imperfect information are unsurprisingly more difficult to analyze.

5. *Static and dynamic games*

Static games involve **simultaneous moves**; the PD game is a simultaneous game, meaning that the players make their moves simultaneously, without knowing the move of the other player. In terms of analysis the moves do not have to be simultaneous in chronological terms, as long as each player is ignorant of the moves of the other player(s). Many life situations involve **dynamic games**; these involve **sequential moves**, where one player moves first and the other player moves afterward, knowing the move of the first player. The ultimatum bargaining game is an example of a dynamic game. The order of play can make a big difference to the outcome in such situations.

6. *Discrete and continuous strategies*

Discrete strategies involve situations where each action can be chosen from a limited number of alternatives. In the PD game there are only two choices for each player, to confess or not confess; thus this is a discrete strategy situation. In contrast, a firm in oligopoly may have a virtually limitless number of prices that it can charge; this is an example of a continuous strategy situation. As a result the analytical approach is somewhat different, in terms of the mathematical techniques involved.

7. *"One-shot" and repetitive games*

Most short-run decision scenarios in business, such as pricing and advertising, are of the repetitive type, in that there is a continuous interaction between competitors, who can change their decision variables at regular intervals. Some of these games may involve a finite number of plays, where an end of the game can be foreseen, while others may seem infinite. Long-run decisions, such as investment decisions, may resemble the "one-shot" situation; although the situation may be repeated in the future, the time interval between decisions may be several years, and the next decision scenario may involve quite different payoffs.

Behavioral game theory and standard game theory

Standard game theory (SGT) involves three main assumptions, which have left it exposed to criticism: (1) people are motivated purely by self-interest; (2) people have unbounded rationality; and (3) equilibria are reached instantly, since there are no time lags due to learning effects or other factors. We will see that, in spite of these assumptions, SGT does not necessarily perform badly in many situations when its predictions are compared with empirical findings. Indeed, in games involving mixed strategies and signaling, its predictions are quite accurate. In other games, like bargaining games and iterated games, its predictions may be way off track; for example, in the ultimatum bargaining game in Figure 7.6, B may be outraged by the uneven offer and reject it because it violates social norms of fairness. We will examine this kind of situation in more detail in the next chapter. However, we often find that by relaxing the SGT assumptions and adding certain new parameters within the basic game-theoretic framework, we can improve fit and prediction significantly. This is in keeping with the general approach of behavioral economics regarding the modification and extension of the SEM.

Thus, throughout the rest of the chapter we will be considering models that tend to be more complex than standard models. In the discussion of these models we will find two strands of analysis in BGT that are additional to SGT:

1. *A sound basis of experimental evidence*

This entails an examination and evaluation of many empirical studies to see what anomalies arise with the relevant SGT model and modifying it accordingly.

2. *A sound basis in the discipline of psychology*
   BGT models are not only constrained by empirical evidence, they are also
   based on theory from psychology.

7.2 Equilibrium

In order to determine strategy or an equilibrium situation, we must first assume
that the players are rational utility maximizers. We can now consider four
main types of equilibrium and appropriate strategies in situations involving
different payoffs: (1) **dominant strategy equilibrium**; (2) **iterated dominant
strategy equilibrium**; (3) **Nash equilibrium**; and (4) **subgame perfect Nash
equilibrium (SPNE)**. It is appropriate to consider these equilibria in this
order, as will be seen. It is also necessary to distinguish between discrete and
continuous strategies, since, although the same conditions apply, the analytical
approach is different. In the next section we will consider another important
type of equilibrium, known as **mixed-strategy equilibrium (MSE)**, and will
discuss other types of equilibrium also. Since discrete strategies are generally
easier to analyze, we will discuss these first.

Discrete strategies

As described earlier, these relate to situations where each action can be chosen
from a limited number of alternatives.

1. *Dominant strategy equilibrium*
   A strategy S_1 is said to strictly dominate another strategy S_2 if, given any
   collection of strategies that could be played by the other players, playing
   S_1 results in a strictly higher payoff for that player than does playing S_2.
   Thus we can say that if player A has a **strictly dominant strategy** in a
   situation, *it will always give at least as high a payoff as any other strategy,
   whatever player B does*. A rational player will always adopt a dominant
   strategy if one is available. Therefore, in any static game involving discrete
   strategies, we should always start by looking for a dominant strategy. This
   is easiest in a two-strategy situation; we can discuss this process in the PD
   situation described earlier. Figure 7.3 is a repeat of this situation. Whatever
   strategy is used by the other player, the best response is always to defect
   (confess). If Suspect B confesses, Suspect A is better off confessing, since
   they will only get a 5-year rather than a 10-year sentence. If Suspect B does
   not confess, Suspect A is still better off confessing, since they will get off

Suspect B

		Confess	Not confess
Suspect A	**Confess**	5, 5	0, 10
	Not confess	10, 0	1, 1

Figure 7.3 Dominant strategy equilibrium

free rather than serving a year. Thus we can say that for each player there is a dominant strategy of confessing or defecting.

When there are many possible strategies, dominant strategies have to be found by a process of eliminating dominated strategies. We could also say that not confessing is in this case a **dominated strategy** for both players; this means that it will always give a lower or equal payoff, whatever the other player does.

Therefore, given the payoffs in Figure 7.3, it is obvious that there is a dominant strategy equilibrium, meaning that *the strategies pursued by all players are dominant.* By individually pursuing their self-interest each player is imposing a cost on the other that they are not taking into account. It can therefore be said that in the PD situation the dominant strategy outcome is **Pareto dominated**. This means that *there is some other outcome where at least one of the players is better off while no other player is worse off.* However, Pareto domination considers total or social welfare; this is not relevant to the choice of strategy by each player.

2. *Iterated dominant strategy equilibrium*
What would happen if one player did not have a dominant strategy? This is illustrated in Figure 7.4, which is similar to Figure 7.3 but with one payoff changed. There is now an asymmetry in the matrix of payoffs, because a confession by A if B does not confess results in a 2-year sentence, maybe because A has had a prior conviction. Although B's dominant strategy is unchanged, A no longer has a dominant strategy. If B confesses (or defects), A is better off also confessing, as before; but if B does not confess (or cooperates), A is better off also not confessing.

In this case A can rule out B not confessing (that is a dominated strategy for B), and conclude that B will confess; A can therefore iterate to a dominant strategy, which is to confess. Thus the equilibrium is the same as before. The general rule for determining the iterated dominant strategy equilibrium is to identify all the dominated strategies first and eliminate

Suspect B

	Confess	Not confess
Confess	5, 5	2, 10
Not confess	10, 0	1, 1

Suspect A (rows: Confess, Not confess)

Figure 7.4 Iterated dominant strategy equilibrium

them. With games involving a greater number of possible strategies it is more difficult to determine an iterated dominant strategy equilibrium, since it can take a while to work out all the strategies that are dominated.

3. *Nash Equilibrium*

The situation becomes more complicated when neither player has a dominant strategy. This means that we are no longer considering a PD, since the structure of the payoffs has changed, as shown in Figure 7.5. Now the table is symmetrical again, but both suspects now get a 2-year sentence if they confess when the other suspect does not confess.

There is no single equilibrium here, meaning that there is no universal tendency for either player to take either action. Instead, we have to use the concept of **Nash Equilibrium**. This represents *an outcome where each player is pursuing their best strategy in response to the best-reply strategy of the other player*. This is a more general concept of equilibrium than the two equilibrium concepts described earlier; while it includes dominant strategy equilibrium and iterated dominant strategy equilibrium, it also relates to situations where the first two concepts do not apply. There are two such equilibria in Figure 7.5:

Suspect B

	Confess	Not confess
Confess	5, 5	2, 10
Not confess	10, 2	1, 1

Suspect A (rows: Confess, Not confess)

Figure 7.5 Game with no dominant strategy

1. If B confesses, A is better off confessing; and given this best response, B's best reply is to confess.

2. If B does not confess, A is also better off not confessing; and given this best response, B's best reply is not to confess.

The same equilibria could also be expressed from the point of view of determining B's strategy:

1. If A confesses, B is better off confessing; and given this best response, A's best reply is to confess.

2. If A does not confess, B is also better off not confessing; and given this best response, A's best reply is not to confess.

Both A and B will clearly prefer the second equilibrium, but there is no further analysis that we can perform to see which of the two equilibria will prevail. This presents a problem for strategy selection if the game is repeated, as will be seen later.

The concept of Nash equilibrium is an extremely important one in game theory, since frequently situations arise where there is no dominant strategy equilibrium or iterated dominant strategy equilibrium. In the next section we will examine cases where none of the three kinds of equilibrium situation exist, and mixed strategies are involved.

4. *Subgame perfect Nash equilibrium*

This kind of equilibrium is relevant in extensive-form games. We will use the ultimatum game in Figure 7.2 for illustration. This is repeated in Figure 7.6.

A **subgame** is the continuation game from a **singleton node** (a node with no other nodes in its information set) to the end nodes which follow from that node. Thus there is a subgame at the decision node for B. **Subgame perfection** means that players play their equilibrium strategies if the subgame is reached. **Subgame perfect Nash equilibrium (SPNE)** is

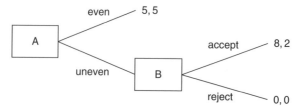

Figure 7.6 Extensive form of ultimatum game

an equilibrium for the complete game where players play their equilibrium strategies in each subgame. In order to determine the SPNE for a game, we have to use the method of **backwards induction**. This means thinking forward and working backward, and we will see that this often unnatural method is the key to successful strategy in many situations. In the ultimatum game in Figure 7.6 it means that in order to determine A's optimal, or equilibrium, strategy, we must first consider B's situation. B must make a decision if A goes for an uneven split. According to SGT (ignoring social preferences), a rational B will accept the uneven split, since a payoff of 2 is better than 0 from rejecting the offer. Working backwards, we can now say that A will therefore decide to go for an uneven split, since a payoff of 8 is better than the 5 from an even split. Thus the SPNE for the game is (uneven, accept|uneven).

It should be noted that SPNE is more restrictive than Nash equilibrium. In the ultimatum game above there are two Nash equilbria, but only the one determined above is subgame perfect. The other Nash equilibrium is (even, reject|uneven). In the second case, if A anticipates that B will reject an uneven offer, A will decide to go for an even split, so this is a best response. If A goes for an even split, B does not get a chance to respond (it is assumed in this game). However, although (even, reject|uneven) is a Nash equilibrium, it is not subgame perfect, since B should not reject an uneven split according to SGT.

Continuous strategies

Strategies in this case relate to a continuous variable rather than a discrete one. Price and quantity of output are frequent examples in economics. We will take two examples from oligopoly theory here, both of which involve competition in the form of output. The first relates to the Cournot case, where moves are simultaneous, and the second relates to the Stackelberg case, where moves are sequential. We will assume the same parameters for market demand and cost conditions in each case, which will allow us to see the advantages of being the first mover in such oligopoly situations.

Cournot oligopoly

This model, originally developed in 1838, initially considered a market in which there were only two firms, A and B (Cournot 1838). In more general terms we can say that the Cournot model is based on the following assumptions:

1. There are few firms in the market and many buyers.
2. The firms produce homogeneous products; therefore each firm has to charge the same market price (the model can be extended to cover differentiated products).
3. Competition is in the form of output, meaning that each firm determines its level of output based on its estimate of the level of output of the other firm. Each firm believes that its own output strategy does not affect the strategy of its rival(s).
4. Barriers to entry exist.
5. Each firm aims to maximize profit, and assumes that the other firms do the same.

Because strategies are continuous in the Cournot model, this allows a more mathematical approach to analysis.

The situation can be illustrated by using the following example, involving two firms A and B:

1. Market demand is given by $P = 400 - 2Q$ (where P is the price in $ and Q is quantity of output in units).
2. Both firms have constant marginal costs of $40 and no fixed costs.

The analytical procedure can be viewed as involving the following steps.

Step 1

Transform the market demand into a demand function that relates to the outputs of each of the two firms. Thus we have

$$P = 400 - 2(Q_A + Q_B)$$
$$P = 400 - 2Q_A - 2Q_B \tag{7.1}$$

Step 2

Derive the profit functions for each firm, which are functions of the outputs of both firms. Bearing in mind that there are no fixed costs and therefore marginal cost and average cost are equal, the profit function for firm A is as follows:

$$\Pi_A = (400 - 2Q_A - 2Q_B)Q_A - 40Q_A = 400Q_A - 2Q_A^2 - 2Q_B Q_A - 40Q_A$$
$$\Pi_A = 360Q_A - 2Q_A^2 - 2Q_B Q_A \tag{7.2}$$

Step 3
Derive the optimal output for firm A as a function of the output of firm B, by differentiating the profit function with respect to Q_A and setting the partial derivative equal to zero:

$$\frac{\partial \Pi_A}{\partial Q_A} = 360 - 4Q_A - 2Q_B = 0$$

$$4Q_A = 360 - 2Q_B$$

$$Q_A = 90 - 0.5Q_B \qquad (7.3)$$

Strictly speaking, the value of Q_B in this equation is not known with certainty for firm A, but is an estimate. Equation 7.3 is known as the **best response function** or **response curve** of firm A. It shows how much firm A will put on the market for any amount that it estimates firm B will put on the market.

The second and third steps above can then be repeated for firm B to derive firm B's response curve. Because of the symmetry involved, it can be easily seen that the profit function for firm B is given by

$$\Pi_B = 360Q_B - 2Q_B^2 - 2Q_B Q_A \qquad (7.4)$$

And the response curve for firm B is given by

$$Q_B = 90 - 0.5Q_A \qquad (7.5)$$

This shows how much firm B will put on the market for any amount that it estimates firm A will put on the market. The situation can now be represented graphically, as shown in Figure 7.7.

Step 4
Solve the equations for the best response functions simultaneously to derive the **Cournot equilibrium**. The properties of this equilibrium will be discussed shortly.

$$Q_A = 90 - 0.5Q_B$$

$$Q_B = 90 - 0.5Q_A$$

$$Q_A = 90 - 0.5(90 - 0.5Q_A)$$

$$Q_A = 90 - 45 + 0.25Q_A$$

$$0.75Q_A = 45$$

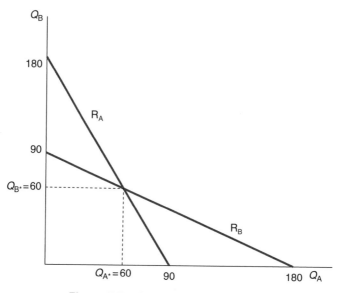

Figure 7.7   Cournot response curves

$$Q_A = 60$$

$$Q_B = 90 - 0.5(60) = 60$$

The equilibrium obtained here is also referred to as **Cournot–Nash Equilibrium**, since each firm is making a best response to the other firm's strategy, and there is no tendency for either firm to deviate from this strategy.

Stackelberg oligopoly

Although this model was originally developed in non-game theory terms, we will apply a game-theoretic analysis to the situation. The basic assumptions underlying the Stackelberg model are as follows:

1. There are few firms and many buyers.
2. The firms produce either homogeneous or differentiated products.
3. A single firm, the leader, chooses an output before all other firms choose their outputs.
4. All other firms, as followers, take the output of the leader as given.
5. Barriers to entry exist.
6. All firms aim to maximize profit, and assume that the other firms do the same.

We shall now refer to the same situation, in terms of demand and cost functions, as that assumed earlier for the Cournot duopoly and examine how equilibrium is determined. We shall then draw certain conclusions regarding the differences in outcomes.

Market demand was given by $P = 400 - 2Q$

Both firms have a cost function given by $C_i = 40Q_i$

Thus we can write the market demand as

$$P = 400 - 2(Q_L + Q_F)$$
$$P = 400 - 2Q_L - 2Q_F \qquad (7.6)$$

Where Q_L is the output of the leader and Q_F is the output of the follower.

Because the Stackelberg situation is a dynamic or sequential game, we need to analyze the situation by using the same foldback method described for the ultimatum bargaining game, even though that game involved discrete strategies. Therefore we must first consider the situation for the follower. They are essentially acting in the same way as a Cournot duopolist. Thus their profit function is given by

$$\Pi_F = (400 - 2Q_L - 2Q_F)Q_F - 40Q_F = 400Q_F - 2Q_F^2 - 2Q_LQ_F - 40Q_F$$
$$\Pi_F = 360Q_F - 2Q_F^2 - 2Q_LQ_F \qquad (7.7)$$

The next step is to obtain the response function for the follower, by deriving the optimal output for the follower as a function of the output of the leader; thus we differentiate the profit function with respect to Q_F and set the partial derivative equal to zero:

$$\frac{\partial \Pi_F}{\partial Q_F} = 360 - 4Q_F - 2Q_L = 0$$
$$4Q_F = 360 - 2Q_L$$
$$Q_F = 90 - 0.5Q_L \qquad (7.8)$$

It should be noted that this is the same as the Cournot result as far as the follower is concerned. However, the leader can now use this information regarding the follower's response function when choosing the output that maximizes its own profit. Thus it will have the demand function given by

$$P_L = 400 - 2Q_L - 2(90 - 0.5Q_L) \qquad (7.9)$$

or

$$P_L = 220 - Q_L \tag{7.10}$$

The leader's profit function is given by

$$\Pi_L = (220 - Q_L)Q_L - 40\,Q_L \tag{7.11}$$

$$\frac{\partial \Pi_L}{\partial Q_L} = 220 - 2Q_L - 40 = 0$$

$$Q_L = 90 \tag{7.12}$$

We can now obtain the output of the follower by using the response function in Equation (7.8), giving us $Q_F = 45$.

These outputs allow us to obtain the market price:

$$P = 400 - 2(90 + 45) = \$130 \tag{7.13}$$

We can now obtain the profits for each firm:

$$\Pi_L = (130 - 40)90 = \$8100$$

and

$$\Pi_F = (130 - 40)45 = \$4050$$

Total profit for the industry is $12 150.

These results can be compared with the Cournot situation (CS), yielding the following conclusions:

1. Price is not as high as in the CS ($130 compared with $160).
2. Output of the leader is higher and output of the follower lower than in the CS.
3. Profit of the leader is higher and profit of the follower lower than in the CS.
4. Total profit in the industry is lower than in the CS ($12 150 compared with $14 400).

Thus we can see that in the Stackelberg situation there is an advantage to being the first mover. However, we should not think that there is always an advantage to being first mover, as we shall see later.

7.3 Mixed strategies

Pure and mixed strategies

All the strategies so far discussed have involved what are called "pure" strategies. A pure strategy always responds in the same way to a given situation, or, in more technical terms, it involves the selection of exactly one action at each decision node. However, there are many games where there is no Nash equilibrium in pure strategies. This applies to "trivial" games like matching pennies and rock-paper-scissors, and to real-life games like poker, tennis, and football (both American and soccer). For example, in rock-paper-scissors, if A plays rock, B's best response is to play paper (paper wraps rock); however, A's best reply to B's best response is to play scissors (scissors cuts paper), not rock, and thus there is no Nash equilibrium here, or if any other action is taken by either player, in terms of pure strategies. On the other hand, we will see shortly that there is an equilibrium in terms of mixed strategies.

We can introduce the idea of a mixed strategy by considering the generic game referred to as "**Battle of the Sexes**" (**BOS**). The nature of this game is that a pair of players, one of each sex, want to spend an evening out together, but they have different interests. A wants to watch a boxing match, but B wants to go to the ballet. In this situation a simplified payoff table can be illustrated by Figure 7.8. As before, row payoffs are given first and column payoffs second.

If both players go to the ballet, B has a fine time, but A does not enjoy himself, except for having the company of his partner. The situation is reversed if they both watch boxing. On the other hand, if each does their own thing, it is assumed that they are miserable without each other's company. In this situation the reader should be able to verify that there are two Nash equilibria in terms of pure strategies: either they both go to the ballet, or they both watch boxing.

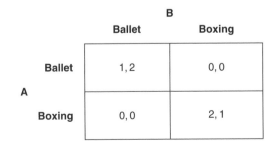

Figure 7.8 Battle of the sexes

There is also another equilibrium in terms of mixed strategies. This should be easy to see in common sense terms, at least if the situation is a repeated game: half the time they go to the ballet, and half the time they watch boxing. This type of equilibrium is referred to as **MSE**, since there is no tendency or incentive for the players to depart from it. In this case there is no mathematical computation necessary to determine the MSE, since the payoff table is symmetrical. If the payoffs are asymmetrical, the MSE is more complex to determine, as we will see in the next section.

Unpredictability

In spite of the title "Battle of the sexes," this game is essentially a game involving cooperation, as is the PD. In both cases the players are trying to coordinate their actions. However, in competitive games the key to success is often unpredictability. If an opponent can detect a pattern in your behavior then they will beat you. This applies to the games mentioned earlier where there is no equilibrium in pure strategies. For example, if your opponent knows that you are going to play rock each time, they will always play paper and beat you. Equally, if they detect that you play an alternating pattern of rock, then scissors, then paper, they will also be able to beat you by selecting the appropriate responses of paper, rock, and scissors. Any detectable pattern can thus be beaten.

Let us consider the well-known situation in tennis where one player is serving and the other is receiving. This is a good example to use for several reasons: (1) both players have two main possible actions: server can serve to forehand or backhand, and receiver can move to forehand or backhand; (2) these actions are repeated many times between the same two players in a match, enabling any pattern to be detected; and (3) an extensive field study (Walker and Wooders 2001) has been conducted to compare theoretical predictions with empirical observations. We can consider this a simultaneous game, since, at least at the top level of the game, the receiver must anticipate the direction of the serve and decide what direction to move in before the server hits the ball if they are to have a reasonable chance of making a return.

A simplified form of this situation is illustrated in Figure 7.9, where the server's payoff is 0 if the serve is returned and 1 if it is not. This is a zero-sum game, so the receiver's payoff is 1 if a return is made and 0 if not. It is assumed at this point that if the receiver anticipates wrongly he or she will fail to make a return, but if he or she anticipates correctly this will result in a successful return.

	Receiver's move	
	Forehand	Backhand
Forehand	0, 1	1, 0
Backhand	1, 0	0, 1

Server's aim

Figure 7.9 Game with no Nash equilibrium in pure strategies

In terms of Nash equilibrium, if the server aims to the forehand, the receiver's best response is to move to the forehand; obviously the server's best reply to this best response is to serve to the backhand. The situation is reversed if the server aims to the backhand, so there is no Nash equilibrium in pure strategies. This means that there are two significant differences between this situation and the Battle of the Sexes game discussed earlier. We have already noted that in this case the players are in competition with each other, rather than trying to cooperate with each other. The game in this case is a zero-sum game: if one player gains, the other automatically loses the same amount (ignoring loss-aversion). This situation arises in more general terms whenever one player wants a coincidence of actions, while the other player does not. This happens in many real-life situations, not just in recognized games: employers want to monitor employees who shirk, while shirkers want to avoid being monitored; the tax authorities want to audit those who evade taxes, while evaders want to avoid being audited; attacking armies want to gain an element of surprise, while defenders want to avoid being surprised. The question therefore arises: how does each player determine an optimal strategy, maximizing payoffs, in this kind of situation?

Randomization

As stated earlier, the key to success is unpredictability. This is achieved by a process of randomization. In the example in Figure 7.9 the optimal strategy for each player, that is the MSE, is to randomize their actions so that half of the time they serve or move in one direction and half of the time they go the other way. Randomization in this case means that the players must each act in such a way that it is as if they are tossing a coin to determine their action at each play. Only by randomizing their actions can they avoid their opponent detecting a pattern in their play, allowing the opponent to anticipate their actions and beat them.

However, it is important to realize that the tossing-a-coin analogy is only appropriate when payoff matrices are symmetrical, as in the simple tennis example and the Battle of the Sexes game (randomization is not necessary there, since the players are trying to cooperate rather than compete, and a simple alternating scheme would suffice). When payoffs are asymmetrical the MSE involves a more complex type of randomization, and it has to be calculated. Randomization may seem like "madness" in terms of being the basis of a strategy, but there must be method in it if it is going to be a sensible, or optimizing, strategy. There must be a pattern in one's lack of pattern. This seeming paradox can be illustrated by a more realistic development of the tennis example in Figure 7.9. We will now consider the situation where payoffs are no longer either "succeed/fail" or (1, 0), but allow for degrees of success. In other words, we are now going to consider a game involving continuous rather than discrete payoffs. Figure 7.10 indicates the probabilities of the server beating the receiver and the complementary probabilities of the receiver returning. This table is adapted from the excellent and highly readable book by Dixit and Nalebuff (1991), *Thinking Strategically*.

This situation is still a zero-sum game (the probabilities or payoffs in each cell always add up to 100 %), but it is not symmetrical since the receiver's forehand is stronger than their backhand. This can be seen from the fact that if the receiver correctly anticipates a serve to their forehand, they will make a successful return 90 % of the time; while if they correctly anticipate a serve to their backhand, their success rate is only 60 %. In order to understand how the MSE is derived from the optimal strategies for each player, let us consider first of all the pattern of 50/50 randomization so far discussed, which we will see is suboptimal for both players. The server wants to maximize the percentage of winning serves (minimize the percentage of successful returns) and the receiver wants to do the opposite.

If the server serves to the forehand half the time and to the backhand half the time, the server's success rate when the receiver moves to their forehand will be 0.5(10 %) + 0.5(80 %) = 45 %, while their success rate when the receiver moves to their backhand will be 0.5(70 %) + 0.5(40 %) = 55 %. Thus

Figure 7.10 Mixed Strategy Equilibrium

the average success rate for the server is 50% (and it is also 50% for the receiver). However, this figure assumes that the receiver is moving to forehand and backhand on a 50/50 basis. We can now see that this is not optimal for the receiver, since by moving to their forehand all the time they can improve their success rate from 50% to 55%, and thus reduce the server's success rate to 45%. How then can we derive an optimization strategy for each player?

The key intuition here is to see that when a player is optimizing their strategy there is no incentive for the opponent to change their strategy. As long as the opponent can gain by changing their strategy, one is not optimizing one's own strategy, as seen in the example above where both players start with a 50/50 randomization pattern. Thus player A (the server) maximizes their payoffs when B (the receiver) is indifferent between their actions (moving to forehand or backhand). The solution can be obtained by using some simple algebra. Let A serve to the forehand in the proportion p and to the backhand in the proportion $(1 - p)$. Similarly, let B move to the forehand in the proportion q and to the backhand in the proportion $(1 - q)$. In order to compute the optimal strategy for A, therefore, we must equate B's payoffs from moving in either direction:

Average payoff from moving to forehand $= p(90) + (1 - p)(20) = 70p + 20$
Average payoff from moving to backhand $= p(30) + (1 - p)(60) = -30p + 60$
$$70p + 20 = -30p + 60$$
$$100p = 40$$
$$p = 0.4 \text{ or } 40\%$$

Thus the server's optimal strategy is to serve to forehand 40% of the time and to backhand 60% of the time. Only with these proportions is the receiver unable to exploit the situation to their own advantage and to the server's disadvantage.

The optimal strategy for the receiver can be calculated in a similar way. In this case the server's payoffs from serving in either direction must be made equal:

Average payoff from serving to forehand $= q(10) + (1 - q)(70) = -60q + 70$
Average payoff from serving to backhand $= q(80) + (1 - q)(40) = 40q + 40$
$$-60q + 70 = 40q + 40$$
$$-100q = -30$$
$$q = 0.3 \text{ or } 30\%$$

Thus the receiver's optimal strategy is to move to forehand 30% of the time and to backhand 70% of the time. Only with these proportions is the server unable to exploit the situation to their own advantage and to the receiver's disadvantage.

We can also compute the overall success rate (s) for the server if they use their optimal strategy and the receiver reacts accordingly:

$$s = 0.4[0.1(0.3) + 0.7(0.7)] + 0.6[0.8(0.3) + 0.4(0.7)] = 0.52 \text{ or } 52\%$$

The corresponding success rate for the receiver is therefore 48 %.

A number of things can be observed regarding the MSE of optimal strategies here. The first general point is that the MSE is always identical to both a **maximin** and a **minimax** strategy for each player. This means that the server is trying to maximize their own minimum payoff, which will result if the opponent is optimizing their own strategy. We have seen, for example, that if the server randomizes on a 50/50 basis, the receiver can exploit this to reduce the server's overall success rate to 45 %. Therefore the 50/50 pattern is not a maximin strategy; the minimum payoff is maximized at 52 %. A similar line of reasoning applies to the receiver. Likewise, a minimax strategy (sometimes called "minimax regret") means that each player is trying to minimize the maximum payoff for their opponent; this follows from the zero-sum nature of the game.

Another observation is that, like many predictions of game theory, the solution is not an intuitive one. While it is not as counterintuitive as some predictions we will come across, it may seem strange that the receiver should move to their stronger forehand so little, only 30 % of the time. This is because the server is serving more to the more vulnerable backhand, and it therefore pays the receiver to move to that side more often.

Empirical studies of mixed-strategy equilibrium

It is all very well to say that a server should serve to the forehand 40 % of the time on a random basis, but how can the server actually achieve this? A number of empirical studies have been performed going back to the 1950s examining this randomization process, and how successful it is in achieving MSE. Almost all of these studies have involved experiments, and these have become more sophisticated and more revealing over time, as various design flaws have been eliminated.

Many psychologists and neuroscientists believe that the brain incorporates some kind of randomizing mechanism (for a survey see Glimcher 2003), but the precise operation of this has not yet been studied in detail at the physiological level. What has emerged from empirical studies, however, is that this mechanism is far from perfect. Although results from different studies vary in their conclusions, the general pattern is that departures from MSE, while often small, are usually statistically significant. These departures can be observed both in games requiring randomization and in direct randomization tasks where subjects are asked to generate a sequence of random responses. There are three main aberrations from a correct pattern of randomization:

1. *People produce too many runs of numbers in a sequence*
   A run is a succession of similar responses. In order to explain this factor it is helpful to give an example. Take the sequence THHTHTTH. This sequence has eight responses and six runs. The maximum number of runs of eight is obtained if the responses alternate each time.

2. *People alternate their responses too much*
   This observation is similar to the first, and probably has the same psychological foundation, as we will see later. This phenomenon is also commonly observed in real life; for example, people avoid betting on lottery numbers that have recently won, until it is "their turn" to win again.

3. *People generate samples that are too balanced*
   There is a tendency for people to assume that large sample properties are also observed in small samples. We can use the previous example of the heads-and-tails sequence to illustrate this phenomenon. Obviously, in a large sample one would expect the total numbers of heads and tails to be approximately equal; however, in a small sample there is statistically a relatively high probability of the sample being biased. The probability of obtaining an exactly 50/50 distribution of heads and tails in a sequence of 8 coin tosses is only .27.

In spite of these general findings there are some interesting results regarding learning. As mentioned earlier, there have been some field studies examining the performance of professional players in certain games in terms of their abilities to randomize successfully. We have seen that successful randomization can be judged by observing whether expected payoffs are equal with each action. For example, if a tennis player is randomizing properly, their success rate will be the same serving to the forehand as serving to the backhand. Several studies have now been performed in this area, one in tennis (Walker and Wooders 2001) and two in European football (Palacios-Heurta 2001; Chiappori, Levitt, and Groseclose 2001). Walker and Wooders studied ten big tennis matches in the period 1974–1997, concentrating on long matches in order to provide a larger sample of points. They observed in particular the proportions of winning points when servers served to the right or left. The football studies examined both the direction of penalty kicks and the direction of goalkeeper moves. The main finding in all studies is that win rates from different actions are approximately the same, supporting the hypothesis that professional players at least can successfully randomize to achieve MSE. Walker and Wooders note that the pro tennis players still have a tendency to over-alternate, although much less than the results observed in experimental studies.

As a final comment regarding these empirical studies it is relevant to consider the conclusion of Walker and Wooders:

> The theory (of MSE) applies well (but not perfectly) at the "expert" end of the spectrum, in spite of its failure at the "novice" end. There is a very large gulf between the two extremes, and little, if anything, is presently known about how to place a given strategic situation along this spectrum.

Behavioral conclusions

At this point the main question we have to ask concerns the causes of the aberrations from MSE observed in empirical studies. What is the psychological foundation for such aberrations? Rapoport and Budescu (1997) propose two factors: (1) limited working memory; and (2) the representativeness heuristic.

Limited working memory essentially relates to the concept of bounded rationality. In their model, subjects remember only the previous m elements in their sequence and use the **feature-matching heuristic**, which is an aspect of the representativeness heuristic, a phenomenon discussed in more detail in Chapter 9. This means that they choose the $m + 1$st element to balance the number of heads and tails choices in the last $m + 1$ flips, ignoring small sample variation. If the memory length is not very long, subjects will tend to over-alternate when asked to generate a random sequence. In binary experiments with coin tosses, this model suggests that memory length is about seven characters. As an illustration of this model, in the sequence of heads and tails given earlier, the first seven results involve 4T and 3H; therefore feature-matching requires that the eighth result be H.

An interesting observation concerning the over-alternation tendency is that this tendency is *not* present in young children. Contrary to many other psychological errors, where people improve as their minds develop, this is one case where the opposite occurs. It seems that only the prolonged experience and exposure to harsh market forces of seasoned professionals can overcome this tendency, at least to some extent.

One interpretation of MSE that is commonly favored in terms of explaining the observed aberrations is that players do not need to actually randomize with perfection, as long as other players cannot guess what they will do. This implies that bounded rationality is symmetrical. In this case, MSE can be described as being an **equilibrium in beliefs**. This means that players' beliefs about the probable frequency with which their opponent will choose different strategies are correct on average, and make them indifferent about which strategy to play. For example, in our tennis scenario described earlier, if a receiver estimates that there is a 40 % chance the server will serve to their forehand, they will be indifferent about which way to move. Empirical studies where players have been given the opportunity to randomize explicitly, but have declined to do so, have indicated that a population of such players can still achieve aggregate results close to those predicted by MSE (Bloomfield 1994; Ochs 1995; Shachat 2002). These findings lend some support to the "equilibrium in beliefs" hypothesis.

A final question arises at this point. Is there any rival theory that can produce better predictions than MSE? Some results indicate that a model involving **quantal response equilibrium (QRE)** may achieve this. According to QRE, players do not choose the best response with certainty (as is the case with the other equilibria so far discussed), but "**better respond**" instead. This means that they choose better responses (with higher payoffs) with higher probabilities. There is some psychological foundation underlying such a model, given the existence of bounded rationality, "noise," uncertainty, and problems of encoding and decoding information. The jury is still out on the virtues of QRE versus MSE.

7.4 Bargaining

Bargaining refers to the process by which parties agree to the terms of a transaction. It has been a focus of attention for economists certainly since the time of Edgeworth (1881), with his well-known "Edgeworth box," which showed the range of outcomes which represented optimality for both parties. In the 1950s, economists, notably Nash (who was really a mathematician), began to use game theory in their approach to the problem of determining optimal outcomes. Nash in many ways foreshadowed the work of more recent researchers using a two-level approach. At one level he investigated the ways in which parties determined how to come to an agreement (unstructured bargaining), and at another level he examined the nature of the solution that the parties would arrive at, given a certain set of rules for the bargaining procedure (structured bargaining).

From the 1960s, economists began to apply the methods of experimental economics to these twin problems, comparing empirical results with theoretical predictions. This then allowed theories to be modified in line with such results, suggesting certain psychological processes and phenomena which have become incorporated into the body of BGT.

It should also be stated at this point that bargaining games are considered in more detail in the next chapter, since they involve the concepts of social norms and fairness.

Unstructured bargaining

This kind of bargaining allows the players to use any kind of communication, not restricting the type of message or the order of offers made. Nash (1950) had proposed a unique Pareto-optimal solution that maximized the product of the utility gains for each player above the so-called "disagreement point." However, many early experimental studies in the 1970s produced results that did not agree with the Nash solution. The reason for this finding was that these studies did not consider how monetary payoffs mapped into utilities as far as attitudes to risk were concerned (they usually assumed risk-neutrality).

Roth and Malouf (1979) used a "**binary lottery**" technique to induce risk-neutrality. This method requires some explanation. Players are asked to bargain over the distribution of a number of lottery tickets. For example, if they bargain for 60 tickets out of 100, they have a .6 probability of winning a fixed cash prize. This technique assumes that players are indifferent between compound lotteries and their single-stage equivalents, for example if they are indifferent between a .5 chance of having 60 tickets and having 30 tickets with certainty. However, the experiments of Kahneman and Tversky have shown that this assumption is highly dubious, as we have seen in the discussion of PT in Chapter 3. Therefore the use of lottery tickets as payoffs may not in itself yield different results from using monetary payoffs.

The study by Roth and Malouf indicated that when tickets gave the same monetary prize ($1) to each player, the players bargained nearly universally to a 50/50 split with a negligible amount of disagreement. However, when the prize of a ticket to the second player was three times the value of the prize to the first player ($3.75 to $1.25), there tended to be two **focal points** for the bargaining solution. The main focal point was the split of 75/25 in favor of the first player, which equalized the expected payoffs (the first player had three times as many tickets, but for a prize of a third of the amount of the second player). However, there was a second focal point, again involving a 50/50 split. One result of having two focal points rather than one was that the average rate of disagreement was higher, at 14 % of the transactions. Roth and Murnighan (1982) duplicated this result.

Another focal point effect was found in a study by Roth and Schoumaker (1983), relating to the past history of the players. The experiment began with some players playing against a computer that was programed to give a generous share to these players, without the players' knowledge. When these players began to play against other human players, with all players' histories being known, there was a **reputation effect**, such that players who had been successful in the past were able to negotiate more favorable outcomes later.

Other studies have shown that focal points can be determined purely by chance, meaning by factors that are totally irrelevant to the bargaining trans-action. Mehta, Starmer, and Sugden (1992) found that allocating playing cards on a chance basis to players affected their demands in bargaining situations. When both players had equal numbers of aces they easily bargained to a single focal point of a 50/50 split. However, unequal allocations of ace cards resulted in dual focal points, one with a 50/50 split and another according to the "irrelevant" distribution of aces, so that a player with 3 aces out of 4 often demanded 3/4 of the pot, and players with only 1 ace often demanded only 1/4 of the pot.

We shall see that the underlying factor behind these different focal points is the phenomenon of **self-serving bias**, discussed in more detail in Chapter 9 because of its implications regarding rationality. People tend to prefer interpret-ations of information that are favorable to themselves – a good example being that the vast majority of people believe they are better-than-average drivers. In the Roth and Malouf study, it was the second players, with the higher prize, who were proposing 50/50 splits, rather than splits which gave the players the same expected payoff. Self-serving bias is a major factor preventing the nego-tiation of agreements in many real-life bargaining situations in business and international relations. The question is, can the problem be solved and how?

There is certainly evidence that the problem can be solved in experimental situations. The first case study at the end of chapter reviews a series of studies by Loewenstein *et al.* (1993), Babcock *et al.* (1995), and Babcock, Loewenstein, and Issacharoff (1997) relating to legal situations where a plaintiff is suing a defendant for damages relating to an accident, with the legal costs to each party mounting as the case takes longer to settle. The authors find various ways in which the probability of settlement can be increased, for example by assigning the roles of plaintiff and defendant *after* the players have read the relevant information about the facts of a case.

It may be objected at this point that these results relate to experiments, not to field studies, and it is difficult, if not impossible, to apply the different protocols used to real-life situations. Obviously, plaintiffs and defendants in real legal cases do not get assigned roles after accidents and similar events have already occurred. However, there are certain policy implications arising from the Babcock, Loewenstein, and Issacharoff (1996) study, where subjects were asked to list weaknesses in their case. The resulting large increase in settlement rate suggests that mediation can be very useful in many situations, where mediators can point out all aspects of the case, including weaknesses overlooked by the different parties. They may also be able to suggest compromise solutions in complex situations, when there are many variables involved, that the principals in the transaction may not be able to envisage on their own. Certainly, organizations like the World Trade Organization and United Nations can play a role here in conflicts in international relations. Given recent perceived "failures" by both these institutions, it must be noted that the success of such organizations depends on the will of parties outside the main conflict to find a solution.

Structured bargaining

The general nature of the structure used in experiments has been for the players to alternate offers over a finite or infinite period. It is usually not advisable for a player to make two consecutive offers, since this tends to be viewed as a sign of weakness. There is also a cost of delay if an offer is rejected, since continued negotiations in reality tend to involve some kind of opportunity cost, such as lost profit and wages in an industrial dispute. A factor of major importance in the outcome of these situations is the discount rate/discount factor of each player. Players with lower discount rates (higher discount factors) have an advantage in such games, if discount rates are common knowledge, since they can afford to be more patient.

Since the 1980s, many experiments have been conducted using a number of variations in procedures: the most important variables have been the number of rounds of offers, the size of discount rate, and the relationship between the rates of the players. Initial experiments by Binmore, Shaked, and Sutton (1985) used a protocol that involved two two-round games, with a common discount factor (δ) of .25, and in the repetition of the game player 1 in the first game became player 2 in the second game. The results again indicated that there were two focal points: one involving a "fair" 50/50 split and another involving the SPNE of 75/25. This split is a SPNE since the pot of £1 was reduced to £0.25 in the second round of both games if player 1's initial offer was refused; thus it makes no sense (ignoring social preferences and reciprocity) for player 2 to refuse any offer above £0.25. Another notable finding was that in the second game initial offers shifted to the single focal point of the SPNE, suggesting a learning effect. It was suggested that player 1 in the second game, having experienced the situation of being player 2 in the first game, now realized that it made no sense to make an initial offer of more than £0.25. Further studies involving a similar kind of "role-reversal" protocol have indicated a similar learning effect, but not as rapid as in situation above.

A later study by Neelin, Sonnenschein, and Spiegel (1988) used an experimental protocol which involved two-round, three-round, and five-round alternating offer games, with common discount factors of 25%, 50%, and 34% respectively, and with the SPNE being $1.25 in each case. Although the study found that initial offers in the two-round game were heavily concentrated around the SPNE, initial offers in the three-round and five-round games were not. In all three types of game the initial offers tended to be concentrated around the size of the pie in the second round. This suggests that the subjects, as business and economics students, had learned about backward induction or had worked it out for themselves for one step, but were unable to apply the technique beyond this to determine the SPNE for three-round and five-round games.

Experiments by Ochs and Roth (1989) provided some evidence, though still weak, that transactions do approximately attain SPNE. The most important finding concerns counter-offers. Not only were these commonly refused in the second and third rounds, but they were frequently "disadvantageous." In other words a majority of players were making counter-offers that would leave them less well-off than if they had accepted the original offer. For example, it makes no sense to reject an offer of $3 out of a $10 pot if this rejection then reduces the size of the pot to $2.50 in the next round. Similarly, it makes no sense to reject the offer of $3 if the pot is then reduced to $3.50 and one makes the counter-offer of $1, since one would only gain $2.50 even if the counter-offer is accepted. There are two possible explanations for this phenomenon of disadvantageous counter-offers:

1. Players had social preferences that inclined them to reject unequal offers.
2. Players had limited computation abilities, failing to realize that rejecting an offer in one round would limit their gains to less than this in later rounds.

As stated earlier, the first explanation is discussed in the next chapter. There have been several studies investigating the second factor, and in particular the strength of the learning effect. Although the original study by Binmore, Shaked, and Sutton (1985) suggested a strong learning effect over just two games, later studies (Ochs and Roth 1989; Bolton 1991; Harrison and McCabe 1992; Carpenter 2000) indicated much slower or insignificant learning rates.

Camerer *et al.* (1994) and Johnson *et al.* (2002) have designed experiments to achieve two aims: (1) isolate social preferences by having players play against a computer; and (2) investigate the thinking processes of subjects by tracking their demands for information in the different rounds of the game. They have reported three main findings:

1. Players tend not to make equilibrium offers even when social preferences are not involved.
2. Players tend not to look ahead one or two periods to consider what will happen if an offer is rejected.
3. Players can learn to look ahead, using backward induction, if they are explicitly taught to do so, since this process appears not to occur naturally.

The experimental protocols discussed up to this point have all involved fixed-discounting games. Other studies have examined situations where there are fixed costs of delay. This situation may apply in legal cases or industrial disputes where costs are generally independent of the size of the pie. The most interesting finding here that has been consistently reported (Binmore, Shaked, and Sutton 1989; Rapoport, Weg, and Felsenthal 1990; Forsythe, Kennan, and Sopher 1991) is that divisions of the relevant pies tend to be very uneven, more in keeping with SPNE, unlike the frequent even splits in fixed-discounting games. The challenge for researchers is that social preferences should apply equally to each situation, so why the difference? More research needs to be conducted regarding learning in each situation; differences in learning may account for the observed disparity.

Bargaining with incomplete information

In many real-life situations the players have asymmetrical information, typically knowing more about their own payoffs than about those of the other player. For example, in auctions buyers know their own valuation of the item, but not often that of the seller, and vice versa. This makes the bargaining situation more complicated, since not only are players trying to maximize their utilities, but they are also aware that the offers and bids that they make and accept or reject convey information regarding their valuations that are often detrimental to their interests. However, once again we have two main aspects to consider: (1) how to organize these situations in terms of bargaining structure; and (2) how to determine solutions in terms of the kind of equilibrium that will prevail.

In terms of the first aspect, Valley *et al.* (2002) have found that communication improves the efficiency of trade. A trade is efficient if a transaction occurs when a buyer's valuation exceeds a seller's valuation. In typical sealed-bid mechanisms, where both parties submit a threshold price that they will trade at, trade will not be 100 % efficient, since both parties will tend to "shave" their bids according to the predictions of game theory. This means that buyers will bid less than their true valuation, while sellers will bid more than their true valuations. The crucial finding in the Valley *et al.* study was not so much the fact that communication improves trade efficiency, but the manner in which it does so. It appears that bargainers tend to coordinate on a single price that they will both bid. This coordination takes the form of "feeling each other out," searching for clues regarding the other player's valuation, while still maintaining a fair amount of bluffing as to their own valuation – we are not talking about mutual truth telling here for the most part. It also seems from this pioneering study that face-to-face communication is more successful at improving trade efficiency than written communication.

Solutions in terms of bidding tend to conform surprisingly well to game-theoretical predictions. The reason that this is surprising is that the predictions are hardly intuitive, as we shall see shortly. Most studies have focussed on the **sealed-bid mechanism**, or **bilateral call market**, as it is often referred to in financial markets. In this kind of market both buyers and sellers make sealed bids, and a transaction occurs at the halfway price if the buyer's bid exceeds that of the seller. If the buyer's bid (v) is below that of the seller (c), no transaction takes place. We will take an example used by Daniel, Seale, and Rapoport (1998). If the buyers' and sellers' valuations (V and C) are uniformly distributed over the space (0, 200) for the buyer and (0, 20) for the seller, the game-theoretic predictions will be as follows:

Sellers' bids will be a linear function of their valuations, according to the equation

$$c = 50 + 2/3C$$

Buyers' bids will follow a **piecewise linear** pattern. This means that, when drawn graphically, the function consists of three linear segments joined together. In mathematical terms, the buyer's predicted bidding pattern is shown below:

When $V \leq 50$, $v = V$
When $50 \leq V \leq 70$, $v = (50 + 2V)/3$
When $V > 70$, $v = 63.3$

These predictions suggest that sellers should ask a price much higher than their actual valuation or costs, while buyers should mostly make a flat bid of 63.3, as long as their valuation is at least 70; these predictions are both strong and counter-intuitive, making for a revealing empirical test. Although the empirical findings from the study by Daniel, Seale, and Rapoport (1998) do not indicate a sharp piecewise linearity in buyers' valuations, they do confirm the predictions in two main ways:

1. Buyers bid a smaller fraction of their valuations when their valuations are high.
2. Sellers mark up their costs very considerably.

The authors replicated these results, in terms of generally confirming game-theoretical predictions, when the parameters of the experiments were somewhat changed, for example with a larger range of sellers' valuations. They also found a significant learning effect in that buyers started by bidding too high and then after ten rounds learned to reduce their offers substantially.

7.5 Iterated games

Iteration and dominance

We have seen in the first section of the chapter that it is often easy to solve games with a dominant equilibrium, particularly if there are only two strategies available for each player in a two-player game. In more complex situations we can iterate to a dominant equilibrium by eliminating dominated strategies. We shall see that some situations can involve many steps of iteration, even an infinite number. The main objective here is to examine how players conduct iterations in different game situations, in particular how many steps they take, using empirical investigation; we can then draw certain conclusions regarding the underlying psychological mechanisms involved, particularly relating to beliefs about other players.

It is useful to start with a simple two-step game using an example from Beard and Beil (1994). They used a sequential game with two players, and by varying the payoffs in a number of ways, they were able to investigate how much player 1 was willing to bet on player 2 obeying dominance. The basic version of the game is shown in Figure 7.11.

Player 1 moves first, and if they move left that ends the game; they earn $9.75 for themselves and $3 for player 2. On the other hand, if player 1 moves right, player 2 then gets to move next. If they act in pure self-interest, they

Figure 7.11   Iterated dominance game

will also move right, earning $5 rather than $4.75 from moving left. This response will also earn $10 for player 1, which is slightly higher than the $9.75 they would receive if they had moved left at the start. Thus the iterated dominant equilibrium is (right, right). However, there is a risk to player 1 in playing right, since if player 2 does not obey dominance then they will only get $3.

In this baseline experiment 66 % of player 1s played left, showing a general mistrust of player 2. In the event this mistrust proved justified, since when player 1 played right, player 2 only responded by playing right 83 % of the time. This percentage means that the expected payoff for player 1 from playing right turned out to be only $(3 \times .17) + (10 \times .83) = \$8.81$, worse than the payoff from playing left.

The investigators then varied the payoffs as follows:

1. Less risk – lower payoff for player 1 moving left.
2. More assurance – lower payoff for player 2 if (right, left).
3. More resentment – higher payoff for player 2 if player 1 moves left.
4. Less risk, more reciprocity – higher payoff for player 1 if (right, left), and higher payoffs for player 2 if player moves right.

When there was less risk, more assurance, or more reciprocity for player 1, this increased the willingness to play right; when playing right created more resentment, they were less likely to play right. However, it was notable that in all the scenarios above player 2s always responded by playing right if player 1 had played right; in other words, player 2s obeyed dominance. This experiment leads to a general conclusion that has since been confirmed by many other studies: players tend to believe that other players are less likely to obey dominance than they actually are. On the basis of the experiment above there could be a number of explanations for this; for example, player 1s may have incorrect beliefs regarding the social preferences of player 2s.

However, this explanation tends to be ruled out by empirical findings from "beauty contest" games, described next.

Beauty contest games

The name for this revealing type of game originated with Keynes's *General Theory of Employment, Interest, and Money* in 1936. He likened investment on the stock market to a beauty contest where competitors have to pick out the prettiest faces, the prize being awarded to the competitor whose choice most nearly corresponds to the average preference of the competitors as a whole. As Keynes explained the situation,

> each competitor has to pick, not those faces which he himself finds prettiest, but those which he thinks likeliest to catch the fancy of the other competitors, all of whom are looking at the problem from the same point of view. It is not a case of choosing those which, to the best of one's judgment are really the prettiest, nor even those which average opinion genuinely thinks the prettiest. We have reached the third degree where we devote our intelligences to anticipating what average opinion expects the average opinion to be.

This situation can be easily modeled into a simple game for experimental purposes. The standard form of this game is to ask a group of players to select a number from 1 to 100. The winner is the player whose number is closest to a certain fraction (p), say 2/3, of the average of all the players. The purpose of the experiment is to examine how many rounds of iteration players perform. If players choose randomly or uniformly then the average will be 50, so 2/3 of this number gives 33. This choice reveals one step of reasoning. The second step is to reason that if other players use one-step reasoning and choose 33 then their best choice is 22. A third step would be to assume that other players use two steps and therefore choose 15. It can be seen that there are an infinite number of possible iterations in this game, and the resulting iterated dominant Nash equilibrium is 0. Nagel (1995) found that the average choice was about 35, with frequency "spikes" at 33 and 22. More comprehensive experiments were carried out by Ho, Camerer, and Weigelt (1998), confirming the general finding that players performed only one or two steps of iteration. Camerer (1997) found similar results with different types of subjects: psychology undergraduates, economics PhDs, portfolio managers, and CEOs. In field studies involving contests for readers of financial magazines offering substantial prizes, the results also tend to be similar, with spikes at 33 and 22, but with a somewhat lower average number. About 8 % of contestants chose the equilibrium of 0.

There are two possible conclusions from these experiments: either people are generally unable to iterate beyond a couple of steps, or they do not believe that other people are capable of doing so. In order to come to more definite conclusions we have to examine results from other games.

Iterations leading to decreased payoffs

A good example where further iteration reduces payoffs is a so-called **centi-pede** game. This is a sequential game involving two players and a repeated number of moves. At each move a player can take 80 % of a growing pie (leaving the other player with 20 %) and end the game, or they can "pass" and let the other player move, with the pie doubling with each move. This kind of game is also known as a **trust** game, since the players can benefit by trusting the other players, at least to some extent. Experiments were carried out with this game by McKelvey and Palfrey (1992) using an initial pie of $0.50 and four moves. A game tree for this game is shown in Figure 7.12.

If the players pass on all four moves, they end up with $6.40 and $1.60, a substantial improvement over the initial situation of $0.40 and $0.10. However, if we solve the game by backward induction, the dominant strategy at the last move is to take; the same is true at the second-to-last move, and so on right back to the first node. Thus the iterated dominant solution is to take at the first move. Passing at the first node would violate four steps of iterated dominance. We can see that this is a kind of game that "unravels," resulting in a PD-type of result, meaning one that is Pareto-dominated by passing on all moves. It also resembles PD in that self-interest causes a mistrust of cooperation by the other player.

So much for the theoretical equilibrium according to SGT. In practice, McKelvey and Palfrey found that the game tended not to unravel until toward the end. In 4-move games only 6–8 % of players took on the first move, with this percentage increasing at each node reaching 75–82 % on the last move. In 6-move games, where the end pie is 2^6 or 64 times the initial amount, only

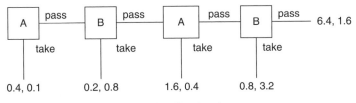

Figure 7.12 Centipede game

1 % or less of players took on the first move. Only with high stakes, and after learning through five trials, did the fraction of players taking at the first move increase significantly, to 22 %.

Similar results have been found in other experimental games that have a similar structure to the centipede game, for example multiple-strategy PD games. Experiments have also been conducted involving continuous strategies (like the beauty contest game), rather than discrete strategies, for example pricing in imperfect competition. In general, players tend to demonstrate two to four steps of iterated dominance in their initial choices.

A similar kind of unraveling effect was noted in the previous chapter, in relation to the dual-self model. When sophisticated consumers are aware that eventually they will most likely succumb to temptation of some kind, they may decide to give in now and indulge themselves. This is one situation where sophisticated consumers may end up worse off than naïve consumers, who may resist temptation for a while, being unable to predict that they will eventually give in.

Iterations leading to increased payoffs

In some games further iteration improves payoffs. A good example is the so-called **dirty faces** game, which has been posed as a riddle for many decades. In its original form (Littlewood 1953) there are three ladies, A, B and C, in a railway carriage, all of whom have dirty faces and all of whom are laughing. A then realizes from the reactions of her companions that she must be laughable. Her reasoning is that, if B saw that A's face was clean, she would infer that C was laughing at her, and therefore stop laughing. Since she is still laughing, this must mean that A's face is dirty. In this situation, A is assuming that B is sufficiently rational to draw inferences from the behavior of C.

This kind of situation can be modeled experimentally by constructing a game where players know the "types" of other players, but not their own type. Such an experiment was performed by Weber (2001). Players are of two types, X and O, with probabilities of .8 and .2. There are two possible strategies, Up or Down. An Up move gives no payoff to either type. A Down move gives a payoff of $1 to type X and −$5 to type O. Players take it in turn to move, and the game ends when one player plays Down. If players know nothing of their type, the expected payoff of playing Down is negative, so they should choose Up (assuming risk-neutrality). Being in state X is like having a dirty face, and playing Down is equivalent to knowing you have a dirty face. The players are commonly told that at least one of them is type X. If a player observes that the other player is O, they can infer immediately that they are type X and play Down on the first move. If a player observes that the other player is X, they cannot infer their own type on the first move of the game. They will both therefore play Up on the first move. This will then inform each player that the other has observed that they are type X. Therefore both players should play Down on the second move.

Weber observed that in the XO protocol 87% of the subjects displayed rationality, using one step of iterated reasoning. However, in the XX situation, only 53% of subjects played Down on the second move, using two steps of iterated reasoning. Camerer (2003) notes that the subjects in this experiment were Caltech students, who are selected for their skills at doing logic puzzles, so that this result of only about half of people performing two steps of iteration may be an upper bound in abstract games like this.

Behavioral conclusions

The results of the games like the "dirty faces" tend to indicate that the reason why people do not generally perform multiple iterations is not just that they doubt the ability of others to perform in this way; they often have "limited computability." However, to obtain really decisive evidence on this issue, experiments have to be performed which examine not just people's choices of strategy, but the decision rules that they use to arrive at such choices. Such experiments have been conducted by Stahl and Wilson (1995) and Costa-Gomes, Crawford, and Broseta (2001).

These experiments are similar in nature to those performed by Camerer (1994) and Johnson et al. (2002) described in the discussion of mixed strategy equilibrium, in that they require subjects to look at certain information in specific locations on a computer screen, thus revealing the information used and steps performed in arriving at decisions. Stahl and Wilson (1995) classified subjects into five main types:

1. Level-0 (choosing each strategy equally often).
2. Level-1 (assuming others are level-0 and best responding to them).
3. Level-2 (assuming others are level-1 and best responding to them).
4. Naïve Nash (assuming others will play Nash equilibrium).
5. Worldly Nash (assuming some others play Nash, but that others are level-1 or level-2).

The study estimated from using 12 different games that about 18 % of players were in the first category, 20 % in the second, only 2 % in the third, 17 % in the fourth, and 43 % in the fifth.

The study by Costa-Gomes, Crawford, and Broseta (2001) reported that 45 % of subjects were naïve, meaning choosing strategies with the highest average payoff, while many were classified as optimistic, meaning using a maximax strategy (maximizing their maximum payoff). They also noted that 10 % of subjects violated one step of iterated dominance, with this fraction rising to 35 % and 85 % for two and three steps.

Camerer, Ho, and Chong (2004) have proposed a **cognitive hierarchy theory**, which is based on both the theory and the empirical evidence in many of the studies described in this section. Their model proposes a Poisson frequency distribution to describe the proportions of players using different numbers of steps in thinking (K). The objective here was to provide a model which has both a sound psychological basis and a sound empirical basis in order to predict equilibrium conditions in iterated games. The model can also be used to predict initial situations for learning models. The model is parsimonious and easy to use, because the Poisson distribution involves only a single parameter: its mean and variance are identical (τ). Those players using 0 steps correspond to level-0 in the Stahl and Wilson classification; those using K steps anticipate the decisions of lower-step thinkers, and best respond to the mixture of those decisions using normalized frequencies. Empirical studies suggest that a value of τ around 1.5 is appropriate in many games. The authors have tested the model using first-period data from a large number of experimental games, and it has always predicted at least as well as the SGT Nash equilibrium. When the cognitive hierarchy model is compared with QRE, which also tends to predict better than Nash equilibrium, it has two main advantages: (1) it is more sophisticated in psychological terms; and (2) it has more empirical appeal, since it can account for probability "spikes" in choosing strategies that are often observed in experiments.

In summary, although patterns of iteration vary somewhat from game to game, people usually do not perform more than two or three steps of iterated dominance, where the elimination of one's own dominated strategies is counted as the first step. However, there is evidence from some experimental games, particularly more complex ones where people are far from equilibrium at first, that learning takes place and that they perform further iterations as successive rounds of the game take place (Rubinstein 1989). These learning aspects are discussed in the final section of the chapter.

7.6 Signaling

Nature and functions of signaling

Many types of game feature asymmetric information, where one player wants to convey information to the other player(s). Such information does not necessarily have to be true. Actions taken by players that are designed to influence the beliefs and behavior of other players in a way favorable to themselves are often referred to as **commitments** or **strategic moves**. In order to be effective these signals or strategic moves must have **credibility**. This characteristic requires two factors:

1. *Affordability by the signaler's type*
   Someone wanting to obtain a good job may want to signal that they are this "type" of person by investing in an expensive education or training program. A union striking for higher wages must be able to afford to go on strike, taking into consideration the foregone wages.

2. *Non-affordability by other types*
   A firm producing an inferior, unreliable product cannot afford to give a decent warranty for it. Thus good warranties are credible signals that products are of high quality. Profitable firms may use advertising as a signal of this type. Firms lacking a sound financial foundation may be unable to spend on advertising, so consumers may view advertising as a signal that a firm is well established.

Signaling is widely used, not just in situations commonly related to economics and business, but also in politics, international relations, sport, warfare, and biology. In general it may be used to achieve either competitive or cooperative objectives.

Signaling and competition

One of the most interesting aspects of signaling in a competitive context is that it may appear to be inefficient or self-defeating, since it limits the actions of the signaler. Some examples from the various fields mentioned above may help to illustrate the seemingly paradoxical nature of much signaling.

We have just observed that much advertising seems wasteful of a firm's resources, particularly if it is not directly aimed at increasing awareness or perceptions of the quality of the product advertised. A similar type of business activity, which may superficially seem to be against a firm's interests, is the use of a **Most Favored Customer Clause** (MFCC). Essentially, what this involves is a guarantee to customers that the firm will not charge a lower price to other customers for some period in the future; if it does, it will pay a rebate to existing customers for the amount of the price reduction, or sometimes double this amount. This is particularly important in consumer durable markets. The reason why this strategy is ingenious (and disingenuous) is that it serves a dual purpose:

1. Ostensibly, it creates good customer relations – many customers are concerned when they are considering buying a new consumer durable that the firm will reduce the price of the product later on. This applies particularly when there are rapid changes in technology and products are phased out over relatively short periods, like computers and other electronics products.

2. The MFCC creates a price commitment – it would be expensive for the firm to reduce price at a later stage, since it would have to pay rebates to all its previous customers. Thus other firms are convinced that the firm will maintain its price, and this causes prices to be higher than they would be without such commitment, contrary to consumer expectations.

In politics it is common for people to make statements like they will never raise taxes, or they will limit immigration. Of course it can always be maintained that talk is cheap, but politicians may have much to lose by reneging on such commitments, and making embarrassing U-turns, especially if the relevant policies form a major part of their electoral platform (their "type"). Their reputations may be irredeemably tarnished by such actions.

In the field of international relations, countries, or groups of countries, often try to influence other countries that are noncompliant in certain regards (like researching and building nuclear weapons), by imposing trade sanctions. These sanctions may hurt the countries imposing them, for example by reducing the availability of oil and increasing its price. On the other hand, if they hurt the noncompliant country more, they may be successful in forcing it to act in the intended manner. However, it is notable that in practice many sanctions have failed to achieve the intended response. When imposed against poor countries, like Iraq and Iran, they mainly affect the poor and can be transformed by dictatorial leaders into a different signal, meaning that the Western counties imposing them want to damage their welfare. It might be said that Western leaders in this situation are not using enough iterations of strategic thought.

Moving on to the field of sport, we can use an example from tennis that was described earlier in the discussion of mixed strategies. It was seen that a server who knows that their opponent's backhand is relatively weak will tend to serve in that direction more frequently (but not exclusively, since their moves then become predictable). If their opponent then improves their backhand with practice, in a later match this may be signaled by moving more to the backhand. The server's response is to serve more to the opponent's forehand, which is stronger. The nonintuitive conclusion can be generalized to other sporting (and non-sporting) situations: by improving our weak points we force our opponents to deal more with our strengths.

Some of the most dramatic examples of signaling come from the field of warfare. The example frequently given here is that of Cortes burning his boats when he invaded Mexico to conquer the Aztec empire. This drastic form of commitment had two effects. First, it caused his soldiers to fight harder than otherwise, since they knew that they had no alternative. The second effect involves a further iteration in strategic thought: the natives lost morale, since they knew that their enemy was now implacable and would not stop until they had either conquered their land or were completely wiped out.

Signaling also seems to play an important role in evolutionary biology. Biologists were stumped to find an evolutionary explanation for the peacock's tail, until Zahavi (1975) proposed the "**handicap principle**." The puzzle was that the lavish tail of the peacock was very expensive to maintain in terms of scarce resources; surely natural selection would eliminate such an extravagance? Zahavi proposed that the peacock's tail, by indeed being a handicap, served as a signal to potential mates that the owner must be very healthy, and therefore desirable, in order to be able to afford to maintain such an extravagance. This aspect of sexual selection has also attracted the attention of social scientists. Some have suggested that certain self-destructive habits of young people in particular, like smoking, binge drinking, doing drugs, or reckless driving, may also be interpreted as a similar signal; only "hard," and therefore desirable, individuals can maintain such habits.

It should be noted at this stage that not all signals involve commitments of the type illustrated here. We shall see in the next section that signals can also be used to ensure coordination and cooperation.

Signaling and cooperation

Many games involve more than one equilibrium, as we have seen in the section on mixed strategies. Even PD situations, when repeated under certain conditions, may give rise to different equilibrium strategies. In terms of everyday situations, one of the most simple is determining which side of the road to drive on. The original situation here must have arisen thousands of years ago, with people driving wagons along trails. Obviously there are two possible equilibria, left or right for both players, with roughly equal payoffs in each case. There are a number of stories which claim to explain the origin of driving on one side or the other. In the United States, for example, the fact that wagon-drivers held whips mainly in their right hand may have caused a preference for driving on the right to avoid hitting passers-by. In the United Kingdom, the prevalent practice of mounting one's horse from the left side may have accounted for the opposite equilibrium being selected.

What these examples demonstrate is that different equilibria may offer different payoffs, with one being preferred over the other in terms of favoring both players. However, there is no principle (like dominance or iterated dominance) that guarantees the attainment of the favorable equilibrium. This situation is modeled by the stylized "**stag hunt**" game, which is described in Figure 7.13.

The essence of this game is that hunting a stag successfully requires the coordination of two hunters. Success brings a big payoff, but hunting stag is risky, since if the other hunter does not cooperate, the payoff is zero. Hunting rabbit is safer, since this can be done on one's own, and one is guaranteed a payoff of one. There are two Nash equilibria in this game: both hunters hunt stag, or both hunters hunt rabbit. Hunting stag is clearly preferred by both, since it is Pareto-dominant. However, the hunters may be risk-averse, pursuing the maximin or **risk-dominant strategy** of hunting rabbit. A risk-dominant strategy is defined as one that minimizes joint risk, measured by the product of the cost of deviations by other players to any one player who does not deviate (Harsanyi and Selten 1988). In the example above, if a hunter plays stag and the other hunter deviates and plays rabbit, the cost to the hunter not deviating is 2. The same applies if the roles are reversed, so the joint risk of the stag–stag strategy is 4. If both hunters hunt rabbit, there is no cost to deviation and therefore zero joint risk.

When empirical tests have been performed in stag-hunt situations, it appears that people tend to be risk-averse. In experiments by Cooper *et al.* (1990),

| | | Hunter B | |
		Stag	Rabbit
Hunter A	Stag	2, 2	0, 1
	Rabbit	1, 0	1, 1

Figure 7.13 Stag hunt game

97 % of players played the inefficient equilibrium, with no players going for the efficient one. It should be noted that in this experiment the efficient equilibrium only gave a payoff of 25 % more for the efficient equilibrium, not 100 % more, as in the example in Figure 7.13. Increasing the difference in payoffs may change the results significantly, but the author is not aware of any experiments with efficient equilibria awarding payoffs in the order of twice the inefficient payoffs.

The only way that the preferred equilibrium can be reached (ignoring outside options) is by signaling. The Cooper *et al.* study found that signaling by just one player, in effect allowing them to indicate that they intended to play stag, resulted in an increase in the number of players playing the payoff-dominant equilibrium from 0 % to 55 %. When both players were allowed to signal, this fraction increased to 91 %.

A note of caution is necessary here regarding the benefits of signaling for the purposes of coordination in cooperative games. Two-way communication does not always improve payoffs compared with one-way communication in games with more than one equilibrium. In Battles of the Sexes (BOS) games the key difference in the structure of the game compared with "stag hunt" is that preferences are asymmetrical. Players again want to match strategies, for example by both going to the ballet or both watching boxing, but each player has a different preference. Cooper *et al.* (1990; 1994) found that, without signaling, players mismatched strategies 59 % of the time. One-way signaling allowed one player to indicate that they would play their preference, and this reduced mismatching to just 4 %. However, when both players signaled, there was a conflict as both indicated their different preferences, resulting in mismatching rising back up to a 42 % rate.

Empirical findings from signaling games

Many signaling games are complex in structure compared to the games so far discussed. This is because, in competitive situations, at least one player has a type, and some players want to reveal their type while others want to hide it. Other players must try to guess this type from the actions of these players, using iterated thinking. A relatively simple illustration is where an employee is hired by an employer. The employee knows their type in terms of whether they are a high productivity (H) worker or a low productivity (L) worker, but the employer cannot observe this directly. At the start the employer is only able to use **prior probabilities** of each type occurring based on past experience. For example, there may be a 50/50 chance of the employee being either H or L. During their employment workers may put in varying degrees of effort (E). The employer has to judge the type of worker from the amount of effort that they put in, using effort, which they can observe, as a signal of productivity. An employer can use this information regarding effort to revise the prior probabilities, a process known as **Bayesian updating**. Employers sack workers whom they perceive to be L, but to do this they have to monitor workers, which is costly. L workers may put in more costly effort in order to persuade the employer that they are really of the H type. In turn, H workers may work harder than otherwise in order to distinguish themselves from the L workers, increasing their effort to a level that is unsustainable or too costly for the L workers.

In general, equilibria in these situations are often referred to as **pooling equilibria** or **separating equilibria**. A pooling equilibrium occurs when the different types make the same move; for example, if both types of worker put in the same effort and then it becomes impossible for the other player to detect type. A separating equilibrium occurs if different types make different moves, in this case putting in different amounts of effort. It may be too costly for L workers to exert a lot of effort, but not for H workers, who may find it worthwhile to put in the extra effort to distinguish or separate themselves from the L type. An example of experiments related to monopoly and new firm entry is given in Case 7.2, relating to a situation modeled by Cooper, Garvin, and Kagel (1997a, b). These experiments manipulated the payoff variables for both the new entrant and the monopolists in order to examine how this would affect the type of equilibrium observed.

We can see from these experiments that separating equilibria are more likely when dominance violation prevents one type from successfully imitating the move of another type. In this case, high-cost monopolists found it unprofitable to produce as much output as low-cost monopolists. However, it does take some time for the low-cost monopolists to learn to produce more output than they would otherwise do, because of the iterations involved. Similar experiments, for example those by Camerer and Weigelt (1988) on trust and reputation and by Chaudhuri (1998) on production quotas and ratchet effects, also indicate the importance of learning processes, as players take time to adjust their beliefs and behavior. Furthermore, they do not always do so in the optimal direction, or by the same extent as is predicted by theory. We therefore now need to examine these learning processes.

7.7 Learning

Learning and game theory

We have seen that learning, meaning changing behavior through experience, occurs in many different types of game, although it is ignored by SGT. However, up to this point we have been examining behavior in these different classes of game in order to draw conclusions about empirical behavior. This involves studying game behavior for its own sake, as an end in itself. For example, we have examined stag hunt and BOS games in order to see how people coordinate their behavior and cooperate. The objective at this final stage is different. We want to use games in general, rather than a particular class of games, as a means to an end: the fitting and testing of different models of learning. In this situation we are not so much concerned with the observation that, for example, people tend to form a separating equilibrium in the monopoly/entry game under certain conditions. Instead, we are interested in how this observation sheds light on different models of learning.

Learning theories and models

Many different theories of learning have been proposed over the years. These include evolutionary dynamics, reinforcement learning, belief learning, anticipatory (sophisticated) learning, imitation, direction learning, rule learning, and experience-weighted attraction (EWA) learning. Although all of these will be described to some extent, and the relationships between them explained, we will focus attention on four main classes of learning theory: reinforcement learning, belief learning, EWA, and rule learning.

Most learning models involve the concept of "**attraction**." Strategies are evaluated according to certain criteria discussed shortly to calculate attraction values which are updated in response to experience. Learning models differ in terms of the basis of these criteria or elements of attraction. It is helpful at this stage to introduce some notation regarding these elements. It is assumed here for simplicity that other players all use the same strategy as each other, for example the kth strategy; otherwise s_{-i} is a vector.

$$s_i^j = \text{the } j\text{th strategy (out of } m_i \text{ strategies) of player } i$$
$$s_{-i}^k = \text{the } k\text{th strategy (out of } n_i \text{ strategies) of other players}$$
$$s_i(t) = \text{the actual strategy chosen by player } i \text{ in period } t$$
$$s_{-i}(t) = \text{the actual strategy chosen by other players in period } t$$
$$\pi_i(s_i^j s_{-i}^k) = \text{the payoff to player } i \text{ from playing } s_i^j \text{ when others played } s_{-i}^k$$
$$b_i(s_{-i}(t)) = \text{player } i\text{'s best response to the other players' strategies in period } t$$

We can now move on to describing these elements of attraction, using the stag hunt game from Figure 7.13 for illustration. There are seven pieces of information that may be relevant in different learning models; it is assumed in this example that Player i is A and that they decide to hunt stag while the other player B hunts rabbit:

1. i's choice $\quad\quad\quad\quad$ $s_i(t)$ $\quad\quad\quad\quad\quad\quad$ hunt stag (S)
2. $-i$'s choice $\quad\quad\quad\quad$ $s_{-i}(t)$ $\quad\quad\quad\quad\quad\quad$ hunt rabbit
3. i's received payoff $\quad$ $\pi_i(s_i(t), s_{-i}(t))$ $\quad\quad$ 0
4. i's foregone payoff $\quad$ $\pi_i(s_i^j, s_{-i}(t))$ $\quad\quad$ 1
5. i's best response $\quad$ $b_i(s_{-i}(t))$ $\quad\quad\quad\quad$ hunt rabbit
6. $-i$'s received payoff $\quad$ $\pi_{-i}(s_i(t), s_{-i}(t))$ $\quad$ 1
7. $-i$'s foregone payoff $\quad$ $\pi_{-i}(s_i(t), s_{-i}^k)$ $\quad\quad$ 1

Camerer (2003) illustrates how these elements form the basis of attraction for different strategies according to different learning models in a very useful table, reproduced as Table 7.1.

This table clearly and concisely indicates the relevant elements in each learning theory, and allows easy comparisons between the different models. For example, we can now say that the attraction of the strategy of hunting stag before period $t+1$, according to **reinforcement theory**, can be represented as,

$$A_S(t) = f\{s_i(t), \pi_i[s_i(t), s_{-i}(t)]\} \quad\quad\quad (7.14)$$

while according to **belief learning theory**

$$A_S(t) = f\{s_{-i}(t), \pi_i[s_i(t), s_{-i}(t)], \pi_i[s_i^j, s_{-i}(t)]\} \quad\quad\quad (7.15)$$

The differences between these different theories of learning are described shortly.

Table 7.1 Information requirements for different learning theories

Information	Reinforcement	Beliefs	EWA	Sophistication	Direction Learning	Imitate Average	Imitate Best
i's choice	X		X		X		
$-i$'s choice		X	X	X		X	X
i's received payoff	X	X	X				
i's foregone payoff		X	X	X			
$-i$'s best response					X		
$-i$'s received payoff				X			X
i's foregone payoff				X			

Unfortunately, this is where the easy part ends. In order to estimate a particular learning model, the attractions have to be mapped into probabilities of choosing different strategies using some statistical rule, usually involving a fairly complex mathematical function like "logit." An explanation of this process goes beyond the scope of this book, but further details are given in Camerer's (2003) excellent book *Behavioral Game Theory: Experiments in Strategic Interaction.*

All the models are intuitively plausible in general terms, so the next issue concerns the testing of models against each other in empirical terms. This can be done in several ways:

1. *Direct testing*
   Subjects can be asked what types of information they use in making strategy decisions.

2. *Indirect testing*
   Experiments can be set up, using computer formats, to observe what information people use.

3. *Statistical testing*
   This involves using statistical techniques like logit regression and MLE to find models that both fit the data best and make the most accurate predictions. These two desirable criteria do not necessarily go together, as we will see in the discussion of EWA.

Each of these kinds of test will be considered in comparing the different models, which can now be explained in more detail.

Reinforcement learning

This theory became popular as an essential component of the behaviorism movement in psychology in the 1920s, being associated with the figures of Watson, Pavlov, and Skinner. This extreme view of human nature dominated the field until the 1960s. Since then it has largely become discredited because the theory fails all the tests described above.

As can be seen from Table 7.1, reinforcement learning theories propose that subjects use very little information in making strategy choices, just their own previous choices, and the resulting payoffs. While such behavior may occur in many non-human animals, various empirical studies have indicated that people use further information than this relating to other elements in the table.

As far as statistical tests are concerned, reinforcement models may predict the direction of learning correctly, but are usually too slow to match the pace of human learning. This is because in many situations, both in experiments and in real life, there is little reinforcement. Reinforcement can only occur if a subject chooses a good strategy (like a dog responding to the sound of a dinner bell); when a bad strategy is chosen, the subject is left searching for a better one with little guidance. Even if a good strategy is selected, this may still be suboptimal, but the subject has no indication of this.

Belief learning

Well-known examples of belief learning in economics go back to Cournot's model of oligopoly in 1835, described earlier. The Bertrand (1883) and von Stackelberg (1934) models of oligopoly are also early examples, and all these oligopoly models feature a best response to behavior observed in the previous period. Thus we have seen that equilibrium in the Cournot case is frequently referred to as a Cournot–Nash equilibrium. In the 1950s, models featuring **fictitious play** were proposed (Brown 1951; Robinson 1951). In fictitious play, players keep track of the relative frequencies with which other players play different strategies over time. These relative frequencies then lead to beliefs about what other players will do in the next period. Players then calculate expected payoffs for each strategy based on these beliefs, and choose strategies with higher expected payoffs more frequently. The basic fictitious play model weights all past observations equally, but more recent variations of the model give different weights to past observations, reducing weights for observations further back in time. The Cournot model is at the extreme end of this spectrum, where only the most recent observation is taken into consideration. A more recent variation of belief learning has been proposed by Jordan (1991), and involves **Bayesian learning**. In this scenario, players are uncertain regarding the payoffs of other players, but have prior probabilities which are updated over time regarding which payoff matrix the other players are using.

As far as empirical testing is concerned, direct measures of the information used by subjects indicate that fictitious play does not explain learning well. Nyarko and Schotter (2002) showed that stated beliefs often deviated from those proposed by fictitious play, even though fictitious play predicts behavior by other players more accurately than the beliefs stated by the experimental subjects. The predictions of the Jordan model have also been tested, with mixed results. The model appears to predict well in a simple situation, but is unlikely to perform well in more complex games. It is difficult to draw definite conclusions in comparing the merits of reinforcement learning compared with belief learning. Different studies have favored different models, and results depend on the type of game used, the precise specification of the learning model used, and the econometric methods used to test goodness of fit and prediction.

Experience-weighted attraction learning

This model was introduced by Camerer and Ho (1999a, b) in response to the perceived weaknesses of both the reinforcement and the belief learning models. The most obvious problems were that reinforcement learning models assumed players ignored information about foregone payoffs, while belief learning models assumed players ignored information about what they had chosen in the past. Since empirical testing indicated that players seem to use both types of information, the EWA model was created as a hybrid to take into account all the relevant information.

The EWA model is therefore mathematically complex in its construction, containing four parameters. These parameters relate to the following:

1. the weight placed on foregone payoffs;
2. the decay of previous attractions (due to forgetting or being given less importance as the environment changes);
3. the rate at which attractions grow, which affects the spread of choice probabilities for different strategies;
4. the strength of initial attractions, which depends on prior beliefs. This is updated in Bayesian fashion.

It goes outside the scope of this book to describe the details of the EWA model, and the interested reader is directed to the original papers and to Camerer (2003).

When it comes to empirical testing, statistical analysis involving 31 data sets has shown that EWA is generally superior in terms of goodness of fit compared with either reinforcement learning or the weighted fictitious play version of belief learning (Camerer, Ho, and Chong 2002). The model has been criticized as being unnecessarily complex and including so many parameters that it was bound to fit data better than other models; however, these criticisms ignore the three main strengths of the model:

1. The EWA parameters are not really additional to those in other models. Other models simply implicitly assume certain values for these parameters.
2. The EWA model illustrates the relationship between the reinforcement and the belief learning models. By letting certain parameters take on extreme values, EWA can become identical with these models.

3. The EWA model not only has a better fit, but also predicts better (in 80–95 % of the studies where comparisons have been made). It is often assumed that these two criteria for a good theory go together, but this is not necessarily true. It is an important point in statistical analysis that the incorporation of additional parameters in a model can improve goodness of fit. However, the ultimate test of the model is **out-of-sample prediction**. It has been shown in a number of studies that models with better fit do not necessarily produce better out-of-sample prediction. The rule used by Camerer, Ho, and Chong (2002), which is fairly common, is to use only 70 % of the data for estimating goodness of fit (assuming this allows sufficient degrees of freedom). Then the resulting model based on the 70 % sample is tested for goodness of prediction against the remaining 30 % of the data.

Rule learning

The learning models proposed so far all involve a single "rule" and sticking to it. Stahl (1996; 1999a, b; 2000a, b) has proposed a model, again a hybrid, that allows people to switch from one rule to another, depending on how these rules perform. A rule is essentially a way of weighting various pieces of evidence, relating to the seven elements of information described in Table 7.1. These rules in turn determine strategies, and the probability that a strategy is played depends on the weight attached to a particular rule; these weights are updated according to how each rule performs over time.

Like EWA, this is a complex, multi-parameter model that is difficult to estimate econometrically. However, it does have a sound psychological basis, and is very flexible. Stahl has shown that, in terms of predicting relative frequencies of choices in a population, rule learning predicts better than other models, including EWA (again using out-of-sample methods).

Conclusions regarding learning theory

The SGT does not take learning into consideration at all. This means that the equilibrium predicted by SGT does not involve any change in strategies over time as a game is played repeatedly. This prediction provides a benchmark for comparison of learning models, albeit one that should not be difficult to improve on. Indeed, Stahl (2001) has shown that all the models discussed in this section predict considerably better than the standard equilibrium model. As might be expected, the learning models that fit and predict better tend to be more complex, incorporating more information and more parameters. Empirical results are difficult to compare, since different models perform differently in different games. For example, reinforcement models tend to do better than belief models in simple MSE games, but belief learning models perform better in coordination games, market games, and iteration games. Good learning models should be flexible enough to perform well in terms of fit and prediction on a universal basis. In view of this problem, Camerer (2003) suggests three main challenges for learning theory in the future:

1. Models should allow for **sophistication**. This means they should take into account that players understand how other players learn; in turn this involves taking into account the last two elements of information in Table 7.1, the actual and foregone payoffs of other players.

2. Models should allow for incomplete information regarding foregone payoffs. This again requires greater complexity.

3. Models should allow a greater range of possible strategies, combined with some algorithm for reducing these to a feasible number for comparison purposes. The determination of an appropriate algorithm poses a major challenge, since it relies on research from neuroscience. An example of such an algorithm is the "somatic marker" hypothesis proposed by Damasio (1994).

7.8 Summary

- The SGT involves three main assumptions: (1) people are motivated purely by self-interest; (2) people have unbounded rationality; and (3) equilibria are reached instantly, since there are no time lags due to learning effects or other factors. BGT relaxes all three of these assumptions.

- Simultaneous games can be represented in normal form, as matrices, while sequential games are best represented in extensive form, in a game tree.

- There are various forms of equilibrium that may be found in games: dominant equilibrium, iterated dominant equilibrium, Nash equilibrium, SPNE, and MSE.

- MSE means that players randomize between different strategies in response to a given strategy of an opponent; the objective is to avoid predictability.

- Empirical studies indicate that people make certain general errors in randomization: they generate too many runs in a sequence, alternate too frequently, and generate samples that are too balanced. The representativeness heuristic may be largely responsible for this.

- QRE means that players do not choose the best response with certainty, as is the case with other equilibria, but "better respond" instead, meaning that they choose better strategies with higher probabilities.
- Focal points are outcomes in bargaining where the players tend to settle. If a game has multiple focal points the probability of disagreement is much greater.
- In bargaining games involving iteration, it is observed that people display social preferences and limited ability to look ahead. Both factors cause departures from SGT equilibrium.
- In games involving iteration, players do not often perform more than two steps of iteration; they also tend to believe that other players perform less iterations than they do, suggesting self-serving bias.
- The cognitive hierarchy theory may provide the best model of initial equilibrium in games involving iterations, in terms of both psychological and empirical foundation.
- Signaling may be used in both competitive and cooperative situations.
- Signals must be both affordable by the signaler and non-affordable by other types in order to be credible.
- Signals in competitive situations may be counterintuitive in nature, restricting the player's possible future moves.
- In cooperative situations, like the stag hunt game, the Pareto-dominant equilibrium (both players hunting stag) may be deemed inferior to the risk-dominant equilibrium (both players hunting rabbit).
- Empirical studies indicate that signaling serves a vital role in helping to achieve the Pareto-dominant equilibrium.
- A pooling equilibrium means that different types of player pool together and settle on the same strategy, as "inferior" types try to hide their type; a separating equilibrium means that the different types will settle at different focal points, allowing the other player to distinguish between types and adjust strategy accordingly.
- There are a variety of different learning theories and models: reinforcement learning, belief learning, EWA learning, and rule learning are the main types.
- More complex models, like EWA and rule learning, tend to both fit empirical data better and predict better out-of-sample. However, at present there are problems comparing different models, in particular because they tend to perform differently in different types of game situation.

7.9 Applications

Case 7.1   Bargaining and self-serving bias

In much of the literature on bargaining, failure to reach agreement has often been put down to the problem of incomplete or asymmetric information. The resulting uncertainty was alleged to cause bargaining impasse, since bargainers used costly delay as a signaling device regarding their own reservation values (Kennan and Wilson 1990; Cramton 1992). This theory is difficult to test in terms of field studies, and experimental studies have proved difficult because of problems in controlling aspects of the experimental environment.

Loewenstein *et al.* (1993), Babcock *et al.* (1995), and Babcock, Loewenstein, and Issacharoff (1996) have proposed a different theory regarding failure to reach agreement. This theory relates to the existence of self-serving bias, where subjects conflate what is fair with their own self-interest. They have conducted various experiments relating to legal situations where a plaintiff is suing a defendant for damages. They developed a tort case based on a trial in Texas, in which an injured motorcyclist sued the driver of the car that collided with him for $100 000.

In the first experiment, subjects were randomly assigned the roles of plaintiff and defendant. They then had the experiment explained to them, along with the rules of negotiation and the costs of failing to reach agreement. Both subjects were then given 27 pages of materials from the original legal case, including witness testimony, police reports, maps, and the testimony of the parties. Subjects were informed that the identical materials had been given to a judge in Texas, who reached a judgment between $0 and $100 000 in terms of compensation.

Before negotiation, the subjects were asked to guess the damages awarded, with the incentive of a monetary bonus if their guess was within $5000 of the actual amount. They were also asked to state what they considered a fair amount of compensation for an out-of-court settlement. None of this information was available to the other party. Subjects were then allowed to negotiate for 30 minutes, with the legal costs to each party mounting as the case took longer to settle, at the rate of $5000 for every 5 minutes' delay. If no agreement was reached after 30 minutes, the judge's decision determined the plaintiff's compensation.

Apart from being paid a fixed fee for participation, the 160 student subjects received additional rewards according to the bargaining outcome, with $1 corresponding to each $10 000 of outcome.

Under normal negotiation conditions, where pairs of players are assigned roles as either plaintiff or defendant from the outset before reading the details of the case, there was a large average difference in estimates of damages, with plaintiffs estimating the judge's award to be about $14 500 higher than defendants. However, this study did not itself demonstrate self-serving bias, since other factors might possibly have caused the discrepancy. Therefore a second study, by Babcock *et al.* (1995), varied the protocol. In this experiment there were two groups of subjects. The first group acted as a control group; roles were again randomly assigned, and the subjects had the same instructions as in the first experiment. The estimates of the judge's award were even further apart than in the first experiment, averaging

---

Case 7.1 *continued*

about $18 500. Furthermore, 28 % of the pairs of bargainers failed to reach agreement. In the second group, the roles of the subjects were only assigned *after* they had read all the case materials. This had a dramatic effect on outcomes: estimate of the judge's award now varied by an average of less than $7000, and only 6 % of the subjects failed to reach agreement.

This second study, therefore, demonstrated that self-serving bias occurs in the encoding of information; other studies have confirmed this process, as bias causes people to ignore information that is not favorable to their interests.

Babcock, Loewenstein, and Issacharoff (1996) found another way of removing self-serving bias in the above situation. After the players were assigned roles and had read the case information, they were told about the possibility of bias and asked to list weaknesses in their position. Again the results were quite dramatic: there was no significant difference in the estimates of damages by both sides; 96 % of the pairs settled, and settled more quickly than in either of the previously described protocols.

Questions

1. What other factors might improve settlement rates in the type of legal dispute described above? Suggest other experimental protocols that might be used to investigate these factors.
2. Self-serving bias has sometimes been called the opposite: "self-defeating" bias. Why?
3. What might be the role of self-serving bias in evolutionary terms, bearing in mind that it can be self-defeating?

Case 7.2 Market entry in monopoly

Cooper, Garvin, and Kagel (1997a) performed an interesting and revealing study of market entry in a monopolistic situation. In their experiment, monopolists were classified into two types: high-cost (*H*) and low-cost (*L*). A potential entrant was considering entry, but did not know the monopolist's type. The game was a simple sequential game, with the monopolists moving first by determining output, and then the potential entrant moved by deciding whether or not to enter.

The study was performed in China, using both students and factory managers as subjects, and it was therefore able to use high stakes (in terms of domestic purchasing power) as an incentive to improve performance and thus obtain reliable results. The game was repeated over a number of periods and cycles in order to gain some insight into the learning process.

Monopolists moved by determining an output in the range of 1–7 units. *H* firms maximized profit at the output of 2 units and made losses if output exceeded 5 units, regardless of whether the other firm entered. L firms maximized profit at 4 units, and continued to make profit up to the maximum output. Profits were obviously much higher for both H and L firms if the other firm did not enter. For entrants there were two different playing protocols. In the first one low payoff (LP), payoffs from entering were generally lower, and the expected value of entry (based on the prior probability of the monopolist being H of .5) was less than the payoff from staying out. In the second protocol high payoff (HP), payoffs were generally higher for the entrant, and the expected value of entry based on prior probabilities was greater than the payoff from staying out.

In both protocols the monopolist moves first, determining output. A high output in the initial move acts as a signal that the monopoly is of the L type, and therefore the other firm should stay out in order to maximize its own payoff. This signal is obviously more costly for H firms than for L firms, but there is some incentive for H firms to hide their type and aim for a pooling equilibrium, where E cannot see what type of firm the monopolist is. If E cannot distinguish between the two types of monopolist, he is forced to use prior probabilities, and in the LP protocol this will deter E from entry (based on expected values), giving greater payoffs to both H and L firms.

According to SGT, there are several equilibria in the LP protocol. There are two pure-strategy separating equilibria, where H produces an output of 2, while L produces either 6 or 7, deterring entry. There are also several pooling equilibria, with both H and L types producing the same output, any level from 1 to 5. In this case, since E cannot observe type, they are deterred from entry, as explained above.

In the HP protocol the SGT equilibrium is different, since it now becomes profitable for L firms to produce 6 or 7 units, an unprofitable output for H firms, resulting in a separating equilibrium. The higher output is necessary to convince E that they are indeed low-cost firms and that entry is therefore not worthwhile. In this situation there are also several partial pooling equilibria where the H and L types do not make exactly the same choices, but the sets of choices they sometimes make overlap.

In a second version of the experiment (Cooper, Garvin, and Kagel 1997b), the payoffs of H firms at outputs of 6 and 7 were increased so that they were still positive at the highest levels of output instead of making losses as previously. This made it more difficult for L firms to give a credible signal and separate, and therefore more difficult for E firms to decide whether or not to enter. The objective here was to see how the rate of convergence and the learning rate would be affected; they were predicted to be slower than in the first experiment.

A number of important empirical findings emerged from both of these experiments:

1. Players played as "myopic maximizers" at the start, maximizing payoffs without regard to how their opponent would perceive this action. This applied in both protocols.

2. In the first LP protocol, H players soon learned to increase output to conceal their type, leading to a pooling equilibrium at the output of 4 units. By the end of all the sessions nearly 70% of the H players settled on this output, and nearly all the L players. Only 6% of potential entrants entered.

Case 7.2 *continued*

3. In the second HP protocol, *H* players again learned to increase their output from 2 to 4 units to try to pool with the *L* players. However, the *L* players then gradually learned to increase their own output to 6 units, to separate themselves from the *H* players, who could not make a profit at such a high output. By the end of the game there was essentially a separated equilibrium, with 80 % of *L* players producing 6 units, and nearly half the *H* players producing 2 units. However, there was another spike of *H* players, with 32 % of them still trying to conceal their type by producing 4 units. This turned out to be a failed strategy, since all the *E* players entered at all outputs up to and including 5 units.

4. In the second experiment, not only was convergence slower, as predicted, but there was no real pattern of convergence at all. *H* players tended to average an output of 3 throughout the periods, while *L* players usually produced 4 units, with a gradual upward trend. The result was a partial pooling equilibrium with overlapping outcomes. Instead of all *E* players entering at the output of 4, as in the first experiment, only 72 % entered at this output, as it became more difficult for *E* players to observe type.

5. When steps of iterated dominance are explained to the subjects, the rate of equilibration is faster.

Questions

1. How do the empirical findings from the experiments compare with the predictions of SGT? What new light do they add to our knowledge of game behavior?

2. Explain what is meant by a credible signal, using the experiments as an illustration.

3. Explain the relationship between iteration and learning in the context of these experiments.

8 Fairness and Social Preferences

8.1 The standard economic model

Nature

As with other aspects of economic behavior discussed in previous chapters, our starting point is the SEM and its shortcomings. In the case of social preferences and fairness the key assumption in the SEM is that economic agents are motivated purely by self-interest. Indeed, the SEM is often referred to as a self-interest model. As we will discuss in the next chapter, this assumption is closely related to the rationality assumption. Advocates of this model tend to agree with an often-quoted statement by Stigler (1981):

> when self-interest and ethical values with wide verbal allegiance are in conflict, much of the time, most of the time in fact, self-interest theory . . . will win.

Behavioral economists, for example Fehr and Gächter (2001), tend to take issue with this stance, appealing to a large amount of evidence for reciprocity. Before we begin to consider the meaning of reciprocity and any related evidence, however, it is necessary to clarify one fundamental and often overlooked point in the burgeoning literature relating to this alleged conflict. "Pure" self-interest models are in many ways a straw man; they represent a simplified situation which is easy to model and apply in a similar way to the model of pure competition. It is this simplicity which makes the model attractive, not its realism, since only pathological individuals have no consideration for the effects of their behavior on others. Furthermore, such individuals, while motivated by pure self-interest, are extremely unlikely to achieve their objectives, because they alienate others. All normal individuals, even those we would describe as "selfish," take into account the effects of their behavior on others to some extent. As we shall see, this "taking into account" may not be deliberate, but be a result of emotions such as guilt, anger, envy, pity, outrage, or even disgust. It is important to understand that *all* behavioral models are essentially extensions of the self-interest model, not negations of it, in the same way that some intertemporal choice models extend and modify the instantaneous utility function. The analogy is a close one, since the pure self-interest model assumes that people maximize utility functions that are not affected by the utility of others, whereas behavioral models modify this utility function to take into account social preferences. We shall return to this point a number of times in this chapter, since it is the cause of a number of confusions.

Anomalies

There is an impressive list of anomalies relating to the "self-interest" aspect of the SEM, which arise both from field studies and from experiments. The following examples give some flavor to the kinds of behavior that will be examined in the course of the chapter:

- tipping waiters;
- giving to charity;
- voting;
- completing tax returns honestly;
- voluntary unpaid work;
- working harder when there are no monetary incentives than when there are monetary incentives;
- firms laying off workers in a recession rather than cutting wages;
- monopolies not raising prices when there are shortages;
- contributing to the provision of public goods;
- punishing "free riders" even when there is a cost in doing so;
- cooperating in prisoner's dilemma (PD) games;
- investing in others, and trusting them to repay;
- making generous offers in ultimatum bargaining games; and
- rejecting ungenerous offers in ultimatum bargaining games.

These anomalies relate to aspects of behavior that can be described as either **altruistic** or **spiteful**. While altruism can be defined in many ways, some of which will be examined later, a basic definition is that it relates to behavior which confers a benefit to others, while involving a cost to the originator of the behavior, with no corresponding material benefit. Tipping waiters at restaurants where one is unlikely to return is an example. Spiteful behavior can be viewed as the flip side of altruistic behavior. This is behavior that imposes a cost on others, while also involving a cost to the originator of the behavior, with no corresponding material benefit. An example is punishing those who throw litter out of their car by yelling at them (the cost may be small in terms of effort, but there is a risk of a hostile altercation). It should be noted that spiteful behavior is not necessarily bad for society; in the above example it may help to enforce valued social norms. It is notable that both altruistic behavior and spiteful behavior involve benefits that are nonmaterial, or psychological. Case 1.3 gave an illustration of this. We will see, as in that case, that neuroeconomic studies are particularly revealing in understanding this kind of behavior.

It can also be seen that a number of the anomalies above relate to games, some of which were discussed in the previous chapter. As we saw, games in this context refer to situations where there is an interdependency in decision-making. The essence of these interdependent decision-making situations is that when player A makes a decision (for example regarding price, entry into a market, whether to take a job) it will consider the reactions of other persons or firms to its different strategies, and how these reactions will affect their own utility or profit. It must also take into account that the other parties or players, in selecting their reactive strategies, will consider how A will react to their reactions. As we have also seen in games like the "beauty contest," this can continue in a virtually infinite progression. In this situation there is often a considerable amount of uncertainty regarding the results of any decision.

Many elements of real-life strategic situations can be simulated in game experiments, which have the considerable advantage of isolating a particular behavioral factor and simplifying analysis. In this chapter we will discuss games related to social preferences, in particular involving trust, bargaining, and punishment. In each case the predictions of SGT are examined, and we will consider how the standard model can be improved by modification and extension. Now that the basic tools of game-theoretic analysis have been described in the previous chapter, it will be easier to understand both the basic model and the appropriate extensions.

In order to appreciate the basis of BGT, it is important to understand the nature of inferences from empirical studies. If empirical data do not "fit" the predictions of a particular theory involving the use of game-theoretical analysis, this does not mean that game theory as a method of analysis is wrong. There are a number of possible conclusions: (1) the utility functions of the players were mis-specified; (2) bounded rationality prevented the players from using the game-theoretical analysis properly; (3) learning factors caused a time lag in terms of reaching an equilibrium situation; or (4) the players misunderstood the nature of the game, or played a different game from that intended by the experimenters.

While game theory is an important element of the SEM, in its standard form (sometimes confusingly called "analytical" game theory), we have seen that it makes a number of important assumptions related to the conclusions above: (1) people are motivated purely by self-interest; (2) people have unbounded rationality; and (3) equilibria are reached instantly, since there are no time lags due to learning effects or other factors. BGT relaxes all three of these assumptions. The second and third assumptions were discussed in the previous chapter, along with the implications of relaxing them; in this chapter we will focus on the first assumption.

8.2 Fairness

The nature of fairness

It is not proposed here to discuss what is fair and what is not. Indeed that would be contrary to the approach of this book, which takes the view that "fairness is in the eye of the beholder." A society's view of what is fair can change hugely over the course of centuries and even decades; 200 years ago slavery and hanging people for stealing a sheep were acceptable in many countries. Some societies today regard the stoning of adulterers to death and "honor killings" of family members for unapproved love affairs as being acceptable, or even as moral obligations. Even over relatively short periods of time, people tend to adjust their values of fairness as circumstances change. The purpose of this section is to examine the factors that determine judgments of fairness in general terms. It is useful to follow the approach of Kahneman, Knetsch, and Thaler (1986), who identify and describe three of these, based on empirical research. Although their discussion relates to the context of profit-seeking by firms, the factors can be applied to more general situations. The key concept in this approach is **dual entitlement**, meaning that both parties in a transaction are entitled to certain considerations. There are three main elements in this concept of dual entitlement:

1. *Reference transactions*
   This transaction can relate to a price, a wage, or a rent. It is normally determined by the past history of a particular type of transaction, or by prevailing competitive rates. Thus it may not be regarded as fair for a landlord to increase the rent of an existing tenant, unless rents for similar properties in the area are also increasing, but it may be acceptable to charge a higher rent for a new tenant. The new tenant does not have the same entitlement as an existing one. The basis for this judgment may involve the concept of **moral hazard**, or post-contract opportunism. Once a transactor has made a commitment, like renting a property or taking a job, it may be regarded as unfair if the other transactor takes advantage of this commitment. Sometimes this is referred to as the "holdup" problem.

   Conflicts may arise in particular when there is more than one reference point. For example, in a wage dispute a union may claim that their wage

is unfair because workers of a similar skill in another industry are higher paid, but an employer may claim that their wages have risen faster in recent years than similar workers.

Two observations can be made regarding the reference transaction factor. First, it is in line with PT's emphasis on reference points as far as the perception of gains and losses is concerned. Second, it illustrates that fairness judgments are based on what is normal, or "norms," rather than what is "just." It should be noted that this runs contrary to the well-known Rawlsian theory of justice (Rawls 1971; 2001). The consequence of this is that not only does the yardstick of what is fair change over time, but agents also tend to perform, and be expected to perform, fairly in the marketplace. For example, a majority of people tip around 15 % in restaurants. An interesting sidelight on this issue is that "ticket touting," or charging above the standard ticket price in the secondary market, is generally regarded as unfair and indeed criminal. Theatre tickets in London's West End are regularly sold at below a market-clearing price, resulting in continuing shortages for popular shows. In 2006 a tout was fined £9000 for selling tickets at a 500 % markup. Even though people are obviously willing to pay the higher price, and may not have been able to purchase tickets earlier at the standard price, the below-equilibrium standard price is regarded as the reference price and the huge excess causes outrage.

2. *Outcomes to the transactors*
The general principle of dual entitlement means that it is usually regarded as unfair if one transactor makes a gain by imposing a similar loss on the other transactor. Thus if there is a shortage of snow shovels after a big snowfall, an increase in the selling price may be regarded as "gouging," since such a gain comes at the expense of the buyer. However, it is usually perceived as fair to pass on any increase in cost to the customer, since the seller is not perceived to make a gain in this case. It should be noted that empirical findings suggest that there is an asymmetry here, since reductions in cost are not necessarily expected to be passed on to the customer; the seller's gain is not perceived to be at the buyer's expense.

Once again concepts from PT are relevant here, along with concepts from mental accounting theory. The phenomenon of loss-aversion means that overall welfare is reduced if gains are made at the expense of equal losses in monetary terms, since losers tend to lose more in utility than winners gain. The accounting rules used to make judgments also suggest a lack of fungibility between different types of expense. Out-of-pocket costs, for example paying higher prices, are not judged in the same way as opportunity costs, like not receiving a price reduction. Furthermore, framing effects are important in terms of how the transactors code gains and losses. A loss is perceived as worse than the cancellation of a gain. For example, firms may prefer to offer a discount in a low season rather than reduce prices, since later on it is more acceptable to customers to remove the discount than increase the price. Similarly, it is more acceptable for firms not to pay bonuses to employees, however much these were expected, than to cut wages.

3. *Circumstances of changing transaction terms*
Kahneman, Knetsch, and Thaler (1986) discuss these in a price-setting situation, classifying occasions for change into the three categories of profit reductions, profit increases, and increases in market power. However, a more useful general classification, which would fit the empirical findings equally well, may relate to controllable and uncontrollable factors. For example, if a firm has an increase in demand that may increase both profit and market power, this may have occurred because of factors outside the control of the firm, and in this case it may be perceived as unfair to increase price. However, an increase in demand caused by the firm producing a better quality product or providing better service may justify a price increase. Similarly, increases in cost outside the firm's control causing a fall in profit may justify a price increase, but increases in cost due to inefficiency may not. The same rules apply to changes in wages and rents.

In general, exploitation of market power is judged to be unacceptable. What may be relevant to the judgment here is how a transactor gained such market power. Market power based on a superior product or technology may be acceptable, while market power gained by restrictive practices may not. Research findings are limited on this aspect, but it appears that some forms of price discrimination are not regarded as fair, even when substitutes are available.

Fairness games

Much insight can be gained into people's perceptions of fairness by examining the results of various games in an experimental setting. Common games that are used to investigate fairness and social preferences are **ultimatum bargaining games**, **dictator games**, **trust games**, **prisoner's dilemma games**, and **public goods games**. Some games are one-shot games and some are conducted on a repeated basis, and the importance of this distinction will be discussed later, since it is a source of debate and confusion. Games can be varied in a number of ways to observe differences in behavior, and this aspect is discussed in the next section. The purpose here is to observe differences between the predictions of "analytical" game theory in the SEM and empirical findings. With these empirical results in mind we can then move on to consider how fairness can be modeled into a game-theoretic analysis in such a way that the findings can be predicted. The different game situations are now discussed.

1. *Ultimatum bargaining games*

These are two-player games, and, as with most games, involve a proposer (P) and a responder (R). An example was given in the previous chapter. We saw that, in its standard form, a certain sum of money, frequently $10, represents a value of the gain to exchange, or surplus, that would be lost if no trade was made. P offers the sum x to R, leaving themselves with $10 − x$. R can either accept the offer, or reject it, in which case both players receive nothing.

The basic form of the game is so simple that it does not faithfully represent the more complex bargaining situations in real life, which often involve several stages, but it does offer some important insights as far as fairness is concerned. The SEM, based on "pure" self-interest, predicts that R will be happy to receive even the smallest amount of money rather than nothing and that therefore P will propose the smallest amount of money possible (maybe one cent), with R accepting this offer. However, the original study by Güth, Schmittberger, and Schwarze (1987) observed that proposers sometimes offered 50 % of the surplus and that responders often rejected positive offers. Empirical findings in experiments have consistently confirmed this result, contradicting the predictions of the SEM. Some of these studies use the method of eliciting responses described above, while others have asked responders to state a **minimal acceptable offer** (MAO). The latter method has the advantage that more exact information can be provided, particularly regarding infrequent low offers; a possible disadvantage is that this method may cause an upward bias in responses, meaning that people may demand more (there is a lack of evidence here).

These studies generally indicate that between 60 % and 80 % of offers are between 0.4 and 0.5 of the surplus and that there are almost no offers below 0.2. Furthermore, low offers are frequently rejected, with offers below 0.2 being rejected about half of the time. The above findings are also robust as far as increased stakes are concerned. For example, an experiment was conducted with Arizona students where the stakes were $100, and a couple of students rejected offers of $30 (Hoffman, McCabe, and Smith 1996). A similar result has been found with a $400 stake (List and Cherry 2000), and in countries with low disposable income where the stake was equivalent to 3 months' income for the subjects (Camerer 1995).

In summary, the results can be interpreted as showing that responders are angered by proposals that they regard as unfair, and are prepared to punish such unfair behavior at a cost to themselves (being "spiteful"). At this point we will not explore the issue of what causes such feelings of unfairness, and how much they are innate or determined by culture. This is better left until later in the chapter, after a discussion of variations of this game, other games, and empirical findings.

2. *Dictator games*

These are games where the responder's ability to reject an offer is removed, and thus are even simpler. In a one-shot situation they do not even involve strategic thinking (at least in the SEM), since the proposer does not have to consider the reaction of the responder. However, the value of such games is that they establish whether proposers make generous offers because they fear rejection, or whether they are altruistic. Any positive offer by a proposer is altruistic rather than strategic, meaning caused by the fear of rejection. The first comprehensive comparison of ultimatum and dictator games (Forsythe *et al.* 1994) indicated that dictators offered on average about 20 %, much lower than proposers in ultimatum games. Early studies also indicated that average offers are close to the offer that maximizes expected payoffs given the actual pattern of rejections in ultimatum games (Roth *et al.* 1991), suggesting strategic behavior, but later more sophisticated analyses showed that offers were more generous than payoff-maximizing offers, even allowing for risk-aversion (Hoffman, McCabe, and Smith 1996; Heinrich *et al.* 2001). In the Hoffman, McCabe, and Smith study, "dictators" still shared their wealth in about 40 % of the observed bargains when the anonymity of the offerer was preserved.

However, these results have also been called into question, on the basis that the wealth of the dictators was not earned. In real life, earned wealth may be the more likely situation. Cherry, Frykblom, and Shogren (2002) controlled for this factor in an experiment involving three treatments: baseline (unearned wealth), earned wealth, and double-blind with earned wealth. Subjects, who were undergraduate students, "earned" wealth by answering a sample of GMAT questions correctly. In the baseline situations a zero offer was only made in an average of 17 % of the bargains. In contrast, in situations where wealth was "earned," zero offers occurred in about 80 % of the bargains. This increased to around 96 % in the double-blind situations where the dictators acted in complete anonymity from both the other transactor and the experimenter. The authors therefore concluded that strategic concerns and not fairness were the motivation for other-regarding behavior.

In summary, it appears that positive offers are mainly strategic, but there is some altruism involved. Again, variations on these games and a more detailed discussion of the implications are given later in the chapter.

3. *Trust games*

Trust is the basis of any transaction that does not involve a complete contract that specifies all possible outcomes of the transaction, that is the vast majority of transactions. This is because most transactions involve costs and benefits in the future where there is always an element of uncertainty. When we buy a good we assume that it will provide the benefits that we expect; the seller assumes that he will be paid in full. Other types of transaction like renting a property, taking a job or hiring an employee, and lending money involve similar assumptions. Other activities not normally considered as relating to economic behavior – such as leaving one's front door unlocked, parking on the street, giving to charity, and getting married – also are based on an element of trust. Economists regard trust as a means of reducing transaction costs, since engaging in legal contracts or other forms of commitment is costly; thus it can be viewed as being "social capital." Some economists believe that countries and cultures that are more trusting have higher rates of growth and development; certainly there appears to be a strong correlation here (Knack and Keefer 1997), but the causation may be more complex.

The essence of all these activities, and games relating to them, is that some kind of investment by the truster (I) in the trustee (T) is involved. This investment is risky because it may not be repaid by the trustee. However, if the return from investment is sufficient and the investment is repaid sufficiently, the investor will benefit in terms of making a net gain compared with not investing. A typical investment game involves I having an amount x which they can choose to invest or keep. If I invests the amount y (and keeps $x - y$), this earns a return so that it becomes $y(1 + r)$. T must then decide how much of this amount to share with I, playing a dictator game at this stage. If T keeps z and returns $y(1 + r) - z$ to I then the total payoffs are z to T and $(x - y) + y(1 + r) - z$, or $x - z + ry$, to I. It is therefore possible to measure the amount of trust and the amount of trustworthiness: trust is measured by the size of investment y, while trustworthiness is measured by the amount returned, $x - z + ry$.

The SEM predicts that there will be no trust, for the reason that trustees will never return anything. Empirical findings have invariably contradicted this. A study by Berg, Dickhaut, and McCabe (1995) used an initial amount x of \$10 and a rate of return r of 2. On average, investors invested about 50 %; 16 % of investors invested the entire amount; and only 6 % invested nothing (zero trust). The average amount repaid was about 95% of the amount invested (or a third of the tripled amount), although there was a wide variation. This indicates that the return to trust is around zero, and this result has been confirmed by later studies. There appear to be some cross-cultural variations, and these are discussed in the following section.

Trust games are interesting since they allow reciprocity, or at least positive reciprocity, to be measured. This is because the second stage of the game is, as we have seen, a dictator game on the part of the trustee. Therefore, if trustees repay more than they would pay in an ordinary dictator game, any excess must be related to reciprocity. The concept of reciprocity is discussed in detail in Section 8.5, but at this point we can think of positive reciprocity as arising from some feeling of moral obligation on the part of the trustee. In terms of empirical findings, a study by Cox (1999) found that repayments were significantly larger than allocations in a similar dictator game, but that the difference was small, about 10%. Dufwenberg and Gneezy (2000) also found that returns were larger than allocations in a similar dictator game, but in this case the difference was insignificant. Thus it seems that positive reciprocity is not a major factor in trust games.

As with the other games described above, there are variations on trust games, in particular involving many persons or groups. These are discussed in the next section.

4. *Prisoner's dilemma games*

The prisoner's dilemma is perhaps the most well-known game of all, and was discussed in some detail in the previous chapter. The classic PD situation involves two prisoners who are held in separate police cells, accused of committing a crime. They cannot communicate with each other, so each does not know how the other is acting. If neither confesses, the prosecutor can only get them convicted on other minor offences, each prisoner receiving a 1-year sentence. If one confesses while the other does not, the one confessing will be freed while the other one receives a 10-year sentence. If both confess, they will each receive a 5-year sentence. The normal form is shown in Figure 8.1, which is a repeat of Figure 7.1.

The values in the table represent payoffs, in terms of jail sentences; the payoffs for Suspect A are the left-hand values, while the payoffs for Suspect B are the right-hand values. The objective for each suspect in this case is obviously to minimize the payoff in terms of jail time. The problem that they have in this case is that the best combination payoff for the pair of them is for them both to not confess, in other words to "cooperate" with each other; in this case each suspect will receive a 1-year sentence.

	Suspect B	
	Confess	**Not confess**
Confess	5, 5	0, 10
Not confess	10, 0	1, 1

Figure 8.1   Prisoner's Dilemma

However, as was shown in the previous chapter, this is not an equilibrium strategy according to the SGT of the SEM. The equilibrium is for both suspects to confess, or to "defect," since this is a dominant strategy for players. This equilibrium situation represents a paradox, since they will both end up receiving longer sentences, 5 years, than if they had cooperated. The equilibrium still applies even if the suspects had agreed to cooperate beforehand; they will still tend to defect once they are separated and do not know how the other is acting.

The reader may wonder at this stage how the type of situation described above relates to social preferences. This is more easily understood if we examine the payoff structure. In any PD situation there is a hierarchy of payoffs, which are frequently labeled as "temptation," "reward," "punishment," and "sucker's payoff." The relationship between strategies and payoffs is shown in Table 8.1.

In this light we can see that the PD situation is more related to reciprocity than to fairness. Extensive empirical studies have been conducted for over two decades, and they generally show that in one-shot situations players cooperate about half of the time. Although this plainly contradicts the predictions of SGT, it is not clear whether the cooperation is caused by altruism or the expectation of matching cooperation. Therefore the analysis of PD games is a blunt tool for predicting real-world behavior. One interesting finding is that pre-play communication, which according to

Table 8.1   Structure of payoffs in Prisoner's Dilemma

Strategy Pair (self/other)	Name of Payoff
Defect/cooperate	Temptation (0)
Cooperate/cooperate	Reward (1)
Defect/defect	Punishment (5)
Cooperate/defect	Sucker's payoff (10)

the SEM should not affect outcomes at all, has a significant effect in terms of increasing cooperation.

As with other games, there are many variations of the standard PD situation. The game as described above involves simultaneous play, or at least each player determines their action without knowing what the other player has decided. If the game is transformed into a sequential play, it resembles a trust game, with the second player acting as a dictator. As we shall see later, many experiments have also been conducted with repeated PD games, sometimes using the same pair of players each time and sometimes changing the pairs.

5. *Public goods games*

Economists define public goods as those goods which have the characteristics of **nonexclusivity** and **nondepletion**. This means that they cannot be easily provided to one person without automatically being provided for others, and the consumption of the good by one person does not reduce the amount of the good available to others. Street lighting is a common example. There are also many examples of semi-public goods, like libraries, stadiums, hospitals, roads, and fish stocks, which satisfy these characteristics up to a point. In each case, one person's consumption or activity causes a negative externality on others. Essentially, public goods games are multiple-player PD situations, where the Pareto-optimal solution is for all players to contribute to the maximum (cooperation), but the equilibrium solution according to the pure self-interest of the SEM is to contribute nothing and defect.

Therefore these goods present a problem for public policy, since few people will volunteer to pay for them, or refrain from consumption, hoping to get a **free ride** by enjoying the goods that others have paid for. The situations can be easily modeled in experimental games as follows: each of N players has an endowment of x_i and invests y_i of this resource in a public good that is shared by everyone, and has a total per-unit value of m. Player i receives the benefit $x_i - y_i + m\Sigma y_j/N$, where Σy_i represents the sum of the contributions of all the other players. The dominant strategy is to defect by making no contribution, in spite of the fact that all players could collectively benefit most by cooperating and contributing the maximum to the common pool of resources. A number of assumptions are made in this simple model regarding the value of m and the shape of the common utility function.

Empirical evidence again contradicts the SEM, since generally subjects in experiments contribute about half of their resources. There is, however, a wide range of responses, with a majority of players contributing either all their resources or nothing (Ledyard 1995; Sally 1995). As with PD games it is difficult to conclude whether people contribute from altruism or because of expectations of cooperation. Furthermore, it is impossible to say whether people defect out of self-interest or whether they have reciprocal social preferences but expect others to free ride. In order to draw sharper conclusions, the structure of the game needs to be tweaked and the consequences examined, as will be seen in the next section. In particular it is interesting to introduce the possibility of punishment at a cost. A detailed example of a public goods experiment with such variations is given in Case 8.2.

Neuroeconomics and preferences for fairness

When discussing altruistic and spiteful behavior earlier, we were careful to distinguish between material and nonmaterial benefits. Until the beginning of this century the measurement and even the identification of nonmaterial benefits and costs were highly speculative and introspective. Furthermore, many people are reluctant to admit that they actually get a kick out of punishing or reducing the welfare of others. However, over the last few years, and with the benefit of various types of neural scanning, both identification and measurement of psychic costs and benefits are possible, and this has added significantly to the science of economics in terms of both theory and empirical evidence. We can now consider the implications of certain neuroeconomic studies regarding some of the games described above.

First of all, researchers need to know where in the brain to look as far as the recording of rewards from decisions is concerned. O'Doherty (2004) found that not only was the dorsal striatum activated in decisions involving expected monetary rewards, but this activation increases as the expected monetary gain grows. Therefore we would expect rewards from punishment or cooperation to be associated with a similar activation. A study by De Quervain *et al.* (2004) examined rewards from punishment in trust games. They used a PET scanning technique and three treatments:

1. Free punishment (F), where player A can punish player B for defecting at the rate of $2 per point at no cost to themselves.

2. Costly punishment (C), where A can still punish B at the rate of $2 per point, but at a cost of $1 per point to themselves.

3. Symbolic punishment (S), where there is just an assignment of punishment points, but no monetary cost to either A or B.

The last treatment was important as a baseline control measure, since neuroimaging scans always measure brain activations in one condition relative to another condition.

The study found that the dorsal striatum was strongly activated in both the F–S contrast and the C–S contrast, indicating that subjects experienced rewards in both situations. Furthermore, subjects in the C condition who exhibited higher dorsal striatum activation also tended to punish more. The authors concluded that the level of striatum activation was related to the *anticipated* satisfaction from punishment rather than to the actual punishment. This was because subjects who experienced higher striatum activation in the F condition, even though they were punishing to the same maximal level as subjects with less activation, were willing to spend more on punishment in the C condition.

Studies relating to rewards from cooperation as opposed to punishment have also been revealing. Rilling *et al.* (2002, 2004) have examined mutual cooperation with a human partner compared to mutual cooperation with a computer in repeated and one-shot social dilemma games. Results were essentially the same in both studies, but the one-shot situation gives more reliable results, since the repeated game involves a number of confounding influences. The studies show that mutual cooperation with a human partner promotes more striatum activation than cooperation with a computer; the use of the computer partner controls for other influences like the size of reward and effort, so it can be concluded that the observed reward arises entirely from mutual cooperation in the normal sense, meaning with another person.

A final area of note in this area of social interaction is the influence of the neuropeptide oxytocin on trust and social behavior. Neurobiologists have suspected for some time that this chemical promotes bonding behavior, including maternal care and trust, in a variety of species. A study reported by Fehr, Fischbacher, and Kosfeld (2005) and Kosfeld *et al.* (2005) supported this hypothesis; it found that the percentage of players who trusted maximally in a social dilemma game increased from 21 % to 45 % after treatment with oxytocin. The issue then raised was whether oxytocin operated at the level of subjects' beliefs about others' trustworthiness, or whether it operated at the level of the subjects' preferences. The authors concluded that oxytocin does not significantly affect beliefs about the trustworthiness of others, but instead renders subjects less averse to being exploited, thus changing their preferences. This instability of preferences in response to various chemical influences, both internal and external, is discussed further in the next chapter, since it has an important bearing on the notion of rationality.

8.3 Factors affecting social preferences

The different games described in the last section have been studied under a wide variety of different conditions that help to shed light on a number of issues related to social preferences. These conditions relate to three main categories of variable: methodological and structural, descriptive, and demographic. These variables and their effects are now discussed.

Methodological and structural variables

These change how experiments are conducted, and include the following factors: repetition and learning, stakes, anonymity, communication, entitlement, competition, available information, number of players, intentions, and the opportunity and cost of punishment. These constitute the most important single variable, particularly since they are to a large extent controllable. This means that, by using clever variations in experiments, individual factors and their effects can be isolated.

1. *Repetition and learning*
   When ultimatum games are repeated with strangers, there is mixed evidence whether there is a learning effect. Bolton and Zwick (1995) report no learning effect, but other studies have found a slight but usually insignificant tendency for both offers and rejections to fall over time (Roth *et al.* 1991; Knez and Camerer 1995; Slonim and Roth 1998; List and Cherry 2000).
   Learning can also occur when players know the offers and MAOs of other players. A study by Harrison and McCabe (1996) indicated that providing such information reduces offers and MAOs to around 15 % by the fifteenth round of play. There may be several reasons for this: responders may cease punishing unfair proposers if they see that others are not doing so; they may "tire" of punishing if the desire to punish is a visceral impulse that can be satiated; or they may adjust their perceptions of what is fair. Although it is possible in principle to test if there is a "tiring" effect by pausing the game for a while and then restarting it, there is at present a lack of research regarding the contributions of any of the above factors.
   There is a similar pattern with trust games, PD games, and public goods games. When these are repeated with strangers, trust, cooperation, and contributions all tend to decline over time (Fehr and Gächter 2000). The situation is different if punishment is allowed, as seen later. It is also

different when games are repeated with the same partners. In this case, trust and cooperation become greater over time and contributions become higher (Andreoni and Miller 1993). Much research has been done with repeated PD games, and various forms of "**tit-for-tat**" (TFT) strategy tend to evolve (Axelrod 1985). Such strategies invoke repaying like-for-like, so defection is punished by defection and cooperation is rewarded with cooperation. The main problem with a simple TFT strategy is that a single defection by one player leads to a debilitating cascade of defections; this is an even more severe problem in real life where errors of both judgment and interpretation of responses can easily occur.

The success of different strategies in repeated PD situations can be tested by computer simulation, the method pioneered by Axelrod (1985). More recent studies have introduced further complications related to real-life situations, such as playing the game sequentially as opposed to simultaneously, and allowing players to have the option of choosing which other players to play with. Successful strategies tend to be easily understood, "nice" (tending to cooperate), but prepared to punish (defecting where necessary as a deterrent). Stability over time is not easy to achieve, given the dynamics of different strategies. For example, in a population of players using different strategies against different players, the nastiest strategy, "always defect" (AD), will do well at first, but then starts to fail as more AD players play each other and get low payoffs. TFT then gains ground, but because of the weakness of tending to spiral into mutual defection mentioned above, it also starts to lose out to more "forgiving" strategies, like "generous" TFT, which occasionally (but unpredictably) forgives defection. "Generous" in turn allows the rise of even more forgiving strategies, like "always cooperate" (AC). However, as such strategies spread, this in turn allows the return of the parasitic AD strategy, and a cycle may be initiated (Nowak, May, and Sigmund 1995).

What can be concluded from existing research regarding PD, trust, and public goods games in a repetitive context? The general consensus is that in environments where people have frequent interactions with others, recognize these others, remember the outcomes of these interactions, and are in a position to punish these others either by defection or by refusing to play with them (social ostracism in real life), successful strategies tend to be "nicer" or more cooperative. It should be noted that the threat of being excluded from playing (and not receiving any payoff at all) may be enough to force people to cooperate. We have to be seen to be nice to get people to trust us.

There is one final observation to be made regarding repetition and learning. It has been assumed so far that players are human, and therefore intellectually capable of calculating the effects of strategies in terms of outcomes. It is important to understand that this is not a necessity. There is a branch of game theory in biology, commonly called **evolutionary game theory**, where the players do not have to be intelligent beings in the normal sense. This aspect of game theory was pioneered by Maynard-Smith (1976; 1982). For example bats (Wilkinson 1984) and fish (Milinski 1987; Dugatkin 1991) have been observed to behave according to the predictions of the theory. In the words of Ridley (1996),

> there is, in fact, no requirement in the theory that the fish understand what it is doing. Reciprocity can evolve in an entirely unconscious automaton, provided it interacts repeatedly with other automata in a situation that resembles a PD – as the computer simulations prove. Working out the strategy is the job not of the fish itself, but of evolution, which can then program it into the fish.

Thus in evolutionary biology it is the blind mechanistic force of natural selection, not the purposeful behavior of intelligent forward-thinking individuals, which leads to equilibrium. The significance of this phenomenon will be discussed more fully in Section 8.6.

2. *Stakes*

The importance and effect of the size of stakes has been discussed before, in both this chapter and earlier ones. One might expect based on this previous discussion that, in ultimatum games, as stakes rise, the *amount* that responders reject should rise, but the *percentage* of the surplus they reject should fall. For example, responders should reject $4 out of $50 more often than $4 out of $10, but should accept 20 % out of $50 more often than 20 % of $10.

In fact there is only weak evidence that stakes have such an effect, with most studies indicating no significant effect (Roth *et al.* 1991; Forsythe *et al.* 1994; Straub and Murnighan 1995; Hoffman, McCabe, and Smith 1996). Even in the study by Camerer (1999), where stakes were as high as 1 month's wages, there was little effect. Only two studies (Slonim and Roth 1998; List and Cherry 2000) find fewer rejections for larger stakes. Furthermore, the studies also indicate little effect on proposers' offers with higher stakes. The probable reason for this is that subjects may offer closer to 50 % rather than much less than 50 %, for fear of costly rejection.

This fear may well be justified: in the study by List and Cherry (2000) a quarter of the subjects rejected offers of $100 out of $400.

In trust, PD and public goods games the effects of increasing stakes, in terms of the relative size of monetary payoffs, are predictable. When the "temptation" (defect when other player cooperates) payoff is reduced, and the "sucker" (cooperate when other player defects) payoff is increased, there is a greater tendency to cooperate. Similarly, when m, the marginal rate of social return, is increased in public goods games, contributions increase.

3. *Anonymity*

One recurring problem with experimental studies in general is that the behavior of the subjects can be influenced by lack of anonymity. The knowledge, or suspicion, that their identity may be known either to the investigator or to other subjects may cause subjects to want to appear "nice" or to please the investigator. Hoffman *et al.* (1994) found that dictator allocations averaged only about 10 % in a double-blind study, significantly less than in other dictator games where the protocol did not involve double-blindness. A similar result was found in Hoffman, McCabe, and Smith (1998), although Bolton, Katok, and Zwick (1998) did not find any significant difference between double-blind and other conditions. In ultimatum games it appears that anonymity may reduce rejections slightly but not significantly (Bolton and Zwick 1995).

4. *Communication*

Several studies show that in dictator games, communication by recipients, for example talking about themselves, increases allocations (Frey and Bohnet 1995; Bohnet and Frey 1999). In the later study, average allocations rose to half, and 40 % of dictators gave *more* than half. Even simply being able to identify their recipients had some effect, in terms of reducing the number of dictators leaving nothing. However, in three-person games where there are two recipients for each dictator, but communication only occurs with one of them, dictators are generous only to the recipient with whom they have communicated (allocations being around twice as large). This indicates that communication elicits a target-specific sympathy rather than a general feeling of generosity (Frey and Bohnet 1997).

5. *Entitlement*

We have already seen that entitlement has important effects on behavior, for example the endowment effect. When dictators or proposers in ultimatum games feel entitled in some way, for example by winning a contest, they make less generous offers (Hoffman *et al.* 1994; List and

Cherry 2000; Cherry, Frykblom, and Shogren 2002). In the Hoffman *et al.* study the right to propose an offer was allocated to the person who answered more general knowledge questions. Offers in ultimatum games were reduced by about 10 %, while dictators' allocations fell by about half. The Cherry, Frykblom, and Shogren study found that the tendency of dictators to make zero offers increased from about 17 % to around 80 %, with the proportion rising still further in double-blind studies to around 96 %. However, it is interesting that recipients did not appear to share the entitlement attitudes of proposers in ultimatum games, since rejection rates increased, even with $100 stakes. There may be a self-serving bias here as far as legitimacy of entitlement is concerned.

6. *Competition*

We have already observed that competition has significant effects on judgments of fairness. For example, it is judged to be fair for firms to cut wages if their survival is threatened by competition, but not otherwise (Kahneman, Knetsch, and Thaler 1986). Furthermore, in ultimatum games proposer competition increases offers significantly. Roth *et al.* (1991) conducted a market game where nine players proposed offers (as sellers), and a single recipient (buyer) had the right to refuse the highest offer. Only one offer could be accepted, as is the case where a buyer only wants to buy a single unit. After five or six rounds of play, proposals converged on 100 %, meaning that all the surplus from trade goes to the buyer. This is in fact the equilibrium according to the SGT of the SEM. In a study of responder competition, Güth, Marchand, and Rullière (1997) found a similar result, but with the effect working in the opposite direction. When a single proposer (seller) was selling a single unit to many competing recipients (buyers), the MAO was found to fall to below 5 % of the surplus by the fifth round, while the average offer had fallen to 15 %. The gap between offer and MAO indicates that the game had still not found its equilibrium by this fifth stage. Again this confirms the prediction of SGT, where the equilibrium is zero, or the smallest unit of money available. These results are discussed further in the following sections.

Some experiments have added outside options to ultimatum games, meaning that players earn nonzero payoffs if offers are rejected (Knez and Camerer 1995). For example, if a proposer's division of a $10 pie was rejected, the proposer earned $2 and the responder earned $3. A variation of this game awarded half of the surplus ($10 minus the sum of the gains of $2 and $3) to each player. The main result was that the rate of disagreement between proposer and responder rose considerably, to nearly

50 % compared with the range of 10–15 % in most experiments. It appears that this change in the game's structure affects the players' perceptions of fairness in different ways, with self-serving bias again causing the conflict.

7. *Available information*

Another structural variable that can be manipulated in experiments concerns the information possessed by the players. In ultimatum games, for example, respondents may be in any one of three situations in terms of knowledge about the size of the pie to be divided: (1) perfect information – they know for certain the amount to be divided; (2) incomplete information – they know the possible payoff sizes and their probability distribution; and (3) no information at all. Most studies indicate that responders tend to accept a smaller amount under conditions of incomplete or zero information (Mitzkewitz and Nagel 1993; Straub and Murnighan 1995; Croson 1996; Rapoport, Sundali, and Potter 1996). This can be interpreted as giving proposers the benefit of the doubt, since low offers could indicate a small pie. Proposers also tend to take advantage of the situation by offering less. However, a study by Camerer and Loewenstein (1993) found a contrasting result. In this case some respondents had perfect information, while others only knew that the possible pies were $1, $3, $5, $7, and $9, with equal probabilities. In the perfect information situation the average MAO was a typical 30 %, but in the incomplete information situation the average MAO was $1.88, which represents about 38 % of the average pie of $5. Disagreements were therefore much more common in the imperfect information case.

Information can also be provided regarding the past history of players in terms of their previous offers or behavior. This can provide a reference point as far as judgments of fairness are concerned. In both ultimatum games (Knez and Camerer 1995) and dictator games (Cason and Mui 1998) there was some positive correlation between the size of offers made by others and that of own offers, indicating some social influence. In PD games, knowledge of the previous behavior of other players has an important effect, particularly if players can choose which other players to play with. As we have seen, a "bad record" of defection is likely to cause social ostracism in these circumstances, so "nasty" players will not get a chance to play much and will therefore earn little after a few rounds of play.

8. *Multi-person games*

The addition of other players to games which normally involve only two players provides a number of new insights regarding reciprocity and fairness. One general result is that players tend to be mainly concerned with fairness or equality in terms of their own payoffs relative to those of a proposer, rather than compared with the payoffs of third parties. Thus allocations of only 12–15 % to other players who are inactive recipients in a three-person game do not seem to concern active responders; overall rejection rates of around 5 % have been recorded, showing that they do not care much about how inactive third parties are treated (Güth and Van Damme 1998). Furthermore, when trust games are played in three-person groups, groups give and repay less, and appear to be disproportionately influenced by the least trusting and trustworthy members (Cox 1999). In multi-person PD games the likelihood of defection increases, since there is often a race to defect first. This is essentially a "tragedy of the commons" situation, which can result in global problems like pollution and the depletion of fish stocks. At a more mundane level it can explain why at parties common resources of food and drink are often soon exhausted. If a player trusts some players but not others, he or she may defect to preempt defection by others. These findings, in both experiments and real-world situations, do not present an optimistic outlook for cooperation. However, and fortunately, they are counterbalanced by the following two factors.

9. *Intentions*

Humans, and human institutions like legal systems, place great importance on the intentions behind a person's actions as well as on the consequences. Harm caused by accident is not punished as harshly as harm caused deliberately. Furthermore, the intention to cause harm ("conspiracy") is usually punished even if there is no harmful consequence. This view is a universal one in different societies, and therefore appears to be deeply rooted in evolutionary psychology. SGT experiments have established that in ultimatum games MAOs are lower when players are paired with random devices like computers, rather than human proposers (Blount 1995). Thus it appears that there is a difference in attitude toward inequality compared with attitude toward inequity. It is the latter, meaning a person's perception of being treated unfairly, which seems to cause outrage, more than the perception of inequality. The importance of this distinction will be examined in the next two sections, when inequality-aversion (IA) models are compared with reciprocity models that incorporate intentions.

10. *Opportunity and cost of punishment*

Punishment is a vital method of enforcing social norms, in particular cooperation. Some writers distinguish between punishment as negative **reciprocity** and punishment as **retaliation** (Fehr and Gächter 2001).

Retaliation is described as relating to situations where players or agents expect future material benefits from their actions. Negative (and positive) reciprocity on the other hand does not entail any expected material benefits. For example, rejecting offers in an ultimatum game represents negative reciprocity on the part of the responder. We have seen that the rewards here are psychological and neurophysiological, as evidenced by neural scanning. A number of studies have shown that a large proportion of subjects, between 40 % and 66 %, exhibit reciprocity in one-shot situations; the one-shot nature of the situation indicates that this behavior is reciprocal rather than retaliatory (Berg, Dickhaut, and McCabe 1995; Fehr and Falk 1999; Gächter and Falk 1999; Abbink, Irlenbusch, and Renner 2000). Furthermore, studies also show that the desire to punish harmful behavior is stronger than the desire to reward friendly behavior (Offerman 1999; Charness and Rabin 2002), indicating that negative reciprocity is stronger than positive reciprocity. This has important consequences for multi-person games.

We have seen that public goods games are particularly prone to defection, or free riding. Defection may occur out of self-interest, or it may arise because reciprocal types want to punish self-interested types, and this may be the only practical way of doing so. However, as Fehr and Gächter (2000) have shown, if the behavior of players is observable and if the direct punishment of individual players is possible (at a cost to the punisher), the results of public goods games are radically different. In this study there were four different protocols, all involving four players:

- perfect strangers in each game and no punishment;
- perfect strangers with punishment;
- same players in repeated game and no punishment; and
- same players with punishment.

In the punishment protocols players could punish any other player by reducing the number of their tokens by x, at a cost of $x/3$ to themselves. The existence of a cost is important not only because it is realistic, but because it enables a distinction to be made between reciprocal and self-interested players. Purely self-interested players will never pay a cost to punish others when there is no material reward.

The results of the four different protocols were vastly different. In the first case, perfect strangers and no punishment, cooperation falls to very low levels in later rounds, with average contribution levels being only

10 % of available tokens, and 79 % of subjects free riding and contributing nothing. Even when games were played repeatedly with the same players, cooperation tended to fall, with contributions averaging only about 30 % for the last five rounds of the ten-period game. However, when the opportunity for punishment existed, contributions *increased* throughout the rounds, even with perfect strangers. In this case contributions started at 50 % and increased to 60 %. When games were repeated with the same players, contributions started at 65 % and rose to 90 % by the end of ten rounds. This is a clear and dramatic demonstration of the power of punishment to enforce cooperation by self-interested individuals. Fehr and Schmidt (1999) have shown theoretically that even a minority of reciprocal subjects is capable of inducing a majority of selfish subjects to cooperate.

There are a number of important policy implications that arise from the above observations that will be discussed at the end of the chapter.

Descriptive variables

As we have seen at some length in previous chapters, framing effects are a common phenomenon. It should therefore be no surprise that they play a part in causing differential responses in various games. For example, when ultimatum games are framed in terms of a buyer–seller transaction, where sellers ask a price for a good that buyers can take or leave, offers are reduced by almost 10 % while rejection rates remain unchanged (Hoffman *et al.* 1994). When ultimatum games are framed as dilemmas where resources are shared, with players making sequential claims on a common pool of resources and receiving nothing if the claims add up to more than the pool, then players tend to be more generous, with rejections less frequent (Larrick and Blount 1997). This may be because the language of "claiming" creates a sense of common ownership thus inducing a greater tendency to cooperate. It also appears that prompting proposers to consider the likely reactions of responders reduces offers, possibly by increasing the fear of rejection. Hoffman, McCabe, and Smith (2000) found that this reduction was in the order of 5–10 %.

Framing effects can also be observed in PD and public goods games. For example, when a PD game is framed as a "social event game," as opposed to an "investment game," this engenders more cooperation (Pilutla and Chen 1999). It appears that different terms can trigger different expectations regarding the behavior of other players, leading to reciprocal behavior. This framing effect is particularly noticeable in the case of the Wason Test situation, described in Case 8.1.

Demographic variables

A considerable body of research has examined the effects of various demographic variables on social preferences. The variables most frequently studied are gender, age, academic major, and culture.

1. *Gender*

   Although there are a number of significant differences between the genders in terms of fairness and social preferences, there is no simple pattern. Instead, there are complex interactions with a number of other factors. Here are some of the main findings:

   - In ultimatum games both sexes make similar offers (Eckel and Grossman 2001).
   - In ultimatum games women reject less often.
   - In dictator games there appear to be no differences (Frey and Bohnet 1995; Bolton, Katok, and Zwick 1998).
   - Both sexes demand more from women and offer more to men (Solnick 2001).
   - Females generally punish more (Eckel and Grossman 1996b).
   - Females are cost-conscious punishers; they punish more than males when it is cheap, but less when it is expensive.
   - While men are not especially generous to attractive women, women offer about 5 % more to attractive men than to unattractive men. In fact Schweitzer and Solnick (1999) report that the average female offer to good-looking men was over 50 % of the pie, with 5 % of females offering almost the whole pie!

   This last interaction is particularly interesting, since it supports field data that looks, and in particular height, are positively correlated with income.

2. *Age*

   Although few studies have been conducted in this area, it appears that children go through three main stages of development as far as social preferences are concerned (Damon 1980; Murnighan and Saxon 1998). Before the age of five, they are highly self-interested. Between five and seven they become very concerned with equality, mainly as a method of preventing conflict. After seven they become more interested in equity, for example by relating rewards to inputs or some other measure of entitlement.

Some researchers have indicated that this constitutes evidence against the evolutionary psychology approach. For example, Camerer (2003) states,

> These facts cast doubt on a strong version of the hypothesis that an instinct for acting tough in repeated interactions evolved because it was adaptive in our ancestral past.

As we shall see, this conclusion can cause misunderstanding, and it is the "weaker" version of the hypothesis which is important. This is discussed in the section on the role of evolutionary psychology.

3. *Academic major*

The evidence appears somewhat mixed in this area. A study by Carter and Irons (1991) found that economics majors offered 7 % less and demanded 7 % more in ultimatum games than other majors. This difference applied to both first- and final-year undergraduates, causing the authors to conclude that economics majors are born self-interested rather than made that way by the subject matter. A side issue is raised here: is this conclusion an example of self-serving bias by economists who want to defend their subject against the alternative conclusion that studying economics makes people more selfish?

Other studies indicate that economics and business students are no different from other majors in terms of offers and MAOs (Eckel and Grossman 1996a; Kagel, Kim, and Moser 1996), and a couple of studies have even indicated that economics and business students are *more* generous in their offers (Kahneman, Knetsch, and Thaler 1986; Frey and Bohnet 1995). It is therefore impossible to come to any definite conclusion on this issue at present.

4. *Culture*

Cultural effects are notoriously difficult to test for because of problems related to language, experimenter interaction, and confounds with other factors. Most cross-cultural studies have involved ultimatum bargaining games. The first detailed study in 1991 by Roth *et al.* examined subjects in four countries: America, Japan, Israel, and Yugoslavia. The main finding was that offers were on average about 10 % lower in Japan and Israel, yet rejection rates were also lower. The conclusion was that there appeared to be a different conception in these countries regarding what constitutes a "fair" offer. It is interesting that a study by Buchan, Johnson, and Croson (1997) found an opposite result as far as Japan was concerned, with average offers being higher than in the United States. This may be due to methodological variations, since the latter study used the MAO method, whereas the earlier study used the specific-offer method. However, there may be confounding factors here related to the two samples of students.

The most interesting studies of cultural differences in social preferences have been conducted by Heinrich *et al.* (2001; 2002), which examined 20 different cultures, including many primitive cultures in Africa and Asia. An important aspect of this research is that an interdisciplinary approach is involved, with contributions from both anthropologists and economists. The research found some very different results regarding average offers in ultimatum games. The Machiguenga in Peru had the lowest average offer rate, with 26 % of the pie, whereas two cultures actually had average offer rates above 50 %: the Ache in Paraguay and the Lamelara in Indonesia.

How can such large differences be explained? It appears that two variables explain the variations to a considerable extent, with a multiple R^2 of 68 %. These variables are as follows:

a) *The amount of cooperative activity or economies of scale in production.*
   For example, when members of a society hunt in a group this factor is high, and offers tend to be higher. It is notable that the Machiguenga have a very low level of such cooperation, since the most important social group is the family, and business transactions outside the family are rare.

b) *The degree of market integration*
   Markets are integrated when there is a national language and national or large-scale markets for goods and labor. Such integration is also associated with higher offers. There is an important conclusion here: well-developed markets that are more likely to be efficient are less likely to be dominated by pure self-interest.

One final point regarding the Heinrich *et al.* findings is worthy of comment, and that concerns the two cultures with average offers above 50 %. This appears to involve the **potlatch syndrome**. A potlatch is essentially an exhibition or competition of gift-giving which is designed to cause embarrassment or a feeling of obligation in the receiver, and it is, or has been, a feature of some primitive societies in both the South Pacific and the Pacific Northwest. There are also aspects of the same syndrome in many advanced countries. In this case gifts are used as weapons, and what may appear to be positive reciprocity is actually negative reciprocity. The reason why the practice is effective, however, is that it relies on the basic psychological mechanism of the feeling of reciprocity, which appears to be universal in all societies.

Modeling social preferences

We have now seen that the SEM, using SGT, fails to predict many empirical outcomes, both in real life and in experiments, and in some cases fails badly. It is important to emphasize again that this is not necessarily a failure of game theory as a technique of analysis. There are in general two possible reasons for failing to predict accurately: either people do not engage in strategic thinking in practice (meaning game theory is an inappropriate analytical technique); or the situations are not being modeled realistically, in particular by failing to incorporate social preferences into utility functions. We shall see that there is some truth in both of these factors. For example, we have already seen in the previous chapter that there are some situations where empirical findings indicate a failure to think strategically, as in the "beauty contest" game. However, we will see in the remainder of this chapter that improved modeling of situations can lead to accurate predictions of many of the empirical findings, indicating that game theory is still useful as a predictive and explanatory tool.

There is a further point to be made, or rather to be repeated, in this regard. Just as birds do not need to understand the theory of aerodynamics in order to be able to fly, people may behave according to the principles of game theory without necessarily following the logical steps involved. This kind of "as if" behavior can evolve under the pressures of natural selection, as we have noted earlier in the discussion relating to repetition and learning; recall the apparent mathematical sophistication of woodpeckers. As we have also noted on several occasions, from the first chapter, this "as if" justification is very commonly used in economics, particularly by supporters of the SEM. However, if SGT fails to predict accurately, we may conclude that the "as if" inference is incorrect, and the model needs to be respecified. This point is further elaborated under the second feature below.

In the modeling context, the challenge that is posed is that a good model must have two main features:

1. It must be able to explain the results of a wide variety of different games in terms of *endogenous* parameters. As we have seen earlier in this section, changes in the structure of games can lead to very different empirical results. For example, the introduction of proposer competition and responder competition in ultimatum bargaining games has drastic effects on responses. A good model must be able to account for such differences in a *parsimonious* way, without resorting to *ad hoc* complications. A further related feature of such a model is that it can make interesting new predictions.

2. It must have a sound psychological basis. This means that models must be based on known psychological mechanisms. It does not necessarily mean that the model actually explicitly incorporates psychological or neurological processes in its mathematical formulation, but it must at least be compatible with such processes and also be compatible with the results of other studies. This issue will become clearer as we move on to discussing particular models.

In general, current models of social preferences fall into two main categories: inequality-aversion models and reciprocity models. Both of these models maintain the basic assumption in the SEM that players aim to maximize utility and that players also assume that other players do the same. Both the models differ from the SEM in that they enrich or modify the utility function to take into account social preferences.

The next two sections will examine these different models in detail, discussing their psychological foundation, the resulting differences in structure, and their abilities to explain empirical results.

8.4 Inequality-aversion models

These models assume that people care about their own payoffs, and the relative size of these payoffs compared to the payoffs of others. It should be noted that sometimes such models are referred to as "inequity-aversion" models. The latter term is less appropriate. The distinction between inequality and inequity was touched on earlier, in the discussions of both intentions and the age factor. The most important point here is that "inequality" is a neutral term and implies no value judgment, while "inequity" is a value-laden or normative term involving the subjective notion of fairness. Thus, if a human proposer offers less than 50 % of the pie in an ultimatum game, this may be rejected by the responder either because of inequality aversion or because of inequity aversion. As we have seen, this ambiguity can be removed by using a random proposer, like a computer. If rejections occur in this situation, the cause must be inequality aversion.

Before examining IA models in detail, it is useful to consider the nature of altruism more closely, since altruism is sometimes regarded as the basis of social preferences. This will also aid an understanding of the relevance of the terms "endogenous," "parsimonious," and *ad hoc*, used earlier in the description of the characteristics of a good model.

Some authors distinguish between **pure altruism**, where a player's utility increases as the utility of other players increases, and **impure altruism**, where a player's utility increases from the act of contributing to others (Margolis 1982). Thus, if I am made happier by lending you my car (and thus making you happier), but not if my neighbor lends you their car, this is impure altruism.

Two fundamental points need to be made at this stage. First, neither of the above types of altruism constitutes pure altruism in the sense that it is sometimes used in psychology (Batson 1991). **Psychological altruism** refers to the objective of increasing the welfare of others *without* any increase in one's own welfare, either material or psychological. Such a phenomenon is alien to economics, since it cannot be incorporated into any utility maximization model, whether in the SEM or the BEM. In any kind of economic model no factor can affect an individual's behavior unless it can be incorporated in some way into that person's utility function, although Amartya Sen (1977) seems to envisage the reality of psychological altruism. However, current neurological research tends to support the economic model, as illustrated in Case 1.3.

The second point is that altruism can only explain positive reciprocity; it cannot explain the widespread negative reciprocity observed in empirical findings reported earlier. Any model explaining empirical findings only in terms of altruism would have to incorporate *ad hoc* complications like changing signs related to the utilities of others. These complications are not explained within the structure of the model itself, meaning that they are exogenous rather than endogenous. This would also make the model lack parsimony, since the model would have to be adjusted to explain different situations.

Therefore any successful model of social preferences must go beyond altruism, since it also has to be able to explain spiteful behavior, like the various forms of punishment we have already observed in different types of game.

The Fehr–Schmidt model

Fehr and Schmidt (1999) proposed a model (FS model), sometimes referred to as a "guilt/envy" model, but which the authors actually referred to as a model of inequity aversion. They use the term "inequity" on the basis that fairness judgments are based on some "neutral" reference point. They refer to the literature in social psychology regarding social comparisons (Stouffer *et al.* 1949; Festinger 1954; Homans 1961; Adams 1963), noting that a key insight in this research is that relative material payoffs affect people's well-being and behavior. They also note a number of empirical findings that directly support their hypothesis (Loewenstein, Thompson, and Bazerman 1989; Agell and Lundborg 1995; Clark and Oswald 1996; Bewley 1998). In real-life situations the determination of the relevant reference group and outcome tends to pose modeling problems, but in experimental situations it seems justifiable to assume that the relevant reference group is the other subjects in the study and that the reference outcome is the average income of these subjects.

In the FS model it is therefore assumed that, in addition to purely selfish subjects, some subjects will also dislike inequitable outcomes. Such inequity could arise from being either worse off or better off than others. An individual's utility function therefore depends not only on their own monetary payoff, but on differences between this payoff and those of others.

This situation can be modeled mathematically as follows:

In a set of n players the social allocation is given by the vector of payoffs:

$$x = (x_1, x_2, \ldots, x_n)$$

The utility function of player i is a function of this vector and is given by

$$U_i(x) = x_i - \alpha_i/(n-1)\Sigma \max (x_j - x_i, 0) - \beta_i/(n-1)\Sigma \max (x_i - x_j, 0)$$
$$(8.1)$$

where α_i is a measure of player i's aversion to disadvantageous inequality, and β_i is a measure of their aversion to advantageous inequality. Thus the second term in Equation (8.1) measures the utility loss from disadvantageous inequality and the third term measures the utility loss from advantageous inequality. Two further assumptions are involved:

1. $\beta_i \leq \alpha_i$, meaning that players suffer less from advantageous than disadvantageous inequality. This certainly seems a reasonable assumption in the light of direct empirical evidence (Loewenstein, Thompson, and Bazerman 1989).

2. $0 \leq \beta_i < 1$, the lower boundary meaning that players do actually suffer from advantageous inequality, rather than feeling a benefit from it. This assumption is certainly questionable (Frank 1985; Wilkinson 2004), and Fehr and Schmidt admit the possibility of status-seeking players with negative values of β_i, but they justify the assumption on the grounds that such players 'have virtually no impact on equilibrium behaviour.' The upper boundary $\beta_i = 1$ can be interpreted as meaning that a player is willing to throw away a dollar in order to reduce their relative advantage over player j of the same amount, which seems unlikely.

Using the utility function in Equation (8.1), Fehr and Schmidt then apply game-theoretic analysis (similar to that used in the previous chapter in relation to continuous strategies) to derive values of α and β, sometimes referred to as the "envy" and "guilt" coefficients, which are necessary to explain the various empirical results.

The FS model derives a number of conclusions regarding different variations of ultimatum and public goods games. While the SEM predicts complete free-riding in public goods games (zero contributions) and no willingness to engage in costly punishment, the FS model predicts that both contributions and punishment will occur if players are sufficiently envious and guilty. The model derives specific conclusions regarding the conditions under which people will free ride ($\beta_i \leq 1 - m$, where m is the marginal return to the public good); how many free riders (k) it takes to cause everyone to free ride ($k > m(n-1)/2$); and how much guilt and envy are necessary for an equilibrium to emerge where there are some positive contributions and punishment (again determined in terms of the endogenous parameters α_i, β_i, m, and c, the cost of punishment).

The twin strengths of the FS model are as follows:

1. *Simplicity*
   The model is simple in form, in terms of the number of parameters involved and the linearity of the function (although the latter feature can easily be modified).

2. *Robustness*
   This characteristic refers to the ability to explain the wide variation in results that are observed from different games. For example, it fits the normal ultimatum game, and the variations with both proposer and responder competition. As far as competition is concerned, the model produces an interesting prediction: in proposer competition, the number of proposers does not affect the equilibrium offer of almost zero, while in responder competition a greater number of responders will reduce the highest equilibrium offer. These contrasting predictions have yet to be confirmed empirically.

The Bolton–Ockenfels model

This model (BO), proposed by Bolton and Ockenfels (2000), is often referred to as an ERC model, because it relates to equity, reciprocity, and competition. It is similar to the FS model in many respects, since players care about their own payoffs and their relative share. It is assumed that players prefer a relative payoff that is equal to the average payoff, meaning that they will sacrifice to move their share closer to the average if they are either above or below it.

This situation can be modeled mathematically as follows:

$$U_i(x) = U(x_i, x_i/\Sigma x_j) \tag{8.2}$$

The BO model, like the FS model, uses game-theoretic analysis to derive specific conclusions regarding equilibria in various different games. For example, it predicts that in ultimatum games responders will reject zero offers all the time and that the rejection rate will fall with increasing percentage offers. It also predicts that ultimatum offers will be larger than dictator offers and that in three-person games the allocation to inactive recipients will be ignored. These predictions are largely confirmed by empirical findings.

There are three main differences between the BO model and the FS model:

1. The BO model is concerned with relative shares, whereas the FS model is concerned with absolute differences.

2. The BO model does not compare each player's payoffs with the maximum and minimum of the other payoffs, as the FS model does; it only makes a comparison with the average payoff.

3. The BO model proposes a symmetrical attitude toward inequality, where guilt and envy are equal in force ($\alpha_i = \beta_i$), whereas the FS model proposes that envy is stronger than guilt.

In all three respects the FS model appears to be superior, in terms of both fitting empirical findings and psychological foundation. A simple demonstration can be given by using a three-person game where the payoff allocation is given by $(x, x - \varepsilon, x + \varepsilon)$. According to the BO model the preferences of the first player should be independent of ε, since the sum of the payoffs will be constant and therefore the relative share of the first player is not affected. However, according to the FS model, as ε increases, both the envy of the third player's payoff and the guilt regarding the second player's payoff increase, causing the first player's utility to fall. A study by Charness and Rabin (2002) has confirmed this prediction.

Another advantage of the FS model is that it correctly predicts that in public goods games it is the biggest free riders who are punished, whereas the BO model makes no prediction regarding who is punished.

A final advantage to be mentioned here concerns predictions in variations of the ultimatum game, where rejections result in payoffs of 10 % of the original offer. The BO model predicts that since relative shares are not affected by acceptance or rejection, but payoffs are larger with acceptance, responders will never reject unequal offers, like 80 %/20 %. In contrast, the standard linear FS model predicts indifference, but modification of the model, to allow concave utilities for money, guilt, and envy, can predict rejection. This is much more consistent with empirical results, where the rejection rate by responders of 80 %/20 % offers may be as high as 50 %. However, this conclusion does not mean that the FS model can explain all empirical results in such games, or that it is complete in capturing all the relevant psychological factors, as we shall now see.

8.5 Reciprocity models

Reciprocity is based on the idea that people's conception of fairness depends not only on equality or inequality but on people's intentions. As explained in the previous section, altruism only explains positive reciprocity, but any realistic model must also be able to explain and predict the negative reciprocity that is widely observed empirically. A good starting point for this discussion is the model proposed by Rabin (1993).

The Rabin model

The central basis of the Rabin model is expressed by the following statement:

> If somebody is being nice to you, fairness dictates that you be nice to him. If somebody is being mean to you, fairness allows – and vindictiveness dictates – that you be mean to him.

The model is a two-player model, in which utilities depend upon beliefs. Player 1's strategy, a_1, depends on his or her belief about the strategy of the other player, b_2, and his or her belief about player 2's belief regarding player 1's strategy, c_1. A similar description can be applied to player 2's strategy. On the basis of these beliefs two important constructs can be determined: (1) player 1's "kindness" to player 2; and (2) player 1's perception of player 2's "kindness" toward him. The determination and interpretation of these constructs requires a certain amount of intellectual effort, and a fairly detailed exposition of the relevant analysis follows, using a PD situation as an illustration.

1. *Player 1's kindness to player 2*
   Given that player 1 has belief b_2 regarding player 2's strategy, his or her own strategy consists of allocating a payoff to player 2 out of a set of possible payoffs. Let the highest and lowest of these payoffs for player 2 be $\pi_2^{\max}(b_2)$ and $\pi_2^{\min}(b_2)$. We then need to define a fair payoff, $\pi_2^{\text{fair}}(b_2)$, which Rabin does by taking an average of the highest and lowest payoffs

(although this particular definition does not affect the basic analysis). Player 1's kindness to player 2 can now be expressed as follows:

$$f_1(a_1, b_2) = \frac{\pi_2(b_2 \cdot a_1) - \pi_2^{\text{fair}}(b_2)}{\pi_2^{\text{max}}(b_2) - \pi_2^{\text{min}}(b_2)} \qquad (8.3)$$

This can be interpreted by saying that player 1's fairness to player 2 is a function of his or her own strategy (a_1) and his or her belief regarding player 2's strategy (b_2), and is determined by the fraction of the way above or below the fair point that player 2's actual payoff lies (the numerator), scaled by the range of payoffs player 1 could have dictated (the denominator). Thus if player 2 received a higher payoff than the fair one, the numerator is positive and player 1 is being kind. If, on the other hand, player 2 receives a lower payoff than the fair one, the numerator is negative and player 1 is being unkind.

2. *Player 1's perception of player 2's kindness*
This perception depends on what player 1 believes player 2 believes player 1 will do (c_1). It can therefore be written as follows:

$$f\sim_2(b_2, c_1) = \frac{\pi_1(c_1 \cdot b_2) - \pi_1^{\text{fair}}(c_1)}{\pi_1^{\text{max}}(c_1) - \pi_1^{\text{min}}(c_1)} \qquad (8.4)$$

Rabin then assumes that player 1's social preferences are given by a three-component utility function:

$$U_1(a_1, b_2, c_1) = \pi_1(a_1, b_2) + \alpha f\sim_2(b_2, c_1) + \alpha f\sim_2(b_2, c_1) f_1(a_1, b_2) \quad (8.5)$$

The first component of the function, $\pi_1(a_1, b_2)$, represents player 1's direct monetary payoff. The second component, $\alpha f\sim_2(b_2, c_1)$, represents the utility of player 1's perception of player 2's kindness, where α is a weight showing how fairness converts into money utility (players with no social preferences have $\alpha = 0$). The third component, $\alpha f\sim_2(b_2, c_1) f_1(a_1, b_2)$, represents the utility of reciprocity; it is a function of the product of the kindness they expect and their own kindness. It should be noted that this term is positive if player 1's generosity is reciprocated by player 2, or if their meanness is reciprocated by player 2. Thus both positive and negative reciprocity yield positive utility, unlike an altruism model.

An equilibrium for the model can then be derived on the basis that players maximize social utilities, assuming rational expectations, $a_1 = b_2 = c_1$. This means that beliefs about the other player's strategy are correct and that beliefs about the other player's beliefs are also correct. An illustration of the operation

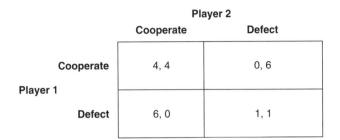

Figure 8.2 Prisoner's Dilemma – monetary payoffs

of the model can be given in terms of a PD situation, assuming the monetary payoffs are those shown in Figure 8.2.

It can be seen that the monetary payoffs correspond to the conditions described in Table 8.1, so that the dominant strategy for each player is to defect, if social utilities are ignored. We now have to calculate social utilities by adjusting the monetary payoffs to incorporate fairness or "kindness" factors, according to the utility function in Equation (8.5). These calculations are shown for each of the four possible pairs of strategies confronting player 1 (player 2's strategies are identical since the monetary payoffs in Figure 8.2 are symmetrical).

1. *Cooperate/cooperate*

$$U_1 = 4 + \alpha(4-2)/(4-0) + \alpha(4-2)/(4-0) \times (4-2)/(4-0)$$
$$= 4 + 0.5\alpha + 0.25\alpha = 4 + 0.75\alpha$$

The second term above (0.5α) is positive because it is perceived that the other player is being kind, and the third term (0.25α) is also positive because there is positive reciprocity.

2. *Cooperate/defect*

$$U_1 = 0 + \alpha(0-2)/(4-0) + \alpha(0-2)/(4-0) \times (6-3.5)/(6-1)$$
$$= 0 - 0.5\alpha - 0.25\alpha = 0 - 0.75\alpha$$

In this case both the second and the third terms are negative. Not only is the other player mean, but they are not reciprocating player 1's kindness.

3. *Defect/cooperate*

$$U_1 = 6 + \alpha(6-3.5)/(6-1) + \alpha(6-3.5)/(6-1) \times (0-2)/(4-0)$$
$$= 6 + 0.5\alpha - 0.25\alpha = 6 + 0.25\alpha$$

The second term is positive since the other player is perceived to be kind, but the third term is negative because player 1's meanness is not reciprocated.

		Player 2 Cooperate	Defect
Player 1	Cooperate	$4+0.75\alpha,\ 4+0.75\alpha$	$0-0.75\alpha,\ 6+0.25\alpha$
	Defect	$6+0.25\alpha,\ 0-0.75\alpha$	$1-0.25\alpha,\ 1-0.25\alpha$

Figure 8.3 Prisoner's Dilemma – social utilities

4. *Defect/defect*

$$\begin{aligned} U_1 &= 1+\alpha(1-3.5)/(6-1)+\alpha(1-3.5)/(6-1)\times(1-3.5)/(6-1) \\ &= 1-0.5\alpha+0.25\alpha = 1-0.25\alpha \end{aligned}$$

The second term is negative because the other player is perceived as mean, but the third term is positive since player 1 is reciprocating the other player's meanness.

We can now construct a new payoff table with the social utilities for each pair of strategies. This is shown in Figure 8.3.

In the revised situation the dominant strategy for each player need not necessarily be to defect. The payoff for cooperation given that the other player cooperates is greater than the payoff for defection if $4+0.75\alpha > 6+0.25\alpha$, that is if $\alpha > 4$.

The Falk–Fischbacher model

Falk and Fischbacher (1998) constructed another reciprocity model, which proposes a social utility function that incorporates four elements as opposed to the three in Rabin's model. As well as including monetary or "material" payoffs, kindness, and reciprocity, it also takes into account how intentional the kindness of a player is. The FF model has two important variations from the Rabin model: (1) kindness is measured in terms of differences between the payoffs of the different players, rather than in terms of possible payoffs for a single player; and (2) intentions are treated as being dependent on available allocations, both chosen and unchosen. These two variations are now explained in more detail.

1. *Measurement of kindness*

   In the Rabin model, kindness is judged in terms of how much players receive relative to some "fair" payoff for themselves, which in turn depends on the range of their own possible payoffs. In contrast, the FF model proposes that players judge fairness in terms of the difference between their own expected payoffs and the other player's payoff.

2. *Measurement of intentions*
   In the FF model there is an intention function, which compares a set of possible payoffs with alternative payoffs. In this case the opportunity cost to the decision-maker is relevant in terms of judging the fairness of their allocation. For example, in an ultimatum game, offering 80%/20% may be regarded as unfair in some situations, but fair in others, depending on what alternatives were open to the decision-maker. If the only alternative was 90%/10% then the 80%/20% split is likely to be judged fair.

Further details of the FF model are not given here, since it was developed to analyze extensive-form games, rather than the normal-form games illustrated in the tables we have so far used. We saw in the previous chapter that the analysis of extensive-form games was more complicated than the analysis of simultaneous games, involving the use of the foldback method. In this respect the FF model is a variation of the model proposed by Dufwenberg and Kirchsteiger (1998). Like the FF model and unlike the Rabin model, the Dufwenberg and Kirchsteiger (DK) model also measures fairness in terms of the difference between a player's own expected payoff and the other player's payoff.

The main advantage that reciprocity models have over IA models is that they capture an important psychological factor omitted from the latter type of model. Empirical evidence suggests that people do not just care about inequality, they also care about reciprocity and intentions. For example, responders in an ultimatum game may reject 80%/20% offers by a human proposer who stands to gain by making such an offer, but may accept the same split if it is determined by a random process. The result is that reciprocity models, especially the FF model, are analytically more complex since they have to take into account unchosen options as well as those selected. However, the greater mathematical complexity of the analysis may well be worth the trouble, in the light of the greater accuracy of explanation and prediction.

8.6 The role of evolutionary psychology

As we have seen in other areas of economic behavior, evolutionary psychology plays an important role in understanding social behavior. As far as social behavior is concerned, evolutionary psychology (EP) proposes that the human brain developed significantly as people started to live in hunter-gatherer bands or tribes over the last few million years. Cooperation yielded significant advantages in such an ancestral environment, since repeated interactions between people in the same group were frequent, and people learned to recognize others and remember debts. Cooperation was also necessary to provide public goods, including food from big game hunting. Punishment of defectors and free riders, often in the form of exclusion from the group or ostracism, was also important in enforcing cooperation. However, there are a number of misunderstandings concerning the role of evolutionary psychology, and it is important to clarify these.

Competing versus underlying theories

The most fundamental misunderstanding is that evolutionary explanations are an alternative to the theories described in the preceding sections. Evolutionary theory is in no way a substitute for these theories; rather it has a comple- mentary role, in terms of explaining how underlying social preferences are formed in the first place. All the theories discussed so far make certain assump- tions regarding how conceptions of fairness are determined, and how these conceptions affect our choices in terms of other concepts such as reciprocity and intentions. The fundamental role of evolutionary psychology is to explain how such conceptions developed in our intellectual decision-making processes. Evolutionary psychology, therefore, is best regarded as an underlying theory rather than a competing theory as far as theories of social preferences are concerned. In terms of the hierarchical reductionism explained in Chapter 1, an evolutionary psychology explanation is at a lower level in the hierarchy than the theories described in this section.

Questionable status as a scientific theory

Related to the first criticism is the accusation that evolutionary psychology suffers from an inability to be falsified or to make precise predictions. These are two basic requirements for any scientific theory. However, although evol- utionary psychology can be difficult to falsify in some cases, this is because of a lack of available evidence in practice, not because of any principle (unlike, for example, string theory in physics, or religious "theories" like the existence of Heaven and Hell). As far as precise predictions are concerned, evolutionary psychology does indeed lead to some very precise, and surprising, predictions, as will be seen in Case 8.1.

Individual development variations

One line of criticism of evolutionary psychology is that people are not born with a sense of social responsibility. As we have seen, this takes a number of years to develop, and in the first few years of life infants are almost entirely "purely" selfish. This is often taken as evidence that the capacities of judging fairness and calculating strategic behavior are inculcated by cultural factors rather than being innate. The falsehood of this argument can be seen by making a direct comparison with sexuality. Most modern psychologists agree that human sexuality does not really develop until puberty (although Freudians dispute this to some extent). However, it is absurd to argue that this is evidence that sexuality is a cultural concept and is not innate. It must be recognized that not all our innate instincts are present at birth; even innate instincts may take some time to fully develop.

Cross-cultural variations

We have also seen that there are considerable variations between cultures as far as certain characteristics like offers and rejections in ultimatum games are concerned. Such variations are also often seen as evidence that evolutionary psychology is not a powerful predictor of social behavior. The essential point here is that evolutionary psychology should not always be seen as a competing explanation for behavior compared with cultural factors (although it may often be). It is not always a case of "nature versus nurture"; frequently phenomena are best explained in terms of "nature via nurture," as Matt Ridley (2004) has proposed. Thus, although our brains may be hardwired with certain innate propensities and preferences, these are to some extent malleable by culture. The phenomenon of suicide bombing is an extreme case, where an evolved psychological mechanism geared to improve survival (belief in purpose and supernatural powers) has been hijacked into serving an entirely opposite purpose.

One-shot and repeated games

It is sometimes argued that the tendency to cooperate or reciprocate in one-shot games is evidence against evolutionary psychology. For example, Camerer (2003) makes the point that "subjects are usually well aware that one-shot games are strategically different than repeated ones," implying that this awareness should discourage them from cooperating in such one-shot games. This implication overlooks the fact that awareness is not sufficient to deter certain behavior in all cases. To take an extreme example, an alcoholic may be very aware that indulgence after a long period of abstinence may cause a relapse into self-destructive behavior, but this does not deter them any more than the knowledge that fatty foods cause heart disease discourages people from going to McDonalds. As Camerer also states, "when our caveman brains play one-shot games in modern laboratories, we cannot suppress repeated-game instincts." The point to recognize here is that repeated-game instincts involve guilt and envy, anger and indignation, all emotions that are now hardwired into our psychological makeup. Such emotions cannot be simply disengaged in one-shot situations.

The real challenge for evolutionary psychology, in analyzing social behavior as in other areas, is to produce precise and testable predictions. Evolutionary psychology is certainly capable of meeting this challenge, and often produces surprising and interesting results, as seen in Case 8.1.

8.7 Policy implications

As with other areas of behavior the factors discussed in this chapter have important policy implications for individuals, firms, and governments. In all cases the implications point to different courses of action compared to those suggested by the SEM.

Market clearing

According to the SEM, markets tend to clear because any shortage or surplus will cause prices to change to eliminate any disequilibrium. Thus, if there is a shortage of shovels after a big snowfall, market forces will cause prices to rise as sellers take advantage of the situation to make additional profit. However, empirical evidence suggests that such an action may be judged unfair; in the survey by Kahneman, Knetsch, and Thaler (1986), 82 % of subjects responded in this way to this specific situation. Buyers may regard such temporary price rises as "gouging," and boycott the seller in the future. As we have seen, anger and indignation are caused because the offending firm is seen as violating customers' perceived entitlement to a particular reference price. Some states have laws against "gouging," particularly for essential products like gasoline. In fact, such laws may not be necessary if firms are conscious of likely unfavorable public reactions. An example is given by Olmstead and Rhode (1985), relating to a severe gasoline shortage in California in 1920. SOCal, the dominant supplier, implemented allocation and rationing schemes, with the result that the price was actually lower in California than in the East, where there was no shortage. It appears that management at SOCal was concerned about their public image and wanted to appear "fair."

Similar considerations may apply when there are surpluses. Overproduction or seasonal factors, for example, may cause a temporary surplus of a product. Of course durable products may be withdrawn from the market and added to inventory, but there is a cost involved in such action. Rather than reducing the price in this situation, which would reduce the reference price, it may be better or more profitable for a firm to offer a discount. Later, when the surplus has disappeared, the discount may be revoked. Revoking a discount involves less hostile consumer reaction than raising price, since it is merely a case of returning to the previous reference price rather than exceeding it; therefore loss-aversion does not occur to the same extent.

Public goods

The main problem relating to public goods relates to free riding. According to the standard game-theoretic analysis of the SEM it is difficult to prevent free riding unless contributions are enforced by public authorities, usually in the form of taxes of some kind. The reason for this, as we have seen, is that it is the "pure" self-interest of players in such a game situation to defect in terms of not contributing, while it is also in the "pure" self-interest of other players to defect by not punishing free riders, since punishment involves some type of cost. Behavioral models which incorporate social utility tend to be more optimistic regarding provision of public goods for two reasons:

1. People may contribute out of altruism, "pure" or "impure." They may also contribute because they expect others to contribute, and therefore they are prepared to contribute themselves out of positive reciprocity.
2. People may be prepared to punish others for not contributing. Such punishment may be in the form of "whistle blowing" to the authorities in the case of social benefit fraud. Alternatively it may take the form of social ostracism, for example by yelling at people who throw trash on the street. Although there is a cost in punishing others, in the form of time spent or the threat of violent confrontation, this cost may be outweighed by a positive social utility of imposing negative reciprocity.

The empirical studies of Fehr and Gächter (2000), referred to earlier, provide confirmation that the opportunity for punishment makes a big difference to the outcome of public goods games. Punishment of course does rely on the ability to observe behavior and contributions. The effectiveness of punishment may also depend on the ability to observe who is being punished.

There is a considerable body of research that emphasizes the importance of **social norms** in the provision of public goods (Elster 1989; Ostrom 1998; 2000; Fehr and Gächter 2000). Fehr and Gächter define social norms in terms of the following three characteristics: (1) behavioral regularities; (2) based on a socially shared belief regarding how one ought to behave; and (3) enforcement is by informal social sanctions. An example of the application of the social norms is given in Case 6.3 relating to the desire for rising consumption profiles.

One main implication here for public policy is that a "naming and shaming" policy may be effective. Some US cities fight prostitution by posting pictures of convicted "johns" and prostitutes on websites or on local-access television. As Levitt and Dubner (2005) ask rhetorically in their popular book *Freakonomics*, "Which is a more horrifying deterrent: a $500 fine for soliciting a prostitute, or the thought of your friends and family ogling you on www.HookersAndJohns.com."

Another implication for public policy is that a "whistle blowing" facility may be beneficial. This is, however, a controversial issue, since it can lead to a "big brother" state, with neighbors spying on each other. For example, the introduction of ASBOs in the United Kingdom has been greeted with mixed enthusiasm by the public.

Crowding out of intrinsic incentives

Another controversial issue is whether explicit incentives crowd out intrinsic incentives. Some empirical results have been observed that defy explanation in terms of the SEM. These results often relate to situations where implicit moral incentives are pitted against explicit economic incentives. One study that is often quoted was conducted by Gneezy and Rustichini (2000). The study examined a situation at 10 Israeli day-care centers, where there was a problem with parents being late picking up their children. The centers had a policy that children were supposed to be picked up by 4 p.m., and delays caused anxiety among the children, and teachers had to wait around for parents to arrive. The study lasted for 20 weeks, and for the first 4 weeks the investigators simply recorded the number of late parents. On average there were 8 late pickups per week per day-care centre. After week 4 a fine was introduced at 6 of the 10 centers, which was the equivalent of $2.5 for a delay of 10 minutes or more. This fine was added to the monthly fee of about $380 per child. In the 4 centers with no fine, which acted as a control group, the number of late pickups stayed about the same. However, in the 6 centers where the fine was enforced the number of late pickups *increased* steadily for 4 weeks, and then stabilized at an average level of about 18 per week, more than twice the original level!

Another study regarding the relative importance of moral and economic incentives was conducted by Titmuss (1971) and related to blood donation. Most people donate blood for altruistic reasons, and are not paid a fee. When a small fee was offered, people tended to give *less* blood than without the fee.

Similar counterintuitive results have been found in labor markets. Experiments by Fehr and Gächter (2000) examined the work effort of workers under two conditions: one in which there were explicit incentives in the form of fines if workers were observed shirking, and another where there were no incentives. The relationship between work effort and offered rents was observed, where offered rents are defined as the wage minus the cost of providing a certain desired effort level. In the condition with explicit incentives, the actual work effort did not vary significantly with the rent offered, averaging about 2.5 on a scale of 1–10. However, when there were no explicit incentives in the form of fines, work effort increased steadily with the rent offered, reaching a level of 7. Only at low rent levels was work effort lower in the absence of incentives; at moderate and high rent levels, work effort was *higher* than when incentives were offered. This result has been confirmed by a later study by Fehr, Klein, and Schmidt (2004), as discussed in Case 8.3.

How can these findings be interpreted? A number of possible explanations have been proposed. One explanation is that the imposition of a fine changes the amount of information available to the players in the game. For example, parents may interpret the fine in terms of the economic and legal options that are feasible for the manager of the center. They may infer from the low value of the fine that the actual cost to the center of a late pickup is low. Blood donors may interpret any fee paid to them in terms of the value of their donation, and therefore may be discouraged from making a donation if they perceive that this value is small.

However, a more likely explanation is that the introduction of fines and rewards causes a shift in the way that the activities in the game are perceived. Fines and rewards transform the meaning of activities into commercial commodities, to which people attach different monetary values than when such activities are performed out of moral incentives. It also appears that this shift in perception can only occur in situations where subjects had not previously considered monetary rewards and punishments as an option. Once subjects have had their perceptions changed in this direction, they cannot be unchanged. This conclusion is supported by the fact that when fines were discontinued in the day-care centers after the sixteenth week, the number of late pickups remained at a high level.

We should not conclude from the findings above that monetary incentives in the form of fines and rewards are ineffective. In the day-care center situation the fines were too low to be effective, and were simply seen as representing a low price for being late. To put this into perspective, we should consider the fine of 10 shekels, $2.5, against the fine for illegal parking of 75 shekels, and the fine for not collecting dog droppings of 360 shekels. Monetary incentives may need to be larger in order to be effective. It should also be noted that being effective is not necessarily desirable; it simply means changing behavior in an expected direction. Levitt and Dubner (2005) note that, in the case of blood donation, large fees may indeed cause not only more donations, but also some highly undesirable side effects, like taking the blood of others by force and donating the blood of animals. These effects have already been observed in the market for replacement body organs.

A final important conclusion relating to all the observed behavior is that **incomplete contracts** may be preferable to complete, or more complete, contracts in many situations. Such incomplete contracts would not specify fines and rewards, but would rely on moral or social incentives for changing behavior in the desired direction. For example, the original contract in the Israeli day-care centers was incomplete, since it did not specify any sanctions for late pickups. This issue is discussed further in Case 8.3.

8.8 Summary

- The SEM is based on the assumption that people are motivated by "pure" self-interest. The main advantage to this model is its simplicity, but there are many empirical anomalies.

- Behavioral models are also based on self-interest, but modify and extend this concept to include altruistic and spiteful behavior.

- Altruistic behavior relates to behavior which confers a benefit to others, while involving a cost to the originator of the behavior, with no corresponding material benefit. Self-interest is still involved, since there is a psychic benefit.

- Spiteful behavior can be viewed as the flip side of altruistic behavior. This is behavior that imposes a cost on others, while also involving a cost to the originator of the behavior, with no corresponding material benefit. Again the benefit is psychic. Such behavior may sometimes be seen as beneficial to society, since it aids the enforcement of social norms.

- Game theory is an essential tool of analysis in understanding social behavior. This area of theory is involved when there is a strategic interaction between individuals, meaning that each individual has to consider the reactions of others to one's own actions, and is aware that others are considering one's own reactions to their actions.

- Fairness must be regarded as a subjective concept not an objective one; different people and cultures have different attitudes toward fairness, and these attitudes can change greatly over time.

- All attitudes regarding fairness involve the concept of dual entitlement regarding the transactors. Dual entitlement relates to three main factors: reference transactions, outcomes to the transactors, and the circumstances of changing transaction terms.

- Experimental games are useful in establishing attitudes toward fairness; examples are ultimatum bargaining games, dictator games, trust games, PD games, and public goods games. Empirical findings related to these games reveal extensive anomalies in the SEM.

- There are three main categories of variable that affect social preferences: methodological and structural, descriptive, and demographic. The first category is particularly important since it relates to variables that can be manipulated experimentally to reveal the key factors involved.

- Inequality-aversion models are based on the assumption that people are not only envious of others who have more utility than themselves, but also feel guilty if they have more utility than others.

- Reciprocity models are more complex, taking into account how "kind' people judge others to be, and basing their own kindness on the perceived kindness of other players. This approach has a stronger psychological foundation.

- Evolutionary psychology should not be viewed as an alternative approach to economic models; rather it is complementary to them, helping to lend understanding to the underlying psychological foundation of economic models. The real challenge for evolutionary psychology is to provide precise falsifiable predictions.

- There are a number of important policy implications of the behavioral approach which differ from the SEM. In particular, these relate to market clearing, public goods, and the crowding out of intrinsic incentives.

8.9 Applications

The first case study involves a detailed examination of the empirical findings regarding the Wason Test and the implications. This is designed to give the reader a better understanding of the role of evolutionary psychology. The second case study involves the policy implications of social preferences. The third case study involves a quantitative game-theoretic analysis relating to an experiment that supports a behavioral inequality-aversion model over the SGT model.

Case 8.1 The Wason Test

One of the main themes of this book is that the human brain is a highly fallible machine, but is fallible in certain predictable ways due to the manner in which it evolved. For example, we have seen that we tend to be bad at calculating and using probabilities, but work much better when probabilities are expressed in terms of frequencies. Similarly, the human brain is often bad at performing **logic**. Logic refers to inferring the truth of one statement from the truth of other statements based only on their form, not their content. A standard example that is normally used relates to the following reasoning: P is true, P implies Q, and therefore Q is true. Being based on form rather than content, logic is not empirically based. Thus it does not matter what P means; to use the example of Pinker (1997), P could be "my car has been eaten by rats."

Why do so many tests show that people are bad at problems involving logic? One factor concerns the ambiguity of certain logical words. For example, the word "or" can either mean "and/or," as in A or B or both, or it can mean "exclusive or," as in "A or B, but not both." The correct or intended meaning can only be inferred from the context, so our knowledge of the empirical world becomes relevant. For example, when we see a restaurant advertising "a free soda or hot beverage with your meal," we immediately understand the "or" in this context to mean "exclusive or"; we can have either a soda or hot beverage, but not both.

The psychologist Peter Wason was particularly interested in Popper's criterion of scientific hypotheses, that they should be falsifiable. He wondered whether everyday learning was in fact hypothesis testing, in terms of looking for evidence that contradicts a hypothesis. In 1966 he devised a test that was designed to see how people perform when it comes to falsifying hypotheses. This well-known test can be described as follows. A set of four cards has letters on one side and numbers on the other. The objective is to test the rule "if a card has D on one side, it has a 3 on the other side," in other words a simple P-implies-Q statement. Subjects are shown four cards, as in Figure 8.4, and are asked which ones they would have to turn over to see if the rule is true.

Figure 8.4 Wason Test

A hypothesis of the form "If P then Q" is violated only when P is true and Q is false. This means that the first and the fourth cards must be turned over. However, in numerous tests over the last 40 years only about 10% of subjects select the right cards. Most subjects pick either just the first card or the first and third cards. It should be seen that picking the third card cannot falsify the hypothesis; if the reverse side is not-D, this does not constitute a falsification, since the hypothesis does not say that only D cards have a 3 on the other side. Furthermore, the ambiguity factor mentioned above cannot account for the observed findings. If people interpreted the hypothesis as "if D then 3 *and vice versa*," they would have to turn over all four cards.

According to Cosmides and Tooby (1992) the results can be explained in terms of evolutionary psychology: humans have not evolved to solve abstract logical problems, but rather to respond to problems structured as social exchanges when they are presented in terms of costs and benefits. More specifically, we have evolved to detect cheaters in social contract situations. A cheater can be defined as a person who receives a benefit without paying a cost (i.e. a free rider). They supported this hypothesis by performing a number of Wason-like tests with subtly designed variations. The basic variation was to pose the situation where the subject was a bouncer in a bar: their job is to eject underage drinkers (cheaters). The problem can be posed logically as "if a person is drinking alcohol, they must be over 18." In general terms this is again an "if P then Q" statement, where P refers to drinking alcohol and Q refers to being of a legal age. The four cards in this case appear as shown in Figure 8.5.

Figure 8.5   Wason Test in terms of a social contract

Given the test in this form the vast majority of subjects (about 75 %) picked the correct first and fourth cards, even though the logic is identical with the original problem. However, it should be noted that the Cosmides and Tooby hypothesis regarding social contracts is not the only explanation for these findings. There are two main alternative theories: availability and facilitation theories.

1. *Availability theory*

   Although this theory comes in different forms, they all essentially argue that framing the logic of the problem in terms of a familiar real-world situation rather than in abstract terms accounts for the difference in performance. Therefore Cosmides and Tooby performed various other experiments to test this alternative hypothesis.

   The first kind of experiment involved using familiar real-world situations that did not involve social contracts. For example, subjects were asked to test the statement "if a person travels to Boston, then he takes a subway." Performance on such descriptive/causal tests was better than on the abstract form of the problem, with 48 % of subjects responding correctly, but it was still well below the level of performance on the social contract version of the test. Furthermore, even when the social contract was expressed in unfamiliar terms, such as "if a man eats cassava root, he must have a tattoo on his face," performance was still higher than in descriptive situations.

2. *Facilitation theory*

   This essentially states that social contracts facilitate logical reasoning. The results of the experiments described above could still be explained by the fact that the correct answer in terms of evolutionary adaptation also happens to be the logically correct answer. In order to test this theory, Cosmides and Tooby devised an experiment with a "switched" form of social contract. In the standard

Case 8.1 *continued*

form, a social contract can be expressed as "if the other party takes the benefit, then it pays the cost"; in switched form the contract becomes "if the other party pays the cost, then it takes the benefit." For example, the same social contract is expressed in the following two statements:

- If you give me your watch, I'll give you $20 (standard form).
- If I give you $20, you give me your watch (switched form).

In the first statement, from your point of view, taking the benefit (me receiving the watch) constitutes the logical category P, whereas in the second statement it relates to Q. However, in either case cheating (from your point of view) means that I receive the watch without paying you the $20. This experiment is represented in Figure 8.6.

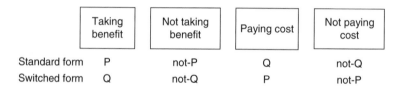

	Taking benefit	Not taking benefit	Paying cost	Not paying cost
Standard form	P	not-P	Q	not-Q
Switched form	Q	not-Q	P	not-P

Figure 8.6   Wason Test in terms of a switched social contract

In the standard social contract the first and fourth cards should again be selected, since they are required in order to detect cheating, and they also happen to be the logically correct answer. However, in the switched form of the contract, the logically correct answer involving P and not-Q means selecting the second and third cards. Thus there is a difference between the solution for cheater detection (first and fourth cards) and the logically correct solution, and it is this factor that allows the facilitation theory to be tested. It should be noted that evolutionary psychology supports the cheater detection hypothesis, since consistently altruistic persons who pay the cost without receiving a benefit would not have been likely to survive in our evolutionary past; there would thus have been no selection pressure for "altruist detection," unlike the strong pressure for cheater detection.

Cosmides and Tooby found that when presented with the switched form of social contract, about 70 % of subjects gave the valid solution for cheater detection but logically incorrect answer. This result validates the prediction arising from evolutionary psychology that we are not attuned to detect altruistic, or foolish, acts such as people paying costs and not receiving benefits in the same way that we are attuned to detecting cheaters. Other experiments by the same authors have confirmed these findings.

It is clear from the above example that the concept of cheating depends on whose perspective is taken, mine or yours. Gigerenzer and Hug (1992) utilized this difference in perspective to conduct further tests of facilitation theory against the cheater detection theory of Cosmides and Tooby. They asked subjects to test the statement "if an employee gets a pension, then that employee must have worked for the firm for at least 10 years." The subjects were divided into two groups, one being told they were the employer and the other being told that they were the employee. For employers, providing a pension is a cost, whereas getting the pension is a benefit to the employee. Likewise, working for at least 10 years is a benefit to the employer but a cost to the employee. The situation is shown in Figure 8.7, assuming a standard form of contract where the logical construct P corresponds to the other party receiving the benefit.

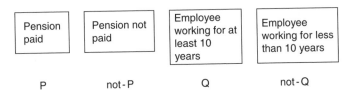

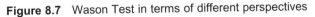

Figure 8.7 Wason Test in terms of different perspectives

Thus, each group defined cheating in a different way: for employers cheating constituted paying a pension without the employee working for 10 years (P and not-Q). However, for employees cheating relates to working for at least 10 years and not being paid a pension (Q and not-P). The logically correct answer for either group is "P and not-Q," as always, since this is independent of content or perspective. Facilitation theory predicts no difference between the two groups regarding the proportion of correct responses, while the cheater detection hypothesis predicts a higher correct response rate from the employer group. Gigerenzer and Hug found that for the employer group about 75% gave the correct "P and not-Q" response, with a negligible proportion responding with "not-P and Q." However, for the employee group, only about 15% gave the logically correct response "P and not-Q," with about 60% giving the incorrect, but cheater-detecting, response "not-P and Q." These results provide another strong vindication of the cheater detection hypothesis.

Questions

1. Give examples of familiar and unfamiliar social contracts. What does the cheater detection hypothesis predict regarding responses testing the breaking of such contracts?

2. Explain why using the switched form of social contract is a useful way of testing facilitation theory against the cheater detection hypothesis.

3. Explain why the use of different perspectives is a useful tool in testing the cheater detection hypothesis.

4. Explain why evolutionary psychology predicts cheater detection much better than altruist detection.

Case 8.2 Public goods and free riding

We have already seen that the provision of public goods presents problems in the SEM, both because people are unwilling to contribute and because they are unwilling to punish other noncontributors due to the cost involved. This case study examines the results of a series of public goods experiments by Fehr and Gächter (2000), showing how reciprocity, both positive and negative, affects the situation.

The basic form of the experiment involves a group of four members, each of whom is given 20 tokens. All four people decide simultaneously how many tokens to keep for themselves and how many tokens to invest in a common public good. For each token that is privately kept there is a return of the same amount. For each token that is invested in the public good each of the subjects earns 0.4 tokens, regardless of whether they have contributed or not. Thus the private return for investing a token is 0.4 tokens, while the social return is 1.6 tokens (since there are four players). According to the SEM, nobody will want to invest in the public good in this situation, since it is more profitable to keep the tokens privately (i.e. defect), and therefore each individual player will earn 20 tokens altogether. However, we can see that this is in effect a multi-player PD situation. If all the players cooperate, with each one contributing all their tokens to the public good, they will each end up with a return of 32 tokens (it is assumed in the simple model that there are constant returns to investment). This optimal solution cannot ever be an equilibrium in the SEM.

If we now introduce positive reciprocity into the model, this means that players are willing to contribute if others are also willing to contribute. However, in order to sustain such contributions there has to be a high proportion of players with such a motivation. In reality we know that there is a significant proportion of people who are motivated by pure self-interest, and this makes it difficult to achieve an equilibrium with positive contributions.

How does introducing negative reciprocity affect the situation? In this case negative reciprocity means retaliating against defectors or noncontributors who are free riding. In the simplest version of the game the only form retaliation can take is to free ride also. This punishes everyone else, whether they are free riding or not. Thus people may free ride either out of pure self-interest or because they are demonstrating negative reciprocity. The result is that negative reciprocity is even more likely to lead to a solution where there are no positive contributions, since "selfish" players are inducing reciprocal players to defect.

This situation changes radically if players can observe the contributions of others, and punish specifically those who do not contribute. The experiment can be modified so that players can reduce the number of tokens of any other player, at a cost of 1/3 token for every token reduced. It is important to impose a cost here not only for realism, but also because this allows a distinction to be made between "selfish" players and reciprocal players. Selfish players will never be willing to punish others because of the cost involved, and the punishment opportunity will not affect the outcome of the game. However, those players with negative reciprocity may be willing to punish free riders, and this in turn may induce selfish players to cooperate and contribute. Thus the end result may be the opposite of that achieved without the punishment opportunity, with reciprocal types ensuring general cooperation rather than selfish types ensuring general defection.

In the experiments performed by Fehr and Gächter (2000) the various forms of the game described above were used, using two versions. One version was called the "Perfect Stranger" version; this involved 24 subjects formed into 6 groups of 4 players each, with the game being repeated 6 times. Every time the game was repeated the groups were shuffled so that no player ended up playing with any other more than once. This ensures that people treat the game as essentially a "one-shot" game so that their actions have no consequences for later games. In the "Partner" version, on the other hand, the same 4 players played 10 times; thus this was a "repeated" game, where actions in one time period could have consequences in later periods. Both versions of the game were implemented with and without the punishment opportunity, and all interactions were anonymous. Where applicable, the punishment in each period occurred after observing the contributions in that period.

The results of the experiments are illustrated in Figure 8.8. NP refers to the "no punishment" version, while WP refers to the version with punishment.

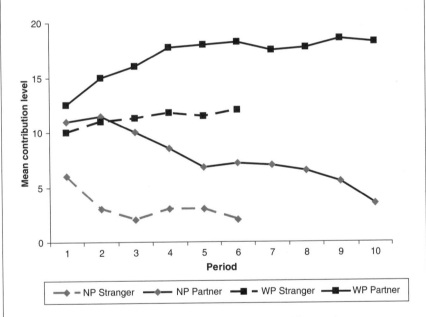

Figure 8.8 Evolution of cooperation in public goods game

Questions

1. Interpret the graph in terms of cooperation in the absence of a punishment opportunity.
2. Explain how the opportunity for punishment affects the development of cooperation.
3. What are the implications of the above findings as far as public policy is concerned?

Case 8.3 Sales force compensation

The issue of determining the optimal structure for sales force compensation essentially involves a sequential game between manager and salesperson. It is an example of the principal-agent problem. The essential problem for the manager (as principal) is that if the effort of the salesperson (as agent) cannot be contracted on or is not fully observable, a self-interested salesperson will always shirk, assuming that effort is costly. Therefore the manager has to design a contract that prevents moral hazard, or post-contract opportunism by the salesperson. The situation is complicated by inequality-aversion and reciprocity, which allows us to test the SEM against a behavioral model incorporating social preferences. If salespeople feel guilty about shirking, or repay kindness with reciprocal effort, they will not shirk as often as pure self-interest and the SEM would predict.

Fehr, Klein, and Schmidt (2004) therefore propose a contract involving a bonus scheme (BC) as being more effective than a standard incentive contract that imposes a penalty for shirking (IC). The parameters of the situation are modeled as follows:

$c(e)=f(e)$ cost of salesperson's effort is a function of the level of effort, with rising marginal cost from 1 to 4 in the permissible range of e (1–10). This is shown in Table 8.2.

Table 8.2 Effort costs for salesperson

e	1	2	3	4	5	6	7	8	9	10
$c(e)$	0	1	2	4	6	8	10	13	16	20

In the first stage the manager offers contract; in the second stage the salesperson decides whether to accept or reject. If they accept, they receive w immediately, and choose effort e in the third stage. In the fourth and final stage the manager observes effort e accurately, and may impose a penalty in the IC or award a bonus in the BC.

Under the IC: effort can be monitored at the cost of K

$w = g(e^*, f)$ where w = wage offered, e^* is effort demanded, and f = penalty for being caught shirking, meaning that $e < e^*$

Probability of monitoring technology working = 1/3

Under the BC: $w = h(e^*, b^*)$ where w = wage offered, e^* is effort demanded, and b^* = promised bonus for salesperson

neither e^* nor b^* is binding; the manager may award a bonus either greater or lesser than b^*.

The expected payoffs for both manager and salesperson can now be calculated for each contract.

With IC: if $e \geq e^*$, $\pi_M = 10 \times e - w - K$ $\pi_S = w - c(e)$
     If $e < e^*$, $\pi_M = 10 \times e - w - K + .33f$ $\pi_S = w - c(e) - .33f$

With BC: $\pi_M = 10 \times e - w - b$ $\pi_S = w - c(e) + b$

Note that the bonus here is not necessarily the promised bonus of b^*.

There is a large gain from exchange here if the salesperson gives high effort, because the marginal gain to the manager of a unit of effort is 10, while the marginal cost to the salesperson is only 1–4 units. Therefore the optimal outcome is for the manager not to invest in the monitoring technology and for the salesperson to choose $e=10$, giving a combined surplus of $10 \times e - c(e) = 80$, since the cost of $e=10$ is 20. However, this is not an equilibrium outcome.

Under the IC the optimal contract would be ($w = 4$, $e^* = 4$, $f = 13$), resulting in $\pi_M = 26$ and $\pi_S = 0$.

Under the BC the purely selfish manager will never pay a bonus in the last stage, and the salesperson, knowing this, will only supply the minimum work effort, $e = 1$. Thus the optimal contract will be ($w = 0$, $e^* = 1$, $b^* = 0$), resulting in $\pi_M = 10$ and $\pi_S = 0$.

Under the above conditions managers will always choose the IC over the BC, according to the SEM. This is basically saying that if managers realize that salespeople do not expect to get bonuses and are therefore likely to shirk, it is better to use an IC and set the demanded level of work at a moderate level, enforced by a probabilistic fine.

However, when Fehr, Klein, and Schmidt tested this model empirically in an experiment, the results did not support the SEM. The investigators asked a group of subjects to act as managers and choose either a BC or an IC. They then had to make offers to another group of subjects acting as salespeople, who then chose their level of effort. Managers chose the BC 88 % of the time, and salespeople reciprocated by supplying a greater effort than necessary. Managers in turn reciprocated by paying higher bonus payments. As a result of the greater effort, payoffs to both manager and salesperson were higher under the BC than under the IC. The study concluded that the empirical findings supported the FS inequality-aversion model described earlier.

Questions

1. Explain how the empirical results could be interpreted as supporting the IA model as far the behavior of the subjects was concerned.

2. The IA model predicts that there will be a pooling equilibrium for managers under the BC, with both purely selfish and fair-minded managers offering the same wage. Why would this happen?

3. The IA model predicts that fair-minded salespersons will put in less effort than purely selfish ones under a BC. Why would this happen?

4. Discuss other forms of contract that a manager might use to motivate salespeople, given the existence of inequality-aversion and reciprocity.

Part V
Conclusion

9 Rationality

9.1 Nature of rationality

Defining rationality

Many references have been made throughout the previous chapters to the notion of rationality. But what does it mean? Maybe it is easiest to start with its opposite, irrationality. People do all sorts of things that tend to be harmful or costly to themselves: they have unsafe sex, smoke cigarettes (maybe afterwards), commit suicide, neglect to wear seat belts, and hurt those that they love, to name just a few. Some or all of these acts may be termed "irrational"; in this case we tend to mean that people are not acting in their self-interest. The psychologist Baumeister (2001) refers to such behavior as being "self-defeating."

When we refer to people acting rationally in the everyday sense, we usually mean that they are using reason. This kind of action is often contrasted with people being prompted either by emotional factors or by unconscious instinct. However, this kind of meaning, although still favored by many in the social sciences, is far too broad and imprecise for most economists. Traditionally they have tended to use the term "rationality" in a far narrower context to refer to actions that are coherent, in the sense of individuals making consistent choices. This in turn involves the concept of transitive preferences: if A is preferred to B, and B is preferred to C, then a rational individual will prefer A to C.

Thus so far we can identify three different meanings of rationality: self-interested behavior, using reasoning, and having transitive preferences. In the context of behavioral economics all these senses of rationality have sometimes been used and others as well. However, it is important to realize that there is still no consensus regarding a universal definition. In fact one can go so far as to say that there is no single *correct* definition of rationality; there are simply a number of different working definitions or interpretations, and some are more useful than others in terms of aiding analysis, meaning explanation, and prediction. One reason it is important to appreciate this is that much of the disagreement about what constitutes rational action is based on differences in definition. Bearing this in mind, it is also important to note that one should not equate the SEM and its neoclassical foundations with rationality. It is possible for people to act irrationally, by some definitions, and find that the predictions of the SEM are still valid; this tends to be the view of Vernon Smith, who has been particularly concerned with examining the predictions of the SEM in terms of long-run market equilibria. Smith, following Simon, does not accept the norms of the SEM in terms of individual behavior, and believes that individuals can violate these norms and still act rationally according to his view of rationality. This view equates rationality with the end results of the decision-making process as far as market efficiency is concerned. For Smith, if markets are efficient, for example in terms of market clearing, then this is evidence that individuals are rational.

On the other hand, by other definitions of rationality, people may act rationally and the predictions of the SEM may prove incorrect; this tends to be the view of Kahneman and Tversky, whose approach was discussed in detail in Chapter 3. Unlike Smith, Kahneman, and Tversky do accept the norms of the neoclassical SEM as a benchmark for judging rationality. By these standards they claim that individuals frequently act irrationally. However, they also argue that the systematic errors and biases that they find in their empirical studies do not necessarily constitute irrational behavior. Not surprisingly, these contrasting views and uses of the term "rationality" tend to cause some confusion.

At one extreme we have a view, which was perhaps first formulated by Ludwig von Mises (1949), that any action must by definition be rational. This approach essentially defines rationality in terms of revealed preference. If we perform a certain act, it must be because we have a preference for doing so; if we did not have such a preference then we would not perform the act. Associated with this approach is the view that "a pronouncement of irrational choice might seem to imply nothing more than our ignorance about another's private hedonic priorities . . . individual tastes are not a matter for dispute, nor can they be deemed rational or irrational" (Berridge 2001). The problem with such an approach is that it obscures the important factors involved in terms of the determination of revealed preference, and therefore, while it is a coherent view, it is not very useful in terms of aiding analysis and understanding.

Similar to the above view is the argument that evolution has necessarily produced organisms that form true beliefs and that reason rationally (Fodor 1975; Dennett 1987). However, this view has been much criticized as misunderstanding the role of natural selection in the evolutionary process. Most evolutionary biologists agree that natural selection does not guarantee that rational beings will evolve, or even intelligent beings for that matter.

A more useful starting point is provided by Baumeister (2001). According to Baumeister, "A rational being should *pursue enlightened self-interest.*" This definition draws attention to three crucial concepts: "pursue," "enlightened," and "self-interest." However, it is only a starting point, since all of these concepts lack clarity and need further examination. This is where much of the disagreement begins.

First, the description "enlightened" implies that an individual has perfect knowledge, something that is obviously not realistic. Sometimes the term "long-run self-interest" is employed, which is definitely more useful, since we have observed many instances of conflicts between short-run and long-run considerations, in Chapters 5 and 6. However, an even more useful qualification in this context is the term "perceived self-interest." Many behavioral economists take the view that if we misjudge what is in our self-interest then this is not a failure of rationality; it may not even be a failure of "bounded rationality," as we will explain shortly. There may be many reasons why we fail to judge what is in our "self-interest" (leaving until later a discussion of how this term can or should be interpreted). We may have incomplete knowledge or we may have cognitive failures in terms of the processing of information within the given time constraints. These failures are often ascribed to "bounded rationality," and behavior which fails to achieve self-interest because of bounded rationality is therefore not irrational according to this criterion.

We now need to focus on a second concept: is pursuing the same as maximizing? The SEM is a normative model in the prescriptive sense of achieving optimality because it equates pursuing perceived self-interest with maximizing expected utility. Again the constraints of bounded rationality are relevant. The work of Kahneman and Tversky in particular concludes that people tend to take a **heuristic** approach to decision-making. The term "heuristic" means that people use simple "rules-of-thumb," often unconsciously, in order to make decisions when there is a lot of information involved, much uncertainty, and a realistic time constraint. Thus we may have a personal rule always to pay by cash for purchases of less than $100 even if we have a credit card handy. Sometimes this can result in inconsistent or incoherent behavior, as we have seen, particularly in the various examples of preference reversals. What can be said at this stage is that bounded rationality is not concerned with optimality, or even sub-optimality; the heuristics involved in the decision-making processes of bounded rationality are more related to **satisficing**. We have seen a number of examples of this in various contexts: the multiple elements involved in editing in PT; the simplified representations of information in fuzzy-trace theory; and the procedural approach to understanding intertemporal choice.

What about cases where we misjudge what is in our self-interest even according to the more forgiving criterion of bounded rationality? Such instances tend to relate to the influence of "self-serving" biases, another term that has been mentioned in several contexts. An often-quoted example of **self-serving bias** is the "above average" effect: well over half of survey respondents typically rate themselves in the top 50% of drivers (Svenson

1981), ethics (Baumhart 1968), managerial prowess (Larwood and Whittaker 1977), productivity (Cross 1997), and health (Weinstein 1980). Some economists and psychologists would claim that such acts are irrational, and this aspect is discussed later in the section.

We can now focus on the third concept; the term "self-interest" also lends itself to different interpretations. Economists have traditionally measured this concept in terms of utility, where utility is a measure of subjective value. While this emphasizes the characteristic of subjectivity, it does not clarify the term "value," which again can have different interpretations. The von Mises interpretation mentioned earlier interprets value in **hedonic** terms, meaning that it should be measured in terms of pleasure or happiness. However, both of these concepts are notoriously difficult to measure. As we saw in Chapter 2, economists tend to steer clear of talking in hedonic terms about happiness, concentrating instead on welfare, which they define more precisely. There are two problems of using the concept of happiness that will be discussed at this stage. The first is that there are frequently conflicts between short-run and long-run happiness. We tend to associate the term "pleasure" with the short run, while the term "happiness" tends to be associated with a long-run state of mind. A typical example of a conflict is that eating a tasty dessert may give us pleasure in the short run, but it may make us unhappy later, both by making us regret our expanding waistline and by causing us to lose self-esteem by demonstrating a lack of self-discipline. These conflicts were discussed in Chapter 6.

A second problem with the concepts of pleasure and happiness is that it is possible for people to feel both happy and sad at the same time. This is supported by neuroscientific evidence that different parts of the brain are activated in each case. We cannot consider happiness and sadness on the same scale, with happiness being the positive side and sadness the negative side, and the happiness and sadness associated with different events in our lives cancelling each other out to result in some overall "score." In short-run terms, it is also possible to feel both pleasure and pain simultaneously. This is not because the pain *causes* pleasure (although this can be the case with masochism), but because of what can be termed the "no pain no gain" syndrome. Look at the faces of winners of distance running or cycling races to see this mixture of pain and pleasure in abundance. Neural imaging studies again confirm that the sensations of pleasure and pain are processed in different locations in the brain. The result of this phenomenon is that there is no single scale or dimension that is possible to use for measurement purposes. Happiness and pleasure, along with their opposites of sadness and pain, are also subject to the problems of anchoring effects, reference points, and framing effects, and these have been discussed in Chapters 2 and 3.

As we have seen, economists usually attempt to measure value in terms of "well-being," rather than in strictly hedonic terms. While well-being is not necessarily associated with happiness or pleasure, it is difficult to measure this vague concept subjectively and this approach tends to suffer from similar problems to the hedonic approach. Kahneman, Wakker, and Sarin (1997) distinguish between four different kinds of utility as measures of value. Of particular relevance to the discussion of rationality is the distinction between two of these: predicted utility, representing expected liking for an outcome in the future; and decision utility, representing the actual choice of outcome. Berridge (2001) defines rational choice as referring to situations where decision utility equals predicted utility. Irrational choice thus occurs when decision utility is greater than predicted utility. This essentially means that we want something more than we expect to like it. The kind of situation where this occurs is discussed in more detail later in this section, in connection with the influence of visceral factors.

There is one final aspect that merits discussion in this context. There is generally universal agreement that actions where no deliberation is involved, sometimes called instinctive, are neither rational nor irrational. These actions tend to occur on the spur of the moment, like ducking a flying object likely to cause harm. Such actions are sometimes referred to as **arational**.

However, even here there are analytical problems which raise a vital philosophical issue. The issue here is the concept of volition, or what is often called "free will." In everyday terms we use the term "free will" to refer to situations where we make a choice that is unconstrained by others. However, philosophers and neuroscientists raise the issue of internal constraints when we make such choices, in terms of brain physiology and function. Of particular relevance here are experiments carried out by Libet et al. (1983) and Libet (1985; 1993). These showed that brain electrical activity occurred at a significant interval (about 300 milliseconds) before conscious willing of finger movements. There has been much speculation and criticism regarding Libet's research findings and their interpretation, but there is a strong suggestion that our sensation of conscious will as a cause of action is an illusion (Wegner 2002). Wegner and others hold the view that the sensation of will is not the real cause of our actions, but is merely an accompanying or following phenomenon, or **epiphenomenon** in philosophical terms. The implication of this is that many or indeed all of our actions may be arational in terms of not being caused by any kind of conscious deliberation. This is not to assert that conscious deliberation does not take place in many cases, but raises the possibility that, contrary to our intuitions, such deliberation merely accompanies events, rather than causing them. Wilson, Lindsay, and Schooler (2000) have proposed that we may have dual attitudes toward many things in our lives, one a rapid response and the other a more studied reaction that takes into account the context and our personal theory of what we ought to be feeling. Wegner (2002) adds, "The conscious attitude will only govern our responses when we have had time to consider the situation and get past the automatic reaction."

Economists generally try to eliminate the many ambiguities surrounding the notion of "pursuing enlightened self-interest" by using a more precise and formal model of rational behavior, EUT, discussed at length in Chapters 2 and 3. We have now seen the shortcomings of the SEM in this respect.

Action and attitude

The preceding discussion introduces another factor into the discussion of rationality: does rationality relate just to decision-making, involving choice and actions, or does it relate to attitudes, preferences and beliefs? In general, economists have tended to concentrate on decision-making and actions, while psychologists have often taken the view that while decision-making involves deliberate choice, the formation of attitudes and beliefs may be beyond our conscious control, and therefore outside a discussion of rationality. If, as evidence like Libet's experiments suggests, our decisions involving action are also outside conscious control, then attitude and belief formation can be claimed to be arational in the same way.

Where does this leave us in terms of defining rationality? As stated earlier, there is no single widely accepted interpretation of rationality once terms come to be precisely defined. This will be made clear with various examples as we proceed through the remaining topics. It is important to realize that this is not in itself a problem, apart from the confusion it inevitably causes. The purpose of defining rationality in any given way is to gain insights into decision-making processes and results and make predictions. These insights and predictions may have policy implications for individuals, firms, and governments, as we have seen at various points; these implications are summarised in the next chapter. The existence and usage of different definitions and interpretations does not prevent us from gaining such insights, making useful predictions and drawing policy conclusions. EUT is the component of the SEM that provides the criterion for decision-making, but many economists and psychologists are also concerned with the reasoning, attitudes, and preferences underlying this model.

This leads us to one other view of rationality which can be considered at this point. Sen (1990) is perhaps the best-known proponent of this view, stating that

> Rationality may be seen as demanding something other than just consistency of choices between different subsets. It must, at least, demand cogent relations between aims and objectives actually entertained by the person and the choices that the person makes.

It may appear that this focus on the correlation between objectives and choices has the advantage that it no longer makes any assumptions regarding the nature of the objectives; these are simply taken as given. Sen thus considers the nature of our objectives to be outside the realm of rationality, on the grounds that people are concerned with more than well-being and happiness. The fundamental flaw in this view is that it takes an excessively narrow view of well-being. Our well-being does not just include material factors, it includes psychological aspects that relate to our emotions. Furthermore, these aspects are becoming easier to identify and measure using neural imaging.

Criteria for rationality

In the light of this discussion, a particularly useful view of the rationality of attitudes and beliefs involves the following four criteria:

1. Attitudes and preferences should adhere to the basic rules of **logic and probability theory.**
2. Attitudes and preferences should be **coherent.**
3. Attitudes and preferences should not be formed or changed based on **immaterial or irrelevant factors**.
4. Attitudes and beliefs should not be **incompatible with empirical observations** known to the individual, including their own conscious actions.

The first three of these criteria have been outlined and utilized by Shafir and LeBoeuf (2002), and in conjunction with the fourth one they are useful in discussing different types of irrational behavior in the next section. Before moving on to this, however, it is useful to note various similarities between these criteria and the axioms of consumer preference described in Chapters 2 and 3 relating to EUT. In particular the first three criteria above relate closely to completeness, transitivity, independence, monotonicity (or dominance), and invariance.

The one exception is the final criterion for rationality, relating to compatibility with empirical observations. This is not explicitly covered by either EUT or the scheme of Tversky and Kahneman (1986) relating to cancellation, transitivity, dominance, and invariance. It has to be said that this is a controversial addition. For example, it does not coincide with Baumeister's description of irrational behavior as being self-defeating. People could violate this fourth criterion, but still not necessarily engage in behavior that is self-defeating. This aspect is discussed later in the context of causes of irrational behavior in relation to cognitive dissonance.

However, the inclusion of the fourth criterion can be justified by comparing it with the second one. The second criterion for judging attitudes and beliefs is whether they are **coherent**, in the sense of being consistent with each other. This criterion can be regarded as relating to internal consistency. The last criterion for judging the rationality of beliefs relates to external consistency, meaning whether they are supported by empirical evidence known by that individual. An individual may hold a set of beliefs that are mutually consistent, but are contrary to known empirical evidence. In this case it may be claimed that the person is acting irrationally by clinging on to such beliefs. This aspect of rationality is the one involved in the commonly used economic concept of **rational expectations**, and it was also implied in Alan Greenspan's often-quoted expression "irrational exuberance," in referring to the stock-market boom in 1996. It is relevant that the empirical evidence must be known by the individual, for otherwise the fault is ignorance, not irrationality. However, it is not relevant that a person may not have any "free will" in choosing what to believe; such a choice can still be regarded as a decision-making action. Of course this kind of phenomenon, which we will see may be extremely widespread, raises the issue of why people would cling on to their beliefs in the face of contrary empirical evidence. This aspect is discussed in the section on causes of irrationality.

Therefore the structure of the remainder of the chapter is, first, to discuss types of alleged violation of rationality; second, to consider objections to these alleged violations; third, to discuss causes of irrationality; fourth, to discuss consequences of irrationality; and finally, to give a critique of EUT in the light of this discussion.

9.2 Types of violation of rationality

There are various kinds of violation of rationality according to the four criteria above. The main categories involve reasoning, choice, the nature of utility, the role of visceral factors, and self-deception. We will now discuss these in turn, attempting at this stage merely to describe the relevant attitudes and behavior rather than attempting to explain them. The explanation is again the subject of the section on causes of irrationality.

Reasoning

Faults in reasoning relate primarily to the first criterion for rationality described above. There have been many observations over a long period of time that have documented systematic defects in logical reasoning. Evidence suggests that people tend to use simple probabilistic rules, or **heuristics**, to guide decision-making, particularly in the context of bounded rationality (Kahneman, Slovic, and Tversky 1982).

An example of such a heuristic is the **representativeness** heuristic; this refers to the tendency to evaluate the likelihood that a subject belongs to a certain category based on the degree to which the subject resembles a typical item in the category. Although this strategy may be effective in certain circumstances, the basic principles of probability and set theory are often ignored by people in making judgments involving representativeness (Kahneman and Tversky 1972; 1973; Tversky and Kahneman 1983). An illustration of this phenomenon is where respondents are given a description of a personality of a woman, Linda, who has the characteristics of a typical feminist. The majority of respondents rank the statement "Linda is a bank teller" as less likely than the conjunctive statement "Linda is a bank teller and an active member of the feminist movement" (Tversky and Kahneman 1983). In this case the strong representativeness of feminism overcomes the basic probability rule that $P(A \text{ and } B)$ can never be higher than $P(A)$. The difficulties that people have in reasoning related to connectives and conditionals have been observed in a number of studies (Johnson-Laird, Byrne, and Schaeken 1992; Johnson-Laird *et al.* 2000).

There exists a large number of studies illustrating various systematic faults in our assessment and calculation of probabilities, discussed in Chapter 3. One notable example is called the **gambler's fallacy**, and relates to situations where a particular outcome of an event has been repeated several times consecutively with the result that an opposite outcome now comes to be expected. For example, if a coin lands heads several times in a row, people may now expect a tail to be more likely on the next toss. There is an opposite syndrome of this kind of misjudgment, sometimes referred to as the **hot hand** (referring to basketball shooting). This involves seeing a pattern in repeated occurrences that is not really there, and concluding that a random process is really nonrandom. For example, people may conclude after several consecutive coin tosses resulting in heads that the coin is biased; likewise, after a player shoots several baskets in a row, people may conclude that he or she will continue to do so. Both the gambler's fallacy and the hot hand are examples of the **law of small numbers**. Essentially, this means drawing unwarranted inferences from small samples about large samples or populations.

The fact that heuristic rules sometimes lead to errors does not necessarily mean that heuristics are a bad decision-making device. This aspect is discussed further in the next section.

Choice

In this case we are referring to decision-making and action, rather than merely judgment. The irrationality here relates primarily to the second and third criteria. We will consider first of all situations where people's choices display a lack of coherence or consistency. The most prominent theory in this area is **prospect theory**, discussed in Chapter 3. The four main elements of prospect theory relate to reference points, loss-aversion, diminishing marginal sensitivity, and nonlinear decision or probability weighting.

Another aspect of irrationality has been discussed in **support theory**, developed by Tversky and Koehler (1994). According to this theory, subjective probability judgments are based on descriptions of events rather than the events themselves. The findings suggest that if the description of an event is separated out into distinct components, the event appears to be better supported in terms of evidence and therefore is perceived to be more likely. This phenomenon involves "event-splitting" effects, also discussed in Chapter 3, and identified by Starmer (2000) as being a significant area where PT predicts better than EUT. Support theory and prospect theory are complementary in a number of ways. We can thus observe that different descriptions of the same events can give rise to different judgments. This is also an example of the phenomenon of "framing effects," discussed in Chapters 3 and 4. A classic example of framing effects is the "Asian disease" problem, although we have also seen that the empirical findings here can be interpreted in different ways.

As well as illustrating framing effects, the "Asian disease" example also illustrates loss-aversion (saving lives is seen as a gain, while dying is seen as a loss), and the widely observed phenomenon of "preference reversal" (Slovic and Lichtenstein 1983; Tversky, Slovic, and Kahneman 1990). This term refers to situations where A is preferred to B using one method of eliciting preferences, while B is preferred to A using a different elicitation method. We saw in Chapter 3 that the nature and implications of the Asian disease problem are a controversial subject area, because of the confounding of framing and reflection effects.

We have seen that preference reversal can occur in a variety of contexts. Perhaps the best-known example relates to gambling situations. If a bet A offers a high probability of a small payoff and bet B offers a low probability of a large payoff, the normal finding is that people choose bet A over the riskier bet B. However, when asked to price the bets, people are normally prepared to pay more for bet B than bet A. Preference reversals have been observed among professional gamblers in a Las Vegas casino (Lichtenstein and Slovic 1973).

Another area where preference reversals are common is in intertemporal choice. We saw in Chapter 6 that various theories have been proposed to explain time-inconsistent choices, like hyperbolic discounting.

Another related example of preference reversal involves the **evaluability effect**. This occurs when attributes are difficult to evaluate in isolation, leading people to evaluate an item A higher than another item B when the two items are evaluated independently, but evaluate B more highly than A when the two items are compared and evaluated together (Hsee 1996). An example concerns the situation where subjects were presented with two second-hand music dictionaries: one contained 20 000 entries but had a damaged cover, while the other only contained 10 000 entries but had a new-looking cover. When they evaluated the items separately, respondents were willing to pay more for the second item with the new cover; however, when the items were evaluated together, most people preferred the first item, with more entries, in spite of the damaged cover (Hsee 1996; Hsee *et al.* 1999).

The examples of choice described so far have involved violations of the second criterion for rationality, coherence. There are also many studies showing situations involving violations of the third criterion, where choice is influenced by immaterial or irrelevant factors. One important type of this kind of violation involves **anchoring effects**, which affect both judgment and choice. In general these effects occur when subjects are exposed to some kind of process generating random values, and are then asked to specify the price they would pay for certain items or prospects. The price people are prepared to pay tends to be influenced by the previous random values. A study by Ariely, Loewenstein, and Prelec (2003) illustrates this effect. Students were presented with various products and asked whether they would buy it for a price equal to the last two digits of their own social security number (a roughly random number). The students were then asked to state the most they would pay. In spite of being reminded that social security numbers were random, students with numbers in the bottom half of the distribution priced a particular bottle of wine at $11.62, while those with social security numbers in the top half of the distribution were prepared to pay $19.95 for the same item.

Another example of a general effect of irrelevant factors is **context** effects. These refer to the influence of other options in the set. For example, people tend to be attracted to options that dominate other options (Huber, Payne, and Puto 1982) and to options that represent compromise options with attribute values that lie between those of other options (Simonson and Tversky 1992). One study has shown that in playing a game of chance, involving drawing a card from a pack with the higher card winning, players wagered 47 % more when playing against meek poorly dressed opponents than against confident well-dressed opponents (Kahneman, Slovic, and Tversky 1982).

Nature of utility

Utility can be measured in a variety of ways, as discussed in Chapter 2. For example, we can talk of predicted utility, decision utility, experienced utility, and remembered utility, amongst others (Kahneman 1994). Many studies have shown that people tend to mispredict utility for a number of reasons, many of which are related to the visceral factors discussed shortly. These mispredictions mainly violate the fourth criterion for rationality, since they frequently show that people fail to take into account past experience in decision-making. For example, people tend to neglect the dissipation of satiation, or how quickly satisfaction is reduced over time, and how quickly desires resurface (Simonson 1990). They also often fail to anticipate increases in liking due simply to exposure (Kahneman and Snell 1992), and fail to foresee the effects of a number of other factors on their future valuation of objects. In general there is a tendency to overestimate the impact of present factors on future hedonic experience (Schkade and Kahneman 1998; Kahneman, Diener, and Shwarz 1999; Wilson, Lindsay, and Schooler 2000).

The role of visceral factors

We have seen that visceral factors relate to emotions like anger, fear, joy, surprise, envy, and pity. Along with these emotions, visceral factors also include what are sometimes called "drives," like hunger, thirst, and sex, as well as cravings and pain. Psychologists tend to use the term "visceral factors" to refer to the combination of all of these feelings. At sufficient levels of intensity, these feelings tend to cause people to behave in ways contrary to their long-run self-interest, often with the full awareness that they are doing so. This behavior violates the fourth criterion for rationality. The following discussion focusses on attention, consciousness, and impulsivity.

Visceral factors like drives tend to be recurring states, which increase in intensity until they are assuaged, when they temporarily fall to a low level before rising again. This inevitable roller-coaster ride has a number of important implications for decision-making. First of all, as they increase in intensity, they narrow our **attention** onto the satisfaction of the drive. Starving people become obsessed with food, prison inmates become obsessed with sex, drug addicts become obsessed with getting a "fix"; all other desires fade into obscurity. In economic terms the MRS between the desired object and other goods approaches zero.

Furthermore, the increase in intensity also focusses attention on the present at the expense of the future, causing a lapse in self-regulation, at least as far as that particular visceral factor is concerned. Shortsighted decisions tend to occur in such circumstances as future consequences are ignored. In the more technical terms of the hyperbolic discounting model, the value of β, the additional discounting factor for the next period, may be substantially less than unity. Other implications here are that the values of both β and δ may vary from one situation to another; in particular they may be different for different goods and at different times.

Another kind of narrowing of attention occurs as individuals experiencing intense levels of visceral factors tend to become more selfish. They are less likely to cooperate with others, unless they see that such cooperation is likely to achieve the satisfaction of their needs. The other side of this coin is that they are also more likely to "defect," in game-theoretic terms. For example, under duress like interrogation they are more likely to betray friends and family.

In moderation, visceral factors tend to prompt us to take sensible actions, but as they increase in intensity and narrow our attention excessively they tend to cause us to make self-defeating choices, as Loewenstein (1996) has noted. Thus extreme fear may produce a panic that causes people to "freeze" rather than adopting a more healthy "fight or flight" reaction (Janis 1967). Likewise, extreme anger can result in impulsive and destructive behavior that is regretted soon afterwards.

Sometimes even moderate anxiety may cause us to make irrational decisions, by focussing our attention unduly on certain factors. For example, it has been observed that earthquake insurance purchases rise after earthquakes, when the objective probability is probably at a low-point (Palm *et al.* 1990). Similarly, purchases of flood and earthquake insurance are influenced more by whether friends have experienced the event than by the experience of one's immediate neighbors, even though the experience of neighbors should provide a better guide to the probability of experiencing flood or earthquake (Kunreuther *et al.* 1978). We tend to give friends more attention than neighbors. The problems here relate to the calculation of subjective probabilities, an issue discussed in Chapter 3.

Visceral factors, particularly when they are intense, tend to affect behavior directly, without any **conscious** deliberation process (Bolles 1975). Brain centers are activated, either chemically or electrically, which often bypass conscious or cognitive mediation, and action results. This mechanistic language indicates once again the irrelevance of volition as far as at least some behavior is concerned, as we have already seen with Libet's experiments. A more dramatic example is people falling asleep at the wheel; nobody makes a conscious decision to do this, but an intense desire for sleep can override the instinct for survival in this case. The extreme sensitivity of the brain's pleasure centers to stimulation is a vital factor in understanding drug addiction. It has long been known that laboratory animals will continue to administer electrical stimulation to pleasure centers in preference to food, water, and sex until the point of collapse and even death (Olds and Milner 1954).

Visceral factors also play an important role in influencing **impulsivity**. In general terms, we tend to think of impulsivity as relating to situations where people depart from prior decision plans. Usually the departure is prompted by some trigger factor, and this has an immediate effect. Impulsivity is often explained in terms of nonconstant discounting, discussed in Chapter 6, but there are certain aspects that cannot be easily explained in such terms. These aspects relate particularly to the effects of visceral or emotional states such as hunger, sexual desire, anger, or fear, which are frequent causes of impulsive behavior. We have seen that modification of the instantaneous utility function may be necessary in order to account for such factors.

We can also consider impulsivity in terms of the distinction drawn by Loewenstein (1996) between **actual** and **desired** value, which parallels the distinction of Kahneman, Wakker, and Sarin (1997) between predicted and decision utility. As the intensity of the relevant visceral factor increases, this increases the desired value (or decision utility), and thus the discrepancy between actual and desired value, increasing the probability of impulsive behavior. Another way of describing the situation is that we want something more than we expect to like it. As discussed earlier, this is how Berridge (2001) defines irrationality.

Impulsivity is also strongly influenced by situational factors. Temporal or physical proximity or sensory contact (sight, sound, touch, or smell) can elicit visceral cravings. In a series of experiments carried out by Mischel (1974) and Mischel, Skoda, and Rodriguez (1992) children were placed in a room by themselves and taught that they could summon the experimenter by ringing a bell. They would then be shown a superior and an inferior prize and told that they would receive the superior prize if they could wait successfully for the experimenter to return. One main finding was that the children found it harder to wait for a delayed reward if they were made to wait in the presence of either the immediate or the delayed reward objects. This finding is particularly important since it provides evidence for the visceral factor theory as against the nonconstant discounting theory. According to the latter, children should be more willing to wait in the presence of the superior delayed reward.

Visceral cravings may even be relevant in decision-making situations where the relevant drive or emotion may not be directly related to the decision. For example, people showing their homes to prospective buyers may do well to bake bread or cakes beforehand to create a more "homely" environment, even though buying a home is not normally considered to be an impulsive purchase.

Self-deception

Self-deception is sometimes neglected as a type of irrationality, but it is more widespread than most people might suspect, and it is clearly a violation of the fourth criterion for rationality. It can take many forms, and have many causes that will be considered in the next section. A psychological theory that is particularly relevant here is **self-perception theory**. It could be claimed that this theory was pioneered by the philosophers Bertrand Russell and Gilbert Ryle in the first half of the twentieth century, but the theory is normally ascribed to the psychologist Bem (1967; 1972). The essence of the theory is that people tend to infer their intentions from their actions, after the fact. It is as if people are unconscious of their original intentions and can only infer them from their actions. One implication of this well-supported theory is that people's preferences can be distorted, leading them to make bad, maybe irrational, decisions. An example of this comes from a study by Wilson and Schooler (1991). They found that students evaluating a series of different strawberry jams gave ratings that were less consistent with that of a panel of experts when they were asked to give reasons for their ratings than when they did not have to give reasons. It seems as if reflection on our reasons leads us to make nonoptimal judgments, by obscuring the unconscious realities of the situation. Thus the often-given advice "go with your gut feeling" may indeed be sound.

A similar example of self-deception is that people may **confabulate** their intentions, meaning that they invent them after they have taken some action, because of **cognitive dissonance**. This psychological theory is discussed in the next section on causes of irrationality, but it often involves people changing their beliefs in order to reconcile them with their past actions and behavior. The situation is demonstrated by Aesop's fable of the fox and the sour grapes. The fox wanted the grapes, but when she found she could not reach them she decided that they were probably sour, so she revised her original intention and believed that she never really wanted the grapes in the first place.

Another type of self-deception was mentioned earlier in the chapter, in connection with **self-serving bias**. People tend to have a higher opinion of their own abilities and actions than is justified by objective observation. This relates not only to the above average effect already described, but also to the fact that people tend to overestimate their contribution to joint or team projects (Ross and Sicoly 1979), and to attribute their successes to ability and skill, while attributing their failures to bad luck (Zuckerman 1979). Over-confidence is also most pronounced for difficult tasks, whereas easy tasks occasionally involve underconfidence; this is sometimes referred to as the **hard–easy effect** (Lichtenstein and Fischhoff 1977). A further aspect of this general phenomenon is that self-serving bias relates not just to individuals' evaluations of themselves, but also to groups with which they are affiliated. Observe any team game with partisan spectators; the different fans will inter-pret the play and, in particular, aspects involving foul play or penalties, quite differently.

9.3 Objections to violations of rationality

As more studies claiming and documenting the violations of rationality described above have been published, there have also been a number of attempts to reestablish the status of rationality, by defending the notion that people do generally behave rationally. These defences make various objections to the claims of irrationality. Shafir and LeBoeuf (2002) have classified these objections into three main categories: trivializations, misinterpretations, and inappropriate tests. We will follow this useful classification in the following discussion.

Trivializations

This category of objection relates to the claim that the alleged violations of rationality are unsystematic and unreliable. There are five main aspects that can be considered here: randomness, incentives, justification, expertise, and need for cognition (NC).

1. *Randomness*
   Sometimes it is claimed that deviations from the norms prescribed by the SEM of rationality are purely random errors, commonly observed in statistical distributions. This claim is easily refuted, however, since a

closer look at the evidence in a large number of studies shows systematic errors of overwhelming statistical significance. We have seen that systematic errors are in a predictable direction, for example many preference reversals.

2. *Incentives*

A common claim is the participants in studies often lack the required motivation to provide true or reliable results. In general, however, it has been observed that incentives do not reduce, let alone eliminate, the observed violations of rationality. This is not to say that incentives do not affect behavior in experiments. For example, we have seen that by using earned as opposed to unearned rewards in a dictator game, many subjects do behave purely selfishly, as the SEM predicts (Cherry, Frykblom, and Shogren 2002). However, in the extensive review by Camerer and Hogarth (1999) of 74 studies that manipulated incentives, the authors concluded that "there is no replicated study in which a theory of rational choice was rejected at low stakes... and accepted at high stakes." Most violations persist in the face of even large incentives, for example the amount of one month's salary in a study involving Chinese workers (Kachelmeier and Shehata 1992). Furthermore, incentives do not prevent a large proportion of small businesses failing. Neither do incentives help to reduce the incidence of optical illusions. It should also be noted that even if incentives are successful in increasing motivation, people still need to apply the correct insights in order to improve their performance; mere enthusiasm does not suffice for good decision-making.

3. *Justification*

Another method that can be used to increase the involvement of participants is to ask them to justify their responses. Although this sometimes reduces inconsistencies like framing effects (Takemura 1994; Sieck and Yates 1997), such effects often persist even when justification is provided (Fagley and Miller 1987; Levin and Chapman 1990; Miller and Fagley 1991; Takemura 1993). As with incentives, greater involvement does not ensure better performance; insight is still required.

4. *Expertise*

It is sometimes claimed that more expert subjects are more likely to exhibit rational choice, having more relevant knowledge and familiarity with the tasks involved. A variation of this objection is that people learn from their mistakes, and thus become more expert. An example of a study reporting this finding is List (2004), who found that experience in the market eliminated the endowment effect. The problem with this "learning effect" objection is that learning relies on feedback. In real life this feedback is problematical because many situations are unique, outcomes are often delayed, and they are often influenced by multiple factors. People do not frequently sell their houses, for example, and even when they do repeat this process, it is often under quite different circumstances from previously. Even when people do learn from experience, there is much evidence that experts make the same sort of violations that nonexperts do. For example, physicians and nurses have been found to make preferences and choices violating the first two criteria for rationality, involving the laws of probability and consistency (Casscells, Schoenberger, and Grayboys 1978; Redelmeier and Shafir 1995; Redelmeier, Shafir, and Aujla 2001). Financial experts have been prone to making judgments and choices involving preference reversal and framing effects (Tversky and Kahneman 1992; Benartzi and Thaler 1995; Siegel and Thaler 1997). Professional gamblers have also been observed to exhibit preference reversal (Lichtenstein and Slovic 1973). It appears that experts are subject to certain judgmental biases discussed earlier, like overconfidence (Faust, Hart, and Guilmette 1988) and hindsight bias (Arkes et al. 1981). It is therefore highly improbable that such violations can be attributed to lack of motivation or understanding.

5. *Need for cognition*
This factor relates to the notion that people differ in their tendency to engage in and enjoy thinking. It has been proposed that people with a greater need for cognition (NC) are more motivated to make better decisions, and are more likely to give proper consideration to the relevant aspects. There is indeed some evidence that certain violations may be reduced with high-NC participants, for example framing effects, with improved judgments in conditional probability situations, and less consideration of irrelevant factors like sunk costs (Smith and Levin 1996; Stanovich and West 1999). However, in spite of these results, there is no evidence that high-NC participants have better insight in judgments involving hypothesis testing and PD situations (Stanovich and West 1999).

There are some studies that combine a number of the above objections. For example, the **discovered preference hypothesis** (DPH) developed by Plott (1996) proposes that people's preferences are not necessarily revealed in their decisions, as we saw in discussing criticisms of PT in Chapter 3. According to this theory, preferences have to be discovered through a process of information gathering, deliberation, and trial-and-error learning. Subjects must therefore have adequate opportunities and incentives for discovery, and it is claimed that studies lacking these factors are unreliable. It has been argued that the best type of experimental design to ensure that the requirements of the DPH are met is a **single-task individual-choice** design (Cubitt, Starmer, and Sugden 2001). Such a design can ensure that subjects get an opportunity to practice a single task repeatedly, with the requisite learning effect, and it can also ensure simplicity and transparency, which are difficult to achieve in market-based studies, where tasks are more complex and involve interactions with others. However, when Cubitt, Starmer, and Sugden reviewed the results of nine different experiments involving such a design, they found that the results still violated the criteria for rationality, specifically in terms of the independence axiom for consistent choices in Allais-type situations, again discussed in Chapter 3.

In summary, it seems fair to say that violations of rationality cannot be dismissed as trivial errors in performance. Such violations persist even with highly motivated experts who give serious consideration to the problems involved.

Misinterpretations

A second objection to the rationality violations is that the irrationality perceived by researchers arises because participants tend to adopt a different understanding of the tasks from that intended, and that in the light of the participants' understanding their responses are rational (Macdonald 1986; Hilton 1995; Levinson 1995; Schwarz 1996; Slugoski and Wilson 1998; Hertwig and Gigerenzer 1999). We will discuss four main aspects of this objection.

1. *The conjunction error*

   It is sometimes claimed that subjects may infer that the researcher only gives relevant and nonredundant information. This is particularly important in tasks relating to the representativeness heuristic, like the Linda problem discussed earlier, involving conjuncts and conjunctives. When comparing the statements "Linda is a bank teller" and "Linda is a bank teller and is active in the feminist movement," subjects may infer that in the first statement Linda is *not* active in the feminist movement, and therefore rate the statement as less probable than the second statement. In more general terms, subjects may, after seeing the statement with the conjunctives A and B, infer that the conjunct statement involving just A refers to "A and not B." Indeed, some studies have found that rewording the construct and giving some logical clues like saying "Linda is a bank teller whether or not she is active in the feminist movement," do tend to reduce the conjunction error

(Dulany and Hilton 1991; Politzer and Noveck 1991). Another study has found that the tendency to make the error was correlated with a person's conversational skill (Slugoski and Wilson 1998). However, other studies have found that the conjunction error occurs across a wide variety of problems, and persists in a majority of subjects even when reinterpretations of the conjuncts are given to aid subjects in understanding the logic (Morier and Borgida 1984; Tversky and Kahneman 1983).

2. *Under-reliance on base rates*

Another kind of error relating to representativeness concerns the insufficient reliance on base rates in likelihood judgments. A good example is the AIDS diagnosis situation (Tversky and Kahneman 1982), where a base rate of one in a thousand people have the disease, but people, even medical experts, are over-influenced by the representativeness description that the positive test is 95% accurate. The critique here is that conversational inferences are again important. When the base rate is stated *after* the representativeness description, rather than before, this increases the reliance on base rates and improves the normativeness of responses, meaning that they conform more closely to the rationality model (Krosnick, Li, and Lehman 1990). When descriptions are said to be randomly sampled and unreliable, reliance on base rates increases significantly (Ginossar and Trope 1987; Schwarz *et al.* 1991). Also, when base rates are varied in the experiment, reliance on base rates improves (Fischhoff, Slovic, and Lichtenstein 1979). In spite of these improvements in performance, however, the evidence suggests that an under-reliance on base rates persists (Fischhoff, Slovic, and Lichtenstein 1979; Schwarz *et al.* 1991).

3. *Framing effects*

It has also been claimed that conversational factors may be involved in framing effects, like the Asian disease situation discussed earlier. Some researchers have suggested that the frames in options A and C, supposedly identical, may not be seen as such by some subjects (Berkely and Humphreys 1982; Macdonald 1986). For example, option A, "saving 200 lives with certainty," may be construed as meaning "saving *at least* 200 lives," while option C, "400 dying with certainty," may be construed as "*at least* 400 people dying." Obviously, under this construal option A is preferable to option C, and the apparent preference reversal disappears. However, evidence also suggests that the majority of subjects do not interpret the options in this manner, and do in fact interpret the options as identical (Stanovich and West 1998).

4. *Interpretations of probability*

A further area where different interpretations of terms may be involved concerns the general concept of probability. There are three main interpretations of the term "probability":

1. Classical – probabilities are determined *a priori*; typical situations involve gambling, like tossing a coin, rolling a die, or drawing a playing card from a pack.
2. Empirical – probabilities are determined *a posteriori*; past similar situations are observed and relative frequencies are used to calculate probabilities. A typical example is the probability of rain in September in London.
3. Subjective – probabilities are estimated based on intuition and experience. An example is the probability that firm A will increase its price next month.

However, it should be stressed that in all three cases the general mathematical maxims of probability hold true; for example, the probability of any event must be between 0 and 1, 0 referring to impossible and 1 referring to certain.

It has been objected that some subjects do not interpret probability in mathematical terms, and this causes them to make certain errors, like the conjunction fallacy (Hertwig and Gigerenzer 1999). This study showed that this error could be reduced by adding further information in the tasks involved. However, other studies have shown that subjects do not have different interpretations of probability than researchers, and that the conjunction fallacy persists even when further information is given to aid judgments (Tversky and Kahneman 1983; Kahneman and Tversky 1996; Stanovich and West 1998).

It should also be stated in summary that we have to be careful not to legitimize all misinterpretations by subjects, for this tends to beg the issue. We must ask *why* subjects tend to misinterpret certain terms in certain ways.

Inappropriate tests

The last, and most fundamental, group of objections to violations of rationality are based on the appropriateness of tests for rationality. Shafir and LeBoeuf (2002) classify these objections into three main categories: computational limitations, inappropriate problem formats, and inappropriate norms.

1. *Computational limitations*

   Some researchers have objected that computational limitations are the source of many violations, and that it is not useful to define rationality in such a way that it is out of reach for the majority of people. This is really the easiest objection to counter. Most of the tasks involved in the experiments described earlier are computationally very simple. It appears to be the conceptual aspects that cause problems and errors (Agnoli and Krantz 1989; Fong and Nisbett 1991; Frank, Gilovich, and Regan 1993). Furthermore, when the source of the errors is pointed out, subjects quickly learn to avoid them (Fiedler 1988; Tversky and Kahneman 1986; Tversky and Shafir 1992). It seems therefore that the problem lies in the heuristic procedures used. More will be said about this in the summary of the section.

2. *Inappropriate problem formats*

   It has been suggested, in particular by evolutionary psychologists, that the type of problem used in many experiments has been the cause of many problems, and that if the nature of the problems set is changed to coincide more with the types of problem encountered during our Pleistocene past, then the errors will tend to disappear (Cosmides and Tooby 1996; Gigerenzer 1996b). This point is discussed in more detail in the next section, where causes of violations of rationality are examined; at this stage it is sufficient to point out that, indeed, general performance on many tasks, like the Wason Test discussed in Case 8.1, is improved when the terms of the problem are restated to resemble realistic situations in our past, like enforcing social contracts (Cosmides and Tooby 1992; Gigerenzer and Hug 1992). However, this objection is really only valid if the problems set in experiments do not resemble current everyday problems, and this is not the case. Most of the tasks and problems are not entirely abstract, and the interesting point is that while people may be proficient at solving problems related to our evolutionary past, they are not nearly as proficient at solving current problems. In this situation it appears to make sense to define rationality as relating to current problems, not those of our past. However, this does not invalidate the most important point of the evolutionary psychologists, that our minds evolved to solve past, not current, problems.

3. *Inappropriate norms*

   The most fundamental of all objections to the rationality violations is that inappropriate normative standards of rationality are imposed (Wetherick 1971; Smith 1990; Gigerenzer, Hoffrage, and Kleinbolting 1991; Lopes and Oden 1991; Gigerenzer 1996a; Plott 1996; Binmore 1999). This objection relates to the definition of rationality and the discussion in the first section of the chapter. In essence, this objection proposes a relaxation of some of the normative rules in the SEM to accommodate certain aspects of choice and behavior that violate principles such as independence and transitivity.

The essential problem with this approach is that the suggestions as to which principles to relax are often somewhat arbitrary. Furthermore, if rationality is redefined in order to allow such a relaxation, rational choice will then involve violations of simple laws of probability, with the result that "rational" individuals will engage in gambles that in general they are bound to lose (Resnik 1987; Osherson 1995; Stein 1996).

It can be argued that there are at least two approaches here that are not arbitrary. A first approach essentially limits the application of EUT to situations involving risk and excludes situations involving uncertainty (Binmore 1999; Plott 1996). This therefore excludes all new situations decision-makers might encounter, like buying a house. In principle there is nothing incorrect about this approach, but in practice it imposes severe limits on the application of EUT. Furthermore, it can still be claimed that violations of rationality will occur even in the more limited scenario.

A second approach is that of Vernon Smith (1990; 1991), described briefly earlier in the chapter. Smith's views have much in common with the work of one of the founding fathers of behavioral economics, Simon (1956; 1957; 1959; 1978). Both reject the norms of the SEM as far as rationality is concerned. Smith claims that the appropriate norms for judging rationality are the end results of decision-making, in terms of long-run market efficiency. He also stresses that short-run errors and biases may be corrected in the long run by experience and learning.

The most obvious problem here is that short-run errors and biases are often not corrected by learning, as mentioned earlier. Furthermore, there are some glaring systematic and long-run inefficiencies in the market; perhaps the best example is a phenomenon referred to as the "equity premium puzzle," discussed at length in Case 4.1. Equities in the United States have over the long run (since 1926) yielded an annual return about 6 % higher than bonds, which is a much greater difference than can be explained by any reasonable degree of risk-aversion. Other examples, such as the tendency to bet on long shots in the last race of the day, were also discussed in Chapter 4.

A different type of problem, both with Smith's approach and with the general approach regarding the use of inappropriate norms, is that the normative standards of the SEM which are so widely violated in practice are actually generally adhered to in principle by the majority of people. It therefore seems to make little sense to abandon them. One might even say that it appears irrational to abandon them. This aspect is developed further in the following summary to this section.

By way of summary we can say that in general the above objections relating to trivializations, misinterpretations, and inappropriate tests cannot explain the large body of systematic evidence documenting a wide variety of violations of the standard model of rationality; nor does it make sense to redefine rationality in order to allow for such choices and preferences. However, it may make sense to formulate **dual-process models** of reasoning and judgment, which involve the operation of different decision-making systems in different situations (Epstein 1994; Osherson 1995; Evans and Over 1996; Sloman 1996; Stanovich 1999). The essence of such models is that in certain situations people use analytical, logical, rule-based systems with a relatively high computational burden, while in other situations people use various types of heuristic procedures. The use of heuristics can be viewed as a shortcut; frequently it results in an efficient use of personal resources, leading if not to optimization at least to satisficing. However, like many shortcuts, the use of heuristics can also lead to many bad decisions in situations where a more cognitive, analytical approach is desirable. Thus heuristics are both a good and a bad method of decision-making, depending on the circumstances.

9.4 Causes of irrationality

Baumeister (2001) has identified five different causes of irrational, or what he terms "self-defeating," behavior. We can really equate self-defeating behavior with behavior that is not in a person's long-run self-interest. One can of course question whether it is legitimate to equate irrational behavior with self-defeating behavior, and this aspect was discussed in the first section of the chapter. However, what is important here is the usefulness of the categories that he proposes in terms of analysis. These categories are emotional distress, threatened egotism, self-regulation failure, rejection and belongingness, and decision fatigue. The first of these categories involves a variety of factors, and it is helpful to discuss memory and cognitive dissonance as separate categories.

Emotional distress

The general impact of emotions on preferences and choices has been discussed in the second section. We now need to explain how and why these effects occur, recognizing that this remains a highly controversial area in psychology.

There has been a lot of research into the effects of emotions on decision-making. The conventional attitude taken by economists, and also by philosophers in the Kantian tradition, is that emotions tend to cloud good judgment, resulting in "irrational" decisions or self-defeating behavior. However, this raises the issue mentioned in the previous section in relation to evolutionary psychology: how can emotions serve as an adaptive evolved psychological mechanism? If they were a maladaptation people with genes for emotional behavior would not have passed them on to succeeding generations, and we would now be living in a world full of unemotional people, like Doctor Spock from Star Trek; this is clearly not the case. In the late 1980s the economist Robert Frank proposed a theory that emotions served as a commitment mechanism, and thus were a useful adaptation. Frank's theory was supported by independent research by Jack Hirshleifer. The neuroscientist Damasio (1994) also researched the role of the emotions in decision-making, by examining patients with brain damage, again concluding that emotions could be an aid as well as a hindrance. These theories are discussed in more detail later in this section. At this stage we can summarize the situation by saying that emotions can lead to either better or worse decisions, depending on the circumstances.

While the effects may be unpleasant and destructive, the evolutionary advantages of such changes in behavior are obvious. The need to satisfy or reduce basic drives is fundamental to survival and reproduction. This also applies to the sensation of pain; its unpleasantness is a signal that something is wrong with the biological system, and we should be doing something to remedy the situation (get out of the heat/cold, rest an injured limb, defend ourselves against the person attacking us, and so on).

One aspect of emotional distress where research has indicated a bad effect on decisions is the role of anger in risk-taking. Leith and Baumeister (1996) found that people who were upset were more inclined to take foolish risks, like betting on long shots in a lottery. There were various possible explanations for this; for example, people who were already upset had less to lose by taking a long shot and more to gain, while people who were in a good or neutral mood had more to lose by taking a long shot. However, Leith and Baumeister were able to eliminate this explanation by further experimentation, requiring respondents to reflect on their decisions for about a minute before choosing. Although the respondents were still angry when they made their decision, they now became more risk-averse. Thus it seems that emotional upset does indeed cloud judgment of risk, and that when upset people are forced to think about things they make better decisions.

In the above situation, emotional distress can lead to irrational decisions or self-defeating behavior. At the same time we have indicated that our emotions may be an aid to good decision-making. This now needs to be discussed further.

The theory of emotions as an evolved psychological mechanism or mental adaptation was described by Frank (1988) in the seminal work *Passions within Reason*. According to Frank, our emotions serve as **commitment** devices, meaning that they commit us to perform certain actions at a later time if other people behave in certain ways. The nature of commitment in general was considered in Chapter 7 in relation to game theory, with the famous example of Cortez burning his boats. Frank's insight was to see the role of emotions in prompting us to perform actions which we would not carry out if we were acting on purely "rational" grounds. A simple example can illustrate the situation. Imagine that we make an agreement with another person such that we perform some work for them now in exchange for being paid afterward. Such "delayed exchange" contracts have been extremely common in human history, on both a formal and an informal basis. The person doing the work first is always subject to a **holdup** problem (unless the details are formalized in a written contract), in that the other party can renege on the deal. Without any formal contract the cheated party has no comeback, and a "rational" person may simply write off the loss, and put it down to experience. An "emotional" person, on the other hand, would be angry with the cheat and take steps to gain revenge, at risk and cost to himself, which the "rational" person would be unwilling to take. However, the knowledge that an emotional person may react in this way might well be enough to prevent the other party from cheating in the first place. This is an example of what is called a **reputation effect**; emotional people may gain a reputation for not standing for any nonsense or backsliding in their dealings, thus encouraging others to be straight with them.

This example illustrates how our emotions can serve our long-run self-interest, but Pinker (1997) has gone a step further, showing how our emotions can backfire on us, referring to them as **doomsday devices**, after the movie *Doctor Strangelove*. The problem with doomsday devices is that they cannot be disarmed, even if they are activated by mistake, and will explode regardless of the consequences. Thus they may lead to futile and self-destructive reactions; a well-known example is the successive rounds of retaliation that occur with feuds between gangs or clans. It is possible that the reaction to social rejection, discussed in more detail later, is of this type. Emotions are indeed a two-edged sword.

Memory – homeostasis and allostasis

As far as our emotional states over time are concerned there are two important factors that need to be discussed, in terms of both their causes and their implications:

1. People tend to revert to a "normal emotional state" after any kind of emotional experience, whether it be pleasant or unpleasant.

2. People tend to overestimate the length of time that it will take to revert to this normal state.

The first aspect of human nature has long been known. According to Adam Smith in *The Theory of Moral Sentiments* of 1759,

> The mind of every man, in a longer or shorter time, returns to its natural and usual state of tranquillity. In prosperity, after a certain time, it falls back to that state; in adversity, after a certain time, it rises up to it.

This "certain time" turns out to be a shorter rather than a longer time in general. There is now a substantial body of research showing that emotional reactions to life-changing events are surprisingly short-lived (Suh, Diener, and Fujita 1996; Frederick and Loewenstein 1999). When people win large amounts of money in a lottery, they do not remain happy for very long (Brickman, Coates, and Janoff-Bulman 1978; Kaplan 1978). In the opposite direction, the majority of bereaved spouses reported themselves to be doing well 2 years after the death (Lund, Caserta, and Diamond 1989; Wortman, Silver, and Kessler 1993). Similarly, people who have suffered serious injury confining them to a wheelchair have recovered equanimity within a period of a year.

The second aspect is less well known. However, experiments have been performed that measure people's forecasts of emotional events and compare these with their actual duration, and there is evidence of a consistent **durability bias** in both directions. Thus there is a tendency for people to overestimate the duration of their reactions to both positive and negative emotional events (Gilbert *et al.* 1998; Wilson *et al.* 2000).

A number of theories have been proposed to explain both of the above factors. Let us take the short-lived nature of emotional reactions first. Five main theories emerge:

1. Happiness is a dispositional trait rather than a reaction to external events (Costa and McCrae 1984; Lykken and Tellegen 1996).

2. People adapt to repeated experiences of the same event, as that experience becomes a reference point to which new experiences are compared (Brickman and Campbell 1971; Kahneman and Tversky 1979; Parducci 1995).

3. Happiness results more from pursuing a goal rather than attaining a goal (Davidson 1994; Diener 2000).

4. People possess a psychological immune system that speeds recovery from negative emotional events (Freud 1937; Festinger 1957; Taylor 1991; Gilbert *et al.* 1998; Vaillant 2000).

5. People reduce the emotional power of events by "making sense" of them; this is also referred to as **ordinization**, meaning making events ordinary, predictable, and explainable (Wilson, Gilbert, and Centerbar 2003).

Although each theory may explain some aspects of the empirical data observed, the first four all tend to leave certain aspects unexplained. The first theory does not explain why external events do affect happiness or why this effect is short-lived. The second theory does not explain why single occurrences of an event cause adaptation or a return to the original emotional state. The third theory does not explain why people recover rapidly from negative events, and is therefore asymmetrical. The fourth theory is asymmetrical in the other direction: it cannot explain why people recover quickly from positive events.

The fifth theory is in many ways the most satisfactory in terms of explaining the different findings. In order to understand it further the concepts of homeostasis and allostasis need to be explained. **Homeostasis** is a well-known biological principle, whereby various systems in the body have an optimal set point, and deviations from this point trigger negative feedback processes that attempt to restore it. Examples are body temperature, the level of blood sugar, and electrolyte balance. The term **allostasis** was introduced by Sterling and Eyer (1988) to refer to a different type of feedback system whereby a variable is maintained within a healthy range, but at the same time is allowed to vary in response to environmental demands. Heart rate, blood pressure, and hormone levels are variables in this category. Thus when we exercise, both heart rate and blood pressure are allowed to rise in order to optimize performance. Wilson, Gilbert, and Centerbar (2003) suggest that happiness is also a variable in this category.

Wilson, Gilbert, and Centerbar (2003) also give an explanation regarding why an allostatic system represents a functional adaptation as far as happiness is concerned; in fact they give three reasons. First, they claim that it is dysfunctional for people to remain in an extreme emotional state, since they cannot adjust to new emotional events. Second, people in extreme emotional states tend to make less rational decisions, resulting in self-harming results, as already discussed. Third, extreme emotional states are physiologically debilitating when they continue for sustained periods; a good example of such situations occurs in wartime, when soldiers may be under extreme stress for prolonged periods, resulting in neurasthenia, "shellshock," and similar conditions.

The theory also maintains that the ordinization process evolved as a cognitive mechanism in order to maintain affective or emotional stability. This aspect involves the **uncertainty aversion principle**, a fundamental factor in many psychological theories. The principle is described by Gilovich (1991):

> We are predisposed to see order, pattern, and meaning in the world, and we find randomness, chaos, and meaninglessness unsatisfying. Human nature abhors a lack of predictability and the absence of meaning.

Again it is easy to see evolutionary advantages in uncertainty aversion. It drives people to take steps to reduce uncertainty by trying to explain and predict their environment, thus furthering their chances of survival and reproduction. Reducing uncertainty also plays a large part in increasing pleasure and decreasing pain, relating the principle to the SEM. The implications of the uncertainty aversion principle for the SEM were discussed further in Chapter 5.

The implications of the principle are very general. It has been argued that the main function of religion and art is to help people make sense out of a confusing, unpredictable world (for example, Jobes 1974; Pfeiffer 1982; Dennett 1995; Pinker 1997). We now need to consider more specifically how ordinization involves uncertainty aversion, how the ordinization process operates, and finally what its implications are for decision-making.

Ordinization is the process of assimiliation, accommodation, and "sense making" (Wilson, Gilbert, and Centerbar 2003), and it is a process that occurs automatically, without any conscious awareness. As time goes on, painful events become part of our life story, making them seem less novel and surprising. The events cause us less sadness, both because we think about them less and because when we do, the emotional reaction is less strong. In this situation, ordinization and uncertainty aversion result in positive hedonic consequences, as pain is reduced. A similar process occurs for positive effects, but in this case there is a paradox, since the hedonic consequences are negative: we seek positive experiences that increase pleasure, but by doing so we rob these experiences of their future hedonic power. This paradox will be discussed further at the end of the section, in connection with EUT, but we can give an example here for illustration. We may have a goal of seeking promotion, which, when achieved, gives intense satisfaction in the immediate aftermath. As time progresses we think about the event less, and it becomes an accepted and normal part of our life history. It may even come to appear inevitable in retrospect, a phenomenon known as **hindsight bias**. More generally this bias means that events become more predictable in retrospect than in prospect, and this is an important feature of ordinization, again being a result of nonconscious, automatic mental processes (Pohl and Hell 1996). However, the paradox is that sometime after gaining the promotion we are essentially in the same emotional state as before the promotion, and in order to increase pleasure and happiness we now have to progress to the next rung. Of course, if and when that is achieved, the same phenomenon will occur again. We are in the situation of the Red Queen from *Alice in Wonderland*, who has to run faster and faster just to stay still. As Matt Ridley has noted in his book of the same title, this phenomenon is ubiquitous in biological systems, because of homeostasis and "arms races."

We can now consider the implications for decision-making as far as emotions and memory are concerned. There are three that we can outline here:

1. Currently experienced emotional or visceral states tend to influence decisions relating to the future, even when those states will not persist for long into the future. For example, we buy consumer durables like TV sets and furniture because we anticipate that these goods will bring us lasting pleasure. Durability bias suggests, therefore, that we tend to pay too much for such goods, since the resulting pleasure will not last as long as we anticipated. Similarly, negative states may influence behavior, so that when we are angry we may make elaborate plans on taking revenge, which turn out to be a waste of time after our anger has cooled off. Another example is given in Case 9.2, where the relevant visceral state is hunger.

2. People underestimate the effect of future emotional or visceral states on future behavior. Thus if we fail to predict tomorrow's pain of awakening, we may fail to anticipate the need to place the alarm clock on the other side of the room, to prevent our switching it off immediately in the morning and going back to sleep. Even if we can predict the intensity of a visceral state, like the desire to smoke or eat chocolate, we may not be able to anticipate the effect on behavior (driving for an hour to find an open shop). This factor is also of importance in understanding the relapse behavior of addicts, who, after a period of abstinence, believe that they can indulge in low-level consumption (of alcohol, drugs, gambling) without relapsing. This situation, which also involves the third factor discussed next, is examined in Case 9.1.

3. People forget the influence that emotional or visceral states had on their past behavior. This can mean that they find past behavior influenced by such states to be increasingly perplexing as time goes on. For example, pregnant women can get food cravings very different from their normal tastes, and find it very difficult months later to understand such past cravings. People

also tend to remember pain and fear badly, probably because it is difficult to re-experience, as opposed to merely recall, these states. Again, pregnant women tend to forget the pain of previous childbirth; they may initially decide to forgo anaesthesia, but when labor starts they often reverse this decision (Christensen-Szalanski 1984). An important policy implication of this phenomenon is that the kinds of scare tactics which are sometimes used in promotional programs to deter people from smoking, taking drugs, or committing crimes often prove ineffective over a sustained period, and sometimes even prove counterproductive (Finkenauer 1982; Lewis 1983).

The discussion of ordinization explains why emotional reactions tend to be short-lived. But why do we consistently tend to underestimate the effects? One reason for this durability bias is that the relevant mental processes are automatic and nonconscious. A second reason is that we may fail to generalize from our experiences; we may come to believe that there was a specific factor involved (we bought a bad TV set, or we were not really that angry), rather than a general process. A final reason involves the phenomenon of **retrospective durability bias**. For example, we may forget that the product did not make us happy for as long as we had originally anticipated. Both prospective and retrospective durability bias may be caused by **focalism**, meaning that people think too much about the event in question and fail to consider the consequences of the many other events that are either likely to be going on, or were going on, in their lives (Schkade and Kahneman 1998; Wilson *et al.* 2000).

Cognitive dissonance

Self-deception is an important category of irrational behavior, as discussed in the previous section. It can be the result of a type of emotional distress discussed earlier. The most important psychological theory that is relevant here is that of **cognitive dissonance**, originated by Festinger (1957). This theory states that people are motivated to avoid having their attitudes and beliefs in a dissonant or conflicting relationship, and they feel uncomfortable when dissonance occurs. This discomfort can cause people to do many things that could be classed as "irrational." Thus cognitive dissonance generally involves people justifying their actions by changing their beliefs. This is because it is often easier to change one's beliefs than to change actions that have already been taken. However, cognitive dissonance may also involve situations where beliefs are held steadfastly in spite of contrary evidence. This is the kind of situation where the fourth criterion for rationality is relevant. These violations of rationality occur when it is harder to change an ingrained belief system than to change one's interpretation of empirical evidence. There may be a variety of ways to explain away uncomfortable empirical findings, as many smokers can attest.

We can of course ask the question as to why such behavior, or the mental processes leading to such behavior, can have evolved as an adaptive response. It might initially seem that such processes would be maladaptive, obscuring the realities of situations and leading to bad decisions. While self-deception may certainly lead to bad decisions, as we will see in more detail in some case studies, it may also be advantageous in other respects. In particular it may bolster confidence and self-esteem, increasing one's sense of well-being, and, if one can also deceive others, it may have the effect of increasing one's status in society. The evolutionary psychologist Pinker (1997) has gone so far as to claim that self-deception can be adaptive because it makes it easier to deceive others. If we really believe that we are the best person to do a certain job, in spite of our lack of ability, then we are more likely to convince others and be offered the job.

Threat to self-esteem

There is considerable evidence that concern with self-esteem can affect the quality of decision-making. In particular there appears to be a relationship between low self-esteem and self-defeating behavior such as self-handicapping, binge eating, and alcohol abuse. These consequences are discussed later in the section. However, research also indicates that the relationship is not a straightforward one. People with high, but misplaced, self-esteem may also indulge in alcohol and drug abuse, believing that they are strong enough to withstand the harmful physical effects and the tendency to addiction. This can be referred to as the **peacock's tail** syndrome, after the theory of the evolutionary biologist Zahavi, that the seemingly useless and wasteful peacock's tail evolved as a sign of health for its owner, who was strong enough to withstand the waste of resources.

Baumeister, Heatherton, and Tice (1993) also found evidence of a more complicated relationship between self-esteem and quality of decision-making. In general they found that people with high self-esteem made better decisions in risk-taking experiments, in terms of judging their own performance better than people with low self-esteem, and gambling in an appropriate manner. However, when people with high self-esteem received a blow to their pride they started to make bad decisions, worse even than those with low self-esteem, by making large bets that were not justified by their own performance. They seemed to be anxious to wipe out the loss of face involved.

Failure of self-regulation

Self-regulation in the current context refers to the need for individuals to reflect on advantages and disadvantages before making decisions rather than acting impulsively. One aspect of this has already been described, in connection with emotional distress. Another aspect of self-regulation involves the weighing of long-run costs against short-run benefits of decisions. This aspect is often referred to as intertemporal decision-making, and was discussed in Chapters 5 and 6. Self-regulation in this situation involves the delay of gratification. The ability for self-regulation is obviously a useful adaptation, enabling our ancestors to withstand temptations that would have resulted in early death, and encouraging them to make long-run investments in the health of themselves and their families.

There may be different reasons why self-regulation breaks down, as we have seen in various contexts. One factor that can be repeated at this stage is that the capacity for self-regulation is an exhaustible resource, much like physical strength (Muraven and Baumeister 2000; Muraven, Tice, and Baumeister 1998). This phenomenon was discussed in Chapter 6, in connection with the study by Shiv and Fedorikhin (1999). The study showed that cognitive load reduced self-control, as people who had to remember longer numbers were more likely to eat chocolate cake. The similarity between the capacity for self-regulation and physical strength is twofold. First, it is easily depleted in the short run so that people cannot continue to resist temptation indefinitely; also as they have to deal with more stress in one situation, they tend to lose control in other situations, for example by smoking, drinking, or eating more. Second, the capacity for self-regulation appears to be something that can be increased in the long run, just as a muscle adapts to physical exercise by becoming stronger in the long run. For example, Muraven, Baumeister, and Tice (1999) found that repeated exercises in self-control, such as trying to improve posture, over a period of 2 weeks led to improvements in self-control in laboratory tasks relative to people who did not exercise.

Decision fatigue

It seems that people not only tire when it comes to self-control, but also tire of making decisions in general. This may well be the main reason that people are creatures of habit; having a routine avoids the need to expend scarce resources by making choices. A good illustration of this phenomenon is provided by the research of Twenge *et al.* (2000). They found that a group of respondents who had to make a series of product choices had a reduced capacity for self-regulation compared with a control group. The capacity for self-regulation was measured by asking the respondents to drink as much as they could of an unpleasant, bitter-tasting beverage. This finding suggests that people tire of making decisions, and when they do so it is possible that any further decisions that are forced on them before they have had time to recover may result in a fall in quality. Military psychologists have found a similar tendency with commanders in battle (Dixon 1976).

Interpersonal rejection

Humans have a strong innate desire to belong to a social group that is virtually universal. The evolutionary advantages of this are obvious, which is why this desire tends to be even greater and more fundamental than the desire for self-esteem. However, if people feel rejected socially, this appears to be such a psychological blow that they cease to function effectively in a number of ways. Experimental research indicates that they make poorer decisions, making more unhealthy choices, gambling foolishly, and also becoming more aggressive and less cooperative. Even performance on intelligence tests is adversely affected. The reasons for this general loss of effective function are not clear at present; further research needs to be performed in this area, probably of a neuroscientific nature. It is likely that rejection causes a change in the body's output of hormones and neurotransmitters. Research has already established, for example, that both the winning teams and their supporters enjoy an increase in testosterone output following victory, while the losers and their supporters suffer from a drop in testosterone.

Foundations in evolutionary neurobiology

We now need to say something in general about all the above causes of irrationality, which apply to many of the observed features of behavior discussed in earlier chapters. Our starting point is to take a reductionist approach. We must examine how the human brain evolved if we are to gain a real understanding of behavior. The brain did not evolve in order to be a rational decision-making system, or to maximize utility, well-being, or hedonic pleasure. The forces of natural selection have caused the brain to be designed as a *system that maximizes biological fitness*. **Biological fitness** relates not only to our own individual survival and reproduction, but also in broader terms to the survival of our relatives who share the same genes. Those of our ancestors who were most successful in achieving biological fitness were most able to spread their genes, ensuring the survival of more people with the same genetic abilities. In order to achieve this end, however, the brain and other body mechanisms must have a signaling system to guide the brain to make the correct decisions. This is where pain and pleasure enter the picture. Pain generally can tell us we have made a bad decision as far as biological fitness is concerned, whereas pleasure can tell us we have made a good decision. Thus we can say that the individual is prompted to maximize hedonic pleasure as a means to the ultimate end of maximizing biological fitness. It is largely the indirect nature of this mechanism that leads to the objection described earlier that inappropriate norms are used to judge rationality.

Furthermore, it should be recognized that this hedonic pleasure relates not only to conventional goods but also to what we call "moral sentiments." This point was made earlier in the chapter, but it is important to realize that talk about "life being about more than happiness" misunderstands this crucial insight. Although morality has been heavily influenced by cultural factors over the last few thousand years, it originally evolved for the same reason as the brain to maximize biological fitness. Ultimately, this involves the same signaling system in terms of pain and pleasure. If we feel the pain of guilt, this may be a signal that we have made a bad decision; others may punish us if they discover our actions. Likewise the pleasure of performing a virtuous action or "doing our duty" may signal a good decision; we may be rewarded by others.

The essential problem with this mechanism is that our hedonic system can be easily hijacked. One main reason for this is that there is always a time lag between the optimal design and the demands of the current environment. Just as the military are often accused of preparing to fight the last war, our brains and physiological systems are geared to dealing with the demands of a past environment. Thus we have cravings for salt and sugar, which in the past were vital nutrients necessary for survival, but which now cause all kinds of health problems when consumed in excess. Our endorphin receptors in the brain can be fooled into craving opiates as a source of pleasure, getting us addicted to hard drugs. It can also be argued that our hedonic system may be hijacked in the case of our moral sentiments as well; for example, a bad or brutal environment may eliminate feelings of guilt for performing antisocial actions.

Another reason why our hedonic systems can be hijacked is that they use **heuristic devices** to achieve their ends. Natural selection is a "blind watchmaker," as Dawkins (1986) has elegantly described it, and is a **mechanistic** rather than a **teleological** process. This means that it has no "purpose"; it builds on what has developed from the past, rather than by looking ahead to the future and setting a goal. The implications of this mechanistic process are often misunderstood even by educated and intelligent commentators, so it is worthwhile expanding on this aspect. The maximization of biological fitness, or **selfish gene theory** as it is frequently described in reductionist terms (Dawkins 1976), is sometimes rejected out-of-hand on the basis that it cannot explain why we use contraceptive devices and other nonreproductive sexual practices. The response to this is that our brains are not designed to further reproduction *directly*. This would involve fantastically complicated neural machinery, which may well not adapt well to changes in the environment, and which would use great resources of precious energy. Instead, our brains operate using basic heuristic processes, so that sexual activity in general gives pleasure, regardless of whether it results in reproduction. The association of sexual activity with pleasure is generally sufficient to promote reproduction, and certainly has been throughout evolutionary history until very recently.

It is true that there is a minority who dispute the mechanistic nature of the theory of natural selection, supporting the idea (it would be presumptuous to call it a theory) of **Intelligent Design** (ID), which proposes that the process of evolution is indeed teleological in nature, engineered by an Intelligent Designer (God), who just happens to be the God of Christianity. However, most scientists do not regard ID as a serious contender in terms of being a legitimate scientific theory. It is generally seen as a cloak for creationism and the political agenda of the religious right in the United States. ID contains some fundamental flaws in terms of scientific argument, both at the level of molecular biochemistry and at the cosmological level (Shanks 2004; Kirschner and Gerhart 2006). Quite apart from this, it makes some heroic assumptions about the nature of the Intelligent Designer. Crews (2006) gives the following critique:

> Intelligent design awkwardly embraces two clashing deities – one a glutton for praise and a dispenser of wrath, absolution, and grace, the other a curiously inept cobbler of species that need to be periodically revised and that keep getting snuffed out by the very conditions he provided for them. Why, we must wonder, would the shaper of the universe have frittered away some fourteen billion years, turning out quadrillions of useless stars, before getting around to the one thing he really cared about, seeing to it that a minuscule minority of earthling vertebrates are washed clean of sin and guaranteed an eternal place in his company?

Such observations lead one to question whether the adjective "intelligent" is an apposite descriptive term in this context; "irrational design" may be deemed a more appropriate description, in keeping with Dawkins's concept of a "blind watchmaker."

If we accept the abundant evidence of the mechanistic nature of evolution and the way it builds structures without purpose, the implication of the use of heuristic devices is that they provide simple rules for appropriate action in a given situation, but they tend to be highly fallible. Many of the anomalies that we have now observed with the SEM are a result of this factor. Therefore, because of the way in which our brains and minds have evolved, we may be bad at performing what may seem simple abstract tasks, using inappropriate heuristic devices. However, these are tasks that have never been required in our ancestral past. On the other hand, human beings are extremely good at performing complex tasks that we take for granted, like visually following an object, changing focus and perceptions of colour, speed, and distance as it moves, and making the necessary biomechanical adjustments involved in catching a ball. Even the most advanced artificial intelligence systems designed cannot rival this performance. The moral appears to be that we are good at what we need to be good at, or, more correctly, we are good at what we needed to be good at in our evolutionary past. This kind of behavior may then not be so "irrational" after all; again the issue of appropriate norms is relevant.

At the psychological level, the kind of "irrationality" that we observe in human belief systems may not really be irrational in evolutionary terms either, in spite of initial appearances. Hood (2006) has claimed that the human mind has adapted to reason intuitively, in order to develop theories about how the world works even when mechanisms cannot be seen or easily deduced. This adaptation has had huge benefits in terms of the development of scientific theories related to invisible forces like gravity and electromagnetism. However, according to Hood, it also results in people being prone to making irrational errors, in particular relating to superstition and religion. This is because in our evolutionary past it has been more advantageous from a survival viewpoint to believe in a cause-and-effect relationship that does not exist (for example, God punishing people with bad weather) than not to believe in a cause-and-effect relationship that does exist (for example, the growl behind the nearby bush being caused by a lurking predator). Thus people tend to be overly fond of positing cause-and-effect relationships, even when none exists. Hood claims that it is therefore unlikely that we will evolve a rational mind, and that religion and superstition are here to stay.

After this albeit brief survey of evolutionary underpinnings, we can now turn our attention to consider the consequences of irrationality.

9.5 Consequences of irrationality

In the previous discussion we have already described many consequences of "irrationality," depending on how the term is defined or interpreted. However, it can be useful to classify these into three main categories, as suggested by Baumeister (2001):

1. deliberate self-harm.

2. trade-offs.

3. counterproductive strategies.

Deliberate self-harm

Baumeister (2001) claims that "systematic reviews of research literature on normal, adult human behavior has found little or no evidence of the first category of deliberate self-harm." This claim depends on how one interprets the term "normal." There is a category of people who can be classed as "thrill-seekers"; such people revel in taking risks, like base-jumping, that "normal" people would shrink away from. Medical evidence suggests that such people are abnormal in the sense that they are either lacking in dopamine receptors or that dopamine is reabsorbed too rapidly back into the cells. All humans have evolved to thrive on some dopamine "rush," which is what we get when we take certain normal risks, like driving fast. Evidence suggests that these normal risks do not produce a sufficient dopamine "rush" in thrill-seekers, and they are therefore compelled to take greater risks simply to get the same dopamine effect as normal people. However, even with this group of "abnormal" people, it is difficult to substantiate the claim that thrill-seekers have a "death wish"; they certainly deny it when interviewed, and they can be observed to take a variety of precautions to ensure that the risks that they do take do not result in death or serious harm.

On the other hand, there is certainly one type of self-destructive behavior that has had a large impact on the world since Baumeister's claim: suicide attacks. Of course it may be claimed that even such an extreme form of self-destruction is still in the pursuit of perceived self-interest and is therefore rational. In this case perceived self-interest involves glory in a heavenly afterlife. This in turn raises the issue regarding whether it is rational to believe in such religious dogma, according to either of the criteria for rational belief discussed earlier: coherence and consistency with empirical observation. Such a discussion goes beyond the scope of this book.

There are two other types of deliberate self-harm that can be discussed here. One type involves that resulting from guilt. Guilt can sometimes cause people to punish themselves in various ways in order to expiate the guilt. The form of punishment can be obvious, such as self-flagellation, or it may be more subtle, involving some kind of deprivation. Again, it can be claimed that such acts are still in the pursuit of perceived self-interest, since the punishment has the effect of improving the person's psychological well-being.

The other type of deliberate self-harm often discussed in the literature is **self-handicapping**. This kind of behavior occurs when people take steps that they know are likely to reduce future performance in some way. For example, a student may party all night the day before a test. The purpose of such behavior is that it provides an excuse for later poor performance, and tends to be found in those lacking confidence or self-esteem. Of course, there may well be other reasons for partying all night before a test: the student may on the contrary be overconfident; they may be lacking in self-regulation; they may be lazy; or they may regard the test as unimportant, at least compared to the benefits of partying.

However, one conclusion does arise from the foregoing discussion: the definition of rationality as pursuing perceived self-interest is too vague to be useful, since all acts, even deliberate self-destruction, can be interpreted in such terms. Berridge's definition is superior in that it does not suffer from this problem.

Trade-offs

Many decisions are intertemporal in nature, as already mentioned. In many situations, the benefits of choices precede the costs, and there may also be a considerable amount of uncertainty surrounding such costs. The decision to smoke is a typical example. The benefits in terms of pleasure are immediate, while the nonmaterial costs, in terms of worse health and the possibility of future disease and premature death, may be decades away.

It may well be that the decision to smoke or, more generally, to trade off long-run costs against short-run benefits could be "rational," again depending on how the term is interpreted. This involves the concept of discounting, as discussed in Chapters 5 and 6. More specifically, the kind of trade-off situation where rationality is most in question is where visceral factors are present, and decision utility exceeds predicted utility. Again, smoking is a behavior that can easily fit this pattern also, since it involves cravings and addiction. Situational factors, like the proximity of other smokers, may increase the intensity of the visceral factor to the point where an irrational choice is made.

Another example of a trade-off situation where visceral factors may be relevant concerns **procrastination**, an activity (or inactivity) with which most of us are familiar. Tice and Baumeister (1997) did a couple of longitudinal studies over a semester of procrastination among students in a class. Procrastination involves getting a short-run benefit, with a long-run cost as the work piles up at the end of the semester. Visceral factors, like the attraction of partying, may be the cause. The researchers measured both performance and health. In terms of performance, the procrastinators got lower grades on all assignments. In terms of health, the results were more ambiguous. The procrastinators had better health earlier in the semester, but they suffered from more illness later on in the semester compared with other students; furthermore, they were so much sicker that they ended up being sicker overall.

Counterproductive strategies

This third category relates to situations where a person is pursuing their self-interest, but chooses a misguided strategy. The fault therefore is with perception. There are a number of reasons why such faults may occur, many of which are related to bounded rationality as discussed earlier. Baumeister gives the example of a person drinking alcohol to cheer themselves up; this is likely to be self-defeating, since alcohol is actually a depressant. In this case ignorance is the cause of the fault. We have also seen that self-serving bias and self-deception may be causes of bad strategies.

However, with most of these examples it is difficult to argue that the problem is irrationality. It has already been argued that bounded rationality does not result in irrational choice. The situation is different with self-serving bias and self-deception. In this case it is attitudes and beliefs that are in question. Therefore the two criteria discussed earlier in this connection, coherence, and consistency with empirical observation, are relevant.

9.6 Critique of expected utility theory as a normative theory

As stated in the first section, the motive of pursuing perceived self-interest can be translated into more technical terms as the assumption that people act in such a way as to maximize their expected utility. This is the most fundamental neoclassical pillar underlying the SEM. However, because of the various problems already discussed relating to rationality, substantial doubts are cast regarding the validity of this model. Even if we extend the standard economic measure of welfare to include the hedonic aspects of happiness, there still remain problems with EUT as a normative theory. Schooler, Ariely, and Loewenstein (2003) classify these problems into three categories:

1. limits to hedonic introspection.
2. the adverse effects of hedonic introspection on well-being.
3. the self-defeating nature of happiness-seeking.

These problems will now be discussed in turn.

Limits to hedonic introspection

Hedonic introspection refers to the subjective measurement of one's own happiness or utility by the individual. It might initially seem self-evident that the individual is in the best position to report their own state of happiness, and relying on self-reports is certainly the easiest way to measure happiness. Furthermore, studies indicate that such measurements have relatively stable qualities of **validity** and **reliability**. In order for a measure to possess validity it has to measure the variable that it is supposed to measure. Lyubomirsky and Lepper (1999) have shown that individuals' self-reports of their overall happiness are reasonably well correlated with assessments made by friends and spouses. The quality of reliability means that repeated tests yield similar results. Again, correlations were quite high.

However, there are various problems related to measuring happiness by relying on self-reports, some of which have already been discussed in previous sections. The first point to note here is that there is a fundamental distinction between individuals' continuous hedonic experience and their intermittent reflective appraisal (sometimes referred to as meta-awareness or meta-consciousness). Thus, although every waking moment involves a hedonic experience, registered as visceral feelings, we only consciously assess these experiences intermittently. We cannot spend our whole lives consciously asking ourselves how happy we feel; sometimes we only realize after the event that we were happy, or unhappy, during that period of time.

When we do intermittently reflect on our happiness state there is then the issue of how we infer it. This is not as simple as it may sound, for it is not like taking a pulse; as we have already seen, there is no single scale we can use here, for we can experience both happiness and sadness simultaneously. There appear to be two main influences here which may not be intuitively obvious. One, which again has already been discussed, relates to the self-perception theory attributed to Bem (1972). Bem's central premise is that people often lack meta-awareness of their own internal states, with the result that they tend to infer these states, attitudes, and preferences from their behavior. This process is subject to considerable error, in terms of misattribution. Not only do people make inferences from their behavior that may be in error, but they may also misattribute sources of visceral arousal. For example, a study by Zillman (1978) showed that arousal induced by exercise could be misattributed to anger, and a study by Dutton and Aaron (1974) showed that arousal induced by fear could be misattributed to sexual attraction.

The second influence on our self-report of happiness is the situational context. Research indicates that people's valuation of experiences is strongly affected by prior questions they are asked. Such effects are known as anchoring effects, as we have seen. For example, a study by Strack, Martin, and Stepper (1988) asked college students how many times they had gone out on a date in the last month, and then asked how happy they had been overall. Other students were asked the same questions but in the reverse order. For the first group who were asked about dates first, the correlation between the two responses was .66; for the second group who were asked about happiness first, the correlation was close to zero. Thus the happiness response for the first group was anchored to the question about dating, indicating that the students were inferring the dating question was a cue to their happiness.

In another study by Ariely, Loewenstein, and Prelec (2000) a group of students were asked if they were willing to pay $10 to listen to poetry, while another group were asked if they were willing to be paid $10 to listen to the same poetry. Then both groups were asked to indicate how much they would want to pay or need to be paid to listen for different periods of time. The first group were willing to pay, but the second group had to be paid. Thus the students had no idea whether the listening experience was going to be a positive or a negative one; they simply took their cue from the prior question. The only consistent result was that they named higher amounts of money for longer periods, regardless of whether they considered the experience to be positive or negative.

In summary, it can be seen that the results of the hedonic introspection research in general shed considerable doubt on our abilities to measure our subjective happiness at all accurately.

The adverse effects of hedonic introspection on well-being

There are a variety of studies that indicate that hedonic introspection reduces the experience of happiness compared with situations where such introspection is absent. Some of these studies relate to specific hedonic experiences, some relate to happiness in general.

Taking the specific studies first, one body of research has exposed subjects to a series of painful stimuli of varying intensities, profiles, and durations, comparing the reports of those subjects who gave frequent online appraisals with those who simply evaluated the whole experience in retrospect (Ariely 1998; Ariely and Zauberman 2000). The result was that the first group was less sensitive in general to various aspects of the experience.

Another study with similar implications was discussed earlier, in connection with self-deception, and relates to preferences for different strawberry jams (Wilson and Schooler 1991). It appears that the requirement to reflect on judgment reduced the ability of the participants to evaluate the jams, by "muffling" their hedonic experience. Wilson *et al.* (2000) found a similar result in a study examining the evaluation of the quality of relationships with a significant other. Rapid judgments, without time for reflection, gave more reliable results, showing the importance of "gut feeling."

A final area of well-being worth mentioning in this context concerns humor. One study has shown that when people were asked to reflect on why they found certain cartoons funny, they actually found them less funny (Cupchik and Leventhal 1974). Thus there appear to be a variety of hedonic experiences where reflection spoils enjoyment.

Various reasons have been proposed to explain the above findings. First, introspection, by focussing on the self, automatically detracts from attention to the experience. Subtle features of the experience may therefore be overlooked, detracting from the hedonic appraisal. A second reason is that increased reflection and evaluation may cause the subject to consider features of the experience that were lacking in some way, thus also detracting from enjoyment.

Another group of studies has examined the overall happiness levels of different types of people. The general finding is that happy people tend to be less introspective (for example Veenhoven 1988; Lyubomirsky and Lepper 1999). Furthermore, unhappy people tend to be more self-conscious and ruminative (Musson and Alloy 1988; Ingram 1990). However, there is one main problem in interpreting these results: the relationships are correlational, which gives no indication of causation. It may well be that, rather than introspection causing unhappiness, unhappiness may cause introspection. Likewise, happy people may have no motive for introspection.

The self-defeating nature of happiness-seeking

A number of philosophers and writers have claimed that the pursuit of happiness is self-defeating. An example can be found in John Stuart Mill:

Those only are happy who have their minds fixed on some object other than their own happiness; on the happiness of others, on the improvement of mankind, even on some art or pursuit, followed not as a means, but as itself an ideal end. Aiming thus at something else, they find happiness by the way.

Schooler, Ariely, and Loewenstein (2003) propose three reasons for the self-defeating nature of seeking happiness:

1. *People have faulty theories of happiness*
   In particular this relates to the phenomenon already discussed in connection with homeostasis and allostasis. People who are motivated by increasing their material wealth tend to underestimate the short-term nature of the increased happiness that results. Studies have shown that such people tend to be less happy than people with other goals, such as achieving psychological growth, having satisfying personal relationships and improving the world (Kasser and Ryan 1993; 1996). Once again it should be realized that these studies are correlational, and do not prove causation. It may well be that unhappiness may motivate people to increase material wealth, and Kasser and Ryan (1996) have found that people experiencing troubled childhoods are more likely to pursue wealth as a primary goal than people with normal childhoods.

2. *Loss of intrinsic value of activities*
   Considerable research indicates that when people perform activities for external reward, for example money, the activities lose their intrinsic appeal. It is therefore plausible that if people perform activities, like going to a concert, with the primary goal of achieving happiness, they may obtain less enjoyment than if they performed the same activities for their intrinsic value, meaning in this example enjoying the music.

3. *Increased monitoring of happiness*
   It is likely that people pursuing happiness will monitor their happiness more frequently, and we have already seen that increased monitoring may well reduce happiness.

One approach to the empirical investigation of the issue of the self-defeating nature of happiness-seeking is to examine the relationship between selfishness and happiness, using selfishness as a proxy variable for intensity of happiness-seeking. A study by Konow (2000) revealed that people who were more selfish in a dictator game showed markedly lower levels of happiness than people who were more generous to teammates.

Another empirical approach has been used by Schooler, Ariely, and Loewenstein (2003). They performed an extensive study with 475 participants to examine their goals, plans, and the realization of these goals for New Year's Eve 2000. This study has particular value since it was not an experiment, and therefore the goals and plans of the participants were self-determined, not determined by an experimenter. One main conclusion of the study was that those who had made the most ambitious plans and devoted the most energy to their celebrations, presumably meaning those most concerned with the pursuit of happiness, were most likely to be disappointed.

The conclusion from all the studies on the pursuit of happiness therefore appears to be a paradox: if we explicitly pursue happiness and monitor the results, we are not likely to achieve our goal. Yet, if we never evaluate our experiences, we can have no idea what kind of activities to pursue at all, and are also unlikely to achieve happiness. Thus it seems that we are damned if we do and damned if we don't. Schooler, Ariely, and Loewenstein, however, are reasonably optimistic. They point to evidence that our unconscious automatic psychological mechanisms may be highly effective at both pursuing goals and monitoring our effectiveness in achieving them (Wegner 1994; Bargh and Chartrand 1999). In practice we may be like pilots who can fly most of the time on automatic pilot and only occasionally have to engage in manual control. As Schooler, Ariely, and Loewenstein conclude, "the challenge is determining when it is best to man the controls, and when it is better to simply enjoy the ride."

What is the significance of these three problems discussed above? As stated in the first section, it is possible to take the view that we can be rational from the point of view of the four criteria considered in terms of attitudes and preferences, but still not follow the norms of EUT. However, there is one final important point to make at the end of this section, which was also made in Chapter 3 in relation to PT. Criteria for normativeness are not the same, or should not be the same, as criteria for descriptiveness. The fact that there are various problems associated with the pursuit of happiness does not mean that EUT is necessarily flawed from the point of view of predicting behavior, at either the individual level or at the aggregate level. It may not be a good model to follow in terms of its policy implications, but it may in principle still be a good predictor of actual behavior, which is what of course economists are largely concerned with. However, as we have seen in practice throughout the previous chapters, EUT often fails as a good descriptive model also.

9.7 Summary

- Rationality can be defined and interpreted in many ways; there is no correct definition, but some definitions are more useful than others, particularly those stressing consistency.

- Rationality is normally applied to decision-making and actions; this has been the focus of most economists, and the neoclassical SEM equates rationality with the norm of expected utility maximization.

- Rationality can also be applied to attitudes, preferences, and beliefs; this has been the focus of most psychologists. Thus their criteria for rationality are different from those of economists, stressing logic, coherence or consistency, and relevance.

- There are various types of violation of rationality, relating to reasoning, choice, the nature of utility, the role of visceral factors, and self-deception.

- Objections to these violations have been made on the grounds of triviality, misinterpretation, and the use of inappropriate tests. However, even taking these into account, evidence suggests that violations still seem to exist.

- There are a variety of causes of irrational behavior: emotional distress, memory-related factors, cognitive dissonance, threat to self-esteem, failure of self-regulation, decision fatigue, and interpersonal rejection.

- The theory of cognitive dissonance states that people feel uncomfortable holding attitudes and beliefs that conflict with each other, and take steps to avoid this that may involve confabulation and self-deception.

- The theory of self-perception states that people tend to be unaware of their values and infer these from their actions, after the fact.

- Emotions can be both an aid and a hindrance to good decision-making; usually extreme emotions tend to have harmful effects.

- Memory for visceral states tends to be shorter than expected. This is known as durability bias. We recover from both negative and positive events quickly, involving a homeostatic or allostatic psychological mechanism.

- Recovery may be quick because of the psychological mechanism of ordinization, which refers to the assimilation, accommodation, and sense-making.

- The function of ordinization appears to be to restore emotional stability because of the uncertainty aversion principle.

- Hindsight bias refers to the phenomenon that events that seemed uncertain beforehand appear inevitable after the fact.

- Visceral factors can often cause impulsive behavior, where decision utility exceeds predicted utility.

- Impulsive behavior is influenced by the intensity of visceral factors and by situational factors.

- Evolutionary factors are ultimately responsible for irrational behavior, natural selection being a mechanistic rather than teleological process, leading to the use of heuristics.

- Irrational behavior can lead to deliberate self-harm, tradeoffs, and counter-productive strategies.

- Reflection on situations can often result in worse decisions, compared with going with "gut feeling."

- There are a number of problems with EUT as a normative as well as a descriptive model; in particular, the explicit pursuit of happiness tends to be self-defeating.

9.8 Applications

Case 9.1   Drug addiction

Drugs can take many forms. They may bring to mind immediately substances like cocaine, heroin, marijuana, and ecstasy, but they also include alcohol, tobacco, and caffeine products; performance-enhancing substances like anabolic steroids, growth hormone, EPO, and amphetamines; and medicines like beta-blockers, analgesics, corticosteroids, antibiotics, and tamoxifen. Not all of these substances are addictive, and some are much more addictive than others; similarly, there may be other products, not classed as "drugs," which may have addictive properties, like chocolate. Our concern here is with the concept of addiction rather than with the product.

Addiction involves cravings, which may be either psychological, physiological, or both. However, recent medical research indicates that all kinds of craving are ultimately physiological in nature, by having some effect on neural processes. These cravings are of a visceral nature, and for the regular user tend to be predictable, in the sense that the intensity of the cravings tends to increase steadily after each "fix," until the next one. The cravings also tend to increase according to the duration of usage, largely because users tend to increase their dosages over time.

The phenomenon of increasing dosages has been explained by Solomon (1980) in terms of an **opponent process theory**. This essentially involves an allostasis mechanism whereby physical events that cause extreme affective responses trigger an opponent process that produces the opposite affective response to avoid prolonged, extreme reactions. For example, when people take cocaine, the extreme emotional high that is caused in turn is followed by an opponent process

---

Case 9.1 *continued*

that neutralizes the reaction, as physiological processes take place to remove the chemicals from the brain. This process is initially weak, but is strengthened with repeated usage, thus explaining habituation and the need for ever-higher doses. Similar effects are known to occur with anabolic steroids, as muscle cell receptor sites become saturated, reducing the effectiveness of given dosages. In addition, the body's endogenous production of testosterone is shut down, offsetting the effect of the exogenous testosterone being administered.

Furthermore, the opponent process continues to occur after usage of the drug has ceased. This explains withdrawal symptoms, as the cocaine addict no longer obtains a pleasure-inducing response, but still suffers from the opponent pleasure-reducing response. The steroid user who comes off anabolics suffers a similar fate: there is no longer any exogenous testosterone, but it takes time for the body's endogenous production to kick back in. In the meantime they shrink in size and strength and lose their libido.

The hardships of withdrawal make it hard for addicts to abstain from usage. Visceral factors are intense, making it easy to relapse, particularly if situational factors are unfavorable. Even if addicts do manage to abstain for some time, two factors go against them. First, the longer they abstain, the weaker the memory of the negative consequences of addiction. Secondly, they fail to anticipate the strength of the future visceral states that will occur if they relapse. These two effects are neatly summarized by the organization Alcoholics Anonymous in the saying "the further away one is from one's last drink, the closer one is to the next one." When addicts abstain for a while, they may then revert to a low level of consumption, believing that they can maintain this. However, they tend to underestimate the strength of the cravings produced by even small levels of consumption, and frequently rapidly resume their previous addictive pattern of consumption (Stewart and Wise 1992).

Questions

1. What are the implications for an organization like Alcoholics Anonymous in terms of strategies they can adopt to counter addiction?
2. How applicable is the above analysis to other "addictions" like food, sex, and gambling?
3. How applicable is the opponent process theory in dealing with psychological responses to emotional events like winning the lottery or losing a loved one?

Case 9.2   Don't go to the supermarket when you are hungry

Impulsivity is a terrible thing; it can cause us to do all sorts of things that we regret soon afterward. Apart from being involved in drug addiction, it also leads to bad habits in terms of eating, drinking, sex, spending money, and sleeping. We have now seen that impulsivity is related to situations where we want something more than we expect to like it, or in more technical terms, where the decision utility is greater than the predicted utility of a decision. We have also seen that visceral factors are responsible, and that it is when these reach high levels of intensity that the impulsive and "irrational" behavior occurs. The key question we now address is, what strategies can we adopt to prevent ourselves from falling prey to impulsivity?

Preempting strategies are much easier if the visceral factors are predictable, for example when they recur at regular intervals. All of the visceral factors mentioned above fall into this category, whereas other factors like anger and fear tend not to be so predictable. However, even here human nature works against us, since we have also seen that people tend to be bad at predicting the strength of these factors in the future, just as they are bad at remembering how strong these factors were in the past. Thus, although we know tonight that we will be sleepy tomorrow morning when the alarm clock goes off, we underestimate our strength of feeling, and therefore fail to anticipate that we will slam the alarm off as soon as it rings and then oversleep.

Preempting strategies involve **commitment**. This means taking actions in the present that will automatically prevent us from pursuing impulsive behavior in the future. In the case of the alarm clock, *if* we can train ourselves to anticipate the strength of our future feelings, then we can place the clock across the room. Similar strategies are available for many bad and impulsive habits, and often make creative use of situational factors.

Let us start off with eating. There are a number of things we can do to cure ourselves of bad eating habits. It is well known to many of us from personal experience that it is disastrous to go to the supermarket when you are hungry. We end up putting all kinds of tasty but ultimately undesirable items into our shopping carts, and the next day at home we find our shelves stacked with goodies that have us scratching our heads and wondering why we ever bought them. This is because we failed to realize when we were in the supermarket that once we have satisfied our hunger, we will no longer want these items. In general we tend to think that our current visceral states will endure into the future; this is durability bias at work.

When we go to the supermarket after a meal we will tend not to buy many things that would otherwise tempt us. Later, at home after dinner, when we suffer from cravings for something sweet, we cannot be tempted by a large plate of pie and ice cream, because there is none in our fridge. Nor are there any of the tasty snacks to which we might otherwise succumb.

There are many variations on such preempting strategies as far as food is concerned. An interesting one is mentioned by Jay Phelan in *Mean Genes*. When he travels by plane he is often presented with a food tray containing a tempting brownie. His strategy is to immediately smear the brownie with the mayonnaise usually provided before starting his meal.

As with the above example and the alarm clock example, preempting strategies may often appear strange, but this is often a necessity in order for them to involve effective commitments. Similar considerations apply to spending. As discussed in Case 6.2, the savings rate in the United States has for many years been very low, less than 1%. Yet Americans on average say they would like to save around 10% of their income. There are a number of factors at the root of this problem, but impulse buying is certainly one of them. One aspect of this that we have seen in

Case 9.2 *continued*

this chapter is that people tend to overestimate the duration of the pleasure that they will obtain from buying consumer durables, and therefore tend to buy more of these than is ultimately in their self-interest. So what preempting strategies can we use to prevent impulse buying?

Again, there are a variety of things we can do here. A brief list follows:

- making a commitment to have a certain amount of money deducted each month from our salary at source, and placed in some kind of savings account;
- keeping a minimum amount of money in easily accessible current accounts;
- carrying small amounts of cash;
- leaving credit cards at home;
- committing to contribute to Christmas clubs;
- requesting low credit card limits;
- throwing away credit card application forms as soon as they arrive in the mail.

Sexual behavior is another area where our visceral impulses often get the better of us. The most radical preemptive strategies tend to be taken by some religious sects. Isolation in monasteries and nunneries is one example; an even more extreme strategy is voluntary castration. However, most people lack the motivation to opt for such radical measures.

There are also implications for government policy as far as impulsive behavior is concerned. Tax incentives can be used to encourage saving for example. Promotional campaigns can be used to encourage contraception, and to discourage crime, drinking and driving, and smoking. Antismoking campaigns in particular have sometimes focussed on scare tactics, but, as we have seen, these tend not to be effective because the fear created does not last very long. Cognitive dissonance may also play a part in reducing the effectiveness of such tactics. The UK government has recently changed its strategy in terms of attempting to discourage smoking, playing on another visceral factor: the message is that smoking ruins your sex appeal. Thus it is trying to implement one visceral factor to combat the effects of another. Whether this new strategy proves to be effective remains to be seen.

Questions

1. Why are preemptive strategies difficult for us to adopt in general?
2. Outline the preemptive strategies that one might use to prevent impulsive sexual behavior.
3. Explain whether you think that the new United Kingdom antismoking campaign is likely to be successful.

Case 9.3 Pursuing happiness

It's the pursuit, rather than the end-product, that makes Americans so American

ONE of the most striking things about the document that Americans celebrate with such gusto on July 4th is that so much of it is dull—hardly worthy of the tons of fireworks and barbecue that are sacrificed in its honour. There are lists of complaints about the administration of the courts and the quartering of British troops. There is an angry passage about King George's habit of summoning legislators "at places unusual, uncomfortable, and distant from the depository of their public records". But all this tedium is more than made up for by a single sentence—the one about "life, liberty and the pursuit of happiness".

The sentence was remarkable at the time—a perfect summary, in a few pithy words, of exactly what was new about the new republic. Previous countries had been based on common traditions and a collective identity. Previous statesmen had been exercised by things like the common good and public virtue (which usually meant making sure that people played their allotted roles in the divinely established order). The Founding Fathers were the first politicians to produce the explosive combination of individual rights and the pursuit of happiness. It remains equally remarkable today, still the best statement, 230 years after it was written, of what makes America American. The Book of Job gives warning that "man is born unto trouble, as the sparks fly upward." Americans, for all their overt religiosity, have dedicated their civilisation to proving Job wrong.

Everywhere you look in contemporary America you see a people engaged in that pursuit. You can see it in work habits. Americans not only work harder than most Europeans (they work an average of 1,731 hours a year compared with an average of 1,440 for Germans). They also endure lengthy commutes (who cares about a couple of hours a day in a car when you have a McMansion to come home to?). You can see it in geographical mobility. About 40m of them move house every year. They are remarkably willing to travel huge distances in pursuit of everything from bowling conventions to factory outlets. You can see it in religion: Americans relentlessly shop around for the church that most suits their spiritual needs. And you can see it in the country's general hopefulness: two-thirds of Americans are optimistic about the future.

Since Americans are energetic even in deconstructing their own founding principles, there is no shortage of people who have taken exception to the happiness pursuit. They range from conservatives such as Robert Bork, who think the phrase encapsulates the "emptiness at the heart of American ideology", to liberals who think that it is a justification for an acquisitive society.

One criticism is that the pursuit is self-defeating. The more you pursue the illusion of happiness the more you sacrifice the real thing. The flip side of relentless mobility is turmoil and angst, broken marriages and unhappy children. Americans have less job security than ever before. They even report having fewer close friends than a couple of decades ago. And international studies of happiness suggest that people in certain poor countries, for instance Nigeria and Mexico, are apparently happier than people in America.

Case 9.3 *continued*

Another criticism is that Americans have confused happiness with material posses-sions (it is notable that Thomas Jefferson's call echoes Adam Smith's phrase about "life, liberty and the pursuit of property"). Do all those pairs of Manolo Blahnik shoes really make you happy? Or are they just a compensation for empty lives à la "Sex in the City"?

If opinion polls on such matters mean anything—and that is dubious—they suggest that both these criticisms are flawed. A 2006 Pew Research Centre study, "Are we happy yet?" claims that 84% of Americans are either "very happy" (34%) or "pretty happy" (50%). The Harris Poll's 2004 "feel good index" found that 95% are pleased with their homes and 91% are pleased with their social lives. The Pew polls show that money does indeed go some way towards buying happiness: nearly half (49%) of Americans with annual incomes of more than $100,000 say they are very happy compared with just 24% of people with incomes of $30,000 or less. They also suggest that Amer-icans' religiosity makes them happier still: 43% of Americans who attend reli-gious services once a week or more report being very happy compared with 31% who attend once a month or less and 26% of people who attend seldom or never.

Weep, and you weep alone

The pursuit of happiness explains all sorts of peculiarities of American life: from the $700m that is spent on self-help books every year to the irritating dinner guests who will not stop looking at their BlackBerries. It also holds a clue to understanding American politics. Perhaps the biggest reason why the Republicans have proved so successful in recent years is that they have established a huge "happiness gap". Some 45% of Republicans report being "very happy" compared with just 30% of Democrats. The Democrats may be right to give warning of global warming and other disasters. But are they right to give the impression that they relish all the misery? The people's party will never regain its momentum unless it learns to relate to the guy on the super-sized patio, happily grilling his hamburgers and displaying his American flag.

The pursuit of happiness may even help to explain the surge of anti-Americanism. Many people dislike America because of its failure to live up to its stated ideals. But others dislike it precisely because it is doing exactly what Jefferson intended. For some Europeans, the pursuit of happiness in the form of monster cars and mansions is objectionable on every possible ground, from aesthetic to ecological. You cannot pursue happiness with such conspicuous enthusiasm without making quite a lot of people around the world rather unhappy.

Questions

1. Discuss the proposition that the pursuit of happiness is self-defeating, commenting on relevant empirical evidence.

2. "For some Europeans, the pursuit of happiness in the form of monster cars and mansions is objectionable on every possible ground." Explain this statement, commenting on differences between the American and the European viewpoints.

3. "Religiosity appears to make people happier; therefore I should become religious." Discuss.

Source: *The Economist* print edition, June 29, 2006

The Future of Behavioral Economics

10.1 The agenda of behavioral economics

Good theories

The purpose of any science is to develop theories that can accurately explain and predict phenomena. Perhaps the most prevalent criticism of economics is that it fails to do this very well in so many cases. Of course, economists are often put in the spotlight, making public forecasts regarding the state of the economy, growth, inflation and unemployment rates, stock-market indices, currency values, and so on. When these forecasts go awry, as they often do, the status of economics as a valid science is called into question. If the forecasts are wrong, then the underlying theory must be wrong too, no matter how complex it may be.

All theories are based on assumptions, or axioms. If a theory is wrong, it is often an indication that these assumptions are misplaced. We have also seen that assumptions are made not because they are necessarily believed to be true (unlike axioms that represent "truths" regarded as self-evident), but because they simplify the analysis. Economic theories should not be criticized simply because they make unrealistic assumptions; some theories can make some surprisingly accurate predictions even when they are based on unrealistic assumptions. However, when a theory fails to explain and predict well because its underlying assumptions are unrealistic, then it is time to reject or revise the theory by constructing it on a sounder base of assumptions.

Let us recall at this point the main criteria, discussed in the first chapter, that are generally agreed to be important in establishing any scientific theory as being good and useful:

1. *Congruence with reality*
   This relates to explaining existing empirical observations, and thus having good fit. The effect of this should be to produce more accurate predictions (although we have seen that goodness of fit and prediction do not necessarily go together).

2. *Generality*
   Theories are more useful when they have a greater range of application. Sometimes this attribute is referred to as fruitfulness.

3. *Tractability*
   This characteristic refers to how easily a theory can be applied to different specific situations in terms of making predictions. Mathematical complexity is often an issue in this regard.

4. *Parsimony*

We have now seen that some theories are more parsimonious than others, meaning that they are based on fewer assumptions or parameters. However, excessive parsimony may adversely affect both congruence with reality and generality.

Behavioral economics criticizes the SEM for being excessively parsimonious, resulting in a lack of congruence with reality or empirical fit. We saw in the first chapter that Ho, Lim, and Camerer (2006) have proposed the addition of two more criteria: precision and psychological plausibility. They, and other behavioral economists, perceive their task as involving the revision of the basic assumptions underlying the SEM, and placing them on a sounder psychological foundation. This should, and does, improve congruence with reality, at the cost of reduced parsimony and sometimes analytical tractability. However, another benefit of the addition of more complex assumptions and parameters is that this often leads to more precise, as well as more accurate, predictions than those of the SEM. It is helpful at this stage if we illustrate the agenda of behavioral economics by using some of the examples discussed throughout the book.

Examples of behavioral revisions to the SEM

The examples given below illustrate that in some cases modeling a situation in behavioral terms and using the model to make predictions is relatively easy, while in other cases the relevant behavioral factors are much more difficult to incorporate into a model capable of precise prediction. We will start with those examples where the use of additional parameters is more obvious and straightforward.

- *Game theory*
  This example is taken first, since it relates to the point in the previous paragraph regarding predictions. The standard model often predicts multiple equilibria, like in the market entry situation discussed in Case 7.2. Learning theory, thinking steps, and other behavioral concepts of equilibrium like QRE can be introduced into the analysis by adding new parameters into the relevant models. BGT can then provide more precise predictions about what will happen.
- *Loss-aversion*
  We have seen that this is a widespread phenomenon. It appears to provide the best explanation for the equity premium puzzle, along with choice bracketing. Loss-aversion can be modeled using a loss-aversion coefficient.

- *Impatience and time-inconsistent preferences*
  These factors are often modeled using hyperbolic discounting models. These models add the parameter β to the standard discounting model, where β represents a preference for immediacy.

- *Inequality-aversion and reciprocity models*
  By taking into account social preferences, these models can explain many seemingly irrational or unselfish actions, like refusing small offers in ultimatum bargaining games or cooperating in public goods games. For example, the inequality-aversion model of Fehr and Schmidt (1999) uses the coefficients α and β as envy and guilt coefficients respectively.

- *Choice bracketing*
  This aspect of mental accounting means that people select certain accounting periods over which they measure gains and losses. The choice of shorter periods results in a greater chance of making a loss in any given period.

- *Lack of fungibility*
  This factor explains why people may simultaneously borrow at high rates of interest, such as on a credit card, when they have current assets earning a much lower interest rate.

- *The representativeness heuristic*
  This and other heuristics have a profound effect on people's judgments of probability, causing severe errors.

- *Anchoring effects*
  These affect both judgment and choice. Purely random influences, like social security numbers, have been shown to affect people's valuation of items.

- *Endowment effects*
  Owners, or sellers, often place a higher value on items than buyers, reducing frequency of transactions. Again loss-aversion coefficients may be relevant.

- *Framing effects*
  We have seen that different ways of presenting identical information can cause preference reversals, like in the "Asian disease" situation.

Obviously this list is not exhaustive, but it does review a wide variety of situations where behavioral theories can improve on the SEM in terms of congruence with reality.

However, there are claimed to be two problems with the behavioral approach that we have come across in relation to accounting for the above factors, and these have led to some criticisms of behavioral economics.

10.2 Criticisms of behavioral economics

A profusion of models

One alleged problem, described by Fudenberg (2006), is that there are too many behavioral models, many of which have few applications. Fudenberg gives the example of modeling mistakes in inference, quoting various different models:

1. The "confirmatory bias" models of Rabin and Schrag (1999) and Yariv (2005), which propose that agents miscode evidence that their prior beliefs indicate is unlikely.
2. The model of Rabin (2002), which proposes that agents update as Bayesians in terms of modifying prior probabilities in the light of new evidence, but that they treat independent draws as draws with replacement. For example, if a lottery number has just come up, people would regard it as unlikely to come up again next week, even though lottery draws are independent from one week to the next.
3. The model of Barberis, Shleifer, and Vishny (1998), which proposes that agents mistakenly see trends in independent and identically distributed data, such as spins of a roulette wheel or daily stock market fluctuations.

All of these models may be applicable in principle to a particular situation. Thus we cannot use as a response here the "power drill" analogy of Camerer and Loewenstein (2004) discussed in the next section, where different tools are appropriate for different jobs. However, there are still two points that can be made in response to the Fudenberg criticism. First, behavioral economics is hardly unique in terms of being a science where there are many conflicting theories regarding the explanation of a given set of phenomena. One example from psychology quoted in the previous chapter relates to the phenomenon where emotional reactions to life-changing events are surprisingly short-lived. There is now a substantial body of research in this area, but we have seen that there are still five main competing theories relating to it. We agree with Fudenberg and grant that this is not an ideal situation from a scientific point of view. However, the second response is that behavioral economics is a relatively new science; it is going through what may be termed the "growth phase" of its product life cycle (PLC). Using the PLC analogy, the growth phase is characterised by a profusion of product variations and firms, and then, as the maturity phase is reached, these products and firms are winnowed down by the market forces of competition. A similar process can be applied to the development of models in behavioral economics. As further research is carried out, some models are likely to be winnowed out as lacking support, while others have their status confirmed.

Lack of normative status

We discussed this criticism in Chapter 3 in comparing PT with EUT. It is alleged that, by attempting to describe reality better, behavioral economics has lost its normative status. This is important because normative status is necessary in order for individuals, firms, and governments to make good policy decisions.

As we have seen, the term "normative" is ambiguous when it is used in an economic context. The ambiguity arises from the interpretation of the word "should," as, for example, in the expression "people should contribute toward public goods." For our purposes here, no moral or value judgment is implied by the term "should." The normative aspect implies a prescriptive status: what is necessary in order to achieve optimization? Therefore the statement involves a conditional, and can be interpreted as meaning "people should contribute toward public goods *if they want to maximize their utilities.*" Obviously a utility function incorporating social preferences is required here. In this example behavioral economics is able to provide a normative statement in the prescriptive sense.

The area of behavioral economics where such prescriptive status is most inclined to break down is where individuals are making judgments and choices, and was discussed in Chapters 2 and 3. We saw, for example, that preferences and choices are not necessarily based simply on attitudes and judgments. This complication arises from the violation of certain assumptions in the SEM relating to description invariance, procedural invariance, and extensionality. There are also different concepts of utility: decision utility; experienced utility, which may be either remembered utility or real-time utility; anticipatory utility, which is based on predicted utility; residual utility, arising from reminiscence; and diagnostic utility, which people infer from their actions. The SEM only considers decision utility, which it assumes is based on attitudes and preferences, which in turn are assumed to be consistent.

Once these demonstrated anomalies in the SEM are taken into account, the simple utility maximization model involving indifference curve analysis is no longer applicable. We have also seen that under conditions of risk a similar situation occurs, in that we can no longer use a simple EUT preference function that is to be maximized. However, in spite of the problems raised by the violation of basic SEM assumptions, this does not mean that the behavioral model cannot be prescriptive in principle. Although the analysis is more complicated, and often difficult to achieve in practical terms, it was shown in Chapters 2 and 3 that prescriptive statements can still be possible. We have also seen that in prospect theory various components, such as the weighting and utility functions, have axiomatic foundations. If we use the concepts of real-time, or moment-based, utility and psychological utility in order to provide an all-inclusive measure of utility then we can draw some conclusions about maximizing welfare. For example, we can attempt to resolve the paradox in the SEM that people may value more highly a job with a higher relative salary but lower absolute salary, because they think it will make them happier, but actually choose a job with lower relative salary and higher absolute salary. Only by becoming aware of these paradoxes to which behavioral economics draws attention can better policy decisions be made.

10.3 Methodology

We have seen at the start of this book that some aspects of this issue are highly controversial in science. For example, reductionism is often opposed in the social sciences, since practitioners find that their authority is being usurped by disciplines lower down the hierarchy or causal chain. It is not proposed here to revisit the methodological issues described in the first chapter, relating in particular to experimental design, but to focus instead on even more fundamental issues.

Assumptions and conclusions

Students frequently misinterpret and misuse these two terms. It is a basic of the scientific method that in any science one starts off with certain assumptions, and based on theory and empirical evidence, one proceeds to form certain conclusions. These conclusions may involve a rejection of some original theory or hypothesis, a confirmation of it, or a modification and refinement of it. Where matters become confusing is that in the causal sequence of events, and this involves the relationships between different sciences, conclusions in one area become assumptions in another. We have seen some examples of this in the first chapter, but more specific examples are needed here to illustrate this phenomenon in terms of how it relates to behavioral economics.

The SEM assumes that people are purely self-interested. As we have seen, this is an example of an assumption that is made for convenience, to simplify analysis, rather than because it is believed to be universally true. It is obviously a useful assumption, enabling a wide variety of predictions to be made, many of which are reasonably accurate. Behavioral economics attempts to find a sounder psychological foundation for economic theorizing, and therefore takes into account social preferences when trying to explain behavior. In attempting to build this better foundation the behavioral approach aims to search for **psychological regularity**. For example, it may find psychological regularity in the empirical evidence that people tend to reject low offers in ultimatum bargaining games, and that people also tend not to make such offers. This finding, a contradiction to the SEM, then provides a basis for a behavioral theory incorporating social preferences. In this context this aspect of psychological regularity becomes an "assumption" on which the development of different behavioral theories, like inequality-aversion and reciprocity, can be based.

However, this analysis only goes one level down the causal sequence. We can then ask, what causes people to have both positive and negative reciprocity? Behavioral economics leaves many questions with this status. For example:

- Why are people influenced by framing effects?
- Why do people exhibit loss-aversion?
- Why do people show self-serving bias?
- Why do people have endowment effects?
- Why do people make choices that do not appear to make them happy?

Some behavioral economists do not regard it as part of their agenda to answer these questions. I disagree. The key underlying theme is this book is that behavioral economics is multidisciplinary in nature. These effects, or psychological regularities, are taken as being the building blocks or "assumptions" on which alternative theories to the SEM must be constructed. The task of answering these questions is "delegated" to psychology, where these regularities are treated as being "conclusions" that must be explained by underlying psychological theories. Psychologists in turn make certain assumptions regarding neuroscience, in terms of how the brain works at a physiological level. Thus we move one further level down the causal sequence into the realm of neuroscience. As explained in the first chapter, this is the nature of hierarchical reductionism, which has proven to be extremely effective over the last few centuries in terms of developing theories with wide and deep explanatory and predictive powers.

The role of evolutionary psychology

The discussion of reductionism, assumptions and conclusions, leads us once more to the equally controversial role of evolutionary psychology, which has been touched on several times throughout the book. Not even the most extreme evolutionary psychologist would claim that *all* human behavior can be explained by examining, and guessing, what our ancestral lives and environments were like and theorizing about how human brains adapted to this. Unfortunately this is a straw man that has become popular in much of the social science literature critiquing the discipline. More realistically, the problem of evolutionary psychology is summarized by Camerer and Loewenstein (2004) as follows:

> it is easy to figure out whether an evolutionary story identifies causes sufficient to bring about particular behaviour, but it is almost impossible to know if those causes were the ones that actually did bring it about.

This problem leads to the main criticism of evolutionary psychology as a science: that it fails to make testable, meaning falsifiable, predictions. It is useful to illustrate this problem by taking one particular example, concerning the tendency to cooperate rather than defect in "one-shot" situations like PD games. The claim in evolutionary psychology is that subjects in these "one-shot" games are unable to switch off their inbuilt cooperation mechanisms. Thus, even when they are told explicitly that they are playing a one-shot game, and acknowledge this, in psychological terms they are still playing a repeated game. As Camerer and Loewenstein point out, this makes the evolutionary psychology hypothesis unfalsifiable if one is trying to predict comparative behavior in one-shot games with behavior in repeated games.

Certainly there is a need to be aware of this problem. Indeed, evolutionary psychologists will always face the problem that concrete evidence from our ancestral Pleistocene past is flimsy. The archaeological and biological record is sparse and is likely to remain so, although progress in molecular biology and genetics may make some progress in the latter area. Therefore conjecture and speculation, despised by "hard" scientists in particular, is inevitable. Much theory in evolutionary psychology proceeds on the basis of examining modern observations and making the following comparison:

$$\text{Prob (theory X from EP|observed values)}$$
$$> \text{or} <$$
$$\text{Prob (other theory Y|observed values)}$$

The evolutionary psychology theory is regarded as being vindicated if the evolutionary psychology theory has greater probability of generating the observed data than any other theory. In many situations there is no other recognized theory. For example, we have seen from Kahneman and Tversky (1973) that people are much better at solving problems when given data involve frequencies rather than probabilities. Single-event probabilities are often nonsensical in practical terms. For example, it may make little sense to say that there is a 35% chance that a woman is pregnant: either she is or she isn't pregnant. Similarly, in evolutionary terms it may seem strange to say that there is a probability of .375 of finding berries in a particular valley. On the other hand, people understand more readily the statement that in the last eight visits to the valley, one found berries three times. This may be regarded as another "just so" story, but the author is not aware of any other comparable theory in cognitive psychology which can explain this phenomenon.

In addition, it should also be pointed out that evolutionary psychology predictions are falsifiable in a number of areas. If experiments were to observe a widespread tendency to defect in one-shot games, this would falsify the hypothesis. We have also given an example in Case 8.1 related to the Wason Test, where evolutionary psychology can make some sharp and falsifiable predictions. Let us take a final example from a different area, regarded as being the domain of cultural influences. Parasites are known to degrade physical appearance. Evolutionary psychologists Gangestad and Buss (1993) therefore made a prediction that people living in ecologies with a high prevalence of parasites should place a greater value on physical attractiveness in a mate than people living in ecologies with a low prevalence of parasites. This hypothesis was tested by collecting data from 29 cultures relating to the prevalence of parasites and the importance that people in those cultures attached to physical attractiveness in a marriage partner. The results confirmed the hypothesis, finding significant positive correlation between the two variables. This example is taken because it illustrates how cultural differences, often assumed to be nonevolutionary in nature, can be explained by universal evolved psychological mechanisms that are differentially activated across cultures. Of course, other theories may be developed to explain the same observed relationship, but the essential point is that evolutionary psychology, when used carefully and thoughtfully, can provide testable hypotheses.

Parsimony and universality

Another criticism leveled at evolutionary psychology is that the explanations that it provides lack universality, and appear to have an *ad hoc* nature about them. We have come across these terms before in connection with the evaluation of theories. The term *ad hoc* means "for a particular purpose," and scientists tend to use the term disapprovingly, since it often implies that a theory is being twisted or convoluted in an unnatural way to explain away undesirable observations that cannot be explained by any standard form of the theory. The result is a loss of parsimony, as the theory becomes more cumbersome. A good example from the field of astronomy is the invention in medieval times of the concept of "epicycles" (circular orbits centered on other circular orbits). The purpose was to explain aberrations in the observed movements of the planets that could not be explained by the standard Ptolemaic theory of the geocentric universe. Copernicus's theory of the heliocentric universe, combined with elliptical planetary orbits, turned out to be a much more parsimonious theory, as well as being more accurate.

However desirable parsimony and universality may be to our structure-loving minds, the irony is that the human mind appears to be good at some things, but is surprisingly incapable of performing other functions. Evolutionary psychologists explain this behavior in terms of the modularity of the brain; it is not a universal problem-solving device. In order for the brain to develop such a broad capacity, enormous resources would be required, and this would be very wasteful, since many of the capabilities of such a brain would never be required in real life. The evolutionary psychology model, expressed most clearly in various contributions from Cosmides and Tooby, is that the brain did indeed develop in an *ad hoc* fashion, as it adapted to deal with the problems that it actually had to face in reality. They liken the mind to a Swiss army knife, with many blades designed for specific tasks.

Evolutionary psychology, by proposing that the mind is a device with *ad hoc* functions, is not alone in terms of appearing to involve *ad hoc* explanations. The same accusation is often leveled at behavioral economics; this is essentially the criticism of Fudenberg (2006) that was discussed earlier. Camerer and Loewenstein (2004) admit that the discipline is not a unified theory, but is rather "a collection of tools or ideas." They also claim that the same is true of neoclassical economics. They repeat the claim of Arrow (1986) that economic models do not derive much predictive power from the single general tool of utility maximization. They then claim that behavioral economics is more like a power drill, which uses a wide variety of drill bits to perform different jobs. Thus the concept of social utility may be the appropriate analytical tool when examining public goods provision and bargaining games; the concept of time-additive separable utility may be relevant in asset pricing; remembered utility (or disutility) may be relevant in the decision to have a colonoscopy; anticipatory utility may be relevant in considering the decision to postpone a pleasurable experience; and loss-aversion may be relevant in explaining asymmetrical price elasticities.

This discussion may seem to lead to a messy, even contradictory, conclusion regarding the desirability of parsimony and generality. There are two points that may clarify this:

1. If we accept that the mind is modular (and certainly more evidence is needed regarding the nature of this modularity) then it should come as no surprise that a variety of tools is necessary to study its functions and operations, as they are manifested in human attitudes and behavior.

2. This variety of tools may still have some commonality, just as all the various drill bits can be used with the same drill. In behavioral economics there are various commonalities; in particular the concepts discussed in PT and mental accounting have a very general application to a wide variety of human behaviors.

10.4 Future directions for behavioral economics

There have been various indications throughout the book where either areas of research or types of research are necessary in order to take the discipline forward. Appropriate topics to discuss at this stage are decision-making heuristics, the formation of social preferences, learning processes, the theory of mental representations, the role of the emotions in decision-making, and the role of neurobiology.

Decision-making heuristics

We have seen, particularly in the earlier chapters, that people frequently use heuristics or simplifying rules when they make decisions, and we have seen that the root cause of this is the existence of bounded rationality. These heuristic devices are of wide variety, including the representativeness heuristic, the availability heuristic, the $1/n$ principle, fuzzy trace theory, and the procedural approach. It is not intended here to review all the heuristics discussed and their shortcomings. However, there is one area of heuristics that has not been discussed so far. This relates to the case-based decision-making approach. Whereas the SEM examines future outcomes and their associated probabilities, the case-based approach is based on assessing the similarity of the current situation with various past decision situations, evaluating average outcomes from particular actions in these past situations, and weighting them by the similarity of previous cases to the current one (Gilboa and Schmeidler 1995; 2001). The approach is therefore based on the common observation that we all use past experience in some way as a guide to future experience. However, the choice of relevant criteria for judging similarity, and assessment using these criteria, obviously involves a heuristic process. This is best illustrated by an example. Say that we are offered a new job and are deciding whether to take it. We may have been in a similar situation in the past on several occasions.

What outcomes were important? These may include salary, or salary relative to one's reference group, working hours, amount of time traveling, working conditions, type of boss, quality of working environment, and so on. If we took a job based just on salary in the past, and this proved to be a bad experience, we may discount this criterion in our current decision.

The formation of social preferences

We have reviewed various models incorporating social preferences in Chapter 8 and have also seen that these can explain behavior in both real-life situations and experimental studies better than the simplistic "pure" self-interest model of the SEM. However, more research needs to be carried out on the underlying psychology involved. For example, it would be useful to know the relative importance of negative and positive reciprocity, and the relative importance of both of these compared with inequality-aversion. The importance of intentions also needs to be studied further, which means taking into account foregone payoffs. These can be studied by various methods of experimental psychology, and the results incorporated into modified social preference models. These can be tested by using further game-theoretical experiments in an ongoing process of refinement and increased understanding. This increased understanding may have significant benefits for public policy, as will be discussed shortly.

Learning processes

These processes were examined in Chapter 7. As with social preference models (and many other economic models), better models, in terms of goodness-of-fit and prediction, are likely to be more complex, taking into account all of the elements of information that people seem to use in the learning process. Once again, foregone payoffs, both one's own and those of other players, are likely to be of importance here in improving our understanding. Learning strategies and processes such as randomization is another area where further research is needed. This research also has important implications for equilibrium analysis. Most conventional and nonconventional approaches assume some kind of equilibrium in their analysis, but, if learning takes a long time, a nonequilibrium type of analysis may be more appropriate. A wider range of experimental situations may also help understanding. Most of the game theory models used to test learning have involved competitive or cooperative situations in a highly stylized manner. Different types of experiment may be required if we are to understand better how children learn language, for example, and also how child learning is different from adult learning. This last aspect is considered further in the last area of direction, neurobiology.

The theory of mental representations

This is a relatively new area in psychology, and is concerned with how people form mental models or perceptions of a situation, in particular the elements in a game situation. In the words of Camerer (2003),

> The theory of mental representations maps raw descriptions of social situations into the kinds of familiar games theorists study and the kinds of rules people use to decide what to choose.

This theory is currently not well developed, but it has certain elements in common with the equally new area of case-based decision-making, discussed earlier.

The relevance and importance of developing theory in this area can be illustrated by an example from Camerer (2003). One of his student subjects commented after an experimental session playing the stag hunt game: "I can't believe you guys are still studying the prisoners' dilemma!" The confusion of these two games is interesting. The common element is that rationality can lead to inefficiency, in terms of not resulting in a Pareto-dominant outcome. However, the "uppity, trigger-happy" student had ignored that in stag hunt, unlike PD, there are two Nash equilibria and one of them is Pareto-dominant, while in PD, unlike stag hunt, there is a dominant strategy equilibrium. His confusion led him to "defect" in each round of play, a rational solution in PD, but not in stag hunt. The student had failed to undertake an essential basic task in any game situation: examine payoffs to see if there are any dominated strategies. The performance of this task would have differentiated between the two types of game.

There is insufficient evidence at present to draw any general conclusions regarding the extent of the type of confusion above, or other types of error in mental representation. It would be interesting to see whether subjects make the same errors when such games are presented in more realistic situations rather than abstract ones. A prediction of evolutionary psychology would be that errors would be substantially reduced in situations that resembled real life, in the same manner as the Wason test variations. This would make a good topic for a PhD dissertation for any enterprising reader!

The role of the emotions in decision-making

This subject was discussed in Chapter 6 in relation to time-inconsistent preferences and again in Chapter 9 in connection with rationality. It is also related to the more general area of decision-making heuristics discussed earlier, and to the role of neurobiology, discussed next. As far as the issue of whether the emotions have a beneficial or detrimental effect on decision-making, the evidence is mixed. Traditionally, since at least the days of Descartes, rationality, in the sense of the absence of emotion, has been regarded as being optimal. However, since the late 1980s, various researchers in economics, notably Frank and Hirshleifer, have suggested that emotions are an evolutionary adaptation and serve an important beneficial role, in that they serve as credible commitments. This theory is also supported by evidence in neurobiology, in particular the work of Damasio (1994). The issue is discussed in more detail in Case 10.1, in the context of patients suffering brain damage.

The role of neurobiology

No discussion of future directions for behavioral economics would be complete without a reference to the role of neurobiology. This aspect has been touched on at various points in the book, with the importance of neuroeconomic evidence being discussed in the contexts of mental accounting, intertemporal choice, and social preferences. Many social scientists are wary of the encroachment of neurobiology on their disciplines, being suspicious of a reductionist agenda. However, as was made clear in the first chapter, there have been a number of recent technological developments, particularly in terms of brain scanning and imaging techniques like PET (positron emission tomography), fMRI (functional magnetic resonance imaging), EEG (electroencephalography), and rCBF (regional cerebral blood flow). These can shed considerable light on various topics of interest in behavioral economics, and are especially relevant in decision-making heuristics, learning processes, and the role of emotions. We are finding that different types of thinking or mental process are performed in different parts of the brain, indicating the importance of brain structure or anatomy. We are also finding that different chemicals and hormones have dramatic effects on behavior, although of course the effects of alcohol on behavior and decision-making have been known in general terms for thousands of years. The proportion of the populations in developed countries who are now taking regular prescription drugs, for example Prozac and Ritalin, to improve mental performance has increased enormously over the last two decades. Thus the importance of brain physiology is becoming better recognized.

Libet's experiments (1985; 1993) represent another area of great importance, although the interpretation of these is still controversial. They certainly appear to show that many, if not all, of our actions are unconscious, even those that we think are conscious, in that the electrical impulses causing such actions start to occur before we become conscious of willing the actions. The implications are enormous in terms of the role of conscious will (Wegner 2002).

Another controversial area, again relating to the nature of free will, concerns the role of genetic factors. Ongoing research in this area is continually finding links between genetic makeup and behavior. Examples include the tendency to commit various criminal acts, tendencies to addictive behavior, tendencies for thrill-seeking, tendencies to certain diseases, various personality traits and disorders like autism, and of course intelligence. The phenomenon of homosexuality, sometimes misleadingly referred to as a life "choice," is discussed in Case 10.2. The antireductionist lobby views this trend toward genetic explanations as distasteful, or politically incorrect, labeling the findings as "genetic determinism," but there is no doubt that the trend is gathering scientific momentum. As with evolutionary psychology, one has to ward against the "straw man" accusations. The label "genetic determinism" is such a straw man, since it implies an extreme view that behavior is completely controlled by genetic factors, with no environmental influences (and this is ignoring the interactions between genetics and environment, such as developments in the womb). What the scientific findings are usually implying is that genetic factors have a predisposing influence, making certain behavioral effects more likely.

10.5 Policy implications

This issue has been discussed in many chapters, in connection with specific behavioral areas. It is useful now to summarize some of the most important implications, as far as individuals, firms, and governments are concerned.

Individuals

Two main aspects of special importance will be summarized here, relating to happiness and intertemporal conflicts in decision-making.

1. *Happiness*
   We have seen that happiness is both difficult to define and measure, and difficult, if not self-defeating, to pursue. There are many different factors involved, and the implications of Pinker's "three-act tragedy" are of fundamental importance. In evolutionary terms we must remember that we did not evolve as happiness-maximizing beings, but rather use happiness as a proxy for how good our chances of survival and reproduction are at any point in time. So, in short, food and sex make us happy, and in that order according to some recent research. The fundamental problem that we find

is that this proxy mechanism is easily hijacked and sent off the rails. This can be caused by three main factors: (1) our evolved mechanisms may no longer be suited to our current environment (causing us to like fatty and sugary foods); (2) bounded rationality (causing us to use easily fooled heuristics); and (3) intertemporal conflicts, discussed next. The author must add that, after writing this book, he is more conscious of the notion of happiness, monitoring it more often on a personal basis. I cannot say whether this has reduced my overall level of happiness, as the research reviewed in Chapter 9 suggests, but this may be a cost of study and analysis! As stated earlier, evidence suggests that introverted and introspecting people tend to be less happy than extraverts. Another general finding seems to be that we are at our happiest in retrospect when we are not thinking about our happiness. The problem with both observations lies in establishing causation: are we happier because we are not thinking about being happy, or are we not thinking about being happy because we are too busy actually being happy?

2. *Intertemporal conflicts*

These conflicts were discussed in Chapter 6, as an important anomaly in the DUM. According to the DUM there will be a time-consistency in preferences, but in reality time-inconsistent preferences are often observed. Continuing with our food example above, we may decide now that we will not have a tasty dessert after dinner at the restaurant tomorrow, but when the dessert trolley comes around we succumb to temptation. The problem is exacerbated by two other related tendencies that we have discussed: we tend to underestimate the strength of future temptations, and overestimate our ability to overcome these temptations.

There may be many possible explanations for this behavior, and various alternative models to the DUM have been discussed, but where does this leave the individual in terms of optimizing their behavior or happiness? We have seen that the main policy implication here is that we need to make credible commitments. In the above example this may mean eating something healthy before going to the restaurant, designing specific rewards for "good" behavior, only taking enough money for a main course, or even wearing tight clothes that make it uncomfortable to eat too much. The reader may suspect that I have had plentiful experience of this particular problem!

Another area where intertemporal conflicts frequently arise is saving habits (money and wealth can be viewed as a means of acquiring food and sex). Many people do not save enough during their working lives to afford a comfortable retirement. Again credible commitments are important in overcoming this problem. We have seen that the use of automatic savings devices (having amounts deducted from our salaries) and the use of illiquid savings accounts that are costly and inconvenient to withdraw from may serve as effective commitments. This aspect of behavior is also a problem for public policy, as will be discussed later.

The other fundamental area where intertemporal conflicts occur relates to sexual behavior. A high proportion of people have indulged in sexual relations that they have later regretted. Again, commitment devices are important. Marriage does not appear to be one of them, at least in many present societies; in the United States about 44% of marriages currently end in divorce. One important point here is that sexual appetite is like appetite for food in at least one respect: it tends to build over time, until it is satisfied; it then falls to a low level and gradually builds again in a series of cycles. We have also seen that, as far as food is concerned, commitment often involves satiating the appetite before temptation takes hold; hence it may be best to go to the supermarket just after eating, not when one is hungry. A similar logic can be applied to developing ways of preempting sexual temptation. The main problem in this case is that sexual temptation is often less predictable in timing compared with food temptation.

Firms

Some of the behavioral aspects discussed above also have policy implications for firms. Three main factors are discussed here: intertemporal conflicts, loss-aversion, and game theory.

1. *Intertemporal conflicts*

   If firms know that people succumb easily to temptations in terms of inter-temporal preferences, they may take advantage of this in a number of ways. We have already mentioned the wheeling around of dessert trolleys in restaurants, which plays on the urgency of visceral factors. The distinction between investment goods and leisure goods has also been seen to be important in terms of contract design. It is better for firms to charge below marginal cost for investment goods like health club memberships, and above marginal cost for leisure goods like mobile phone usage. As far as saving and spending is concerned, financial organizations can make attractive offers of loans, sometimes framing these in particular ways: "no money down"; "no payments for eighteen months"; "pay all your debts with one low monthly payment"; and flexible repayment schemes that allow lower repayments when a borrower's income falls, balanced by higher repayments when income rises. Some of these practices may be regarded as ethically questionable of course, since they take advantage of human frailties and may cause unhappiness later. However, they are certainly frequently used.

2. *Loss-aversion*

This is another important behavioral concept that firms can profitably employ, especially when coupled with framing effects. We have seen, for example, that it may be better for firms to reduce prices by framing the reduction in terms of a discount. This means that if a firm later wants to raise prices, it can then frame this rise as an ending of the discount, causing less loss-aversion and adverse consumer reaction than a standard price rise. Another method of raising prices in a latent way and avoiding loss-aversion is to reduce the quantity offered for a given price. Consumers are less likely to notice that their cereal box is now 350 grams instead of 375 grams than if the price goes up from £1.99 to £2.13, although the effect is exactly the same in terms of price per unit weight.

3. *Game theory*

There are a number of lessons to be learned here, particularly as far as bargaining and negotiation are concerned. These situations can arise with employees, customers, and competitors. One example we have discussed is the use of a most-favored-customer-clause (MFCC), which has the twin advantages to the firm of reassuring customers regarding prices, and para-doxically serving as a signaling device to other firms that the firm intends to maintain higher prices. The appropriate use and interpretation of signaling devices is particularly important for firms in both competitive and cooper-ative environments. As another example, a firm may expand its capacity as a signal that it intends to produce more output in the future, discour-aging entry into the market. In oligopolistic markets, direct communication between firms that may imply cooperation is illegal in many countries; for example, a number of private schools in the United Kingdom have recently been prosecuted for sharing information regarding costs, because it was suspected that this led to higher fees being charged. In this kind of situation firms can effectively use signals regarding price-setting, without needing any direct communications. Many economists suspect that the tobacco and airline industries use such signals effectively.

As far as relationships with employees are concerned, firms need to understand concepts of fairness in determining salaries and salary differen-tials. In many financial firms, where salaries can be extremely high, it is strictly against company policy for employees to reveal their individually negotiated salaries to other employees, for fear of causing resentment and envy. As we have seen, an employee may be delighted to learn that they have just been given a 10% raise, until they learn that a colleague has been given a 20 % raise. An understanding of social preferences, reference points, and focal points, along with self-serving bias, is necessary for a firm to have satisfactory negotiations with employees.

Governments

The behavioral concepts and principles applied in the situations above are also applicable as far as government policy is concerned. We will start this time with perhaps the obvious example, loss-aversion.

1. *Loss-aversion*

   If a government wants to stay in power and retain votes, having a vital and growing economy is extremely helpful. In a recession, people are losing jobs and income, and even a stagnant or slowing economy can have adverse electoral implications if conditions are worse than people had expected.

2. *Intertemporal conflicts*

   Time-inconsistent preferences are important for governments for a number of reasons. First of all many people would charge the government with the duty of helping to increase their state of happiness. How far a government should interfere with the freedom of individuals in order to further their own interests is of course a controversial topic. We are not going to consider the arguments of parochial government versus "nanny" state here. However, there are some areas of policy where governments can help people overcome their tendencies to succumb to temptation resulting in regrets later which are relatively uncontroversial. One broad area concerns pensions and saving for retirement. In view of the well-established tendency for people to save insufficient funds for a comfortable retirement, there are various routes that governments can take to reduce this problem. One method, used in more socialist countries, is simply to collect higher tax revenues in order to pay a moderate government pension to everyone. This creates a problem of moral hazard, in that people lose the incentive to save, relying solely on government-provided pensions. Many countries with developed economies and aging populations are finding it increasingly difficult to fund pensions in this way. Some of the more market-oriented of these economies, like the United Kingdom, are trying to provide incentives for people to take out sufficient private pensions on a voluntary basis. In order to encourage participation it is better to frame such participation as the default option, rather than require people to actively opt into such a scheme. Another means of encouraging saving for retirement is to use the tax system, by offering tax breaks on retirement accounts like IRAs in the United States.

As far as the effects of paying pensions on government budgets are concerned, one possible way of reducing the burden is to offer people the option of receiving a lump sum rather than an ongoing payment. We have seen evidence that, in the case of public employees, this may save a considerable sum for the state, as people tend to opt for lump-sum payments in spite of the high implicit discount rate. Of course, if this practice were to be implemented on a large scale for all government-provided pensions, the savings involved would have to be balanced against the likelihood of hardship later for those people with time-inconsistent preferences, who fritter away their lump sums without planning for the future.

There is one other area of government policy where time-inconsistent preferences are of particular importance. This concerns addiction. The term "addiction" in this context is applied in the broadest sense to include not just recreational drugs, with which it is most commonly associated, but also alcohol, tobacco, gambling, and even food. We have seen that visceral influences play a large role here. Addiction not only causes unhappiness and suffering for addicts themselves, but also imposes heavy externalities. These relate to the effects on the families of addicts, the resulting increase in crime, and additional costs imposed on the state in terms of care and rehabilitation. Tackling the causes of addiction is a formidable task. It involves a sociocultural approach; for example, examining the causes of the drug culture among the young, which appears particularly prevalent in the United Kingdom. It also involves a psychological approach: researching the factors that cause particular individuals to be vulnerable to different types of addiction is important here. Finally, it involves a neurophysiological approach: this may also help to identify those people most vulnerable, but it should also lead to the development of medical treatments and drugs which counter the effects of addiction.

An important policy implication here, discussed in Chapter 6, is that making the production and distribution of addictive substances illegal may be counterproductive. This is because it increases transactions costs for suppliers, encouraging larger transactions and greater consumption. High excise taxes may be a more effective method of discouraging consumption. However, this conclusion is controversial. Gul and Pesendorfer (2007) argue that taxes on drugs decrease welfare while prohibitive policies may increase welfare.

3. *Game theory*

A final area of application concerns the use of BGT by governments. There are a number of policy areas which have possible applications; three of these are discussed here, but this is not intended as an exhaustive list:

a) *Auctions*

Governments and government agencies are sometimes in a position to sell business operations or licenses to businesses to operate in certain areas. Large sums of money are usually involved, so it is important for governments to raise a maximum amount. The amount raised is highly sensitive to the method used for the sale. The various privatizations by the UK government in the 1980s and 1990s did not manage this efficiently. The general method was to invite the public to tender for a number of shares at a fixed price. In some cases the share offer was oversubscribed by a factor of four, indicating that the government, and its investment bank advisers, had considerably underestimated the market value of the operations being sold. When shares were later sold on the secondary market at much higher prices than the par value, often within days of the original issue, huge profits were made by speculators at the expense of the government.

An alternative approach is to auction operations to the highest bidder or bidders. An example of a successful auction relates to the sale of radio licenses by the Federal Communications Commission (FCC) in the United States, in 1994. The FCC took the advice of game theorists, notably Binmore, in establishing the rules for the auction's structure. These were complicated, following a simultaneous, multiple-round format. The end result was that, after 46 rounds of bidding over a 5-day period, 10 nation-wide licenses were sold for a total of over $600 million. This sum was over 10 times the highest estimates that had appeared in the press.

b) *International trade*

Governments frequently have to negotiate trade deals on a bilateral or multi-lateral basis. They also often unilaterally determine import tariffs and export subsidies, as well as other less obvious trade barriers. They may even appear to take actions which harm their own country, like imposing voluntary export restraints (VERs). The effects of all of these actions are generally counterintuitive: tariffs and subsidies often reduce overall welfare within the country imposing them, while VERs may improve welfare (at least compared with the likely alternatives). This is not the context to explore the effects of these policy measures in detail, but frequently a major problem is a lack of game theoretic analysis: how are other governments and other firms likely to react?

This failure is particularly evident in the imposition of trade sanctions. As we have seen, when these are imposed on poor countries ruled by dictators, they often backfire, causing unnecessary hardship and bolstering the regime at which they are aimed. The problem is again a lack of iterative thought.

c) *Mediation*

Bargaining impasses are often caused by self-serving bias and multiple focal points. However, we have seen that one way to resolve these problems is to have some form of mediation where the bargaining parties can have the weaknesses of their positions explained. Governments, or their agencies, can serve as independent arbiters in industrial relations or employment disputes in particular. An example of such an agency is the Advisory, Conciliation and Arbitration Service (ACAS) in the United Kingdom. There is some evidence that the existence of this organization has helped to reduce the number and length of industrial disputes over the last two decades.

10.6 Applications

Case 10.1   The effects of brain damage on decision-making

The following story might be called "the curious case of Phineas Gage." The year was 1848. Gage, 25 years old, was a construction foreman involved in building a railway in Vermont. It was customary in the course of construction to use explosives to blast and clear away rock, in order to build a straighter and more level track. Gage was an expert in such a task and was described by his bosses as "the most efficient and capable" man in their employ. However, in the course of tamping an explosive charge, there was an accident, and the ensuing explosion caused the iron rod used to tamp the charge to be blown right through Gage's head. The rod entered through his left cheek, pierced the base of his skull, traversed the front of his brain and exited through the top of his head. The rod measured just over a metre in length, had a diameter just over three centimetres, and weighed about six kilograms. It was tapered, and it was the pointed end which entered first, or the story may well have been different.

We do not need to dwell on the gory details, but some description of the incident is necessary in order to understand its implications. First of all, Gage not only survived the accident, but made a remarkable recovery, returning in terms of outward appearances to close to his previous self. Indeed, he was talking within a few minutes of the accident, and, having been carried in an ox cart about a kilometer to get medical assistance, he was able to get out of the cart himself, with only a little help from his men. He was then able to explain "perfectly rationally" to the doctor the nature and circumstances of the accident. Gage was pronounced cured in less than 2 months. According to his doctor, Gage's physical recovery was complete. He could touch, hear, and see, and was not paralysed "of limb or tongue." He had lost the sight in his left eye, but his vision was perfect in the right. He walked firmly, used his hands with dexterity, and had no noticeable difficulty with speech or language.

However, Gage's unfortunate story was only just beginning. According to his doctor, "the equilibrium or balance, so to speak, between his intellectual faculty and animal propensities" had been destroyed. He was now "fitful, irreverent, indulging at times in the grossest profanity which was not previously his custom, manifesting but little deference for his fellows, impatient of restraint or advice when it conflicts with his desires, at times pertinaciously obstinate, yet capricious and vacillating, devising many plans of future operation, which are no sooner arranged than they are abandoned ... A child in his intellectual capacity and manifestations, he has the animal passions of a strong man."

This description marks a dramatic change in Gage's personality. Before the accident he was reported to have "temperate habits" and "considerable energy of character." He had possessed "a well balanced mind and was looked upon by those who knew him as a shrewd, smart businessman, very energetic and persistent in executing all his plans of action." In short, as his friends and acquaintances noted, "Gage is no longer Gage." After the accident his employers were not willing to take him back because of the changes in him, and he drifted from job to job, unable to secure and maintain the type of steady, remunerative job that he had once held. He died at the age of 38, after a series of epileptic fits.

The reason for telling this harrowing tale is that it illustrates a vital point. In the words of Damasio (1994), there are

> systems in the human brain dedicated more to reasoning than to anything else, and in particular to the personal and social dimensions of reasoning.

After exhuming Gage's body, his skull was examined using the latest neuroimaging techniques, and it is now possible to draw certain conclusions regarding the extent of his brain damage. It was concentrated in the prefrontal cortices, mainly in the ventromedial sector. According to Damasio, this damage "compromised his ability to plan for the future, to conduct himself according to the social rules he previously had learned, and to decide on the course of action that ultimately would be most advantageous to his survival."

One can only draw limited conclusions from a single medical case study. It was obvious that certain parts of the brain had specialized functions, and could function independently of others, but more detailed conclusions are only possible by examining other similar cases. Damasio, as a professor of neurology and a practitioner, has been in an ideal environment in which to encounter such cases. He describes a modern equivalent, whom he refers to as "Elliot," who suffered similar damage after a surgical operation to remove a brain tumor. The damage was again largely in the ventromedial sector of the prefrontal cortices, the main difference from Gage being that the damage was more on the right side. Like Gage, Elliot's physical capacities were not affected, nor were most of his intellectual faculties, including language and memory. His IQ was tested and showed no impairment, being in the superior range. He appeared charming, knowledgeable, and with a laconic sense of humor. However, after the operation, his personality and judgment were severely affected. He became easily distracted, engrossing himself in the detail of trivial or irrelevant tasks, and became incapable of maintaining a normal schedule, time management, or forward planning. He lost his job, and various others. Simple and

Case 10.1 *continued*

basic decisions, like whether to take an umbrella when going out, would take ages to make, as he would tediously weigh up all the pros and cons. He made a string of consistently bad business, financial, and personal decisions, and proved incapable of learning from his past mistakes. Most important of all, from Damasio's point of view as a diagnostic, Elliot appeared emotionally flat, describing his fall from grace and disastrous personal experiences with a wry and detached tone.

It was this last characteristic that provided Damasio with the material from which he developed a new theory, which he refers to as the **somatic marker hypothesis**. Essentially, this states that the emotions are necessary in order for us to make good decisions, not just in a social environment, but in any real-life setting. The somatic markers act as a decision-making heuristic, enabling us to narrow down possible strategies from an initially huge range of possibilities. Without this heuristic we tend, like Elliot, to waste a lot of time evaluating courses of action that are simply not worthy of consideration. For example, if we are faced with a decision whether to take a new and highly paid job in a different country, we may immediately be overcome by the emotion that we cannot leave our friends or relatives behind. This somatic marker prevents us from considering and evaluating all the other factors related to the decision, and we immediately make the decision to refuse the position.

This hypothesis is in direct contrast to the belief of Descartes that we need to use reason alone, and not the emotions, if we are to make the best decisions. Hence the title of Damasio's book: *Descartes' Error*.

Questions

1. What do the cases of Gage and Elliot tell us about the nature of rationality?
2. What does this case study reveal regarding the relationship between the brain and the mind?
3. Behavioral economics seeks a sound psychological foundation; what then is the relevance of neuroscience?

Case 10.2 Born gay?

Brothers in arms

Some men are gay because their mothers have already had many sons

RAY BLANCHARD, a researcher at Toronto's Centre for Addiction and Mental Health, was reviewing some data a few years ago when he noticed something odd: gay men seemed to have more older brothers than straight men.

Intrigued—and sceptical—he decided to investigate. He recruited 302 gay men and the same number of heterosexual controls and inquired about their families.

How many siblings did they have, of what sex, and how had the births been spaced? How old had their parents been when they had had them? Dr Blanchard found that only one detail seemed to predict sexual orientation: the more elder brothers a man had, the more likely he was to be gay. Neither elder sisters nor younger siblings of either sex had any effect, but each additional elder brother increased his chance of being gay by about 33 % from the population average of one man in 50.

It was a rather perplexing discovery. It implied either that being brought up with a lot of elder brothers affects a boy's sexual orientation, or that a mother's body is somehow able to keep count of how many sons she has conceived, and that this count affects the orientation of future children. Hard as it was to explain, though, the finding was replicated again and again, across different cultures, eras and even psychiatric groups.

Those who argued for a social explanation suggested that having lots of elder brothers makes a boy more likely to engage in same-sex play, and might also increase the chance he is a victim of sexual abuse. But, regardless of whether either of these conjectures is true, neither playing with other boys nor sexual abuse has been scientifically linked to homosexuality.

Anthony Bogaert of Brock University in St Catharines, Ontario, therefore decided to examine the other hypothesis—that the phenomenon is caused by something that happens in the womb. He has just published his results in the *Proceedings of the National Academy of Sciences*.

Dr Bogaert reasoned that if the effect were social, elder brothers would wield the same power even if they had not been born to the same mother. Lots of half- or step-siblings, or adopted brothers, for instance, would also cause their younger brothers to be gay. On the other hand, if the effect were really due to birth order, biological brothers would make their younger brothers more likely to be gay even if they did not grow up together; indeed, even if the younger boy grew up without any older boys around at all.

Dr Bogaert collected a new sample of several hundred men, this time specifically recruiting those who had grown up with "brothers" to whom they were not biologic- ally related. He collected information on how long they had been reared with each sibling, as well as about biological siblings from whom they had been separated.

He found that only the number of biological elder brothers had an impact on a later-born boy's sexual orientation; non-biological siblings had no effect. This was true even when a boy had grown up surrounded by an enormous gaggle of non- biological elder brothers. By contrast, elder brothers raised in a separate household "influenced" their younger brothers' sexual orientation in exactly the same way as they would have done had they been living with them.

Like many of the best pieces of research, this one raises questions, as well as answering them. One is, how does the mother's body keep count of how many sons she has conceived? A second is, how does that change the environment in the womb? A third is, how does that change affect sexual orientation? And a fourth is, is this an accidental effect, or has it evolved for some reason?

To these questions, Dr Bogaert has no answers, though in some cases he has his suspicions. He speculates that, for reasons as yet unknown, a mother's immune

---

Case 10.2 *continued*

system takes note of the number of male offspring and that each succeeding male fetus is subjected to increased levels of antibodies. These somehow affect its development. Clearly, something strange is going on, because things other than sexual orientation are also affected by birth order. Boys with elder brothers are also likely to have larger-than-normal placentas while in the womb. And despite that apparent nutritional advantage (for a larger placenta should be able to draw more food from the mother's bloodstream), they are also likely to have lower birth-weights than would otherwise be expected.

Dr Blanchard, meanwhile, calculates that about one gay man in seven can chalk his orientation up to having elder brothers. But to the question of whether there is some evolutionary advantage for a mother who has many sons to include a gay one among them, neither he nor Dr Bogaert has an answer.

Questions

1. Explain how the "elder brother" theory emerged, comparing the circumstances with the development of other theories.
2. Explain the methodology and purpose underlying Dr Bogaert's study.
3. Why is this case relevant as far as the study of decision-making processes is concerned?

Source: *The Economist* print edition, June 29, 2006, Toronto

---

Case 10.3 The bioeconomic causes of war

The title of this case comes from an article by Hirshleifer (1998). His article relates to many of the concepts discussed in the book, although I have rarely mentioned the phenomenon of warfare. The case study is included here to indicate the broad range of phenomena that the tools of behavioral economics are able to analyze. Thus we will be able to see the relevance of bargaining, game theory, self-serving bias and focal points, social preferences, reciprocity, and evolutionary psychology.

Hirshleifer states that the premise of bioeconomics is that

> Our preferences have themselves evolved to serve economic functions in a very broad sense: those preferences were selected that promoted survival in a world of scarcity and competition.

The most fundamental drives in both nonhuman animals and humans concern food and sex. Most conflict between animals is on an individual basis, and is directly related to these objectives. When male animals fight over territory, territory represents resources of food, and also females are often only attracted to males who possess a territory. Territory always represents more access to females.

Chimpanzees are the only nonhuman animals known to fight in groups (although dolphins may also do so), and the objective of the kinds of raid that they carry out into other territories is always to gain access to females.

It may be claimed that humans have the dubious distinction of being the only species that conducts organized warfare. However, in human warfare between primitive tribes the objectives in fighting are usually again food and sex. Chagnon (1983; 1988) studied the warlike Yanomamo tribe at length and concluded that female capture was the primary motive. He also noted that Yanomamo men who have killed more enemies in battle also produce more offspring. Keeley (1996) noted that wars were often caused by multiple factors, and estimated that, among American Indian societies, material motives (land, booty, poaching, and slaves) contributed to 70 % of wars, while women contributed to 58 %.

In much of human history the same appears to have been true. Genghis Khan was certainly more concerned with access to women than with access to material resources. It is a tribute to his phenomenal success in this regard that it has been estimated that one in twenty Asians can now claim descent from him. In many ancient wars the vanquished males were universally slaughtered, while females became slaves/concubines/wives.

Food and sex may have been the dominant issues, but why does war break out? War represents the ultimate breakdown of a bargaining process. An individual or group of individuals wants something (food or sex) possessed by another individual or group, and they cannot agree to the terms of a transaction. Of course, in this impasse one party can just walk away dissatisfied, and this frequently occurs in the animal kingdom when one animal backs down from a confrontation. So why do animals and humans fight? For physical combat to occur both parties must evaluate the benefits from fighting to be greater than the costs. If only one party does so but the other does not then the second party will back down, and combat is avoided. One method animals have of avoiding costly combat is to have some display of arms first; the purpose, unconscious though it may be, is to increase both parties" information regarding the strengths and weaknesses of the opponent. If both parties have perfect information, and encode it correctly, no combat can occur. Combat therefore tends to occur when the two combatants are pretty evenly matched, as well as the stakes being high in order to justify the potential high costs.

A factor that is therefore clearly relevant in the outbreak of human warfare is overconfidence, or self-serving bias, which in this case may not be so self-serving, since it may lead to costly defeat or death. Many wars have been fought and lost through underestimating either the strength of the enemy or the costs involved in fighting in terms of resources. Certainly this accusation can be leveled at both Germany and Japan in World War II.

Historically, most wars were fought between groups of people who were related in terms of kinship. The same is still true of tribal wars today. As civilizations grew in size, often due to returns to scale from industrialized production and increased productivity, kinship was greatly diluted and the related concept of affiliation became important. Many social scientists have noted that even when assignment to different groups is purely arbitrary, bonds of affiliation are soon formed (Sherif and Sherif 1964). Experiments dividing subjects into "prisoners" and "guards" have had frightening consequences, as the "guards" come to regard

---

Case 10.3 *continued*

the prisoners as inferior beings to be punished and humiliated. An essential part of our human psychological makeup is an "us and them" mentality, which evolved from kinship ties.

Affiliation can occur on the basis of many kinds of tie: class, interest, age, and location are common. Nationality, ethnicity, and religion are particularly important in causing strong bonds – bonds strong enough to kill and risk being killed for. Diamond (1997) argues that a key factor in the formation of large warlike groups has been religion. He defines religion as an ideology that manipulates group members to become peaceful and obedient internally, and suicidally brave when it comes to external warfare. It is also notable that in societies where affiliation is particularly strong, the members often use kinship terms, like "brother" and "sister," in referring to other members; the leader of the group may be referred to as "father" or "mother."

As affiliation has become more important and kinship less so, the issues of food and sex appear to have disappeared into the background. Material welfare is still important, although this is often referred to in abstract terms. For example, in 1914 German war aims were linked to finding its "place in the sun." In the 1930s, the war movement was linked to a similar concept, *lebensraum*, but by this time there was a strong feeling of aggrievement, particularly related to racial hatred. As the importance of food and sex has declined in explicit terms, the concepts of dominance, prestige, and honour appear to have taken their place.

In the twentieth century in particular, it seemed that biological motives were no longer relevant in warfare. The historian Ferguson (1998) has claimed that in World War I the main motive for ordinary men fighting was that war was regarded as sport, as fun. Certainly there is a primitive, visceral thrill of the hunt involved, often evoked by soldiers' writings of the time. However, it might well be that this was a minority view, considering the massive slaughter, appalling conditions, and futility of the fighting. Writers and poets like Graves, Sassoon, and Owen were certainly more affected by the latter factors.

Ferguson further contends,

> Today's neo-Darwinian genetic determinism may be more scientifically respectable than Freud's mixture of psychoanalysis and amateur anthropology, but the latter seems better able to explain the readiness of millions of men to spend four and a quarter years killing and being killed. (It is certainly hard to see how the deaths of so many men who had not married and fathered children could possibly have served the interests of Dawkins's 'selfish genes'.)

This passage displays a misunderstanding of "genetic determinism" and the operations of "selfish genes." As explained in the previous chapter, genes do not operate in the teleological manner suggested by Ferguson, but in a purely mechanistic way. We have seen that this is the main reason why they can so easily be fooled or hijacked to serve irrational and self-destructive ends.

Hirshleifer (1998), on the other hand, claims that one main factor why sex has become less important as an issue in war is that war leaders have far greater internal opportunities than before; they do not need to invade other countries in order to obtain access to females. Maybe this is why President Clinton never declared war.

Questions

1. Explain the fundamental flaw in the argument by Ferguson: "It is certainly hard to see how the deaths of so many men who had not married and fathered children could possibly have served the interests of Dawkins's 'selfish genes.' "
2. Explain why self-serving bias is important in causing war.
3. How have the aims of war changed over time?

References

Abbink, K., Irlenbusch, B., and Renner, E. (2000). The moonlighting game: An experimental study on reciprocity and retribution. *Journal of Economic Behavior and Organization, 42* (2), 265–77.

Abdellaoui, M. (1998). Parameter-free eliciting of utilities and probability weighting functions. Working paper, GRID, ENS, Cachan, France.

Adams, J.S. (1963). Toward an understanding of inequity. *Journal of Abnormal and Social Psychology, 67*, 422–36.

Agell, J. and Lundborg, P. (1995). Theories of pay and unemployment: Survey evidence from Swedish manufacturing firms. *Scandinavian Journal of Economics, 97*, 295–308.

Agnoli, F. and Krantz, D.H. (1989). Suppressing natural heuristics by formal instruction: The case of the conjunction fallacy. *Cognitive Psychology, 21*, 515–50.

Ainslie, G.W. (1975). Specious reward: A behavioral theory of impulsiveness and impulsive control. *Psychological Bulletin, 82*, 463–96.

Ainslie, G.W. (1986). Beyond microeconomics: Conflict among interest in a multiple self as a determinant of value. In J. Elster (Ed.), *The Multiple Self*. Cambridge: Cambridge University Press, 133–75.

Ainslie, G.W. (1991). Derivation of 'rational' economic behaviour from hyperbolic discount curves. *American Economic Review, 81*, 334–40.

Ainslie, G.W. (1992). *Picoeconomics: The Strategic Interaction of Successive Motivational States within the Person*. Cambridge: Cambridge University Press.

Ainslie, G.W. (2001). *Breakdown of Will*. Cambridge: Cambridge University Press.

Ainslie, G.W. and Haendel, V. (1983). The motives of the will. In E. Gottheil, K. Durley, T. Skodola, and H. Waxman (Eds), *Etiology Aspects of Alcohol and Drug Abuse*. Springfield, IL: Charles C. Thomas.

Ainslie, G.W. and Haslam, N. (1992). Hyperbolic discounting. In G. Loewenstein and J. Elster (Eds), *Choice Over Time*. New York: Russell Sage.

Algom, D. and Lubel, S. (1994). Psychophysics in the field: Perception and memory for labor pain. *Perception and Memory, 55*, 133–41.

Ali, M. (1977). Probability and utility estimates for racetrack bettors. *Journal of Political Economy, 85*, 803–15.

Allais, M. (1953). Le comportement de l'homme rationnel devant le risque, critique des postulats et axioms de l'école américaine. *Econometrica, 21*, 503–46.

al-Nowaihi, A. and Dhami, S. (2006). A simple derivation of Prelec's probability weighting function. *Journal of Mathematical Psychology*, 50(6), 521–524.

Aloysius, J.A. (2005). Ambiguity aversion and the equity premium puzzle: A re-examination of experimental data on repeated gambles. *Journal of Socio-Economics, 34*(5), 635–55.

Andreoni, J. and Miller, J.H. (1993). Rational cooperation in the finitely repeated prisoner's dilemma: Experimental evidence. *Economic Journal, 103*, 570–85.

Argyle, M. (1999). Causes and correlates of happiness. In D. Kahneman, E. Diener, and N. Schwarz (Eds), *Well-being: The Foundation of Hedonic Psychology.* New York: Russell Sage, 353–73.

Ariely, D. (1998). Combining experiences over time: The effects of duration, intensity changes and on-line measurements on retrospective pain evaluations. *Journal of Behavioral Decision Making, 11*, 19–45.

Ariely, D., Huber, J., and Wertenbroch, K. (2005). When do losses loom larger than gains? *Journal of Marketing Research, 42*(2), 134–38.

Ariely, D., Loewenstein, G., and Prelec, D. (2000). Coherent arbitrariness: Duration-sensitive pricing of hedonic stimuli around an arbitrary anchor. Working paper, Department of Social and Decision Sciences, Carnegie Mellon University, Pittsburgh.

Ariely, D., Loewenstein, G., and Prelec, D. (2003). Coherent arbitrariness: Stable demand curves without stable preferences. *Quarterly Journal of Economics, 118*, 73–105.

Ariely, D. and Wertenbroch, K. (2002). Procrastination, deadline, and performance: Self-control by precommitment. *Psychological Science, 13*(3), 219–24.

Ariely, D. and Zauberman, G. (2000). On the making of an experience: The effects of breaking and combining experiences on their overall evaluation. *Journal of Behavioral Decision Making, 13*, 219–32.

Arkes, H.R. (1991). Costs and benefits of judgment errors: Implications for debiasing. *Psychological Bulletin, 110*, 486–98.

Arkes, H.R. and Blumer, C. (1985). The psychology of sunk cost. *Organizational Behavior and Human Decision Processes, 35*(1), 124–40.

Arkes, H.R., Wortmann, R.L., Saville, P.D., and Harkness, A.R. (1981). Hindsight bias among physicians weighing the likelihood of diagnoses. *Journal of Applied Psychology, 66*, 252–54.

Arrow, K.J. (1986). Rationality of self and others in an economic system. In R.M. Hogarth and M.W. Reder (Eds), *Rational Choice: The Contrast between Economics and Psychology.* Chicago: Chicago University Press.

Ausubel, L.M. (1999). Adverse Selection in the Credit Card Market. Mimeo, University of Maryland, College Park.

Axelrod, R. (1985). *The Evolution of Cooperation.* New York: Basic Books.

Ayduk, O., Mendoza-Denton, R., Mischel, W., Downey, G., Peake, P.K., and Rodriguez, M. (2000). Regulating the interpersonal self: Strategic self-regulation for coping with rejection sensitivity. *Journal of Personality & Social Psychology, 79*(5), 776–92.

Babcock, L., Loewenstein, G., and Issacharoff, S. (1996). Debiasing litigation impasses. Unpublished paper.

Babcock, L., Loewenstein, G., and Issacharoff, S. (1997). Creating convergence: Debiasing biased litigants. *Law and Social Inquiry, 22*, 913–25.

Babcock, L., Loewenstein, G., Issacharoff, S., and Camerer, C. (1995). Biased judgments of fairness in bargaining. *American Economic Review, 85*, 1337–43.

Ballinger, T.P. and Wilcox, N.T. (1997). Decisions, error and heterogeneity. *Economic Journal, 107*(443), 1090–105.

Bansal, R. and Yaron, A. (2004). Risks for the long run: A potential resolution of asset pricing puzzles. *Journal of Finance, 59*(4), 1481–509.

Barberis, N. and Huang, M. (2001). Mental accounting, loss-aversion, and individual stock returns. *Journal of Finance, 56*(4), 1247–92.

Barberis, N., Shleifer, A., and Vishny, R. (1998). A model of investor sentiment. *Journal of Financial Economics, 49*(3), 307–43.

Bargh, J.A. and Chartand, T.L. (1999). The unbearable automaticity of being. *American Psychologist, 54*, 462–79.

Batson, C.D. (1991). *The Altruism Question*. Chicago: Chicago University Press.

Baumeister, R.F. (2001). The psychology of irrationality: Why people make foolish, self-defeating choices. In Isabelle Brocas and Juan D. Carillo (Eds), *The Psychology of Economic Decisions*. Oxford: Oxford University Press, 3–16.

Baumeister, R.F., Heatherton, T.F, and Tice, D.M. (1993). When ego threats lead to self-regulation failure: Negative consequences of high self-esteem. *Journal of Personality and Social Psychology, 64*, 141–56.

Baumhart, R. (1968). *An Honest Profit*. New York: Prentice-Hall.

Beard, T.R. and Beil, R. (1994). Do people rely on the self-interested maximization of others? An experimental test. *Management Science, 40*, 252–62.

Bechara, A., Tranel, D., Damasio, H., and Damasio, A.R. (1996). Failure to respond automatically to anticipated future outcomes following damage to prefrontal cortex. *Cerebral Cortex, 6*, 215–25.

Becker, G.S. (1976). Altruism, egoism, and genetic fitness: Economics and sociobiology. *Journal of Economic Literature, 14*(3), 817–26.

Becker, G.S. and Murphy, K.M. (1988). A theory of rational addiction. *Journal of Political Economy, 96*(4), 675–701.

Becker, J.L. and Sarin, R.K. (1987). Gamble dependent utility. *Management Science, 33*, 1367–82.

Bell, D. (1985). Disappointment in decision making under uncertainty. *Operations Research, 33*, 1–27.

Bem, D.J. (1967). Self-perception: An alternative interpretation of cognitive dissonance phenomena. *Psychological Review, 74*(3), 183–200.

Bem, D.J. (1972). Self-perception theory. In L. Berkowitz (Ed.), *Advances in Experimental Social Psychology*, Vol. 6. New York: Academic Press.

Benartzi, S. and Thaler, R.H. (1995). Myopic loss aversion and the equity premium puzzle. *Quarterly Journal of Economics, 110*(1), 73–92.

Benartzi, S. and Thaler, R.H. (1998). Illusory diversification and retirement savings. Working paper, University of Chicago and UCLA.

Benartzi, S. and Thaler, R.H. (1999). Risk aversion or Myopia? Choices in repeated gambles and retirement investments. *Management Science, 45*(3), 364–81.

Benjamin, J., Li, L., Patterson, C., and Greenberg, B.D. (1996). Population and familial association between the D4 dopamine receptor gene and measures of novelty seeking. *Nature Genetics, 12*, 81–4.

Bentham, J. (1789/1948). *An Introduction to the Principle of Morals and Legislations*. Oxford: Blackwell.

Benzion, U., Rapoport, A., and Yagil, J. (1989). Discount rates inferred from decisions: An experimental study. *Management Science, 35*, 270–84.

Berg, J., Dickhaut, J., and McCabe, K. (1995). Trust, reciprocity, and social history. *Games and Economic Behavior, 10*, 122–42.

Berkely, D. and Humphreys, P. (1982). Structuring decision problems and the 'bias' heuristic. *Acta Psychologica, 50*, 201–52.

Bernheim, B. and Scholz, J.K. (1993). Do Americans save too little? Business Review (Federal Reserve Bank of Philadelphia), Sep/Oct, 3–20.

Bernoulli, D. (1738/1954). Exposition of a new theory on the measurement of risk. *Econometrica, 22*, 23–36.

Berridge, K.C. (2001). Irrational pursuits: hyperincentives from a visceral brain. In Isabelle Brocas and Juan D. Carillo (Eds), *The Psychology of Economic Decisions*. Oxford: Oxford University Press, 17–40.

Bertrand, J. (1883). Book review of *Recherche sure les principes mathématiques de la théorie des richesses*. *Journal des Savants, 67*, 499–508.

Bewley, T. (1998). Why not cut pay? *European Economic Review, 42*, 459–90.

Bi, L. and Montalto, C. (2005). Is there a credit card puzzle? An exploratory study. *Consumer Interests Annual, 51*, 72.

Binmore, K. (1999). Why Experiment in Economics? *The Economic Journal, 109* (453), 16–24.

Binmore, K., Shaked, A., and Sutton, J. (1985). Testing noncooperative bargaining theory: A preliminary study. *American Economic Review, 75*, 1178–80.

Bloomfield, R. (1994). Learning a mixed strategy equilibrium in the laboratory. *Journal of Economic Behavior and Organization, 25*, 411–36.

Blount, S. (1995). When social outcomes aren't fair: The effect of causal attributions on preference. *Organizational Behavior and Human Decision Processes, 63*, 131–44.

Bodner, R. and Prelec, D. (1997). *The diagnostic value of actions in a self-signaling model*, MIT mimeo.

Bodner, R. and Prelec, D. (2001). Self-signaling and diagnostic utility in everyday decision making. In I. Brocas and J.D. Carillo (Eds), *The Psychology of Economic Decisions*. New York: Oxford University Press, 105–23.

Böhm-Bawerk, E.V. (1970/1889). *Capital and Interest*. South Holland: Libertarian Press.

Bohnet, I. and Frey, B. (1999). The sound of silence in prisoner's dilemma and dictator games. *Journal of Economic Behavior and Organization, 38*, 43–57.

Bolles, R.C. (1975). *The Theory of Motivation*. 2nd ed. New York: Harper and Row.

Bolton, G.E. (1991). A comparative model of bargaining: Theory and evidence. *American Economic Review, 81*, 1096–1136.

Bolton, G.E., Katok, E., and Zwick, R. (1998). Dictator game giving: Rules of fairness versus acts of kindness. *International Journal of Game Theory, 27*, 269–99.

Bolton, G.E. and Ockenfels, A. (2000). ERC: A theory of equity, reciprocity, and competition. *American Economic Review, 90*, 166–93.

Bolton, G.E. and Zwick, R. (1995). Anonymity versus punishment in ultimatum bargaining. *Games and Economic Behavior, 10*, 95–121.

Bostic, R., Gabriel, S., and Painter, G. (2006). Housing wealth, financial wealth and consumption: New evidence from microdata, Lusk Center for Real Estate, University of Southern California, July.

Bowman, D., Minehart, D., and Rabin, M. (1999). Loss-aversion in a savings model. *Journal of Economic Behavior and Organization, 38*(2), 155–78.

Brickman, P. and Campbell, D.T. (1971). Hedonic relativism and planning the good society. In M.H. Appley (Ed.), *Adaptation-level Theory*. New York: Academic Press, 287–305.

Brickman, P., Coates, D., and Janoff-Bulman, R. (1978). Lottery winners and accident victims: Is happiness relative? *Journal of Personality and Social Psychology, 36*, 917–27.

Brocas, I. and Carrillo, J.D. (2004). Entrepreneurial boldness and excessive investment. *Journal of Economics and Management Strategy, 13*(2), 321–50.

Brookshire, D. and Coursey, D. (1987). Measuring the value of a public good: An empirical comparison of elicitation procedures. *American Economic Review, 77*, 554–66.

Broome, J. (1993). QALYs. *Journal of Public Economics, 50*, 149–67.

Brown, G. (1951). Iterative solution of games by fictitious play. In T.C. Koopmans (Ed.), *Activity Analysis of Production and Allocation*. New York: Wiley.

Buchan, N.R., Johnson, E., and Croson, R.T.A. (1997). Culture, power, and legitimacy: Contrasting influences on fairness beliefs and negotiation behavior in Japan and the United States. University of Wisconsin Department of Marketing working paper.

Burgstahler, D. and Dichev, I. (1997). Earnings management to avoid earnings decreases and losses. *Journal of Accounting and Economics, 24*, 99–126.

Burnham, T. and Phelan, J. (2001). *Mean Genes: Can We Tame Our Primal Instincts?* London: Simon and Schuster.

Buss, D.M. (1999). *Evolutionary Psychology: The New Science of the Mind*. Needham Heights, MA: Allyn and Bacon.

Cacioppo, J.T., Gardner, W.C., and Berntson, G. (1999). The affect system has parallel and integrative processing components: Form follows function. *Journal of Personality and Social Psychology, 76*, 839–55.

Cairns, J.A. (1994). Valuing future benefits. *Health Economics, 3*, 221–29.

Cairns, J.A. and van der Pol, M.M. (1997). Constant and decreasing timing aversion for saving lives. *Social Science and Medicine, 45*(11), 1653–59.

Cairns, J.A. and van der Pol, M.M. (1999). Do people value their own future health differently than others' future health? *Medical Decision Making, 19*(4), 466–72.

Camerer, C.F. (1989). An experimental test of several generalised utility theories. *Journal of Risk and Uncertainty, 2*(1), 61–104.

Camerer, C.F. (1992). Recent tests of generalizations of expected utility theories. In W. Edwards (Ed.), *Utility Theories: Measurement and Applications*. Dordtrecht, The Netherlands: Kluwer Academic Publishers.

Camerer, C.F. (1995). Individual decision making. In J.H. Kagel, and A.E. Roth (Eds), *Handbook of Experimental Economics*. Princeton, NJ: Princeton University Press.

Camerer, C.F. (1997). Progress in behavioral game theory. *Journal of Economic Perspectives, 11*, 167–88.

Camerer, C.F. (2000). Prospect theory in the wild: Evidence from the field. In D. Kahneman, and A. Tversky (Eds), *Choices, Values, and Frames*. New York: Cambridge University Press and the Russell Sage Foundation, 288–300.

Camerer, C.F. (2003). *Behavioral Game Theory: Experiments in Strategic Interaction*. New York: Russell Sage Foundation, 67.

Camerer, C.F. (2005). Three cheers – psychological, theoretical, empirical – for loss-aversion. *Journal of Marketing Research, 42*(2), 129–33.

Camerer, C.F., Babcock, L., Loewenstein, G., and Thaler, R. (1997). Labor supply of New York city cabdrivers: One day at a time. *Quarterly Journal of Economics, 112*(2), 407–41.

Camerer, C.F. and Ho, T. (1994). Violations of the betweenness axiom and nonlinearity in probability. *Journal of Risk and Uncertainty, 8*, 167–96.

Camerer, C.F. and Ho, T. (1999a). Experience-weighted attraction learning in games: Estimates from weak-link games. In D. Budescu, I. Erev, and R. Zwick (Eds), *Games and Human Behavior: Essays in Honor of Amnon Rapaport*. Mahwah, NJ: Erlbaum.

Camerer, C.F. and Ho, T. (1999b). Experience-weighted attraction learning in normal-form games. *Econometrica, 67*, 827–74.

Camerer, C.F., Ho, T., and Chong, K. (2002). Sophisticated experience-weighted attraction learning and strategic teaching in repeated games. *Journal of Economic Theory, 104*, 137–88.

Camerer, C.F., Ho, T., and Chong, K. (2004). A cognitive hierarchy model of games. *Quarterly Journal of Economics, 119*(3), 861–98.

Camerer, C.F. and Hogarth, R.M. (1999). The effects of financial incentives in experiments: a review and capital-labor-production framework. *Journal of Risk and Uncertainty, 19*, 7–42.

Camerer, C.F., Johnson, E., Rymon, T., and Sen, S. (1994). Cognition and framing in sequential bargaining for gains and losses. In K. Binmore, A. Kirman, and P. Tani (Eds), *Frontiers of Game Theory*. Cambridge, MA: MIT Press, 27–47.

Camerer, C.F. and Loewenstein, G. (1993). Information, fairness, and efficiency in bargaining. In B. Mellers and J. Baron (Eds), *Psychological Perspectives on Justice: Theory and Applications*. Cambridge: Cambridge University Press.

Camerer, C.F. and Loewenstein, G. (2004). Behavioral Economics: Past, Present and Future. In C.F. Camerer, G. Loewenstein, and M. Rabin (Eds), *Advances in Behavioral Economics*. Princeton: Princeton University Press, 3 and 40.

Camerer, C.F., Loewenstein, G., and Prelec, D. (2005). Neuroeconomics: How neuroscience can inform economics. *Journal of Economic Literature, 43*, 9–64.

Camerer, C.F. and Weigelt, K. (1988). Experimental tests of a sequential equilibrium reputation model. *Econometrica, 56*, 1–36.

Campbell, R. and Sawden, L. (Eds) (1985). *Paradoxes of Rationality and Cooperation*. Vancouver: Vancouver University.

Canova, F. and De Nicoló, G. (2003). The properties of the equity premium and the risk-free rate: an investigation across time and countries. *International Monetary Fund Staff Papers, 50*(2), 222–49.

Cantor, N. and Sanderson, C.A. (1999). Life task participation and well-being: The importance of taking part in daily life. In D. Kahneman, E. Diener, and N. Schwarz (Eds), *Well-being: The Foundations of Hedonic Psychology*. New York: Cambridge University Press, 220–43.

Carillo, J.D. (2004). To be consumed with moderation. *European Economic Review, 49*(1), 99–111.

Carpenter, J.P. (2000). Bargaining outcomes as the results of coordination expectations: An experimental study of sequential bargaining. Middlebury College Department of Economics working paper.

Carroll, C.D., Otsuka, M., and Slacalek, J. (2006). How large is the housing wealth effect? A new approach. German Institute for Economic Research, October.

Carter, J.R. and Irons, M.D. (1991). Are economists different, and if so, why? *Journal of Economic Perspectives, 5*, 171–77.

Case, K.R., Quigley, J.M., and Shiller, R.J. (2005). Comparing wealth effects: The stock market versus the housing market. *Advances in Macroeconomics, Berkeley Electronic Press, 5*(1), article 1. http://www.bepress.com/bejm/advances/vol5/iss1/art1.

Cason, T.N. and Mui, V.-L. (1998). Social influence and the strategy method in the sequential dictator game. *Journal of Mathematical Psychology, 42*, 248–65.

Casscells, W., Schoenberger, A., and Grayboys, T. (1978). Interpretation by physicians of clinical laboratory results. *New England Journal of Medicine, 299*, 999–1001.

Chagnon, N.A. (1983). *Yanomamo: The Fierce People.* 3rd ed. New York: Holt, Rinehart and Winston.

Chagnon, N.A. (1988). Life histories, blood revenge, and warfare in a tribal population. *Science, 239,* 985–92.

Chakravarti, D., Krish, R., Pallab, P., and Srivastava, J. (2002). Partitioned presentation of multicomponent bundle prices: Evaluation, choice and underlying processing effects. *Journal of Consumer Psychology, 12*(3), 215–29.

Chang, C.J., Yen, S.-H., and Duh, R.-R. (2002). An empirical examination of competing theories to explain the framing effect in accounting-related decisions. *Behavioral Research in Accounting, 14,* 35–64.

Chapman, D.A. (2002). Does intrinsic habit formation actually resolve the equity premium puzzle. *Review of Economic Dynamics, 5*(3), 618–45.

Chapman, G.B. (1996). Temporal discounting and utility for health and money. *Journal of Experimental Psychology: Learning, Memory, Cognition, 22*(3), 771–91.

Chapman, G.B. (2000). Preferences for improving and declining sequences of health outcomes. *Journal of Behavioral Decision Making, 13,* 203–18.

Chapman, G.B. and Elstein, A.S. (1995). Valuing the future: Temporal discounting of health and money. *Medical Decision Making, 15*(4), 373–86.

Chapman, G.B., Nelson, R., and Hier, D.B. (1999). Familiarity and time preferences: Decision making about treatments for migraine headaches and Crohn's disease. *Journal of Experimental Psychology: Applied, 5*(1), 17–34.

Chapman, G.B. and Winquist, J.R. (1998). The magnitude effect: temporal discount rates and restaurant tips. *Psychonomic Bulletin and Review, 5*(1), 119–23.

Charness, G. and Rabin, M. (2002). Understanding social preferences with simple tests. *Quarterly Journal of Economics, 117,* 817–69.

Chaudhuri, A. (1998). The ratchet principle in a principal agent problem with unknown costs: An experimental analysis. *Journal of Economic Behavior and Organization, 37,* 291–304.

Cheema, A. and Soman, D. (2002). Consumer responses to unexpected price changes: Affective reactions and mental accounting effects. *Advances in Consumer Research, 29,* 342.

Cheema, A. and Soman, D. (2006). Malleable mental accounting: The effect of flexibility on the justification of attractive spending and consumption decisions. *Journal of Consumer Psychology, 16*(1), 33–44.

Chen, C., Burton, M., Greenberger, E., and Dmitrevea, J. (1999). Population migration and the variation of dopamine D4 receptor (DRD4) allele frequencies around the globe. *Evolution and Human Behavior, 20*(5), 309–24.

Cherry, T.L., Frykblom, P., and Shogren, J.F. (2002). Hardnose the dictator. *American Economic Review, 92*(4), 1218–21.

Chesson, H. and Viscusi, W.K. (2000). The heterogeneity of time-risk trade-offs. *Journal of Behavioral Decision Making, 13,* 251–58.

Chew, S.H. (1983). A generalization of the quasilinear mean with applications to the measurement of income inequality and decision theory resolving the Allais paradox. *Econometrica, 51,* 1065–92.

Chew, S.H., Epstein, L.G., and Segal, U. (1991). Mixture symmetry and quadratic utility. *Econometrica, 59,* 139–63.

Chew, S.H. and MacCrimmon, K. (1979). Alpha-nu choice theory: A generalisation of expected utility theory. Working paper 669, University of British Columbia.

Chiappori, P., Levitt, S., and Groseclose, T. (2001). Testing mixed strategy equilibria when players are heterogeneous: The case of penalty kicks. University of Chicago working paper.

Christensen-Szalanski, J.J. (1984). Discount functions and the measurement of patients' values: Women's decisions during child birth. *Medical Decision Making, 4*, 47–58.

Chung, S.H. and Herrnstein, R.J. (1967). Choice and delay of reinforcement. *Journal of the Experimental Analysis of Behavior, 10*, 67–74.

Clark, A.E. and Oswald, A.J. (1996). Satisfaction and comparison income. *Journal of Public Economics, 61*, 359–81.

Coller, M. and Williams, M.B. (1999). Eliciting individual discount rates. *Experimental Economy, 2*, 107–27.

Conlisk, J. (1989). Three variants on the Allais example. *American Economic Review, 79*, 392–407.

Constantinides, G.M. (1990). Habit formation: A resolution of the equity premium puzzle, term premium, and risk-free rate puzzles. *Journal of Political Economy, 98*, 519–43.

Cooper, R., DeJong, D., Forsythe, R., and Ross. T. (1990). Selection criteria in coordination games: Some experimental results. *American Economic Review, 80*, 218–33.

Cooper, R., DeJong, D., Forsythe, R., and Ross. T. (1994). Alternative institutions for solving coordination problems: Experimental evidence on forward induction and preplay communication. In J. Friedman (Ed.), *Problems of Coordination in Economic Acitivity*. Dordrecht, Netherlands: Kluwer.

Cooper, D., Garvin, S., and Kagel, J. (1997a). Signalling and adaptive learning in an entry limit pricing game. *RAND Journal of Economics, 28*, 662–83.

Cooper, D., Garvin, S., and Kagel, J. (1997b). Adaptive learning versus equilibrium refinements in an entry limit pricing game. *Economic Journal, 107*, 553–75.

Cosmides, L. and Tooby, J. (1992). Cognitive adaptations for social exchange. In J. Barkow, L. Cosmides, and J. Tooby (Eds), *The Adapted Mind: Evolutionary Psychology and the Generation of Culture*. New York: Oxford University Press, 163–228.

Cosmides, L. and Tooby, J. (1996). Are humans good intuitive statisticians after all? Rethinking some conclusions from the literature in judgment under uncertainty. *Cognition, 58*, 1–73.

Costa, Jr, P.T. and McCrae, R.R. (1984). Personality is a lifelong determinant of well-being. In C. Malatesta and C. Izard (Eds), *Affective Processes in Adult Development and Aging*. Beverly Hills, CA: Sage, 141–56.

Costa-Gomes, M., Crawford, V., and Broseta, B. (2001). Cognition and behavior in normal-form games: An experimental study. *Econometrica, 69*(5), 1193–1235.

Cournot, A. (1838/1897). On the competition of producers. In N.T. Bacon (Trans.), *Research into the Mathematical Principles of the Theory of Wealth*. New York: Macmillan.

Coursey, D., Hovis, J., and Schulze, W. (1987). The disparity between willingness to accept and willingness to pay measures of value. *Quarterly Journal of Economics, 102*, 679–90.

Cox, J.C. (1999). Trust, reciprocity and other-regarding preferences of individuals and groups. University of Arizona Department of Economics.

Cramton, P. (1992). Strategic delay in bargaining with two-sided uncertainty. *Review of Economic Studies, 59*, 205–25.

Crews, F. (2006). *Follies of the Wise*. New York: Shoemaker and Hoard.

Croson, R.T.A. (1996). Information in ultimatum games: An experimental study. *Journal of Economic Behavior and Organization, 30*, 197–212.

Cross, P.K. (1997). Not can, but will college teaching be improved? *New Directions for Higher Education*, 17, 1–15.

Cubitt, R.C., Starmer, C., and Sugden, R. (2001). Discovered preferences and the experimental evidence of violations of expected utility theory. *Journal of Economic Methodology*, 3(8), 385–414.

Cupchik, G.C. and Leventhal, H. (1974). Consistency between expressive behavior and the evaluation of humorous stimuli: The role of sex and self-observation. *Journal of Personality and Social Psychology*, 30, 429–42.

Czikszentmihalyi, M. (1990). *Flow: The Psychology of Optimal Experience*. New York: Harper and Row.

Damasio, A.R. (1994). *Descartes' Error: Emotion, Reason, and the Human Brain*. New York: Putnam Berkley.

Damon, W. (1980). Patterns of change in children's social reasoning: A two-year longitudinal study. *Child Development*, 51, 1010–17.

Daniel, T.E., Seale, D.A., and Rapoport, A. (1998) Strategic play and adaptive learning in the sealed-bid bargaining mechanism. *Journal of Mathematical Psychology*, 42, 133–66.

Dasgupta, P. and Maskin, E. (2005). Uncertainty and Hyperbolic Discounting. *American Economic Review*, 95(4), 1290–1299.

Davidson, R.J. (1994). Asymmetric brain function, affective style, and psychopathology: The role of early experience and plasticity. *Development and Psychopathology*, 6, 741–58.

Davidson, R.J. (1998). Affective style and affective disorders: Perspectives from affective neuroscience. *Cognition and Emotion*, 12, 307–30.

Davidson, R.J. and Fox, N.A. (1989). Frontal brain asymmetry predicts infants' response to maternal separation. *Journal of Abnormal Psychology*, 98, 127–31.

Davidson, R.J. and Tomarken, A.J. (1989). Laterality and emotion: An electrophysiological approach. In F. Boller and J. Grafman (Eds), *Handbook of neuropsychology*. Amsterdam: Elsevier.

Dawkins, R. (1976). *The Selfish Gene*. Oxford: Oxford University Press.

Dawkins, R. (1986). *The Blind Watchmaker*. London: Longman.

Della Vigna, S. and Malmendier, U. (2003). Self-Control in the Market: Evidence from the Health Club Industry, mimeo.

Della Vigna, S. and Malmendier, U. (2004). Contract design and self-control. *Quarterly Journal of Economics*, 119(2), 353–402.

Dennett, D. (1987). Cognitive wheels: the frame problem of AI. In K.M. Ford and Z.W. Pylyshyn (Eds), *The Robot's Dilemma Revisited: The Frame Problem in Artificial Intelligence*. Norwood, NJ: Ablex Publishing Corporation.

Dennett, D. (1995). *Darwin's Dangerous Idea*.

de Quervain, D., Fischbacher, U., Treyer, V., Schellhammer, M., Schyder, U., Buck, A., and Fehr, E. (2004). The neural basis of altruistic punishment. *Science*, 305, 1254–58.

Desvousges, W., Johnson, R., Dunford, R., Boyle, K.J., Hudson, S., and Wilson, K.N. (1992). *Measuring non-use damages using contingent valuation: An experimental evaluation accuracy*. Research Triangle Institute Monograph 92–1.

Dhami, S. and al-Nowaihi, A. (2007). Why do people pay taxes? Expected utility versus prospect theory. *Journal of Economic Behavior & Organization*, 64, 171–192.

Diamond, J. (1997). *Guns, Germs, and Steel*. New York: Norton.

Diamond, P. and Köszegi, B. (2003). Quasi-hyperbolic discounting and retirement. *Journal of Public Economics*. 87, 9/10, 1839–72.

Diener, E. (2000). Subjective well-being: The science of happiness and a proposal for a national index. *American Psychologist, 55*, 34–43.

Dixit, A. and Nalebuff, B. (1991). *Thinking Strategically*. New York: Norton.

Dixon, N.F. (1976). *The Psychology of Military Incompetence*. Jonathan Cape.

Dolan, P. and Gudex, C. (1995). Time preference, duration and health state valuations. *Health Economics, 4*, 289–99.

Dreyfus, M.K. and Viscusi, W.K. (1995). Rates of time preference and consumer valuations of automobile safety and fuel efficiency. *Journal of Law and Economics, 38*(1), 79–105.

Drumwright, M.E. (1992). A demonstration of anomalies in evaluations of bundling. *Marketing Letters, 3*, 311–21.

Duesenberry, J. (1949). *Income, Saving, and the Theory of Consumer Behavior*. Cambridge, MA: Harvard University Press.

Dufwenberg, M. and Gneezy, U. (2000). Measuring beliefs in an experimental lost wallet game. *Games and Economic Behavior, 30*, 163–82.

Dufwenberg, M. and Kirchsteiger, G. (1998). A theory of sequential reciprocity. Tilburg Center for Economic Research discussion paper 9837.

Dugatkin, L.A. (1991). Dynamics of the tit for tat strategy during predator inspection in guppies. *Behavioral Ecology and Sociobiology, 29*, 127–32.

Dulany, D.E. and Hilton, D.J. (1991). Conversational implicature, conscious representation, and the conjunction fallacy. *Social Cognition, 9*, 85–110.

Dutton, D.G. and Aaron, A.P. (1974). Some evidence for heightened sexual attraction under conditions of high anxiety. *Journal of Personality and Social Psychology, 30*, 510–17.

Duxbury, D., Keasey, K., Zhang, H., and Chow, S.L. (2005). Mental accounting and decision making: Evidence under reverse conditions where money is spent for time saved. *Journal of Economic Psychology, 26*(4), 567–80.

Eagly, A. and Chaiken, S. (1996). Attitude structure and function. In D. Gilbert, S. Fiske, and G. Lindzey (Eds), *The Handbook of Social Psychology*. 4th ed. New York: McGraw-Hill.

Easterlin, R.A. (1995). Will raising the incomes of all increase the happiness of all? *Journal of Economic Behavior and Organization, 29*(1), 35–47.

Easterlin, R.A. (2001). Income and happiness: Towards a unified theory. *Economic Journal, 111*, 464–84.

Eckel, C.C. and Grossman, P. (1996a). Altruism in anonymous dictator games. *Games and Economic Behavior, 6*, 181–91.

Eckel, C.C. and Grossman, P. (1996b). The relative price of fairness: Gender differences in a punishment game. *Journal of Economic Behavior and Organization, 30*, 143–58.

Eckel, C.C. and Grossman, P. (2001). Chivalry and solidarity in ultimatum games. *Economic Inquiry, 39*, 171–88.

Economist (2005). Loss aversion in monkeys. June 23.

—— (2005). The rational response to terrorism. July 21.

—— (2006). Soothing the savage breast. January 12.

—— (2006). Brothers in arms. June 29.

—— (2006). Pursuing happiness. June 29.

—— (2006). The joy of giving. October 12.

Edgeworth, F.Y. (1881). *Mathematical Psychics*. London: Kegan Paul.

Edwards, W. (1955). The prediction of decisions among bets. *Journal of Experimental Psychology. 50*, 201–14.

Edwards, W. (1962). Subjective probabilities inferred from decisions. *Psychological Review, 69*, 109–35.

Ellsberg, D. (1961). Risk, ambiguity and the Savage axioms. *Quarterly Journal of Economics, 75*, 643–69.

Elster, J. (1979). *Ulysses and the Sirens: Studies in Rationality and Irrationality.* Cambridge: Cambridge University Press.

Elster, J. (1985). Weakness of will and the free-rider problem. *Economics and Philosophy*, 231–65.

Elster, J. (1989). When rationality fails. In K. Cook and M. Levi (Eds), *Limits of Rationality.* Chicago: University of Chicago Press.

Elster, J. (1998). Emotions and economic theory. *Journal of Economic Literature, 36*(1), 47–74.

Engen, E.M., Gale, W.G., and Uccello, C.E. (1999). The adequacy of household saving. *Brookings Papers on Economic Activity, 2*, 65–187.

Epstein, S. (1994). Integration of the cognitive and the psychodynamic unconscious. *American Psychologist, 49*, 709–24.

Epstein, L.G. and Zin, S.E. (1989). Substitution risk aversion, and the temporal behaviour of consumption growth and asset returns I: A theoretical framework. *Econometrica, 57*, 937–69.

Evans, D.J. and Sezer, H. (2004). Social discount rates for six major countries. *Applied Economics Letters, 11*, 557–60.

Evans, J. St B.T. and Over, D.E. (1996). *Rationality and Reasoning.* Hove, UK: Psychology Press.

Fagley, N.S. and Miller, P.M. (1987). The effects of decision framing on choice of risky versus certain options. *Organizational Behavior and Human Decision Processes, 39*, 264–77.

Fagley, N.S. and Miller, P.M. (1997). Framing effects and arenas of choice: Your money or your life? *Organizational Behavior and Human Decision Processes, 71*, 355–73.

Falk, A. and Fischbacher, U. (1998). A theory of reciprocity. University of Zurich, IEER working paper.

Faust, D., Hart, K.J., and Guilmette, T.J. (1988). Pediatric malingering: The capacity of children to fake believable deficits on neuropsychological testing. *Journal of Consulting and Clinical Psychology, 56*, 578–82.

Feenberg, J. and Skinner, J. (1989). Sources of IRA saving. In L. Summers (Ed.), *Tax Policy and the Economy*, Vol. 3. Cambridge, MA: MIT Press.

Fehr, E. (2002). The economics of impatience. *Nature, 415*, 269–272.

Fehr, E. and Falk, A. (1999). Wage rigidity in a competitive incomplete contract market. *Journal of Political Economy, 107*, 106–34.

Fehr, E., Fischbacher, U., and Kosfeld, M. (2005). Neuroeconomic foundations of trust and social preferences: Initial evidence. AEA Papers and Proceedings, May.

Fehr, E. and Gächter, S. (2000). Cooperation and punishment in public goods experiments. *American Economic Review, 90*(4), 980–94.

Fehr, E. and Gächter, S. (2001). Fairness and retaliation. *Journal of Economic Perspectives, 3*, 159–181.

Fehr, E., Klein, A., and Schmidt, K.M. (2004). Contracts, fairness and incentives. Discussion Paper No. 2004–07, Department of Economics, University of Munich.

Fehr, E. and Schmidt, K.M. (1999). A theory of fairness, competition and cooperation. *Quarterly Journal of Economics, 114*, 817–68.

Fehr, E. and Tyran, J.-R. (2003). What causes nominal inertia? Insights from experimental economics. In Isabelle Brocas and Juan D. Carillo (Eds), *The Psychology of Economic Decisions*. Oxford: Oxford University Press, 299–314.

Ferguson, N. (1998). *The Pity of War*. London: Allen Lane, 358.

Ferson, W.E. and Constantinides, G.M. (1991). Habit persistence and durability in aggregate consumption: Empirical tests. *Journal of Financial Economics, 29*, 199–240.

Festinger, L. (1954). A theory of social comparison processes. *Human Relations, 7*, 117–40.

Festinger, L. (1957). *A Theory of Cognitive Dissonance*. Stanford, CA: Stanford University Press.

Fiedler, K. (1988). The dependence of the conjunction fallacy on subtle linguistic factors. *Psychological Research, 50*, 123–29.

Finkenauer, J. (1982). *Scared Straight! And the Panacea Phenomenon*. Englewood Cliffs, NJ: Prentice Hall.

Fischhoff, B., Slovic, P., and Lichtenstein, S. (1979). Subjective sensitivity analysis. *Organizational Behavior and Human Performance, 23*, 339–59.

Fishburn, P.C. (1970). *Utility Theory and Decision Making*. New York: Wiley.

Fishburn, P.C. (1983). Transitive measurable utility. *Journal of Economic Theory, 31*, 293–317.

Fisher, I. (1928). *The Money Illusion*. New York: Adelphi.

Fisher, I. (1930). *The Theory of Interest*. New York: Macmillan.

Fiske, A.P. and Tetlock, P. (1997). Taboo trade-offs: reactions to transactions that transgress the domain of relationships. *Political Psychology, 18*, 255–97.

Fodor, J. (1975). *The Language of Thought*. New York: Crowell.

Fong, G.T. and Nisbett, R.E. (1991). Immediate and delayed transfer of training effects in statistical reasoning. *Journal of Experimental Psychology, 120*, 34–45.

Forsythe, R., Horowitz, J.L., Savin, N.E., and Sefton, M. (1994). Fairness in simple bargaining experiments. *Games and Economic Behavior, 6*, 347–69.

Forsythe, R., Kennan, J., and Sopher, B. (1991). Dividing a shrinking pie: An experimental study of strikes in bargaining games with complete information. In R.M. Isaac (Ed.), *Research in Experimental Economics*, Vol. 4. Greenwich, CN: JAI Press, 223–67.

Frank, R.H. (1985). *Choosing the Right Pond – Human Behavior and the Quest for Status*. Oxford: Oxford University Press.

Frank, R.H. (1988). *Passions within Reason: the Strategic Role of the Emotions*. New York: Norton.

Frank, R.H., Gilovich, T., and Regan, D.T. (1993). Does studying economics inhibit cooperation? *Journal of Economic Perspectives, 7*, 159–71.

Frank, R.H. and Hutchens, R.M. (1993). Wages, seniority, and the demand for rising consumption profiles. *Journal of Economic Behavior and Organization, 21*, 251–76.

Frederick, S. and Loewenstein, G. (1999). Hedonic adaptation. In D. Kahneman, E. Diener, and N. Schwarz (Eds), *Well-Being: The Foundations of Hedonic Psychology*. New York, NY: Russell Sage Foundation Press.

Frederick, S., Loewenstein, G., and O'Donoghue, T. (2002). Time discounting and time preference: A critical review. *Journal of Economic Literature, 40*(2), 351–401.

Frederick, S. and Read, D. (2002). The empirical and normative status of hyperbolic discounting and other DU anomalies. Working paper, MIT and London School of Economics, Cambridge, MA and London.

Fredrickson, B.L. (2000). Extracting meaning from past affective experiences: The importance of peaks, ends, and specific emotions. *Cognition and Emotion, 14*, 577–606.

Freud, A. (1937). *The Ego and the Mechanisms of Defense*. London: Hogarth Press.

Frey, B. and Bohnet, I. (1995). Institutions affect fairness: Experimental investigations. *Journal of Institutional and Theoretical Economics, 151*(2), 286–303.

Frey, B. and Bohnet, I. (1997). Identification in democratic society. *Journal of Socio-Economics, 26*, 25–38.

Friedman, M. (1953). The methodology of positive economics. In M. Friedman, *Essays in Positive Economics*. Chicago: University of Chicago Press, 343.

Friedman, M. (1957). *A Theory of Consumption Function*. Princeton, NJ: Princeton University Press.

Friedman, M. and Savage, L.J. (1948). The utility analysis of choices involving risks. *Journal of Political Economy, 56*, 279–304.

Fuchs, V. (1982). Time preferences and health: An exploratory study. In V. Fuchs (Ed.), *Economic Aspects of Health*. Chicago: University of Chicago Press.

Fudenberg, D. (2006). Advancing beyond 'Advances in Behavioral Economics'. *Journal of Economic Literature, 44*(3), 694–711.

Fudenberg, D. and Levine, D.K. (2006). A dual self model of impulse control. *American Economic Review, 96*(5), 1449–76.

Gabaix, X. and Laibson, D. (2001). The 6D bias and the equity premium puzzle. *NBER/Macroeconomics Annual, 16*(1), 257–312.

Gächter, S. and Falk, A. (1999). Reputation or reciprocity? Working paper no. 19, Institute for Empirical Research in Economics, University of Zurich.

Galanter, E. and Pliner, P. (1974). Cross-modality matching of money against other continua. In H.R. Moskowitz *et al.* (Eds), *Sensation and Measurement*. Dordrecht, the Netherlands: Reidel, 65–76.

Gangestad, S.W. and Buss, D.M. (1993). Pathogen prevalence and human mate preferences. *Ethology and Sociobiology, 14*, 89–96.

Ganiats, T.G., Carson, R.T., Hamm, R.M., Cantor, S.B., Sumner, W., Spann, S.J., Hagen, M., and Miller, C. (2000). Health status and preferences: Population-based time preference for future health outcome. *Medical Decision Making, 20*(3), 263–70.

Gateley, D. (1980). Individual discount rates and the purchase and utilization of energy-using durables: Comment. *Bell Journal of Economics, 11*, 373–74.

Genesove, D. and Mayer, C. (2001). Loss-aversion and seller behavior: Evidence from the housing market. *Quarterly Journal of Economics, 116*(4), 1233–60.

Gertner, R. (1993). Game shows and economic behaviour: Risk taking on "Card Sharks." *Quarterly Journal of Economics, 106*, 507–21.

Gigerenzer, G. (1996a). On narrow norms and vague heuristics: A reply to Kahneman and Tversky. *Psychological Review, 103*, 592–96.

Gigerenzer, G. (1996b). Rationality: Why social context matters. In P.B. Baltes and U. Staudinger (Eds), *Interactive Minds: Life-Span Perspectives on the Social Foundation of Cognition*. Cambridge: Cambridge University Press, 319–46.

Gigerenzer, G., Hoffrage, U., and Kleinbolting, H. (1991). Probabilistic mental models: A Brunswikian theory of confidence. *Psychological Review, 98*, 506–28.

Gigerenzer, G. and Hug, K. (1992). Domain-specific reasoning: Social contracts, cheating and perspective change. *Cognition, 43*, 127–71.

Gigliotti, G. and Sopher, B. (1993). A test of generalized expected utility theory. *Theory and Decision, 35*, 75–106.

Gilbert, D.F., Pinel. E.C., Wilson, T.D., Blumberg, S.J., and Wheatley, J.P. (1998). Immune neglect: A source of durability bias in affective forecasting. *Journal of Personality and Social Psychology, 75*, 617–38.

Gilboa, I. and Schmeidler, D. (1995). Case-based decision theory. *Quarterly Journal of Economics, 110*, 605–39.

Gilboa, I. and Schmeidler, D. (2001). *A Theory of Case-Based Decisions*. Cambridge: Cambridge University Press.

Gilovich, T. (1991). *How we know what isn't so: The Fallibility of Human Reason in Everyday Life*. New York: The Free Press.

Ginossar, Z. and Trope, Y. (1987). Problem solving in judgment under uncertainty. *Journal of Personality and Social Psychology, 52*, 464–74.

Glassner, B. (1999). *The Culture of Fear: Why Americans are Afraid of the Wrong Things*. New York: Basic Books.

Glimcher, P.W. (2003). *Decisions, Uncertainty, and the Brain: The Science of Neuroeconomics*. Cambridge, MA: MIT Press.

Gneezy, U., Kapteyn, A., and Potters, J. (2003). Evaluation periods and asset prices in a market experiment. *Journal of Finance, 58*, 821–38.

Gneezy, U. and Potters, J. (1997). An experiment on risk taking and evaluating periods. *Quarterly Journal of Economics, 112*, 631–46.

Gneezy, U. and Rustichini, A. (2000). A fine is a price. *Journal of Legal Studies, 29*, 1–17.

Gonzalez, R. and Wu, G. (1999). On the shape of the probability weighting function. *Cognitive Psychology, 38*, 129–66.

Gourville, J. (1998). Pennies-a-day: The effect of temporal reframing on transaction evaluation. *Journal of Consumer Research, 24*, 395–408.

Gourville, J. and Soman, D. (1998). Payment depreciation: The effects of temporally separating payments from consumption. *Journal of Consumer Research, 25*(2), 160–74.

Green, J., and Jullien, B. (1988). Ordinal independence in nonlinear utility theory. *Journal of Risk and Uncertainty, 1*, 355–87.

Green, J., Myerson, J., and McFadden, E. (1997). Rate of temporal discounting decreases with amount of reward. *Memory and Cognition, 25*(5), 715–23.

Green, L., Fry, A., and Myerson, J. (1994). Temporal discounting and preference reversals in choice between delayed outcomes. *Psychonomic Bulletin and Review, 1*(3), 383–89.

Greenspan, A. and Kennedy, J. (2005). Estimates of home mortgage originations, repayments, and debt on one-to-four family residences. Federal Reserve Board Finance and Economics Discussion Paper. 2005–41.

Gruber, J. and Köszegi, B. (2001). Is addiction rational? Theory and evidence. *Quarterly Journal of Economics, 116*(4), 1261–1303.

Gul, F. (1991). A theory of disappointment in decision making under uncertainty. *Econometrica, 59*, 667–86.

Gul, F. and Pesendorfer, W. (2001). Temptation and self-control. *Econometrica, 69*(6), 1403–36.

Gul, F. and Pesendorfer, W. (2005). The case for "mindless economics." Working paper, Princeton University, November.

Gul, F. and Pesendorfer, W. (2007). Harmful Addiction. *Review of Economic Studies, 74*(1).

Güth, W., Marchand, N., and Rullière, J.L. (1997). On the reliability of reciprocal fairness – An experimental study. Discussion paper, Humboldt University Berlin.

Güth, W., Schmittberger, R., and Schwarze, B. (1987). An experimental analysis of ultimatum bargaining. *Journal of Economic Behavior and Organization, 3*, 367–88.

Güth, W. and Van Damme, E. (1998). Information, strategic behavior and fairness in ultimatum bargaining: An experimental study. *Journal of Mathematical Psychology, 42*, 227–47.

Haigh, M.S. and List, J.A. (2005). Do professional traders exhibit myopic loss-version? An experimental analysis. *Journal of Finance, 60*(1), 523–34.

Hamer, D. (1998). *Living with our Genes*. New York: Doubleday.

Handa, J. (1977). Risk, probability, and a new theory of cardinal utility. *Journal of Political Economy, 85*, 97–122.

Hardie, B.G.S., Johnson, E.J., and Fader, P.S. (1993). Modeling loss-aversion and reference dependence effects on brand choice. *Marketing Science, 12*, 378–94.

Harless, D.W. (1992). Predictions about indifference curves inside the unit triangle: A test of variants of expected utility. *Journal of Economic Behavior and Organisation, 18*, 391–414.

Harrison, G., Lau, M.I., and Williams, M.B. (2002). Estimating individual discount rates in Denmark: A field experiment. *American Economic Review, 92*, 5, 1606–17.

Harrison, G. and McCabe, K. (1992). Testing noncooperative bargaining theory in experiments. In R.M. Isaac (Ed.), *Research in Experimental Economics*, Vol. 5. Greenwich, CN: JAI Press.

Harrison, G. and McCabe, K. (1996). Expectations and fairness in a simple bargaining experiment. *International Journal of Game Theory, 25*, 303–27.

Harsanyi, J.C. and Selten, R. (1988). *A General Theory of Equilibrium in Games*. Cambridge, MA: MIT Press.

Harvey, C.M. (1986). Value functions for infinite-period planning. *Management Science, 32*, 1123–39.

Hausch, D.B. and Ziemba, W.T. (1995). Efficiency in sports and lottery betting markets. In R.A. Jarrow, V. Maksimovic, and W.T. Ziemba (Eds), *Handbook of Finance*. Amsterdam: North-Holland.

Hausman, J. (1979). Individual discount rates and the purchase and utilization of energy-using durables. *Bell Journal of Economics, 10*(1), 33–54.

He, H. and Modest, D.M. (1995). Market frictions and consumption-based asset pricing. *Journal of Political Economy, 103*, 94–117.

Heath, C. and Fennema, M.G. (1996). Mental depreciation and marginal decision making. *Organizational Behavior and Human Decision Processes, 68*, 95–108.

Heath, C. and Soll, J.B. (1996). Mental budgeting and consumer decisions. *Journal of Consumer Research, 23*, 40–52.

Heberlein, T.A. and Bishop, R.C. (1985). Assessing the validity of contingent valuation: Three field experiments. Paper presented at the International Conference on Man's Role in Changing the Global Environment, Italy.

Hedesström, T.M., Svedsäter, H., and Gärlin, T. (2004). Identifying heuristic choice rules in the Swedish premium pension scheme. *Journal of Behavioral Finance, 5*(1), 32–42.

Heilman, C., Nakamoto, K., and Rao, A. (2002). Pleasant surprises: Consumer response to unexpected in-store coupons. *Advances in Consumer Research, 29*, 342.

Heinrich, J., Boyd, R., Bowles, S., Camerer, C., Fehr, E., Gintis, H., and McElreath, R. (2001). In search of Homo Economicus: Behavioral experiments in 15 small-scale societies. *American Economic Review, 91*(2), 73–78.

Heinrich, J., Boyd, R., Bowles, S., Camerer, C., Fehr, E., Gintis, H., and McElreath, R., Alvard, M., Barr, A., Ensminger, J., Hill, K., Gil-White, F., Gurven, M., Marlowe, F., Patton, J.Q., Smith, N., and Tracer, D. (2002). 'Economic Man' in cross-cultural perspective: Behavioral experiments in 15 small-scale societies. Working paper. http://webuser.bus.umich.edu/henrich/gameproject.htm.

Helson, H. (1964). *Adaptation Level Theory: An Experimental and Systematic Approach to Behavior*. New York: Harper.

Herrnstein, R. (1981). Self-control as response strength. In C.M. Bradshaw, E. Szabadi, and C.F. Lowe (Eds), *Quantification of Steady-State Operant Behavior*. North Holland: Elsevier.

Hertwig, R. and Gigerenzer, G. (1999). The 'conjunction fallacy' revisited: how intelligent inferences look like reasoning errors. *Journal of Behavioral Decision Making, 12,* 275–305.

Hertwig, R. and Ortmann, A. (2001). Experimental practices in economics: A methodological challenge for psychologists. *Behavioral and Brain Sciences, 24*(3), 383–403.

Hesketh, B. (2000). Time perspective in career-related choices: Applications of time discounting principles. *Journal of Vocational Behavior, 57,* 62–84.

Hey, J.D. and Orme, C. (1994). Investigating generalizations of expected utility theory using experimental data. *Econometrica, 62,* 1291–326.

Hilton, D.J. (1995). The social context of reasoning: Conversational inference and rational judgment. *Psychological Bulletin, 118,* 248–71.

Hirshleifer, J. (1987). On the emotions as guarantors of threats and promises. In J. Dupre (Ed.), *The Latest on the Best.* Cambridge, MA: MIT Press, 307–26.

Hirshleifer, J. (1998). The bioeconomic causes of war. *Managerial and Decision Economics,* 19, 457–66. Reproduced in J. Hirshleifer (2001), *The Dark Side of the Force: Economic Foundations of Conflict Theory,* 26–27.

Ho, T., Camerer, C., and Weigelt, K. (1998). Iterated dominance and iterated best-response in experimental p-beauty contests. *American Economic Review, 88,* 947–69.

Ho, T., Lim, N., and Camerer, C. (2006). Modeling the psychology of consumer and firm behaviour with behavioural economics. *Journal of Marketing Research, 43,* 307–31.

Hodgson, D. (1999). Hume's mistake. *Journal of Consciousness Studies, 6,* 201–24.

Hoffman, E., McCabe, K., Shachat, K., and Smith, V. (1994). Preferences, property rights and anonymity in bargaining games. *Games and Economic Behavior, 7,* 346–80.

Hoffman, E., McCabe, K., and Smith, V. (1996). On expectations and monetary stakes in ultimatum games. *International Journal of Game Theory, 25,* 289–301.

Hoffman, E., McCabe, K., and Smith, V. (1998). Behavioral foundations of reciprocity: Experimental economics and evolutionary psychology. *Economic Inquiry, 36,* 335–52.

Holcomb, J.S. and Nelson, P.S. (1992). Another experimental look at individual time preference. *Rationality and Society, 4*(2), 199–220.

Holden, S.T., Shiferaw, B., and Wik, M. (1998). Poverty, market imperfections and time preferences of relevance for environmental policy? *Environmental Developmental Economics, 3,* 105–30.

Homans, G.C. (1961). Social Behavior: Its Elementary Forms. New York: Harcourt, Brace and World.

Hood, B. (2006). Talk given at the British Association Festival of Science, September 4.

Houston, D.A. (1983). Implicit discount rates and the purchase of untried energy-saving durable goods. *Journal of Consumer Resources, 10,* 236–46.

Hsee, C.K. (1996). The evaluability hypothesis: An explanation of preference reversals between joint and separate evaluations of alternatives. *Organizational Behavior and Human Decision Processes, 46,* 247–57.

Hsee, C.K., Abelson, R.P., and Salovey, P. (1991). The relative weighting of position and velocity in satisfaction. *Psychological Science, 2*(4), 263–66.

Hsee, C.K., Loewenstein, G., Blount, S., and Bazerman, M.H. (1999). Preference reversals between joint and separate evaluations: A review and theoretical analysis. *Psychological Bulletin, 125*(5), 576–90.

Huber, J., Payne, J.W., and Puto, C. (1982). Adding asymmetrically dominated alternatives: Violations of regularity and the similarity hypothesis. *Journal of Consumer Research, 9,* 90–98.

Hung, M.-W. and Wang, Jr-Y. (2005). Asset prices under prospect theory and habit formation. *Review of Pacific Basin Financial Markets & Policies, 8*(1), 1–29,

Ibbotson, R.G. and Chen, P. (2003). Long-run stock returns: Participating in the real economy. *Financial Analysts Journal, 59*(1), 88–98.

Ingram, R.E. (1990). Self-focused attention in clinical disorders: Review and a conceptual model. *Psychological Bulletin, 109*, 156–76.

Insurance Information Institute (1992). *No-fault Auto Insurance.* New York: Insurance Information Institute.

Janakiraman, N., Meyer, R., and Morales, A. (2002). The mental accounting of price shocks: The effects of unexpected price changes on cross-category purchase patterns. *Advances in Consumer Research, 29*, 342–43.

Janis, I. (1967). Effects of fear arousal on attitude change. In L. Berkowitz (Ed.), *Advances in Experimental Social Psychology.* New York: Academic Press.

Jevons, H.S. (1905). *Essays on Economics.* London: Macmillan.

Jevons, W.S. (1888). *The Theory of Political Economy.* London: Macmillan.

Jha-Dang, P. and Banerjee, A. (2005). A theory based explanation of differential consumer response to different promotions. *Advances in Consumer Research, 32*, 235–36.

Jobes, J. (1974). A revelatory function of art. *The British Journal of Aesthetics, 14*, 24–133.

Johanneson, M. and Johansson, P.-O. (1997). Quality of life and the WTP for an increased life expectancy at an advanced age. *Journal of Public Economics, 65*, 219–28.

Johnson, E.J., Camerer, C., Sen, S., and Rymon, T. (2002). Detecting failures of backward induction: Monitoring information search in sequential bargaining experiments. *Journal of Economic Theory, 104*, 16–47.

Johnson, E.J., Hershey, J., Meszaros, J., and Kunreuther, H. (1992). Framing, probability distortions, and insurance decisions. *Journal of Risk and Uncertainty, 7*, 35–51.

Johnson, M.D., Herrmann, A., and Bauer, H.H. (1999). The effects of price bundling on consumer evaluations of product offerings. *International Journal of Research in Marketing, 16*, 129–42.

Johnson-Laird, P.N., Byrne R.M.J., and Schaeken, R.S. (1992). Propositional reasoning by model. *Psychological Review, 99*, 418–39.

Johnson-Laird, P.N., Legrenzi, P., Girotto, V., and Legrenzi, M.S. (2000). Illusions in reasoning about consistency. *Science, 288*, 531–32.

Jones, C.P. and Wilson, J.W. (2005). The equity risk premium controversy. *Journal of Investing, 14*(2), 37–43.

Jones-Lee, M.W., Loomes, G., and Philips, P.R. (1995). Valuing the prevention of non-fatal road injuries: Contingent valuation versus standard gambles. *Oxford Economic Papers, 47*, 675–95.

Jordan, J.S. (1991). Bayesian learning in normal-form games. *Games and Economic Behavior, 3*, 60–81.

Jullien, B. and Salanié, B. (1997). Estimating preferences under risk: The case of racetrack bettors. IDEI and GREMAQ, Working paper, Toulouse University.

Kachelmeier, S.J. and Shehata, M. (1992). Examining risk preferences under high monetary incentives: Experimental evidence from the People's Republic of China. *American Economic Review, 82*, 1120–41.

Kagel, J., Kim, C., and Moser, D. (1996). Fairness in ultimatum games with asymmetric information and asymmetric payoffs. *Games and Economic Behavior, 13*, 100–10.

Kahneman, D. (1986). Comments on the contingent valuation method. In R.G. Cummings, D.S. Brookshire, and W.D. Schulze (Eds), *Valuing Environmental Goods: An Assessment of the Contingent Valuation Method.* Totowa, NJ: Rowman and Allanheld.

Kahneman, D. (1994). New challenges to the rationality assumption. *Journal of Institutional and Theoretical Economics, 150,* 1836.

Kahneman, D. (2000). Experienced utility and objective happiness: A moment-based approach. Ch. 37 in D. Kahneman, and A. Tversky (Eds), *Choices, Values, and Frames.* New York: Cambridge University Press and the Russell Sage Foundation.

Kahneman, D., Diener, E., and Schwartz, N. (Eds) (1999). *Well-Being: The Foundations of Hedonic Psychology.* New York: Russell Sage Foundation.

Kahneman, D., Knetsch, J.L., and Thaler, R.H. (1986). Fairness as a constraint on profit seeking: Entitlements in the market. *American Economic Review, 76*(4), 728–41.

Kahneman, D., Knetsch, J.L., and Thaler, R.H. (1990). Experimental tests of the endowment effect and the Coase theorem. *Journal of Political Economy, 98*(6), 1352–75.

Kahneman, D. and Ritov, I. (1994). Determinants of stated willingness to pay for public goods – A study in the headline method. *Journal of Risk and Uncertainty, 9*(1), 5–38.

Kahneman, D., Ritov, I., and Schkade, D.A. (1999). Economic preferences or attitude expressions? An analysis of dollar responses to public issues. *Journal of Risk and Uncertainty, 19,* 203–35.

Kahneman, D., Schkade, D.A., and Sunstein, C.R. (1998). Shared outrage and erratic awards: The psychology of punitive damages. *Journal of Risk and Uncertainty, 16,* 49–86.

Kahneman, D., Slovic, P., and Tversky, A. (1982). *Judgement under Uncertainty: Heuristics and Biases.* Cambridge: Cambridge University Press.

Kahneman, D. and Snell, J. (1992). Predicting a changing taste: Do people know what they will like? *Journal of Behavioral Decision Making, 5,* 187–200.

Kahneman, D. and Tversky A. (1972). Subjective probability: A judgement of representativeness. *Cognitive Psychology, 3,* 430–54.

Kahneman, D. and Tversky A. (1973). On the psychology of prediction. *Psychological Review, 80,* 237–51.

Kahneman, D. and Tversky A. (1979). Prospect theory: An analysis of decision under risk. *Econometrica, 47,* 263–91.

Kahneman, D. and Tversky A. (1982). Judgement of and by representativeness. In D. Kahneman, P. Slovic, and A. Tversky (Eds), *Judgement under Uncertainty: Heuristics and Biases.* New York: Cambridge University Press, 84–100.

Kahneman, D. and Tversky A. (1984). Choices, values, and frames. *The American Psychologist, 39,* 341–50.

Kahneman, D. and Tversky A. (1992). Advances in prospect theory: Cumulative representation of uncertainty. *Journal of Risk and Uncertainty, 5,* 297–324.

Kahneman, D. and Tversky A. (1996). On the reality of cognitive illusions. *Psychological Review, 103,* 582–91.

Kahneman, D., Wakker, P. and Sarin, R. (1997). Back to Bentham? Explorations of experienced utility. *Quarterly Journal of Economics, 112,* 375–405.

Kaplan, H.R. (1978). *Lottery Winners: How they Won and how Winning changed their Lives.* New York: Harper and Row.

Kasser, T. and Ryan R.M. (1993). A dark side of the American dream: Correlates of financial success as a central life aspiration. *Journal of Personality and Social Psychology, 65*(2), 41–42.

Kasser, T. and Ryan R.M. (1996). Further examining the American dream: Differential correlates of intrinsic and extrinsic goals. *Journal of Personality and Social Psychology, 22*(3), 280–87.

Katz, J., Redelmeier, D., and Kahneman, D. (1997). Memories of painful medical procedures. Paper presented at the American Pain Society 15th Annual Scientific Meeting.

Keeley, L.H. (1996). *War Before Civilization*. New York: Oxford University Press.

Kennan, J. and Wilson, R. (1990). Theories of bargaining delays. *Science, 249*, 1124–28.

Keren, G. and Roelofsma, P. (1995). Immediacy and certainty in intertemporal choice. *Organizational Behavior and Human Decision Processes, 63*(3), 287–97.

Keynes, J.M. (1936). *The General Theory of Employment, Interest, and Money*. London: Macmillan, 156.

Kirby, K.N. (1997). Bidding on the future: Evidence against normative discounting of delayed rewards. *Journal of Experimental Psychology: General, 126*, 54–70.

Kirby, K.N. and Marakovic, N.N. (1995). Modeling myopic decisions: Evidence for hyperbolic delay-discounting with subjects and amounts. *Organizational Behavior and Human Decision Processes, 64*, 22–30.

Kirby, K.N. and Marakovic, N.N. (1996). Delay-discounting probabilistic rewards: Rates decrease as amounts increase. *Psychonomic Bulletin and Review, 3*(1), 100–104.

Kirby, K.N., Petry, N.M., and Bickel, W. (1999). Heroin addicts have higher discount rates for delayed rewards than non-drug-using controls. *Journal of Experimental Psychology: General, 128*(1), 78–87.

Kirschner, M.W. and Gerhart, J.C. (2006). *The Plausibility of Life: Resolving Darwin's Dilemma*. New Haven, CT: Yale University Press.

Knack, S. and Keefer, P. (1997). Does social capital have an economic payoff? A cross-country investigation. *Quarterly Journal of Economics, 112*, 1251–88.

Knetsch, J.L. (1989). The endowment effect and evidence of nonreversible indifference curves. *American Economic Review, 79*, 1277–84.

Knetsch, J.L. and Sinden, J.A. (1984). Willingness to pay and compensation demanded: Experimental evidence of an unexpected disparity in measures of value. *Quarterly Journal of Economics, 99*, 507–21.

Knez, M.J. and Camerer, C. (1995). Social comparison and outside options in 3-person ultimatum games. *Games and Economic Behavior, 10*, 165–94.

Knez, P., Smith, V.L., and Williams, A. (1985). Individual rationality, market rationality, and value estimation. *American Economic Review, 75*, 397–402.

Knutson, B., Rick, S., Wimmer, E., Prelec, D., and Loewenstein, G. (2007). Neural predictors of purchases. *Neuron, 53*, 147–56.

Kocherlakota, N.R. (1996). The equity premium: It's still a puzzle. *Journal of Economic Literature, 34*(1), 42–71.

Konow, J. (2000). Fair shares: Accountability and cognitive dissonance in allocation decisions. *American Economic Review, 90*(4), 1072–91.

Koopmans, T.C. (1960). Stationary ordinal utility and impatience. *Econometrica, 28*, 287–309.

Kooreman, P. (1997). The labeling effect of a child benefit system. Unpublished working paper, University of Groningen.

Kosfeld, M., Heinrichs, M., Zuk, P., Fischbacher, U., and Fehr, E. (2005). Oxytocin increases trust in humans. *Nature, 435*(7042), 673–76.

Krosnick, J.A., Li, F., and Lehman, D.R. (1990). Conversational conventions, order of information acquisition, and the effect of base rates and individuating information on social judgments. *Journal of Personality and Social Psychology, 59*, 1140–52.

Kühberger, A. (1995). The framing of decisions: A new look at old problems. *Organizational Behavior and Human Decision Processes*, 62, 230–40.

Kuhnen, C.M. and Knutson, B. (2005). The neural basis of financial risk-taking. *Neuron, 47*, 763–70.

Kunreuther, H., Ginsberg, R., Miller, L., Slovic, P., Bradley, B., and Katz, N. (1978). *Disaster Insurance Protection: Public Policy Lessons*. New York: Wiley.

Laibson, D.L. (1996). Hyperbolic discounting, undersaving, and savings policy. NBER Working Paper No. 5635.

Laibson, D.L. (1997). Golden eggs and hyperbolic discounting. *Quarterly Journal of Economics, 112*, 443–77.

Laibson, D.L. (1998), Life-cycle consumption and hyperbolic discount functions. *European Economic Review, 42*(3–5), 861–87.

Lancaster, K.J. (1963). An axiomatic theory of consumer time preference. *International Economic Review, 4*, 221–31.

Lang, P. (1995). The emotion probe: studies of emotion and attention. *American Psychologist, 50*, 372–85.

Langer, E.J. (1982). The illusion of control. In D. Kahneman, P. Slovic, and A. Tversky, (Eds), *Judgment under Uncertainty: Heuristics and Biases*. Cambridge University Press, Chapter 16.

Langer, T. and Weber, M. (2001). Prospect theory, mental accounting, and differences in aggregated and segregated evaluation of lottery portfolios. *Management Science, 47*(5), 716–33.

Langer, T. and Weber, M. (2005). Myopic prospect theory versus myopic loss-aversion: How general is the phenomenon? *Journal of Economic Behavior and Organization, 56*(1), 25–38.

Larrick, R.P. and Blount, S. (1997). The claiming effect: Why players are more generous in social dilemmas than in ultimatum games. *Journal of Personality and Social Psychology, 72*, 810–25.

Larwood, L. and Whittaker, W. (1977). Managerial myopia: Self-serving biases in organizational planning. *Journal of Applied Psychology, 62*, 194–98.

Lattimore, P.K., Baker, J.R., and Witte, A.D. (1992). The influence of probability on risky choice: A parametric examination. *Journal of Economic Behavior and Organization, 17*, 377–400.

LeBoeuf, R.A. (2006). Discount rates for time versus dates: The sensitivity of discounting to time-interval description. *Journal of Marketing Research, 43*, 59–72.

Leclerc, F., Schmidt, B., and Dube, L. (1995). Decision making and waiting time: Is time like money? *Journal of Consumer Research, 22*, 110–19.

LeDoux, J.E. (1996). *The Emotional Brain: The Mysterious Underpinnings of Emotional Life*. New York: Simon and Schuster.

Ledyard, J. (1995). Public goods: A survey of experimental research. In J. Kagel and A. Roth (Eds), *Handbook of Experimental Economics*. Princeton: Princeton University Press.

Leith, K.P. and Baumeister, R.F. (1996). Why do bad moods increase self-defeating behaviour? Emotion, risk-taking, and self-regulation. *Journal of Personality and Social Psychology, 71*, 1250–67.

Levin, I.P. and Chapman, D.P. (1990). Risk taking, frame of reference, and characterization of victim groups in AIDS treatment decisions. *Journal of Experimental and Social Psychology, 26*, 421–34.

Levin, I.P., Schneider, S.L., and Gaeth, G.J. (1998). All frames are not created equal: A typology and critical analysis of framing effects. *Organizational Behavior and Human Decision Processes, 76*, 149–88.

Levinson, S.C. (1995). Interactional biases in human thinking. In E. Goody (Ed.), *Social Intelligence and Interaction*. Cambridge: Cambridge University Press, 221–60.

Levitt, S.D. and Dubner, S.J. (2005). *Freakonomics*. London: Allen Lane.

Levy, M. and Levy, H. (2002). Prospect theory: Much ado about nothing? *Management Science, 48*(10), 1334–49.

Lewis, R.J. (1983). Scared straight – California style. *Criminal Justice and Behavior, 10*, 209–26.

Libet, B. (1985). Unconscious cerebral initiative and the role of conscious will in voluntary action. *Behavioural and Brain Sciences, 8*(4), 529–66.

Libet, B. (1993). The neural time factor in conscious and unconscious events. *Experimental and Theoretical Studies of Consciousness* (Ciba Foundation Symposium, 174), 123–46.

Libet, B., Gleason, C.A., Wright, Jr, E.W., and Pearl. D.K. (1983). Time of conscious intention to act in relation to onset of cerebral activity (readiness-potential). *Brain, 106*, 623–42.

Lichtenstein, S. and Fischhoff, B. (1977). Do those who know more also know more about how much they know? The calibration of probability judgments. *Organizational Behavior and Human Performance, 16*, 1–12.

Lichtenstein, S. and Slovic, P. (1973). Response-induced reversals of preference in gambling: An extended replication in Las Vegas. *Journal of Experimental Psychology, 101*, 16–20.

Lima, S. (1984). Downy woodpecker foraging behavior: Efficient sampling in simple stochastic environments. *Ecology, 67*, 377–85.

List, J.A. (2004). Neoclassical theory versus prospect theory: evidence from the marketplace. *Econometrica, 72*(2), 615–25.

List, J.A. and Cherry, T.L. (2000). Learning to accept in ultimatum games: Evidence from and experimental design that generates low offers. *Experimental Economics, 3*, 11–31.

Littlewood, J.E. (1953). *A Mathematician's Miscellany*. London: Methuen.

Loewenstein, G. (1987). Anticipation and the valuation of delayed consumption. *Economic Journal, 87*, 666–84.

Loewenstein, G. (1988). Frames of mind in intertemporal choice. *Management Science, 34*, 200–14.

Loewenstein, G. (1996). Out of control: Visceral influences on behaviour. *Organizational Behavior and Human Decision Processes, 65*, 2.

Loewenstein, G. (2000). Emotions in economic theory and economic behavior. *American Economic Review Papers and Proceedings, 90*, 426–32.

Loewenstein, G., Issacharoff, S., Camerer, C., and Babcock, L. (1993). Self-serving assessments of fairness and pretrial bargaining. *Journal of Legal Studies, 22*, 135–59.

Loewenstein, G., O'Donoghue, T., and Rabin, M. (2003). Projection bias in predicting future utility. *Quarterly Journal of Economics, 118*(4), 1209–48.

Loewenstein, G. and Prelec, D. (1992). Anomalies in intertemporal choice: Evidence and interpretation. *Quarterly Journal of Economics, 107*, 573–97.

Loewenstein, G. and Prelec, D. (1993). Preferences for sequences of outcomes. *Psychological Review, 100*(1), 91–108.

Loewenstein, G. and Sicherman, N. (1991). Do workers prefer increasing wage profiles? *Journal of Labor Economics, 9*(1), 67–84.

Loewenstein, G., Thompson, L., and Bazerman, M.H. (1989). Social utility and decision making in interpersonal contexts. *Journal of Personality and Social Psychology, 62*(3), 426–41.

Loewenstein, G., Weber, R., Flory, J., Manuck, S., and Muldoon, M. (2001). Dimensions of time discounting. Paper presented at Conference on Survey Research on Household Expectations and Preferences. Ann Arbor, MI. November 2–3.

Loomes, G., Starmer, C., and Sugden, R. (2003). Do anomalies disappear in repeated markets? *The Economic Journal, 113*, C153–C166.

Loomes, G. and Sugden, R. (1982). Regret theory: An alternative theory of rational choice under uncertainty. *Economic Journal, 92*, 805–24.

Loomes, G. and Sugden, R. (1986). Disappointment and dynamic consistency in choice under uncertainty. *Review of Economic Studies, 53*(2), 271–82.

Loomes, G. and Sugden, R. (1987). Some implications of a more general form of regret theory. *Journal of Economic Theory, 41*(2), 270–87.

Loomes, G. and Sugden, R. (1995). Incorporating a stochastic element into decision theories. *European Economic Review, 39*, 641–48.

Lopes, L.L. and Oden, G.C. (1991). The rationality of intelligence. In E. Eels and T. Maruszewski (Eds), *Probability and Rationality: Studies on L. Jonathan Cohen's Philosophy of Science*. Amsterdam: Editions Rodopi, 199–223.

Lund, D.A., Caserta, M.S., and Diamond, M.F. (1989). Impact of spousal bereavement on the subjective well-being of older adults. In D.A. Lund (Ed.), *Older Bereaved Spouses: Research with Practical Implications*. New York: Hemisphere, 3–15.

Luttmer, E.G.J. (1996). Asset pricing in economies with frictions. *Econometrica, 64*, 1439–67.

Lykken, D. and Tellegen, A. (1996). Happiness is a stochastic phenomenon. *Psychological Science, 7*, 186–9.

Lyubomirsky, S. and Lepper, H.S. (1999). A measure of subjective happiness: Preliminary reliability and construct validation. *Social Indicators Research, 46*, 137–55.

Macdonald, R.R. (1986). Credible conceptions and implausible probabilities. *British Journal of Mathematical and Statistical Psychology, 39*, 15–27.

Machina, M.J. (1982). 'Expected utility' theory without the independence axiom. *Econometrica, 50*, 277–323.

Machina, M.J. (1983). The economic theory of individual behaviour toward risk: Theory, evidence, and new directions. Technical Report 433, Dept. of Economics, Stanford University.

MacKeigan, L.D., Larson, L.N., Draugalis, J.R., Bootman, J.L., and Burns, L.R. (1993). Time preference for health gains versus health losses. *Pharmacoeconomics, 3*(5), 374–86.

Madden, G.J., Petry, N.M., Badger, G.J., and Bickel, W. (1997). Impulsive and self-control choices in opioid-dependent patients and non-drug-using control participants: Drug and monetary rewards. *Experimental and Clinical Psychopharmacology, 5*(3), 256–62.

Madrian, B.C. and Shea, D.F. (2001). The power of suggestion: Inertia in 401(k) participation and savings behavior. *Quarterly Journal of Economics, 116*(4), 1149–87.

Maital, Shloma and Maital, Sharon (1978). Time preference, delay of gratification, and intergenerational transmission of economic inequality: A behavioral theory of income distribution. In O. Ashenfelter and W. Oates (Eds), *Essays in Labor Market Analysis*. New York: Wiley.

Mankiw, N.G. and Zeldes, S. (1991). The consumption of stockholders and nonstockholders. *Journal of Financial Economics, 29*(1), 97–112.

Margolis, H. (1982). *Selfishness, Altruism and Rationality: A Theory of Social Choice.* Cambridge: Cambridge University Press.

Markowitz, H. (1952). The utility of wealth. *Journal of Political Economy, 60,* 151–58.

Mayer, T. and Russell, T. (2005). Income smoothing and self-control: The case of school teachers. *Economic Enquiry, 43*(4), 823–30.

Maynard-Smith, J. (1976). Evolution and the theory of games. *American Scientist, 64,* 41–45.

Maynard-Smith, J. (1982). *Evolution and the Theory of Games.* Cambridge: Cambridge University Press.

McClure, S.M., Laibson, D.L., Loewenstein, G., and Cohen, J.D. (2004). Separate neural systems value immediate and delayed monetary rewards. *Science, 306*(5695), 503–07.

McGlothlin, W.H. (1956). Stability of choices among uncertain alternatives. *American Journal of Psychology, 69,* 604–15.

McKelvey, R.D. and Palfrey, T.R. (1992). An experimental study of the centipede game. *Econometrica, 58,* 1321–39.

Mehra, R. (2003). The equity premium: Why is it a puzzle? *Financial Analysts Journal, 59*(1), 54–69.

Mehra, R. and Prescott, E.C. (1985). The equity premium: A puzzle. *Journal of Monetary Economics, 15,* 145–61.

Mehta, J., Starmer, C., and Sugden, R. (1992). An experimental investigation of focal points in coordination and bargaining: Some preliminary results. In J. Geweke (Ed.), *Decision Making under Risk and Uncertainty: New Models and Findings.* Norwell, MA: Kluwer, 211–20.

Meyer, D.J. and Meyer, J. (2005). Risk preferences in multi-period consumption models, the equity premium puzzle, and habit formation utility. *Journal of Monetary Economics, 52*(8), 1497–515.

Meyer, R.F. (1976). Preferences over time. In R. Keeney and H. Raiffa (Eds), *Decisions with Multiple Objectives.* New York: Wiley.

Milinski, M. (1987). Tit for tat and the evolution of cooperation in sticklebacks. *Nature, 325,* 433–35.

Miller, P.M. and Fagley, N.S. (1991). The effects of framing, problem variations, and providing rationale on choice. *Personality and Social Psychology Bulletin, 17,* 517–22.

Mischel, W. (1974). Process in delay of gratification. In D. Berkowitz (Ed.), *Advances in Experimental Social Psychology*, Vol. 7. New York: Academic Press.

Mischel, W., Grusec, J., and Masters, J.C. (1969). Effects of expected delay time on subjective value of rewards and punishments. *Journal of Personality and Social Psychology, 11*(4), 363–73.

Mischel, W. and Metzner, R. (1962). Preference for delayed reward as a function of age, intelligence, and length of delay interval. *Journal of Abnormal Psychology, 64*(6), 425–31.

Mischel, W., Skoda, Y., and Peake, P.K. (1988). The nature of adolescent competencies predicted by preschool delay of gratification. *Journal of Personality and Social Psychology, 54*(4), 687–96.

Mischel, W., Skoda, Y., and Rodriguez, M.L. (1992). Delay of gratification in children. In G. Loewenstein and J. Elster (Eds), *Choice Over Time.* New York: Russell Sage.

Mitzkewitz, M. and Nagel, R. (1993). Experimental results on ultimatum games with incomplete information. *International Journal of Game Theory, 22,* 171–98.

Modigliani, F. and Brumberg, R. (1954). Utility analysis and the consumption function: An interpretation of cross-section data. In K.K. Kurihara (Ed.), *Post Keynesian Economics.* New Brunswick: Rutgers University Press.

Moore, M.J. and Viscusi, W.K. (1988). The quantity-adjusted value of life. *Economic Inquiry, 26*(3), 369–88.

Moore, M.J. and Viscusi, W.K. (1990a). Discounting environmental health risks: New evidence and policy implications. *Journal of Environmental Economics and Management, 18*, S51–S62.

Moore, M.J. and Viscusi, W.K. (1990b). Models for estimating discount rates for long-term health risks using labor market data. *Journal of Risk and Uncertainty, 3*, 381–401.

Morier, D.M. and Borgida, E. (1984). The conjunction fallacy: A task specific phenomenon? *Personal and Social Psychology Bulletin, 10*, 243–52.

Munasinghe, L. and Sicherman, N. (2000). Why do dancers smoke? Time preference, occupational choice, and wage growth. Working paper, Columbia University and Barnard College, New York.

Muraven, M. and Baumeister, R.F. (2000). Self-regulation and depletion of limited resources: Does self-control resemble a muscle? *Psychological Bulletin, 126*, 227–59.

Muraven, M. and Baumeister, R.F., and Tice, D.M. (1999). Longitudinal improvement of self-regulation through practice: Building self-control through repeated exercise. *Journal of Social Psychology, 139*, 446–57.

Muraven, M., Tice, D.M., and Baumeister, R.F. (1998). Self-control as a limited resource. *Journal of Personality and Social Psychology, 74*(3), 774–89.

Murnighan, J.K. and Saxon, M.S. (1998). Ultimatum bargaining by children and adults. *Journal of Economic Psychology, 19*, 415–45.

Musson, F.F. and Alloy, L.B. (1988). Depression and self-directed attention. In L.B. Alloy (Ed.), Cognitive Processes in Depression. New York: Guilford Press, 193–220.

Myers, D.G. and Diener, E. (1995). Who is happy? *Psychological Science, 6*, 10–19.

Nagel, R. (1995). Unravelling in guessing games: An experimental study. *American Economic Review, 85*, 1313–26.

Nash, J. (1950). The bargaining problem. *Econometrica, 18*, 155–62.

Nash, J. (1951). Non-cooperative games. *Annals of Mathematics, 54*, 286–95.

Neelin, J., Sonnenschein, H., and Spiegel, M. (1988). A further test of noncooperative bargaining theory: Comment. *American Economic Review, 78*, 824–36.

Neilson, W.S. (1992). A mixed fan hypothesis and its implications for behavior toward risk. *Journal of Economic Behavior and Organisation, 19*, 197–211.

Newell, R.G. and Pizer, W.A. (2003). Discounting the distant future: How much do uncertain rates increase valuations? *Journal of Environmental Economics and Management, 46*(1), 52–71.

Novemsky, N. and Kahneman, D. (2005a). The boundaries of loss-aversion. *Journal of Marketing Research, 42*, 119–28.

Novemsky, N. and Kahneman, D. (2005b). How do intentions affect loss-aversion? *Journal of Marketing Research, 42*, 139–40.

Nowak, M.A., May, R.M., and Sigmund, K. (1995). The arithmetics of mutual help. *Scientific American, 272*, 50–55.

Nussbaum, M.C. and Sen, A.K. (Eds) (1993). *The Quality of Life.* Oxford: Clarendon Press.

Nyarko, Y. and Schotter, A. (2002). An experimental study of belief learning using elicited beliefs. *Econometrica, 70*, 971–1005.

Ochs, J. (1995). Games with unique, mixed strategy equilibria: An experimental study. *Games and Economic Behavior, 10*, 202–17.

Ochs, J. and Roth, A.E. (1989). An experimental study of sequential bargaining. *American Economic Review, 79*, 355–84.

O'Curry, S. (1997). Income source effects. Working paper, Department of Marketing, DePaul University, Chicago.

Odean, T. (1998). Are investors reluctant to realize their losses? *Journal of Finance, 53*, 1775–98.

Odean, T. (2004). Do investors trade too much? In C. Camerer, G. Loewenstein, and M. Rabin (Eds), *Advances in Behavioral Economics*. Princeton, NJ: Russell Sage Foundation.

O'Doherty, J.P. (2004). Reward representations and reward-related learning in the human brain: Insights from neuroimaging. *Current Opinion in Neurobiology, 14*(6), 769–76.

O'Donoghue, T. and Rabin, M. (2001). Choice and procrastination. *Quarterly Journal of Economics, 116*(1), 121–60.

OECD (2004). Comparison of Household Saving Ratios, OECD Statistics Brief No. 8, June.

Oehler, A., Heilmann, K., Läger, V., and Oberländer, M. (2003). Coexistence of disposition investors and momentum traders in stock markets: experimental evidence. *Journal of International Financial Markets, Institutions and Money. 13*(5), 503–24.

Offerman, T. (1999). Hurting hurts more than helping helps: The role of the self-serving bias. Mimeo, CREED, University of Amsterdam.

Okada, E.M. (2001). Trade-ins, mental accounting, and product replacement Decisions. *Journal of Consumer Research, 27*(4), 433–46.

Olds, J. and Milner, P. (1954). Positive reinforcement caused by electrical stimulation of septal area and other regions of rat brain. *Journal of Comparative and Physiological Psychology, 47*, 419–27.

Olmstead, A.L. and Rhode, P. (1985). Rationing without government: The West Coast gas famine of 1920. *American Economic Review, 75*, 1044–55.

Olsen, R.A. and Troughton, G.H. (2000). Are risk premium anomalies caused by ambiguity? *Financial Analysts Journal, 56*(2), 24–31.

Osherson, D.N. (1995). Probability judgment. In E.E. Smith and D.N. Osherson (Eds), *Thinking: An Invitation to Cognitive Science*, Vol. 3. Cambridge, MA: MIT Press. 2nd ed., 35–75.

Ostrom, E. (1998). A behavioural approach to the rational choice theory of collective action. *American Political Science Review, 92*, 1–22.

Ostrom, E. (2000). Collective action and the evolution of social norms. *Journal of Economic Perspectives, 14*, 137–58.

Oyefeso, O. (2006). Would there ever be consensus value and source of the equity risk premium? A review of the extant literature. *International Journal of Theoretical and Applied Finance, 9*(2), 199–215.

Palacios-Heurta, I. (2001). Professionals play minimax. Brown University working paper.

Palm, R., Hodgson M., Blanchard, D., and Lyons, D. (1990). *Earthquake insurance in California*. Boulder, CO: Westview Press.

Parducci, A. (1995). *Happiness, Pleasure, and Judgment: The Contextual Theory and its Applications*. Mahway, NJ: Erlbaum.

Payne, J.W., Schkade, D.A., Desvousges, W., and Aultman, C. (1999). Valuation of multiple environmental programs: A psychological analysis. Unpublished manuscript, Duke University.

Pender, J.L. (1996). Discount rates and credit markets: Theory and evidence from rural India. *Journal of Developmental Economics, 50*(2), 257–96.

Pfeiffer, J.E. (1982). *Explosion: An Enquiry into the Origins of Art and Religion.* New York: Harper and Row.

Phelps, E.S. and Pollak, R.A. (1968). On second-best national saving and game-equilibrium growth. *Review of Economic Studies, 35,* 185–99.

Pidgeon, N., Hood, C., Jones, D., Turner, B., and Gibson, R. (1992). Risk perception. In *Risk analysis, perceptions and management.* Report of a Royal Society Study Group. London: The Royal Society.

Pigou, A.C. (1920). *The Economics of Welfare.* London: Macmillan.

Pilutla, M.M. and Chen, X.-P. (1999). Social norms and cooperation in PDs: The effect of context and feedback. *Organizational Behavior and Human Decision Processes, 78,* 81–103.

Pinker, S. (1997). *How the Mind Works.* New York: Norton.

Platt, M.L. and McCoy, A.N. (2005). Risk-sensitive neurons in macaque posterior cingulate cortex. *Nature Neuroscience, 8*(9), 1220–27.

Plott, C.R. (1996). Rational individual behavior in markets and social choice processes: The discovered preference hypothesis. In K.J. Arrow, E. Colombatto, M. Perlman, and C. Schmidt (Eds), *The Rational Foundations of Economic Behavior.* New York: St. Martin's Press, 225–50.

Plott, C.R. and Zeiler, K. (2005). The willingness to pay-willingness to accept gap, the 'endowment' effect, subject misconceptions, and experimental procedures for eliciting valuations. *American Economic Review, 95*(3), 530–45.

Plutchik, R. and Conte, H.R. (Eds) (1997). *Circumplex Models of Personality and Emotions.* Washington, DC: American Psychological Association.

Pohl, R.F. and Hell, W. (1996). No reduction in hindsight bias after complete information and repeated testing. *Organizational Behavior and Human Decision Processes, 67,* 49–58.

Politzer, G. and Noveck, I.A. (1991). Are conjunctional rule violations the result of conversational rule violations? *Journal of Psycholinguistic Research, 20,* 83–103.

Prelec, D. (1989). Decreasing impatience: Definition and consequences. Working paper 90-015, Harvard Business School.

Prelec, D. (1998). The probability weighting function. *Econometrica, 60,* 497–528.

Prelec, D. and Loewenstein, G. (1998). The red and the black: Mental accounting of savings and debt. *Marketing Science, 17*(1), 4–27.

Prelec, D. and Simester, D. (2001). Always leave home without it: A further investigation of the credit-card effect on willingness to pay. *Marketing Letters, 12*(1), 5–12.

Putler, D. (1992). Incorporating reference price effects into a theory of consumer choice. *Marketing Science, 11,* 287–309.

Quattrone, G.A., and Tversky, A. (1984). Causal versus diagnostic contingencies: On self-deception and on the voter's illusion. *Journal of Personality and Social Psychology, 46,* 237–48.

Quiggin, J. (1982). A theory of anticipated utility. *Journal of Economic Behavior and Organisation, 3*(4), 323–43.

Rabin, M. (1993). Incorporating fairness into game theory and economics. *American Economic Review, 83,* 1281–302.

Rabin, M. (2000). Risk-aversion and expected utility theory: A calibration theorem. *Econometrica, 68*(5), 1281–92.

Rabin, M. (2002). The law of small numbers. *Quarterly Journal of Economics, 117,* 775–816.

Rabin, M. and Schrag, J.C. (1999). First impressions matter: A model of confirmatory bias. *Quarterly Journal of Economics, 114,* 37–82.

Rae, J. (1905/1834). *The Sociologicial Theory of Capital*. London: Macmillan.

Rapoport, A. and Budescu, D.V. (1997). Randomization in individual choice behavior. *Psychological Review, 104*, 603–17.

Rapoport, A., Sundali, J.A., and Potter, R.E. (1996). Ultimatums in two-person bargaining with one-sided uncertainty: Offer games. *International Journal of Game Theory, 25*, 475–94.

Rapoport, A., Weg, E., and Felsenthal, D.S. (1990). Effects of fixed costs in two-person sequential bargaining. *Theory and Decision, 28*, 47–71.

Rawls, J. (1971). *A Theory of Justice*. Cambridge, MA: Harvard University Press.

Rawls, J. (2001). *Justice as Fairness*. Cambridge, MA: Belknap, Harvard University Press.

Read, D., Frederick, S., Orsel, B., and Rahman, J. (2005). Four score and seven years from now: The date/delay effect in temporal discounting. *Management Science, 51*(9), 1326–35.

Read, D. and Loewenstein, G. (1995). Diversification bias: Explaining the discrepancy in variety seeking between combined and separated choices. *Journal of Experimental Psychology: Applied, 1*, 34–49.

Read, D. and Read, N.L. (2004). Time discounting over the lifespan. *Organizational Behavior and Human Decision Processes, 94*(1), 22–32.

Read, D. and Roelofsma, P. (2003). Subadditive discounting versus hyperbolic discounting: A comparison of choice and matching. *Organizational Behavior and Human Decision Processes, 91*(2), 140–53.

Redelmeier, D.A. and Heller, D.N. (1993). Time preference in medical decision making and cost-effectiveness analysis. *Medical Decision Making, 13*(3), 212–17.

Redelmeier, D.A and Kahneman, D. (1996). Patients' memories of painful medical treatments: Real-time and retrospective evaluations of two minimally invasive procedures. *Pain, 116*, 3–8.

Redelmeier, D.A. and Shafir, E. (1995). Medical decision making in situations that offer multiple alternatives. *Journal of the American Marketing Association, 273*, 302–05.

Redelmeier, D.A., Shafir, E., and Aujla, P. (2001). The beguiling pursuit of more information. *Medical Decision Making, 21*(5), 376–87.

Redelmeier, D.A. and Tversky, A. (1992). On the framing of multiple prospects. *Psychological Science, 3*(3), 191–93.

Resnick, M.D. (1987). *Choices: An Introduction to Decision Theory*. Minneapolis: University of Minnesota Press.

Restak, R. (1984). *The Brain*. New York: Bantam.

Reyna, V.F. and Brainerd, C.J. (1991). Fuzzy-trace theory and framing effects in choice: gist extraction, truncation, and conversion. *Journal of Behavioral Decision Making, 4*, 249–62.

Rha, J.-Y. and Rajagopal, P. (2001). Is time like money? Consumers' mental accounting of time. *Consumer Interest Annual, 47*, 1–2.

Ridley, M. (1993). *The Red Queen: Sex and the Evolution of Human Nature*. London: Viking.

Ridley, M. (1996). *The Origins of Virtue*. London: Penguin, 79.

Ridley, M. (2004). *Nature via Nurture*. London: Harper Perennial.

Rilling, J.K., Gutman, D.A., Zeh, T.R., Pagnoni, G., Berus, G.S., and Kilts, C.D. (2002). A neural basis for social cooperation. *Neuron, 35*(2), 395–405.

Rilling, J.K., Sanfey, A.G., Aronson, J.A., Nystrom, L.E., and Cohen, J.D. (2004). Opposing bold responses to reciprocated and unreciprocated altruism in putative reward pathways. *Neuroreport, 15*(16), 2539–43.

Robinson, J. (1951). An iterative method of solving a game. *Annals of Mathematics, 54,* 296–301.

Rockenbach, B. (2004). The behavioral relevance of mental accounting for the pricing of option contracts. *Journal of Economic Behavior and Organization, 53,* 513–27.

Roelofsma, P. (1994). *Intertemporal Choice.* Amsterdam: Free University.

Ross, M. and Sicoly, F. (1979). Egocentric biases in availability and attribution. *Journal of Personality and Social Psychology, 37,* 322–36.

Roth, A.E. and Malouf, M. (1979). Game-theoretic models and the role of information in bargaining. *Psychological Review, 86,* 574–94.

Roth, A.E. and Murnighan, J.K. (1982). The role of information in bargaining: An experimental study. *Econometrica, 50,* 1123–42.

Roth, A.E. and Schoumaker, F. (1983). Expectations and reputations in bargaining: An experimental study. *American Economic Review, 73,* 362–72.

Roth, A.E., Prasnikar, V., Okuno-Fujiwara, M., and Zamir, S. (1991). Bargaining and market behavior in Jerusalem, Ljubljana, Pittsburgh and Tokyo: An experimental study. *American Economic Review, 81,* 1068–95.

Rubinstein, A. (1989). The electronic mail game: Strategic behavior under "almost common knowledge". *American Economic Review, 79,* 385–91.

Rubinstein, A. (2003). "Economics and Psychology"? The case of hyperbolic discounting. *International Economic Review, 44*(4), 1207–16.

Russell, J.A. (1980). A circumplex model of affect. *Journal of Personality and Social Psychology, 39,* 1161–78.

Russell, J.A. and Carroll, J.M. (1999). On the bipolarity of positive and negative affect. *Psychological Bulletin, 125,* 3–30.

Sally, D. (1995). Conversation and cooperation in social dilemmas: A meta-analysis of experiments from 1958 to 1992. *Rationality and Society, 7,* 58–92.

Samuelson, P.A. (1937). A note on measurement of utility. *Review of Economic Studies, 4,* 155–61.

Samuelson, P.A. (1963). Risk and uncertainty: A fallacy of large numbers. *Scientia,* 108–13.

Schelling, T.C. (1960). *The Strategy of Conflict.* Cambridge: Harvard University Press.

Schelling, T.C. (1984). Self-command in practice, in policy, and in a theory of rational choice. *American Economic Review, 74,* 1–11.

Schkade, D. and Kahneman, D. (1998). Does living in California make people happy? A focusing illusion in judgements of life satisfaction. *Psychological Science, 9,* 340–46.

Scholz, J.K., Seshadri, A., and Khitatrakun, S. (2003). Are Americans saving 'optimally' for retirement? Working paper, University of Wisconsin at Madison.

Schooler, J.W., Ariely, D., and Loewenstein, G. (2003). The pursuit and assessment of happiness can be self-defeating. In Isabelle Brocas and Juan D. Carillo (Eds), *The Psychology of Economic Decisions.* Oxford: Oxford University Press, 41–70.

Schwartz, J.M. (1999). A role for volition and attention in the generation of new brain circuitry: Toward a neurobiology of mental force. *Journal of Consciousness Studies, 6,* 115–42.

Schwarz, N. (1996). *Cognition and Communication: Judgmental Biases, Research Methods, and the Logic of Conversation.* Mahwah, NJ: Erlbaum.

Schwarz, N., Strack, F., Kommer, D., and Wagner, D. (1987). Soccer, rooms, and the quality of your life: Mood effects on judgments of satisfaction with life in general and with specific domains. *European Journal of Social Psychology, 17,* 69–79.

Schwarz, N., Strack, F., Hilton, D., and Naderer, G. (1991). Base rates, representativeness, and the logic of conversation: The contextual relevance of "irrelevant" information. *Social Cognition, 9,* 67–84.

Schweitzer, M. and Solnick, S. (1999). The influence of physical attractiveness and gender on ultimatum game decisions. *Organizational Behavior and Human Decision Processes, 79*, 199–215.

Sen, A.K. (1977). Rational fools: A critique of the behavioral foundations of economic theory. *Philosophy and Public Affairs, 6*, 317–44.

Sen, A.K. (1987). *On Ethics and Economics*. Oxford, UK: Blackwell.

Sen, A.K. (1990). Rational Behavior. In J. Eatwell, M. Milgate, and P. Newman (Eds), *The New Palgrave: Utility and Probability*. New York: Norton, 198–216.

Senior, N.W. (1836). *An Outline of the Science of Political Economy*. London: Clowes and Sons.

Shachat, J.M. (2002). Mixed strategy play and the minimax hypothesis. *Journal of Economic Theory, 104*, 189–226.

Shafir, E., Diamond P., and Tversky A. (1997). Money Illusion. *Quarterly Journal of Economics, 112*(2), 341–74.

Shafir, E. and LeBoeuf, R. (2002). Rationality. *Annual Review of Psychology, 53*, 491–517.

Shanks, N. and Dawkins, R. (2004). *God, the Devil, and Darwin: A Critique of Intelligent Design Theory*. New York: Oxford University Press.

Shapiro, J.M. (2005). Is there a daily discount rate? Evidence from the food stamp nutrition cycle. *Journal of Public Economics, 89*(2/3), 303–25.

Shea, J. (1995a). Myopia, liquidity constraints, and aggregate consumption. *Journal of Money, Credit, Banking, 27*(3), 798–805.

Shea, J. (1995b). Union contracts and the life cycle/permanent income hypothesis. *American Economic Review, 85*, 186–200.

Shefrin, H.M. and Statman, M. (1984). Explaining investor preference for cash dividends. *Journal of Financial Economics, 13*, 253–82.

Shefrin, H.M. and Statman, M. (1985). The disposition to sell winners too early and ride losers too long. *Journal of Financial Economics, 40*, 777–90.

Shefrin, H.M. and Thaler, R.H. (1992). Mental accounting, saving, and self-control. In G. Loewenstein and J. Elster (Eds), *Choice Over Time*. New York: Russell Sage Foundation.

Shelley, M. (1993). Outcome signs, question frames and discount rates. *Management Science, 39*, 806–15.

Shelley, M. (1994). Gain/loss asymmetry in risky intertemporal choice. *Organizational Behavior and Human Decision Processes, 59*, 124–59.

Sherif, M. and Sherif, C.W. (1964). *Reference Groups: Exploration into Conformity and Deviation of Adolescents*. New York: Harper and Row.

Shiv, B. and Fedorikhin, A. (1999). Heart and mind in conflict: The interplay of affect and cognition in consumer decision making. *Journal of Consumer Research, 26*(3), 278–92.

Shoda, Y., Mischel, W., and Peake, P.K. (1990). Predicting adolescent cognitive and self-regulatory competencies from preschool delay of gratification. *Developmental Psychology, 26*(6), 978–86.

Shogren, J.F., Shin, S.Y., Hayes, D.J., and Kliebenstein, J.B. (1994). Resolving differences in willingness to pay and willingness to accept. *American Economic Review, 84*, 255–70.

Sieck, W. and Yates, J.F. (1997). Exposition effects on decision making: Choice and confidence in choice. *Organizational Behavior and Human Decision Processes, 70*, 207–19.

Siegel, J. and Thaler, R. (1997). Anomalies: The equity premium puzzle. *Journal of Economic Perspectives, 11*, 191–200.

Simon, H.A. (1956). Rational choice and the structure of the environment. *Psychological Review, 63*, 129–38.

Simon, H.A. (1957). *Models of Man: Social and Rational.* New York: Wiley.

Simon, H.A. (1959). Theories of decision making in economics and behavioral science. *American Economic Review, 49*, 252–83.

Simon, H.A. (1978). Rationality as process and as product of thought. *American Economic Review, Papers and Proceedings, 68*, 1–16.

Simonson, I. (1990). The effect of purchase quantity and timing on variety-seeking behaviour. *Journal of Marketing Research, 17*, 150–62.

Simonson, I. and Tversky, A. (1992). Choice in context: Tradeoff contrast and extremeness aversion. *Journal of Marketing Research, 29*(3), 281–95.

Slacalek, J. (2006). What drives personal consumption? The role of housing and financial wealth. German Institute for Economic Research. September.

Sloman, S.A. (1996). The empirical case for two systems of reasoning. *Psychological Bulletin, 119*, 3–22.

Slonim, R.L. and Roth, A.E. (1998). Learning in high-stakes ultimatum games: An experiment in the Slovak republic. *Econometrica, 66*, 569–96.

Slovic, P., Fischhoff, B., and Lichtenstein, S. (1982). Response mode, framing, and information-processing effects in risk management. In R. Hogarth (Ed.), *New Directions for Methodology of Social and Behavioural Science: Question Framing and Response Consistency.* San Francisco: Jossey-Bass, 21–36.

Slovic, P. and Lichtenstein, S. (1983). Preference reversals: A broader perspective. *American Economic Review, 73*, 596–605.

Slugoski, B.R. and Wilson, A.E. (1998). Contribution of conversation skills to the production of judgmental errors. *European Journal of Social Psychology, 28*, 575–601.

Smith, A. (1759/1892). *The Theory of Moral Sentiments.* New York: Prometheus.

Smith, S.M. and Levin, I.P. (1996). Need for cognition and choice framing effects. *Journal of Behavioral Decision Making, 9*, 283–90.

Smith, V.L. (1990). *Schools of Economic Thought: Experimental Economics.* Aldershot, UK: Edward Elgar.

Smith, V.L. (1991). Rational choice: the contrast between economics and psychology. *Journal of Political Economy, 99*, 877–97.

Solnick, S.J. (2001). Gender differences in the ultimatum game. *Economic Inquiry, 39*, 189–200.

Solomon, R.L. (1980). The opponent-process theory of acquired motivation. *American Psychologist, 35*, 691–712.

Soman, D. (1997). Contextual effects of payment mechanism on purchase intention: check or charge? Unpublished working paper, University of Colorado.

Soman, D. (2004). The effect of time delay on multi-attribute choice. *Journal of Economic Psychology, 25*(2), 153–75.

Soman, D. and Cheema, A. (2002). The effect of credit on spending decisions: The role of the credit limit and credibility. *Marketing Science, 21*(1), 32–53.

Soman, D. and Gourville, J.T. (2001). Transaction decoupling: How price bundling affects the decision to consume. *Journal of Marketing Research, 38*(1), 30–44.

Stahl, D.O. (1996). Boundedly rational rule learning in a guessing game. *Games and Economic Behavior, 16*, 303–30.

Stahl, D.O. (1999a). Sophisticated learning and learning sophistication. University of Texas at Austin working paper.

Stahl, D.O. (1999b). Evidence based rules and learning in symmetric normal-form games. *International Journal of Game Theory, 28*, 111–30.

Stahl, D.O. (2000a). Rule learning in symmetric normal-form games. *Games and Economic Behavior, 32*, 105–38.

Stahl, D.O. (2000b). Action-reinforcement learning versus rule learning. University of Texas at Austin working paper.

Stahl, D.O. (2001). Population rule learning in normal-form games: Theory and evidence. *Journal of Economic Behavior and Organization, 45*, 19–35.

Stahl, D.O. and Wilson, P. (1995). On players' models of other players: Theory and experimental evidence. *Games and Economic Behavior, 10*, 218–54.

Stanovich, K.E. (1999). *Who is Rational? Studies of Individual Differences in Reasoning.* Mahwah, NJ: Erlbaum.

Stanovich, K.E. and West, R.F. (1998). Individual differences in framing and conjunction effects. *Thinking and Reasoning, 4*, 289–317.

Stanovich, K.E. and West, R.F. (1999). Discrepancies between normative and descriptive models of decision making and the understanding/acceptance principle. *Cognitive Psychology, 38*, 349–85.

Starmer, C. (1999). Cycling with rules of thumb: An experimental test for a new form of non-transitive behaviour. *Theory and Decision, 46*, 141–58.

Starmer, C. (2000). Developments in non-expected utility theory: The hunt for a descriptive theory of choice under risk. *Journal of Economic Literature, 38*, 332–82.

Starmer, C. (2005). Normative notions in descriptive dialogues. *Journal of Economic Methodology, 12*(2), 277–89.

Starmer, C. and Sugden, R. (1989). Violations of the independence axiom in common ratio problems: An experimental test of some competing hypotheses. *Annals Operational Res., 19*, 79–102.

Starmer, C. and Sugden, R. (1998). Testing alternative explanations of cyclical choices. *Economica, 65*(259), 347–61.

Stein, E. (1996). *Without Good Reason: The Rationality Debate in Philosophy and Cognitive Science.* New York: Oxford University Press.

Sterling, P. and Eyer, J. (1988). Allostasis: A new paradigm to explain arousal pathology. In S. Fisher and J. Reason (Eds), *Handbook of Life Stress, Cognition and Health.* Chichester, UK: Wiley, 629–48.

Stewart, J. and Wise, R.A. (1992). Reinstatement of heroin self-administration habits: Morphine prompts and naltrexone discourages renewed responding after extinction. *Psychopharmacology, 108*, 779–84.

Stigler, G. (1965). The development of utility theory. In *Essays in the History of Economics.* Chicago: University of Chicago Press.

Stigler, G. (1981). Economics or ethics? In S. McMurrin (Ed.), *Tanner Lectures on Human Values.* Cambridge: Cambridge University Press.

Stone, A.A. (1995). Measures of affective response. In S. Cohen, R. Kessler, and L. Gordon (Eds), *Measuring Stress: A Guide for Social and Health Scientists.* New York: Cambridge University Press, 148–71.

Stone, E.R., Yates, F., and Parker, A.M. (1994). Risk communication: Absolute versus relative expressions of low-probability risks. *Organizational Behavior and Human Decision Processes, 60*, 387–408.

Stouffer, S.A., Lumsdaine, A.A., Lumsdaine, M.H., Williams, Jr, R.M., Smith, I.L., and Cottrell, Jr, L.S. (1949). *The American Soldier*. Princeton: Princeton University Press.

Strack, F., Martin, L.L., and Stepper, S. (1988). Inhibiting and facilitating conditions of the human smile: A nonobtrusive test of the facial feedback hypothesis. *Journal of Personality and Social Psychology, 54*(5), 768–77.

Straub, P. and Murnighan, K. (1995). An experimental investigation of ultimatum games: Information, fairness, expectations, and lowest acceptable offers. *Journal of Economic Behavior and Organization, 27*, 345–64.

Strotz, R.H. (1955). Myopia and inconsistency in dynamic utility maximization. *Review of Economic Studies*, 23, 165–80.

Suh, E. Diener, E., and Fujita, F. (1996). Events and subjective well-being: Only recent events matter. *Journal of Personality and Social Psychology, 70*, 1091–102.

Sunstein, C.R., Kahneman, D., and Schkade, D.A. (1998). Assessing punitive damages. *Yale Law Journal, 107*, 2071–153.

Sutton, S.K. and Davidson, R.J. (1997). Prefrontal brain asymmetry: A biological substrate of behavioral approach and inhibition systems. *Psychological Science, 8*, 204–10.

Svenson, O. (1981). Are we all less risky and more skilful than our fellow drivers? *Acta Psychologica, 9*, 143–48.

Takemura, K. (1993). The effect of decision frame and decision justification on risky choice. *Japanese Psychological Research, 35*, 36–40.

Takemura, K. (1994). Influence of elaboration on the framing of decisions. *Journal of Psychology, 128*, 33–39.

Taylor, S.E. (1991). Asymmetrical effects of positive and negative events: The mobilization-minimization hypothesis. *Psychological Bulletin, 110*, 67–85.

Tetlock, P.E., Kristel, O.V., Elson, B., Green, M., and Lerner, J. (2000). The psychology of the unthinkable: Taboo trade-offs, forbidden base rates, and heretical counterfactuals. *Journal of Personality and Social Psychology, 78*, 853–70.

Thaler, R.H. (1980). Toward a positive theory of consumer choice. *Journal of Economic Behavior and Organization*, 1, 39–60.

Thaler, R.H. (1981). Some empirical evidence on dynamic inconsistency. *Economic Letters, 8*, 201–07.

Thaler, R.H. (1985). Mental accounting and consumer choice. *Marketing Science, 4*, 199–214.

Thaler, R.H. (1999). Mental accounting matters. *Journal of Behavioral Decision Making, 12*, 183–206.

Thaler, R.H. and Johnson, E.J. (1990). Gambling with the house money and trying to break even: The effects of prior outcomes on risky choice. *Management Science, 36*(6), 643–60.

Thaler, R.H. and Shefrin, H.M. (1981). An economic theory of self-control. *Journal of Political Economy, 89*(2), 392–406.

Thaler, R.H., Tversky, A., Kahneman, D., and Schwartz, A. (1997). The effect of myopia and loss-aversion on risk taking: An experimental test. *Quarterly Journal of Economics, 112*, 647–61.

Thaler, R.H. and Ziemba, W. (1988). Parimutuel betting markets: Racetracks and lotteries. *Journal of Economic Perspectives, 2*, 161–74.

Tice, D.M. and Baumeister, R.F. (1997). Longitudinal study of procrastination, performance, stress, and health: The costs and benefits of dawdling. *Psychological Science, 8*, 454–58.

Titmuss, R.M. (1971/1987). The gift of blood. In B. Abel-Smith and K. Titmuss (Eds), *The Philosophy of Welfare: Selected Writings by R.M. Titmuss*. London: Allen and Unwin.

Tobin, J. (1972). Inflation and unemployment. *American Economic Review, 42*, 1–18.

Tooby, J. and Cosmides, L. (1984). The psychological foundations of culture. In J.H. Barkow, L. Cosmides, and J. Tooby (Eds), *The Adapted Mind*. Oxford: Oxford University Press, 19–136.

Train, K.E. (1991). *Optimal regulation*. Cambridge, MA: MIT Press.

Tversky, A. and Griffin, D. (2000). Endowments and contrast in judgments of well-being. In D. Kahneman and A. Tversky (Eds), *Choices, Values and Frames*. New York: Cambridge University Press and the Russell Sage Foundation.

Tversky, A. and Kahneman, D. (1971). Belief in the law of small numbers. *Psychological Bulletin, 76*, 105–10.

Tversky, A. and Kahneman, D. (1973). Availability: A heuristic for judging frequency and probability. *Cognitive Psychology, 5*, 207–32.

Tversky, A. and Kahneman, D. (1981). The framing of decisions and the psychology of choice. *Science, 211*, 453–58.

Tversky, A. and Kahneman, D. (1982). Evidential impact of base rates. In D. Kahneman, P. Slovic, and A. Tversky (Eds), *Judgement under Uncertainty: Heuristics and Biases*. New York: Cambridge University Press, 153–60.

Tversky, A. and Kahneman, D. (1983). Extensional versus intuitive reasoning: the conjunction fallacy in probability judgement. *Psychological Review*, 90, 293–315.

Tversky, A. and Kahneman, D. (1986). Rational choice and the framing of decisions. *Journal of Business, 59*, S251–S278.

Tversky, A. and Kahneman, D. (1992). Advances in prospect theory: Cumulative representation of uncertainty. *Journal of Risk and Uncertainty, 5*, 297–323.

Tversky, A. and Koehler, D.K. (1994). Support theory: A nonextensional representation of subjective probability. *Psychological Review, 101*, 547–67.

Tversky, A., Sattath, S., and Slovic, P. (1988). Contingent weighting in judgment and choice. *Psychological Review, 93*(3), 371–84.

Tversky, A. and Shafir, E. (1992). Choice under conflict. The dynamics of deferred decision. *Psychological Science, 3*(6), 358–61.

Tversky, A., Slovic, P., and Kahneman, D. (1990). The causes of preference reversal. *American Economic Review, 80*, 204–17.

Twenge, J.M., Baumeister, R.F., Tice, D.M., and Schmeichel, B. (2000). Decision Fatigue: Making Multiple Personal Decisions Depletes the Self's Resources. Manuscript submitted for publication, Case Western Reserve University, Cleveland, OH.

Vaillant, G. (2000). Adaptive mental mechanisms: Their role in positive psychology. *American Psychologist, 55*, 89–98.

Valley, K., Thompson, L., Gibbons, R., and Bazerman, M.H. (2002). How communication improves efficiency in bargaining games. *Games and Economic Behavior, 38*, 127–55.

van der Pol, M.M. and Cairns, J.A. (1999). Individual time preferences for own health: Application of a dichotomous choice question with follow-up. *Applied Economic Letters, 6*(10), 649–54.

van der Pol, M.M. and Cairns, J.A. (2001). Estimating time preferences for health using discrete choice experiments. *Social Science and Medicine, 52*, 1459–70.

Varey, C.A. and Kahneman, D. (1992). Experiences extended across time: evaluation of moments and episodes. *Journal of Behavioral Decision Making, 5*(3), 169–85.

Varian, H.R. (2006). *Intermediate Microeconomics*. New York: Norton.

Veenhoven, R. (1988). Utility of happiness. *Social Indicators Research, 20*, 333–54.

Venti, S.F. and Wise, D.A. (1987). Aging, moving, and housing wealth. Cambridge, MA: National Bureau of Economic Research Working Paper.

Viscusi, W.K. and Moore, M.J. (1989). Rates of time preference and valuation of the duration of life. *Journal of Public Economics, 38*(3), 297–317.

von Mises, L. (1949). *Human Action: A Treatise on Economics*. San Francisco: Fox and Wilkes.

von Neumann, J. and Morgenstern, O. (1944). *The Theory of Games and Economic Behavior*. Princeton: Princeton University Press.

von Stackelberg, H. (1934). *Marktform und Gleichgewicht*. Vienna: Julius Springer.

Wahlund, R. and Gunnarsson, J. (1996). Mental discounting and financial strategies. *Journal of Economic Psychology, 17*(6), 709–30.

Wakker, P.P. (2003). The data of Levy and Levy (2002) "Prospect theory: Much ado about nothing?" actually support prospect theory. *Management Science, 49*(7), 979–81.

Wakker, P.P., Thaler, R.H., and Tversky, A. (1997). Probabilistic insurance. *Journal of Risk and Uncertainty, 15*, 5–26.

Walker, M. and Wooders, J. (2001). Minimax play at Wimbledon. *American Economic Review, 91*, 1528–38.

Wang, X.T. (1996). Framing effects: Dynamics and task domains. *Organizational Behavior and Human Decision Processes, 68*, 145–57.

Wang, X.T. and Johnston, V.S. (1995). Perceived social context and risk preference: A re-examination of framing effects in a life-death decision problem. *Journal of Behavioral Decision Making, 8*, 279–93.

Warner, J.T. and Pleeter, S. (2001). The personal discount rate: Evidence from military downsizing programs. *American Economic Review, 91*(1), 33–53.

Warr, P. (1999). Well-being and the workplace. In D. Kahneman, E. Diener, and N. Schwarz (Eds), *Well-being: The Foundations of Hedonic Psychology*. New York: Cambridge University Press, 392–412.

Wason, P.C. (1966). Reasoning. In B.M. Foss (Ed.), *New Horizons in Psychology*. Harmondsworth: Penguin.

Weber, R. (2001). Behavior and learning in the 'dirty faces' game. *Experimental Economics, 4*, 229–42.

Wegner, D.M. (1994). Ironic processes of mental control. *Psychological Review, 101*, 34–52.

Wegner, D.M. (2002). *The Illusion of Conscious Will*. Cambridge, MA: MIT Press.

Weil, P. (1989). The equity premium puzzle and the risk-free rate puzzle. *Journal of Monetary Economics, 15*, 145–61.

Weinstein, N.D. (1980). Unrealistic optimism about future life events. *Journal of Personality and Social Psychology, 39*, 806–20.

Wertenbroch, K. (1996). Consumption self-control via purchase rationing. Working paper, Yale University.

Wetherick, N.E. (1971). Representativeness in a reasoning problem: A reply to Shapiro. *Bulletin of the British Psychologal Society, 24*, 213–14.

Wilkinson, G.S. (1984). Reciprocal food sharing in the vampire bat. *Nature, 308*, 181–84.

Wilkinson, J.N. (1996). Marketing in the health club industry. Ph.D. dissertation, City University, London.

Wilkinson, J.N. (2003). Frequency of price promotion: A consumer deadline model. Working paper, Department of Business and Economics, Richmond the American International University in London.

Wilkinson, J.N. (2004). Utility theory and evolutionary psychology: Some implications and empirical evidence. Working paper, Department of Business and Economics, Richmond the American International University in London.

Williams, A.C. (1966). Attitudes toward speculative risks as an indicator of attitudes toward pure risks. *Journal of Risk and Insurance, 33*, 577–86.

Williams, G.C. (1966). *Adaptation and Natural Selection: A Critique of Some Current Evolutionary Thought*. Princeton: Princeton University Press.

Wilson, E.O. (1998). *Consilience*. London: Little, Brown, 57.

Wilson, T.D., Gilbert, D.T., and Centerbar, D.B. (2003). Making sense: The causes of emotional evanescence. In I. Brocas and J.D. Carrillo (Eds), *The Psychology of Economic Decisions, Volume 1: Rationality and Well-Being*. Oxford: Oxford University Press.

Wilson, T.D., Lindsay, S., and Schooler, T.Y. (2000). A model of dual attitudes. *Psychological Review, 107*, 101–26.

Wilson, T.D., and Schooler, T.Y. (1991). Thinking too much: Introspection can reduce the quality of preferences and decisions. *Journal of Personality and Social Psychology, 60*(2), 181–92.

Wilson, T.D., Wheatley, T., Meyers, J.M., Gilbert, D.T., and Axsom, D. (2000). Focalism: A source of durability bias in affective forecasting. *Journal of Personality and Social Psychology, 78*, 821–36.

Winkler, R. (2006). Does 'better' discounting lead to 'worse' outcomes in long-run decisions? The dilemma of hyperbolic discounting. *Ecological Economics, 57*(4), 573–82.

Winston, G.C. (1980). Addiction and backsliding: A theory of compulsive consumption. *Journal of Economic Behavior and Organization, 1*, 295–324.

Wortman, C.B., Silver, R.C., and Kessler, R.C. (1993). The meaning of loss and adjustment to bereavement. In M.S. Stroebe, W. Stroebe, and R.O. Hansson (Eds), *Handbook of Bereavement: Theory, Research, and Intervention*. New York: Cambridge University Press, 349–66.

Wu, G. and Gonzalez, R. (1996). Curvature of the probability weighting function. *Management Science, 42*, 1676–90.

Yariv, L. (2005). I'll see it when I believe it: A simple model of cognitive consistency. Mimeo.

Yates, J.F. and Watts, R.A. (1975). Preferences for deferred losses. *Organizational Behavior and Human Performance, 13*(2), 294–306.

Yoo, K.-Y. and de Serres, A. (2004). Tax Treatment of Private Pension Savings in OECD Countries and the Net Tax Cost Per Unit of Contribution to Tax-Favoured Schemes. OECD Economics Department Working Paper No. 406, October.

Zahavi, A. (1975). Mate selection – A selection for a handicap. *Journal of Theoretical Biology, 53*, 205–14.

Zhou, C. (1999). Informational asymmetry and market imperfections: Another solution to the equity premium puzzle. *Journal of Financial and Quantitative Analysis, 34*(4), 445–69.

Zillman, D. (1978). Attribution and misattribution of excitatory reactions. In J.H. Harvey, W.J. Ickes, and R.F. Kidd (Eds), *New Directions in Attribution Research, Vol. 2*. Hillsdale: Erlbaum, 335–68.

Zuckerman, M. (1979). Attributions of success and failure revisited, or: The motivational bias is alive and well in attribution theory. *Journal of Personality, 47*, 245–87.

Index